PATHOLOGY	CHANGE	ILLUSTRATIVE CASE
Infantile sexuality; fixation and regression; conflict; symptoms.	Transference; conflict resolution; "Where id was, ego shall be."	Little Hans
Defensive maintenance of self; incongruence.	Therapeutic atmosphere: congruence, unconditional positive regard, empathic understanding.	Mrs. Oak
Disordered functioning of construct system.	Psychological reconstruction of life; invitational mood; fixed-role therapy.	Ronald Barrett
Heredity and environment; conflict; anxiety.	Change in trait structure.	Jim Hersh
Maladaptive learned response patterns.	Extinction; discrimination learning; counter-conditioning; positive reinforcement; imitation; systematic desensitization; behavior modification.	Peter; Joey
Learned response patterns; excessive self-standards; problems in self-efficacy.	Modeling; guided participation; increased self-efficacy.	Reinterpretation of bombardier case.

PERSONALITY

Theory and Research

Fifth Edition

PERSONALITY
Theory and Research

Lawrence A. Pervin
Rutgers, The State University

WILEY

JOHN WILEY & SONS, INC.
New York Chichester Brisbane Toronto Singapore

Acquisitions Editor, Deborah Moore
Managing Editor, Joan Kalkut
Production Manager, Linda Indig
Production Supervisor, Elizabeth Austin
Editorial Supervisor, Gilda Stahl
Manufacturing Manager, Robin Garmise
Photo Research Manager, Stella Kupferberg
Photo Researcher, Anne Manning
Interior & Cover Designer, Dawn L. Stanley

Library of Congress Cataloging-in-Publication Data

Pervin, Lawrence A.
   Personality : theory and research / Lawrence A. Pervin.—5th ed.
     p.   cm.
   Bibliography: p.
   Includes index.

   1. Personality.   I. Title.
BF698.P375 1989
155.2—dc19   88-28355
                                                                   CIP

Printed in Singapore

10 9 8 7 6 5 4 3

To Bobbie, David, and Levi

Preface

The publication of the fifth edition of this book brings to a close 20 years of involvement with presenting the field of personality to students. During this time there have been important changes in the field of personality, most notably developments associated with the cognitive revolution, but the goal that guided the original edition of this text remains the same — to present to the student the many fascinating efforts psychologists have made to understand the complexity of the human personality.

Since my days as a graduate student I have been particularly struck with the interplay between research and applied clinical work. It is my sense that each has something to offer the field, and I have tried to capture these contributions in this book. Theory puts research in a broader context, research is the arena in which the science of personality evolves, and clinical work is the area in which individuals are most appreciated in their full complexity. Thus, in this book I have attempted to present research supportive of each theory as well as cases that illustrate the application of that theory to the understanding of an individual. At the end of the book a college student is considered from the standpoint of each of the major theoretical perspectives, providing the opportunity for review of the theories and comparisons among them.

This book is an outgrowth of my experiences as a student, teacher, researcher, and clinician. I have attempted to be comprehensive in my coverage of the many theories in the field of personality, and at the same time discuss particular theories in sufficient depth to appreciate each point of view. It is important to learn about a particular theory, but it also is important to understand that the field of personality includes many different points of view, each with its own strengths and limitations. We all have preferred ways of understanding people, and thus some of the theories presented will make more sense than others. At the same time, it is important to understand and appreciate each theory on its own terms. The effort here, then, has been to avoid an ideological position and instead to present as accurate a picture as possible of each point of view. It is up to the student then to weigh the evidence and come up with a personal conclusion concerning which theory has the most to offer, or how elements of various theories may be brought together to offer an even richer understanding of people.

Finally, coverage of each theory includes "Current Applications" boxes to illustrate the relevance of emphasized concepts to issues we face in our daily lives. Students often approach the field of personality expecting to learn more about themselves and are disappointed that the theories presented seem so removed from their personal experiences. The theories of personality presented in this text, however, *have* relevance for the student, and hopefully the cases and Current Applications boxes will help to draw the connecting link between theory and application.

What is it, then, that I hope students will gain from reading this book? It is an appreciation for the mystery of people and the efforts of psychologists to unravel this mystery, an appreciation for the contributions that come from work in the clinic, and, finally, the discovery of a particular theory that makes a lot of personal sense as well as respect for the insights offered by alternative approaches.

Personality, in individuals and in the field, is always in a state of evolution. I hope that this edition captures this dynamic aspect of people and the field.

INSTRUCTOR'S MANUAL

Often an instructor's manual merely contains multiple-choice test questions. While including such items, the current manual attempts to go beyond this in terms of being a full teaching resource for the instructor.

The instructor's manual for the fifth edition of the text includes four sections: (1) Suggested Lecture Topics and Resource Materials; (2) Instructional Aids; (3) Questions for Thought and Discussion; (4) Multiple-Choice Test Items. With an occasional exception, each chapter in the text contains these four sections.

There are suggested lecture topics in each chapter that either expand upon material presented in the text or bring in new material that remains directly related to the text. In this way, areas that remain confusing to the student can be clarified and content valued by the instructor and not included in the text can be brought to the attention of the student. Following such a format, the lectures do not duplicate the text but remain integrated with it. In most cases the suggestions include a brief description of the content that might be included in the lecture and a number of references (bibliography included at the end of the manual) that can be reviewed for discussion of the issue under consideration.

The instructional aids section includes films, tapes, and demonstrations that can be presented in conjunction with the text and lectures. For the films and tapes there is a brief description of the content, a listing of the distributor, and, in most cases, price information. The addresses of the distributors are included at the end of the manual.

The questions for thought and discussion section includes items that are designed to challenge the student to make use of what has been learned and to think critically about its implications for further inquiry. The questions are designed to make the student build on and go beyond the information presented. They may serve as a basis for lecture material, as a basis for large or small group discussions, or for essay test questions.

Finally, the multiple-choice items provide a testing resource to check on the progress being made by students. The items are mainly drawn from the original sets developed by Raymond Higgins, Alan Marlatt, and Hanna Levenson, but new items are included to cover new material presented in the fourth edition.

ACKNOWLEDGMENTS

In my efforts to present a comprehensive, scholarly, and interesting textbook I have been assisted by many. Students in my classes have been a constant source of stimulation and useful feedback. The assistance of my son Levi, who has reached the age where he can share with me his critical thoughts and evaluations from the student point of view, has been particularly meaningful. The helpful reviews and suggestions for revision of the following professors is gratefully acknowledged:

Norman R. Simonson
University of Massachusetts at
    Amherst

Daniel Cervone
The University of Illinois at Chicago

Vincent Adesso
The University of Wisconsin at
    Milwaukee

Richard Davison
University of Wisconsin

Jim Council
North Dakota State University

Larry Hjelle
SUNY Brockport

Thomas Schoeneman
Lewis & Clark College

Arnold Buss
University of Texas at Austin

I'm also grateful for the efforts of all of the people at John Wiley & Sons who contributed their skills and talents to the fifth edition, particularly those of my editor, Deborah Moore.

LAWRENCE A. PERVIN

Contents

Chapter Five

Chapter Six

Chapter Ten

Chapter Eleven

Chapter Twelve

Social Cognitive Theory: Applications and Evaluation 405

Chapter Thirteen

A Cognitive, Information-Processing Approach to Personality 429

Chapter Fourteen

A Cognitive, Information-Processing Approach to Personality: Applications and Evaluation 467

Chapter Fifteen

Chapter Sixteen

PERSONALITY

Theory and Research

Chapter One
Personality Theory

CHAPTER FOCUS: How can we define personality, organize what is known, and point to future directions for research? What do we want a theory of personality to do? How can we know when we have a good theory? These are some of the questions we address in this chapter. We discuss what a theory is, what a theory of personality should include, and how to tell how good a theory is. Although theories are based on facts, they are also influenced by the personalities of the psychologists who develop them and by the social times in which they are developed. We therefore approach theories from a human as well as a scientific viewpoint. Finally, we discuss how competition among theories leads to scientific progress.

> *Every person is in certain respects*
> *a. like all other people.*
> *b. like some other people.*
> *c. like no other person.*
>
> *Adapted from* KLUCKHOHN AND MURRAY, 1953, p. 53

> *Probably no field of psychology has been more perplexing to its students with respect to theory than that of personality.*
>
> SEARS, 1950, p. 115

To one extent or another, we all are personality psychologists. That is, we all develop some ideas about people in general, some terms for describing and differentiating among people, and some rules for understanding and predicting the behavior of others. Rarely do we make these ideas and principles explicit, but they nevertheless enter into our thinking and influence our behavior. We describe people we meet in personality terms and, based on our assessment of their personality, make early judgments of whether or not we like them. Our interactions with others are governed, at least in part, by what we feel we can expect of them, based on our understanding of their personality. This is true for us in small decisions, and even more true when we are making major life decisions in relation to others. Yet, again, rarely do we make explicit the framework we are using and open it up for serious investigation. In our everyday functioning, our theories of personality are lived but not scientifically tested.

In a sense, the work of the personality scientist and theorist is not fundamentally different from the work conducted by all of us in our daily lives. The task for each is to develop some model of human functioning, some means for differentiating among people, and some rules for predicting behavior. This model, and the rules for prediction that follow from it, forms the essence of the personality scientist's theory as much as it forms the essence of our theories in our everyday existence. The difference is that personality scientists make their models more explicit, define their terms more clearly, and conduct systematic research to evaluate the quality of their predictions. Whereas in our everyday lives we may be accepting of fuzzy theories and are capable of distorting events or biasing the data to conform to our beliefs, as personality scientists we must be clear about our concepts and as objective as possible about our findings.

DEFINING PERSONALITY

Every person and event is unique. However, there is enough similarity among many people and the events of their lives to consider what they have in common. It is these patterns of human behavior that the psychologist attempts to understand.

In psychology, the field of **personality** is concerned with the total individual and with individual differences. Although recognizing that all people are similar in some ways, those interested in personality are particularly concerned with the ways people differ from one another. Why do some achieve and others not? Why do some perceive things one way and others in a different way? Why do talents vary? Why do some people become mentally ill whereas others do not under similar conditions?

Personality theorists also are concerned with the total person. Thus they attempt to understand the complex relationships among the different aspects of an individual's functioning, including such aspects as learning, perception, and motivation. Personality research is not the study of perception but rather of how individuals differ in their perceptions and how these differences relate to their total functioning. The study of personality focuses not only on a particular psychological process but also on the relationships among different processes. Understanding how these processes act together to form an integrated whole often involves more than an understanding of each of them separately. People function as organized wholes, and it is in the light of such organization that we must understand them.

There are few aspects of human functioning that do not reflect and express an individual's personality. How, then, are we to define personality? To the general public it may represent a value judgment—if you like someone, it is because he or she has a "good" personality. To the scientist and student of personality, the term *personality* is used to define a field of study. A definition of personality reflects the kinds of problems to be studied and the methods to be used in studying these problems.

At present there is no generally agreed-on single definition of personality. Some personality psychologists study the biochemical and physiological aspects of how individuals function and use methods appropriate to these areas of investigation. Other personality psychologists look at individuals and observe their overt behavior. Still others define personality in terms of characteristics, such as unconscious processes, which must be inferred from behavior and cannot be observed directly. Finally, some psychologists define personality strictly as the ways in which individuals interact with other individuals or as the roles that individuals use to function in society. Thus, these and other possible definitions of personality range from processes internal to the organism to overt behavior in an interpersonal context.

It is clear that various definitions of personality are possible and have been used. Each leads to a concentration on different kinds of behavior and to the use of different methods of study. These definitions may be more concrete or more abstract. They may describe what goes on inside individuals, or how individuals interact with each other. They may describe what is directly observable or what must be inferred. They may define what is unique to particular individuals or what is characteristic of most, or all, individuals.

In considering definitions of personality it is important to keep two issues in mind. First, a definition reflects the kinds of behavior the psychologist will pay attention to and the kinds of methods that will be used to study this behavior. Second, there is no one right or wrong definition of personality. Definitions of personality are not necessarily true or false but are more or less useful to psychologists in assessing personality, in pursuing research, and in communicating their findings to others. Insofar as they lead to an increase in our ability to understand, predict, and influence behavior, they are more or less useful to psychology as a science.

For the present, the following is suggested as a working definition of personality: *Personality represents those characteristics of the person or of people generally that account for consistent patterns of behavior.* A number of points can be made in this context. First, personality concepts must be defined in terms that permit psychologists to agree on ways to observe and measure behavior. To study personality systematically we must be able to agree on what we are looking at and how we are to measure it. Second, personality is characterized by regularities in one individual's functioning as well as by regularities that are similar from person to person. Although we are each unique in some ways, in other ways we are like some other people and in some ways we are like all other people. Personality is a concept that expresses such regularities within a person and similarities between people. Personality represents the attributes of individuals that distinguish them from other individuals and make them unique as well as the attributes of functioning that are common to all humans. Third, personality includes both the more stable, unchanging aspects of the person's functioning—sometimes called *structure*—and the more fluid, changing aspects—sometimes called *process*. Just as the system of the physical organism consists of parts of the body and various processes relating these parts to one another, so the psychological organism consists of stable parts and fluid processes that relate the parts to one another. In this sense, the personality is a system. Fourth, personality includes cognitions (thought processes), affects (emotions), as well as overt behaviors. Perhaps most of all, personality concerns the complex relationships among cognitive, affective, and overt behavioral processes in the person. Finally, it may be noted that these processes occur in relation to stimuli and situations, some created by the surrounding environment and others created by the person. What is important to recognize is that people do not operate in a vacuum, but rather that they respond to and express themselves in relation to situations and circumstances.

To understand people in terms of such complexity is a tall order. As noted, it is something that each of us attempts to do, more or less successfully, on a daily basis. The task for personality theorists and researchers, however, is to be more objective in their observations and more open to public evaluation in the theories they develop.

Our working definition is based on certain assumptions about the nature of human personality:

1. *The human organism has characteristics distinct from those of other species that are particularly important for the study of personality.* Compared with members of other species, we are less dependent on biological influences and more dependent on psychosocial factors. We are less dependent than members of other species on primary sources of motivation such as hunger and thirst. Our considerable ability for thinking and language means that we can communicate and transmit learned patterns of behavior (culture) to a degree unique among the species. This ability also means that we have a lengthened perspective of past and future, and therefore we need not be bound by immediately present stimuli. Further, it means that we can reflect upon ourselves—we can consider ourselves as objects, so to speak. We can both experience and reflect on our experience; we can be ourselves and think about being ourselves. Finally—and very important for understanding personality—the human organism has a slower rate of maturation than members of other species.

2. *Human behavior is complex.* An understanding of personality must include an appreciation of the complexity of human behavior. Often there are many reasons for an individual's behavior, which may vary from person to person, although the observable behavior

may be the same. The same events may be understood differently by different individuals, and the same behavior may have different roots in different individuals. Complexity also exists because behavior arises not only from personalities but also in relation to situations and circumstances.

3. *Behavior is not always what it appears to be.* There is no fixed relationship between a certain behavior and its causes; there may be different causes for the same behavior shown by two individuals at one time or by the same individual at different times. To understand the significance or meaning of an act for the individual, we must know something about that individual and about the situation in which the act occurred.

4. *We are not always aware of or in control of the factors determining our behavior.* This follows from the concept of the unconscious, although it is not necessary to accept all aspects of the Freudian view of the unconscious to agree with it. This simply suggests that at times people cannot explain why they act in ways contrary to their own expressed wishes. Whether these acts are significant or minor, frequent or infrequent, they occur and remain to be accounted for in some way.

These qualities of human functioning greatly complicate our efforts to measure, interpret, and predict behavior. They suggest that often we capture only glimpses of a person. Although they make the study of personality frustrating, frequent surprises and occasional insights into patterns of behavior also make it exciting.

The scientific exploration of personality, then, attempts to understand how people are alike while recognizing that individuals are unique in some ways. It attempts to discover, understand, and explain regularities in human behavior. Further, it develops theories to help order phenomena and to suggest strategies for further research. There are many theories of personality. They range from those believed by the general public and used by them in their daily living to those developed through the use of sophisticated mathematical techniques and computer technology. Each theory tends to look at different behavior or to study the same behavior in different ways. Therefore, it is hardly surprising that the field often is so perplexing to students of human behavior.

PERSONALITY THEORY AS AN ANSWER TO THE QUESTIONS OF WHAT, HOW, AND WHY

If we study individuals intensively, we want to know *what* they are like, *how* they became that way, and *why* they behave as they do. Thus, we want a theory to answer the questions of *what*, *how*, and *why*. The "what" refers to the characteristics of the person and how they are organized in relation to one another. Is the person honest, persistent, and high in need for achievement? The "how" refers to the determinants of a person's current personality. To what extent and in what ways did genetic and environmental forces interact to produce this result? The "why" refers to the reasons for the individual's behavior. Answers refer to the motivational aspects of the individual—why he or she moves at all, and why in a specific direction. If an individual seeks to make a lot of money, why was this particular path chosen? If a child does well in school, is it to please parents, to use talents, to bolster self-esteem, or to show up friends? Is a mother overprotective because she happens to be affectionate, because she seeks to give her children what she missed as a child, or because she seeks to avoid any expression of the resentment and hostility she feels for the child? Is a person depressed as a result of humiliation, because of the loss of a loved one, or because of feelings of guilt? A theory should help us understand to what extent depression is characteristic of a person, how this personality characteristic developed, why depression is experienced in specific circumstances, and why the person behaves in a certain manner when depressed. If two people tend to be depressed, why does one go out and buy things whereas another withdraws into a shell? Let us consider questions such as these in more systematic detail.

Structure

Theories can be compared in terms of the concepts they use to answer the what, how, and why of personality. **Structural concepts** refer to the more stable and enduring aspects of personality. They represent the building blocks of personality theory. In this sense they are comparable to parts of the body or to concepts such as atoms and molecules in physics. Such structural concepts as *response*, *habit*, *trait*, and *type* have been popular in efforts to conceptualize what people are like. The concept of trait refers to the consistency of individual response to a variety of situations, and approximates the kind of concept the layman uses to describe people. Examples of traits are rigidity, honesty, and emotionality. The concept of type refers to the clustering of many different traits. Compared to the trait concept, that of type implies a greater degree of regularity and generality to behavior. Although people can have one or another degree of many traits, they are generally described as being a specific type. For example, individuals have been described as being introverts or extroverts—and in terms of whether they move toward, away from, or against others (Horney, 1945).

It is possible to use conceptual units other than trait or type to describe personality structure. Theories of personality differ in the kinds of units or structural concepts they use. They also differ in the way they conceptualize the organization of these units. Some theories involve a *complex* structural system, one in which many component parts are linked to one another in a variety of ways. Other theories involve a *simple* structural system, in which a few component parts have few connections to one another. The human brain is a far more complex structure than the brain of a fish because it has more parts, which can be distinguished from one another, and more linkages or interconnections among these parts. Theories of personality also differ in the extent to which they view the structural units as organized in a hierarchy, that is, in the extent to which some structural units are seen as higher in order and therefore as controlling the functioning of other units. The human nervous system is more complex than that of other species, not only because it has more different parts and more linkages among them but also because some parts, like the brain, regulate the functioning of other parts in the system. An analogy can be found in business structures. Some business organizations are more complex than others. Complex business organizations have many units, with many linkages among the units, and a ranking of people who have responsibility for making decisions. Simple business organizations have few units, few linkages among the units, and few levels in the chain of command — General Motors, say, as opposed to a mom-and-pop store. Similarly, personality theories differ in the numbers and kinds of structural units they emphasize and in the extent to which they emphasize complexity or organization within the system.

Process

Just as theories can be compared in their structures, so they can be compared in the dynamic, *motivational concepts* they use to account for behavior. These concepts refer to the **process** aspects of human behavior.

Again think of the human body. It can be considered both as an organization of parts and as processes that relate those parts one to another. Similarly, a business organization consists of units and processes through which the units function in relation to one another and to the outside world. Organizational processes could, for example, be described in terms of how much conflict exists among the parts and how that conflict is handled.

Some theories view personality processes as resulting from efforts of the individual to reduce tension. Other theories emphasize the efforts of the organism toward growth and self-fulfillment. According to the former view, physiological needs within the organism create tensions that the individual seeks to reduce by satisfying needs. Hunger or thirst creates tension that can be relieved by eating or drinking. According to the latter view, individuals seek to grow and realize their inner potentials even at the cost of increased tension.

The most widely accepted model for earlier theories of motivation was, in fact, that of tension reduction. The organism was viewed as seeking a state of rest, quiet, or balance—often called *homeostasis* or *equilibrium*. Pleasure was to be derived from satisfying needs or reducing tension. Recently, research on animals and humans has suggested that organisms often seek tension. Monkeys, for example, will work to solve puzzles independent of any reward—in fact, rewards may interfere with their performance. The exploratory and play behavior of members of many species is well known. Observations such as these led R. W. White (1959) to formulate a process in human functioning that he called **competence motivation.** According to this view, a significant process in personality functioning is the motivation toward dealing competently or effectively with the environment. Individuals appear to take pleasure in increasing tension or excitement and in trying out new behaviors. As individuals mature, more of their behavior appears to be involved with developing skills merely for the sake of mastery or for dealing effectively with the environment, and less of their behavior appears to be exclusively in the service of reducing tension.

The concept of competence motivation has served to emphasize behaviors neglected by earlier theorists, but we need not choose between the tension reduction and the competence motivation models of person-

Motivation—Personality theories emphasize different kinds of motivation (e.g., tension-reduction, self-actualization, power, etc.)

ality dynamics. As one leading motivational theorist (Maslow, 1954) suggests, it is likely that at times the individual is stimulated by physiological needs and seeks to reduce tension, at other times is stimulated by self-fulfilling tendencies, and at yet other times is stimulated by social needs for praise and respect. Such an integrated view is possible, but theorists have tended to use one or another model to account for the more momentary, fluid aspects of human behavior.

Growth and Development

Growth and *development* are related to the concepts of structure and process in personality theory. An interpretation of growth and development must account for changes in structure from infancy to maturity, and for the corresponding developments in process. Significant among the *environmental determinants of personality* are experiences individuals have as a result of membership in a particular culture. Each culture has its own institutionalized and sanctioned patterns of learned behaviors, rituals, and beliefs. The institutionalization of some behavior patterns means that most members of a culture will have certain personality characteristics in common. Even in a complex society like ours, one in which the number and rigidity of institutionalized patterns of behavior are minimal, the importance of cultural forces in shaping personality functioning is considerable. These forces influence our needs and means of satisfying them, our relationships to authority, our self-concepts, our experiences of the major forms of anxiety and conflict, and our ways of dealing with them. They affect what we think is funny and sad, how we cope with life and death, what we view as healthy and sick. In the words of an eminent anthropologist: "Culture regulates our lives at every turn. From the moment we are born until we die there is, whether we are conscious of it or not, constant pressure upon us to follow certain types of behavior that other men have created for us" (Kluckhohn, 1949, p. 327).

Although certain patterns of behavior develop as a result of membership in a culture, others develop as a result of membership in some social class of the population. Few aspects of an individual's personality can be understood without reference to the group to which that person belongs. One's social class group—whether lower class or upper class, working class or professional—is of particular importance. Social class factors help determine the status of individuals, the roles they perform, the duties they are bound by, and the privileges they enjoy. These factors influence how they see themselves and how they perceive members of other social classes, how they earn and spend money. Like cultural factors, social class factors influence the ways individuals define situations and how they respond to them. There is evidence that social class factors are related in a population to the prevalence of mental illness and to the types of mental disorders found. In a study of social class and mental illness, Hollingshead and Redlich (1958) found that although each type of mental disorder occurs in all social classes, proportions in the various classes differ. For example, upper-class patients tended to be neurotic and lower-class patients to be psychotic. Within the neurotic and psychotic categories, members of different classes tended to behave differently.

Beyond the similarities determined by environmental factors such as membership in the same culture or social class, environmental factors lead to considerable variation in the personality functioning of members of a single culture or class. Of particular significance among these is the influence of the family. Parents may be warm and loving or hostile and rejecting, overprotective and possessive or aware of their children's need for freedom and autonomy. Each pattern of parental behavior affects the personality development of the child. For some time personality researchers mainly were interested in environmental differences between families. However, more recently attention has focused on differences within a family. Thus, while clearly family environments differ from one another, children within the same family experience different environments depending, for example, on their birth order or on parental relationships at the time they were maturing.

Some theories of personality attach particular importance to early social interaction between infant and mother. The interpersonal relations theory of Sullivan (1953), for example, suggests that a significant component of personality is the *self-system* (a person's perceptions of the

Genetic Influences on Personality Development—Personality development reflects the interaction of environmental and genetic forces. The triplets pictured here had been separated in infancy and discovered one another as young men. They found that they not only looked alike but smiled and talked in the same way.

self), which develops out of relationships with significant figures in the environment. During infancy the developing self-system is influenced by the amount of anxiety the mother communicates, often in a subtle way, to the child. In later years, the self-system is influenced by reflected appraisals — how the individual perceives others as perceiving and responding to him or her. Of particular significance here is whether the person sees the self as good or bad as a result of perceptions of the evaluative judgments made by others.

Parents influence their children's behavior in at least three important ways:

1. Through their own behavior they present situations that elicit certain behavior in children (e.g., frustration leads to aggression).
2. They serve as role models for identification.
3. They selectively reward behaviors.

Along with environmental factors, genetic factors play a major role in determining personality, particularly in relation to what is unique in the individual. Although many psychologists historically have argued the relative importance of environmental and genetic factors in shaping personality as a whole, recent theorists have recognized that the importance of these factors may vary from one personality characteristic to another. Genetic factors are generally more important in such characteristics as intelligence and temperament, and less important in regard to values, ideals, and beliefs. Theorists have also begun to explore possible interactions between genetic and environmental factors. Thus, for example, the concept of *reaction range* (Gottesman, 1963) suggests that although heredity fixes a number of possible behavioral outcomes, environment ultimately determines the behavior. That is, heredity may set a range within which the further development of the characteristic is determined by the environment. However, the relationship may be even more complicated than this since genetically influenced characteristics may lead the person to act upon, and in return be influenced by, the environment in a particular way. For example, the hyperactive child evokes different responses from parents than does the tranquil child. Thus, rather than a simple cause–effect relationship we have an ongoing interaction or reciprocal process between heredity and environment.

In summary, personality is determined by many interacting factors, including genetic, cultural, social class, and familial forces. Heredity sets limits on the range of development of characteristics; within this range, characteristics are determined by environmental forces. Heredity provides us talents that a culture may or may not reward and cultivate. It is possible to see the interaction of these many genetic and environmental forces in any significant aspect of personality. Theories of personality differ in the importance attributed to questions of growth and development, in the relative weight given to genetic and environmental factors, and in interpretations of the mechanisms through which personality development occurs. Ultimately, however, it is the task of any personality theory to account for the development of structures and patterns of behaving. A theory of personality should explain what is developed, how it is developed, and why it is developed.

Psychopathology and Behavior Change

In attempting to account for these varied aspects of human behavior, a complete theory of personality must include analyses of why some people are capable of coping with the stresses of daily life and generally experience satisfaction, whereas others develop psychopathological responses (abnormal behavior due to psychological causes). Further, such a theory should suggest psychotherapies or means by which pathological forms of behavior can be modified. Although not all personality theorists are therapists, a complete theory of personality should suggest how and why people change or resist change.

Summary

This section has explored five areas that a complete theory of personality must take into account and in relation to which theories of personality can be compared: structure, process, development, psychopathology, and change. These areas represent conceptual abstractions: A person is not structure or process, and what appears as structure at one moment may appear as process at another. For example, someone may be said to have a strong conscience (structure) that makes him or her feel guilty (process). Such conceptual abstractions, convenient devices for understanding and explaining human behavior, are found in biology as well as psychology. Similarly, development and change are neither independent of structure or process nor independent of one another. They represent an effort to find pattern and regularity in human behavior, ways in which individuals are similar and ways in which they are unique. The concepts developed by a theory represent efforts toward accounting for the organization of personality characteristics—what we have labeled the what, how, and why of personality.

IMPORTANT ISSUES IN PERSONALITY THEORY

A theory of personality must conceptualize the varied areas of functioning that have been described. A number of theories have attempted this difficult task. Throughout the relatively brief history of personality theory, a number of issues have confronted theorists repeatedly. The ways in which they treat these issues do much to define the major characteristics of each theoretical position. Thus, in reviewing various personality theories we need to keep certain issues in mind, to see how much attention each theorist gives to these issues and how that theorist resolves each issue.

Philosophical View of the Person

A philosophical view concerning the fundamental nature of the human organism tends to underlie current personality theories. One theory emphasizes the instinctual aspect of humans, another the social; one theory stresses free will, another determinism; one theory discusses simple and mechanistic relationships, another complex and dynamic ones; one theory views the person as an organism that reasons, chooses, and decides (rational view), another views the person as an organism that is driven, compelled, irrational (animal view). A third theory views the person as automatically responding to outside stimuli (machine view), whereas a fourth views the person as processing information like a computer (computer view). Philosophical assumptions concerning human nature are important because they focus on specific problems and lead to particular forms of research.

Proponents of different points of view have had different life experiences and have been influenced by different historical traditions. Thus, beyond scientific evidence and fact, theories of personality are influenced by personal factors, by the spirit of the time (Zeitgeist) and by philosophical assumptions characteristic of members of a given culture (Pervin, 1984). Although based on observed data, theories selectively emphasize certain kinds of data and go beyond what is known, and therefore can be influenced by personal and cultural factors. In developing a personality theory, individuals are influenced by important events in their own lifetimes. To some extent, in developing psychological theories we talk about ourselves. This in itself is not a problem. Only when personal experiences become more important than other kinds of experience and ignore research evidence do personal determinants of a theory become a problem.

Along with these personal determinants are the influences on the theorist of the prevailing mood or spirit within the field at the time — the **Zeitgeist.** There are phases in psychology during which one topic of research is emphasized and one point of view stressed. For example, for some time personality theory emphasized the importance of drives or needs that appeared to have some physiological basis. More recent theory has tended to emphasize cognitive factors — how individuals come to organize and conceptualize their environment. Reflecting the Zeitgeist, both types of theory emphasize certain kinds of empirical observations and suggest that research follow a defined path.

Internal and External Determinants of Behavior

One critical issue that tends to express an underlying philosophical view concerns the relationship between internal and external behavior determinants. All theories of personality recognize that factors inside the organism, and events in the surrounding environment, are important in determining behavior. However, the theories differ in the level of importance given to internal and external determinants and in their interpretation of the relationship between the two (Pervin & Lewis, 1978). Consider, for example, the difference between Freud's view that we are controlled by unknown, internal forces and Skinner's suggestion that "a person does not act upon the world, the world acts upon him" (1971, p. 211). Whereas the Freudian views the organism as active and responsible for behavior, the Skinnerian views it as a passive victim of controlling events in the environment. The Freudian view suggests that we focus our attention on what is going on *inside* the person; the Skinnerian view suggests that such efforts are foolhardy and that we would be wise to concentrate on environmental variables.

Although the Freudian and Skinnerian views may represent extremes that many psychologists avoid, most psychologists nevertheless weight their theories in the direction of internal or external factors. Periodically there is a shift in emphasis from internal to external factors or vice versa, with an occasional call for investigation of the relationship between the two. For example, in the 1940s one psychologist spoke out against the prevalent tendency to overestimate the importance of internal (person) relative to external (environmental) factors in personality (Ichheiser, 1943); in the 1970s another psychologist was asking "Where is the person in personality research?" (Carlson, 1971). Most recently debate concerning the role of internal and external forces in governing behavior has been highlighted in the *person–situation controversy*. In 1968, the social learning theorist Walter Mischel wrote a book, *Personality and Assessment*, that criticized traditional personality theories for their emphasis on stable and enduring internal structures, which leads to the perception of people's behavior as fairly unchanging over time and across situations. Instead of emphasizing broad personality characteristics that function independently of external factors, Mischel suggested that changes in environmental or external conditions modify how people behave. Such changes result in relatively situation-specific behavior: each environmental situation acts independently to affect individual behavior.

Since the publication of Mischel's book and its development of this issue, considerable attention has been given to the internal–external (or person–situation) controversy. First there was debate about whether persons or situations control behavior, then about whether persons or situations are more important, and, finally, acceptance of the view that both are important and interact with one another (Endler & Magnusson,

1976; Magnusson & Endler, 1977). Almost all researchers today suggest an emphasis on person–situation interaction, even though fundamental disagreements remain. Even when persons, situations, and interactions are all accepted as important, there are theoretical differences about *what* in the person interacts *how* and with *what* in the situation. Thus, the internal–external debate remains lively and is an issue to be kept in mind in considering various theoretical points of view (Pervin, 1985).

The Unity of Behavior and the Concept of the Self

Most psychologists agree that human behavior results not only from the operation of specific parts but also from the relationships among these parts. To a certain extent this is true for a mechanical system such as an automobile; it is even truer for a living system such as the human body. Rather than being made up of isolated responses, human behavior generally expresses *pattern, organization,* and *integration.* Like a smooth-running car, the parts are operating in harmony with one another. They all seem to function together toward their common goals, instead of each part functioning independently toward different goals that may be in conflict with one another. Indeed, when behavior appears disorganized and disintegrated, we suspect that something is drastically wrong with the person. How, then, are we to formulate this pattern and organization? What is it that gives an integrative quality to behavior? The concept of the **self** has often been used in this regard, but whereas many personality theorists give major attention to this concept, others choose to disregard it entirely.

Traditionally the concept of the self has been emphasized for three reasons. First, our awareness of ourselves represents an important aspect of our phenomenological or subjective experience. Second, considerable research suggests that how we feel about ourselves influences our behavior in many situations. Third, the concept of the self is used to express the organized, integrated aspects of human personality functioning. In asking whether the concept of the self is necessary, the noted theorist Gordon Allport suggested that many psychologists have tried in vain to account for the integration, organization, and unity of the human person by not making use of the concept of the self. For example, many behavioral psychologists have found it difficult to discuss the person as a whole because they deny the importance of internal factors. Other psychologists, after struggling with a fragmented conceptualization of personality, have returned to the concept of self as a way of representing the coherence, unity, and goal-directedness of human behavior (Allport, 1955).

Without a concept of self, the theorist is left with the task of developing an alternative concept to express the integrated aspects of human functioning. On the other hand, reliance on the concept of the self leaves the theorist with the task of defining self in a way that makes it possible to be studied systematically rather than leaving it vaguely defined as

The Concept of Self—Personality psychologists are interested in how the concept of self develops and helps to organize experience.

some strange inner being. Thus, how to account for the organized aspects of personality, and the utility of the concept of the self in this regard, remains a major issue of concern for personality psychologists.

Varying States of Awareness and the Concept of the Unconscious

A fourth issue of continuing concern to most personality theorists is how to conceptualize the role of varying states of consciousness in individual functioning. Most psychologists grant that the potential for different states of consciousness exists. The effects of drugs, along with interest in Eastern religion and techniques of meditation, have served to heighten the concern of personality theorists with the whole range of altered states of consciousness. Most theorists also accept the view that we are not always attentive to or aware of factors that influence our behavior. However, many are uncomfortable with Freud's theory of the unconscious. They feel that it is used to account for too much, and that it does not lend itself to empirical investigation. But how are we to account for such diverse phenomena as slips of the tongue, dreams, occasional inability to give a "rational" explanation for our behavior, and our ability under special circumstances to remember events of the past that appeared to have been forgotten? Are these related or separate phenomena? Must they be understood in terms of the working of an unconscious, or are alternative explanations possible? As we shall see, the issue here is important not only in relation to personality theory but also in relation to personality measurement. To what extent can we rely on people to give accurate reports concerning themselves? Are they aware of some things, but unaware of others? Does such lack of awareness serve a protective

Important Issues in Personality Theory

function for the individual? In relation to the concept of the self, are people aware of all their feelings about and perceptions of themselves or are some of these feelings and perceptions unconscious? If we cannot recognize some important feelings about and perceptions of ourselves, what are the implications of this fact on attempts at measurement of the self concept?

Relationships among Cognition, Affect, and Overt Behavior

Earlier in this chapter personality was defined as including cognitions (thought processes), affects (emotions, feelings), and overt behavior. Not all psychologists agree that these are all worthy of investigation and, even where such agreement exists, there are major differences concerning relationships among them. As we shall see later in the text, radical behaviorism led to a focus on overt behavior and the rejection of investigation of internal processes such as thoughts and feelings. Then, starting in the 1950s, a cognitive revolution took place in psychology that led to the field being dominated by cognitive theories. For some time the area of affect was ignored, though in recent years there are signs of a strong developing interest in affect, both in its own right and in its implications for thought and action.

Personality psychologists differ in the relative weight or attention they give to each of these areas of functioning. This is of particular interest since it concerns what is investigated, how research is conducted, and how we assess personality. That is, different methods of personality investigation and assessment are involved in the study of human thoughts, feelings, and behaviors. Personality psychologists also differ in their views of the causal relations among thoughts, feelings, and behaviors.

It is interesting to think about one's own personality and consider the relevance of these phenomena. For example, how much of your personality is expressed in overt behavior? Could we know all there is to know about you from observing your overt behavior? From knowing your thoughts? From knowing your feelings? Or, does personality involve all three and, most significantly, relationships among what you are thinking, what you are feeling, and how you behave?

For some time cognitive psychologists have argued that cognitions are primary in causal relationships, that is, they cause both feelings and behaviors. Other psychologists, however, have argued that affects or emotions are primary and can direct thought processes. Such psychologists also argue that affects are important in the development and channelizing of motivation. Finally, there has lately been a growing acceptance of the view that thought, feeling, and overt behavior influence each other mutually or reciprocally (Pervin, 1983, 1984).

The Influence of the Past, Present, and Future on Behavior

A final issue that may be noted here is the importance of the past, present, and future in governing behavior. Theorists would undoubtedly agree that behavior can be influenced only by factors operating in the present. In this sense, only the present is important in understanding behavior. But the present can be influenced by experience of the remote past or of the recent past. Similarly, what one is thinking about in the present can be influenced by thoughts about the immediate future or about the distant future. People vary in the extent to which they worry about the past and the future. And personality theorists differ in their concern with and conceptualization of the past and the future as determinants of behavior in the present. At one extreme lies psychoanalytic theory, which attaches importance to early learning experiences. At the other extreme lies cognitive theory, which emphasizes the individual's plans for the future. However, the issue is not whether events that happened in the past can have lasting effects or whether anticipations about the future can have effects in the present (theorists undoubtedly would agree that both are possible and occur), but how to conceptualize the role of past experiences and future anticipations and connect their influence to what is occurring in the present.

Summary

In attempting to account for the *what*, *how*, and *why* of human functioning, personality theorists are confronted with many issues. Six issues of particular importance have been mentioned here: (1) the philosophical view of the person; (2) the relation between internal (person) and external (situation) influences in determining behavior; (3) the concept of the

The Effects of Early Experience—The suggestion has been made that some historic figures, such as Fidel Castro, have been driven to achieve greatness to overcome the stigma associated with their being born out of wedlock (Bourne, 1986). Psychologists generally agree that early experiences can be important for personality development, but they disagree on whether these experiences lead to the development of relatively fixed personality characteristics.

self and how to account for the organized aspects of personality functioning; (4) the role of varying states of awareness and the concept of the unconscious; (5) the relationships among cognition, affect, and behavior; and (6) the role of the past, present, and future in governing behavior. Of course, many other issues concern personality theorists and account for differences among them, but the purpose here has been to point to the main ones. The importance of these and other issues will become increasingly clear as we consider the positions of the various theorists in the chapters that follow.

THEORY AND THEORETICAL ISSUES

A theory of personality suggests ways of bringing together and systematizing a wide variety of findings. It also may suggest which directions in research are potentially the most useful. Stated most simply, theories help to pull together what we know and to suggest how we may discover what is yet unknown. Stated more systematically, a **theory** consists of a set of assumptions and concepts that tie together various empirical findings and suggest new relationships among them that should obtain under certain defined conditions. Viewed in this light, theories involve systematic ordering of ideas and planned approaches to research.

This description could lead to the assumption that the place of theory in psychology is well accepted and that there is consensus about its desirability. However, just as there is disagreement about the view of the person implied in a theory, so there is disagreement concerning the positive contributions of theory and the proper time for its development in psychology. There are those who emphasize that theories sharpen research objectives, make research more organized, and help the psychologist avoid wasting time on meaningless or irrelevant variables. "My argument is that it is only with the rubble of bad theories that we should be able to build better ones, and without theory of some kind, somewhere, psychological observation and description would at best be chaotic and meaningless" (Hebb, 1951, p. 39).

In contrast, there are those who argue that theories inhibit the search for new variables in a variety of areas. Here theory is seen as masking the discovery of new ideas. Accidental discoveries are used to illustrate how science can progress without—indeed, in spite of—theory. Whereas the former view emphasizes the contributions of theory to the development of new lines of research and new techniques, the latter view emphasizes how much of theory-related research takes a wrong path and eventually is discarded (Skinner, 1950).

Those who choose to use theories suggest that facts acquire significance only in the light of theory and that theory makes research cumulative. Those who choose to operate without theory suggest that we should pay attention to gathering facts and develop theories only after we have a considerable body of knowledge upon which to base them. Although some theorists feel that concepts such as drive and need add to understanding, others do not. "In the final analysis of behavior, is it not simpler to say a man drinks because he has been deprived of water for six hours rather than to say because he is thirsty? Such statements as 'thirsty' are perfectly acceptable in common parlance but cannot be allowed in scientific analysis" (Lundin, 1961, p. 40).

Theory is not something that can be taken lightly. It can be useful or destructive, guiding or misleading, revealing or blinding. Yet is it possible to function without theory? B. F. Skinner, a leading learning theorist, believes that it is and argues for caution in the use of theory. On the other hand, others argue that with all the possible variables and phenomena to be studied, only some are chosen, and that the selectivity involved in choice must assume some theory. If selection is not made on the basis of conscious theory, it is made on the basis of unconscious forces (Miller, 1951). To the extent that this may be the case, it seems reasonable to argue in favor of conscious, well-formulated theories. As noted earlier, the task of personality psychologists is to make their theories explicit and open to scientific examination.

Evaluation of Theories

How can we evaluate theories of personality? The criteria for such an analysis follow from the functions of theory—the organization of existing information and the selection of fruitful areas for investigation. The corresponding criteria for evaluation of theories of personality are *comprehensiveness, parsimony* or *simplicity,* and *research relevance* (Hall & Lindzey, 1957). The first two relate to the organizing function of theory and the third to its guiding function.

A good theory is comprehensive in that it encompasses and accounts for a wide variety of data. Such a theory is directed to each of the realms of behavior discussed previously. It is important to ask how many different kinds of phenomena the theory can account for. However, we must not be merely quantitative. No theory can account for everything, so one must also ask whether the phenomena accounted for by one theory are as important or central to human behavior as the phenomena encompassed by another theory. It is important to recognize that comprehensiveness includes both the number and the significance of the facts accounted for by the theory.

Along with being comprehensive, a theory should be simple and parsimonious. It should account for varied phenomena in an economical, internally consistent way. A theory that makes use of a different concept for every aspect of behavior or of concepts that contradict one another is a poor theory. These goals of simplicity and comprehensiveness in turn raise the question of the appropriate level of organization and abstraction of a personality theory. As theories become more comprehensive and more parsimonious, they tend to become more abstract. It is important that, in becoming abstract, theories retain concepts that relate in clear ways to the behavior studied. In other words, fuzzy or unclear concepts should not be the price paid for a theory becoming more comprehensive.

Finally, a theory is not true or false but useful or not useful. A good theory has research relevance in that it leads to many new hypotheses, which can then be confirmed empirically. It has what Hall and Lindzey call empirical translation: it specifies variables and concepts in such a way that there is agreement about their meaning and about their potential for measurement. Empirical translation means that the concepts in a theory are clear, explicit, and lead to the expansion of knowledge; they must have predictive power. In other words, a theory must contain testable hypotheses about relationships among phenomena. A theory that is not open to the "negative test," one that potentially cannot be shown to be inaccurate, is a poor theory. This would lead to argument and debate, but not to scientific progress. Whatever the life of a theory, if it has led to new insights and new research techniques it has made a valuable contribution to science. "Theories of psychology are seldom disproved; they just fade away. Of course, all present theories of personality are doomed to pass into history. They should be tolerated only in proportion to their heuristic value to research" (Jensen, 1958, p. 295).

These criteria of comprehensiveness, parsimony, and research relevance provide the basis for a comparative evaluation of theories of personality. In comparing theories, however, we should have two questions in mind: Do they address themselves to the same phenomena? Are they at the same stage of development? Two theories that deal with different kinds of behavior may each be evaluated in relation to these three criteria. Nevertheless, we need not choose between the two theories. Each can be allowed to lead to new insights, with the hope that at some point both can be integrated into a single more comprehensive theory. Finally, a new and immature theory may be unable to account for many phenomena but may lead to a few important observations and show promise of becoming more comprehensive with time. Such a theory may be unable to explain phenomena considered to be understood by another established theory but may represent a breakthrough in significant areas formerly left untouched.

Theory and the History of Scientific Progress

We have discussed ways to evaluate theories and the importance of evaluating a theory in relation both to the phenomena it attempts to explain and to its stage of development. A look at the history of developments in most fields of science will help us understand some of the relevant issues. According to Kuhn (1970), there have been three distinct **stages of scientific development:** an early developmental stage, a stage of normal science, and a period of scientific revolution. The *early develop-*

mental stage of scientific activity is characterized by continual competition between a number of distinct schools or views of nature. Each school believes it functions according to the dictates of scientific method and observation. Indeed, what differentiates these competing views is not the degree of commitment to scientific method but rather their differing ways of viewing the world and of practicing science within it. Since at this stage of development there is no common body of data and belief, each school builds the field anew from its own foundation and chooses its own supporting observations and experiments. Fact gathering during this time has a random quality. One rarely observes a systematic accumulation of knowledge. Essentially, during the early development stage, the field is without a commonly accepted model, or **paradigm,** that defines the field of observations and the methods to be used in research.

The *stage of normal science* begins with the acceptance of such a paradigm or model and is based on clear scientific achievement. During this stage there is acceptance of and commitment to a model that defines which problems are legitimate areas of inquiry and points out the appropriate methods of research. A more rigid definition of the field occurs, research is more focused, observations more restricted, and knowledge more cumulative. Each new bit of knowledge serves as a building block for the next. The scientists during this period are somewhat tradition-bound and are committed to the accepted model. Instead of many competing schools in the field, there tend to be relatively few, and frequently only one.

Since no paradigm or theory can ever explain all facts, ultimately there are some observations during the period of normal science that do not fit the accepted models. These observations or *anomalies* create a crisis in which tradition is shattered and, after a period of turmoil, a new paradigm is accepted. Copernicus, Newton, and Einstein were each associated with a stage of scientific revolution. In each case, a time-honored theory was rejected in favor of a new theory. In each case also, the new theory was incompatible with the old one and offered explanations of critical observations that could not be explained within the earlier paradigm. However, typically, acceptance of the new paradigm occurs after a period of intense competition among competing views and a period of wide-open research. This period thus shares some characteristics with the early developmental phase—competition among alternative views, wide-open research, debate over fundamental issues, occasional recourse to philosophy, and additions to knowledge that are noncumulative. What differentiates this state from the early development stage is that it follows a period of articulation of a paradigm and is a response to specific observations that have presented problems for that paradigm. Although the new paradigm may not be very well articulated and may be limited in scope, it is accepted because it offers solution to critical issues in the field. Rather than representing a competing paradigm or point of view, it replaces an old one and involves a reevaluation of prior fact. Once accepted, the new paradigm is associated with a new period of normal science until new observations arise and the stage is set for a further scientific revolution. The successive transition from one paradigm to another via revolution is the usual developmental pattern of a mature science.

The field of personality today is filled with issues that divide scientists along sharply defined lines and that lead to alternative, competing schools of thought. It is important to recognize that such theoretical differences exist and that they may not be readily resolved by debate or soon resolved by experimental proof. Kuhn suggests that the social sciences are still in the early developmental stage and have not yet arrived at their first universally received paradigm. If this is the case, we should not be surprised to find competing views that make a common claim to science and emphasize different observations and modes of research. Unfortunately, there may be nothing in the laws of science that allows us to choose among these views. And, though they compete with one another, each may result in significant contributions to knowledge in the field.

Theory and the Study of Personality

What then is the role of theory in the study of personality? The entire plan of this book suggests that theory is important to our goals of understanding and explaining human behavior. It can be said that the current state of personality theory is at a low ebb and that what is available is hardly worth considering. It is true that we have not had a good personality theory in some time; perhaps we have never had a good one. But it is on the basis of our past failures that we will have to build future successes. As a minimum, at least we know some directions of investigation that are *not* worthy of our efforts. As Kuhn notes, history suggests that the road to a firm research consensus is extraordinarily difficult.

We can be critical of personality theory, as many rightfully have been, and we can even turn away from theory and devote ourselves to detailed research problems, as many psychologists are doing. But, in the final analysis, theory is necessary, and a good theory of personality will be developed. The choice is not between "theories or no theories," but rather in the degree to which a theory is so tightly constructed that it narrows the potential for "play in research." A theory can be abstract or concrete, complex or simple. It can lead to rigorous research or haphazard research, to the investigation of many problems or the investigation of a few. Freedom to explore and theories of lesser abstraction and complexity are most useful during the early stages of the development of a science. Focused, rigorous, and complex theories are more useful when observation and data are well advanced.

Theory, then, is both inevitable and useful in the study of personality. At this point, our concerns are how explicit we make theories, how good they are, and how well we use them. Theories imply views of humans but we must also appreciate that "in truth, man is at once both biological animal and social product, both master and servant of fate, both rational and irrational, both driver and driven. His behavior can be fully explained only by placing each aspect in its proper perspective. Of all the dynamic physical systems constituting the universe, man is the most complex" (Krech & Crutchfield, 1958, p. 272). Ideally, a theory of personality should involve laws that help us understand how each person is different as well as how all people are the same. In the pursuit of such laws, we must develop theories that will permit coherent organization of what is known, *and* leave room for us to move on to insights into the unknown.

Major Concepts and Summary	personality	self
	structure	theory
	process	comprehensiveness, parsimony (simplicity), research relevance
	tension reduction model	
	competence motivation model	stages of scientific development
	Zeitgeist	paradigm
	person–situation controversy	

A theory consists of a set of assumptions and concepts that tie together empirical findings and suggests new relationships that should hold true under defined conditions. Theories define areas of observation and methods of research. In doing so, they focus attention but may also restrict observation. Theories of personality are expected to answer questions concerning the structure of the organism (what), the processes of personality functioning (why), and the growth and development of these structures and processes (how). In evaluating theories we are interested in the criteria of comprehensiveness, parsimony, and research relevance.

Although it is tempting to believe that science is completely objective and free of personal bias, there is evidence that personal values and arbitrariness affect theories of personality and strategies for research: "An apparently arbitrary element, compounded of personal and historical accident, is always a formative ingredient of the beliefs espoused by a given scientific community in a given time" (Kuhn, 1970, p. 4). Such arbitrariness may be particularly evident during the early developmental stage of a science and may help us understand the conflicting positions that arise in relation to significant issues. Finally, an awareness of the history of scientific progress in other disciplines can help us understand the presence of competing theories of personality today and the potential contributions each may make to future advances.

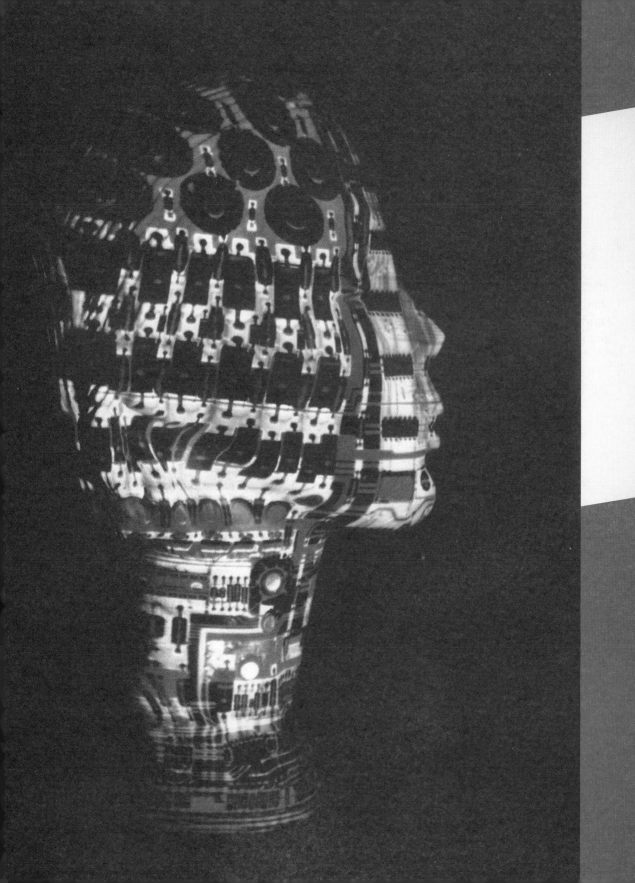

Chapter Two
The
Scientific Study
of People

CHAPTER FOCUS: In this chapter we consider the process of personality research. We discuss alternative approaches as illustrated by research on the concepts of stress, helplessness, and control. The strengths and limitations of each approach are considered as well as the commitments of various investigators to one approach or another. In conclusion, we focus on the human and social forces that influence research, from defining a problem for study to influences on public social policy.

> *The well-known virtue of the experimental method is that it brings situational variables under tight control. It thus permits rigorous tests of hypotheses and confident statements about causation. The correlational method, for its part, can study what man has not learned to control or can never hope to control. . . . The correlator's method is to observe and organize the data from Nature's experiments.*
>
> CRONBACH, 1957, p. 672

> *Different kinds of data and differing levels of information are obtained in the laboratory and the clinic. Each is necessary, useful, and desirable.*
>
> LAZARUS AND DAVISON, 1971, p. 197

In the first chapter it was suggested that all people are personality psychologists in the sense of developing ideas about how to describe people and why they behave as they do. What makes the theories of scientific personality psychologists different is that their theories are more explicit and more open to systematic examination than are those of the ordinary person. Similarly, we are all researchers about personality in the sense of noticing differences between people and observing consistent patterns of behavior within individuals. However, once more there is a difference between the "research" of the ordinary person in the street and that of the personality scientist. As scientists we make our ideas explicit and are systematic in our observations. We follow established procedures to make as sure as possible that our observations are accurate and can be duplicated by others as well. And, as scientists we follow established procedures to determine whether our observations are reliable and stable, as opposed to having occurred by chance or error.

THE SCIENTIFIC STUDY OF PEOPLE

Research has to do with the systematic study of relationships among events. It involves the gathering of data in the search for facts or principles that can be interpreted in a broader theoretical framework. Research forms a connecting link with theory. Theory without research is mere speculation, but unending research without theory is meaningless fact-gathering.

A personality theory attempts to answer the questions of what, how, and why, and suggests that certain relationships should exist among specific phenomena (observed events). Research involves the use of data-gathering techniques to observe relevant phenomena; it attempts to determine whether the suggested relationships do in fact exist. Where there are two competing theories of personality, we look for a crucial test—a place where the two theories predict different relationships and research can determine which relationships exist. This is not to say that our understanding of personality is never advanced by research unrelated to theory or even to "chance" findings; it suggests that the general course of an increase in our understanding is through a relationship between theory and research. This chapter will describe some systematic efforts in personality research, outline some of the issues and problems, and illustrate how personality research tends to reflect differences in theoretical assumptions and styles.

RESEARCH TACTICS AND GUIDING CONCEPTS

Humans are complex animals and research on them is a complex pursuit. Although all personality researchers hold certain goals and scientific values in common, they differ in strategy concerning the best route to these goals. In some cases, the difference in research strategy or tactic is minor, the choice of one experimental procedure or test over another. In other cases, however, the difference is major and expresses a more fundamental difference in approach. In this chapter we will consider three major approaches to personality research—naturalistic observation and clinical research, personality tests and questionnaires, and laboratory research. Before doing so, however, let us consider some of the more general issues that relate to the utilization of one or another approach.

Three General Approaches to Research

Naturalistic observation involves the study of phenomena as they occur in their own environment, without any efforts on the part of the investigator to control what occurs. Ethologists, biologists who study animal behavior in its natural environment, use naturalistic observation as a primary mode of research. Animals are studied in their natural habitats to observe patterns of behavior characteristic of the members of the

Tactics of Research—The psychologist (David Elkin) here illustrates the approach of naturalistic observation by observing children's behavior in an everyday situation.

species. In psychology, the play behavior of children, patterns of mother–infant interaction, aggressive behavior in adolescents, and many other phenomena have been studied through naturalistic observation. **Clinical research** involves the intensive study of individuals in terms of verbal reports, observation of naturally occurring behavior, or the analysis of autobiographical and biographical documents. Verbal reports of what occurred in the natural setting may be used, for example, where direct observation of behavior is impossible. The material gathered by the psychoanalyst Sigmund Freud illustrates this approach.

In considering naturalistic observation and clinical research, it should be noted that they are not identical and do not necessarily follow from one another. Researchers who prefer one of these methods are often critical of the other. However, the two are considered together here because both exemplify a research tradition in which there is minimal experimental control and maximum effort to study phenomena as they occur naturally.

Case studies and the in-depth observations made by clinicians working with patients have played an important role in the development of some major theories of personality. As the theories were evolving, and once they were developed, additional efforts were made to formulate hypotheses that could be tested more systematically, either through the use of personality tests and questionnaires or through experimental means. However, the initial focus of these theorists was on their observations with patients, and it was these clinical observations by them and their followers that continued to play a major role in the further elaboration of the theories.

The approach of **experimental research** involves efforts to gain control over the variables of interest, to manipulate some variables and see the consequences for other variables, and to establish if–then causal relationships. In the experimental approach, for example, the researcher might create conditions of high, moderate, and low anxiety and observe the effects of such varying degrees of anxiety on thought processes or interpersonal behavior. The goal is to produce consistent variation in behavior as a result of specific experimental procedures. It is the consequences that are uniform for all subjects that are of interest. The ideal is to be able to make specific statements about causation, that is, by changing one variable one can produce changes in another variable. The laboratory provides the setting for conducting such research.

In many ways clinical research and experimental research provide a marked contrast with one another. Whereas clinicians make observations as close to life as possible, by and large allow events to unfold, and study but a few individuals, experimental research in the laboratory involves tight control over the variables, the study of many subjects, and interest in the effects on the group of subjects as a whole.

In **correlational research** the investigator seeks to establish an estimate of the relationship between two or more variables that do not readily lend themselves to experimental manipulation and control. Typically the psychologist who follows the correlation tradition is interested

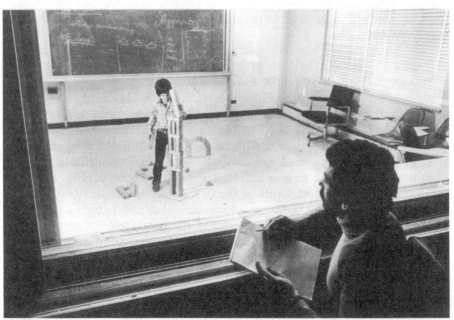

Tactics of Research—The experimenter here is observing the child's behavior through a one-way mirror.

Research Tactics and Guiding Concepts

in differences among individuals, for example, in whether individuals who differ in one personality characteristic also differ in another personality characteristic. Are individuals who are more anxious also less creative? More inhibited in their interpersonal behavior?

Although correlational research can be done with many different types of observations, typically personality tests and questionnaires are used. In such cases the investigator makes use of already developed personality questionnaires or develops a new questionnaire. More will be said later about how this is done, but for now the important point is that in correlational research relationships typically are established between scores on two or more personality tests. This method allows the investigator to study patterns of relationships among individual differences. Although no one individual or group of individuals may be studied as intensively as with the case study approach, the investigator can study many different personality characteristics at one time and determine quantitative relationships among them. The investigator cannot demonstrate control over the variables of interest, as in the experimental method, but relationships among many variables can be studied at one time and there is the opportunity to study variables not easily produced in the laboratory. For these reasons correlational research has been very popular among personality psychologists.

These, then, represent three major approaches to personality research. As we shall see, each is associated with its own advantages and disadvantages. First, however, let us consider the extent to which these approaches have represented different traditions and views among psychologists, and then go on to consider the approaches in relation to some specific research.

Two Disciplines of Scientific Psychology

Periodically a distinguished observer of the field has commented on the existence of two streams of method, thought, and affiliation in psychology—what has been called the two disciplines of psychology (Cronbach, 1957). In 1939 the president of the American Psychological Association distinguished between the *experimental* attitude and the *clinical* attitude, the former emphasizing control over variables and the latter discovery of the totality of the individual (Dashiell, 1939). In 1959, in another presidential address, a contrast was drawn between the *experimental* discipline and the *correlational* discipline, the former again emphasizing control over variables and the latter emphasizing an interest in individual differences and phenomena that do not lend themselves to experimental control (Cronbach, 1957). A contemporary observer of the field of personality notes again the existence of two distinct traditions—each typified by a specific subject matter, methodology, and theoretical orientation (Hogan, 1982). In the one tradition, there is an emphasis on experimental methodology, single aspects of human performance, and what is true for people generally. In the other tradition, there is an emphasis on clinical case study or questionnaire research, individual differences, and relationships among the parts.

In sum, we have evidence of a historical tendency for personality research to follow one of two traditions. In a sense, the traditions differ in attitude or viewpoint. Such a difference need not logically lead to differences in what is studied or how it is studied—subject matter and research methodology. However, these linkages have tended to occur. Thus, historically personality researchers have tended to fall on one or the other side of three basic orientations: (1) "making things happen" in research (experimental) versus "studying what has occurred" (correlational); (2) all persons (experimental) versus the single individual (clinical); and (3) one aspect or few aspects of the person versus the total individual.

RESEARCH ON STRESS AND HELPLESSNESS

The personality theories covered in this text reflect differences in these traditions, and we shall return to this issue later in the chapter. At this point, however, it may be useful to examine the research approaches themselves. The effort here will be to see how data gathered from different research procedures can be consistent and lead to a greater understanding of the phenomena of interest. The topic chosen for illustration —stress and helplessness—was selected because of its intrinsic interest and its current importance in personality research.

Naturalistic Observation and Clinical Research

How have naturalistic observation and clinical research been used in relation to stress and helplessness? The concept of anxiety, related to that of stress, has received considerable clinical attention. The noted psychoanalyst Rollo May, in an early review of the literature, concluded that "the special characteristics of anxiety are the feelings of uncertainty and helplessness in the face of danger" (1950, p. 191). Uncertainty, or lack of cognitive structure, and a sense of helplessness, or lack of control, are mentioned repeatedly in the clinical literature. The former often is expressed in the "fear of the unknown" and is often seen as related to a sense of powerlessness or helplessness—an unknown danger creates a situation where activity cannot be directed toward any one goal, with a resultant feeling of mental paralysis and helplessness (Kris, 1944). Among the many valuable naturalistic and clinical investigations of responses to stress have been the studies by Grinker and Spiegel (1945) of the reactions of World War II flying personnel to battle stress and the studies of Janis (1965) of reactions of individuals to loss and illness.

After World War II, two psychoanalysts (Grinker & Spiegel, 1945) reported on their experiences interviewing and treating individuals engaged in the air battle. Their book, *Men under Stress*, is a fascinating account of the stress that is common for all combatants and the varied reactions that occur among different individuals. After describing the kinds of dangers to which the airmen are exposed and their use of group morale to deal with the constant threats facing them, the authors raise the question: Of what is the airman afraid? Their description of the relationship between helplessness and anxiety runs:

> Although the fear of the aircraft and of human inefficiency are a constant source of stress, the greatest fear is attached to enemy activity. The enemy has only two forms of defense against our combat aircraft: fighter planes and flak [antiaircraft guns]. The enemy's fighter aircraft are efficient and highly respected by our combat crew members. But they are not as great a source of anxiety as flak. Enemy planes are objects that can be fought against. They can be shot down or outmaneuvered. Flak is impersonal, inexorable, and as used by the Germans, deadly accurate. It is nothing that can be dealt with — a greasy black smudge in the sky until the burst is close.
>
> GRINKER AND SPIEGEL, 1945, p. 34

Grinker and Spiegel similarly describe the response of ground forces to enemy air and mortar attack. What is so stressful is that "there is nothing in the environment which can be used to anticipate the approach of danger . . . any stimuli may actually mean the beginning of an attack. Inhibition of anxiety becomes increasingly difficult" (1945, p. 52). According to these psychoanalysts, the initial reaction to such stress is heightened tension and alertness. The person becomes mentally and physically prepared for trouble so as to counteract the threat and avoid loss of control. A variety of means can be used to deal with the threat but, in the final analysis, "mastery, or its opposite, helplessness, is the key to the ultimate emotional reaction" (p. 129). Confidence is lessened by near-misses, physical fatigue, and the loss of friends. Efforts to see the self as invulnerable (incapable of being harmed) become increasingly difficult: "Out of the ensuing helplessness is born the intense anxiety" (p. 129). Some strive to hold on to ideas of personal invulnerability ("It can't happen to me"), whereas others hold on to a faith in magical or supernatural powers ("God is my co-pilot").

Whatever the nature of the efforts, they can be viewed as attempts to deal with the threatened loss of control or experience of helplessness. With prolonged stress, the development of almost any type of neurotic and psychosomatic (psychologically induced illness) reaction is possible. These reactions are grouped under the term *operational fatigue* and generally include a mixture of anxiety, depression, and psychosomatic

Clinical Research—During World War II psychiatrists and psychologists treated and studied combat men under stress, such as flying personnel subjected to enemy flak.

reaction. The depression that is so common in such cases is associated with a sense of failure ("I've let my buddies down") and wounded pride. In sum, the main component of the anxiety is the sense of helplessness in the presence of a perceived danger. Prolonged stress of this sort leads to a psychological and physical breakdown expressed in a variety of neurotic reactions that are often accompanied by fatalism and depression.

These observations of Grinker and Spiegel are interesting, not only in relation to stress and helplessness, but in relation to our understanding of depression as well. Note that they tie depression to prolonged stress, a sense of failure, and wounded pride. Bibring (1953) emphasizes similar factors in his clinical analysis of patient reports of depression as well as other naturally occurring phenomena. Thus, for example, he describes a patient who became depressed whenever his fear of remaining weak was aroused, another patient who became depressed when confronted with a power beyond her reach, and people who became psychologically depressed during the economic depression of the 1930s and the political crises prior to the Second World War. The common theme running throughout trivial and complicated cases of depression is, Bibring suggests, helplessness, a feeling of doom, and a blow to the person's self-esteem. Similarly, two psychiatrists studying suicidal ideation that precedes suicide attempts concluded that it "is associated with a person's feeling of being unable to alter his circumstances through his own actions and also by a narrowing of his span of awareness into the future. This suggests a hopeless, helpless, and narrowed view of the personal future" (Melges & Weisz, 1971, p. 249).

Observations of patients' responses to illness also illustrate this research approach to the study of stress. Individuals about to be examined by a physician are bothered by the uncertainty as to what will be found. During the examination they wonder and worry about each step in the examination and search for clues about what is going on. Psychologist Irving Janis has been interested in how people attempt to master stress. Among his many studies has been research on the responses of patients to long-term illness. Through observation and interview of cancer victims, he has developed some hypotheses concerning the process of the response to their form of stress. The typical process involves a sense of shock and numbness upon being informed of the bad news. Preoccupation with their "doomed" status may then alternate with blaming of others and denial of the implications of the fatal illness. Where a reasonably healthy process is in action, there follows a period of grieving or "working through" of the loss and a gradual readaptation to the life that remains.

Janis has been particularly concerned with the process of "working through" and the anticipatory preparation for the difficulties that will follow some painful event. In one of his early studies he compared the postoperative responses of three groups of patients: those who had extremely high preoperative fear, those who had moderate anticipatory fear, and those who had extremely low anticipatory fear. He found that people who were extremely fearful before the operation were more likely than others to be anxiety ridden after the operation. However, people who were not afraid before the operation had more than minimal distress after the operation. These individuals were found to be more likely than others to express extreme postoperative anger and resentment. The patients who expressed the least postoperative emotional disturbance were those who had displayed a moderate degree of preoperative fear. Janis' conclusion was that the arousal of anticipatory fear prior to confronting the actual stressful situation is necessary for effective psychological coping with stress. Such anticipatory fear and the "working through" process allow for mental rehearsal and inner preparation for the dangers that follow. Such rehearsal and preparation are valuable in precluding an overwhelming sense of helplessness when the full impact of the surgery and illness must be recognized. They are useful in making plans for future action that can greatly reduce feelings of helplessness. In contrast, the person who denies the threat and at first experiences little apparent stress may later experience rage and/or gloom as actual consequences are recognized: "Thus the work of worrying is conceived as increasing the level of tolerance for subsequent threat or danger stimuli. The more thorough the work of worrying, the more reality tested the person's

THE SCIENTIFIC STUDY OF PEOPLE

self-delivered reassurances are likely to be and hence, the more emotional control he will have under conditions of subsequent danger or deprivation" (Janis, 1965, p. 238). One implication is that preparatory communications to patients about to undergo stressful experiences are extremely important in the process of "emotional inoculation" against overwhelming stress.

To summarize the work of Grinker and Spiegel and that of Janis, we may note that in both cases there is the use of firsthand observation and interview material from individuals undergoing periods of extreme stress. Also, both sets of investigations have emphasized the process through which individuals attempt to cope with threat. Finally, in both cases there has been an emphasis on the person's efforts at control and responses to a perceived sense of helplessness.

Laboratory, Experimental Research

We have already defined the experimental tradition as involving efforts to gain control over the variables of interest, to manipulate some variables and see the consequences for other variables, and to establish if–then, causal relationships. To appreciate this approach, let us consider two major research programs directed toward an understanding of the effects of stress and helplessness. The focus here will be on the use of experimental procedures in the laboratory setting, though we shall see that these efforts have been influenced by and expanded into the use of other research procedures as well.

The first example of laboratory research concerns the effects of stress. In the first part of this research two psychologists, Glass and Singer (1972), were concerned with the consequences of adaptation to stress generally and urban stress in particular. They made use of the laboratory because they felt that this was the best way to sort out the effects of different variables. Noise was used as the source of stress, rather than such urban problems as crowding, garbage, crime, and so on, because it could be clearly defined and manipulated in the laboratory. Thus their studies of the problem of urban stress came to focus largely on the consequences of adaptation to unpredictable and uncontrollable high-intensity noise. Prior naturalistic research had suggested that the effects of such stresses as noise depend on cognitive factors associated with unpredictability and uncontrollability. Glass and Singer set out to investigate the relationship between these factors and performance. Two basic questions were asked: Is adaptation to a stress such as noise achieved at such cost to the individual that behavioral aftereffects are observed? Do such consequences vary with the meanings attributed to the noise?

In a number of laboratory studies Glass and Singer manipulated the intensity, predictability, and controllability of noise and examined the effects on performance in tasks of varying complexity. Initially they found that subjects could adapt to the noise under almost all the conditions and that, by and large, performance was disrupted only when subjects had to perform highly complex tasks under conditions of unpredictable or uncontrollable noise. However, other observations led them to believe that the negative effects of noise were more important after termination of the stress than during the process of adaptation or coping itself. Further investigations of the effects of noise on performance clearly indicated that behavioral problems occurred after the noise stopped. Noise was found to have an aftereffect on tasks such as solving puzzles and proofreading even if there was no effect when the noise itself was heard.

The authors speculated that unpredictable noise was particularly stressful because the individual experienced not only the aversiveness of the noise itself but also the anxiety of not being able to do anything to prepare for it because they did not know when it would occur. Was this true and why the aftereffect phenomenon? In some further research, the authors, found that the perception of control reduced the negative aftereffects of unpredictable noise. They concluded that uncontrollable noise (stress) results in a sense of helplessness: "Consider first what an organism experiences during inescapable or unavoidable stress. Nothing he can do will affect the occurrence of the stressor, for there are no available resources that will enable him to counter it. If the aversive event is also unpredictable, there cannot even be preparation for stimulation. The individual is at the mercy of his environment, in which case we may describe his psychological state as one of helplessness" (Glass & Singer, 1972, p. 86). The authors viewed their work as fitting in with the view that it is not only the stressful event that is significant, but also the experience of lack of control or helplessness that may be associated with it. What Glass and Singer demonstrated was that the perception of control alone was enough to make a difference: the individual does not actually have to exert control!

Glass and Singer extended their research to other stresses, such as electric shock and social stress (harassment by an administrative assistant). In each case they found that the negative aftereffects of stress were a function of unpredictability and perceived lack of control. They reasoned that the perception of control reduces the aversive impact of the stress and thereby the behavioral aftereffects. As demonstrated in their studies, belief in actual or potential control reduces feelings of helplessness and thereby the magnitude of the stress response (tension) and the adverse aftereffects. The sequence suggested runs:

unpredictable stress—increased sense of helplessness—greater magnitude of stress response (attempt to cope)—greater negative behavioral aftereffects

Addressing themselves to the questions raised initially, Glass and Singer concluded that adaptation to stress may be achieved at considerable cost to the individual resulting in negative behavioral aftereffects; that is, the cumulative effects of the responses to the stress may go beyond the effects of any single response. Furthermore, the consequences of stress appear to vary with the meanings attributed to the stress. In particular, the perception of lack of control or helplessness seems to result in negative aftereffects. The unpredictability of stress appears to be a critical variable influencing the perception of helplessness. The findings indicated that psychological factors, not simply the physical characteristics of stimuli, are the principal determinants of the adverse aftereffects of aversive stimuli.

As we shall see later, this experimental work on stress provided the foundation for important research on factors contributing to coronary heart disease. Before turning to this research, however, which involves the utilization of correlational methods as well as experimental methods, let us consider another illustration of the experimental approach to personality research. This second illustration of the utility of laboratory research involves the important work of Seligman and the concept of **learned helplessness.** In the course of some early work on fear conditioning and learning, Seligman and his co-workers observed that dogs who had experienced uncontrollable shocks in one situation transferred their sense of helplessness to another situation where shock was avoidable. In the first situation, dogs were put in a situation where no response they made could affect the onset, offset, duration, or intensity of the shocks. When placed in a second, different situation where jumping over a barrier could lead to escape from shock, most of the dogs seemed to give up and accept the shock passively. They had learned in the first condition that they were helpless to influence the shocks and transferred this learning to the second condition. Note that this was true for most of the dogs (about two-thirds), but not for all — an important difference among individuals that will be returned to later.

The behavior of the dogs who had learned that they were helpless was particularly striking in contrast with that of dogs who received no shock or shock under different conditions. Given the situation where escape and avoidance were possible, the latter dogs would run frantically until they accidentally stumbled on the response that led to escape. Thereafter they would progressively learn to move to that response more quickly until, finally, they were able to avoid the shock altogether. In contrast to such "healthy" dogs, the learned helplessness dogs would similarly first run frantically, but then they would stop, lie down, and whine. With succeeding trials the dogs would give up more and more quickly and accept the shock more passively — the classic learned-helplessness response. The depth of their despair would become so great that it became extremely difficult to change the nature of their expectations. The experimenters tried to make it easier for the dogs to escape and tried to get them to come to safety by attracting them with food — to no avail. By and large, the dogs would just lie there. Even outside that situation, the behavior of the helpless dogs was different from that of the nonhelpless dogs: "When an experimenter goes to the home cage and attempts to remove a nonhelpless dog, it does not comply eagerly: it barks, runs to the back of the cage, and resists handling. In contrast, helpless dogs seem to wilt; they passively sink to the bottom of the cage, occasionally even rolling over and adopting a submissive posture; they do not resist" (Seligman, 1975, p. 25).

Further research demonstrated that the same phenomena found in dogs could be produced in humans (Hiroto, 1974). In this research one group of college students heard a loud noise that they could turn off by pushing a button, a second group of students heard the same noise but could not stop it, and a third (control) group did not hear a noise. All three groups of subjects were then put in another situation where in order to escape the noise they had to move their hand from one side of the box to the other once a light signal had gone on. The members of the first and third groups quickly learned to escape the noise by moving their hands whereas the members of the learned-helplessness group failed to escape the noise; most sat passively and accepted the painful noise. The measure of the learned-helplessness effect was response latency or how long it took the subjects to move their hand once the light signal went on. In sum, manipulation of the escape versus no-escape conditions in the first phase of the experiment produced clear evidence of differences in learned helplessness in the second phase of the experiment (Figure 2.1).

Further research demonstrated that such learned helplessness could generalize beyond the initial task to a broad range of behaviors (Hiroto & Seligman, 1975). More recently, studies have demonstrated that learned helplessness can occur through observing helpless models (Brown & Inouye, 1978; DeVellis, DeVellis, & McCauley, 1978). Individ-

Learned Helplessness—Experiences in childhood associated with the feeling of control and competence can help to prevent the development of learned helplessness.

THE SCIENTIFIC STUDY OF PEOPLE

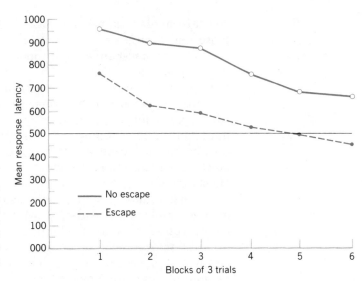

FIGURE 2.1 Learned Helplessness in Humans. As in the animal research, subjects who were first in the no-escape treatment condition took longer to respond and failed to escape more often in the test situation than did subjects who were first in the escape condition. (Hiroto, 1974)

uals will give up more easily if they see themselves as similar to a helpless model than if they observe a successful model or if they perceive themselves as more competent than the observed model.

Seligman's explanation of the learned helplessness phenomenon was that the animal or person learns that outcomes are not affected by its behavior. The expectation that outcomes are independent of the organism's response then has motivational, cognitive, and emotional implications: (1) Uncontrollable events undermine the organism's motivation to initiate other responses that might result in control. (2) As a result of uncontrollability of previous events, the organism has difficulty learning that its response can have an effect on other events. (3) Repeated experiences with uncontrollable events eventually lead to an emotional state similar to that identified in humans as depression.

This is the theory of helplessness, a theory that also leads to suggestions concerning prevention and cure. First, to prevent an organism from expecting events to be independent of its behavior, one should provide it with experiences in which it can exercise control. In particular, the experience of controlling trauma protects the organism from the effects caused by experiences of unescapable trauma. Here Seligman notes that the dogs in the original research who did not become helpless even when exposed to inescapable shock probably had histories of controllable trauma prior to coming to the laboratory. This hypothesis was, in fact, tested and it was found that dogs with little experience in controlling anything were particularly susceptible to helplessness. Finally, in terms of therapy, the depressed person who suffers from expectations of uncontrollability needs to be directed toward experiences that will result in recovery of the belief that responding produces reinforcement. In therapy this involves games and tasks of increasing difficulty, starting with those that ensure success (Beck, 1976).

The learned-helplessness model and associated research are indeed impressive. The negative effects of experience with uncontrollable events have been produced in cats, fish, and rats as well as in dogs and humans. However, further research with humans has suggested that additional factors beyond experience with uncontrollability appear to be important in determining the consequent effects. At least with humans, the effects of experience with uncontrollable events appear to depend on how the person interprets what has occurred. Observation of varying effects depending on modifications in the experimental design or on individual differences in people has led to a reformulated model of learned helplessness. Although we have not yet covered all the experimental research on learned helplessness, much of the research following from the reformulated model has followed correlational rather than experimental procedures. We shall review some of this research in the next section. At this point, however, we may take stock of some of the defining characteristics of experimental research as seen in the efforts of Glass and Singer and of Seligman. In these research programs, we have seen the careful manipulation and control of the relevant variables and, by and large, a focus on systematic influences that are independent of individual differences. We shall consider the strengths of the experimental approach, as well as its limitations, once we have had a chance to place it in perspective relative to the other approaches to research.

Correlational Research and Questionnaires

In correlational research the researcher gives up control over the variables of interest because they cannot be isolated from one another, because practical considerations preclude such an approach, or because there is an interest in individual differences. For example, if one is interested in how stress and helplessness are associated with depression and coronary heart disease in humans, it would be difficult as well as unethical to produce experimentally the phenomena of interest. However, one can take already existent illustrations of the phenomena and try to associate them or correlate them with other variables. Thus, for example, one can see if there is an association or correlation between people being depressed and reporting earlier experiences of helplessness, or between heart attacks and earlier experiences of stress.

An interesting comparison of the experimental and correlational perspectives may be made by returning briefly to the experimental research on learned helplessness in humans (Figure 2.1). Remember that it was demonstrated that human subjects who were first in the no-escape treatment condition took longer to respond to a signal light and more often failed to escape in the test situation than did subjects who were first in the escape condition. The interpretation was that in the no-escape

THE SCIENTIFIC STUDY OF PEOPLE

condition the subjects learned that outcomes were not affected by their behavior. Would subjects who already differ in their beliefs concerning their ability to influence outcomes also differ in their performance in the second situation? In other words, could one find in people differences that occurred naturally and also reproduced the effects of the experimental manipulations? We can now consider another feature of Hiroto's research on learned helplessness in humans. Hiroto not only considered the effects of no-escape and escape treatment conditions on later performance, but he also considered the effects of differences in the personality characteristic known as **locus of control.**

The concept of locus of control is part of Rotter's (1966, 1982) social learning theory of personality and represents a generalized expectancy concerning the determinants of rewards and punishments in one's life. At one extreme are people who believe in their ability to control life's events; that is, internal locus of control. At the other extreme are people who believe that life's events, such as rewards and punishments, are the result of external factors such as chance, luck, or fate; that is, external locus of control. The *Internal–External Scale* (I–E Scale) has been developed to measure individual differences in perception of the extent to which rewards and punishments are generally under internal or external control. Representative items are presented in Figure 2.2. Since the beliefs of external locus of control people sounded very much like the beliefs that are part of learned helplessness, Hiroto suspected that people differing in the personality characteristic of locus of control would perform differently in the test situation. Dividing subjects up into extreme groups of internal and external locus of control on the basis of responses to the I–E Scale, Hiroto exposed members of each group to the no-escape and escape conditions and then looked at their performance in the second or test situation. As expected, he found that external locus of control

1a. Many of the unhappy things in people's lives are partly due to bad luck.

1b. People's misfortunes result from the mistakes they make.

2a. One of the major reasons why we have wars is because people don't take enough interest in politics.

2b. There will always be wars, no matter how hard people try to prevent them.

3a. Sometimes I can't understand how teachers arrive at the grades they give.

3b. There is a direct connection between how hard I study and the grades I get.

4a. The average citizen can have an influence in government decisions.

4b. This world is run by the few people in power and there is not much the little guy can do about it.

FIGURE 2.2 Illustrative Items from Rotter's Internal–External Locus of Control Scale.

subjects, regardless of their pretreatment, were slower to escape or avoid than were the internal locus of control subjects (Figure 2.3). In other words, the personality variable of externality appeared to function like the pretreatment variable of inescapability. An association was found between an already existent personality difference and performance in a test situation.

To illustrate further the correlational approach to personality research, as well as the combined use of questionnaires with experimental procedures, let us continue with the story of research on learned helplessness. Earlier we noted that the original formulation of learned helplessness could not account for the varied consequences of uncontrollability often found in human subjects. This led to a reformulated model of learned helplessness (Abramson, Seligman, & Teasdale, 1978; Abramson, Garber, & Seligman, 1980). According to this reformulation, when people find themselves helpless, they ask *why* they are helpless. People answer the question *why* in terms of *casual attributions*. Three dimensions of causal attribution are suggested as important. First, people may attribute the cause of their helplessness to themselves or to the nature of the situation. In the former case, the cause of helplessness is seen as being internal or personal; in the latter case, it is seen as being external or universal. Second, people may attribute helplessness to factors specific to the situation they are in or to more general conditions in the world around them or in themselves. Third, people may perceive the conditions of their situation to be stable and relatively permanent or to be unstable and perhaps temporary.

In sum, three dimensions of causal attribution are suggested in the

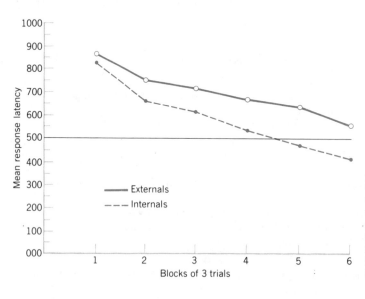

FIGURE 2.3 Locus of Control and Performance. The personality variable of externality appears to function like the pretreatment variable of inescapability. In view of the parallel effects created by inescapability and externality, it is likely that the same underlying process exists in each, that is, the expectancy that responding and reinforcement are independent. (Hiroto, 1974)

THE SCIENTIFIC STUDY OF PEOPLE

reformulated model of learned helplessness: **internal–external, specific–global,** and **stable–unstable.** The attribution made by the person is seen as determining a broad range of important consequences. For example, the attribution of lack of control to internal factors is seen as leading to a greater loss in self-esteem than an attribution to external factors. A student who perceives continuous failure to be due to his or her own stupidity or incompetence will experience a much greater loss of self-esteem than the student who perceives continuous failure to be due to poor teaching. If the person attributes lack of control to global factors, there will be greater generalization of the learned-helplessness response to other situations than if a more situation-specific attribution is made. And, if the person attributes lack of control to stable factors, such as lack of ability or difficulty of the curriculum, there will be greater permanence of the effects over time than if helplessness is attributed to unstable factors such as how the person felt that day or how one was lucky or unlucky. Which attribution is made in response to helplessness will influence, then, whether expectations of future helplessness are chronic or acute, broad or narrow, and whether or not self-esteem is lowered. Of particular import is the suggestion that internal, global, and stable attributions have important implications for the development of depression.

An experimental approach to the reformulated model of learned helplessness would involve the manipulation of casual attributions and observation of the resultant motivational and emotional effects. Thus, for example, subjects could be exposed to conditions that would lead them to make internal or external attributions for failure and differences in consequent effects on self-esteem would be predicted. Although there is some support for the attributional reformulation from experimental research, most such studies have had methodological problems in producing the desired attributions or helplessness effects. To facilitate research in this area, the **Attributional Style Questionnaire** (ASQ) has been developed to measure individual differences in the use of the three specified attributional dimensions (Peterson, Semmel, von Baeyer, Abramson, Metalsky, & Seligman, 1982). In this questionnaire subjects are asked to give a cause for each of 12 hypothetical events and to then rate the cause on scales relevant to the internal–external, stable–unstable, and specific–global dimensions. An illustrative question appears in Figure 2.4. Six of the hypothetical events involve good events (e.g., "You become very rich.") and six involve bad events (e.g., "You go out on a date and it goes badly."). In addition, some events are interpersonal whereas others have to do with achievement. The assumption is that people have characteristic attributional tendencies or styles and that these can be measured with a questionnaire.

According to the reformulated learned helplessness model, attributing uncontrollable bad events to internal, stable, and global factors leads to depression. This would suggest that people scoring high on these dimensions on the ASQ should show more depression than people scor-

You have been looking for a job unsuccessfully for some time.

1. Write down the one major cause_____.

2. Is the cause of your unsuccessful job search due to something about you or to something about other people or circumstances? (circle one number)

   Totally due to
   other people   Totally due
   or circumstances   1 2 3 4 5 6 7   to me

3. In the future when looking for a job, will this cause again be present? (circle one number)

   Will never again   Will always
   be present   1 2 3 4 5 6 7   be present

4. Is the cause something that just influences looking for a job or does it also influence other areas of your life? (circle one number)

   Influences just   Influences
   this particular   all situations
   situation   1 2 3 4 5 6 7   in my life

5. How important would this situation be if it happened to you? (circle one number)

   Not at all   Extremely
   important   1 2 3 4 5 6 7   important

FIGURE 2.4 Illustrative Item—The Attributional Study Questionnaire (ASQ). (Peterson et al., 1982, p. 292)

ing low on these dimensions. Indeed, the authors of the ASQ report an association or correlation between a style in which internal, stable, and global attributions are made for bad events and depressive symptoms in college students, adults, and patients. Scores on the ASQ have been found to be associated with the development of depressive symptoms following poor performance by college students on a midterm examination. Finally, in a study using a similar questionnaire, it was found that depression was associated with blame directed at one's character but not with blame directed at one's behavior (Peterson, Schwartz, & Seligman, 1981). Bad events attributed to character ("I'm that kind of person.") were viewed as less controllable than events attributed to behavior ("I did something."). In addition, characterological blame was associated with more stable and global attributions than was behavior blame. However, self-blame or characterological blame could not be determined to be a cause of depression. That is, characterological self-blame was found to be associated with but not a cause of later depressive symptoms.

The final point made in relation to the above study is important both for the reformulated learned helplessness model of depression and for an appreciation of the limits of correlational research. The above research suggests an association between internal, global, and stable attributions for bad events and depression but the research does not demonstrate that such cognitive attributions cause depression. Could they be a part of depression and caused by the same factors that lead to the depression? Indeed, a major study of people before and after they became depressed found that depression-related cognitions did not predict future depression and appeared to be more of a concomitant of depression than a cause of it. Prior to becoming depressed, the future depressives did not attribute failure to internal causes or perceive themselves as having little control over events in their lives (Lewinsohn, Steinmetz, Larson, & Franklin, 1981).

Another study addresses the same issue and also illustrates how both experimental procedures and questionnaires can be used in the same research (Danker-Brown & Baucom, 1982). In this research, college students were asked to solve problems presented as part of an intelligence test. Students in the experimental group were given false feedback that prevented them from solving any of the problems. This was the learned helplessness condition. Students in the other group were given feedback that indicated successful solution of the problems. Following this, the subjects filled out a cognitions questionnaire designed to measure their explanations for their performance on the intelligence test. Then the subjects filled out a mood questionnaire that is sensitive to mood changes following failure and were asked to solve problems on an anagrams task.

Scores on the mood questionnaire and the anagrams task suggested that the experimental manipulation was effective in producing symptoms of helplessness among the students forced to fail the problems. Thus, the experimental (learned helplessness) group showed significantly more depressive mood on the questionnaire and significantly less productive effort on the anagrams task than did the control group. So much for the experimental part and the effect of learned helplessness on emotion and motivation. What of the relation of the cognitive attributions to the prior conditions and the consequent emotions and motivations? Did the learned helplessness condition lead to differing cognitions, and were these differing cognitions associated with depression and a motivational deficit? The answer to the first question appears to be affirmative. Students in the experimental and control groups responded differently to the questionnaire that asked about their views of their own intelligence and the causes for their performance on the task. However, an association could not be found between responses to this questionnaire and subsequent measures of depression and motivational deficit. In other words, in contrast with what the model would suggest, an association could not be found between the kinds of attributions made by subjects in the experimental group and the magnitude of their subsequent depression and decrease in productive performance: "Results of the current study fail to confirm a relationship between self-statements including attributions and the development of helplessness symptoms in human adults. One must question whether attributions are necessary in explaining the development of helplessness symptoms" (Danker-Brown & Baucom, 1982, p. 800). Thus, we are left with associational evidence for the model but causal linkages among events, attributions, and mood or motivation remain to be demonstrated.

It has now been over twenty years since Seligman began his research on learned helplessness, and over five years since the development of the ASQ. An impressive body of research has been established, including representatives from each of the major research traditions. In reviewing this literature, Seligman remains convinced of the import of attributional style, or what is now called *explanatory style*, for depression (Peterson & Seligman, 1984). Beyond work with adults, research with children also suggests a relation between explanatory style and depression (Nolen-Hoeksema, Girgus, & Seligman, 1986). More recently research has branched out into the realms of job performance and health, with evidence linking an internal, stable, and general explanatory style for negative events to lower performance and poorer health.

At the same time, not all the findings have been supportive of Seligman's views. In particular, questions have been raised in relation to three issues. First, there is the question of whether people have explanatory *styles* as opposed to explanations for *specific* kinds of events (Cutrona, Russell, & Jones, 1985). Whereas Seligman suggests that people tend to develop generalized styles for explaining events, others present evidence to suggest that these explanations are much more situation specific. Second, questions have been raised as to whether the ASQ represents an adequate measure of attributional or explanatory style (Cutrona, Russell, & Jones, 1985). Despite Seligman's suggestions to the contrary, evidence has been presented that responses to the questionnaire may not match actual causal attributions. Further, the ASQ may not actually measure the three dimensions of explanation that it is supposed to measure. Finally, as noted, questions have been raised as to whether explanatory style precedes and causes depression as opposed to it accompanying depression or even being caused by depression (Brewin, 1985; Cochran & Hammen, 1985).

These questions and the evidence in support of them are important. Although the evidence in support of Seligman's views remains impressive, we see that we must be cautious in our evaluations and conclusions. In addition, they illustrate some of the problems associated with correlational research and questionnaires, namely, the difficulty of establishing cause–effect relationships and the difficulty of ensuring that a questionnaire measures what it claims to measure.

And what of the research on the effects of stress? The experimental research of Glass and Singer suggests that continuous efforts at adaptation to stress may result in negative aftereffects. Does correlational research have anything to contribute to our understanding of these or

THE SCIENTIFIC STUDY OF PEOPLE

related phenomena? The experimental work on stress suggests that unpredictable negative events are stressful because they lead to the experience of helplessness. Can correlational research, in particular the study of individual differences, help to clarify some of these relationships?

CURRENT APPLICATIONS   EXPLANATORY STYLE, JOB SUCCESS, AND HEALTH

Seligman's research on explanatory style has expanded beyond depression to the realms of job performance and health, leading to headlines in the mass media of "Research Affirms Power of Positive Thinking" and "Stop Blaming Yourself."

Do life insurance sales agents with an optimistic explanatory style remain on the job longer and sell more life insurance than do agents with a pessimistic style? Since sales agents repeatedly encounter failure, rejection, and indifference from prospective clients, Seligman reasoned that "optimists" would weather the challenge better than "pessimists." ("Optimists" have internal, stable, and global explanations for positive events and external, unstable, and specific explanations for negative events. The opposite pattern holds true for "pessimists.") Evidently the answer to the above question is a clear *yes*. According to Seligman, "I think we've got a test for who can face a stressful, challenging job and who can't. My guess is that this test could save the insurance company millions of dollars a year in training alone since it costs about $30,000 each to train new people, and half of them quit."

In terms of health, Seligman suggests a relation between a helpless explanatory style and subsequent physical illness, both over a short period of time and over an extended period of time. How could this be? There is evidence that the immunological system of "pessimists," or those with a helpless explanatory style, may provide less resistance to disease than does the disease-fighting system of "optimists."

SOURCE: Seligman & Schulman, 1986; *Psychology Today*, February 1987; *New York Times*, February 3, 1987.

Optimism and Job Success—An optimistic explanatory style is associated with success in sales.

Following up on his earlier work, Glass became interested in the role of stress-related psychological factors in heart disease or cardiac disorders. Coronary heart disease is a major cause of death. Although many factors have been found to be associated with high risk for heart disease (e.g., age, sex, hypertension, obesity, heavy cigarette smoking), understanding of the cause of these disorders remains incomplete and no combination of these risk factors predicts the majority of new cases. Clinical investigation suggests that psychological factors play a role in determining the risk of developing cardiac disorders, in particular a relationship between stressful life events and risk of heart disease. Thus, such stressful life events as economic distress, job dissatisfaction, marital unhappiness, and the sudden death of a spouse all have been correlated with increased risk of heart disease. At the same time, not all people react to stress in the same way and the observation was made that there appears to be a particular personality pattern associated with increased risk for heart disease. This personality variable has come to be known as the **Type A behavior pattern,** sometimes as the Type A personality, and it has been the subject of considerable investigation.

As noted, the initial observation of a possible link between a pattern of personality characteristics and risk of heart disease was made on a clinical basis by medical cardiologists. (Friedman & Rosenman, 1974). Indeed, some of the initial observations were made by a secretary who noticed that many of the patients were wearing out the front of the seats while waiting to see the doctors. The cardiologists went on to observe that many younger patients suffering from cardiac disorders had a partic-ular constellation of behavioral characteristics including competitive achievement striving, a sense of time urgency, and aggressiveness (Figure 2.5). Observation of this pattern was followed by the development of a **Structured Interview (SI)** procedure to measure individual differences in this regard. The interview consists of 25 questions about the person's life that are designed to elicit competitiveness, impatience, and hostility from the Type A person. For example, the person is asked about the reaction to working with a slow person or having to wait on line. In addition to content, the SI measures expressive style in terms of characteristics such as vocal speed, volume, and explosiveness. Later, a questionnaire was developed to measure individual differences in Type A characteristics — the **Jenkins Activity Survey** (JAS, Figure 2.5). The questionnaire inquires about competitiveness, the wish for quick action, living a pressured style of life, and hostility. Individuals taking the questionnaire are then scored on a continuum in terms of the extent to which they exemplify the Type A behavior pattern.

Glass and his co-workers modified the JAS for use with college students and set out to clarify the relationship between Type A charac-teristics and stress in the production of coronary disease (Glass, 1977; Glass & Carver, 1980). Observations of behavior in the laboratory and in the natural environment indeed indicated that individuals scoring high

THE SCIENTIFIC STUDY OF PEOPLE

conscientious	fast thinking	expresses bravado
intense	fast acting	aggressive sexually
sets high standards	firm handshake	poor listener
desires power	vigilant	energetic movements
needs to control	self-centered	restless
competitive	easily angered	clipped speech

Illustrative Items and Responses (JAS)

1. *How would your wife (or closest friend) rate you?*
   "*Definitely hard driving and competitive.*" Type A
   "*Definitely relaxed and easy going.*" non-Type A

2. *Do you ever set deadlines or quotas for yourself at work or home?*
   "*Yes, once per week or more often.*" Type A
   "*No.*" "*Only occasionally.*" non-Type A

3. *Has your spouse or some friend ever told you that you eat too fast?*
   "*Yes, often.*" Type A
   "*No.*" non-Type A

FIGURE 2.5   Illustrative Type A Characteristics and Items from the Jenkins Activity Survey (JAS) (Jenkins, 1979; Zymanski, 1972; Surwit, Williams, & Shapiro, 1982)

on the JAS show more achievement striving, a greater sense of time urgency, and more aggressiveness than do low-scoring individuals. In addition, the former display a greater effort to exercise control over the environment and to deny uncontrollability. For example, relative to individuals scoring low on the JAS, Type A individuals:

1. Attempt to solve more problems when no time limit is set.
2. Earn more academic honors.
3. Set higher academic goals.
4. Work at levels closer to the limits of their endurance.
5. Report less fatigue.
6. Report a time interval of one minute as elapsing faster.
7. Respond with greater hostility when provoked or frustrated though they are not necessarily uniformly more aggressive.
8. Respond to stress with a greater increase in motivation.
9. Show greater learned helplessness in an uncontrollable situation if the cues signifying lack of control are salient and cannot be denied.

The conclusion reached from these findings was the following: "At the crux of all of these behavioral effects, we would submit, is an attempt

TYPE A BEHAVIOR—CAN IT LEAD TO BURNOUT?

Recently psychologists have been interested in the phenomenon of job burnout—emotional exhaustion associated with stress on the job. Such burnout has been observed among a variety of helping professionals and associated with stressors such as excessive caseloads, lack of time, and lack of support or appreciation. Although burnout has been studied in relation to job stress, there also are personality characteristics associated with the burnout syndrome. People who "burn out" emotionally on the job often are perfectionistic and try too hard to reach unrealistic goals.

Each year witnesses the retirement of a number of successful professional coaches, many of whom show the burnout syndrome and the Type A pattern of behavior. For example, take the history of Dick Vermeil, the highly successful former coach of the Philadelphia Eagles professional football team. Many years ago he developed the motto: The Best Way to Kill Time Is To Work It To Death. And work he did—up to twenty hours a day. The point was to achieve a lot and fast. In the words of one person: "You couldn't even drink a glass of water slow around him." Winning was the point, but winning only increased the tension and the need for further work. There was a driven quality to it all, as if something inside him was out of control as he tried to control the events around him. Assistant coaches would resign, fearful that they would end up with a heart attack. Ultimately it was too much for him as well, and the decision to get out had to be made. As a fellow coach said: "There are now more factors than ever that an NFL coach cannot control."

What advice do other successful coaches have to offer? Tom Landry, the highly successful coach of the Dallas Cowboys for the past twenty-five years says: "A long time ago I tried to judge what I could and could not control and stopped worrying about what I couldn't."

SOURCE: *Sports Illustrated*, March 28, 1983.

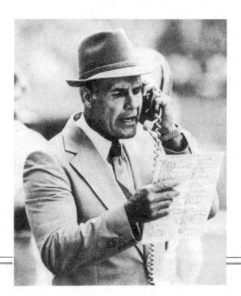

Stress—Dallas football coach Tom Landry.

by the Type A to assert control over environmental demands and requirements . . . The coronary-prone behavior pattern thus might be described as a characteristic type of responding to environmental stressors that threaten the individual's sense of control. The Type A is engaged in a continual struggle for control . . ." (Glass & Carver, 1980, p. 232).

The JAS has been used by other investigators to measure individual differences in the Type A pattern and a number of important relationships have been established (Matthews, 1982). Many of these results fit with Glass' suggestion that Type A individuals strive to assert and maintain control over stressful aspects of their environment. For example, in one study that compared coronary patients with hospitalized (general medical and psychiatric) patients and nonhospitalized controls, it was found that both patient groups had a higher percentage reporting a significant loss during the previous year and that the coronary patients had the highest JAS scores (Theorell & Rahe, 1975). In addition, there are studies that show an association between high scores on the JAS and physiological responses consistent with those predisposing for heart disease as well as with the actual development of heart disease.

A recent fascinating study illustrates the possible implications of Type A behavior for occupational stress and performance. In this cross-cultural study, bus drivers in the United States and India were measured on the JAS for Type A behavior patterns. Type A and Type B bus drivers then were compared in terms of their stress and driving performance. Although not all differences held in both cultures, generally there was evidence that Type A bus drivers experienced more stress, had more accidents, and showed more impatient driving behavior relative to Type B individuals (Evans, Palsane, & Carrere, 1987) (Figure 2.6).

Measure	Indian Sample		U.S. Sample	
	Type A	Type B	Type A	Type B
Workday job stress	3.45	2.20	4.20	2.70
Accidents per month	0.020	0.004	0.020	0.009
Sick days per month	Data unavailable		0.39	0.17
Braking per minute	1.46	1.08	1.15	1.20
Passing per minute	0.78	0.37	0.008	0.011
Horn blowing per minute	.50	.30	0.03	0.02

FIGURE 2.6 Illustrative Differences between Type A and Type B Bus Drivers from Indian and U.S. Samples. (Evans, Palsane, & Carrere, 1987) (Copyright © 1978 American Psychological Association. Reprinted by permission.)

Type A and Stress—Bus drivers possessing the Type A behavior pattern are prone to have more accidents and show more impatient driving behavior than bus drivers not possessing this personality pattern.

It has now been roughly three decades since the first tie between Type A characteristics and risk of coronary heart disease was suggested. Considerable research has been conducted, a recent summary of which suggests the following conclusions (Booth-Kewley & Friedman, 1987).

1. Generally a modest but reliable association has been found between the Type A behavior pattern and risk for the development of heart disease.

2. There is some evidence that some components of the Type A behavior pattern are more critical than others. In particular, there is evidence that the anger/hostility component is the dominant characteristic among the coronary-prone Type A behaviors (Rosenman, 1985). In addition, there is evidence that other characteristics, such as depression and anxiety, may be of equal if not greater significance: "The picture of coronary-proneness revealed by this review is not one of a hurried, impatient workaholic but instead is one of a person with one or more negative emotions."

3. Generally the SI measure of Type A shows a better relationship with the predicted variables than does the JAS.

THE SCIENTIFIC STUDY OF PEOPLE

4. Relationships found between Type A and risk of coronary heart disease have been more substantial in earlier studies than in more recent studies. There are many possible explanations for this, but the exact reason remains to be determined.

As with the learned-helplessness research, with time we have learned more and the area of study has become more complex. In relation to the Type A concept, we can consider four critical questions:

1. *What are the critical ingredients of the Type A behavior pattern?* As indicated above, there is evidence that some ingredients of the Type A pattern are more important than others. Although some suggest that the key ingredient is stress associated with a struggle for control, others focus more on the struggle with negative emotions such as hostility/anger.

2. *How should the Type A behavior pattern be measured?* As noted, generally there is evidence of the superiority of the SI over the JAS. However, even well-trained interviewers can sometimes ask questions in a way that does not lead to a representative reading of the individual's expressive style. Such faulty interviewer behavior has been described as the problem in some studies that have failed to show an association between Type A behavior (SI) and risk for heart disease (Friedman & Powell, 1984).

3. *Is all Type A behavior bad and the alternative good?* Clearly Type A individuals are capable of considerable achievement in school and on the job. If such achievement is considered desirable, the relaxed and easygoing style of the Type B person may not be most adaptive. Furthermore, an emotionally constricted Type C person has been described that shows some poorer prognosis for the course of cancer than does the more emotionally expressive individual (Temoshok, 1985).

4. *Can Type A behavior be changed?* There is evidence that Type A behavior can be changed, without necessarily disturbing some of the positive aspects of this behavioral pattern. Friedman, one of the cardiologists who originally defined the pattern, runs regular programs designed to reduce the stressful aspects of the Type A behavior pattern. In one study of individuals who had already had a heart attack, it was found that those who received the counseling program had almost half the number of further heart attacks as did those who did not receive this program (Friedman, 1984). In another study of officer-students at the U.S. War College, it was found that a training program could reduce the detrimental aspects of the Type A pattern (e.g., hostility and time urgency) without adverse effects on their military leadership qualities (Gill, 1985).

Summary

In general, the above studies are illustrative of research that can be done within the correlational tradition. The main thrust in both the attribution-learned helplessness research and the Type A research was on the establishment of patterns of relations or correlations utilizing groups differing on a particular personality characteristic. In some cases there was the utilization of an experimental procedure in a laboratory setting but even then there was the use of already established differences, measured by questionnaires, to investigate the variables of interest. In other cases, of course, associations were established without any experimental manipulation of the variables at all. Although a causal relationship between internal, global, stable attributions and depression has not been established, correlational research has provided a basis for the investigation of such relationships. Similarly, although causal links between Type A behavior characteristics and heart disease have not been established, a number of potentially important relationships have been discovered. In addition, the studies discussed in this section illustrate the importance of individual differences in causal attribution and response to stress, and thereby the potential value of studying individual differences more generally.

GOALS OF RESEARCH: RELIABILITY AND VALIDITY

Until now, we have considered differing research traditions and alternative research approaches. At the same time, all research efforts share certain goals in common. Earlier we noted that our goal was to make meaningful observations that could be interpreted in a theoretical framework. At this point we can be more specific about the criteria we want to apply in evaluating our data. In research, we are seeking systematic observations that can be replicated and that relate to the concept of interest to us; that is, in research we seek reliable and valid observations.

The concept of **reliability** relates to the extent to which our observations are stable, dependable, and can be replicated. There are many different kinds of reliability and many different factors may contribute to a lack of reliability. However, an essential in all scientific research is that other investigators be able to reproduce or replicate the observations reported by one investigator. We must have stable, consistent observations to even begin to make theoretical interpretations. What are some of the factors that might contribute to unreliable observations? On the subject side, if subject performance is greatly influenced in unsystematic ways by transient factors such as attitude or mood, then unreliable observations are likely. On the experimenter side, variations in instructions to subjects as well as in measuring or interpreting responses can

THE SCIENTIFIC STUDY OF PEOPLE

lead to a lack of reliability. The particular basis for a lack of reliability can vary from research tradition to research tradition and from experiment to experiment. In general, however, a continuing problem for psychologists is that periodically we find that the same data are not obtained by other investigators. Again, for scientific research to be cumulative and of significance we must have reliable observations.

In addition to reliable observations, our data must be valid. The concept of **validity** relates to the extent to which our observations indeed reflect the phenomena or variables of interest to us. What use are reliable observations if they do not relate to what we think they do? Suppose, for example, that we have a reliable test for locus of control or attributional style but there is no evidence that the test measures what it purports to measure. Of what use is such a measure? Suppose we take certain behaviors to be expressive of learned helplessness, but they reflect other phenomena. Of what use is such a measure? Problems such as this may seem trivial in some areas. For example, we know that a scale is both a reliable and a valid measure of weight, and we know that a ruler is both a reliable and a valid measure of height. But how do we know that not solving certain problems is a measure of learned helplessness, that responses to the ASQ are indicative of attributional style, or that responses to the JAS are valid indicators of Type A behavior patterns? Indeed, it is not unusual for different tests or measures of the same concept not to agree with one another. Thus, as noted earlier, the SI interview measure of the Type A behavior pattern and the JAS measure of this pattern agree with one another to a substantial, but by no means a perfect, extent. Which, then, is the true or valid measure of Type A behavior pattern? If there are two different measures of temperature, how can we know which is the true or valid measure? The answer is the measure that gives us the most reliable and theoretically useful results. If there are two different measures of a personality concept, how do we know which is the true or valid measure? Here too we would consider the reliability, meaningfulness, and usefulness of the observations. In sum, validity concerns the extent to which we can be sure that we are measuring the phenomena or variables of interest to us.

The complexities of psychological research are such that certain problems may enter that affect both the reliability and the validity of the data. As a human enterprise, research in personality lends itself to influences that are part of everyday interpersonal behavior. The investigation of such influences might be called the *social psychology of research*. Let us consider here two important illustrations. First, there may be factors influencing the behavior of human subjects that are not part of the experimental design. Among such factors may be cues implicit in the experimental setting that suggest to the subject that the experimenter has a certain hypothesis and, "in the interest of science," the subject behaves in a way that will confirm it. Such effects are known as **demand characteristics** and suggest that the psychological experiment is a form of social interaction in which subjects give purpose and meaning to things (Orne, 1962; Weber & Cook, 1972). The purpose and meaning given to the research may vary from subject to subject in ways that are not part of the experimental design and thereby serve to reduce both reliability and validity.

Complementing these sources of error or bias in the subject are unintended sources of influence or error in the experimenter. Without realizing it, experimenters may either make errors in recording and analyzing data or emit cues to the subjects and thus influence their behavior in a particular way. Such unintended **experimenter expectancy effects** may lead subjects to behave in accordance with the hypothesis (Rosenthal, 1964; Rosenthal & Rubin, 1978). For example, consider the classic case of Clever Hans (Pfungst, 1911). Hans was a horse who by tapping his foot could add, subtract, multiply, and divide. A mathematical problem would be presented to the horse and, incredibly enough, he was able to come up with the answer. In attempting to discover the secret of Hans' talents, a variety of situational factors were manipulated. If Hans could not see the questioner or if the questioner did not know the answer, Hans was not able to come up with the correct answer. On the other hand, if the questioner knew the answer and was visible, Hans could tap out the answer with his foot. Apparently the questioner unknowingly signaled Hans when to start and stop tapping his hoof. The tapping would start when the questioner inclined his head forward, increase in speed when the questioner bent forward more, and stop when the questioner straightened up.

To summarize the above discussion, we can say that in research we are interested in obtaining reliable, valid, and theoretically significant information. From this discussion, it should be clear that we can make reliable observations without their being valid but we cannot make valid observations that are unreliable. We can obtain theoretically inconsequential results that can be replicated and valid, but we cannot obtain theoretically significant results that cannot be confirmed by other investigators or do not appear to relate to what they are supposed to measure. Obtaining data that are reliable, valid, and theoretically meaningful are goals of all research efforts, and we shall keep them in mind as we consider the potential strengths and limitations of each of the approaches discussed thus far.

EVALUATING ALTERNATIVE RESEARCH TACTICS

Having considered the goals of all personality research, we are in a position to evaluate the three major research strategies. We shall see that as a consequence of proceeding along different lines, each tactic may be characterized as having strengths as well as potential limitations.

THE SCIENTIFIC STUDY OF PEOPLE

Naturalistic Observation and Clinical Research

The advantage of naturalistic observation is that one examines the behavior of interest directly and does not have to extrapolate from a somewhat artificial setting to the real world. Naturalistic observation is the only feasible means for the study of some phenomena (e.g., wartime stress), but many psychologists argue that this approach has special merit even when it is possible to study the phenomena of interest in the laboratory. Through naturalistic observation, it is argued, one can observe the full complexity of personality processes and individual–environment relationships. On the other hand, certain phenomena may be very rare or difficult to study in the natural environment and, even when such study is possible, it may be very difficult to disentangle the relationships among the variables. In addition, whenever observations are not made in an objective way, there is the problem of different observers reporting different observations. Insofar as researchers make observations on a subjective basis, they accumulate data that decline considerably in reliability and validity.

Clinical research brings with it its own set of potential strengths and limitations, depending on what is being investigated and how the research is conducted. Most generally, clinical research has the advantage of in-depth study of processes going on in one or a few individuals. Such individualistic or idiographic research has two main features that stand in contrast with research on groups (Pervin, 1983). First, relationships established for a group as a whole may not reflect the way any individual behaves or the way some groups of individuals behave. The average learning curve, for example, may not reflect the way any one individual learns. Second, by considering only group data one may miss some valuable insights into processes going on in particular individuals. Some time ago Henry Murray argued for the utility of individual as well as group studies as follows: "In lay words, the subjects who gave the majority response may have done so for different reasons. Furthermore, a statistical answer leaves unexplained the uncommon (exhibited-by-the-minority) response. One can only ignore it as an unhappy exception to the rule. Averages obliterate the 'individual characters of individual organisms' and so fail to reveal the complex interaction of forces which determine each concrete event" (1938, p. viii).

Clinical research in personality need not involve the use of verbal report by subjects, though clearly it often does. In such cases, we are confronted with special problems associated with such data. Treating what people say as accurate reflections of what has actually occurred or actually going on has come under attack from two very different groups. On the one hand, psychoanalysts and dynamically oriented psychologists (Chapters 3 and 4) argue that people not only consciously lie but often distort things for unconscious reasons: "Children perceive inaccurately, are very little conscious of their inner states and retain fallacious recollections of occurrences. Many adults are hardly better" (Murray, 1938,

p. 15). On the other hand, many experimental psychologists argue that people do not have access to their internal processes and respond to interviewer questions in terms of some inferences they make about what must have been going on rather than accurately reporting what in fact occurred (Nisbett & Wilson, 1977; Wilson, Hull, & Johnson, 1981). For example, despite experimenter evidence that subjects make decisions in accord with certain experimental manipulations, the subjects themselves may report having behaved in a particular way for very different reasons. In a sense, people give their subjective *reasons* for behaving as they do, but they do not give actual *causes*. In sum, the argument is that whether for defensive reasons or because of "normal" problems people have in keeping track of their internal processes, verbal self-reports are questionable sources of reliable and valid data.

Other psychologists argue that verbal reports should be accepted for what they are—data (Ericsson & Simon, 1980). The argument is made that there is no intrinsic reason to treat verbal reports as any less useful data than an overt motor response such as pressing a lever. Indeed, it is possible to analyze the verbal responses of people in as objective, systematic, and quantitative fashion as their other behavioral responses. If verbal responses are not automatically discounted, then the twofold question becomes: "Which kinds of verbal responses are most useful and trustworthy, and how should such data be analyzed?" Here the argument is made that subjects can only report about things they are attending to or have attended to. If the experimenter asks the subject to remember or explain things that were never attended to do in the first place, the subject will either make an inference about what occurred or state a hypothesis about what occurred (White, 1980). Thus, if you later ask persons why they purchased one product over another in the supermarket when they were not attending to this decision at the time, they will give you an inference or a hypothesis rather than an account of what occurred.

Those who argue in favor of the use of verbal reports suggest that when they are elicited with care and the circumstances involved are appreciated, they can be a useful source of information. Although the term introspection (i.e., verbal descriptions of process going on inside a person) was long discredited by experimental psychologists, there is now increased interest in the potential utility of such data: "If introspective reports are sometimes wrong or misleading, there is equally compelling evidence that in some instances they may provide information of truly impressive accuracy and reliability (Lieberman, 1979, p. 319). In accepting the potential utility of verbal reports, we may expand the universe of potential data for rich and meaningful observation. At the same time, we must keep in mind the goals and requirements of reliability and validity. Thus, we must insist on evidence that the same observations and interpretations can be made by other investigators and that the data do reflect the concepts they are presumed to measure. In appreciating the merits and vast potential of verbal reports, we must also be aware of the potential for misutilization and naive interpretation. In sum, verbal reports as data should be held up to the same scrutiny as other research observations.

Laboratory, Experimental Research

In many ways, experimental laboratory research represents the scientific ideal. Ask people for their image of a scientist and they are likely to conjure up the image of a person in a white smock in a laboratory, clipboard in hand, noting meter readings of machines or making minor adjustments to a piece of apparatus. Much of the research in physics and chemistry, two of our most advanced sciences, would approximate this image. What is the basis for this? The strength of the experimental approach to research is the potential for careful manipulation of the variables of interest, the gathering of objective data free from biased or subjective interpretation, and the establishment of cause–effect relationships. In the experiment that is properly designed and carried out, every step is carefully planned to limit effects to the variables of interest. Few variables are studied so that there is not the problem of disentangling complex relationships. Systematic relationships between changes in some variables and consequences for other variables are established so that the experimenter can say: "If X, then Y." Full details of the experimental procedure are reported so that the results can be replicated by investigators in other laboratories.

Psychologists who are critical of laboratory research suggest that too often such research is artificial and limited in relevance to other contexts. The suggestion is that what works in the laboratory may not work elsewhere. Furthermore, although relationships between isolated variables may be established, such relationships may not hold when the complexity of actual human behavior is considered. Also, since laboratory research tends to involve relatively brief exposures to stimuli, such research may miss important processes that occur over time. Finally, for all of its objectivity, experimental research lends itself to the problems of demand characteristics and experimenter expectancy effects. These criticisms are in addition, of course, to the potential limitation due to the fact that not all phenomena can be produced in the laboratory.

Many of these criticisms have themselves been attacked by experimental psychologists. In defending laboratory experiments, the following statements are made: (1) Such research is the proper basis for testing causal hypotheses. The generality of the established relationship is then a subject for further investigation. (2) Some phenomena would never be discovered outside of the laboratory. (3) Some phenomena can be studied in the laboratory that would be difficult to study elsewhere (e.g., subjects are given permission to be aggressive in contrast with the often quite strong restraints in natural social settings). (4) There is little empirical support for the contention that subjects typically try to confirm the experimenter's hypothesis or for the significance of experimental artifacts more generally. Indeed, many subjects are more negativistic than conforming (Berkowitz & Donnerstein, 1982).

Correlational Research and Questionnaires

As previously noted, many of the strengths and limitations of the correlational approach are the opposite of those of experimental research. On the one hand, there may be the opportunity to study a broader range of variables; on the other, there is less control over the variables. Consider the use of personality questionnaires in correlational research. First, many psychologists would question whether we can accept the subjects' responses to questionnaires as accurate statements of what the subjects feel and do. Second, responses to self-report questionnaires are susceptible to particular biases. Research suggests that subjects often respond to qualities in the questionnaire items other than content or that they have a consistent tendency to respond in one or another way to a test—a **response style.** Two illustrative response-style problems can be considered. The first has been called *acquiescence* and involves the tendency to agree or disagree with items regardless of their content. For example, subjects may have a preference for responses such as "Like" and "Agree" (yea-sayers) or for responses such as "Dislike" and "Disagree" (nay-sayers). The second illustrative potential for bias in response to questionnaires involves the *social desirability* of the items. Instead of responding to the intended psychological meaning of a test item, a subject may respond to it as suggesting a socially acceptable or a socially desirable personality characteristic. Finally, a questionnaire thought to measure one variable may in fact be measuring another set of variables—a problem with the validity of the questionnaire.

Those who defend the use of questionnaires suggest that such problems and sources of bias can be remedied through careful test construction and interpretation. For example, testgivers suggest that questionnaire responses need not be considered as true or accurate reflections of the subject's feelings and behaviors but only that the resulting scores relate to phenomena of interest. Also, others suggest that by careful item writing one can remove the potential effects of biases such as acquiescence and social desirability. Finally, still others suggest that test items or scales can be included to measure whether subjects are faking or trying to present themselves in a particularly favorable or socially desirable way. Although such safeguards may be possible, few of them appear in many personality questionnaires. Furthermore, even when a personality test is presented as having reasonable evidence of reliability and validity, it not infrequently gives results that do not agree with those from another equally well structured test that is presumed to measure the same personality concept. Thus, for example, although the structured interview and JAS measures of Type A behavior pattern both have been used with some degree of success in research, scores on the two do not necessarily show perfect agreement with one another, and results from the use of one do not always match those associated with the use of the other. In sum, although personality questionnaires are attractive because they are easy to use and can get at many aspects of personality that would otherwise be difficult to study, the problems in establishing their reliability and validity are often substantial.

Summary

In assessing these alternative research goals we must recognize that we are considering potential, not necessary, strengths and limitations (Figure 2.7). When it comes down to it, each research effort must be evaluated on

Potential Strengths	*Potential Limitations*
NATURALISTIC OBSERVATION AND CLINICAL RESEARCH	
1. Avoid artificiality of laboratory.	1. Lead to unsystematic observation.
2. Study full complexity of person-environment relationships.	2. Encourage subjective interpretation of data.
3. Lead to in-depth study of individuals.	3. Entangled relationships among variables.
EXPERIMENTAL RESEARCH	
1. Manipulates specific variables.	1. Excludes phenomena that can not be studied in the laboratory.
2. Records data objectively.	2. Creates artificial setting that limits generality of findings.
3. Establishes cause-effect relationships.	3. Fosters demand characteristics & experimenter expectancy effects.
CORRELATION RESEARCH AND QUESTIONNAIRES	
1. Study wide range of variables.	1. Establishes relationships that are associational rather than causal.
2. Study relationships among many variables.	2. Problems of reliability & validity of self-report questionnaires.

FIGURE 2.7 Summary of Potential Strengths and Limitations of Alternative Research Methods

its own merits and for its own potential in advancing understanding rather than on some preconceived basis. It is clear that alternative research procedures can be used in conjunction with one another in any single research enterprise. In addition, data from alternative research procedures can be integrated in the pursuit of a more comprehensive theory.

At the same time, it is clear that psychologists do have preferences and biases concerning how research should be conducted. Despite all the objectivity of science, research is a very human enterprise. Furthermore, different research theories of personality often are linked with different research strategies and thereby with different kinds of data. The observations that led to one theory of personality often are different from those that led to another theory. The phenomena of interest to one theory of personality are not as easily studied by the research procedures useful in the study of phenomena emphasized by another theory of personality. Personality psychologists make theoretical decisions concerning *what* should be studied and decide on research strategies for *how* these phenomena should be studied. The point here is important: often the *what* and the *how* are linked with one another, as well as with some aspects of the personality of the researcher. These linkages make one or another approach temperamentally more suitable and aesthetically more appealing.

We shall want to keep these inevitable ties between theory and research in mind as we consider historical theories of personality as well as those that are current today. In future chapters we shall begin with those that rest on clinical procedures, progress to those that rely heavily on the correlational tradition, and conclude with the most current approaches that depend primarily on the experimental tradition. Before beginning this exploration, however, let us turn to consider briefly the ethics of research and the place of research in public policy.

THE ETHICS OF RESEARCH AND PUBLIC POLICY

As a human enterprise, research involves ethical questions, not in terms of the questions we address but in terms of how we address these questions and report our results. Over the past two decades a number of studies have brought into sharp focus some of the issues involved. For example, in one research effort that won a prize from the American Association for the Advancement of Science, subjects were told to teach other subjects ("learners") a list of paired associate words and to punish them with an electric shock when an error was made (Milgram, 1965). The issue investigated was obedience to authority. Although actual shock was not used, the subjects believed that it was being used and

THE SCIENTIFIC STUDY OF PEOPLE

often "administered" high levels despite pleas from the "learners" that it was painful. In another research effort in which a prison environment was simulated, subjects took on the roles of guards and prisoners (Zimbardo, 1973). Subject "guards" were found to be verbally and physically aggressive to subject "prisoners," who allowed themselves to be treated in a dehumanized way. Finally, we are all probably aware of one behavior modification program or another that has been used to shape the behavior of children or patients without their consent or voluntary participation.

Such programs are dramatic in the issues they raise, but the underlying question concerning ethical principles of research is fundamental. Do experimenters have the right to require participation? To deceive subjects? What are the ethical responsibilities of researchers to subjects and to psychology as a science? The former has been an issue of concern to the American Psychological Association, and it has adopted a list of relevant ethical principles (*Ethical Principles of Psychologists*, 1981). The essence of these principles is that "the psychologist carries out the investigation with respect and concern for the dignity and welfare of the people who participate." This includes evaluating the ethical acceptability of the research, determining whether subjects in the study will be at risk in any way, and establishing a clear and fair agreement with research participants concerning the obligations and responsibilities of each. Although the use of concealment or deception is recognized as necessary in some cases, strict guidelines are presented. It is recognized as the responsibility of the investigator to protect participants from physical and mental discomfort, harm, and danger.

The ethical responsibility of psychologists includes the interpretation and presentation of results as well as the conduct of the research. Of late there has been serious concern in science generally with "the spreading stain of fraud" (*APA Monitor*, 1982). Some concern with this issue began with charges that Sir Cyril Burt, a once prominent British psychologist, intentionally misrepresented data in his research on the inheritance of intelligence. In other fields of science there have been reports of investigators intentionally manipulating data to enhance their chances of publication, grant funding, promotion, and public recognition. Recently, there was an investigation of whether psychologists working in the area of alcoholism had intentionally misrepresented their data. The issue of fraud is one that scientists do not like to recognize or talk about because it goes against the very fabric of the scientific enterprise. Although fraudulent data and falsified conclusions are very rare, the profession of psychologists is beginning to face up to their existence and to take constructive steps in solving the problem.

Much more subtle than fraud, and undoubtedly of much broader significance, is the issue of the effects of personal and social bias on the ways in which issues are developed and the kinds of data that are accepted as evidence in support for one or another enterprise (Pervin,

1984, Chapter 10). In considering sex differences, for example, to what extent are research projects developed in a way that is free from bias and to what extent is evidence for or against the existence of sex differences equally likely to be accepted? To what extent do our own social and political values influence not only what is studied but how it is studied and the kinds of conclusions we are prepared to reach (Bramel & Friend, 1981)? As noted, although scientists make every effort to be objective and remove all possible sources of error and bias from their research, this remains a human enterprise with the potential for personal, social, cultural, and political influence.

Finally, we may note in a related way the role of research in the formulation of public policy. Though still in an early stage of development as a science, psychology does relate to fundamental human concerns and psychologists are often called on to suggest the relevance of this research for public policy. This has happened with intelligence tests and immigration policy, child development and the effects of early enrichment programs such as Head Start, and the effects of television violence on aggression in everyday life.

Recently, Seligman's work has been related to societal functioning, with the suggestion that some social programs may operate to increase learned helplessness. For example, many Scandinavian countries have served as a model for social reform and social welfare. While praising these accomplishments, one Swedish psychologist has warned that a potential side effect of overly extensive programs in this area may be the development of a broad learned helplessness phenomenon in the population (Magnusson, 1980, pp. 73–74). In sum, among the issues that concern us as researchers and as consumers of research is that of how the results may be interpreted to direct, support, or refute various social policies.

Major Concepts and Summary	naturalistic observation	Attributional Style Questionnaire (ASQ)
	clinical research	Type A behavior pattern
	experimental research	Structured Interview (SI)
	laboratory research	Jenkins Activity Survey (JAS)
	correlational research	reliability
	learned helplessness	validity
	locus of control	demand characteristics
	Internal–External Scale	experimenter expectancy effects
	causal attribution: internal (personal)–external (universal), specific–global, stable–unstable	response style

This chapter has concerned itself with how psychologists conduct research on important personality phenomena. The goal of research is to establish facts and principles that can be interpreted within a broader theoretical framework. Although psychologists share certain goals in research and certain standards for evaluating research, they differ in the problems they choose for investigation and in the methods they favor in conducting research. Discussion of the two disciplines was followed by a more detailed analysis of the major alternative approaches to research. Three methods of research were emphasized: naturalistic observation and clinical research, laboratory experimentation, and correlational research using questionnaires. All three were considered in relation to the concepts of stress, helplessness, and control.

Naturalistic observation involves the study of phenomena as they occur naturally without any efforts on the part of the researcher to manipulate or control what occurs. Clinical research involves the intensive study of individuals. These approaches were illustrated in relation to the study of stress under conditions of war, in relation to clinical descriptions of patients treated for depression, as well as in observational studies of patient responses to illness. Clinical observations were also noted as important in the original description of the Type A behavior pattern.

Laboratory research involves the manipulation of specific variables and the ability to state if–then causal relationships. The research cited suggests that animals and people who experience conditions where events (reinforcements) are not contingent on their behavior are likely to develop feelings of helplessness and expect that they will be unable to influence the outcomes of events in the future. The expectation that outcomes are independent of responding is seen as having motivational, cognitive, and emotional implications. Also cited was research that demonstrated that stress (noise) may have effects on performance, after the stress is removed, even if there are no observable effects during the period of stress itself. Furthermore, the consequences of stress are influenced by the meanings a person attributes to the stress. If a person experiences a lack of control or sense of helplessness as a result of unpredictability, there will likely be negative behavioral aftereffects.

Work on the concept of locus of control illustrated the use of personality questionnaires in correlational research. The Internal–External Scale was developed to measure generalized expectancies concerning the control of reinforcers. Internals have a generalized belief in their ability to control events whereas externals believe in chance, luck, and fate. Individual differences in this generalized expectancy or belief have been found to be related to differences in effort on tasks, differences in anxiety and maladjustment, and differences in the attribution of blame for failure. It has been demonstrated that there is a relationship between external locus of control and the phenomenon of learned helplessness, both of which probably are related to the same causal factors.

The correlational approach to personality research was further illustrated in discussion of the reformulated model of learned helplessness. This model emphasizes the consequences of various causal attributions made by people: internal (personal)–external (universal), specific–global, stable–unstable. Research involving the Attributional Style Questionnaire (ASQ) suggests that internal (personal), global, and stable attributions have important implications for the development of depression. However, studies of attribution and depression have not yet established a causal relation between the two.

A final illustration of the use of questionnaires in personality research involved discussion of the Type A behavior pattern, which follows from a link between a pattern of personality characteristics (competitive achievement striving, sense of time urgency, aggressiveness) and increased risk of heart disease. Relationships have been found between high scores on the Jenkins Activity Survey (JAS), designed to measure the Type A behavior pattern, and behaviors assumed to put the person at risk for coronary heart disease. One suggestion made is that such people are involved in a continual struggle to control the environment. However, here too causal links remain to be established. Furthermore, there now is some question concerning the adequacy of the relation between scores on the SI and JAS, and some question as to which component of the Type A behavior pattern is most central to producing risk for coronary heart disease.

All research shares the goals of reliability and validity—of obtaining observations that can be replicated and for which there is evidence of a clear relation to the phenomena of interest. All human psychological research may suffer from certain sources of potential error or bias, expressed most clearly in the concepts of demand characteristics and experimenter expectancy effects. Beyond this, however, alternative approaches to personality research can be seen to have specific potential strengths and limitations. Naturalistic observation and clinical research facilitate investigation of the full complexity of human functioning in the real world, but are subject to the problems of unsystematic observation and subjective interpretation. Experimental research can be quite objective and useful in establishing cause–effect relationships, though often it sets limits on what can be observed and studied. Correlational research involving questionnaires facilitates the study of a wider range of variables, as well as interrelationships among many variables, but does not lead to the establishment of cause–effect relationships. In addition, self-report questionnaires are subject to particular sources of error and bias. Thus, alternative strategies to research are available that include within them the potential for particular insights as well as for particular pitfalls.

As a human enterprise, research involves ethical questions concerning the treatment of subjects and the reporting of data. The latter becomes particularly important as findings from psychological research begin to have an impact on public policy.

As we move now to consideration of specific theories of personality, we will have a chance to consider the application of these alternative research strategies and the implications that follow for the observation and conceptualization of personality.

Chapter Three
A Psychodynamic Theory: Freud's Psychoanalytic Theory of Personality

CHAPTER FOCUS: In this chapter we consider psychoanalytic theory as illustrative of a psychodynamic, clinical approach to personality. The psychodynamic emphasis is clear in the interpretation of behavior as a result of the interplay among motives, drives, needs, and conflicts. The clinical qualities are apparent in the emphasis on the individual, in the attention given to individual differences, and in attempts to assess and understand the total individual. The research consists mainly of clinical investigation.

> *It seems like an empty wrangle over words to argue whether mental life is to be regarded as co-extensive with consciousness or whether it may be said to stretch beyond this limit, and yet I can assure you that the acceptance of unconscious mental processes represents a decisive step toward a new orientation in the world and in science.*
>
> FREUD, 1924, p. 26

The first personality theory to be considered is that of psychoanalysis. The psychoanalytic theory of Freud is reviewed because of its prominence in the culture of our society, its place in the history of psychology, and its importance as a model of a psychodynamic theory of personality. Psychoanalysis has reflected changing values in our society and has itself played a role in the changing of these values. As noted by Norman O. Brown: "It is a shattering experience for anyone seriously committed to the Western tradition of morality and rationality to take a steadfast, unflinching look at what Freud has to say. It is humiliating to be compelled to admit the grossly seamy side of so many grand ideals. . . . To experience Freud is to partake a second time of the forbidden fruit" (1959, p. xi). Freud astutely observed that there had been three hurts to human self-love and self-image—the discovery by Copernicus that the earth was not the center of the universe, the discovery by Darwin that we do not exist independent of other members of the animal kingdom, and the discovery of the degree to which we are "influenced" by unknown, unconscious, and at times uncontrollable forces.

Psychoanalytic theory was derived from intensive work with individuals and, in turn, was applied to individuals. Although it involves assumptions relevant to all people, psychoanalytic theory has particular relevance to the study of individual differences as well as the total

A PSYCHODYNAMIC THEORY: FREUD'S THEORY OF PERSONALITY

functioning of individuals. Furthermore, psychoanalysis exemplifies a psychodynamic theory in that it gives a prominent role to the complex interplay among forces in human behavior. In psychoanalytic theory, behavior is a result of struggles and compromises among motives, drives, needs, and conflicts. Behavior can express a motive directly or in a subtle, disguised way. The same behavior can satisfy different motives in different people, or a variety of motives in one person. For example, eating can satisfy a hunger need but it also can symbolically satisfy a need for love; or being a psychoanalyst can satisfy a need to help others, a wish to discover new aspects of psychological functioning, a wish to satisfy one's curiosity about the private lives of others, or some combination of these as well as other motives. Being a doctor can satisfy a need to help others as well as serve as a way of overcoming anxieties about illness and bodily harm. Thus, any behavior or goal can satisfy a variety of motives at the same time. It is this quality of behavior that forms a major aspect of a psychodynamic theory of personality. Finally, behavior occurs at different levels of awareness, with individuals more or less aware of the forces behind their various behaviors. "The deeper we probe in our study of mental processes, the more we become aware of the richness and complexity of their content. Many simple formulas which seemed to us at first to meet the case turned out later to be inadequate. We are incessantly altering and improving them" (Freud, 1933, p. 121).

In this chapter we shall be analyzing and assessing a theory that is significant in its emphasis on individual differences, the entire personality, behavior as the result of an interplay among forces, personality as involving hierarchical organization, and phenomena as "simple" as the slip of the tongue and as "complex" as the development of culture. To increase the breadth and depth of our perspective, we shall turn our attention first to the life of the individual primarily responsible for psychoanalytic theory, and then to the view of the person and science implicit in his theory. Along with its usefulness for putting psychoanalytic theory into personal and historical perspective, a reading of the biography of Freud (Jones, 1953, 1955, 1957) gives one a sense of the genius and courage of the man responsible for the theory.

SIGMUND FREUD (1856–1939): A VIEW OF THE THEORIST

Sigmund Freud was born in Austria in 1856. He was the first child of his parents; although his father, 20 years older than his mother, had two sons by a previous marriage. His birth was followed by the birth and early death of one sibling and the birth of six more siblings. He is described as having been his mother's favorite and later was to say that "a man who has been the indisputable favorite of his mother keeps for life the feeling

Sigmund Freud

of a conqueror, that confidence of success that often induces real success" (Freud, 1900, p. 26). As a boy, he had dreams of becoming a great general or minister of state, but, being Jewish, he was concerned about anti-Semitism in these fields. This led him to consider medicine as a profession. As a medical student (1873–1881), he came under the influence of the noted physiologist Ernst Brücke. Brücke viewed humans in terms of a dynamic physiological system in which they are controlled by the physical principles of the conservation of energy. This view of physiological functioning was the foundation for Freud's dynamic view of psychological functioning (Sulloway, 1979).

After obtaining his medical degree, Freud did research and practiced in the field of neurology. Some of his early research involved a comparison of adult and fetal brains. He concluded that the earliest structures persist and are never buried, a view that was paralleled later by his views concerning the development of personality. Professionally, the years after medical school were filled first with theory and research, but then, for financial reasons, there was a turn toward practice. Personally, Freud experienced periodic depressions and attacks of anxiety, occasionally using cocaine to calm the agitation and dispel the depression. During these years he married and had three daughters and three sons.

In 1886 Freud spent a year with the French psychiatrist Jean Charcot, who was having some success in treating neurotic patients with hypnosis. Although not satisfied with the effects of hypnosis, Freud was stimulated by the thinking of Charcot and, essentially, changed during this time from a neurologist to a psychopathologist. Jones, the biographer of Freud, comments on Freud's development at this time. "All this work would have established Freud as a first class neurologist, a hard worker, a close thinker, but—with the exception perhaps of the book on aphasia —there was little to foretell the existence of genius" (1953, p. 220).

In 1897, the year following his father's death, Freud began his self-analysis. He continued to be bothered by periods of depression and, though intellectual pursuits helped to distract him from his pain, he looked for answers in his unconscious: "My recovery can only come through work in the unconscious; I cannot manage with conscious efforts alone." For the rest of his life he continued self-analysis, devoting the last half hour of the working day to it. In the 1890s, he tried a variety of therapeutic techniques with his patients. First he used hypnotic sugges- tion as practiced by Charcot. Then he tried a concentration technique in which he pressed his hand upon the patient's head and urged the recall of memories. During these years he also collaborated with the Viennese physician Joseph Breuer, learning from him the technique of **catharsis** (a release and freeing of emotion through talking about one's problems) and collaborating with him on a book *Studies in Hysteria*. At this point, already in his forties, Freud had developed little, if any, of what was later to become known as psychoanalysis. Furthermore, his judgments of himself and of his work parallel the comment made by his biographer Jones. "I have restricted capacities or talents. None at all for the natural sciences; nothing for mathematics; nothing for anything quantitative. But what I have, of a very restricted nature, is probably very intense."

The momentum in Freud's work and thinking most clearly dates back to his self-analysis and to the beginnings, in 1896, of his use of the **free-association** method with his patients. This method of allowing all thoughts to come forth without inhibition or falsification of any kind resulted, in 1900, in what many still consider to be Freud's most signifi- cant work, *The Interpretation of Dreams*. In this book, Freud began to develop his theory of the mind and, although only 600 copies were sold in the first eight years after publication, he began to develop a following. In 1902, a Psychoanalytic Society was formed, and was joined by a number of people who went on to become outstanding psychoanalysts—Alfred Adler, Paul Federn, Otto Rank, and Sandor Ferenczi. Freud's writing and development of theory progressed, but with increased public attention, there was increased public abuse. In 1904, Freud wrote on the *Psycho- pathology of Everyday Life*, and in 1905 he published *Three Essays on the Theory of Sexuality*. The latter presented Freud's views on infantile sexuality and its relation to perversions and neuroses. This resulted in ridicule of Freud, who was seen as an evil and wicked man with an obscene mind. Medical institutions were boycotted for tolerating Freud's view; an early follower, Ernest Jones, was forced to resign his neurologi- cal appointment for inquiring into the sexual life of his patients.

In 1909 Freud was invited by G. Stanley Hall to give a series of lectures at Clark University in Worcester, Massachusetts. During this period, Freud was developing his theories of development and infantile fantasies, his theory of the principles of mental functioning, and his views concerning the psychoanalytic process. He had by now achieved sufficient fame and acceptance to have a waiting list of patients.

But Freud had problems, too. By 1919 he had lost all his savings in the war. In 1920, a daughter, age 26, died. Perhaps of greatest significance was his fear for the lives of two sons who were in the war. It is out of such a historical context that Freud in 1920, at age 64, developed his theory of the death instinct—a wish to die, which is in opposition to the life instinct, or wish for survival.

Just as the war appeared to influence his thinking, so apparently did the growth of anti-Semitism during the 1930s. In 1932, for example, the Nazis in Berlin made a bonfire of his books. Shortly thereafter, Freud published his book on *Moses and Monotheism,* in which he suggested that Moses was an Egyptian noble who joined the Jews and gave them a religion. Freud attributed anti-Semitism to resentment against the strict moral code of the Jews and, in this book, appeared to say that it was not a Jew but an Egyptian who bears the onus.

Freud died on September 23, 1939, at the age of 83. Almost to the very end, he was doing analysis daily and continuing his writing. The last 20 years of his life represent a remarkable period of personal courage and productivity. Earlier, it had taken a great deal of courage to go on with his work in spite of considerable attack from the public and his medical colleagues. During this later period, it took considerable courage to go on in spite of the loss of many of his disciples, and in spite of the brutality of the Nazis. During these later years, Freud continued to work despite extreme physical discomfort and pain, including 33 operations for cancer of the jaw. Although not a wealthy man, he turned down lucrative offers that he felt would jeopardize the proper stature of his work. In 1920, he refused an offer from *Cosmopolitan* magazine to write on topics such as "The Husband's Place in the Home," saying to the magazine: "Had I taken into account the considerations that influence your edition from the beginning of my career, I am sure I should not have become known at all, either in America or Europe." In 1924 he turned down an offer of $100,000 by Samuel Goldwyn to collaborate in making films of famous love stories.

Most of what we now recognize as the major elements in Freud's theory were developed during these last 20 years. It was during these later years that Freud developed his final ideas concerning civilization, neuroses, psychoses, and perhaps most significant of all, his theory of anxiety and the mechanisms of defense. As a man he was glorified by some as being compassionate, courageous, and a genius. Others take note of his many battles and breaks with colleagues and see him as rigid, authoritarian, and intolerant of the opinions of others (Fromm, 1959).

Whatever the interpretation of Freud's personality, most, if not all, would agree that he had a passionate thirst for truth and pursued his studies with tremendous courage and integrity. Finally, most students of Freud, and psychoanalysis, would agree that factors in Freud's personal life and related historical factors (e.g., the Victorian era, World War I, and anti-Semitism) played a part in the final formulation of his theory and in the development of the psychoanalytic movement.

FREUD'S VIEW OF THE PERSON AND SOCIETY

It can be argued that implicit in psychoanalysis are a view of the person, a view of society, and perhaps even a total Weltanschauung or philosophy of life. Although Freud struggled to develop a theory based on science rather than philosophy, a theory free of biases from his personal life and the historical period of which he was a part, psychoanalytic theory reflects the themes that were current in the lay and scientific communities of late nineteenth- and early twentieth-century Europe. Freud's theory was based on observations, but these were primarily observations of middle- and upper-class patients of a Victorian era.

What is at the heart of the psychoanalytic view of the person is that the human is an energy system. There is the sense of a system in which energy flows, gets sidetracked, or becomes dammed-up. In all, there is a limited amount of energy, and if it gets used in one way, there is that much less energy to be used in another way. The energy that is used for cultural purposes is withdrawn from the energy available for sexual purposes, and vice versa. If the energy is blocked from one channel of expression, it finds another, generally along the path of least resistance. The goal of all behavior is **pleasure,** that is, the reduction of tension or the release of energy.

Why the assumption of an energy model concerning human behavior? The assumption is traceable to the excitement scientists were then experiencing in the field of energy dynamics. For example, according to the nineteenth-century physicist Helmholtz's principle of the conservation of energy, matter and energy can be transformed but not destroyed. Not only physicists but members of other disciplines were studying intensively the laws of energy changes in a system. As was already noted, while in medical school Freud came under the influence of the physiologist Brücke. Brücke viewed humans as moved by forces according to the principle of the conservation of energy, a view apparently translated by Freud into the psychological realm of behavior. The age of energy and dynamics provided scientists with a new conception of humans, "the view that man is an energy system and that he obeys the same physical laws which regulate the soap bubble and the movement of the planets" (Hall, 1954, pp. 12–13).

Beyond the view of the person as being an energy system, there is the view that humans are driven by sexual and aggressive instincts or drives. Freud's view of the importance of aggression in human behavior was based on observation, but his interpretation of these observations had the definite quality of a philosophical view. For example, in *Civilization and Its Discontents* (1930), Freud commented as follows. "The bit of truth behind all this—one so eagerly denied—is that men are not gentle, friendly creatures wishing for love, who simply defend themselves if they are attacked, but that a powerful measure of desire for aggression has to be reckoned as a part of their instinctual endowment" (p. 85). Freud goes on to comment that the instinct of aggression lies "at the bottom of all relations of affection and love between human beings—possibly with the single exception of that of a mother to her male child" (p. 89). We have already noted that Freud published his theory of aggression and the death instinct in 1920, after the extended and bloody period of the First World War.

Along with the aggressive drive, Freud placed great emphasis on the sexual drive, and on the conflict between expression of these drives and society. The emphasis on sexual inhibition in particular appears to relate to the Victorian period of which Freud and his patients were a part. For Freud, the person in pursuit of pleasure was in conflict with society and civilization. People function according to the **pleasure principle,** seeking "unbridled gratification" of all desires. Yet, such a mode of operation runs counter to the demands of society and the external world. The energy that would otherwise be released in the pursuit of pleasure and gratification must now be inhibited and channeled to conform to the aims of society. Freud believed that scientific activities and artistic endeavors, in fact the whole range of cultural productivity, are expressions of sexual and aggressive energy that is prevented from expression in a more direct way.

Another possible outgrowth of this conflict between the individual and society is misery and neurosis. In fact, according to Freud, the price of progress in civilization is misery, the forfeiting of happiness, and a heightened sense of guilt. It is even worth the possibility of giving up civilization and returning to primitive conditions!

We can see, then, that beyond the formal conceptualization of a theory of personality, there is implicit in psychoanalysis a view of the person. According to this view humans, like other animals, are driven by instincts or drives and operate in the pursuit of pleasure. People operate as an energy system, building, storing, and releasing, in one form or another, what is basically the same energy. All behavior is determined, much of it by forces outside of awareness. In the end, psychoanalysis sides with the instincts and seeks a reduction in the extent to which the instincts are frustrated.

In sum, the person is an energy system, driven by sexual and aggressive drives and operating in the pursuit of pleasure (tension reduction), functioning in a regular, lawful way, but often unaware of the forces determining behavior, and basically in conflict with society's restrictions on the expressions of the instincts.

FREUD'S VIEW OF SCIENCE, THEORY, AND RESEARCH

It is important to note that Freud himself disclaimed any relationship between psychoanalysis and philosophy. Freud found the philosopher's thinking too far removed from the rigors of science and viewed psychoanalysis as a branch of psychology and a part of science.

We know that Freud was trained in medical research and appreciated the relation between theory and research. He felt a need for sharp definition of concepts, but he also accepted the possibility that vague conceptions and speculative theory might be necessary during the early stages of science. Thus, Freud could insist on the importance of the instincts while calling them "mythical beings, superb in their indefiniteness."

Although he developed an elaborate theory of personality, Freud's major contribution was in the nature of the observations he made. He was aware that theories could and would change, and he saw these observations as the ultimate contribution of psychoanalysis to the science of psychology. It is important to note that Freud's observations were based on the analysis of patients and, by and large, he had little use for mechanical efforts to verify psychoanalytic principles in the laboratory. When a psychologist wrote to Freud to tell him of his experimental studies of one psychoanalytic concept, Freud wrote back that psychoanalytic concepts were based on a wealth of reliable observations and thus were not in need of independent experimental verification. He was satisfied using the intensive clinical study of the individual case as his major research method.

It is clear that this research method allows for the accumulation of considerable data about an individual. There is probably no other method in psychology that even approximates the wealth of material gathered about a single person by the psychoanalyst. On the other hand, as Freud himself pointed out, analysts are unlike other scientists in that they do not use experiments as a significant part of their research. Although Freud viewed psychoanalysis as a part of the science of psychology, most of the early research was conducted by medical professionals in a therapeutic setting. It is only within the last 20 to 30 years that psychologists have tried to apply the traditional scientific techniques of the discipline to the concepts of psychoanalysis. As we consider psychoanalytic concepts, we shall continue to see this struggle between the complex, uncontrolled observations of the clinical setting and the systematic, controlled study of phenomena in the laboratory.

PSYCHOANALYSIS: A THEORY OF PERSONALITY

Psychoanalysis is three things—a theory of personality, a method of therapy, and a technique for research. It is important to keep these different aspects in mind, since comments and criticisms appropriate to one may not be relevant to the other. For example, criticism of psychoanalysis as a therapy does not reflect on psychoanalysis as a theory, unless the theory is being tested in the course of therapy. The improvement of a patient in therapy is not critical to the theory, unless the theory makes specific predictions concerning the progress of the patient. Since therapy is such a complex process, and the nature of environmental events outside of therapy can never be predicted, the theory is rarely used to make predictions concerning the outcome of therapy. While keeping these aspects separate, however, we must also seek to see the links between them.

Structure

What are the structural units used by psychoanalytic theory to account for human behavior? In the early development of the theory the concept of levels of consciousness served as a focal point in psychoanalytic thinking. In fact, Freud claimed that "Psychoanalysis aims at and achieves nothing more than the discovery of the unconscious in mental life" (1924, p. 397).

Levels of consciousness

According to the psychoanalytic theory, psychic life can be described in terms of the degree to which we are aware of phenomena: the **conscious** relates to phenomena we are aware of at any given moment, the **preconscious** to phenomena we are able to be aware of if we attend to them, and the **unconscious** to phenomena that we are unaware of, and *cannot* become aware of except under special circumstances.

Although Freud was not the first to pay attention to the importance of the unconscious, he was the first to explore in detail the qualities of unconscious life and attribute major importance to them in our daily lives. Through the analysis of dreams, slips of the tongue, neuroses, psychoses, works of art, and rituals, Freud attempted to understand the properties of the unconscious. What he found was a quality of psychic life in which nothing was impossible. The unconscious is alogical (opposites can stand for the same thing), is disregarding of time (events of different periods may coexist), and is disregarding of space (size and distance relationships are neglected so that large things fit into small things and distant places are brought together). One is reminded of William James's reference to the world of the newly born infant as a "big blooming buzzing confusion."

Within the unconscious, there is a fluidity and plasticity to phenomena that is rarely observed during our rational, waking life. It is in the dream, and in the psychic productions of psychotics, that the workings of the unconscious become most apparent. Here we are exposed to the world of symbols, where many ideas may be telescoped into a single word, where a part of any object may stand for many things. It is through the process of symbolization that a penis can be represented by a snake or nose, a woman by a church, chapel, or boat, and an engulfing mother by an octopus. It is through this process that we are allowed to think of writing as a sexual act—the pen is the male organ and the paper is the woman who receives the ink (the semen) that flows out in the quick up and down movements of the pen (Groddeck, 1923). In *The Book of the It*, Groddeck, gives many fascinating examples of the workings of the unconscious and offers the following as an example of the functioning of the unconscious in his own life.

> I cannot recall her [my nurse's] appearance. I know nothing more than her name, Bertha, the shining one. But I have a clear recollection of the day she went away. As a parting present she gave me a copper three-pfennig piece. A Dreier. . . . Since that day I have been pursued by the number three. Words like trinity, triangle, triple alliance, convey something disreputable to me, and not merely the words but the ideas attached to them, yes, and the whole complex of ideas built up around them by the capricious brain of a child. For this reason, the Holy Ghost, as the Third Person of the Trinity, was already suspect to me in early childhood; trigonometry was a plague in my school days. . . . Yes, three is a sort of fatal number for me.
>
> GRODDECK, 1923, p. 9

The unconscious is never observed directly. What evidence then is there that supports the concept of the unconscious? Let us consider the range of evidence that might be considered supportive of the concept of the unconscious, beginning with Freud's clinical observations. Freud realized the importance of the unconscious after observing hypnotic phenomena. As is well known, people under the effects of hypnosis can recall things they previously could not. Furthermore, they will perform things under posthypnotic suggestion without consciously "knowing" that they are behaving in accordance with that suggestion; that is, in the latter case, they will fully believe that what they are doing is voluntary and independent of any suggestion by another person. When Freud discarded the technique of hypnosis and continued with his therapeutic work, he found that often patients would become aware of memories and wishes of which they previously had been unaware. Frequently, such discoveries were associated with considerable painful emotion. It is indeed a powerful clinical observation to see a patient suddenly experience

FAILURE, UNHAPPINESS, AND UNCONSCIOUS MOTIVATION

In his study of "Those Wrecked by Success," Freud described individuals who, because of feelings of guilt, would fall ill once they had achieved some long-cherished wish. More recently, the psychoanalyst Roy Schafer has described the unconscious meanings success, failure, happiness, and unhappiness can have for people. He suggests that repetitive failure and chronic unhappiness typically are self-inflicted rather than expressions of inescapable events. For example, in one case a male underachieved to ward off the envy of others, whereas in another case a young man pursued failure to protect the self-esteem of his unsuccessful father: "Thus, for this young man, failure

was also a success of a kind, while being a success was also a failure." In a third case, a woman was self-sacrificing to an extreme degree so as to retain the love of others. Although the "pursuit of failure" and the "idealization of unhappiness" are seen as being found in members of both sexes, Schafer suggests that the former is more prevalent in men whereas the latter is more prevalent in women. This is not to say, however, that all cases of failure or unhappiness are motivated or the result of unconscious conflicts.

SOURCE: Schafer, 1984.

Newsweek, May 21, 1984; p. 79 (Copyright © 1980 The New Yorker Magazine, Reprinted by permission.)

"He's mad as hell. He has this need to fail and he keeps getting promoted."

tremendous anxiety, sob hysterically, or break into a rage as they recall a forgotten event or get in touch with a forbidden feeling. Thus, it was clinical observations such as these that suggested to Freud that the unconscious includes memories and wishes that not only are not currently part of our consciousness but are "deliberately buried" in our unconscious.

What of experimental evidence? Let us consider the evidence for unconscious perception or **perception without awareness** wherein "the brain responds to stimuli of which the mind remains oblivious" (Dixon, 1981, p. 17). Can the person "know" something without knowing that they know it? There is considerable research evidence that this is indeed the case. Thus, for example, people can have emotional responses conditioned to sounds they cannot report hearing and may be influenced by messages going into one ear that they cannot report hearing because they are attending to messages in another ear.

Perhaps the easiest way to understand what otherwise may seem like a mystical process is to describe a piece of relevant research. This research may be seen as part of the area of *subliminal stimulation* or the registration of stimuli at a level that is below that required for awareness. In this research each of two groups of subjects was exposed to a picture. The two pictures used, one for each group, are presented in Figure 3.1. How similar do the two seem? Is there a significant difference? Perhaps in this case it is obvious that the one on the right contains a duck image shaped by the branches of the tree. However, in the actual research each group of subjects was shown the picture at a rapid speed so that it was barely visible. This was done through the use of a tachistoscope, an apparatus that allows the experimenter to show stimuli to subjects at very fast speeds, so they cannot be perceived, or at slow speeds. Once the picture had been shown the subjects closed their eyes and imagined a nature scene. They then drew the scene and labeled the parts. Would the two groups, those seeing the picture in Figure 3.1 on the left and those seeing the one on the right, draw different pictures? It was found that more of the subjects viewing the picture on the right had duck-related images ("duck," "water," "birds," "feathers") in their drawings; and as a group, they had significantly more such images than did subjects in the group viewing the picture on the left. Was this because of differences in what could be reported as having been perceived? The subjects did not report seeing the duck during the experiment and the majority even had trouble finding it when they were asked to look for it. The conclusion drawn was that stimuli that are not consciously perceived may still influence the imagery and thoughts of people (Eagle, Wolitzky, & Klein, 1966).

The fact that people can perceive and be influenced by stimuli of which they are unaware does not in itself suggest that there are psychodynamic or motivational forces involved. Is there evidence that such is or can be the case? Two relevant lines of research can be noted. The first

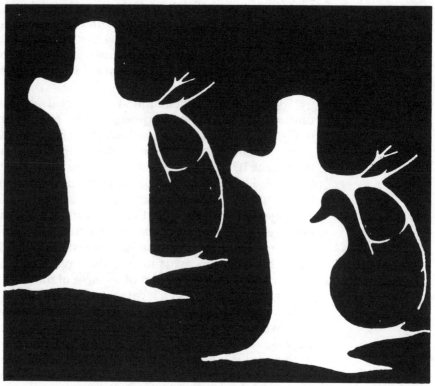

FIGURE 3.1 *The Concept of the Unconscious* (Eagle, Wolitzky, and Klein, 1966, p. 838)

has been called **perceptual defense** and involves a process by which the individual defends against the anxiety that accompanies actual recognition of a threatening stimulus. In a relevant early experiment, subjects were shown two types of words in a tachistoscope: neutral words such as apple, dance, child and emotionally toned words such as rape, whore, penis. The words were shown first at very fast speeds and then at progressively slower speeds. A record was made of the point at which the subjects were able to identify each of the words and their sweat-gland activity (a measure of tension) in response to each word. These records indicated that subjects took longer to recognize the emotionally toned words than the neutral words and that they showed signs of emotional response to the emotionally toned words prior to their being verbally identified (McGinnies, 1949). Despite criticism of such research (e.g., Did subjects identify the emotionally toned words earlier but were they reluctant to verbalize them to the experimenter?), there appears to be considerable evidence that people can, outside of awareness, be selectively responsive to and rejecting of specific emotional stimuli (Erdelyi, 1984).

A related line of research has been called **subliminal psycho-dynamic activation** (Silverman, 1976; 1982). In this research, there is an effort to stimulate unconscious wishes without making them conscious. In general, the experimental procedure involves using a tachistoscope to show subjects material related to wishes that are expected to be either threatening or anxiety alleviating to them and then observing whether the expected effects do occur. In the first case, the material being presented subliminally (below threshold for conscious recognition) is expected to stir up unconscious conflict and thus increase psychological disturbance. In the latter case, the material being presented subliminally is expected to diminish unconscious conflict and thus decrease psychological disturbance. For example, the content "I Am Losing Mommy" might be upsetting to some subjects whereas the content "Mommy and I Are One" might be reassuring. In a series of studies, Silverman and his colleagues have demonstrated that such subliminal psychodynamic activation effects can be produced. In one recent study this method was used to present conflict-intensifying material ("Loving Daddy Is Wrong") and conflict-reducing material ("Loving Daddy Is OK") to female undergraduates. For subjects prone toward conflict over sexual urges, the conflict-intensifying material, presented outside of awareness, was found to disrupt memory for passages presented after the subliminal activation of the conflict. This was not true for the conflict-reducing material or for subjects not prone toward conflict over sexual urges (Geisler, 1986). What is key here is that the content that is upsetting or relieving to various groups of subjects is predicted beforehand on the basis of psychoanalytic theory and that the effects only occur when the stimuli are perceived subliminally or unconsciously.

The research on perceptual defense and subliminal psychodynamic activation has been proclaimed by some as conclusive experimental evidence in support of the importance of psychodynamic, motivational factors in determining what is "deposited into" and "kept in" the unconscious (Dixon, 1981). On the other hand, the experiments have frequently been criticized on methodological grounds and at times some of the effects have been difficult to replicate or reproduce in other laboratories (Condon & Allen, 1980; Heilbrun, 1980, 1982; Oliver & Burkham, 1982).

It is hard to overestimate the importance of the concept of the unconscious to psychoanalytic theory, the moral dilemmas over responsibility that have occurred as a result of it, and the difficulties it has presented to scientists interested in rigorous, controlled investigation. Clearly, acceptance of this concept represents more than just acceptance of the principle that there are aspects of our functioning of which we are not fully aware. Far more than this, the psychoanalytic concept of the unconscious suggests that a significant portion of our behavior, perhaps the major one, is determined by unconscious forces, and that much of our psychic energy is devoted either to finding acceptable expression of unconscious ideas or to keeping them unconscious. The concept of the unconscious is deeply embedded in the rest of psychoanalytic theory. Although many new concepts were added as the theory developed, the concept of the unconscious has always remained as part of the framework for the entire theory.

Almost all psychologists, whether psychoanalytic or otherwise, would agree at this point that unconscious processes are important in influencing what we attend to and how we feel (Glucksberg, 1982; Posner, 1981). One recent review goes so far as to suggest that "no psychological model that seeks to explain how human beings know, learn, or behave can ignore the concept of unconscious psychological processes" (Shevrin & Dickman, 1981, p. 432). What still needs further exploration, however, is the role of specific motivations and conflicts in keeping memories and feelings outside of awareness.

In a sense, psychology has come a long way in taking what Freud described as a decisive step toward a new orientation in the world and in science. At the same time, it should be clear that not all psychologists agree on the importance given by Freud to the unconscious.

Id, ego, and superego

In 1923 Freud developed a more formal structural model for psychoanalysis, defined by the concepts of id, ego, and superego, which refer to different aspects of people's functioning. According to the theory, the **id** represents the source of all drive energy. The energy for a person's functioning originally resides in the life and death, or sexual and aggressive instincts, which are part of the id. In its functioning, the id seeks the release of excitation, tension, and energy. It operates according to the **pleasure principle**—the pursuit of pleasure and the avoidance of pain. In operating this way the id seeks immediate, total release. It has qualities of a spoiled child: it wants what it wants when it wants it. The id cannot tolerate frustration and is free of inhibitions. It shows no regard for reality and can seek satisfaction through action or through imagining that it has gotten what it wants—the fantasy of gratification is as good as the actual gratification. It is without reason, logic, values, morals, or ethics. In sum, the id is demanding, impulsive, blind, irrational, asocial, selfish, and, finally, pleasure loving.

In marked contrast to the id is the **superego,** which represents the moral branch of our functioning, containing the ideals we strive for and the punishments (guilt) we expect when we have gone against our ethical code. This structure functions to control behavior in accordance with the rules of society, offering rewards (pride, self-love) for "good" behavior and punishments (guilt, feelings of inferiority, accidents) for "bad" behavior. The superego may function on a very primitive level, being relatively incapable of reality testing, that is, incapable of modifying its action depending on circumstances. In such cases, the person is unable to distinguish between thought and action, feeling guilty for thinking some-

ARE ALL DREAMS AND SLIPS DETERMINED BY THE MOTIVATED UNCONSCIOUS?

For some time the phenomena of special interest to Freud and psychoanalysts were neglected by psychologists. More recently cognitive psychologists have begun to be interested in unconscious phenomena, dreams, and slips of the tongue, but their approach is different and they are coming to somewhat different conclusions. In relation to awareness, there is substantial evidence that we unconsciously respond to events and feelings that do not reach the level of conscious awareness. There also is evidence that conscious thinking proceeds more rationally and logically than does unconscious thinking and that decisions may be made outside of awareness. What is unclear is whether such decisions are influenced, guided, and directed by *motives* present in the unconscious.

In relation to dreams, it would appear that some dreams have meaning and may serve to disguise secret wishes and conflicts. However, another view is that most, if not all, dreams merely represent an integration of experiences of the day; that is, our dreams represent the weaving together of daily events and experiences into a story, but a story without unconscious meaning. Similarly, although there may be an unconscious, hidden meaning for some slips, others appear to be the result of slips in attention or errors due to competing choices of words.

With increased interest in such phenomena, the underlying question is whether the kinds of unconscious forces emphasized by Freud *can* play a role in determining slips and dreams, and, if so, whether such forces *always* play a role, or whether Freudian explanations make no sense at all and alternative explanations must be considered.

While some slips of the tongue may merely represent a confusion among choice of words, others seem to fit with Freud's suggestion that slips express hidden wishes. (Illustration by Patrick McConnell. *Psychology Today*, February 1987. Copyright © 1987 American Psychological Association. Reprinted by permission from *Psychology Today*.)

"Double Scotches for me and my super-ego, and a glass of water for my id, which is driving."

Psychoanalytic Theory—Freud emphasized the concepts of id, ego, and superego as structures of personality, Drawing by Handelsman; © 1972 The New Yorker Magazine, Inc.

thing even if it did not lead to action. Furthermore, the individual is bound by black–white, all–none judgments and by the pursuit of perfection. Excessive use of words such as good, bad, judgment, and trial are often expressive of a strict superego. But the superego can also be understanding and flexible. For example, people may be able to forgive themselves or someone else if it is clear that something was an accident or done under circumstances of severe stress. In the course of development, children learn to make such important distinctions and see things not only in all-or-none, right-or-wrong, black-or-white terms.

The third structure conceptualized in the theory is that of the **ego.** Whereas the id seeks pleasure and the superego seeks perfection, the ego seeks reality. The function of the ego is to express and satisfy the desires of the id in accordance with reality and the demands of the superego. Whereas the id operates according to the pleasure principle, the ego operates according to the **reality principle**—gratification of the instincts is delayed until an optimum time when the most pleasure can be obtained with the least pain or negative consequences. According to the reality principle, the energy of the id may be blocked, diverted, or released gradually, all in accordance with the demands of reality and the conscience. Such an operation is not in contradiction to the pleasure principle but, rather, represents a temporary suspension of it. It functions, in George Bernard Shaw's words, so as "to be able to choose the line of greatest advantage instead of yielding in the direction of least resistance." The ego is able to separate wish from fantasy, can tolerate tension and compromise, and changes over time. Accordingly, it expresses the development of perceptual and cognitive skills, the ability to perceive more and think in more complex terms. For example, the person can begin to think in terms of the future and what is best in the long run. All these qualities are in contrast with the unrealistic, unchanging, demanding qualities of the id.

In comparison with his investigations into the unconscious and the workings of the id, Freud did relatively little work on the functioning of the ego. He pictured the ego as a weak structure, a poor creature that owed service to three harsh masters—the id, reality, and the superego. The "poor" ego has a hard time serving these masters and must reconcile the claims and demands of each. Of particular significance is the relation of the ego to the tyranny of the id.

> One might compare the relation of the ego to the id with that between a rider and his horse. The horse provides the locomotive energy, and the rider has the prerogative of determining the goal and of guiding the movements of his powerful mount towards it. But all too often in the relations between the ego and the id we find a picture of the less ideal situation in which the rider is obliged to guide his horse in the direction in which it itself wants to go.
>
> FREUD, 1933, p. 108

In sum, Freud's ego is logical, rational, tolerant of tension, the "executive" of personality, but it is a poor rider on the swift horse of the id and is subject to control by three masters.

Just before his death Freud began to give more attention to the importance of the ego in personality. This attention was then developed by his daughter, Anna Freud, and a number of analysts whose work has been categorized under the heading of ego psychology. Whereas in the earlier view the ego was viewed as existing without energy of its own and obliged to guide the id where it wanted to go, the later view emphasized the importance of the ego in conflict resolution as well as in adaptation. This view left room for the possibility that the individual may experience pleasure through the conflict-free functioning of the ego, and not only through the release of the energies of the id. According to ego psychology, the ego has a source of energy of its own and takes pleasure in mastery of the environment. This concept is related to R. W. White's (1959) concept of competence motivation. In its description of personality, this view gave increased importance to the ways in which individuals actively engage their environment and to their modes of thinking and perceiving. Although these modes still could be considered as functioning in the service of the id and serving to reduce conflict, they were now viewed as having adaptive functions and importance independent of these other functions.

It is important to understand the status of the concepts used by the theory. The concepts of conscious, unconscious, id, ego, and superego are at a high level of abstraction and are not always defined with great precision. For example, the unconscious is at times taken to mean a structure, at times refers to forces pushing toward expression in consciousness and behavior, and at times refers to descriptive properties of psychic phenomena. Furthermore, there is some lack of clarity because the meaning of some concepts changed as the theory developed, but the exact nature of the change in meaning was never spelled out (Madison, 1961). Finally, it should be clear that these are conceptualizations of phenomena. Even though the language is picturesque and concrete, we must avoid regarding concepts as real things. There is no energy plant inside us with a little person controlling its power. We do not "have" an id, ego, and superego but, according to the theory, there are qualities of human behavior that are usefully conceptualized in these structural terms. The structures achieve greater definition in relation to the processes implied in them, and it is to these processes that we now turn.

Process
Life and death instincts
We have discussed Freud's view of the person as an energy system obeying the same laws as other energy systems. Energy may be altered and transformed but essentially it is all the same energy. Within such an overall framework, the processes (dynamics) involved in psychoanalytic theory relate to the ways in which energy is expressed, blocked, or transformed in some way. According to the theory, the source of all psychic energy lies in states of excitation within the body that seek expression and tension reduction. These states are called **instincts,** or **drives**, and represent constant, inescapable forces. In the earlier view, there were ego instincts, relating to tendencies toward self-preservation, and sexual instincts, relating to tendencies toward preservation of the race. In the later view, there was the **life instinct**, including both of the earlier ego and sexual instincts, and the **death instinct**, involving an aim on the part of the organism to die or return to an inorganic state. The energy of the life instinct was called **libido**. No name has come to be commonly associated with the energy of the death instinct. In fact, the death instinct remains one of the most controversial and least-accepted parts of the theory, with most analysts instead referring to the **aggressive instinct**. Both sexual and aggressive instincts are viewed as being part of the id.

In psychoanalytic theory, the instincts are characterized as aiming toward the immediate reduction of tension, toward satisfaction and pleasure. They are gratified by means of external stimuli or objects. In contrast to lower animals, the objects for humans that are capable of gratifying an instinct are many and varied. This provides for uniqueness in personality. Furthermore, in humans the instincts can be delayed and modified before they are released.

In the dynamics of functioning, what can happen to one's instincts? They can, at least temporarily, be blocked from expression or expressed without modification. More likely is some change in the quality or direction of the instinct. For example, there may be partial (aim-inhibited) rather than full expression of the instinct. Affection may be a partial, aim-inhibited expression of the sexual instinct, and sarcasm an expression of the aggressive instinct. It is also possible for the object of gratification of the instinct to be changed or *displaced* from the original object to another object. Thus, the love of one's mother may be displaced to the wife, kids, or dog. Each instinct may be transformed or modified, and the instincts can combine with one another. Football, for example, can gratify both sexual and aggressive instincts; in surgery there can be the fusion of love and destruction. It should already be clear how psychoanalytic theory is able to account for so much behavior on the basis of only two instincts. It is the fluid, mobile, changing qualities of the instincts and their many alternative kinds of gratification that allow for such variability in behavior. In essence, the same instinct can be gratified in a number of ways, and the same behavior can have different causes in different people or multiple gratifications for any one individual.

Virtually every process in psychoanalytic theory can be described in terms of the expenditure of energy in an object or in terms of a force inhibiting the expenditure of energy, that is, inhibiting gratification of an instinct. Because it involves an expenditure of energy, people who direct much of their efforts toward inhibition end up feeling tired and bored. The interplay between the expression of instincts and their inhibition forms the foundation of the dynamic aspects of psychoanalytic theory. The key to this is the concept of **anxiety**. In psychoanalytic theory, anxiety is a painful, emotional experience, representing a threat or danger to the organism. In a state of "free-floating" anxiety, individuals are unable to relate their state of tension to an external object, in contrast to a state of fear, where the source of tension is known. Freud had two theories of anxiety. In the first theory, anxiety was viewed as a result of undischarged sexual impulses — dammed-up libido. In the later theory, anxiety represented a painful emotion that acted as a signal of impending danger to the ego. Here, anxiety, an ego function, alerts the ego to danger so that it can act.

The psychoanalytic theory of anxiety states that at some point the organism experiences a trauma, an incident of considerable harm or injury. Anxiety represents a repetition of the earlier traumatic experience, but in miniature form. Anxiety in the present, then, is related to an earlier danger. It is because the earlier trauma is not recalled that anxiety has its free-floating quality. The sources of anxiety may reside in the id, in the superego, or in reality. Where the id is the source of anxiety, the individual feels threatened with being overwhelmed by impulses. Where the superego is the source of anxiety, the individual experiences guilt and self-condemnation. It is as if the id says "I want it," the superego says "How terrible," and the ego says "I'm afraid." Basically, anxiety develops out of a conflict between the push of the id instincts and the threat of punishment by the superego.

Anxiety and the mechanisms of defense

Anxiety is such a painful state that we are incapable of tolerating it for very long. How is it that we are able to deal with such a state? Why are we not anxious more of the time? The answer is that individuals develop **defense mechanisms** against anxiety. Unconsciously, we develop ways to distort reality and exclude feelings from awareness so that we do not feel anxious. What are some of the ways in which this can be done? One of the most primitive defense mechanisms is **projection**. In projection, what is internal and unacceptable is projected out and seen as external. Rather than recognize hostility in oneself, the individual sees others as being hostile. There is in this process a fluidity of boundaries, or a breakdown in the differentiation between what is self and what is other.

In a relevant experimental study, Sears (1936) investigated the degree to which subjects possessed traits such as stinginess, obstinacy, disorderliness, and bashfulness, whether the subjects had insight into their possession of the traits, and the degree to which they attributed the traits to others. He found that subjects who lacked insight into their possession of a trait tended to attribute a greater amount of the trait to others than did subjects who possessed an equal amount of the trait but had insight into this. Furthermore, subjects who lacked insight into their own possession of unacceptable traits gave more extreme ratings on the trait to others and considered the traits to be more unacceptable than did subjects who had insight.

Efforts to produce projection experimentally have been more problematic (Holmes, 1978, 1981). In a semi-experimental study Halpern (1977) tested the psychoanalytic hypothesis that defensive subjects would respond to threat by projecting feared characteristics on to disliked others. First, a measure of sexual defensiveness was obtained by scoring the number of times the subject agreed with questionnaire items such as "I never have sexual fantasies" and "I never have dreams with sexual content." Subjects were thereby divided into a high-defensive group and a low-defensive group. Members of each group were then exposed to one of two conditions. In one, subjects were exposed to pornographic photographs. In the other group, subjects received no stimuli of a sexual nature. Following this, all subjects were asked to rate the most unfavorable person seen in the photographs as well as themselves on a list of traits.

How might projection appear and where? The trait "lustful" was selected as key with the expectation that high-defensive subjects would project this trait onto the unfavorable person when they had been stimulated by the nude photographs. Presumably such stimuli would be threatening to the high sexual defense group and provide the conditions for projection. Indeed, sexually defensive subjects who viewed the nude photographs rated the unfavorable person highest on lustful, whereas the nondefensive subjects who viewed the nude photographs gave this person the lowest lustful ratings. In both conditions, the high-defensive subjects rated themselves lower on the trait lustful than did the low-defensive subjects. The study is noteworthy in demonstrating that certain conditions were required for projection to occur. In addition, the study recognized that according to psychoanalytic theory, people will project only those traits or motives they are seeking to defend against and will associate these characteristics with an unfavorable person; that is *projection as a defense is only used in relation to specific characteristics, under particular conditions, and in relation to specific others.* Unfortunately, many research studies are not so careful in their definition and exploration of this mechanism of defense.

A second defense mechanism is that of **denial**. Here there may be either denial of reality, as in the girl who denies she lacks a penis or in the boy who in fantasy denies the lack of power, or denial of impulse, as when an irate person protests "I do not feel angry." The saying "Thou doth protest too much" gives specific reference to this defense. Denial of reality is commonly seen where people attempt to avoid recognizing the extent of a threat. The expression "Oh no!" upon hearing of the death of a close friend represents the reflex action of denial. Children have been known to deny the death of a loved animal and long afterward to behave as if it were still alive. Denial of reality is also seen when people say, or assume, "It can't happen to me" in spite of clear evidence of impending doom. This defense was seen in Jews who were victims of the Nazis. Steiner (1966), in his book on the Nazi concentration camp Treblinka, describes how the population acted as if death did not exist, in spite of clear evidence to the contrary all around them. He notes that the extermination of a whole people was so unimaginable that the people could not accept it. They preferred to accept lies rather than to bear the terrible trauma of the truth.

Another way to deal with anxiety and threat is to isolate events in memory or to isolate emotion from the content of a memory or impulse. In **isolation**, the impulse, thought, or act is not denied access to consciousness, but it is denied the normal accompanying emotion. For example, a woman may experience the thought or fantasy of strangling her child without any associated feelings of anger. The result of using the mechanism of isolation is *intellectualization*, an emphasis on thought over emotion and feeling, and the development of logic-tight compartments. In such cases, the feelings that do exist may be split, as in the case

Denial and Addiction—One of the most frequently cited characteristics of alcoholics and drug addicts is denial. The former Brooklyn Dodger pitcher, Johnny Podres, describes how he'd come home drunk, his mother would say he's an alcoholic, and he'd say "Not me." Another former Dodger pitcher, Don Newcombe, also a reformed alcoholic, describes how he and his drinking buddies would all deny their problem: "That's part of the syndrome—the denial syndrome." And in seeking to understand why N.Y. Mets pitcher Dwight Gooden would agree to be tested for cocaine use when he was using cocaine, one expert suggested that "massive denial is the hallmark of cocaine addiction. There is some denial in all addictions, but it is probably greatest in cocaine abuse." (*N.Y. Times*, July 30, 1983 and April 4, 1987.)

where a male separates women into two categories, one with whom there is love but no sex and the other with whom there is sex but no love (Madonna–prostitute complex).

People who use the mechanism of isolation also often use the mechanism of **undoing**. Here, the individual magically undoes one act or wish with another act. "It is a kind of negative magic in which the individual's second act abrogates or nullifies the first, in such a manner that it is as though neither had taken place, whereas in reality both have done so" (Freud, 1936, p. 33). This mechanism is seen in compulsive acts in which the person has an unresistible impulse to perform some act (e.g., the person undoes a suicide or homicide fantasy by compulsively turning off the gas jets at home), in religious rituals, and in children's sayings such as "Don't step on the crack or you will break your mother's back."

In **reaction-formation**, the individual defends against expression of an unacceptable impulse by only recognizing and expressing its opposite. This defense is evident in socially desirable behavior that is rigid, exaggerated, and inappropriate. The person who uses reaction-formation cannot admit to other feelings, as in overprotective mothers who cannot allow any conscious hostility toward their children. Reaction-formation is most clearly observable when the defense breaks down, as when the good, model boy shoots his parents, or when the man who "wouldn't hurt a fly" goes on a killing rampage. Of similar interest here are the occasional reports of judges who go on to commit crimes.

A mechanism often familiar to students is that of **rationalization**. Here an action is perceived, but the underlying motive is not. Behavior is reinterpreted so that it appears reasonable and acceptable. What is of particular interest about rationalization is that with this defense the individual can express the dangerous impulse, seemingly without it being frowned on by the superego. Some of the greatest atrocities of humankind have been committed in the name of the Christian God of love. The leaders of the Inquisition tortured persons who were without a "proper" attitude toward Christ. It is through the defense of rationalization that we can be hostile while expressing God's will, that we can be immoral in the pursuit of morality.

Finally, we come to the major primary defense mechanism, **repression**. In repression, a thought, idea, or wish is dismissed from consciousness. It is as if we say "What we don't know or remember can't hurt us." Repression is viewed as playing a part in all the other defense mechanisms and, like these other defenses, requires a constant expenditure of energy to keep that which is dangerous outside of consciousness. There has been more experimental research on repression than on any other defense mechanism and perhaps more than on any other single concept in psychoanalytic theory. An early study in this area was that by Rosenzweig (1941), in which he found that when they were personally involved with the experiment a group of Harvard undergraduates recalled a larger proportion of tasks that they had been able to complete than tasks they had been unable to complete. When the students did not feel threatened, they remembered more of the uncompleted tasks.

More recently, women high in sex guilt and women low in sex guilt were exposed to an erotic videotape and asked to report their level of sexual arousal. At the same time, their level of physiological response was recorded. Women high in sex guilt were found to report less arousal than those low in sex guilt, but to show greater physiological arousal! Presumably the guilt associated with sexual arousal led to repression or the blocking of awareness of the physiological arousal (Morokoff, 1985).

In another fascinating study of repression, subjects were asked to think back to their childhood and recall any experience or situation that

DENIAL—HEALTHY OR SICK? ADAPTIVE OR MALADAPTIVE?

Should we avoid self-deception? Is knowing all there is to know a sign of health? Psychoanalysts generally assume that although the mechanisms of defense are useful in reducing anxiety, they also are maladaptive in turning the person away from reality. For example, consider the potentially damaging effects of denial. A person who denies threatening signs may not be in a position to respond adaptively. Thus, women who discover a lump in their breast and delay going to a doctor because of denial of the possible seriousness of the lump may seriously reduce the chances of surgical success. Or, men who deny the symptoms of a heart attack and continue to exercise or climb stairs may turn out to have made a fatal mistake.

However, there is evidence that denial and self-deception can also be constructive and adaptive. For example, take the person who has had a severe, incapacitating illness such as polio or cancer. Denial and self-deception can provide temporary relief from the emotional trauma and help the person to avoid being overwhelmed by anxiety, depression, or anger. Defensive processes can then facilitate optimism, and thereby allow constructive participation in rehabilitative efforts. In this case, denial as a coping process can be adaptive. It can be good for your health!

What sense can one make out of this conflicting evidence? The suggestion has been made that denial generally is maladaptive where it interferes with action that might otherwise improve the person's condition. However, denial generally is adaptive where action is impossible or irrelevant and where excessive emotion may interfere with recuperative efforts. Should the doctor tell all to the patient? Evidently this depends not only on the above, but also on the patient's personality. Some people seek out information and function best when they are fully informed. On the other hand, other people avoid information and function best when they know only what is essential. In other words, denial may or may not be adaptive depending on the circumstances involved, and information may or may not be helpful depending on the person's coping style.

SOURCES: Lazarus, 1983; Miller & Mangan, 1983.

Denial—How much information is useful to the patient?

came to mind. They also were asked to recall childhood experiences associated with each of five emotions (happiness, sadness, anger, fear, and wonder) and to indicate the earliest experience recalled for each emotion. Subjects were divided into repressors and nonrepressors (high anxious and low anxious nonrepressors) on the basis of response to questionnaires. Did the subjects differ in recall, as would be suggested by the psychoanalytic theory of repression? It was found that repressors recalled fewer negative emotions and were significantly older at the time of the earliest negative memory recalled (Figure 3.2). The authors concluded: "The pattern of findings is consistent with the hypothesis that repression involves an inaccessibility to negative emotional memories and indicates further that repression is associated in some way with the suppression or inhibition of emotional experiences in general. The concept of repression as a process involving limited access to negative affective memories appears to be valid" (Davis & Schwartz, 1987, p. 155).

In considering the status of the concept of repression, we return in many ways to issues considered in relation to the concept of the unconscious, which is not surprising since the two are linked so closely. In a plea that we not sweep repression under the rug, Erdelyi and Goldberg (1979) have given an enlightening discussion of the problems in defining the conept and in demonstrating related phenomena in the laboratory. Consideration begins with a quote from Dostoyevsky's *Notes from Underground:*

> Every man has reminiscences which he would not tell to everyone but only to his friends. He has other matters in his

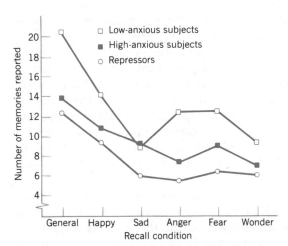

Mean number of memories in each recall condition for low-anxious subjects, high-anxious subjects, and repressors.

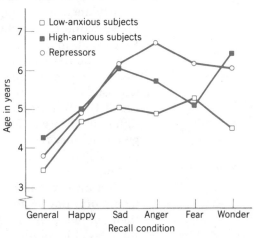

Mean age of earliest memory in each recall condition for low-anxious subjects, high-anxious subjects, and repressors.

FIGURE 3.2 Repression and Affective Memories. (Davis & Schwartz, 1987) (Copyright © 1987 American Psychological Association. Reprinted by permission.)

mind which he would not reveal even to his friend, but only to himself, and that in secret. But there are other things which a man is afraid to tell even to himself, and every decent man has a number of such things stored away in his mind.

In terms of research, they suggest that there is considerable evidence that events or memories apparently hopelessly forgotten can be recovered into consciousness. What is more difficult to demonstrate in the laboratory is the defensive function of repression, that is, the effort to keep ideas repressed from consciousness to minimize psychological pain. However, rather than arguing that a lack of experimental evidence should lead us to discard the concept, they concern themselves instead with the limitations of laboratory efforts to produce the complex phenomena. In a telling discussion of the results of clinical and laboratory data, it is suggested that "the two approaches have had palpably different yields. Such differences, we believe, reflect inherent differences in the two approaches, not some peculiar inconstancy of the phenomenon itself. The genius of the clinical approach is its ability to reveal truly complex cognitive processes. . . . From the clinical standpoint, the evidence for repression is overwhelming and obvious. The weakness of the clinical approach, on the other hand, is its looseness of method . . . the strength of the laboratory-experimental approach, unlike the clinical, is its methodological vigor; its overriding weakness is its inability to deal with truly complex processes" (Erdelyi & Goldberg, 1979, pp. 383–384).

Although these authors are critical of mainstream cognitive psychology for ignoring repression, there is evidence of growing interest in it and related phenomena. Noteworthy here is Bower's (1981) work on mood or **state-dependent memory**. Bower describes anecdotal and clinical evidence suggesting that sometimes people can recall events experienced while in a certain mood only when they are again experiencing that mood. In contrast, they will be unable to recall events experienced in a particular state if their state at attempted recall is different from or incongruent with the original state: "Memories acquired in one state are accessible mainly to that state but are 'dissociated' or not available for recall in an alternate state. It is as though the two states constitute different libraries into which a person places memory records, and a given memory record can be retrieved only by returning to the library, or physiological state, in which the event was first stored" (Bower, 1981, p. 130).

In an effort to produce and study state-dependent learning in the laboratory, Bower and his colleagues used hypnosis to induce moods in their subjects. Once a mood had been induced, the subjects were given some tasks involving learning and recall. In one experiment hypnotized subjects were given a list of words to learn while happy and one to learn while sad. They then were tested for recall while in the same or opposite mood. The data clearly indicated that recall was better for the same-mood list than for the opposite-mood list. In another experiment, subjects recorded emotional events in a daily diary for a week. A week later they were hypnotized, with half the subjects put in a pleasant mood and the remaining half put in an unpleasant mood. They were then asked to recall all the events they could from those recorded in their diary the week before. As expected, the subjects recalled a greater percentage of their pleasant experiences when they were in an induced pleasant mood and a greater percentage of their unpleasant experiences when they were in a congruent unpleasant mood (Figure 3.3). Finally, in another experiment, subjects were asked to recall childhood events while in either a happy mood or a sad mood. The following day, while in a neutral mood, subjects rated the recalled childhood incidents as pleasant, unpleasant, or neutral. Again, a mood-state-dependent memory effect was found—happy subjects retrieved more pleasant than unpleasant memories whereas the reverse was true for sad subjects (Figure 3.3).

What are the implications of such research for the concept of repression and the experimental study of psychoanalytic phenomena? It is clear that Bower is not studying repression directly. However, it also is clear that Bower has been impressed with and influenced by clinical descriptions of amnesia and repression. Second, while acknowledging criticism of cognitive psychologists for ignoring the role of emotion and motivation in thinking and memory, Bower argues that it is possible to study such important phenomena experimentally: "Perhaps that is as it should be—theories developed in one field aiding our understanding of phenomena from another field. Certainly it is the goal of all basic science" (p. 147).

Before ending this discussion of the defenses, it is important to note one further device that is used to express an impulse free of anxiety. This

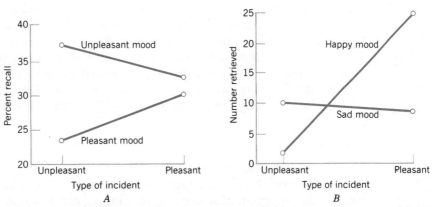

FIGURE 3.3 Mood and Memory. A. Percentage recall of incidents from an emotional diary depending on whether the incident was pleasant or unpleasant and whether the subject was in a pleasant or unpleasant mood during recall. B. Number of pleasant and unpleasant childhood incidents when the recaller was in a happy or sad mood. (Bower, 1981, p. 133)

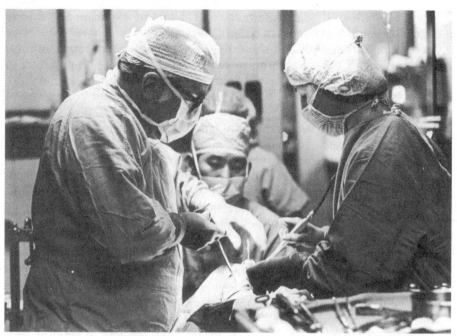

Sublimation—In performing surgery, aggressive impulses can be turned toward useful, constructive ends.

mechanism, of considerable social importance, is that of **sublimation**. In sublimation, the original object of gratification is replaced by a higher cultural goal, one further removed from direct expression of the instinct. Whereas the other defense mechanisms meet the instincts head on and, by and large, prevent discharge, in sublimation the instinct is turned into a new and useful channel. In contrast to the other defense mechanisms, here the ego does not have to maintain a constant energy output to prevent discharge. Freud interpreted DaVinci's Madonna as a sublimation of his longing for his mother. Becoming a surgeon, butcher, or boxer can represent sublimations, to a greater or lesser degree, of aggressive impulses. Being a psychiatrist can represent a sublimation of "peeping tom" tendencies. In all, as noted, Freud felt that the essence of civilization is contained in a person's ability to sublimate sexual and aggressive energies.

Growth and Development

The psychoanalytic theory of development takes into consideration the development of structures, of thinking processes, of the instincts, and in relation to all of these, the development of character (personality). There are two major aspects to the theory of development. The first is that the individual progresses through stages of development that are rooted in

A PSYCHODYNAMIC THEORY: FREUD'S THEORY OF PERSONALITY

the biological processes of the organism. The second, the genetic approach, emphasizes the importance of early events for all later behavior. An extreme psychoanalytic position would go so far as to say that the most significant aspects of later personality have been formed by the end of the first five years of life.

The development of thinking processes

The psychoanalytic theory of the development of thinking processes focuses on the change from **primary process** thinking to **secondary process** thinking. The primary process is the language of the unconscious, in which reality and fantasy are indistinguishable. Aspects of primary process thinking often are seen in dreams. Here events may occur in more than one place at the same time, characteristics of different people and objects may be combined or fused, events shift rapidly back and forth in time and what in waking life is impossible occurs with ease. The secondary process is the language of consciousness, of learning, thinking, remembering, and reality testing. Parallel to this is the development of the ego and, later, that of the superego. With the development of the ego, the individual becomes more differentiated, as a self, from the rest of the world. There is a decrease in self-preoccupation, an increase in motor ability, an increase in the use of language, and a greater ability to anticipate events and to delay gratification. The development of a healthy superego is reflected in an integrated, conflict-free set of values, an ability to accept blows to the self-esteem (to accept limitations without withdrawal into fantasy), and a sense of pride in accomplishment.

The development of the instincts

The most significant part of the psychoanalytic theory of development concerns the development of the instincts. The source of the instincts is in states of bodily tension, which tend to focus on certain regions of the body, called **erogenous zones**. According to the theory, there is a biologically determined development of, and change in, the major erogenous zones of the body. At any one time the major source of excitation and energy tends to focus on a particular zone, with the location of that zone changing during the early developmental years. The first erogenous zone is the mouth, the second the anus, and the third the genitals. The mental and emotional growth of the child are dependent on the social interactions, anxieties, and gratifications that occur in relation to these zones.

Stages of development The first major area of excitation, sensitivity, and energy is the mouth. It is the locus of excitation that leads to the name **oral stage**. Early oral gratification occurs in feeding, thumbsucking, and other mouth movements characteristic of infants. In adult life, traces of orality are seen in chewing gum, eating, smoking, and kissing. In the early part of the oral stage the child is passive and receptive. In the late oral stage, with the development of teeth, there can be a fusion of sexual and aggressive pleasures. In children, such a fusion of instinctual gratification is seen in the eating of animal crackers. In later life, we see traces of orality in various spheres. For example, academic pursuits can have oral associations within the unconscious—one is given "food for thought," asked to "incorporate" material in reading, and "regurgitate" what has been learned on exams.

In the second stage of development, the **anal stage** (ages two and three), there is excitation in the anus and in the movement of feces through the anal passageway. The expulsion of the feces is believed to bring relief from tension and pleasure in the stimulation of the mucous membranes in that region. The pleasure related to this erogenous zone involves the organism in conflict. There is conflict between elimination and retention, there is the conflict between the pleasure in release and the pleasure in retention, and there is the conflict between the wish for pleasure in evacuation and the demands of the external world for delay. This latter conflict represents the first crucial conflict between the individual and society. Here the environment requires the child to violate the pleasure principle or be punished. The child may retaliate against such demands by intentional soiling (diarrhea); associate having bowel movements with losing something important, which leads to depression; or assoicate having bowel movements with giving a prize or gift to others, which may be associated with feelings of power and control.

In the **phallic stage** (ages four and five), excitation and tension come to focus in the genitals. The biological differentiation between the sexes leads to psychological differentiation. The male child develops erections, and the new excitations in this area lead to increased interest in the genitals and the realization that the female lacks the penis. This leads to the fear that he may lose his penis—*castration anxiety*. The father becomes a rival for the affections of the mother, suggestion to which is given in the song "I Want a Girl Just Like the Girl That Married Dear Old Dad." The boy's hostility toward the father is projected onto the father with the consequent fear of retaliation. This leads to what is known as the **Oedipus complex**. According to the Oedipus complex, every boy is fated to kill his father in fantasy and marry his mother. The complex can be heightened by actual seductiveness on the part of the mother. Castration anxiety can be heightened by actual threats from the father to cut off the penis. These threats occur in a surprising number of cases!

For an interesting illustration of an effort at experimental testing of the concept of the Oedipus complex, we can return to the subliminal psychodynamic activation research discussed in relation to the concept of the unconscious. In this research stimuli are presented to subjects subliminally in a tachistoscope. When certain stimuli register subliminally, they activate, it is presumed, unconscious conflicts and either intensify or alleviate these conflicts, depending on the nature of the conflict and the stimulus presented. The point of the current experiment was to manipulate the degree of oedipal conflict in males and to observe the effects on their performance in a competitive situation (Silverman, Ross, Adler & Lustig, 1978). The stimuli chosen to intensify or alleviate oedipal conflict were *"Beating Dad Is Wrong"* and *"Beating Dad Is OK."* In addition, a number of other stimuli were presented, including the neutral stimulus *"People Are Walking."* These stimuli were presented tachistoscopically to male college students after they engaged in dart-throwing competition. The subjects were again tested for dart-throwing performance following exposure subliminally to each of the stimuli. As expected, the two oedipal stimuli had clear-cut effects in different directions. The *"Beating Dad Is OK"* stimulus was followed by significantly higher scores than those following the neutral stimulus, whereas the *"Beating Dad Is Wrong"* stimulus was followed by significantly lower scores than those following the neutral stimulus (Figure 3.4).

What is interesting about his research is that whereas the theoretical formulation was derived from clinical material with patients, the experimental testing involved normal college males. The assumption of the experimenters was that "since most persons are vulnerable to some degree of neurotic behavior and since, according to psychoanalytic understanding, oeidpal conflict often plays a central pathogenic role, we anticipated that the clinically based relationship might apply to a 'normal' college population" (p. 342). Two additional points are worthy of note since there have been difficulties in replicating this type of research. First, the results were not obtained when the stimuli were presented above threshold. The psychodynamic activation effects appear to operate at the unconscious rather than the concious level. Second, the authors emphasize that the experimental stimuli must relate to the motivational state of the subjects and the response measured must be sensitive to changes in this motivational state. Thus, in the experiment above, subjects were first "primed" with picture and story material containing oedipal content and then the task was presented as one involving competition.

The resolution of the Oedipus complex occurs because of frustrations and disappointments by the mother, because of fear of the father,

Tachistoscopic Presentation of Three Stimuli			
Dart Score	*"Beating Dad Is Wrong"*	*"Beating Dad Is OK"*	*"People Are Walking"*
Mean, Prestimulus	443.7	443.3	439.0
Mean, Poststimulus	349.0	533.3	442.3
Difference	−94.7	+90.0	+3.3

FIGURE 3.4 Oedipal Conflict and Competitive Performance. (Partial results adapted from Silverman *et al.*, 1978, p. 346)

and because of the possibility of partial gain through identification with the father. For the male child, the Oedipus complex is resolved through keeping the mother as a love object but gaining her through identifying with the father. In identifying with the father, the child assumes many of the same values and morals. It is in this sense that the superego has been called the heir to the resolution of the Oedipus complex.

The developmental processes during this stage are somewhat different for the female. She realizes the lack of a penis and blames the mother, the original love object. In developing **penis envy**, the female child chooses the father as the love object and imagines that the lost organ will be restored by having a child by the father. Whereas the Oedipus complex is abandoned in the boy because of castration anxiety, in the female it is started because of penis envy. As with the male, conflict during this period is in some cases accentuated by seductiveness on the part of the father toward the female child. And, as with the male, the female child resolves the conflict by keeping the father as a love object but gaining him through identification with the mother. Because the female child develops less fear than does the male child (the little girls considers her penis to be already gone), and because the boy must give up an object (mother) that is more salient than the object (father) for the girl, the female child does not resolve the oedipal issues to the same degree as does the male child. Thus, the female develops a weaker and less harsh superego, which accounts for their being kinder and softer than men.*

The development of an **identification** with the parent of the same sex is a critical issue during the phallic stage and, more generally, is a critical concept in developmental psychology. In identification, individuals take on themselves the qualities of another person and integrate them into their functioning. Freud distinghished among four types of identification. In *narcissistic* (self-love) *identification*, individuals identify with qualities in those who are similar to themselves. This process leads to group membership. In *goal-oriented identification*, the individual identifies with a successful person. For example, the boy may identify with and assume the values of his father. In *object-loss identification*, the individual attempts to recover a lost object (person) through identification with it. The boy who loses a father early in life may develop an exaggerated identification with the father, or with an idealized image of him. Finally, there is *identification with the aggressor*, in which the individual identifies with a figure in authority so as to avoid punishment. This type of identification also occurs in the development of the superego and is a powerful force in socialization. It is also seen in situations of extreme threat, as in the experiences of prisoners in the Nazi concentra-

---

*Psychoanalytic theory has been criticized by feminists on a variety of grounds. Perhaps more than any other concept, the concept of penis envy is seen as expressing a chauvinistic, hostile view toward women. This issue will be addressed in Chapter 4 in the Critical Evaluation section.

tion camps. For example, according to accounts of life in the concentration camps, some of the prisoners started to wear whatever pieces of Nazi clothing they could get and, when put in a position of authority, treated the other prisoners in a cruel, inhumane way. Sarnoff (1951) has done some research that suggests that anti-Semitism among Jews can be accounted for in terms of identification with the aggressor.

Although Freud gave relatively little attention to developmental factors after the resolution of the Oedipus complex, he did recognize their existence. After the phallic stage, the child enters **latency**, during which there is a lessening of the sexual urge and no new libidinal developments. The meaning of the latency stage has never been clear in

Oedipus Complex, Competition, and Identification— For the male child to become competitive there must not be too much anxiety about rivalry with the father. Jim Burt, of the N.Y. Giants football team, carried his son around the field after winning the 1987 Super Bowl. He describes his son, Jim Jr., age 4½, as "So much like me it's frightening. He's got the same fire in his eyes. And like when we wrestle together on the rug, he always wants to win."

psychoanalytic theory. An assumption of a decrease in sexual urges and interest during the ages of 6 through 13 might have fit observations of Victorian children, but it does not fit observations of children in other cultures. A more plausible assumption, and one more difficult to test, is that there are no new developments during this stage in terms of the ways in which children gratify their instincts.

The onset of puberty, with the reawakening of the sexual urges and oedipal feelings, marks the beginning of the **genital stage**. The significance of this period for individuals and for their functioning in society is demonstrated in the initiation rites of many cultures and in the Jewish Bar Mitzvah. Dependency feelings and oedipal strivings that were not fully resolved during the pregenital stages of development now come back to rear their ugly heads. The turmoil of adolescence is partly attributable to these factors.

Erikson's psychosocial stages of development It is probably clear that in the psychoanalytic theory of development, major attention is given to the first five years and to the development of the instincts. Ego psychologists have tried, within this framework, to give greater attention to other developments during the early years and to significant developments that take place during the latency and genital stages. Erik H. Erikson (1950), for example, one of the leading ego psychoanalysts, describes development in psychosocial terms rather than merely in sexual terms (Figure 3.5). Thus, the first stage is significant not just because of the localization of pleasure in the mouth, but because in the feeding situation a relationship of trust or mistrust is developed between the infant and the mother. Similarly, the anal stage is significant not only for the change in the nature of the major erogenous zone, but also because toilet training is a significant social situation in which the child may develop a sense of autonomy or succumb to shame and self-doubt. In the phallic stage the child must struggle with the issue of taking pleasure in, as opposed to feeling guilty about being assertive, competitive, and successful.

For Erikson, the latency and genital stages are periods when the individual develops a sense of industry and success, or a sense of inferiority, and perhaps most important of all, a sense of identity or a sense of role diffusion. For him, the crucial task of adolescence is the establishment of a sense of ego identity, an accrued confidence that the way one views oneself has a continuity with one's past and is matched by the perceptions of others. In contrast to people who develop a sense of identity, people with role diffusion experience the feeling of not really knowing who they are, of not knowing whether what they think they are matches what others think of them, and of not knowing how they have developed in this way or where they are heading in the future. During late adolescence and the college years, this struggle with a sense of identity may lead to joining a variety of groups and to considerable anguish about the choice of a career. If these issues are not resolved

Psychosocial Stage	Age	Positive Outcomes	Negative Outcomes
Basic Trust vs. Mistrust	1	Feelings of inner goodness, trust in oneself and others, optimism	Sense of badness, mistrust of self and others, pessimism
Autonomy vs. Shame and Doubt	2–3	Exercise of will, self-control, able to make choices	Rigid, excessive conscience, doubtful, rigid, self-conscious shame
Initiative vs. Guilt	4–5	Pleasure in accomplishments, activity, direction and purpose	Guilt over goals contemplated and achievements initiated
Industry vs. Inferiority	Latency	Able to be absorbed in productive work, pride in completed product	Sense of inadequacy and inferiority, unable to complete work
Identity vs. Role Diffusion	Adolescence	Confidence of inner sameness and continuity, promise of a career	Ill at ease in roles, no set standards, sense of artificiality
Intimacy vs. Isolation	Early Adulthood	Mutuality, sharing of thoughts, work, feelings	Avoidance of intimacy, superficial relations
Generativity vs. Stagnation	Adulthood	Ability to lose oneself in work and relationships	Loss of interest in work, impoverished relations
Integrity vs. Despair	Later Years	Sense of order and meaning, content with self and one's accomplishments	Fear of death, bitter about life and what one got from it or what did not happen

FIGURE 3.5 Erikson's Eight Psychosocial Stages of Development and Their Implications for Personality

Erik H. Erikson

during this time, the individual is, in later life, filled with a sense of despair—life is too short and it is too late to start all over again.

Continuing with his description of the later stages of life and the accompanying psychological issues, Erikson suggests that some people develop a sense of intimacy, an acceptance of life's successes and disappointments, and a sense of continuity throughout the life cycle, whereas other people remain isolated from family and friends, appear to survive on a fixed daily routine, and focus on both past disappointments and

The Life Cycle—Integrating experiences and achievements gained during the life cycle can lead to wisdom and contentment in later life.

future death. Although the ways in which people do and do not resolve these critical issues of adulthood may have their roots in childhood conflict, Erikson suggests that this is not always the case and that they have a significance of their own (Erikson, 1982). In sum, Erikson's contributions are noteworthy in three ways: (1) He has emphasized the psychosocial as well as the instinctual basis for personality development: (2) He has extended the stages of development to include the entire life cycle and has articulated the major psychological issues to be faced in these later stages: (3) He has recognized that people look to the future as well as to the past, and how they construe their future may be as significant a part of their personality as how they construe their past.

The importance of early experience

Psychoanalytic theory emphasizes the importance of events early in life for later personality development. Others suggest a much greater potential for change across the entire life span (Brim & Kagan, 1980). The issue is complex, the prevailing view changes from time to time, and at no point has a consensus been reached.

The complexities of the issue can be illustrated with two studies. The first, conducted by a psychoanalyst (Gaensbauer, 1982), involved the study of affect development in infancy. The infant, Jenny, was first studied systematically when she was almost four months old. Prior to this time, at the age of three months, she had been physically abused by her father. At that time she was brought to the hospital with a broken arm and a skull fracture. She was described by hospital personnel as being a "lovable baby" — happy, cute, sociable, but also as not cuddling when held and as being "jittery" when approached by a male. Following this history of abuse she was placed in a foster home, where she received adequate physical care but minimal social interaction. This was very much in contrast with her earlier experience with her natural mother, who spent considerable time with her and would breast-feed her "at the drop of a hat." The first systematic observation occurred almost a month after placement in the foster home. At this time her behavior was judged to be completely consistent with a diagnosis of depression — lethargic, apathetic, disinterested, collapsed posture. A systematic analysis of her facial expressions indicated five discrete affects, each meaningfully related to her unique history. Sadness was noted when she was with her natural mother. Fearfulness and anger were noted when she was approached by a male stranger but not when she was approached by a female stranger. Joy was noted as a transient affect during brief play sequences. Finally, interest–curiosity was noted when she interacted with female strangers.

After she was visited in her foster home, Jenny was placed in a different foster home where she received warm attention. Following two weeks in this environment, she was again brought to the hospital for further evaluation, this time by her second foster mother. This time she generally appeared to be a normally responsive infant. She showed no evidence of distress and even smiled at a male stranger. After an additional month at this foster home, she was brought to the hospital *by her natural mother* for a third evaluation. Generally, she was animated and happy. However, when the mother left the room, she cried intensely. This continued following the mother's return despite repeated attempts to soothe her. Apparently separation from her natural mother continued to lead to a serious distress response. In addition, sadness and anger were frequently noted. At eight months old, Jenny was returned to her natural mother who left her husband and received counseling. At the age of twenty months, she was described as appearing to be normal and having an excellent relationship with her mother. However, there continued to be the problem of anger and distress associated with separation from her mother.

The conclusion to be reached from these observations is that there was evidence for both continuity and discontinuity between Jenny's early emotional experiences and her later emotional reactions. In general, she was doing well and her emotional responses were within the normal range for infants her age. At the same time, the anger reactions in response to separations and frustration appeared to be a link to the past. The psychoanalyst conducting the study suggested that perhaps isolated traumatic events are less important than the repeated experiences of a less dramatic but more persistent nature. In other words, the early years are important, but more in terms of patterns of interpersonal relationships than in terms of isolated events.

The second study, conducted by a group of developmental psychologists, assessed the relationship between early attachment relationships and later psychopathology (Lewis, Feiring, McGuffog, & Jaskir, 1984). In this study, the attachment behavior of boy and girl children one year of age was observed. The observation involved a standardized procedure consisting of a period of play with the mother in an unstructured situation, followed by the departure of the mother and a period of the child being alone in the playroom, and then by the return of the mother and a second free play period. The behavior of the children was scored systematically and assigned to one of three attachment categories: avoidant, secure, or ambivalent. The avoidant and ambivalent categories were suggestive of difficulties in this area. Then at six years of age, the competence of these children was assessed through the completion by the mothers of a Child Behavior Profile. The ratings of the mothers were also checked against teacher ratings. On the basis of the Child Behavior Profile the children were classified into a normal group, an at risk group, and a clinically disturbed group.

What was the relationship between early attachment behavior and later pathology? There are two aspects of the results that are particularly noteworthy. First, the relationships were quite different for boys than for girls. For boys, attachment classification at one year of age was significantly related to later pathology. Insecurely attached boys showed more pathology at age six than did securely attached boys. On the other hand, no relationship between attachment and later pathology was observed for girls. Second, the authors noted a difference between trying to predict pathology from the early data (prospective) as opposed to trying to understand later pathology in terms of earlier attachment difficulties (retrospective). If one starts with the boys who at age six were identified as being at risk or clinically disturbed, 80 percent would be found to have been assigned to the avoidant- or ambivalent-attachment category at age one. In other words, a very strong statistical relationship. On the other hand, if one took all boys classified as insecurely attached (avoidant or ambivalent) at age one and predicted them to be at risk or clinically disturbed at age six, one would be right in only 40 percent of the cases. The reason for this is that far more of the boys were classified as insecurely attached than were later diagnosed as at risk or disturbed. Thus, the clinician viewing later pathology would have a clear basis for suggesting a strong relationship between pathology and early attachment difficulties. On the other hand, focusing on the data in terms of prediction would suggest a much more tenuous relationship and the importance of other variables as well. The early attachment relationship, at least for boys, may be critical but not an all-determining factor in later pathology. As Freud himself recognized, when we observe later pathology it is all too easy to understand how it developed. On the other hand, when we look at these phenomena prospectively we are made aware of the varied paths that development can follow. In the words of the authors, "the findings suggest that although the child's attachment relationship plays an important role in the development of pathology, a child is neither made invulnerable by early secure attachment nor doomed to pathology by an insecure attachment."

Another recent study extends even further the possible relationships between early attachment relationships and later emotional bonds (Hazan & Shaver, 1987). In this case the psychologists set out to investigate the possibility of a relationship between the kind of affectional bond a person established in infancy and the affectional bond they established as an adult in love with another person. In particular, the hypothesis was formed that early styles of attachment (secure, avoidant, anxious/ambivalent) would relate to adult styles of romantic love — the kind of continuity of emotional and behavioral patterns suggested by psychoanalytic theory.

Subjects in the study were respondents to a newspaper survey or "love quiz." As a measure of attachment style, the newspaper readers described themselves as fitting one of three categories in terms of their relationships with others. These three categories were descriptive of the three attachment styles (Figure 3.6). As a measure of current style of romantic love, subjects were asked to respond to questions listed under a banner headline in the newspaper: "Tell Us About The Love Of Your

Questions: Which of the following best describes your feelings?

Answers and percentages:

Secure (N = 319, 56%): I find it relatively easy to get close to others and am comfortable depending on them and having them depend on me. I don't often worry about being abandoned or about someone getting too close to me.

Avoidant (N = 145, 25%): I am somewhat uncomfortable being close to others; I find it difficult to trust them completely, difficult to allow myself to depend on them. I am nervous when anyone gets too close, and often love partners want me to be more intimate than I feel comfortable being.

Anxious/Ambivalent (N = 110, 19%): I find that others are reluctant to get as close as I would like. I often worry that my partner doesn't really love me or won't want to stay with me. I want to merge completely with another person, and this desire sometimes scares people away.

Scale Name	Sample Item	Attachment Type Means		
		Avoidant	Anxious/ ambivalent	Secure
Happiness	My relationship with _____ (made/makes) me very happy.	3.19	3.31	3.51
Friendship	I (considered/ consider) _____ one of my best friends.	3.18	3.19	3.50
Trust	I (felt/feel) complete trust in _____	3.11	3.13	3.43
Fear of closeness	I sometimes (felt/feel) that getting too close to _____ could mean trouble.	2.30	2.15	1.88
Acceptance	I (was/am) well aware of _____'s imperfections but it (did/ does) not lessen my love.	2.86	3.03	3.01
Emotional extremes	I (felt/feel) almost as much			

Scale Name	Sample Item	Attachment Type Means		
		Avoidant	Anxious/ ambivalent	Secure
	pain as joy in my relationship with _____.	2.75	3.05	2.36
Jealousy	I (loved/love) _____ so much that I often (felt/feel) jealous.	2.57	2.88	2.17
Obsessive preoccupation	Sometimes my thoughts (were/are) uncontrollably on _____	3.01	3.29	3.01
Sexual attraction	I (was/am) very physically attracted to _____	3.27	3.43	3.27
Desire for union	Sometimes I (wished/wish) that _____ and I were a single unit, a "we" without clear boundaries	2.81	3.25	2.69
Desire for reciprocation	More than anything, I (wanted/want) _____ to return my feelings.	3.24	3.55	3.22
Love at first sight	Once I noticed _____, I was hooked.	2.91	3.17	2.97

FIGURE 3.6 Illustrative Items and Means for Three Attachment Types for Twelve Love Experience Scales. (Hazan & Shaver, 1987) (Copyright © 1987 American Psychological Association. Reprinted by permission.)

Life." Responses to the questions concerning the most important love relationship they ever had formed the basis for scores on twelve Love Experience Scales (Figure 3.6). Additional questions were asked concerning the person's view of romantic love over time and their recollection of childhood relationships with parents and between parents.

Did the different types of respondents (secure, avoidant, anxious/ambivalent) also differ in the way they experienced their most important love relationships? As the means for the three groups on the Love Scales indicate (Figure 3.6), this appears to be the case. Secure attachment styles were associated with experiences of happiness, friendship, and trust; avoidant styles with fears of closeness, emotional highs and lows, and jealousy; and anxious/ambivalent styles with obsessive preoccupation with the loved person, a desire for union, extreme sexual attraction, emotional extremes, and jealousy. In addition, the three groups differed in their views or mental models of romantic relationships: secure lovers viewed romantic feelings as being somewhat stable but also waxing and waning, and discounted the kind of head-over-heels romantic love often depicted in novels and movies; avoidant lovers were skeptical of the lasting quality of romantic love and felt that it was rare to find a person one can really fall in love with; anxious/ambivalent lovers felt that it was easy to fall in love but rare to find true love. Finally, secure subjects, in comparison with subjects in the other two groups, reported warmer relationships with both parents and between their two parents.

A further study by the psychologists with college students confirmed the pattern of these relationships and also suggested differences in the ways members of the three groups described themselves: secure subjects described themselves as easy to get to know and liked by most people, whereas anxious/ambivalent subjects described themselves as having self-doubts and being misunderstood and underappreciated by others. The avoidant subjects were between these two groups, but closer to the latter in their responses.

In sum, the results provided support for a view of romantic love as based on early attachment relationships. Adults differing in attachment style were found to differ in the ways they experienced romantic love, in their views of romantic relationships and themselves in relation to others, and in their views of childhood experiences with and between parents. At the same time, the authors cautioned that although the results suggested connections between current relationships and earlier relationships, they did not indicate that these relationships were fixed in stone or were never to be altered by later experiences. Also, one should note that these results were based on current self-reports of the subjects as opposed to ratings of them in childhood and independent ratings of them again as adults.

As previously noted, the issues relevant to the importance of early experience for later personality development are complex. Perhaps we must seek a more differentiated approach to the question rather than a black-or-white answer. For example, how are we to define consistency, stability, or continuity of development? Do we mean that the personality of the adult is the *same* as that of the child? Or do we mean that the personality of the adult is derived from or represents some clear transformation of characteristics from childhood? the former is a much more stringent test of continuity and by that criterion one could find little supportive evidence. The latter is a more relaxed criterion and provides for more confirming evidence. But which comes closer to the heart of psychoanalytic theory? In addition, we can consider variations in the importance of early experience depending on the personality characteristic being considered and the particular experiences that occur during and following the early years. Thus, for example, the early years might be quite important for the development of what Erikson calls basic trust but less critical for other personality characteristics. The role of early experience might depend on the intensity of particular experiences, their duration, and the extent to which differing experiences occurred earlier and later. Thus, for example, the effects of maternal deprivation may depend on how serious and long lasting the deprivation is as well as on the role of positive experiences both before and following deprivation. Finally, we may note the distinction between what may occur and what must inevitably occur. Psychoanalytic theory can be accurate in portraying the *possible* effects of early experience, particularly as seen in various forms of psychological disturbance where a pattern of relationships is established early and maintained over time, without it being the case that such effects are inevitable.

Major Concepts and Summary	energy system	oral, anal, phallic stages of development
	conscious, preconscious, unconscious	
	id, ego, superego	Oedipus complex
	pleasure principle	castration anxiety
	reality principle	identification
	life and death instincts	oral, anal, and phallic personality types
	sexual and aggressive instincts	
	anxiety	
	mechanisms of defense	
	erogenous zones	

Before turning to the clinical applications of psychoanalytic theory and a final evaluation, let us take stock of the essentials of the theory of personality. The chapter began with a discussion of some of the events in Freud's life that played a role in the development of his theory and that influenced his approach toward science. Illustrative of such events were his concerns about death and destruction during the First World War, the prevailing concerns in physics and medicine with energy models, and the inhibitions concerning sexuality found in Victorian society broadly and in Freud's patients in particular. In attempting both to help his patients and to develop a lasting theory of personality, Freud developed concepts that often appeared to have explanatory value but proved to be difficult to investigate systematically in nonclinical settings. Freud was impressed with the role of *unconscious forces* in the functioning of his patients. In listening to dreams and slips of the tongue, and in trying to understand the symptoms patients brought to treatment, Freud was struck by the importance of *repressed memories and wishes* in the associations of his patients. Similarly, he was impressed with the conflicts faced by his patients between what they wished and what society or their own conscience would permit. This led to the development of Freud's concept of *id* to represent the basic sexual and aggressive urges, the concept of the *superego* to represent the conscience or internalization of parental and societal prohibitions, and the concept of the *ego* or efforts to find gratification and pleasure in accordance with the demands of reality.

Freud attached particular importance to the role of anxiety in the functioning of his patients. Often they came in with feelings of free-floating anxiety. At the same time, he was impressed with the various devices used to ward off anxiety. From this he developed the theory of anxiety and the mechanisms of defense.

The wishes and fears expressed by Freud's patients appeared to relate to experiences they had during their early years. These experiences were seen as centering around various *erogenous zones*. Changes in the region of special sensitivity as well as in the region of special social contact were expressed in the concepts of the *oral, anal,* and *phallic stages of development*. The person's character or basic personality structure was seen as pretty well established by age five, following the struggles associated with the *Oedipus complex*. The theory of development provides links to many diverse aspects of psychoanalytic theory, including a link to the theory of psychopathology, to which we turn in the following chapter.

Chapter Four
A Psychodynamic Theory: Applications and Evaluation of Freud's Theory

CHAPTER FOCUS: In this chapter we continue to examine psychoaı.alytic theory as illustrative of a psychodynamic, clinical approach to personality. Attention is given to associated techniques of personality assessment, particularly projective tests such as the Rorschach Inkblot Test and the Thematic Apperception Test. We then consider Freud's attempts to understand and explain the symptoms presented by his patients and his efforts to develop a systematic method of treatment. After considering developments in psychoanalytic theory since Freud, we turn to a final critical evaluation and summary.

CLINICAL APPLICATIONS

Psychoanalysis started as and continues to be a clinical theory of personality, focusing on individual differences and the intensive study of the person. In addition, central to the theory is an emphasis on unconscious processes and the interplay among motives. A central theme in this book is that a theory of personality does not stand alone but rather is tied to and reflects ways of observing people. In addition, to the extent that the theory is associated with an approach to psychotherapy or change, the theory and therapy will reflect some common basic assumptions. Let us consider, then, how basic psychoanalytic concepts get reflected in approaches to the assessment of people as well as in the understanding and treatment of psychopathology.

Assessment — Projective Techniques

Although many different personality tests can be used in conjunction with psychoanalytic theory, it is *projective techniques* that are most closely linked to the theory. The term *projection* in relation to assessment techniques was first used in 1938 by Henry A. Murray, who developed the Thematic Apperception Test, but emphasis on the importance of projective techniques was first most clearly stated by L. K. Frank in 1939. Frank argued against the use of standardized tests, which he felt classified people but did not tell much about them as individuals. He argued for the use of tests that would offer insight into the private world of meanings and feelings of individuals. Such tests would allow individuals to impose their own structure and organization on stimuli and would thereby be expressive of a dynamic conception of personality.

A PSYCHODYNAMIC THEORY

In this section we consider two projective techniques, the Rorschach Inkblot Test and the Thematic Apperception Test (TAT). Both are unstructured in that they provide considerable freedom for subjects to respond in their own unique ways. Both are also disguised tests in that generally subjects are not aware of the purpose of the test or of how particular responses will be interpreted. The relation of psychoanalytic theory to projective tests can be seen as follows:

1. Psychoanalytic theory emphasizes individual differences and the complex organization of personality functioning. Personality is viewed as a process through which the individual imposes organization and structure on external stimuli in the environment. Projective techniques allow for maximum uniqueness of response, in terms of both the content and organization of the response.

2. Psychoanalytic theory emphasizes the importance of the unconscious and defense mechanisms. Projective tests involve directions and stimuli that provide few guidelines for responding and in which the purposes of the test and interpretations of responses are hidden.

3. Psychoanalytic theory emphasizes a holistic understanding of personality in terms of relationships among parts, rather than the interpretation of behavior as expressive of single parts or personality characteristics. Clinicians who use projective tests generally make holistic interpretations based on the patterning and organization of test responses rather than on interpreting a single response as reflecting a particular characteristic.

Having considered some general relationships between psychoanalytic theory and projective techniques, let us turn now to consideration of two of them in some detail.

The Rorschach Inkblot Test

The Rorschach Inkblot Test was developed by Hermann Rorschach, a Swiss psychiatrist. Although inkblots had been used earlier to elicit responses from individuals, Rorschach was the first to grasp fully the potential for the use of these responses for personality assessment. Rorschach developed stimuli through putting ink on paper and folding the paper so that symmetrical but ill-defined forms were produced. These inkblots were then shown to hospitalized patients. Through a process of trial and error, those inkblots that elicited different responses from different psychiatric groups were kept, while those that did not were discarded. Rorschach experimented with thousands of inkblots and finally settled on ten.

Rorschach was well acquainted with the work of Freud, the concept of the unconscious, and a dynamic view of personality. The development of his test certainly seems to have been influenced by this view. Ror-

Hermann Rorschach

schach felt that the data from the inkblot test would have relevance for an understanding of the unconscious and psychoanalytic theory in general, and he used psychoanalytic theory in his own interpretations of subjects' responses.

The Rorschach test consists of ten cards with inkblots on them. When showing the cards, the experimenter tries to make the subjects relaxed and comfortable while providing them with sufficient information to complete the task. Thus, the test is presented as "just one of many ways used nowadays to try to understand people" and the experimenter volunteers as little information as possible — "It is best not to know much about the procedure until you have gone through it." Subjects are asked to look at each card and tell the examiner what they see — anything that might be represented on the card. Individuals are free to select what they will see, where they will see it, and what determines their perceptions. All responses offered by the subjects are given on the test record.

In interpreting the Rorschach one is interested in the way in which the responses or percepts are formed, the reasons for the response, and its content. The basic asumption is that there is a correspondence between the way individuals form their perceptions and the way they generally organize and structure stimuli in their environments. Perceptions that match the structure of the inkblot suggest a good level of psychological functioning that is well oriented toward reality. On the other hand, poorly formed responses that do not fit the structure of the inkblot suggest unrealistic fantasies or bizarre behavior. The content of subject responses (whether they see mostly· animate or inanimate objects, humans or animals, and content expressing affection or hostility) makes a great deal of difference in the interpretation of the subject's personality. For example, compare the interpretations we might make of two sets of responses, one where animals are seen repeatedly as fighting and a second where humans are seen as sharing and involved in cooperative efforts.

Beyond this, content may be interpreted symbolically. An explosion may symbolize intense hostility; a pig, gluttonous tendencies; a fox, a tendency toward being crafty and aggressive; spiders, witches, and octopuses, negative images of a dominating mother; gorillas and giants, negative attitudes toward a dominating father; and an ostrich as an attempt to hide from conflicts (Schafer, 1954). General categories of content such as food and nurturant animals (cows, mother hen), hostile figures and devouring animals (beasts of prey, vultures, animals clawing), and figures of power and authority (kings, queens, generals) are interpreted in relation to symbolism. Two illustrative stimuli and responses are presented in Figure 4.1.

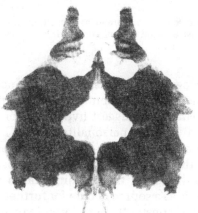

**ILLUSTRATION
NO. 1**

RESPONSE
"Two bears with their paws touching one another playing pattycake or could be they are fighting and the red is the blood from the fighting."

RESPONSE
"Two cannibals. Supposed to see something in this? African natives bending over a pot. Possibly cooking something—hope they're not maneaters. I shouldn't make jokes— always liking humor. (Are they male or female?) Could be male or female. More female because of breasts here. But didn't impress me at first glance as being of either sex."

**ILLUSTRATION
NO. 2**

FIGURE 4.1 Examples from the Rorschach Inkblot Test. The inkblot illustrtions reproduced here are from the Rorschach location chart. The actual inkblot cards contain color. (Reprinted by permission of Hans Huber, Publishers.)

Clinical Applications

Rorschach Inkblot Test—The Rorschach interpreter assumes that the subject's personality is projected onto unstructured stimuli such as inkblots. Drawing by Ross; © 1974 The New Yorker Magazine, Inc.

It is important to recognize that interpretation is not made on the basis of one response alone, but in relation to the total sum of responses. However, each response is used to suggest hypotheses or possible interpretations about the individual's personality. Such hypotheses are checked against interpretations based on other responses, on the total response pattern, and on the subject's behavior while responding to the Rorschach. In relation to the latter, the examiner takes note of all unusual behavior and uses this as a source of data for further interpretation. For example, a subject who constantly asks for guidance may be interpreted as dependent. A subject who seems tense, asks questions in a subtle way, and looks at the back of the cards may be interpreted as suspicious and possibly paranoid.

The Thematic Apperception Test (TAT)

Probably the most widely used projective test is the Thematic Apperception Test (TAT) developed by Henry Murray and Christina Morgan. The test represents an extension of Murray's longstanding interest in the needs or underlying motives of individuals, fantasy behavior, and the intensive study of the individual. The TAT consists of cards with scenes on them. Most of the cards depict one or two people in some important life situation, though some of the cards are more abstract. The subject is asked to make up a story based on the scene on the card, with the story to include what is going on, the thoughts and feelings of the participants, what led up to the scene, and the outcome of what is going on. Since the

A PSYCHODYNAMIC THEORY

Henry Murray

scenes often are ambiguous, they leave considerable room for individuality in the content of stories made up by the subjects: "The test is based on the well-recognized fact that when a person interprets an ambiguous social situation he is apt to expose his own personality as much as the phenomenon to which he is attending" (Murray, 1938, p. 530).

Some TAT cards are shown to both male and female subjects; others are shown to members of one sex only. An illustrative card and responses given to it by two different individuals are shown in Figure 4.2. The card is given to female subjects and is described by Murray as: "The portrait of a young woman. A weird old woman with a shawl over her head is grimacing in the background." Common themes given in response to this card are stories of disappointment with a parent, parental pressure, and sad thoughts about the past. In addition, some women appear to see the younger woman as having a vision of her evil self or of herself in old age (Holt, 1978).

The thinking behind the TAT clearly shows its relation to the psychodynamic view. According to Murray (1938), the TAT is used to discover unconscious and inhibited tendencies. The assumption is that subjects are not aware that they are talking about themselves and that thereby the defenses can be bypassed: "If the procedure had merely exposed conscious fantasies and remembered events it would have been useful enough, but it did more than this. It gave the experimenter excellent clues for the divination of unconscious thematic formations!" (p. 534).

TAT responses of subjects can be scored systematically according to

Sample Card
from the Thematic
Apperception Test.

ILLUSTRATION 1   This is the picture of a woman who all of her life has been a very suspicious, conniving person. She's looking in the mirror and she sees reflected behind her an image of what she will be as an old woman—still a suspicious, conniving sort of person. She can't stand the thought that that's what her life will eventually lead her to and she smashes the mirror and runs out of the house screaming and goes out of her mind and lives in an institution for the rest of her life.

ILLUSTRATION 2   This woman has always emphasized beauty in her life. As a little girl she was praised for being pretty and as a young woman was able to attract lots of men with her beauty. While secretly feeling anxious and unworthy much of the time, her outer beauty helped to disguise these feelings from the world and, sometimes, from herself. Now that she is getting on in years and her children are leaving home, she is worried about the future. She looks in the mirror and imagines herself as an old hag—the worst possible person she could become, ugly and nasty—and wonders what the future holds for her. It is a difficult and depressing time for her.

FIGURE 4.2   Illustrative TAT Card and Responses to It

a scheme developed by Murray or on a more impressionistic basis. It is used both in clinical work and in experimental studies of human motivation (McClelland, 1961). The TAT assumes a close relationship between the expressed fantasy (story about the TAT card) and underlying motivation as well as a relationship between such fantasy and behavior.

Efforts to test these assumptions have met with mixed results. Fantasy can both be associated with the expression of motives in behavior and also serve as a substitute for the expression of motives in behavior. Thus, for example, a person with a strong motive to be aggressive with others may express this motive both in fantasy (TAT) and behavior, but the person may also express it in fantasy and block it from expression in overt behavior.

Illustrative research use and evaluation

Projective techniques have been used for a great variety of research purposes, both in relation to psychoanalytic theory and apart from it. A recent study of comedians, clowns, and actors illustrates the clinical, psychodynamic approach to understanding such phenomena, including the utilization of projective tests (Fisher & Fisher, 1981). The study represented an effort to understand the origins, motivations, and personalities of those who make people laugh as opposed to those who entertain through acting. In it professional clowns, comedians, and actors were interviewed and given projective tests such as the Rorschach and TAT. Participants included such comedians as Sid Caesar, Tommy Smothers, Donald O'Connor, "Professor" Irwin Corey, and Myron Cohen. In addi-

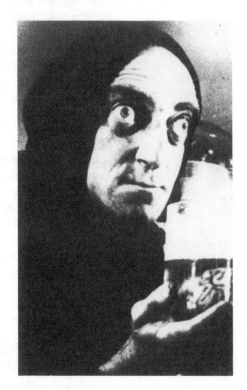

Comedians and Clowns—Research using psychoanalytic theory and projective techniques suggests that comedians and clowns often are sensitive about a part of their body. Here, in a scene from *Young Frankenstein*, the bulging eyes of the comedian Marty Feldman are highlighted.

tion, biographies and autobiographies of comedians such as Charlie Chaplin, Johnny Carson, and Dick Gregory were reviewed.

What can such research contribute to our understanding of comedians and clowns? First, they were found to be funny early in life, particularly in school, despite little support from their parents for their comic endeavors. Second, a number of motivations seemed to be contributing factors to the investment in being a comedian. Among these motivations suggested by the data are the following:

1. *Power* The ability to control an audience and "make" people laugh.
2. *Preoccupation with good–evil and positive presentation of self* "We would propose that a major motive of comedians in conjuring up funniness is to prove that they are not bad or repugnant. They are obsessed with defending their basic goodness" (p. 69).
3. *Concealment and denial* Humor is used to remove themselves from difficulty and as a screen to hide behind when feeling embarrassed or inferior.
4. *Anarchy* Comedians belittle accepted norms, leave nothing sacred, and make everything laughable.

Let us consider illustrative Rorschach evidence for two of these motivations. First, the concern with good–bad or virtue–evil. A scoring system was devised to consider the frequency with which such themes appeared in the Rorschach records. Illustrative responses were those directly referring to good and bad (e.g., bad person, virtuous look), those referring to religious matters (e.g., church, angel, devil, heaven, purgatory), and those referring to persons often linked with good–bad (e.g., policeman, criminal, judge, sinner). The Rorschach records of 35 comedians and clowns were found to have significantly more such good–bad references than did the records of 35 actors who were not comedians. Second, the concern with concealment and denial. Many of the Rorschach responses seemed to express an attitude of denying that things are as bad or threatening as they seem. For example, consider the following responses: "Faces. Evil looking . . . The evil not very evil. A put on." "Mephisto . . . charming character." "Tiger. Loveable tiger." "Monster . . . He's nice." "Wolfman . . . He's misunderstood . . . People are afraid. If you walk up and talk to him, he's a decent thing." "Two devils. Funny devils. Not to be taken seriously." In analyzing the Rorschach records of comics, it was found that they contained significantly more of these "not bad" images than did the records of actors. In addition, the records of comics were found to have significantly more concealment themes (e.g., hiding, mask, disguise, magic, tricks) than did records of actors.

One final theme noted in this study related to the tendency for comedians and clowns to be sensitive about some part of their body or their sense of self generally. Thus, for example, one can think of Jimmy Durante's jokes about his nose. Or, consider the film comic Marty Feldman whose trademark was his bulging eyes. He was quoted as follows in relation to his appearance: "The sum total of the disasters of my life. If I aspired to be Robert Redford, I'd have my eyes straightened and my nose fixed and end up like every other lousy actor, with two lines on Kojak. But this way, I'm a novelty" (*New York Times*, December 4, 1982). In sum, comedy is seen as a way of helping themselves deal with some sense of inferiority.

A review of this study provides us with a brief consideration of the strengths and limitations of such studies and projectives. The Rorschach, as well as projectives generally, is a marvelous instrument for glimpsing individual fantasy and the complexity of organization of individual perception. However, the difficulties in substantiating theoretical hypotheses or in establishing the reliability and validity of the instrument itself are enormous. Those who use projective techniques emphasize that only these tests are capable of capturing the richness of personality. Ambiguous stimuli elicit individual, idiosyncratic responses. Through these responses individuals express their personalities. The Rorschach is seen as being the psychologist's "microscope" or "X ray," able to penetrate to the depths of the individual's personality. The data from other tests are looked on as being trivial and fragmented by comparison. On the other hand, such efforts to give a multidimensional picture of the total personality create problems in empirical investigation. Thus, it is difficult to establish the reliability and validity of the Rorschach as well as other projective tests.

Once more we are involved with the tension between the richness of psychodynamic, clinical data and the scientific requirements of systematic investigation. We have considered this tension before and it will remain with us as we now consider the psychoanalytic interpretation of psychopathology and personality change.

Psychopathology

Frequently it is difficult for people to appreciate psychoanalytic theory without first appreciating the nature of the often strange and puzzling behaviors that were brought to Freud's attention. Freud spent most of his professional time working with patients with neurotic disorders. In fact, the most critical elements in his theory are based on the observations that came from working with these patients. In the course of his work he decided that the processes of psychological functioning found in his patients were not peculiar to those with neurotic disturbances but could be found, to one degree or another, and in one form or another, in all people. Thus, though originally based on observations with patients, his theory is a general theory of personality functioning rather than only a theory of abnormal behavior.

Personality types

As noted, Freud thought that the first five years of life were critical in the development of the individual. During these years, it is possible for a number of failures to occur in the development of the instincts. Such failures in the development are called **fixation**s. If individuals receive so little gratification during a stage of development that they are afraid to go to the next stage, or if they receive so much gratification that there is no motivation to move on, a fixation will occur. If a fixation occurs, the individual will try to obtain the same type of satisfaction that was appropriate for an earlier stage of development during later stages. For example, the individual partially fixated at the oral stage may continue to seek oral gratification in eating, smoking, or drinking. A developmental phenomenon related to that fixation is **regression**. In regression, the individual seeks to return to an earlier mode of satisfaction, an earlier point of fixation. Regression will often occur under conditions of stress, so that people may only overeat, smoke, or drink during periods of frustration and anxiety. It is interesting to note in this regard that although research has not demonstrated a relationship between frustration at the oral stage and smoking, a relationship has been found between such frustration and difficulty in giving up smoking (McArthur, Waldron, & Dickinson, 1958).

The concepts of the stages of development, fixation, and regression are of tremendous importance to the psychoanalytic theory of development. One of its most fascinating aspects is the way in which personality characteristics are developed in early life and maintained thereafter. For each of the early stages of development, there is a corresponding character type that is developed because of partial fixations at that stage (Figure 4.3). The characteristics of the **oral personality**, for example, relate to processes going on during the oral stage of development that the individ-

Personality Type	Personality Characteristics
Oral	demanding, impatient, envious, covetous, jealous, rageful, depressed (feels empty), mistrustful, pessimistic
Anal	rigid, striving for power and control, concerned with shoulds and oughts, pleasure in possessions, anxiety over waste and loss of control, concern with whether to submit or rebel
Phallic	*male:* exhibitionistic, competitive, striving for success, emphasis on being masculine-macho-potent *female:* naive, seductive, exhibitionistic, flirtatious

FIGURE 4.3 Personality Characteristics Associated With Psychoanalytic Personality Types

A PSYCHODYNAMIC THEORY

ual maintains in later life. Oral personalities are narcissistic in that they are only interested in themselves and do not have a clear recognition of others as separate entities. Other people are seen only in terms of what they can give (feed). Oral personalities are always asking for something, either in terms of a modest, pleading request or an aggressive demand.

The **anal personality** stems from the anal stage of development. In contrast to gratification associated with the mouth and oral activity, which can be expressed in adulthood in a relatively unrepressed form, the gratifications of anal impulses must undergo considerable transformation. The general theme here is that the traits of the anal character are related to processes going on at the anal stage of development that have not been completely relinquished. The processes of significance are the bodily processes (accumulation and release of fecal material) and interpersonal relations (the struggle of wills over toilet training). Tying the two together, the anal person sees excretion as symbolic of enormous power. That such a view persists is shown in many everyday expressions such as the reference to the toilet as "the throne." The change from the oral to the anal character is one from "give me" to "do what I tell you," or from "I have to give you" to "I must obey you." The anal character is known by a triad of traits, called the *anal triad:* orderliness and cleanliness, parsimony and stinginess, and obstinacy. The emphasis on cleanliness is expressed in the saying "Cleanliness is next to godliness." The anal-compulsive personality has a need to keep everything *clean* and *in order* representing a reaction-formation against an interest in things that are disorderly and unclean. The second trait of the triad, *parsimony-stinginess,* relates to the anal-compulsive's interest in holding on to things, an interest dating back to a wish to retain the powerful and important feces. The third trait in the triad, *obstinacy,* relates to the anal character's infantile defiance against parting with their stools, particularly on command by others.

Anal personalities are filled with contradictions and ambivalence. Generally, they are persevering, although at times they will put things off to the last minute. This relates to the conflict between doing things when they are supposed to as opposed to waiting and experiencing the pleasure in delay. They are generally orderly, but in most cases there is also some trace of messiness. Thus, it is said that every compulsive housewife has a mess closet. The person who keeps an extremely neat desk generally has at least one drawer for all the waste. Often the anal character is submissive and obedient, but then there is an occasional outburst of defiance and vengence.

Anal characters are sensitive to external encroachments on their actual or supposed field of power. They will hold fast to their own way of doing things, expecting compliance from others. They will refuse a request or demand from others, particularly those in authority, but they will do the same things of their own free choice. The important thing is to be in control. Thus an anal husband may oppose expenditures of his wife, and then give, "of his own free will," in fact, more than his wife had asked for.

Just as the oral and anal character types reflect partial fixations at the first two stages of development, so the **phallic character** represents the result of a partial fixation at the stage of the Oedipus complex. Fixation here has different implications for men and women and particular attention has been given to the results of partial fixation for males. Whereas success for the oral person means "I get," and success for the anal person means "I control," success for the phallic male means "I am a man." The phallic male must deny all possible suggestions that he has been castrated. For him success means that he is "big" in the eyes of others. He must at all times assert his masculinity and potency, an attitude reflected in the Rough Riders of Theodore Roosevelt and in the saying "Speak softly but carry a big stick." The excessive, exhibitionistic quality to the behavior of these people is expressive of the underlying anxiety concerning castration. The female counterpart of the male phallic character is known as a hysterical personality. As a defense against oedipal wishes, the little girl identifies to an excessive extent with her mother and femininity. She uses seductive and flirtatious behavior to maintain the interest of her father but denies their sexual intent. The pattern of behavior then is carried over into adulthood, where she may attract men with flirtatious behavior but deny sexual intent and generally appear to be somewhat naive. Hysterical women idealize life, their partners, and romantic love, often finding themselves surprised by life's uglier moments.

Whereas the phallic person generally strives to be successful, conflicts dating back to the oedipal period may lead to feelings of guilt over success. For such a person, success means winning out over the father or mother, a breaking of an incest taboo. As with many of the derivatives of earlier fixations, the same conflict can express itself in opposite ways. The male phallic personality type may seek success on the job, many sexual conquests, and many children, all as evidence of potency, or he may be impotent in his work and sexual life because of guilt over competitive strivings with the father. Although the behavior found in these two cases may appear to be opposite to one another, they tend to reflect the same issue or conflict in their dynamics.

Conflict and defense

According to Freud, all psychopathology relates to an effort to gratify instincts that have been fixated at an earlier stage of development. Thus, in psychopathology the individual still seeks sexual and aggressive gratification in infantile forms. However, because of its association with past trauma, expression of this wish may signal danger to the ego and lead to the experience of anxiety. As a result, there is a conflict situation in which the same behaviors are associated with both pleasure and pain. For example, the person may seek to be dependent on others but fear that if this is done he or she will be vulnerable to frustration and loss (pain). Another example would be of a wish to indulge in sexual behavior that is blocked by feelings of guilt and fear of punishment or injury. A third example is the conflict between a wish to retaliate against powerful others, representing the parents, and a fear that these figures will themselves retaliate with force and destruction. In each case there is a conflict between a wish and anxiety. In such a situation the result often is that the individual "can't say no," can't be assertive, or otherwise feels blocked and unhappy (Figure 4.4).

As noted in the preceding, a critical part of the conflict is anxiety. To reduce the painful experience of anxiety, defense mechanisms, as outlined in Chapter 3, are brought into play. Thus, for example, the person may deny his or her aggressive feelings or project them onto others. In either case, the person no longer has to be afraid of the aggressive feelings. In sum, in psychopathology there is a conflict between a drive or wish (instinct) and the ego's sense (anxiety) that danger will

ILLUSTRATIVE CONFLICTS		BEHAVIOR CONSEQUENCES OF DEFENSE MECHANISMS
Wish	*Anxiety*	*Defense*
I would like to have sex with that person.	Such feelings are bad and will be punished.	Denial of all sexual behavior, obsessive preoccupation with the sexual behavior of others.
I would like to strike out at all those people who make me feel inferior.	If I am hostile they will retaliate and really hurt me.	Denial of wish or fear: "I never feel angry" or "I'm never afraid of anyone or anything."
I would like to get close to people and have them feed me or take care of me.	If I do they will smother me or leave me.	Excessive independence and avoidance of getting close to people or fluctuations between approaching people and moving away from them; excessive need to take care of others.

FIGURE 4.4 Psychoanalytic Theory of Psychopathology

EMOTIONAL SUPPRESSION AND HEALTH

In Chapter 2 we discussed the relation between personality factors and health. More than fifty years ago psychoanalysts suggested a relation between personality dynamics and health, in particular a relation between specific conflicts and specific somatic difficulties. In developing the area of psychosomatic medicine, each disorder was thought to result from a specific emotional constellation. For example, peptic ulcers, described as the "Wall Street stomach," were thought to result from an unconscious craving for love and dependence, which was defended against by an active, productive, aggressive life-style. Or, hypertension was thought to be associated with individuals who were gentle in outward manner but inside boiled with rage.

This line of psychology fell into disfavor because the relation between psychological factors and bodily illness seemed more complex than was originally suggested. Although different in form, currently there is a return to interest in some of these early psychoanalytic views. In particular, there is evidence that the continued suppression of emotion can be detrimental to one's health. Thus, for example, it has been suggested that the suppression of emotion may play a negative role in the course of cancer, ulcers, and heart disease. Alternatively, the expression of emotion, or nonsuppression of emotion, may represent an active, adaptive style of coping that reduces the risk of illness and bodes well for the course of an illness.

SOURCES: Jensen, 1987; Levy, 1984; Pennebaker, 1985; Temoshok, 1985.

I happen to believe a nasty disposition is good for your health.

A PSYCHODYNAMIC THEORY

ensue if the wish is expressed (discharged). To guard against this, and to ward off anxiety, defense mechanisms are used. In structural terms, a neurosis is a result of conflict between the id and the ego. In process terms, an instinct striving for discharge triggers anxiety, leading to a defense mechanism.

In many cases the conflict between the id and ego, between instinct and defense, leads to the development of a **symptom**. A symptom, such as a tic, psychological paralysis, or compulsion, represents a disguised expression of a repressed impulse. The meaning of the symptom, the nature of the dangerous instinct, and the nature of the defense all remain unconscious. For example, a mother may be painfully obsessed with the fear that something will happen to her child. Underlying the obsession may be rage at her child and anxiety about the harm she may do to the child. The symptom of the obsession expresses both the mother's feelings that she may harm or injure the child and her defense against it in terms of excessive preoccupation with the child's welfare. To take another example, in a hand-washing compulsion, in which the person feels compelled to wash his or her hands continuously, the symptom may express both the wish to be dirty or do "dirty" things and the defense against the wish in terms of excessive cleanliness. In both of these cases the person in unaware of the wish or the defense and is troubled only by the symptom. Many people do not suffer from such specific problems or symptoms but analysts suggest that all psychological problems can still be understood in these terms.

To summarize the psychoanalytic theory of psychopathology, there is an arrest in the development of the person that is associated with conflicts between wishes and fears. The wishes and fears that were part of a specific time period in childhood are now carried over into adolescence and adulthood. The person attempts to handle anxiety that is a painful part of this conflict by using defense mechanisms. However, if the conflict becomes too great, the use of defense mechanisms can lead to neurotic symptoms or psychotic withdrawal from reality. Symptoms express the unconscious conflict between wish or drive and anxiety. In each case of abnormal behavior there is an unconscious conflict between a wish and a fear that dates back to an earlier period in childhood. In this sense, as adults there continue to be childlike parts of us that under some conditions, such as those of stress, may become more active and troublesome.

Behavior Change

How does behavior change come about? Once a person has established a behavioral pattern, a way of thinking about and responding to situations, through what process does a change in personality take place? The psychoanalytic theory of growth suggests that there is a normal course of human personality development, one that occurs because of optimum

ACTUAL SEDUCTION OR FANTASY?

Freud's original theory of psychopathology, his original seduction theory, suggested that neurotics experienced actual childhood seduction by their parents. He came to question this both because such reports of childhood seduction were so common that they were hard to believe, and because patients developed sexual feelings for their therapists that seemed to evolve out of fantasies and wishes that dated back to childhood. Thus, rather than actual seduction, Freud suggested that children develop fantasies of seduction based on their own wishes and desires. Rather than traumatic events of seduction, children experienced anxiety and conflict in relation to oedipal wishes.

Recently, an analyst, Dr. Jeffrey Masson, has suggested that Freud's patients were telling the truth. In his book *The Assault On Truth*, Masson suggests that Freud shifted attention away from the actual external trauma to internal fantasy as the causal agent in mental illness, and that he did this in part because of a personal failure of courage. Aside from the question of Freud's character, the issue is of importance for two reasons. First, it raises the question of whether patient recollections of childhood experiences are generally accurate and whether such data can be used in the formulation of a theory. Second, it raises the question of just how often childhood sexual abuse occurs. Recent reports suggest that it is much more frequent than had previously been suspected, and that many people repress the memory because of the trauma associated with it.

SOURCES: Masson, 1985; *New York Times*, January 24, 1984; *APA Monitor*, June 1987.

degrees of frustration. Where there has been too little or too much frustration at a particular stage of growth, personality does not proceed normally and a fixation takes place. When this occurs, the individual repeats patterns of behavior regardless of other changes in situations. Given the development of such a neurotic pattern, how is it possible to break the cycle and to move forward?

In his early efforts to effect behavioral change, Freud used a method called cathartic hypnosis. The view then held was that relief from neurotic symptoms would come about through the discharge of blocked emotions. Freud did not like using hypnosis, since not all patients could be hypnotized, the results were often transient, and he did not feel that he was learning much about mental functioning. The second development in technique was that of waking suggestion. Here Freud put his hand on the patient's head and assured him that he could recall and face repressed past emotional experiences. With the increased interest in the interpretation of dreams, Freud focused on the **free-association** method as basic to psychoanalysis. In free association the patient is asked to report to the analyst every thought that comes to mind, to delay reporting nothing, to withhold nothing, to bar nothing from coming to consciousness. **Dreams** are the "royal road" to the unconscious. Through the free association method the analyst and patient are able to go beyond the manifest (obvious) content of the dream to the latent content, to the hidden meaning that expresses the unconscious wish. Dreams, like symptoms, are disguises and partial wish–fulfillments. In the dream, the person can satisfy a hostile or sexual wish in a disguised, and thereby safe, way. For example, rather than dreaming of oneself killing someone, one may dream of a battle in which a particular figure is killed. In such a case the wish may remain at least somewhat obvious, but in other cases the wish may be much more disguised. Free association allows for the uncovering of the disguise. When conscious control is relaxed, the impulses, wishes, memories, and fantasies of the unconscious break through into consciousness. It is important to realize, however, that the free-association process, the stream of consciousness, is not in fact free; it is determined, as is all behavior, by the forces within the individual that are striving for expression. It is also important to recognize that ordinarily one cannot easily or immediately understand the meaning of a dream —it requires a process of uncovering or discovery.

At first, Freud thought that making the unconscious conscious was sufficient to effect change and cure. This was in keeping with an early emphasis on repressed memories as the basis for pathology. Freud then realized that more than the recovery of memories was involved. Rather, emotional insight into the wishes and conflicts that had remained hidden was necessary.

The process of therapeutic change in psychoanalysis involves coming to grips with emotions and wishes that previously have been unconscious and struggling with these painful experiences within a relatively safe environment. If psychopathology involves fixation at an early stage of development, then in psychoanalysis individuals become free to resume their normal psychological development. If psychopathology involves the damming up of the instincts and the expenditure of energy for defensive purposes, then psychoanalysis involves a redistribution of energy so that more energy is available for mature, guiltless, less rigid, and more gratifying activities. If psychopathology involves conflict and defense mechanisms, then psychoanalysis involves the reduction of conflict and the freeing of the patient from the limitations of the defensive processes. If psychopathology involves an individual dominated by the unconscious and the tyranny of the id, then psychoanalysis involves making conscious what was unconscious and putting under control of the ego what was formerly under the domination of the id or superego.

Our plan of cure is based upon these views. The ego has been weakened by the internal conflict; we must come to its aid. The position is like a civil war which can only be decided by the help of an ally from without. The analytical physician and the weakened ego of the patient, basing themselves upon the real external world, are to combine against the enemies, the instinctual demands of the id, and the moral demands of the superego. We form a pact with each other.

FREUD, 1940, pp. 62–63

In sum, then, psychoanalysis is viewed as a learning process in which the individual resumes and completes the growth process that was interrupted when the neurosis began. The principle involved is the reexposure of the patient, under more favorable circumstances, to the emotional situations that could not be handled in the past. The vehicle for such reexposure is the transference relationship and the development of a transference neurosis. The term **transference** refers to the development, on the part of the patient, of attitudes toward the analyst that have as their basis attitudes held by the patient toward earlier parental figures. In the sense that transference relates to distortions of reality based on past experiences, transference occurs in everyone's daily life and in all forms of psychotherapy. In expressing transference attitudes toward the analyst, patients duplicate in therapy their interactions with people in their outer lives and their past interactions with significant figures. For example, if patients feel that the analyst's taking notes may lead to exploitation by the analyst, they are expressing attitudes they hold toward both people they meet in their daily existence and earlier figures in their lives. In free associating, oral characters may be concerned about whether they are "feeding" the analyst and whether the analyst gives them enough in return; anal characters may be concerned about who is

Freud's consulting room.

A PSYCHODYNAMIC THEORY

controlling the sessions; phallic characters may be concerned about who will win in competitive struggles. Such attitudes, often part of the unconscious daily existence of the patient, come to light in the course of analysis.

Although transference is a part of all relationships and of all forms of therapy, psychoanalysis is distinctive in its use of it as a dynamic force in behavior change. Many of the formal qualities of the analytic situation are structured to enhance the development of transference. The patient lying on the couch supports the development of a dependent relationship. The scheduling of frequent meetings (up to five or six times a week) strengthens the emotional importance of the analytic relationship to the patient's daily existence. Finally, the fact that patients become so tied to their analysts, while knowing so little about them as people, means that their responses are almost completely determined by their neurotic conflicts. The analyst remains a mirror or blank screen on which the individual projects wishes and anxieties.

The encouragement of transference, or providing the circumstances that allow it to develop, leads to the development of the transference neurosis. It is here that patients play out, full-blown, their old conflicts. Patients now invest the major aspects of their relationship with the analyst with the wishes and anxieties of the past. The goal is no longer to get well, but to gain from the analyst what they had to do without in childhood. Rather than seeking a way out of competitive relationships, they may only seek to castrate the analyst; rather than seek to become less dependent on others, they may seek to have the analyst gratify all their dependency needs. The fact that these attitudes have developed within the context of the analysis allows patients and their analysts to look at and understand the instinctual and defensive components of the original infantile conflict. The fact that the patient invests considerable emotion in the situation allows for the increased understanding to be emotionally meaningful. Change occurs when insight has been gained, when patients realize, on both an intellectual and emotional level, the nature of conflicts and feel free, in terms of their new perceptions of themselves and the world, to gratify their instincts in a mature, conflict-free way.

Whereas guilt and anxiety prevented growth in the past, the analytic situation offers the individual the opportunity to deal anew with the old conflicts. Why should the response be any different at this time? Basically, change occurs in analysis because of the three therapeutic factors. First, in analysis the conflict is less intense than it was in the original situation. Second, the analyst assumes an attitude that is different from that of the parents. Finally, patients in analysis are older and more mature, that is, they are able to use parts of their ego that have developed to deal with the parts of their functioning that have not. These three factors, creating as they do the opportunity for relearning, provide the basis for what Alexander and French (1946) call the "corrective emotional experience." It should be clear that developments such as these in no way suggest that psychoanalysis is an intellectual experience as opposed to an emotional experience, that insight and understanding are given by the analyst rather than gained by the patient, or that there is a denial of moral responsibility and a sanctioning of sin. Rather, psychoanalytic theory suggests that through insight into old conflicts, through an understanding of the needs for infantile gratifications and recognition of the potential for mature gratification, and through an understanding of old anxieties and a recognition of their lack of relevance to current realities, patients may progress toward maximum instinctual gratification within the limits set by reality and their own moral convictions.

A CASE EXAMPLE—LITTLE HANS

Although many psychiatrists and psychologists have spent considerable time treating patients, Freud is one of the very few who have reported cases in detail. Most of Freud's cases come from early in his career. Although these case presentations are useful in understanding many aspects of psychoanalytic theory, it is important to remember that they occurred prior to Freud's development of his theory of the sexual and aggressive instincts, prior to the development of the structural model, and prior to the development of the theory of anxiety and defense mechanisms.

The case of Little Hans, published in 1909, involves the analysis of a phobia in a five-year-old boy. It involves the treatment of the boy by his father and does not represent Freud's direct participation in the therapeutic process. The boy was bothered by a fear that a horse would bite him. Therefore, he refused to leave the house. The boy's father kept detailed notes on his treatment and frequently discussed his progress with Freud. Although the "patient" was not treated by Freud, the case of Little Hans is important because it illustrates the theory of infantile sexuality, the functioning of the Oedipus complex and castration anxiety, the dynamics of symptom formation, and the process of behavior change.

Our account of events in the life of Little Hans begins at age three. At this point he had a lively interest in his penis, which he called his "widdler." What was striking about Hans during this period was his pleasure in touching his own penis and his preoccupation with penises or "widdlers" in others. For example, he wanted to know if his mother had a widdler and was fascinated with the process by which cows are milked. The interest in touching his penis, however, led to threats by his mother. "If you do that, I shall send you to Dr. A. to cut off your widdler. And then what will you widdle with?" Thus, there was a direct castration threat on the part of a parent, in this case the mother. Freud pinpointed this as the beginning of Hans' castration complex.

Hans' interest in widdlers extended to noting the size of the lion's widdler at the zoo and analyzing the differences between animate and inanimate objects—dogs and horses have widdlers, tables and chairs do not. Hans was curious about many things, but Freud related his general thirst for knowledge to sexual curiosity. Hans continued to be interested in whether his mother had a widdler. "I thought you (mother) were so big you'd have a widdler like a horse." When he was three-and-a-half, a sister was born, who also became a focus for his widdler concerns. "But her widdler's still quite small. When she grows up it'll get bigger all right." According to Freud, Hans could not admit what he really saw, namely, that there was no widdler there. To do so would mean that he must face his own castration anxieties. These anxieties occurred at a time when he was experiencing pleasure in the organ, as witnessed in his comments to his mother while she dried and powdered him after his bath.

> HANS: Why don't you put your finger there.
> MOTHER: Because that'd be piggish.
> HANS: What's that? Piggish? Why?
> HANS (*laughing*): But it's great fun.

Thus Hans, now more than four years old, was preoccupied with his penis, experienced pleasure in it and concern about the loss of it, and began some seduction of his mother. It was at this point that his nervous disorders became apparent. The father, attributing the difficulties to sexual overexcitation due to his mother's tenderness, wrote Freud that Hans was "afraid that a horse will bite him in the street" and this fear seemed somehow to be connected with his having been frightened by seeing a large penis. As you remember, he had noticed at a very early age what large penises horses have, and at that time he inferred that, as his mother was so large, she must "have a widdler like a horse." Hans was afraid of going into the street and was depressed in the evenings. He had bad dreams and was frequently taken into his mother's bed. While walking in the street with his nurse, he became terribly frightened and sought to return home to be with his mother. The fear that horses would bite him became a fear that the horse would come into his room. He had developed a full-blown phobia, an irrational dread or fear of an object (horse). What more can we learn about this phobia? How are we to account for its development? As Freud notes, we must do more than simply call this a small boy's foolish fears.

The father attempted to deal with his son's fear of horses by offering him an interpretation. Hans was told that the fear of horses was nonsense, that the truth was that he (Hans) was fond of his mother and the fear of horses had to do with an interest in their widdlers. Upon Freud's suggestion, the father explained to Hans that women do not have widdlers. Apparently there was a period of some relief in Hans, but he continued to be bothered by an obsessive wish to look at horses, though he was then frightened by them. At this point, he had his tonsils taken out and his phobia worsened. He was afraid that a white horse would bite him. He continued to be interested in widdlers in females. At the zoo, he was afraid of all the large animals and was entertained by the smaller ones. Among the birds, he was afraid of the pelican. In spite of his father's truthful explanation, Hans sought to reassure himself. "And everyone has a widdler. And my widdler will get bigger as I get bigger, because it does grow on me." According to Freud, Hans had been making comparisons among the sizes of widdlers and was dissatisfied with his own. Big animals reminded him of this defect and were disagreeable to him. The father's explanation heightened his castration anxiety, as expressed in the words "it does grow on me," as if it could be cut off. Thus, for this reason he resisted the information, and thus it had no therapeutic results. "Could it be that living beings really did exist which did not possess widdlers? If so, it would no longer be so incredible that they could take his own widdler away, and, as it were, make him into a woman."

Around this time, Hans reported the following dream. "In the night there was a big giraffe in the room and a crumpled one; and the big one called out because I took the crumpled one away from it. Then it stopped calling out; and then I sat down on top of the crumpled one." The father's interpretation was that he, the father, was the big giraffe, with the big penis, and the mother was the crumpled giraffe, missing the genital organ. The dream was a reproduction of a morning scene in which the mother took Hans into bed with her. The father warned her against this ("The big one called out because I'd taken the crumpled one away from it") but the mother continued to encourage it. The mother encouraged and reinforced the oedipal wishes. Hans stayed with her and, in the wish–fulfillment of the dream, he took possession of her ("Then the big giraffe stopped calling out; and then I sat down on top of the crumpled one").

Freud's strategy in understanding Hans' phobia was to suspend judgment and to give his impartial attention to everything there was to observe. He learned that prior to the development of the phobia, Hans had been alone with his mother at a summer place. There, two significant events occurred. First, he heard the father of one of his friends tell her that a white horse there bites and she was not to hold her finger to it. Second, while playing as if they were horses, a friend who rivaled Hans for the affection of the little girls fell down, hit his foot, and bled. In an interview with Hans, Freud learned that Hans was bothered by the blinders on horses and the black around their mouths. The phobia became extended to include a fear that horses dragging a heavy van would fall down and kick their feet. It was then discovered that the exciting cause of his phobia, the event that capitalized on a psychological readiness for the formation of a phobia, was the perception of a horse falling down. While walking outside with his mother one day, Hans had seen a horse pulling a van fall down and begin to kick its feet.

A PSYCHODYNAMIC THEORY

The central feature in this case of little Hans was the phobia about the horse. What is fascinating in this regard is how often associations concerning a horse came up in relation to father, mother, and Hans himself. We have already noticed Hans' interest in his mother's widdler in relation to that of a horse. To his father, he said at one point: "Daddy, don't trot away from me." Can father, who wore a mustache and eyeglasses, be the horse that Hans was afraid of, the horse that would come into his room at night and would bite him? Or, could Hans himself be the horse? Hans was known to play horse in his room, to trot about, fall down, kick about with his feet, and neigh. He repeatedly ran up to his father and bit him, just as he feared the horse would do to him. Hans was overfed. Could this relate to his concerns about large, fat horses? Finally, Hans was known to have called himself a young horse and to have a tendency to stamp his feet on the ground when angry, similar to what the horse did when it fell down. To return to the mother, could the heavily laden carts symbolize the pregnant mother and the horse falling down the birth or delivery of a child? Are such associations coincidental or can they play a significant role in our understanding of the phobia?

According to Freud, the major cause of Hans' phobia was his Oedipus conflict. Hans felt considerable affection for his mother, more than he could handle during the phallic stage of his development. Although he had deep affection for the father he also considered him a rival for his mother's affections. When he and mother stayed at the summer cottage and father was away, he was able to get into bed with mother and keep her for himself. This heightened his attraction for his mother and his hostility toward his father. For Freud, "Hans was really a little Oedipus who wanted to have his father 'out of the way,' to get rid of him, so that he might be alone with his handsome mother and sleep with her. This wish had originated during his summer holidays, when the alternating presence and absence of his father had drawn Hans' attention to the condition upon which depended the intimacy with his mother which he longed for." The fall and injury to his friend and rival during one of those holidays was significant in symbolizing the defeat for Hans of his rival.

When he returned home from the summer holidays, Hans' resentment toward his father increased. He tried to suppress the resentment with exaggerated affection. He arrived at an ingenious solution to the oedipal conflict. He and his mother would be parents to children and the father could be the granddaddy. Thus, as Freud notes, "the little Oedipus had found a happier solution than that prescribed by destiny. Instead of putting his father out of the way, he had granted him the same happiness that he desired himself: he made him a grandfather and let him too marry his own mother." But such a fantasy could not be a satisfactory solution, and Hans was left with considerable hostility for his father. The exciting cause of the phobia was the horse falling down. At that moment, Hans perceived a wish that his father might in the same way fall down and die. The hostility toward his father was projected onto the father and was symbolized in the horse, because he himself nourished jealous and hostile wishes against him. He feared the horse would bite him because of his wish that his father should fall down, and fears that the horse would come into his room occurred at night when he was most tempted by oedipal fantasies. In his own play as a horse and in his biting of his father, he expressed an identification with his father. The phobia expressed the wish and the anxiety and, in a secondary way, accomplished the objective of leaving Hans home to be with his mother.

In sum, both his fear that a horse would bite him and his fear that horses would fall down represented the father who was going to punish Hans for the evil wishes he was harboring against him. Hans was able to get over the phobia and, according to a later report by Freud, he appeared to be functioning well. What factors allowed for the change? First, there was the sexual enlightenment by the father. Although Hans was reluctant to accept this and it at first heightened his castration anxiety, it did serve as a useful piece of reality to hold onto. Second, the analysis provided by his father and by Freud was useful in making conscious for Hans what had formerly been unconscious. Finally, the father's interest and permissive attitude toward Hans' expression of his feelings allowed for a resolution of the Oedipus conflict in favor of an identification with the father, diminishing both the wish to rival the father and the castration anxiety, and thereby decreasing the potential for symptom development.

The case of little Hans has many problems with it as a piece of scientific investigation. The interviewing was done by the father in an unsystematic way. The father himself was a close adherent of Freud's and therefore was possibly biased somewhat in his observations and interpretations. Freud himself was dependent on secondhand reports. He was aware of the limitations of the data, but he was also impressed with them. Whereas before he had based his theory on the childhood memories of adult patients, now, in the case of Little Hans, he began to observe the sexual life of children.

It is hard to draw conclusions about the theory in terms of this one case. The presentation does not contain all of Freud's observations on Hans. Furthermore, it is but a single case, and it is taken from an early point (1909) in Freud's work. On the other hand, we do get an appreciation of both the wealth of information available to the analyst and, moreover, the problems inherent in evaluating and interpreting such data. We must necessarily get a feeling for Freud's ability to observe and describe phenomena and his efforts to come to terms with the complexity of human behavior. In this one case alone we have descriptions of phenomena relevant to the following: infantile sexuality, fantasies of children, functioning of the unconscious, the process of conflict development and conflict resolution, the process of symptom formation, symbolization, and the dream process. In reading such a case we cannot fail to be impressed by Freud's courageous efforts to discover the secrets of human functioning and by his willingness to pursue the job that needed to be done, in spite of limitations in his observations and in full recognition of the complexity of the phenomena he was trying to understand.

RELATED POINTS OF VIEW
AND RECENT DEVELOPMENTS

One interesting aspect of the history of psychoanalytic theory has been the development of schools or groups with different, often antagonistic points of view. Freud changed many aspects of psychoanalytic theory during the course of his professional career. However, he and his followers clashed on many issues. To a certain extent there was what has been described as a religious or political quality (Fromm, 1959) to psychoanalysis, with the traditional followers being considered among the faithful and those who deviated from the fundamental principles being cast outside the movement. This pattern started during Freud's lifetime and continued afterward. A theorist such as Erikson is still highly regarded by most traditional psychoanalysts, whereas the theorists considered in the following often are not. Frequently it is hard to determine the basis for the response to one or another theorist. However, as a general rule, a theorist must retain a commitment to the following concepts to be considered a part of Freudian psychoanalysis: the sexual and aggressive instincts, the unconscious, and the stages of development. As we shall see, the theorists considered questioned one or another of these concepts and thereby approached understanding humans somewhat differently.

Two Early Challenges to Freud

Among the many early analysts who broke with Freud and developed their own schools of thought were Alfred Adler and Carl G. Jung. Both were early and important followers of Freud, Adler having been president of the Vienna Psychoanalytic Society and Jung president of the International Psychoanalytic Society. Both split with Freud over what they felt was an excessive emphasis on the sexual instincts. The split with Jung was particularly painful for Freud since Jung was to be his "crown prince" and chosen successor. Other individuals also split with Freud and developed their own schools of thought. However, Adler and Jung were among the earliest and remain among the best known.

Alfred Adler (1870–1937)

For approximately a decade, Alfred Adler was an active member of the Vienna psychoanalytic group. However, in 1911, when he presented his views to the other members of this group, the response was so hostile that he left it to form his own school of *Individual Psychology*. What ideas

Alfred Adler

could have been considered so unacceptable to psychoanalysts? We cannot consider all of Adler's theory, but we can consider some of his early and later views to get a feeling for the important differences between them and psychoanalysis.

Perhaps most significant of all in Adler's split from Freud was his greater emphasis on social urges and conscious thoughts than on instinctual sexual urges and unconscious processes. Early in his career Adler became interested in organ inferiorities and how people compensate for them. A person with a weak organ may attempt to compensate for this weakness by special efforts to strengthen that organ or by efforts to develop other organs. For example, someone who stutters as a child may attempt to become a great speaker, or someone with a defect in vision may attempt to develop special listening sensitivities. Whereas initially Adler was interested in bodily organ weaknesses, gradually he became interested in psychological *feelings of inferiority* and *compensatory strivings* to mask or reduce these painful feelings. Thus, whereas Freudians might see Theodore Roosevelt's emphasis on toughness and carrying a "big stick" as a defense against castration anxiety, Adlerians might see him as expressing compensatory strivings against feelings of inferiority associated with boyhood weaknesses. Whereas Freudians might see an extremely aggressive woman as expressing penis envy, Adlerians might see her as expressing a *masculine protest* or rejection of the stereotyped feminine role of weakness and inferiority. According to Adler, how a

A PSYCHODYNAMIC THEORY

person attempts to cope with such feelings becomes a part of his or her *style of life*—a distinctive aspect of his or her personality functioning.

These concepts already suggest a much more social rather than biological emphasis. This social emphasis increasingly became an important part of Adler's thinking. At first Adler spoke of a *will to power* as an expression of the organism's efforts to cope with feelings of helplessness dating from infancy. This emphasis gradually shifted to an emphasis on *striving for superiority*. In its neurotic form this striving could be expressed in wishes for power and control over others; in its healthier form it expressed a "great upward drive" toward unity and perfection. In the healthy person the striving for superiority is expressed in social feeling and cooperation as well as in assertiveness and competition. From the beginning there is in people a *social interest*, that is, an innate interest in relating to people and an innate potential for cooperation.

Adler's theory is also noteworthy for its emphasis on how people respond to feelings about the self, how people respond to goals that direct their behavior toward the future, and how the order of birth among siblings can influence their psychological development. In relation to the latter, many psychologists have noted the tendency for only sons or first-born sons to achieve more than later sons in a family. For example, twenty-one of the first twenty-three American astronauts were first born or only sons. Although many of Adler's ideas have found their way into the general public's thinking and are related to views later expressed by

Birth Order—Alfred Adler emphasized the importance of birth order in personality development. Twenty-one of the first twenty-three American astronauts were first-born or only sons.

other theorists, the school of individual psychology itself has not had a major impact on personality theory and research.

Carl G. Jung (1875–1961)

Jung split with Freud in 1914, a few years after Adler, and developed his own school of thought called *Analytical Psychology*. Like Adler, he was distressed with what he felt was an excessive emphasis on sexuality. Instead, Jung viewed the libido as a generalized life energy. Although sexuality is a part of this basic energy, the libido also includes other strivings for pleasure and creativity.

Jung accepted Freud's emphasis on the unconscious but added to it the concept of the *collective unconscious*. According to Jung, people have stored within their collective unconscious the cumulative experiences of past generations. The collective unconscious, as opposed to the personal unconscious, is shared by all humans as a result of their common ancestry. It is a part of our animal heritage, our link with millions of years of past experience: "This psychic life is the mind of our ancient ancestors, the way in which they thought and felt, the way in which they conceived of life and the world, of gods and human beings. The existence of these

Carl Jung

A PSYCHODYNAMIC THEORY

historical layers is presumably the source of belief in reincarnation and in memories of past lives" (Jung, 1939, p. 24).

An important part of the collective unconscious are universal images or symbols, known as *archetypes*. Archetypes, such as the Mother archetype, are seen in fairy tales, dreams, myths, and in some psychotic thoughts. Jung was struck with similar images that keep appearing, in slightly different forms, in far-distant cultures. For example, the Mother archetype might be expressed in a variety of positive or negative forms: as life-giver, as all-giving and nurturant, as the witch or threatening punisher ("Don't fool with Mother Nature"), and as the seductive female. Archetypes may be represented in our images of persons, demons, animals, natural forces, or objects. The evidence in all cases for their being a part of our collective unconscious is their universality among members of different cultures from past and current time periods.

Another important aspect of Jung's theory was his emphasis on how people struggle with opposing forces within them. For example, there is the struggle between the face or mask we present to others (*persona*) and the private or personal self. If people emphasize the persona too much there may be a loss of sense of self and a doubting about who they are. On the other hand, the persona, as expressed in social roles and customs, is a necessary part of living in society. Similarly, there is the struggle between the masculine and feminine parts of ourselves. Every male has a feminine part (*anima*) and every female has a masculine part (*animus*) to their personality. If a man rejects his feminine part he may emphasize mastery and strength to an excessive degree, appearing cold and insensitive to the feelings of others. If a woman rejects her masculine part she may be excessively absorbed in "motherhood" and unable to accomplish herself in other ways. Psychologists currently interested in stereotyped sex roles would probably applaud Jung's emphasis on these dual aspects in everyone's personality, although they might question his characterizing some as specifically masculine and others as feminine.

Another contrast in Jung's theory is that between *introversion* and *extroversion*. Everyone relates to the world primarily in one of two directions, though the other direction always remains a part of the person. In the case of introversion, the person's basic orientation is inner, toward the self. The introverted type is hesitant, reflective, and cautious. In the case of extroversion the person's basic orientation is outward, toward the outside world. The extroverted type is socially engaging, active, and venturesome. For each person there is the task of finding unity in the *self*. For Jung an important task of life is to be found in bringing into harmony or integrating the preceding and other opposing forces. The integration of the many opposing aspects of our personality into the self is a lifelong struggle: "Personality as a complete realization of the fullness of our being is an unattainable ideal. But unattainability is no counter argument against an ideal, for ideals are only signposts, never goals" (Jung, 1939, p. 287). The struggle described here can become a particularly important aspect of life once people have passed the age of forty and defined themselves to the outside world in a variety of ways.

As with Adler, we have been able to consider only some of the highlights of Jung's theory. Jung is considered by many to be one of the great creative thinkers of the century and his theory has influenced the thinking of people in many fields outside of psychology. Although periodically there are signs of the development of a strong interest in Jung inside of psychology, his views have yet to have a significant impact on the field.

The Cultural and Interpersonal Emphasis

With the later shift in psychodynamic thinking from Europe to the United States, one finds theorists emphasizing social rather than biological forces in behavior. Collectively, these theorists are called neo-Freudians, recognizing both their theoretical debt to Freud and their development of new theoretical positions. Some of these theorists, such as Karen Horney, emigrated to the United States prior to the Second World War. Other theorists, notably Harry Stack Sullivan, were born and trained in this country.

Karen Horney (1885–1952)

Karen Horney was trained as a traditional analyst in Germany and came to the United States in 1932. Shortly thereafter she split with traditional psychoanalytic thought and developed her own theoretical orientation and psychoanalytic training program. In contrast to Adler and Jung, she felt that her views were built on the tremendous contributions of Freud, and not replacements of them. Perhaps the major difference between her and Freud centers on the question of universal biological influences as opposed to cultural influences: "When we realize the great import of cultural conditions on neuroses, the biological and physiological conditions, which are considered by Freud to be their root, recede into the background" (1937, p. viii). She was led to this emphasis by three major considerations. First, Freud's statements concerning women made Horney think about cultural influences: "Their influence on our ideas of what constitutes masculinity or femininity was obvious, and it became just as obvious to me that Freud had arrived at certain conclusions because he failed to take them into account" (1945, p. 11). Second, she was associated with another psychoanalyst, Erich Fromm, who increased her awareness of the importance of social and cultural influences. Third, Horney's observations of differences in personality structure between patients seen in Europe and the United States confirmed the importance of cultural influences. Beyond this, these observations led her to conclude that interpersonal relationships are at the core of all healthy and disturbed personality functioning.

Horney's emphasis in neurotic functioning is on how individuals

Karen Horney

attempt to cope with *basic anxiety*—the feeling a child has of being isolated and helpless in a potentially hostile world. According to her theory of neurosis, in the neurotic person there is conflict among three ways of responding to this basic anxiety. These three patterns, or *neurotic trends*, are known as moving toward, moving against, and moving away. All three are characterized by rigidity and the lack of fulfillment of individual potential, the essence of any neurosis. In *moving toward* the person attempts to deal with anxiety by an excessive interest in being accepted, needed, and approved of. Such a person accepts a dependent role in relation to others and, except for the unlimited desire for affection, become unselfish, undemanding, and self-sacrificing. In *moving against*, the person assumes that everyone is hostile and that life is a struggle against all. All functioning is directed toward denying a need for others and toward appearing tough. In *moving away*, the third component of the conflict, the person shrinks away from others into neurotic detachment. Such people often look at themselves and others with emotional detachment, a way of not getting emotionally involved with others. Although each neurotic person shows one or another trend as a special aspect of their personality, the problem is really that there is conflict among the three trends in the effort to deal with basic anxiety.

Before leaving Horney, her views concerning women should be considered. These views date back to her early work within traditional psychoanalytic thought and are reflected in a series of papers in *Feminine Psychology* (1973). As has been noted, from the start Horney had

Neurotic Trends—Karen Horney emphasized the neurotic trends of moving toward, moving against, and moving away (as illustrated in the following three photographs) as an attempt to cope with basic anxiety. In more moderate forms such trends exist in most people.

A PSYCHODYNAMIC THEORY

trouble accepting Freud's veiws of women. She felt that the concept of penis envy might be the result of a male bias in psychoanalysts that treat neurotic women in a particular social context: "Unfortunately, little or nothing is known of physically healthy women, or of women under different cultural conditions" (1973, p. 216). She suggested that women are not biologically disposed toward masochistic attitudes of being weak, dependent, submissive, and self-sacrificing. Instead, these attitudes indicated the powerful influence of social forces.

In sum, both in her views of women and in her general theoretical orientation, Horney rejected Freud's biological emphasis in favor of a social, interpersonal one. Partly as a result of this difference she held a much more optimistic view concerning the person's capacity for change and self-fulfillment.

Harry Stack Sullivan (1892–1949)

Of the theorists considered in this section, Sullivan is the only one born and trained in the United States, the only one who never had direct contact with Freud, and the one who most emphasized the role of social, interpersonal forces in human development. In fact, his theory has been known as the *Interpersonal Theory of Psychiatry* (1953) and his followers consider themselves part of the Sullivan school of interpersonal relations.

Sullivan placed great importance on the early relationship between the infant and the mother in the development of anxiety and in the development of a sense of self. Anxiety may be communicated by the mother in her earliest interaction with the infant. Thus, from the start, anxiety is interpersonal in character. The *self*, a critical concept in Sulli-

Harry Stack Sullivan

van's thinking, similarly is social in origin. The self develops out of feelings experienced while in contact with others and from *reflected appraisals* or perceptions on the part of the child as to how it is valued or appraised by others. Important parts of the self, particularly in relation to the experience of anxiety as opposed to security, are the *good-me* associated with pleasurable experiences, the *bad-me* associated with pain and threats to security, and the *not-me* or part of the self that is rejected because it is associated with intolerable anxiety.

Sullivan's emphasis on social influences is seen throughout his views on the development of the person. These views are somewhat similar to Erikson's in their emphasis on interpersonal influences, and in their emphasis on important stages beyond the Oedipus complex. Particularly noteworthy here is Sullivan's emphasis on the *juvenile era* and *preadolescence*. During the juvenile stage, roughly the grammar school years, the child's experiences with friends and teachers begin to rival the influence of parents. Social acceptance becomes important and the child's "reputation" with others becomes an important source of self-esteem or anxiety. During preadolescence a relationship to a close friend of the same sex, or chum, becomes particularly important. This relationship of close friendship, of love, forms the basis for the development of a love relationship with a person of the opposite sex during adolescence. Today, many child psychologists suggest that early relationships with peers may equal in importance the early relationships with the mother (Lewis *et al.*, 1975).

As with the other theorists in this section, we have been able to consider only a few of the major concepts of Sullivan's interpersonal

A PSYCHODYNAMIC THEORY

Peers—Harry Stack Sullivan emphasized the importance of peers and a close friend of the same sex during preadolescence.

theory. Sullivan's work is noteworthy in its social emphasis, in its emphasis on the development of the self, and in the outstanding contributions that he made to the treatment of schizophrenic patients.

Recent Developments within Traditional Psychoanalytic Theory

Turning to developments within traditional psychoanalytic theory, we can consider progress associated with clinical investigations and progress associated with systematic research efforts. From its inception with Freud and continuing to the present, developments within psychoanalytic theory generally have been based on clinical investigation, that is, analysis of individual cases. One important development has been the extension of psychoanalytic investigation to age groups and forms of psychopathology rarely treated by Freud and his followers. As noted, Little Hans was treated by his father. Most psychoanalytic material on childhood and adolescence was based on memories reported by adult parents. The situation changed considerably with the efforts of individuals such as Anna Freud and Melanie Klein, who used psychoanalytic concepts in the treatment of children, so that now a major part of the psychotherapy conducted with children and adolescents in Great Britain and the United States is based on psychoanalytic theory. Modifications are made in the treatment procedure according to the age group being treated (e.g., with children, play therapy is used as a substitute for dream analysis as a route to the unconscious), but the essential theoretical concepts remain the same.

In addition to the expansion of their clinical efforts to treatment of children, psychoanalysts increasingly have been concerned with different types of patient problems than those faced, in the main, by Freud. In the words of one analyst, today's patients come from a different social and cultural context than did Freud's patients and bring with them different problems. Rather than presenting themselves with "typical neuroses," they seek help with depressions, with feelings of emptiness, and with lives "lacking zest and joy" (Wolf, 1977). Such changes in the major problems coming to the attention of analysts have led to new theoretical advances, not from a dissatisfaction with Freudian theory per se but from the need to understand and solve different clinical problems.

Clinical concern with problems of self-definition and excessive vulnerability of one's sense of self-esteem have led psychologists to become increasingly interested in how, during the earliest years, a person develops a sense of self (Kohut, 1977). Thus, many recent theoretical efforts, though not rejecting Freud's views concerning the roles of sex and aggression, have become more concerned with how the person attempts to protect the integrity of the sense of self. To a certain extent, this recent focus on the self represents an extension of the earlier emphasis by other analysts on ego functioning. However, there is a difference. The earlier emphasis in psychoanalytic ego psychology focused on the undefensive, conflict-free aspects of ego functioning. Such functioning is expressed in artistic, creative productions as opposed to disturbed neurotic or psychotic functioning. In contrast, more recently there has been concern with disturbance in the development of ego functioning and the sense of self, and with the implications of such disturbances for the development of psychopathology.

In relation to this interest in the disturbances in the sense of self, psychoanalytic attention has particularly focused on the concept of narcissism and consideration of the *narcissistic personality*. The two figures most important in this area are Heinz Kohut and Otto Kernberg. In the development of a healthy sense of self and a healthy narcissism, the individual has a clear sense of self, a satisfactory and reasonably stable level of self-esteem, takes pride in accomplishments, and is aware of and responsive to the needs of others while responding to his or her own needs. In the narcissistic personality, there is a disturbance in the sense of self, a vulnerability to blows to self-esteem, a need for the admiration of others, and a lack of empathy with the feelings and needs of others. While being vulnerable to intense feelings of worthlessness and powerlessness (shame and humiliation), the narcissistic individual has a grandiose sense of self-importance and is preoccupied with fantasies of unlimited success and power. Such individuals tend to have an exaggerated feeling of being *entitled* to things from others, of *deserving* the admiration and love of others, and of being *special* or unique. They are capable of being very giving to others, though generally not on an emotional or empathic level, but also of being very demanding. They at times idealize others around them, as well as themselves, but at other times may completely devalue others. In therapy it is not unusual for the narcissistic individual to one moment idealize the therapist as extremely insightful and the best around and the next moment berate the therapist as stupid and incompetent.

Henry Murray, who developed the TAT, also developed a questionnaire to measure narcissism (Figure 4.5). More recently a *Narcissistic Personality Inventory* (NPI) (Raskin & Hall, 1979, 1981) has been developed and is beginning to be used in research (Emmons, 1987) (Figure 4.5). In one study, individuals scoring high on the NPI were found to use many more self-references in their speech than did those scoring low on the NPI (Raskin & Shaw, 1987), and in another study a relationship was found between high scores on the NPI and being described by others as exhibitionistic, assertive, controlling, and critical-evaluative (Raskin & Terry, 1987).

Many analysts are skeptical of such efforts to study psychoanalytic concepts. Indeed, some analysts feel that observations from "depth psychology" are part of a theoretical framework different than personality psychology in general (Kohut, 1971). Other analysts and psychologists, however, have attempted to study psychoanalytic phenomena and principles through the use of questionnaires as well as in the laboratory.

Murray's Narcissism Scale (1938, p. 181)

I often think about how I look and what impression I am making upon others.

My feelings are easily hurt by ridicule or by the slighting remarks of others.

I talk a good deal about myself, my experiences, my feelings, and my ideas.

Narcissism Personality Inventory (Raskin & Hall, 1979)

I really like to be the center of attention.

I think I am a special person.

I expect a great deal from other people.

I am envious of other people's good fortune.

I will never be satisfied until I get all that I deserve.

FIGURE 4.5 Illustrative Items from Questionnaire Measures of Narcissism

Often the motives that are part of the narcissistic personality lead them to tremendous accomplishment and the admiration of others. However, when carried to an extreme, some of the characteristics associated with the narcissistic personality can spell trouble. For example, according to Dr. Otto Kernberg, narcissistic business executives often are talented, hardworking, and intelligent, but their narcissistic needs may destroy their potential. Thus, their need for admiration may distract them from their central task and they may surround themselves with "yes men," who play up to their needs for praise, rather than with those who are most competent and perhaps also critical. In addition, their self-centeredness, insensitivity, and outbursts of rage may make others feel that it is impossible to work for them.

In 1987 the difficulties of presidential candidate Gary Hart and PTL leader Jim Bakker brought the concept of narcissism to public attention. The suggestion was made that such leaders often feel the arrogance of power and that rules are made for others, not themselves. In addition, their sense of grandiosity may lead to a self-deceptive sense of invulnerability, so they are surprised when others learn about, and are critical of, their activities. Finally, their preoccupation with their own gratification and lack of empathy for others may lead them to be shocked when they learn that their activities have harmed others.

SOURCES: *New York Times*, May 1, 1984, and May 19, 1987.

Narcissism and Power—Public figures Gary Hart and Jim Bakker

Recent reviews of the experimental testing of Freudian concepts come to a variety of conclusions, ranging from the conclusion that generally the theory has fared well (Fisher & Cleveland, 1977; Kline, 1981) to the conclusion that there is no evidence at all for psychoanalytic theory (Eysenck & Wilson, 1973).

One problem in the experimental testing of psychoanalytic concepts has been the difficulty in producing the phenomena of interest in the laboratory. Perhaps some advances are being made. For example, we considered earlier the work on subliminal psychodynamic activation as well as some evidence of interest on the part of experimental cognitive psychologists in phenomena such as repression. Along with these efforts are those of other psychologists who are attempting to translate Freud's clinical observations into concepts that are free of metaphor and more open to systematic observation (Klein, 1976; Schafer, 1976, 1978). Instead of concepts such as drive, libido, instinct, and force there would be greater emphasis on behavior, including all private psychological activity that can be made public (dreams, fantasies, fears, etc.).

In sum, recent developments have taken two somewhat divergent trends. On the one hand, there is a concern with new kinds of clinical phenomena and a disregard of the potential for systematic, empirical investigation. On the other hand, there is an effort to produce in the laboratory the phenomena emphasized by Freud and to translate Freudian concepts into a language that can better stand the test of scientific criticism. The clinical and laboratory investigators discussed here share a commitment to the basic principles of Freudian psychoanalytic theory.

A CRITICAL EVALUATION

In evaluating psychoanalysis as a theory of personality, we need to keep in mind three points. First, we need to be clear about whether we are considering an early or a later view in the development of the theory. Although the thrust of psychoanalysis, in terms of its emphasis on unconscious forces and on the importance of early events, has remained consistent throughout, major developments in the theory did take place between publication of The Interpretation of Dreams in 1900 and Freud's death in 1939. Second, in evaluating psychoanalysis we need to be clear about whether we are considering a part of the theory or the theory as a whole. Where consideration is given to a part of the theory, is that part basic to the entire structure or is the rest independent to it? For example, the latency period as a stage of development is not as critical to the theory as is the genetic approach. Finally, in considering psychoanalysis as a theory, we must keep it distinct from psychoanalysis as a method of therapy. The issue of therapeutic success with psychoanalysis has not been dealt with here because it is not critical to an understanding of the theory or an evaluation of it. If psychoanalytic theory did in fact lead to specific predictions concerning therapy, predictions that could be tested in a systematic way, then the results of therapy would be related to the validity of the theory. However, predictions of this nature are rarely made and, therefore, psychoanalysis as a theory of personality must be evaluated on grounds other than those of therapeutic effectiveness.

Major Contributions

How good a theory of personality is psychoanalysis? Clearly, Freud made major contributions to psychology and greatly influenced the developmental approach. Psychoanalysis has led to the use of new techniques, such as those of free association and dream interpretation, and has been a significant force in the development and use of special tests in the assessment of personality. There are two outstanding contributions. First, psychoanalysis made a major contribution to the discovery and investigation of phenomena. Whether ultimately these observations remain part of psychoanalytic theory or are integrated into another theory, the importance of the discovery of these phenomena remains. As we go beyond some of the superficialities of human behavior, we are impressed with the observations made by Freud. These become particularly apparent in clinical work with patients. It is striking for the therapist to observe the paranoid patient's fear that the therapist is out to make a homosexual attack upon him. It is striking to observe the chemist with obsessive-compulsive qualities describe how he first became interested in chemistry because of the "smells, stinks, and explosions" he could make. It is striking to observe the patient fantasy in the transference that the therapist is dependent on the patient's money for his groceries. And it is striking to observe how learning blocks in students may be related to fears that the teacher or other students will "castrate" them, to fears that being intelligent will mean that they are sissies, or to unconscious fear that intellectual curiosity will give rise to their sexual curiosity, just as the word "to know," in the Bible, means knowing someone sexually. Whether we choose to interpret these phenomena as characteristic of all human functioning, as Freud did, or merely as idiosyncratic to neurotics, we are forced to take account of these observations as data concerning human behavior. The importance of Freud's emphasis on certain essentials in human functioning was well expressed by the eminent anthropologist Clyde Kluckhohn.

> When I began serious field work among the Navaho and Pueblo Indians, my position on psychoanalysis was a mixed one. I had been analyzed and was thoroughly convinced that Freudian psychology was the only dynamic depth psychology of much importance. . . . On the other hand, I tended to believe that psychoanalysis was strongly culture-bound. . . . But the facts

uncovered in my own field work and that of my collaborators have forced me to the conclusion that Freud and other psychoanalysts have depicted with astonishing correctness many central themes in motivational life which are universal. The styles of expression of these themes and much of the manifest content are culturally determined, but the underlying psychologic drama transcends cultural difference.

This should not be too surprising—except to an anthropologist over-indoctrinated with the theory of culture relativism—for many of the inescapable givens of human life are also universal.

KLUCKHOHN, 1951 p. 120

The first major contribution by Freud, then, was the richness of his observations and the attention he paid to all details of human behavior. The second was the attention he gave to the complexity of human behavior at the same time that he developed an extremely encompassing theory. Psychoanalytic theory emphasizes that seemingly similar behavior can have very different antecedents and that very similar motives can lead to quite different behavior. Generosity can express genuine affection or an effort to deal with feelings of hostility, and the lawyer and the criminal whom he defends or prosecutes may, in some cases, be closer to one another psychologically than most of us care to realize. Out of this recognition of complexity comes a theory that accounts for almost all aspects of human behavior. No other theory of personality comes close to psychoanalytic theory in accounting for such a broad range of behavior. Few others give comparable attention to the functioning of the individual as a whole.

Many, perhaps most, of our theories of personality deal not with personality as a whole, but rather with some selected aspect or process. Freudian theory kept the whole personality more in view. . . . Freud produced this general theory not out of a combination of existing elements, but largely by new creative insights. His theory therefore has a scope, a unity, and a coherence which is unmatched in psychology.

INKELES, 1963, p. 333

Limitations of the Theory

In making these contributions, Freud stands as a genius and an investigator of tremendous courage. What then of the limitations of psychoanalysis as a theory? Comments have been made in relation to parts of the theory but what about the theory as a whole? Two major criticisms are worthy of note. The first involves the psychoanalytic view of the person, and the second involves the scientific status of psychoanalysis as a theory. In essence, these two criticisms suggest that serious questions can be raised about the energy model used by psychoanalysis to account for behavior and the ways in which its concepts are defined.

We already have observed that Freud was influenced by the discoveries of the conservation of matter and the views of Brücke concerning the person as an energy system. Basic to the psychoanalytic model is the view that all behavior can be understood in terms of exchanges and transformations of energy, with the goal of the organism being tension reduction. The pleasure principle, the principle fundamental to all behavioral functioning, states that the organism seeks pleasure in the form of tension reduction. Yet, there is considerable evidence that suggests that the organism does not always seek tension reduction, in fact, it often seeks stimulation. R. W. White (1959), in his review of the relevant literature, notes that there are many behaviors that do not seem to fit the models of physiological drive and tension reduction. These range from the "curiosity of the cat" to the play of children. These behaviors do not appear to be related to any physiological drive, they do not appear to satisfy the organism in the sense that food satisfies a hungry organism, and they do not appear to reduce tension. There is, then, evidence that a tension-reduction model alone is inadequate to account for all aspects of human functioning.

Another problem with Freud's energy model is that it tends to shade differences and make too many things equivalent. There is a simplistic quality to the theory that suggests that everything is a result of the sexual and aggressive instincts. For example, a man's love for a woman is viewed by Freud as an aim-inhibited instinct, as a repetition of the incestuous feelings for the mother. For Freud, the sucking of the infant at the breast of the mother is the model for every love relation. Such a view, however, fails to give adequate attention to differences between a child's love and that of an adult, between the love for a mate and the love for a friend, between the love for a person and the love for one's work. It does seem likely that all these loves have something in common, that in any one individual they share at least some earlier roots and at least some common principles of functioning. On the other hand, to consider all of them partial gratifications of the same instinct hardly seems to do justice to the considerable differences among them.

Thus, the principles concerning the transformations of energy appear to contain both assets and limitations. They provide an appreciation of the possible relationships and similarities among phenomena that might otherwise appear to be isolated and distinct. On the other hand, they tend to reduce too many phenomena to the same thing and thereby neglect the importance of major differences among them.

In many ways it is this noting of similarities and shadings of differences that gives appeal to the clinician and creates difficulties for the experimenter. In many ways it is the looseness and ambiguity of its concepts that allows psychoanalytic theory to account for so much human behavior. But these factors raise questions concerning the status of psychoanalysis as a scientific theory. The terms of psychoanalysis are ambiguous. There are many metaphors and analogies that can, but need not, be taken literally. Examples would be latency, death instinct, Oedipus complex, and castration anxiety. Does castration anxiety refer to the fear of loss of the penis, or does it refer to the child's fear of injury to his body at a time that his body-image is of increased importance to his self-esteem? The language of the theory is so vague that investigators often are hard pressed to agree on precise meanings of the terms. How are we to define libido? Furthermore, the same word, such as repression, was used for different concepts at different times, often without a clear definition of the nature of the change of the concept.

Even where the constructs are well defined, often they are *too removed from observable and measurable behavior* to be of much empirical use. Concepts such as id, ego, and superego have considerable descriptive power, but it is often hard to translate them into relevant behavioral observations. Robert Sears, who for some time worked on problems in child development, in general, and the process of identification, in particular, commented on this problem as follows. "We became acutely aware of the difference between the purely descriptive statement of a psychodynamic process and a testable theory of behavioral development. Psychoanalytic theory contained suggestions for the latter, but it did not specify the conditions under which greater or lesser degrees of any particular behavioral product of identification would occur" (Sears, Rau, & Alpert, 1965, p. 241). Here Sears is emphasizing the difference between a descriptive statement involving the use of a concept and an explicit statement of how the concept translates itself into quantitative relationships among phenomena.

Within psychoanalytic theory, the relationships among phenomena are not always made explicit, and quantitative estimates of relationships are never made. Whereas some suggest that observations drawn from patients in analysis are adequate grounds for testing psychoanalytic concepts (Edelson, 1984), others suggest that clinical data remain suspect and are an inadequate basis for testing the theory (Grunbaum, 1984). Eysenck, a frequent and passionate critic of psychoanalysis, whose views we will consider later in the book, suggests that "we can no more test Freudian hypotheses on the couch than we can adjudicate between the rival hypotheses of Newton and Einstein by going to sleep under the apple tree" (1963, p. 220).

What we have, then, is a theory that is at times confusing and often difficult to test. This problem is complicated further by the way in which psychoanalysts can account for almost any outcome, even opposite outcomes. If one behavior appears, it is an expression of the instinct; if the opposite appears, it is an expression of a defense; if another form of behavior appears, it is a compromise between the instinct and the defense. For example, take Freud's comment on the interpretation of a slip of the tongue. "When a person who commits a slip gives an explanation which fits your views then you declare him to be the final authority on the subject. He says so himself! But if what he says does not suit your book, then you suddenly assert that what he says does not count, one need not believe it. Certainly that is so" (Freud, 1920, p. 46). It does not seem unlikely that such developments take place; that is, that depending on minor shifts in forces, major differences in overt behavior can appear. The problem with the theory is not that it leaves room for such complexity, but that it fails to state which behavior will occur, given a specific set of circumstances. In not providing such statements, psychoanalytic theory does not leave itself open to disproof or the negative test.

Other criticisms are relevant to psychoanalytic theory and the way in which it is defended. Psychoanalysts use observations influenced by the theory to support the theory, without giving adequate consideration to the factors relevant to the social psychology of the experimenter. Committed observers may bias the response of their subjects and bias their own perceptions of the data. It is also true that analysts often respond to criticism of the theory by suggesting that the critics are being defensive in not recognizing phenomena such as infantile sexuality, that they do not understand the theory. To the extent that some psychoanalysts advance such arguments in a routine way, they perpetuate some of the early developments of psychoanalysis as a religious movement rather than as a scientific theory. Kohut, whose influential work on narcissism has been noted, has described the dilemma he faced when he no longer believed in certain traditional aspects of psychoanalysis. Not only did he face difficulties in giving up views formerly dear to him, but he also had to face the condemnation of traditional analysts. Interestingly enough, he attributed dogmatic adherence to Freud's views as part of an idealization of Freud and a devaluation of alternative points of view (Kohut, 1984).

In noting these criticisms of the status of psychoanalysis as a scientific theory, it is important to recognize that Freud was aware of most of these objections. He was not a naive scientist. His position, rather, was that the beginning of scientific activity consists of the description of phenomena, and that at the early stages some imprecision is inevitable. Also, Freud was acutely aware of the difficulties in making use of psychoanalytic insights for predictive purposes. He noted that the analyst was on safe ground in tracing the development of behavior from its final stage backward, but that if he proceeded in the reverse way, an inevitable sequence of events no longer seemed to be apparent. His conclusion was that psychoanalysis does a better job at analysis than at synthesis, at explaining than at predicting. Freud did not believe that a science consists of nothing but conclusively proved propositions but, rather, insisted that the scientist be content with approximations to certainty.

In carrying on his work with that scientific credo, Freud encountered a number of limitations. For the most part, his direct analytic observations were limited to upper- and middle-class patients who presented symptoms relevant to the issues dominant in the culture at the time. It seems likely, therefore, that he exaggerated the importance of Victorian issues such as sex, morality, and guilt relative to other human concerns. Because of his training and the scientific spirit of his time, Freud appears to have relied, to an excessive degree, on a physiological energy model to account for psychological phenomena. Finally, it is unfortunate that, at the time of the development of his theory, Freud did not have the benefit of a discipline in psychology that supported his efforts to develop a scientific theory. Unfortunately, Freud was excessively dependent on a medical, therapeutic environment when he was committed to developing a system with broader relevance.

It is interesting to note that Freud's aim was to be both scientific and humanistic, "to bring concepts and order to human concerns and human concerns into the scientific community" (Havens, 1973, p. 2). We have already noted the arguments raised by scientific critics. Psychoanalysis also has been criticized by humanists as being overly intellectual, excessively abstract, and simplistic. Proponents of the existential point of view in psychology and psychiatry have been particularly critical of psychoanalysis along these lines. As has often been the case in the past, some of the harshest and most cogent criticism comes from individuals who themselves are analysts. Thus R. D. Laing (1967), a British analyst, has been critical of the extent to which psychoanalytic concepts may hide and distort human experience and critical of the tendency to label the patient "sick" as opposed to looking at "sickness" in the patient's family or in the broader society. Thomas Szasz, also an analyst, has argued against the "myth of mental illness" created by the model of abnormal behavior associated with psychoanalysis. Szasz (1961) notes that Freud served a tremendous humanitarian function in demonstrating that mentally "sick" people do not always "will" their pathological behavior and therefore should not be subject to moral outrage. At the same time, Szasz argues that the view of such people as "sick" has led to negative value judgments about them. Furthermore, it has led to serious curtailment of their rights and civil liberties. The criticism by Szasz is not so much against psychoanalytic theory itself as against the medical model of psychopathology that has come to be associated with it and the current social context of that model.

Another aspect of psychoanalytic theory related to the current social context is the criticism it has received from feminists. Although Freud often is misinterpreted, he did see certain traits such as receptivity, dependence on others, sensitivity, vanity, and submissiveness as part of the feminine orientation. These characteristics were seen as part of women because of biological influences and because of psychological reactions to their awareness of the lack of a penis—Freud's concept of penis envy. The concept of penis envy symbolizes for many women a "biology is destiny" view on the part of Freud and an inadequate appreciation of cultural factors. Among others, the analyst Karen Horney questioned many of Freud's views concerning women and feminine sexuality, and, as noted earlier, proposed instead a view of feminine development that emphasized cultural influences. It is an interesting aspect of psychoanalysis that while it has come under attack by feminists, perhaps more than any other theory, it has almost always had major female figures within its ranks (e.g., Anna Freud, Helene Deutsch, Greta Bibring, Margaret Mahler, Clara Thompson, and Frieda Fromm-Reichman).

Summary Evaluation

How, then, are we to summarize our evaluation of Freud and psychoanalytic theory (Figure 4.6)? As an observer of human behavior, and as a person with a creative imagination, Freud was indeed a genius with few, if any, equals. The theory he developed certainly has the virtue of being comprehensive. There is no other personality theory that approximates psychoanalysis in the range of behavior considered and interpretations offered. Given such scope, the theory is economical. The structural and process concepts used by the theory are relatively few in number. Futhermore, the theory has suggested many areas for investigation and has led to a considerable amount of research. Although relevant to the theory, however, much of this research does not offer an explicit test of a theory-derived hypothesis, and little of it has been used to extend and develop the theory. The major problem with psychoanalytic theory is the way in which the concepts are formulated; that is, ambiguity in the concepts and in the suggested relationships among concepts has made it very difficult to test the theory. The question for psychoanalytic theory is

STRENGTHS	LIMITATIONS
1. Provides for the discovery and investigation of many interesting phenomena.	1. Fails to define all its concepts clearly and distinctly.
2. Develops techniques for research and therapy (free association, dream interpretation, transference analysis).	2. Makes empirical testing difficult, at times impossible.
3. Recognizes the complexity of human behavior.	3. Endorses the questionable view of the person as an energy system.
4. Encompasses a broad range of phenomena.	4. Tolerates resistance by parts of the profession to empirical research and change in the theory.

FIGURE 4.6 Summary of Strengths and Limitations of Psychoanalytic Theory

A PSYCHODYNAMIC THEORY

whether it can be developed to provide for specific tests, or whether it will be replaced in the future by another theory that is equally comprehensive and economical but more open to systematic empirical investigation.

<table>
<tr><td rowspan="3">**Major Concepts and Summary**</td><td>[Review concepts from Chapter 3]</td><td>regression</td></tr>
</table>

Major Concepts and Summary	[Review concepts from Chapter 3]	regression
	projective techniques	symptom
	Rorschach Inkblot Test	free association
	Thematic Apperception Test (TAT)	dream interpretation
	fixation	transference

In this chapter and the previous one we have considered psychoanalytic theory as illustrative of a psychodynamic, clinical approach to personality. The psychodynamic emphasis is clear in the interpretation of behavior as a result of the interplay among forces, in the emphasis on anxiety and defense mechanisms, and in the interpretation of symptoms as compromises between instinct and defense. The clinical qualities of psychoanalysis are apparent in the emphasis on the individual, the attention given to individual differences, and the attempt to assess and understand the total individual. The psychoanalytic approach is highly interpretive, making use of many constructs that are not open to direct observation to account for a wide range of individual and group behavior.

Projective techniques, such as the Rorschach Inkblot Test and Thematic Apperception Test (TAT), emphasize disguise and maximum freedom of response and illustrate the relationship between psychoanalytic theory and personality assessment. These assessment devices are widely used in clinical work with patients as well as in systematic research. The latter was illustrated in the study of comedians, clowns, and actors.

In terms of emphasis on the stability of personality, it is not surprising that psychoanalytic theory places great importance on structural concepts. The main structural concepts are those of id, ego, and superego, which roughly represent drives (instincts), an orientation toward reality, and morals (values), respectively. Psychic life is also described in terms of the extent to which thoughts and memories are available to awareness —ranging from unconscious (unavailable to awareness), preconscious (available to awareness), and conscious (part of awareness).

Psychoanalytic theory also places great emphasis on the processes (dynamics) of psychological functioning. Basically, the organism seeks expression or discharge of the life (libido) and death instincts or sexual and aggressive instincts. Because of its association with a past trauma, expression of an instinct may signal danger to the ego and lead to the experience of anxiety. The individual then faces a conflict situation in which he seeks to gratify the instinct but also fears doing so. Often the result is the use of mechanisms of defense (i.e., projection, denial, isolation, undoing, reaction-formation, rationalization, repression) that attempt to give some expression to the instinct in a way that does not produce anxiety. The use of mechanisms of defense always involves some distortion of reality. Only in sublimation is the individual able to express an impulse free of anxiety and without distortion of reality. In such a case id, ego, and superego are acting in unison and with freedom from conflict.

The psychoanalytic theory of development places great emphasis on stages of development (i.e., oral, anal, phallic, latency, genital) that are rooted in the biological processes of the organism. Experiences during the first five years of life are viewed as critical for the determination of later, adult personality characteristics. This is particularly true where frustration has led to fixation at a pregenital stage of development or where, because of later frustration, the individual regresses back to an earlier mode of functioning. Oral, anal, and phallic character types illustrate how adult personality characteristics may be understood in terms of partial fixations at early stages of development.

The above concepts lay the groundwork for an understanding of psychopathology. Whereas all pathology is believed to center in the Oedipus complex, representing fixations at the phallic stage of development, frustration and trauma can lead to regression to an earlier stage of development. Thus, the exact form taken in a neurosis or a psychosis is dependent on the stage to which the individual regresses. In psychopathology there is a struggle between striving of the id instincts for discharge and the efforts of the ego to prevent discharge and defend against anxiety. Behavior change in the direction of growth occurs when individuals are exposed to conditions that allow them to gratify their instincts in new, more mature ways that lead neither to guilt nor to external threat. In psychoanalysis, the free-association method is used to facilitate the process of becoming aware of unconscious wishes and conflicts. The transference situation is used as an opportunity for insight and growth.

Finally, an evaluation of psychoanalytic theory must recognize the richness of observations, the range of behavior covered in a reasonably economical way, and the fertile areas for research suggested by the theory. At the same time the theory suffers from a number of scientific limitations (e.g., terms are ambiguous, constructs are often far removed from observable and measurable behavior, relationships among phenomena are not always made explicit). It also has come under attack from humanists for being too far removed from the actual experiences of individuals and from that which is uniquely human, and from feminists as well as others for being too involved with biological influences to a prejudicial disregard of cultural ones.

Chapter Five

A Phenomenological Theory: Carl Rogers' Person-Centered Theory of Personality

*C*HAPTER FOCUS: In this chapter we consider Rogerian theory as illustrative of a phenomenological, clinical approach to personality. The clinical emphasis is apparent in the attention given to individual differences and the efforts to understand and assess the total individual. The phenomenological approach is apparent in the emphasis on the phenomenal world of the individual—how the person perceives and experiences the self and the world. Assessment and research follow in their emphasis on verbal self-report and concepts such as self and experience. The theory is a part of the humanistic, human potential movement that emphasizes self-actualization and the fulfillment of an individual's growth potential.

> *To me such a highly personal "view from within" is not only the best source of learning, it also points the way, perhaps, toward a new and more human science. . . .*
>
> ROGERS, 1972, p. 3

> *I see the actualizing tendency in the human organism as being basic to motivation. . . . So I reaffirm, even more strongly than when I first advanced the notion, my belief that there is one central source of energy in the human organism; that it is a trustworthy function of the whole organism rather than of some portion of it; and that it is perhaps best conceptualized as a tendency toward fulfillment, toward actualization, not only toward maintenance but also toward the enhancement of the organism.*
>
> ROGERS, 1977, pp. 237, 242–243

In the previous chapter we discussed the psychoanalytic theory of Freud. Psychoanalytic theory was considered in light of its emphasis on individual differences, the total individual, the importance of the unconscious, and human behavior as a function of the interplay among various forces —a dynamic model.

In this second chapter on a specific theoretical position, the focus is on the phenomenological theory of Carl Rogers. Originally, the theory was not one of personality. Rather it was a theory of psychotherapy and the process of behavior change. However, a theory of personality has been an outgrowth of the theory of therapy. The position of Rogers is presented because it typifies an approach to personality that stresses why people can and should be understood in terms of how they view themselves and the world around them—the **phenomenological approach.** Rogers' theory also is presented because it gives attention to the concept of the *self* and experiences related to the self, and because it illustrates a conscious, focused effort to combine clinical intuition with objective research. In his emphasis on human experience and the importance of being a fully functioning human being, Carl Rogers had a tremendous impact on the training of counselors, of teachers, and of managers at the executive level in business. His view of the person is frankly stated, in opposition to the one presented by Freud, and is clearly related to his views of therapy and research. Finally, the total spirit of the theory and the theorist have resulted in the association of Rogers with the human potential movement.

Although the American emphasis on objective and quantitative research influenced Rogers, the theory is derived from intensive work with individuals and, in turn, is applied to individuals. Throughout his career, Rogers spent time in the treatment of individuals and generally began his research efforts by examining clinical material. Like psychoanalytic theory, Rogers' theory involves assumptions relevant to all people, but the theory has particular relevance to the study of individual differences and the total functioning of individuals. For example, Rogers is interested in therapy as a unique experience for each individual. However, the therapy involves a predictable *process* for all individuals. Unlike the psychoanalytic emphasis on the unconscious, the theory of Rogers places emphasis on that which is conscious. For Rogers, the phenomenological world of individuals, the world as it is experienced by them, primarily in conscious terms, contains the data necessary to understand and to predict behavior. Although the private world of the individual can be known only to the individual himself, the psychologist can, by providing a supportive atmosphere, approximate an understanding of the private world of the individual.

In summary, this chapter and the next will analyze and evaluate a theory that is significant in its emphasis on individual differences, the entire personality, and behavior as a function of the private, unique way in which individuals experience their worlds. In particular, the concern is with the importance of the concept of the *self* in personality theory, with the ways in which individuals experience themselves and others, and with the conditions under which individuals are capable of becoming fully functioning people.

CARL R. ROGERS (1902–1987):
A VIEW OF THE THEORIST

"I speak as a person, from a context of personal experience and personal learning." Thus does Rogers introduce his chapter "This Is Me" in his 1961 book *On Becoming A Person*. The chapter is a personal, very moving account by Rogers of the development of his professional thinking and personal philosophy. Rogers states what he does and how he feels about it.

> This book is about the suffering and the hope, the anxiety and the satisfaction, with which each therapist's counseling room is filled. It is about the uniqueness of the relationship each therapist forms with each client, and equally about the common elements which we discover in all these relationships. This book is about the highly personal experiences of each one of us. It is about a client in my office who sits there by the corner of the desk, struggling to be himself, yet deathly afraid of being himself—striving to see his experience as it is, wanting to be that experience, and yet deeply fearful of the prospect. This book is about me, as I sit there with that client, facing him, participating in that struggle as deeply and sensitively as I am able. It is about me as I try to perceive his experience, and the meaning and the feeling and the taste and the flavor that it has for him. It is about me as I bemoan my very human fallibility in understanding that client, and the occasional failures to see life as it appears to him, failures which fall like heavy objects across the intricate, delicate web of growth which is taking place. It is about me as I rejoice at the privilege of being a midwife to a new personality—as I stand by with awe at the emergence of a self, a person, as I see a birth process in which I have had an important and facilitating part. It is about both the client and me as we regard with wonder the potent and orderly forces which are evident in this whole experience, forces which seem deeply rooted in the universe as a whole. The book is, I believe, about life, as life vividly reveals itself in the therapeutic process—with its blind power and its tremendous capacity for destruction, but with its overbalancing thrust toward growth, if the opportunity for growth is provided.

> ROGERS, 1961A, pp. 4–5

Carl R. Rogers was born on January 8, 1902, in Oak Park, Illinois. He was reared in a strict and uncompromising religious and ethical atmosphere. His parents had the welfare of the children constantly in mind and inculcated in them a worship of hard work. From his description of his

Carl R. Rogers

early life, we see two main trends that are reflected in his later work. The first is the concern with moral and ethical matters already described. The second is the respect for the methods of science, particularly where things need to be accomplished. The latter appears to have developed out of exposure to his father's efforts to operate their farm on a scientific basis and Rogers' own reading of books on scientific agriculture.

Rogers started his college education at the University of Wisconsin in the field of agriculture, but after two years he changed his professional goals and decided to enter the ministry. During a trip to the Orient, in 1922, he had a chance to observe commitments to other religious doctrines and to observe the bitter mutual hates of French and German people, who otherwise seemed to be likable individuals. Experiences like these influenced his decision to go to a liberal theological seminary, the Union Theological Seminary in New York. Although he was concerned about questions regarding the meaning of life for individuals, Rogers had doubts about specific religious doctrines. Therefore, he chose to leave the seminary, to work in the field of child guidance, and to think of himself as a clinical psychologist.

Rogers obtained his graduate training at Teachers College, Columbia University, receiving his Ph.D. in 1931. He described his experience as leading to a "soaking up" of both the dynamic views of Freud and the "rigorous, scientific, coldly objective, statistical" views then prevalent at Teachers College. Again, there were the pulls in different directions, the development of two somewhat divergent trends. In his later life Rogers attempted to bring these divergent trends into harmony with one another. Indeed, these years represent an effort to integrate the religious with the scientific, the intuitive with the objective, and the clinical with the statistical. Throughout his career, Rogers tried continually to apply the objective methods of science to what is most basically human.

> Therapy is the experience in which I can let myself go subjectively. Research is the experience in which I can stand off and try to view this rich subjective experience with objectivity, applying all the elegant methods of science to determine whether I have been deceiving myself. The conviction grows in me that we shall discover laws of personality and behavior which are as significant for human progress or human relationship as the law of gravity or the laws of thermodynamics.
>
> ROGERS, 1961A, p. 14

In 1968 Rogers and his more humanistically oriented colleagues formed the Center for the Studies of the Person. The development of the Center expressed a number of shifts in emphasis in the work of Rogers—from work within a formal academic structure to work with a collection of individuals who share a perspective, from work with "disturbed" individuals to work with "normal" individuals, from individual therapy to intensive group workshops, and from conventional empirical research to the phenomenological study of people: "We are deeply interested in persons but are rather 'turned-off' by the older methods of studying them as 'objects' for research" (Rogers, 1972b, p. 67). From this perspective Rogers felt that most of psychology is sterile and generally felt alienated from the field. Yet, the field continues to value his contributions—he was president of the American Psychological Association in 1946–1947, was one of the first three psychologists to receive the Distinguished Scientific Contribution Award (1956) from the profession, and in 1972 was the recipient of the Distinguished Professional Contribution Award.

With Rogers, the theory, the man, and the life are interwoven. In his chapter on "This Is Me," Rogers lists fourteen principles that he learned from thousands of hours of therapy and research. Because the man, his life, and his theory are so interwoven, the principles themselves contain much of the theory. Here are some illustrations:

1. In my relationships with persons I have found that it does not help, in the long run, to act as though I were something that I am not.
2. I find I am more effective when I can listen acceptantly to myself, and can be myself.
3. I have found it of enormous value when I can permit myself to understand another person.
4. I have found it highly rewarding when I can accept another person.

5. Experience is, for me, the highest authority . . . it is to experience that I must return again and again, to discover a closer approximation to truth as it is in the process of becoming in me.

6. The facts are friendly . . . painful reorganizations are what is known as learning.

7. What is most personal and unique in each one of us is probably the very element which would, if it were shared or expressed, speak most deeply to others.

8. It has been my experience that persons have a basically positive direction . . . I have come to feel that the more fully the individual is understood and accepted, the more he tends to drop the false fronts with which he has been meeting life, and the more he tends to move in a direction which is forward.

9. Life, at its best, is a flowing, changing process in which nothing is fixed.

ROGERS, 1961A, pp. 16–27

ROGERS' VIEW OF THE PERSON

For Rogers, the core of our nature is essentially positive. The direction of our movement basically is toward self-actualization, maturity, and socialization. It is Rogers' contention that religion, particularly the Christian religion, has taught us to believe that we are basically sinful. Furthermore, Rogers contends that Freud and his followers have presented us with a picture of the person with an id and an unconscious that would, if permitted expression, manifest itself in incest, murder, and other crimes. According to this view, we are at heart irrational, unsocialized, and destructive of self and others. For Rogers, we may at times function in this way, but at such times we are neurotic and not functioning as fully developed human beings. When we are functioning freely, we are free to experience and to fulfill our basic nature as positive and social animals, ones that can be trusted and basically are constructive.

Aware that others may seek to draw parallels between the behaviors of other animals and the behavior of humans, Rogers draws his own parallels. For example, he observes that, although lions are often seen as "ravening beasts," actually they have many desirable qualities—they kill only when hungry and not for the sake of being destructive, they grow from helplessness and dependence to independence, and they move from being self-centered in infancy to being cooperative and protective in adulthood.

Aware that others may call him a naive optimist, Rogers is quick to point out that his conclusions are based on more than twenty-five years of experience in psychotherapy:

> I do not have a Pollyanna view of human nature. I am quite aware that out of defensiveness and inner fear individuals can and do behave in ways which are incredibly cruel, horribly destructive, immature, regressive, antisocial, hurtful. Yet one of the most refreshing and invigorating parts of my experience is to work with such individuals and to discover the strongly positive directional tendencies which exist in them, as in all of us, at the deepest levels.
>
> ROGERS, 1961A, p. 27

Here is a profound respect for people, a respect that is reflected in Rogers' theory of personality and his person-centered approach to psychotherapy.

ROGERS' VIEW OF SCIENCE, THEORY, AND RESEARCH

Although Rogers' theory and specific research tools changed, he remained a phenomenologist. According to the phenomenological position of Rogers (1951), the individual perceives the world in a unique way. These perceptions make up the individual's **phenomenal field**. Individuals react to the environment as they perceive it. This environment may or may not correspond with an experimenter's definition of the environment. The phenomenal field of the individual includes both conscious and unconscious perceptions, those of which the individual is aware and those of which he is not aware. But the most important determinants of behavior, particularly in healthy people, are the ones that are conscious or capable of becoming conscious. Although the phenomenal field is essentially a world that is private to individuals, we can (particularly with clinical material) attempt to perceive the world as it appears to individuals, to see behavior through their eyes and with the psychological meaning it has for them.

Rogers was committed to phenomenology as a basis for the science of the person and as the method to be used in the development of a theory of subjective phenomena. According to Rogers, research in psychology must involve a persistent, disciplined effort to understand the phenomena of subjective experience. In following the path of science, these efforts need not start in the laboratory or at the calculating machine, and they should not take the advanced stages of theoretical physics as the most helpful model of science.

As has been observed, Rogers believes that clinical material, obtained during psychotherapy, offers a valuable source of phenomenological data. In attempting to understand human behavior, Rogers always starts with clinical observations. He attempts to listen to recorded therapeutic interviews, as naively as possible, with as few preconceptions as possible, and to develop some hypotheses concerning the events he has observed. He attempts to steep himself in the events of the human drama, to soak up clues concerning the mystery of behavior, and then to use these observations to formulate hypotheses that can be tested in a rigorous way. Rogers believes that it is legitimate to start free of concerns for objectivity and rigor, and then to move forward to the process of empirical investigation. As previously stated, Rogers views therapy as a subjective, "letting go" experience and research as an objective effort with its own kind of elegance. He is as committed to one as a source for hypotheses as he is to the other as a tool for their confirmation.

Throughout his career, then, Rogers attempted to bridge the gap between the subjective and the objective, just as in his youth he felt a need to bridge the gap between religion and science. Within this context, Rogers was concerned with the development of psychology as a science and with the preservation of people as individuals who are not simply the pawns of science.

THE PERSONALITY THEORY OF CARL ROGERS

As we stated previously, Rogers' main focus was on the process of psychotherapy. His theory of personality is an outgrowth of his theory of therapy. Also, both the theory and the focus of the related research have changed over time. Throughout, however, there is a concern with how people perceive their worlds, in particular the self, and a concern with the process of change. In contrast to the psychoanalytic emphasis on drives, instincts, the unconscious, tension reduction, and early character development, the phenomenological approach emphasizes perceptions, feelings, subjective self-report, self-actualization, and the process of change.

Structure
The self

The key structural concept in the Rogerian theory of personality is that of the **self**. According to Rogers, the individual perceives external objects and experiences and attaches meanings to them. The total system of perceptions and meanings make up the individual's phenomenal field. Those parts of the phenomenal field seen by the individual as "self," "me," or "I" make up the self. The self-concept represents an organized and consistent pattern of perceptions. Although the self changes, it always retains this patterned, integrated, organized quality to it.

IS THE SENSE OF SELF UNIQUELY HUMAN?

Most dog owners have at some time experimented with placing a mirror in front of their dog. Is there self-recognition? Animal research suggests that species lower than primates do not recognize themselves in mirrors. Chimpanzees are able to do so, provided they have some exposure to mirrors. Given such experience, chimps will use the mirror to examine and groom themselves (self-directed behavior) rather than ignore the image or react to it as if it is another member of the species (e.g., fish showing aggressive displays toward a mirror image).

Research on the development of self-directed mirror behavior in infants suggests that the development of self recognition is a continuous process, starting as early as four months of age. At this point infants show some response to relationships between self-movements and changes in mirror images. And what of recognition of specific features of the self? If an infant looks at itself in the mirror, has rouge placed on its nose, and then looks in the mirror again, will the infant respond to the rouge mark in a way expressive of self recognition? Such specific feature recognition, in terms of self-directed mirror behavior, appears to begin at about the age of one year.

The recognition of self, whether expressed through self-directed mirror behavior or otherwise, can be related to the development of consciousness and mind. Clearly it is a matter of considerable psychological significance. Not only does it mean that we can be aware of ourselves and have feelings about ourselves, but also that we can have knowledge of and empathy for the feelings of others. It would indeed be ironic if the very processes that allow us to feel worst about ourselves also provided us with the opportunity to feel most empathetic with others.

Mirror, mirror on the wall, is that me after all? This appears to be a question that only members of a few species can address. In humans some maturation is required but self recognition begins to develop fairly early and remains a significant part of life thereafter.

LEWIS & BROOKS-GUNN, 1979.

Self-Recognition — Whereas almost all other species are indifferent to their images in a mirror, or react to them as another animal, humans begin to be fascinated with their self-reflection at an early age.

Two additional points are noteworthy in relation to Rogers' concept of the self. First, the self is not a little person inside of us. The self does not "do" anything. The individual does not have a self that controls behavior. Rather the self represents an organized set of perceptions. Second, the pattern of experiences and perceptions known as the self is, in general, available to awareness, that is, it can be made conscious. Although individuals do have experiences of which they are unaware, the self-concept is primarily conscious. Rogers believes that such a definition of the self is accurate and a necessary one for research. A definition of the self that included unconscious material, according to Rogers, could not be studied objectively.

A related structural concept is that of **ideal self**. The ideal self is the self-concept that individual would most like to possess. It includes the perceptions and meanings that potentially are relevant to the self and that are valued highly by the individual.

Measures of the self-concept

Rogers maintained that he did not begin his work with the concept of the self. In fact, in his first work he thought that it was a vague, scientifically meaningless term. However, as he listened to clients expressing their problems and attitudes, he found that they tended to talk in terms of the self. The concept of self finally appeared in his 1947 description of personality.

In that paper, he reported the statements made by a client, Miss Vib, who came for nine interviews. At the outset of counseling, her conscious perception of herself was reflected in statements of this kind: "I haven't been acting like myself; it doesn't seem like me; I'm a different person from what I used to be in the past." "I don't have any emotional response to situations; I'm worried about myself." "I don't understand myself; I haven't known what was happening to me." By the ninth interview, 38 days later, the perception of self had been deeply altered: "I'm taking more interest in myself." "I do have some individuality, some interests." "I can look at myself a little better." "I realize I'm just one person, with so much ability, but I'm not worried about it; I can accept the fact that I'm not always right." Statements like these convinced Rogers, and have continued to convince him, that the self is an important element in human experience and that the goal of individuals is to become their real selves. An illustration of the way in which the self-concept may be discussed in a counseling session is given in Figure 5.1. This interview segment is of particular interest because it illustrates how the person, often a college student, attempts to choose a career that, among other things, fits with some image they have of themselves and the kind of person they would like to be.

Although impressed with the self-statements of clients, and by Raimy's (1948) elaborate consideration of the utility and importance of the concept, Rogers experienced the need for an objective definition of

S: That's why I'm in engineering college. I have an opportunity to — well, just to experiment with myself and see actually what talents I do have in that direction. They're not so bad, but I lack some — some of the very fundamental things that a good engineer should have: that is, being calm, sticking right to it, and forgetting about things that have come up. A good engineer is not emotional, that's about one of the worst things he could — No person who is emotional is a good engineer.

C: So that in some respects you've gone into engineering because you felt it would be awfully good discipline for you, is that right? Make you stop being emotional?

S: That's right.

C: It was that, perhaps, rather than being interested in engineering.

S: Well, it was mingled with a certain genuine interest. There was some that's true. But it was largely due to that, exactly what I said, to a considerable extent.

C: You don't suppose that part of your trouble is that now you're wondering whether you want to be your real self. Could that be part of it?

S: Uh, what's that?

C: Well, I just wondered. You're trying so hard to be some other fellow aren't you?

S: Yeah, because I'm not satisfied with myself.

C: You feel that the self that you are isn't worth being.

S: Yeah, that's right, and unless you can change my mind about that, then I'll continue thinking along the same line.

C: (*Laughing*) Why, that almost sounds as though you were wishing that somebody would change your mind about it.

S: (*Very soberly*) Yeah. Because I don't know how I can solve it the other way.

C: In other words, you're finding it a pretty rough proposition to try to be a calm, unemotional engineer when really you're something quite different.

S: Right. Yeah, that is a very tough position. I find it impossible, and I hate the idea that it's impossible.

C: And you have it partly because you feel there's nothing worthwhile about this real self of yours.

S: Yes.

C: What are some of the things your real self would like to do?

S: Oh, let's see. Well — uh, I told you I was interested in mathematics. That's one thing. Also, I was interested in anthropology. At the same time, I was interested in music and in — well, now, I used to like novels, but I don't care for them anymore, but — I would like — I think I have a gift for writing, too, and I'm ashamed of those gifts.

FIGURE 5.1 Interview Emphasizing Discussion of the Self-Concept in Relation to Occupational Choice (S = Student; C = Counselor). (Rogers, 1942)

the concept, a way to measure it, and a research tool. Rogers began his research by recording therapy interview sessions and then categorizing all words that referred to the self. After the early research with recorded interviews, he made use of the **Q-sort** developed by Stephenson (1953). The Q-sort technique has been used frequently to measure the self-concept. In this approach the experimenter gives the subject a pile of cards, each containing a statement concerning some personality characteristic. One card might say "Makes friends easily," another might say "Has trouble expressing anger," and so on for each of the cards. Subjects are asked to read these statements (generally about a hundred) and then sort the cards according to which statements they feel are most descriptive of them and which are least descriptive. The subjects are asked to arrange the cards into a certain distribution of which one end represents "Most characteristic of me" and the other "Least characteristic of me." Subjects are told how many piles of cards are to be used and how many cards are to go into each pile. For example, with 100 cards the subject might be asked to sort the cards into eleven piles as follows: 2–4–8–11–16–18–16–11–8–4–2. The distribution is a normal one and expresses the subjects' comparative estimates of how descriptive each characteristic is.

Thus, the Q-sort involves a task in which the subject sorts a number of statements, in this case about the self, into categories ranging from most characteristic to least characteristic. In addition, the identical terms can be sorted into the same number of categories in terms of the ideal self—"most like my ideal self" to "least like my ideal self." This provides for a quantitative measure of the difference or discrepancy between self and ideal self. As we shall see (Chapter 6), such concepts and measures are important in relation to psychopathology and therapeutic change. The Q-sort leads to data that represent a systematic expression of subjects' perceptions of parts of their phenomenal fields. However, it does not represent a completely phenomenological report, since subjects must use statements provided by the experimenter, instead of their own, and must sort the statements into prescribed piles, representing a normal distribution, rather than according to a distribution that makes the most sense to them.

Other efforts to obtain subjective reports about the self have made use of the *adjective checklist,* in which subjects check adjectives that they feel are applicable to them, and the *semantic differential* (Osgood, Suci, & Tannenbaum, 1957). Developed as a measure of attitudes and the meanings of concepts, rather than as a specific test of personality, the semantic differential has potential as a useful technique for personality assessment. In filling out the semantic differential, the individual rates a concept on a number of seven-point scales defined by polar adjectives such as good–bad, strong–weak, active–passive. Thus, a subject would rate a concept such as "My Self" or "My Ideal Self" on each of the polar adjective scales. A rating on any one scale would indicate whether the subject felt one of the adjectives was very descriptive of the concept or somewhat descriptive, or whether neither adjective was applicable to the concept. The ratings are made in terms of the meaning of the concept for the individual.

Like the Q-sort, the semantic differential is a structured technique in that the subject must rate certain concepts and use the polar adjective scales provided by the experimenter. This structure provides for the gathering of data suitable for statistical analysis but, also like the Q-sort, the semantic differential does not preclude flexibility as to the concepts and scales to be used. There is no single standardized semantic differential. A variety of scales can be used in relation to concepts such as father, mother, and doctor to determine the meanings of phenomena for the individual.

One example of the way in which the semantic differential can be used to assess personality is its application to a case of multiple personality. In the 1950s two psychiatrists, Corbett Thigpen and Harvey Cleckley, made famous the case of "The Three Faces of Eve." This was the case of a woman who possessed three personalities, each of which predominated for a period of time, with frequent shifts back and forth. The three personalities were called Eve White, Eve Black, and Jane. As part of a research endeavor, the psychiatrists were able to have each of the three personalities rate a variety of concepts on the semantic differential. The ratings were then analyzed both quantitatively and qualitatively by two psychologists (C. Osgood and Z. Luria) who did not know the subject. The analysis by the psychologists included both descriptive comments and interpretations of the personalities that went beyond the objective data. For example, Eve White was described as being in contact with social reality but under great emotional stress, Eve Black as out of contact with social reality but quite self-assured, and Jane as superficially very healthy but quite restricted and undiversified. A more detailed, though still incomplete description of the three personalities based on the semantic differential ratings is presented in Figure 5.2. The analysis on the basis of these ratings turned out to fit quite well with the descriptions offered by the two psychiatrists (Osgood & Luria, 1954).

The Q-sort, adjective checklist, and semantic differential all approach the Rogerian ideal of phenomenological self-report; they provide data that are statistically reliable and theoretically relevant. It can be argued that there are many self-concepts rather than a single self-concept, that these tests do not get at unconscious factors, and that the tests are subject to defensive distortion. Rogers felt, however, that these tests provide useful measures for the concepts of self and ideal self (as he has defined them) and that they have been a necessary part of a productive research effort. We shall not discuss the status of the concept of self and its measurement until the critique and evaluation section of the next chapter. In the meantime, we explore its relationship to other parts of the theory and its place in the related research.

EVE WHITE	Perceives the world in an essentially normal fashion, is well socialized, but has an unsatisfactory attitude toward herself. The chief evidence of disturbance in the personality is the fact that ME (the self-concept) is considered a little bad, a little passive, and definitely weak.
EVE BLACK	Eve Black has achieved a violent kind of adjustment in which she perceives herself as literally perfect, but, to accomplish this break, her way of perceiving the world becomes completely disoriented from the norm. If Eve Black perceives herself as good, then she also has to accept HATRED and FRAUD as positive values.
JANE	Jane displays the most "healthy" meaning pattern, in which she accepts the usual evaluations of concepts by her society yet still maintains a satisfactory evaluation of herself. The self concept, ME, while not strong (but not weak, either) is nearer the good and active directions of the semantic space.

FIGURE 5.2 Brief Personality Descriptions, Based on Semantic Differential Ratings, in a Case of Multiple Personality. (Osgood & Luria, 1954)

Process

Self-actualization

Freud viewed the essential components of personality as relatively fixed and stable, and he developed an elaborate theory of the structure of personality. Rogers' view of personality emphasizes change, and he used few concepts of structure in his theory. Freud considered the person as an energy system. Thus, he developed a theory of dynamics to account for how this energy is discharged, transformed, or "dammed up." Rogers thought of the person as forward moving. Therefore, he tended to deemphasize the tension-reducing aspects of behavior, in favor of an emphasis on **self-actualization**. Whereas Freud placed great emphasis on drives, for Rogers there was no motivation in the sense of drives per se. Instead, the basic tendency is toward self-actualization: "The organism has one basic tendency and striving—to actualize, maintain, and enhance the experiencing organism" (Rogers, 1951, p. 487). "It should be noted that this basic actualizing tendency is the only motive which is postulated in this theoretical system" (Rogers, 1959, p. 196).

Rogers chose to postulate a single motivation to life and to stay close to that idea rather than to be tied to abstract conceptualizations of many motives. But the conceptualization of a self-actualizing tendency is highly abstract and as yet has not been measured objectively. In a poetic passage, Rogers (1963) described life as an active process, comparing it to the trunk of a tree on the shore of the ocean as it remains erect, tough, resilient, maintaining and enhancing itself in the growth process: "Here in this palm-like seaweed was the tenacity of life, the forward thrust of life, the ability to push into an incredibly hostile environment and not only to hold its own, but to adapt, develop, become itself" (Rogers, 1963, p. 2).

The concept of actualization involves the tendency on the part of the organism to grow from a simple structure to a complex one, to move from dependence toward independence, from fixity and rigidity to a process of change and freedom of expression. The concept involves tendencies on the part of the organism toward need reduction or tension reduction, but emphasizes the pleasures and satisfactions that are derived from activities that enhance the organism.

Although Rogers was generally concerned with measures for his concepts, he never did develop a measure of the self-actualizing motive. Over the years a number of scales have been developed to measure self-actualization. The most recent such effort involves a fifteen-item scale that measures the ability to act independently, self-acceptance or

Self-actualization — Rogers emphasizes the basic tendency of the organism toward self-actualization.

self-esteem, acceptance of one's emotional life, and trust in interpersonal relations (Figure 5.3). Scores on this questionnaire measure of self-actualization have been found to be related to other questionnaire measures of self-esteem and health, as well as to independent ratings of individuals as self-actualizing persons (Jones & Crandall, 1986).

Self-consistency and congruence

The concept of an organism moving toward actualization has not been the subject of empirical investigation. Much more critical to the process aspects of the theory and to research has been Rogers' emphasis on **self-consistency** and **congruence** between self and experience. Accord-

---

It is always necessary that others approve of what I do. (F)

I am bothered by fears of being inadequate. (F)

I do not feel ashamed of any of my emotions. (T)

I believe that people are essentially good and can be trusted. (T)

FIGURE 5.3 Illustrative Items from an Index of Self-Actualization. (Jones & Crandall, 1986)

The Personality Theory of Carl Rogers

ing to Rogers, the organism functions to maintain consistency (an absence of conflict) among self-perceptions and congruence between perceptions of the self and experiences: "Most of the ways of behaving which are adopted by the organism are those which are consistent with the concept of the self" (Rogers, 1951, p. 507). The concept of self-consistency was developed by Lecky (1945). According to Lecky, the organism does not seek to gain pleasure and to avoid pain but, instead, seeks to maintain its own self-structure. The individual develops a value system, the center of which is the individual's valuation of the self. Individuals organize their values and functions to preserve the self-system. For Lecky, people can be true only to themselves. Individuals will behave in a way that is consistent with their self-concept, even if this behavior is otherwise unrewarding to them. Thus, if you define yourself as a poor speller you will try to behave in a manner consistent with this self-perception.

Does the individual ever experience inconsistencies in the self, a lack of congruence between self and experience? If so, how does the individual function to maintain consistency and congruence? According to Rogers, we experience a state of **incongruence** when there is a discrepancy between the perceived self and actual experience. For example, if you view yourself as a person without hate and you experience hate, you

"Hi, there, the me nobody knows!"

Incongruence—A discrepancy between the perceived self and actual experience is experienced as a state of incongruence. Drawing by H. Martin; © 1971 The New Yorker Magazine, Inc.

are in a state of incongruence. The state of incongruence is one of tension and internal confusion. When it exists, and the individual is unaware of it, he or she is potentially vulnerable to anxiety. Anxiety is the result of a discrepancy between experience and the perception of the self. For the most part, we are aware of our experiences and allow them into consciousness. However, we also are capable of making experiences unavailable to awareness. Here Rogers made reference to the process called **subception** (McCleary & Lazarus, 1949). The individual can experience a stimulus without bringing it into awareness. The individual can discriminate an experience as threatening, as being in conflict with the self-concept, and not allow it to become conscious. In the interest of maintaining congruence between self and experience, the individual denies certain experiences to awareness. The price for this is anxiety—the "subception" of the organism that the discrepant experience may enter awareness and force a change in the self-concept. Again, the person whose self-concept is that they never hate anyone will experience anxiety whenever hateful feelings are experienced to any degree at all.

The organism seeks to maintain the self-concept. Its response to a state of incongruence—to the threat presented by recognition of experiences that are in conflict with the self—is that of **defense**. An experience is dimly perceived as incongruent with the self-structure, and the organism reacts defensively to deny awareness of the experience. Two defensive processes are described—**distortion** of the meaning of experience and **denial** of the existence of the experience. Denial serves to preserve the self-structure from threat by denying it conscious expression. Distortion, a more common phenomenon, allows the experience into awareness but in a form that makes it consistent with the self: "Thus, if the concept of self includes the characteristic 'I am a poor student', the experience of receiving a high grade can be easily distorted to make it congruent with the self by perceiving in it such meanings as, 'That professor is a fool;' 'It was just luck'" (Rogers, 1956, p. 205). What is striking about this last example is the emphasis it places on self-consistency. What is otherwise likely to be a positive experience, receiving a high grade, now becomes a source of anxiety and a stimulus for defensive processes to be set in operation. Events do not have meanings in and of themselves. Meaning is given to events by individuals with past experiences and concerns about the maintenance of a self-system.

Research on self-consistency and congruence Rogers was not clear whether he had in mind actual experiences, such as emotions, or perceptions of these experiences. That is, does a person respond defensively to the experience of hostility per se or to the dim perception of the self as a hostile person that is in conflict with other perceptions of the self? In any case, the related research has tended to focus on perceptions. An early study in this area was performed by Chodorkoff (1954). In a study of self-perception, perceptual defense, and adjustment, Chodorkoff found that subjects were slower to perceive words that were personally threatening than they were to perceive neutral words. This tendency was particularly characteristic of defensive, poorly adjusted individuals. The poorly adjusted individual, in particular, attempts to deny awareness to threatening stimuli.

Additional research by Cartwright (1956) involved the study of self-consistency as a factor affecting immediate recall. Following Rogers' theory, Cartwright hypothesized that individuals would show better recall for stimuli that are consistent with the self than for stimuli that are inconsistent. He hypothesized further that this tendency would be greater for maladjusted subjects than for adjusted subjects. In general, subjects were able to recall adjectives they felt were descriptive of themselves better than they were able to recall adjectives they felt were most unlike themselves. Also, there was considerable distortion in recall for the latter, inconsistent adjectives. For example, a subject who viewed himself as hopeful mis-recalled the word "hopeless" as being "hopeful," and a subject who viewed himself as friendly mis-recalled the word "hostile" as being "hospitable." As predicted, poorly adjusted subjects (those applying for therapy and those for whom psychotherapy had been judged to be unsuccessful) showed a greater difference in recall than did adjusted subjects (those who did not plan on treatment and those for whom psychotherapy had been judged to be successful). This difference in recall scores was due particularly to the poorer recall of the maladjusted subjects for inconsistent stimuli. In a related study, an effort was made to determine the ability of subjects to recall adjectives used by others to describe them (Suinn, Osborne, & Winfree, 1962). Accuracy of recall was best for adjectives used by others that were consistent with the self-concept of subjects and was poorest for adjectives used by others that were inconsistent with the self-concept. In sum, the degree of accuracy of recall of self-related stimuli appears to be a function of the degree to which the stimuli are consistent with the self-concept.

The two studies just discussed related to perception and recall. What of overt behavior? Aronson and Mettee (1968) considered this question and found results that were consistent with Rogers' view that the individual behaves in ways that are congruent with the concept of the self. In a study of dishonest behavior, they reasoned that if people are tempted to cheat they will be more likely to do so if their self-esteem is low than if it is high; that is, whereas cheating is not inconsistent with generally low self-esteem, it is inconsistent with generally high self-esteem. The data gathered indeed suggested that whether or not an individual cheats is influenced by the nature of the self-concept. People who have a high opinion of themselves are likely to behave in ways they can respect whereas people with a low opinion of themselves are likely to behave in ways that are consistent with that self-image.

More recently additional research supports the view that the self-concept influences behavior in varied ways (Markus, 1982). What is particularly noteworthy here is the suggestion that people often behave in ways that will lead others to confirm the perception they have of themselves—a self-fulfilling prophecy (Darley & Fazio, 1980; Swann, 1983). For example, people who believe they are likable may behave in ways that lead others to like them, whereas others who believe themselves to be unlikable may behave in ways that lead others to dislike them (Curtis & Miller, 1986). For better or for worse, then, your self-concept may be maintained by behaviors of others that were influenced in the first place by your own self-concept!

The need for positive regard

We have, then, a number of studies supporting the view that the individual attempts to behave in accordance with the self-concept and that experiences inconsistent with the self-concept are often ignored or denied awareness. In the earlier writing of Rogers, no mention was made of the reasons for the development of a rift between experience and self and, therefore, the need for defense. In 1959 Rogers presented the concept of the **need for positive regard**. The need for positive regard includes attitudes such as warmth, liking, respect, sympathy, and acceptance and is seen in the infant's need for love and affection. If the parents give the

Positive Regard—Healthy personality development is fostered through the communication of unconditional positive regard to the child.

The Personality Theory of Carl Rogers

child *unconditional positive regard*, if the child feels "prized" by his parents, there will be no need to deny experiences. However, if the parents make positive regard conditional, the child will be forced to disregard its own experiencing process whenever it conflicts with the self-concept. For example, if the child feels that it will only receive love (positive regard) for always being loving, it will deny all feeling of hate and struggle to preserve a picture of the self as loving. In this case the feeling of hate not only is incongruent with the self-concept but also threatens the child with loss of positive regard. Thus it is that the imposition of *conditions of worth* on the child leads to the denial of experiences, the rift between organism and self. The origins of inaccuracies in the self-concept, the origins of conflict between the individual's experience and the self-concept, lie in the individual's attempt to retain love.

To summarize, Rogers did not feel a need to use the concepts of motives and drives to account for the activity and goal-directedness of the organism. For him, the person is basically active and self-actualizing. As part of the self-actualizing process, we seek to maintain a congruence between self and experience. However, because of past experiences with conditional positive regard, we may deny or distort experiences that threaten the self-system. The result is a state of incongruence in which we experience anxiety and rigidly hold on to a fixed way of perceiving and experiencing.

Before we leave this section on process, we should raise some questions that are given detailed consideration in the critique and evaluation section of the next chapter. In his conceptualization of the process of awareness and denial to awareness, to what extent does Rogers depart from the Freudian notion of the unconscious? In his description of the development of anxiety and the processes of defensive denial and distortion, to what extent does Rogers depart from the Freudian concepts of anxiety and the mechanisms of defense? Clearly, there are differences in the two points of view. We shall keep these differences in mind as we study the rest of the theoretical network.

Growth and Development

Rogers did not really develop a theory of growth and development and did not do research in the area in terms of long-term studies or studies of parent–child interaction. Basically, Rogers believed that growth forces exist in all individuals. The natural growth process of the organism involves greater complexity, expansion, increasing autonomy, greater socialization—in sum, self-actualization. The self becomes a separate part of the phenomenal field and becomes increasingly complex. The self develops as a total whole, so that each element is part and parcel of the total self-concept. As the self emerges, the individual develops a need for positive regard. If the need for positive regard by others becomes more important than being in touch with one's own feelings, the individual will screen various experiences out of awareness and will be left in a state of incongruence.

Self-actualization and healthy psychological development

Essentially, then, the major developmental concern for Rogers is whether the child is free to grow within a state of congruence, to be self-actualizing, or whether the child will become defensive and operate out of a state of incongruence. A healthy psychological development of the self takes place in a climate in which the child can experience fully, can accept itself, and can be accepted by its parents, even if they disapprove of particular pieces of behavior. This is a point that is emphasized by most child psychiatrists and psychologists. It is the difference between a parent saying to a child "I don't like what you are doing" and their saying to the child "I don't like you." In saying "I don't like what you are doing," the parent is accepting the child while not approving of the behavior. In contrast to this climate is one in which the parents tell the child, verbally or in more subtle ways, that they feel that its behavior is bad and that it is bad. The child then feels that recognition of certain feelings would be inconsistent with the picture of itself as loved or lovable, leading to denial and distortion of these feelings.

Research on parent–child relationships

A variety of studies suggest that acceptant, democratic parental attitudes facilitate the most growth. Whereas children of parents with these attitudes show an accelerated intellectual development, originality, emotional security, and control, the children of rejecting, authoritarian parents are unstable, rebellious, aggressive, and quarrelsome (Baldwin, 1945). What is most critical is the children's perceptions of their parents' appraisals. If they feel that these appraisals are positive, they will find pleasure in their bodies and in their selves. If they feel that these appraisals are negative, they will develop negative appraisals of their bodies and insecurity (Jourard & Remy, 1955). Apparently, the kinds of appraisals that the parents make of their children reflect, to a considerable degree, their own degree of self-acceptance. Mothers who are self-accepting also tend to be accepting of their children (Medinnus & Curtis, 1963).

An extensive study of the origins of **self-esteem** gives further support to the importance of the dimensions suggested by Rogers. Coopersmith (1967) conducted a study of self-esteem, which he defined as the evaluation an individual makes and customarily maintains with regard to the self. Self-esteem, then, is a personal judgment of worthiness. It is a general personality characteristic, not a momentary attitude or an attitude specific to individual situations. Self-esteem was measured by a fifty-item Self Esteem Inventory, with most of the items coming from scales previously used by Rogers. Children in the public schools of central Connecticut filled out the inventory, and their scores were used to define groups of high, medium, and low self-esteem. When compared to children low in self-esteem, those high in self-esteem were found to be more assertive, independent, and creative. The high self-esteem subjects were also less likely to accept social definitions of reality unless they were in accord with their own observations, were more flexible and imaginative, and were capable of more original solutions to problems. In other words, the subjective estimates of self-esteem had a variety of behaviors attached to them.

What of the origins of self-esteem? Coopersmith obtained data on the children's perceptions of their parents, ratings from staff members who interviewed the mothers, and responses from the mothers to a questionnaire relating to child-rearing attitudes and practices. The results indicated that external indicators of prestige such as wealth, amount of education, and job title did not have as overwhelming and as significant an effect on self-esteem as is often assumed. Instead, the conditions in the home and the immediate interpersonal environment had the major effect on judgments of self-worth. Apparently children are influenced in their self-judgments through a process of **reflected appraisal** in which they take the opinions of them expressed by others who are important to them and then use these opinions in their own self-judgments.

What kinds of parental attitudes and behaviors appeared to be important in the formation of self-esteem? Three areas of parent–child interaction seemed to be particularly important. The first area concerned the *degree of acceptance*, interest, affection, and warmth expressed toward the child. The data revealed that the mothers of children with high self-esteem were more loving and had closer relationships with their children than did mothers of children with low self-esteem. The interest on the part of the mother appeared to be interpreted by children as an indication of their significance, that they were worthy of the concern, attention, and time of those who were important.

The second critical area of parent–child interaction related to *permissiveness and punishment*. The data revealed that the parents of children with high self-esteem made clear demands that were firmly enforced. Reward generally was the preferred mode of affecting behavior. In contrast to this pattern, the parents of children with low self-esteem gave little guidance and were harsh and disrespectful in their treatment. These parents did not establish and enforce guidelines for their children, were apt to use punishment rather than reward, and tended to lay stress on force and loss of love.

Finally, differences were found in parent–child interactions in relation to democratic practices. Parents of children with high self-esteem established an extensive set of rules and were zealous in enforcing them, but treatment within the defined limits was noncoercive and recognized the rights and opinions of the child. Parents of children low in self-esteem set few and poorly defined limits and were autocratic, dictatorial, rejecting, and uncompromising in their methods of control. Coopersmith summarized his findings as follows: "The most general statement about the origins of self-esteem can be given in terms of three conditions: total or nearly total acceptance of the children by their parents, clearly defined and enforced limits, and the respect and latitude for individual actions that exist within the defined limits" (Coopersmith, 1967, p. 236). Coopersmith further suggested that it is the perception of the parents by the child and not necessarily the specific actions they express that is important, and that the total climate in the family influenced the child's perception of the parents and their motives.

A recent study further supports the relevance of such child-rearing conditions for the development of creative potential. According to Rogers, children raised by parents who provide conditions of psychological safety and psychological freedom are more likely to develop creative potential than children raised by parents who do not provide these conditions. Conditions of psychological safety are provided by parental expressions of unconditional positive regard for the child and empathic understanding, whereas conditions of psychological freedom are expressed in permission to engage in unrestrained expression of ideas. In a test of this view, measures were taken of child-rearing practices and parent–child interaction patterns for children between the ages of three and five (Figure 5.4). Independent measures of creative potential in the children were obtained prior to their admission to school and in adolescence. In support of Rogers' theory, measures of childhood (preschool) environmental conditions of psychological safety and freedom were

Fostering Creative Potential—Psychological conditions of safety and freedom help to develop the creative potential of children.

Creativity-Fostering Environment

Parents respect the child's opinions and encourage expression of them.

Parents and child have warm, intimate time together.

Children are allowed to spend time with other children or families who have different ideas or values.

Parents are encouraging and supportive of the child.

Parents encourage the child to proceed independently.

The Creative Personality

Tends to be proud of accomplishments.

Is resourceful in initiating activities.

Becomes strongly involved in activities.

Has a wide range of interests.

Is comfortable with uncertainties and complexities.

Perseveres in the face of adversity.

FIGURE 5.4 Illustrative Characteristics of Creativity-Fostering Environments and the Creative Personality. (Adapted from Harrington, Block, & Block, 1987)

found to be significantly associated with creative potential—both in preschool and in adolescence (Harrington, Block, & Block, 1987).

Rogers' views on the parent characteristics and practices that influence the child's development of self-esteem have influenced the thinking of researchers and child-care experts. Although they do not always refer to Rogers, in many cases their emphasis on respect for the child and protection of the child's self-esteem speaks to the influence of Rogers and other members of the human potential movement. His emphasis on the conditions that promote self-actualization and the conditions that block it receives further attention in the next chapter, where we consider the clinical applications of the theory.

Major Concepts and Summary		
phenomenological self	incongruence
ideal self	subception
Q-sort	defense: distortion and denial
self-actualization	need for positive regard
self-consistency	self-esteem
congruence	

Before turning to the clinical applications of Rogers' theory of personality, let us take stock of the theorist and the basic theory of personality. In this chapter we have begun to see how Rogers attempted in his own life and in his theory to combine the religious and the scientific, the philosophical and the pragmatic. The emphasis by Rogers is on what is "good" and self-actualizing in people. Humans are unique among the species. Basic to this uniqueness is the awareness of a sense of self and movement toward self-actualization.

The ways in which we experience events, in particular ourselves, is central in Rogers' theory. The sense of self represents an organized pattern or set of experiences and perceptions. In our daily functioning we seek to preserve the sense of self and, beyond this, to move toward self-actualization, a process of continuing growth and development. It is this emphasis on self-actualization as the central motivation that links Rogers with the human potential movement.

Self-actualization involves continuous openness to experience and the ability to integrate experiences into an expanded, more differentiated sense of self. Self-actualizing, "fully-functioning" people are trusting of themselves as well as others, open to their own experiences as well as those of others, spontaneous and flexible, free to be creative, and able to respond to others in a genuine, nondefensive way. We are most able to self-actualize when we have a sense of self and self-worth that is not easily threatened. During the early years it is up to the parents to provide the basic acceptance and respect for the child that facilitates the development of such a sense of self. If such conditions are not provided, if the child experiences itself as conditionally accepted or rejected, then there is not room for growth and self-actualization. Under such conditions the child, out of a fear of loss of love, must reject experiences that are incongruent with the desired sense of self and that therefore arouse anxiety.

The concept of self was emphasized by Rogers following his observation that clients tend to talk about their problems in terms of the self. Although impressed with self-statements of clients in therapy interviews, Rogers attempted to obtain more objective measures of the concept as well as ones that could be used in research. Illustrative measures of the self-concept include the Q-sort and the semantic differential, both of which provide the potential for comparison of the self and ideal self concepts.

We have here the basic elements of the theory. However, many of these concepts become most meaningful in relation to Rogers' discussions of the problems of his clients and the process of psychotherapy. During most of the development of the theory, Rogers' main commitment was to psychotherapy and the process of effecting change—to understanding the conditions that provide for therapeutic change and self-actualization. The personality theory is really an outgrowth of these clinical and research efforts. Therefore, it should not be surprising to find considerable elaboration of the basic concepts when viewed (Chapter 6) within the context of psychopathology and change.

Chapter Six
A Phenomenological Theory: Applications and Evaluation of Rogers' Theory

CHAPTER FOCUS: Rogers' theory of personality has followed from his work with clients. His major emphasis has been on how individuals are led to deny and distort experience and on the conditions that provide the basis for growth and therapeutic change. Also considered in this chapter are other significant figures in the human potential movement (K. Goldstein, A. H. Maslow), existentialism, and an overall evaluation of Rogers' theory of personality.

> *I wanted only to try to live in accord with the promptings which*
> *came from my true self. Why was that so very difficult?*
>
> HESSE, 1965, p. 80

> *It also means that if the counselor is congruent or transparent, so*
> *that his words are in line with his feelings rather than the two*
> *being discrepant—if the counselor likes the client,*
> *unconditionally, and if the counselor understands the essential*
> *feelings of the client as they seem to the client—then there is a*
> *strong probability that this will be an effective helping relationship.*
>
> ROGERS, 1961A, p. 103

CLIENT: That's why I want to go, 'cause I don't care what happens.

THERAPIST: M-hm, m-hm. That's why you want to go, because you really don't care about yourself. You just don't care what happens. And I guess I'd just like to say—I care about you. And I care what happens. (Silence of 30 seconds) (Jim bursts into tears and unintelligible sobs)

THERAPIST: (Tenderly) Somehow that just makes all the feelings pour out.

ROGERS, 1967, p. 409

CLINICAL APPLICATIONS

In this section on clinical applications we will consider Rogers' views on psychotherapy and personality change. These views are an important part of the theory; in fact, the major part of Rogers' professional life

Client-Centered Therapy—Rogers emphasized the importance of the therapeutic atmosphere in producing positive personality change.

involved these clinical applications. The person-centered approach developed first in counseling and psychotherapy, where it was known as **client-centered therapy,** "meaning that a person seeking help was not treated as a dependent patient but rather as a responsible client" (Rogers, 1977, p. 5). Rather than focusing on an illness model of abnormal behavior and a medical model of a doctor treating a patient, Rogers emphasized the individual's drive toward health, the conditions that may interfere with such growth, and the therapeutic conditions that help to remove obstacles to self-actualization.

Psychopathology

The essential elements of the Rogerian view of psychopathology have been given in the last chapter in the sections on process and growth and development. For Rogers, the healthy person does or can assimilate experiences into the self-structure. In the healthy person, there is a congruence between self and experience, an openness to experience, a lack of defensiveness. In contrast to this, the neurotic person's self-concept has become structured in ways that do not fit organismic experience. The psychologically maladjusted individual must deny to awareness significant sensory and emotional experiences. Experiences that are incongruent with the self-structure are *subceived* as threatening and are either denied or distorted. The result is a rigid, defensive maintenance of the self against experiences that threaten the wholeness of the self and frustrate the need for positive self-regard. Rogers sees no utility in diagnosing different psychopathological illnesses, viewing such diagnoses as meaningless tools. Psychotic behaviors are viewed as behaviors that are inconsistent with the self but that have broken through the defensive processes. "Thus the person who has kept sexual impulses rigidly under control, denying them as an aspect of self, may now make open sexual overtures to those with whom he is in contact. Many of the so-called irrational behaviors of psychosis are of this order" (Rogers, 1959, p. 230).

Although Rogers does not differentiate among forms of pathology, he does differentiate among types of **defensive behaviors.** The defensive

---

CURRENT APPLICATIONS   DRINKING, SELF-AWARENESS, AND PAINFUL FEELINGS

Why do people abuse alcohol and drugs? Why, after treatment, do so many relapse? In Chapter 2 it was suggested that many alcoholics and drug addicts use the mechanism of defense of denial to cope with painful feelings. However, evidence of this relationship was not presented, nor was there analysis of how the self is experienced by substance abusers. This would appear to be important since substance abusers commonly report that they used drugs to handle painful feelings, with alcoholics often reporting that they drink to create a blur that blots out the painful aspects of life.

Though not conducted within a Rogerian framework, some recent research in this area is relevant to Rogers' views. The basic model of this research is that alcohol reduces self-consciousness and that alcoholics high in self-consciousness drink to reduce their awareness of negative life experiences. Individuals high in self-consciousness of inner experiences are those who would describe themselves in terms of statements such as the following: I reflect about myself a lot; I'm generally attentive to my inner feelings; I'm alert to changes in my mood.

In laboratory research with social drinkers it has been found that individuals high in self-consciousness consume more alcohol following failure experiences than do members of three other groups—individuals high in self-consciousness following success experiences and individuals low in self-consciousness regardless of whether they experienced success or failure. Further, in a study of alcohol use in adolescents it was found that increased alcohol use was associated with poor academic performance for students high in self-consciousness but not for those low in self-consciousness.

But what of alcoholics? And what about relapse? The latter would appear to be particularly significant since a half to three-quarters of all treated alcoholics relapse within six months of the end of treatment. In a study of relapse in alcohol abuse following treatment, results comparable to the above were found—relapse appeared to be a joint function of negative events and high self-consciousness.

Across a number of different populations and kinds of studies, a consistent relationship has been found between drinking, high self-consciousness, and experiences of personal failure. The conclusion suggested by the research is that many individuals drink to reduce their level of awareness of painful, negative experiences.

SOURCES: Hull, Young, & Jouriles, 1986; Pervin, 1987.

---

behaviors described are similar to those described by Freud. For example, in *rationalization* the person distorts behavior in such a way as to make it consistent with the self. For example, if you view yourself as a person who does not make mistakes, you are likely to attribute a mistake to some other factor. Another example of defensive behavior is *fantasy*. A man who defensively believes himself to be an adequate person may fantasize that he is a prince, that all women adore him, and he may deny any experiences that would be inconsistent with this image. A third example of defense behavior is *projection*. Here the individual expresses a need, but it is expressed in a form such that the need is denied to awareness and the behavior is viewed as consistent with the self. People whose self-concept involves no "bad" sexual thoughts may feel that others are making them have these thoughts. The descriptions of these defensive behaviors are quite similar to the ones given by Freud. For Rogers, however, the important aspect of these behaviors is their handling of an incongruence between self and experience by denial in awareness or distortion of perception: "It should be noted that perceptions are excluded because they are contradictory, not because they are derogatory" (Rogers, 1951, p. 506). Furthermore, the classification of the defenses is not as critical to Rogerian theory as it is to Freudian theory.

Although Rogers interpreted psychological pathology in terms of disturbed relationships between self and experience, most of the relevant research has been on the relationship between the self and ideal-self concepts. In this research, typically the discrepancy between self and ideal-self ratings is used as a measure of adjustment. Many studies were conducted in support of the view that health and self-esteem are associated with small discrepancies between the self and ideal-self concepts, including a recent study suggesting a relationship between high self-ideal discrepancies and depression (Higgins *et al.*, 1986). Other recent research suggests that even more critical for adjustment may be how close one feels one is to the negative or undesired self (Ogilvie, 1987). In other words, self-esteem and life satisfaction may depend even more on not being like the undesired self than on being like the ideal self.

Later in his career, Rogers (Walker, Rablen, & Rogers, 1960) developed a scale to measure how individuals relate to their feelings and how they experience feelings. The scale relates to statements made by individuals, generally clients in a therapeutic interview, which are then rated by judges according to prescribed rules. For example, according to the scale maladjusted people would express disownership of feelings or a vagueness about their feelings. Statements representative of these states would be "The symptom was—it was—just being depressed" and "I am experiencing something vague and puzzling which I do not understand." In contrast to this mode of experience, healthy people accept their feelings ("I am depressed") and are clearer about them. The scale represents an attempt to gather data, in a systematic way, on the individual's mode of relating to the self and to others. Although still not a measure of the discrepancy between self and experience, the scale does begin to give attention to the way individuals relate to their feelings, a variable that Rogers long felt to be critical to psychopathology.

Change

Although a theory of personality developed out of Rogers' experiences in therapy, his central focus was on the therapeutic process itself. Rogers' main concern is with the manner in which personality change comes about. He committed himself to a continuous subjective and objective involvement with the process of change. It is this process, the process of becoming, that was of greatest concern to him.

The history of client-centered therapy

Seeman (1965) has described three phases in the history of client-centered therapy. In the first phase, Rogers placed great emphasis on the therapist's use of the technique of reflection of feeling. According to this view, there is to be a minimum of therapist activity and guidance of what the client says—the nondirective view. In particular, the therapist was not to offer interpretations about unexpressed attitudes or about the unconscious. The task of the therapist was to recognize and clarify the client's expressed feelings. Research at this point tended to focus on the therapist's behavior. For example, a study by Gump (1944) compared nondirective methods of treatment with psychoanalytic methods. Gump found that psychoanalytic methods involved a greater proportion of interpretation, whereas nondirective methods emphasized more reflection of feelings. In both methods, however, the client did more than 70 percent of the talking.

Rogers believed that a misconception about his goals was developing. Some counselors who thought that they were being nondirective were merely being passive and seemingly uninterested. Also, the emphasis on "technique" led to excessive intellectualizing by some counselors. Rogers began to realize that the same statement on the part of the counselor could be given in a way that expresses indifference and critical judgment rather than empathy and understanding. In the second phase, therefore, Rogers changed his focus from an emphasis on the counselors being nondirective to an emphasis on their being *client centered*. The emphasis shifted from technique to attitude. The counselor was to have an attitude of interest in the phenomenal world of the client. Counselors were to be involved with an active experiencing of their clients' feelings. They were, in an empathic way, to get under the skin of their clients, to understand clients as the clients seem to themselves.

In this second phase, attention was given to process elements in therapy. Emphasis was placed on the client's increased awareness of previously denied attitudes, on the client's increased ability to evaluate phenomena, and on reorganization of the self-concept. His 1954 book contained a variety of studies on changes in the self-concept during therapy. During this period, the Q-sort was used extensively in research. For example, Butler and Haigh (1954) used the Q-sort to compare the self–ideal-self correlations of adult clients at the University of Chicago Counseling Center with a matched group of adults who were not candidates for treatment. They found that the nonclient group had a much closer relationship or correlation between their self and ideal-self Q-sort ratings than was true for the client group. The adults there for counseling were then divided into two groups, one that waited sixty days for treatment to begin and one that completed six or more counseling interviews. Both groups again completed the Q-sort for self and ideal-self concepts — one after the period of counseling and the other after a sixty-day waiting period. The counseling group showed a clear improvement in the self–ideal-self correlation whereas this was not true for the waiting group at all. Indeed, the waiting group showed no change in this relationship over the sixty-day period. Thus, the improvement in the self–ideal-self correlation for the counseling group could not be attributed to time alone. Finally, the group that received counseling and the original matched group (not candidates for therapy) again completed the self and ideal-self Q-sorts at a follow-up time. The counseling group maintained its gains in improved self–ideal-self correlation though this relationship remained below that for the matched, noncounseling group. In sum, the Q-sort data indicated that client-centered counseling results in an increase in congruence between self and ideal-self concepts and that such gains can be maintained over time.

In the third phase of client-centered therapy, there has been an increased emphasis on the therapeutic atmosphere. Rogerian therapists are not detached but involved. They express feelings and are involved in a relationship with their clients. There is an increased emphasis on experiencing rather than verbal self-exploration. Increasingly, there is the sense of a counselor and a client involved in a relationship. There is an emphasis in research on the therapeutic climate and the process of personality change.

Therapeutic conditions necessary for change
It was Rogers' belief that the critical variable in therapy is that of the therapeutic climate (Rogers, 1966). If therapists can provide three conditions in their relationships with their clients, in a way that is phenomenologically meaningful to the clients, then therapeutic change will occur. The three conditions hypothesized by Rogers to be critical to therapeutic movement are **congruence** or genuineness, **unconditional positive regard,** and **empathic understanding.** Genuine therapists are themselves. They do not give a façade but rather are open and transparent. Therefore, clients feel that they can be trusted. Congruent or genuine therapists feel free to be what they are, to experience events in the therapeutic encounter as they occur. They can be with their clients on a person-to-per-

son basis and be themselves. In a genuine relationship, therapists are free to share feelings with their patients, even when negative feelings toward the client are involved: "Even with such negative attitudes, which seem so potentially damaging but which all therapists have from time to time, I am suggesting that it is preferable for the therapist to be real than to put on a false posture of interest, concern, and liking that the client is likely to sense as false" (Rogers, 1966, p. 188).

The second condition essential for therapeutic movement is that of unconditional positive regard. This means that the therapist communicates a deep and genuine caring for the client as a person; the client is prized in a total, unconditional way. The unconditional positive regard provided by the therapist provides a nonthreatening context in which clients can explore their inner selves.

Finally, the third condition of empathic understanding involves the ability of the therapist to perceive experiences and feelings and their meaning to the client during the moment-to-moment encounter of psychotherapy. It is not a diagnostic formulation of the client's experiences, or a rote reflection of what the client says, but instead a "being with" the client while being oneself. It is active listening and understanding of the feelings and personal meanings as they are experienced by the client.

Essentially, Rogers is talking about factors that go beyond all forms of psychotherapy, factors that are independent of the theoretical orientation of the therapist, unless that orientation prevents the development of a helping relationship. In one important study, Fiedler (1950) had judges listen to the recorded interviews of experts and nonexperts of the psychoanalytic, nondirective (Rogerian), and Adlerian schools. The judges then sorted a number of descriptive items according to the extent to which they were characteristic of the interview. Fiedler found that, compared to nonexperts, experts were more successful in creating an "ideal" therapeutic relationship. Independent of orientation, experts were similar to one another in their ability to understand, to communicate with, and to maintain rapport with the client. In a related study, Heine (1950) investigated the relation between the theoretical orientation of therapists and therapeutic progress as viewed by clients. Clients sorted a number of statements to describe the changes they felt had occurred while in treatment and a number of statements to describe the therapeutic factors that they felt were responsible for the changes. Heine found that, according to their own reports, patients from psychoanalytic, nondirective, and Adlerian schools did not differ in the kinds of changes they reported had occurred. Furthermore, the clients who reported the greatest changes described similar factors as being responsible for these changes. A later study by Halkides (1958) found that the existence of the attitudes of genuineness, positive regard, and empathy in the therapist were related to therapeutic success, supporting Rogers' view that these indeed are the conditions necessary for change.

Outcomes of client-centered therapy

One of the landmark contributions of Rogers was his opening up the field of psychotherapy for systematic investigation. During the 1940s and 1950s a number of studies were done by Rogers and others to determine the changes associated with client-centered therapy. Among the changes observed were: a decrease in defensiveness and an increase in openness to experience; development of a more positive and more congruent self; development of more positive feelings toward others; and a shift away from using the values of others to asserting their own evaluations.

In addition to his work with neurotic clients, Rogers undertook a major therapeutic and research effort with schizophrenic patients (Rogers, 1967). In this study scales were developed to measure the critical therapist variables of a therapeutic climate (empathy, congruence, positive regard) and the process of patient experiencing. Once more he found evidence that positive therapeutic climate was associated with positive personality change. Indeed, these conditions seemed even more critical for schizophrenics than for neurotics. However, the therapeutic climate was found to depend on a complex dynamic interaction between patient and therapist, rather than on patient or therapist factors alone. Further, there was evidence that patients of therapists who were unable to establish positive therapeutic conditions sometimes got worse, even though these were generally competent and conscientious therapists.

Summary of distinguishing characteristics

Although client-centered therapy has been changing, it has retained from its inception certain distinguishing characteristics (Rogers, 1946, 1977). First, there is the belief in the capacity of the client. Because the basic strivings of the organism are toward growth, actualization, and congruence, the therapist need not control or manipulate the therapeutic process. Second, there is an emphasis on the importance of the therapeutic relationship. What is important is that the therapist attempt to understand the client and to communicate this understanding. In contrast to the psychoanalytic search for hidden meanings and insights into the unconscious, the Rogerian therapist believes that personality is revealed in what clients say about themselves. Diagnoses are not important since they say little about peoples' view of themselves and do not help to create the necessary therapeutic relationship. Third, there is the belief that client-centered therapy involves a predictable process. Growth occurs as the therapist establishes a helping relationship and is able to help free the strong drive of the individual to become mature, independent, and productive. Finally, with his research emphasis, Rogers tried to maintain ties among theory, therapy, and research. The client-centered theory of therapy is an if–then theory. The theory states that if certain *conditions* exist, then a *process* will occur that will lead to personality and behavioral change.

CASE EXAMPLE—MRS. OAK

As noted, one of Rogers' outstanding contributions to the field of psychotherapy was his leadership in opening it up as an area for investigation. He made available verbatim transcripts of therapy, films of client-centered therapy sessions, and a file of recorded therapy sessions that can be used for research purposes. In his 1954 volume on psychotherapy and personality change, Rogers presented an extensive analysis of a single case, the case of Mrs. Oak. As Rogers observed, it is the individual case that makes a total research investigation come to life, which brings diverse facts together in the interrelated way in which they exist in life. The case of Mrs. Oak is presented here to illustrate the Rogerian approach to an understanding of personality.

Mrs. Oak was a housewife in her late thirties when she came to the University of Chicago Counseling Center for treatment. At that time, she was having great difficulty in her relationship with her husband and her adolescent daughter. Mrs. Oak blamed herself for the daughter's psychosomatic illness. Mrs. Oak was described by her therapist as a sensitive person who was eager to be honest with herself and deal with her problems. She had little formal education but was intelligent and had read widely. Mrs. Oak was interviewed forty times over a period of five-and-one-half months, at which point she terminated treatment.

In the early interviews, Mrs. Oak spent much of her time talking about specific problems with her daughter and her husband. Gradually, there was a shift from these reality problems to descriptions of feelings:

> And secondly, the realization that last time I was here I experienced a-an emotion I had never felt before—which surprised me and sort of shocked me a bit. And yet I thought, I think it has a sort of a . . . the only word I can find to describe it, the only verbalization is a kind of cleansing. I-I really felt terribly sorry for something, a kind of grief.
>
> P. 311

At first the therapist thought Mrs. Oak was a shy, almost nondescript person and was neutral toward her. He quickly sensed, however, that she was a sensitive and interesting person. His respect for her grew, and he described himself experiencing a sense of respect for, and awe of, her capacity to struggle ahead through turmoil and pain. He did not try to direct or guide her. Instead, he found satisfaction in trying to understand her, in trying to appreciate her world, in expressing the acceptance he felt toward her.

MRS. OAK: And yet the-the fact that I—I really like this I don't know, call it a poignant feeling. I mean . . . I felt things that I've never felt before. I like that, too. Uh-Uh . . . maybe that's the way to do it. I-I just don't know today.

THERAPIST: M-hm. Don't feel at all sure, but you know that you somehow have a real, a real fondness for this poem that is yourself. Whether it's the way to go about this or not, you don't know.

P. 314

Given this supportive therapeutic climate, Mrs. Oak began to become aware of feelings she had previously denied to awareness. In the twenty-fourth interview, she became aware of conflicts with her daughter that related to her own adolescent development. She felt a sense of shock at becoming aware of her own competitiveness. In a later interview, she became aware of the deep sense of hurt inside of her.

MRS. OAK: And then of course, I've come to . . . to see and to feel that over this . . ., see, I've covered it up. (*Weeps*) But . . . and . . . I've covered it up with so much bitterness, which in turn I had to cover up. (*Weeps*) That's what I want to get rid of! I almost don't care if I hurt.

THERAPIST: (*Gently*) You feel that here at the basis of it, as you experienced it, is a feeling of real tears for yourself. But that you can't show, mustn't show, so that's been covered by bitterness that you don't like, that you'd like to be rid of. You almost feel you'd rather absorb the hurt than to . . . than to feel bitterness. (*Pause*) And what you seem to be saying quite strongly is, "I do hurt, and I've tried to cover it up."

MRS. OAK: I didn't know it.

THERAPIST: M-hm. Like a new discovery really.

MRS. OAK: (*Speaking at the same time*) I never really did know. But it's . . . you know, it's almost a physical thing. It's . . . sort of as though I-I-I were looking within myself at all kinds of . . . nerve endings and-and bits of-of . . . things that have been sort of mashed. (*Weeping*)

P. 326

At first, this increased awareness led to a sense of disorganization. Mrs. Oak began to feel more troubled and neurotic, as if she was going to pieces. She said she felt as though she were a piece of structure or a piece of architecture that had parts removed from it. In struggling with these feelings, Mrs. Oak began to recognize the dynamics of anxiety that had operated in her and to discover how, in an attempt to cope with anxiety, she had deserted her self. She described her previous inability to recognize and "sort of simply embrace" fear. She described her feeling that the problem for her and for many others is that they get away from self.

Intermittently, Mrs. Oak expressed her feelings toward the therapist. At first she felt resentful that the therapist was not being very helpful and that the therapist would not take responsibility for the sessions. During the course of therapy, she at times felt very strongly that the therapist didn't "add a damn thing." But, also, in the course of therapy, she developed a sense of relationship with the therapist and how this relationship compared with the descriptions her friends had given of the relationship in psychoanalysis. She concluded that her relationship with the therapist was different, was something she would never be casual about—was the basis of therapy.

> I'm convinced, and again I may sound textbookish, that therapy is only as deep as this combination, this relationship, as the need in the client is as deep as the need, and as deep as the willingness for the relationship to grow on the part of the therapist.
>
> P. 399

Progress did not occur in all areas. By the end of therapy, Mrs. Oak still had sexual conflicts. However, significant gains had been made in a number of areas. She began to feel free to be herself, to listen to herself, and to make independent evaluations. Mrs. Oak began to stop rejecting the feminine role and, more generally, began to become accepting of herself as a worthwhile human being. She decided that she could not continue in her marriage, and she arrived at a mutually agreeable divorce with her husband. Finally, she obtained and held a challenging job.

RECENT DEVELOPMENTS

Rogers' Shift in Emphasis: From Individuals to Groups and Society

Over the years, Rogers emphasized consistently the phenomenological approach, the importance of the self, and the change process. Whereas earlier there was a clear effort to combine clinical sensitivity with scientific rigor, later Rogers appeared to move increasingly toward sole reliance on personal, phenomenological types of studies: "To my way of thinking, this personal, phenomenological type of study—especially when one reads all of the responses—is far more valuable than the traditional 'hard-headed' empirical approach. This kind of study, often scorned by psychologists as being 'merely self-reports,' actually gives the deepest insight into what the experience has meant" (Rogers, 1970, p. 133). Apparently Rogers felt that the yield of orthodox scientific studies was minute compared to the insights obtained from clinical work. Rogers' emphasis on experience, particularly private experience, and his disappointments with graduate education in psychology led to a certain disillusionment with current definitions of science: "I'm not really a scientist. Most of my research has been to confirm what I already felt to be true . . . Generally I never learned anything from research" (Rogers, in Bergin & Strupp, 1972, p. 314).

Another shift for Rogers, at least in emphasis, was from the one-to-one therapy relationship to an interest in groups. In his book *On Encounter Groups* (Rogers, 1970), Rogers stated that changes occur more rapidly and clearly in small, intensive groups. Of particular interest to Rogers was the marital partnership group and alternatives to marriage (Rogers, 1972a). This interest is focused on the extent to which there was openness, honesty, sharing, and movement toward awareness of inner feelings in the relationship. Finally, Rogers extended his person-centered approach to administration, minority groups, interracial, intercultural, and international relationships. Rogers expressed a revolutionary spirit in his belief that the person-centered approach could produce a change in the concepts, values, and procedures of our culture: "It is the *evidence* of the *effectiveness* of a person-centered approach that may turn a very small and quiet revolution into a far more significant change in the way humankind perceives the possible. I am much too close to the situation to know whether this will be a minor or a major event, but I believe it represents a radical change" (p. 286).

RELATED POINTS OF VIEW

It was noted in the previous chapter that the tone and spirit of the Rogerian position are apparent in other theories of personality, particularly in the emphasis on the continuous striving of the organism to realize its inherent potential. Together with similar emphases by others, Rogers' position is part of the human potential movement that has been called the "third force" in psychology, offering an alternative to psychoanalysis and to behaviorism.

The Human Potential Movement

According to Riesman (1950), with rapid industrialization the prevailing American personality structure changed from an emphasis on behavior in accordance with tradition to behavior in accordance with individual initiative and an internal set of goals (e.g., accumulation of money, possessions, and power). With the development of bureaucratized, large cities and a consumer orientation, there was a further change in personality structure toward conformity and an anxious concern with being popular and well liked. In recent years, however, this emphasis on conformity and adjustment has changed to an emphasis on fulfillment. Along with Rogers, a number of personality theorists speak to this concern with fulfillment and with being human in the face of large institutions and the demands of society. Although there are theoretical differences among them, many humanist theories of personality are joined in the human potential movement. These theories respond to current concerns (e.g., anxiety, boredom, and lack of meaning) with an emphasis on self-actualization, fulfillment of potential, and openness to experience. Two major figures in this tradition are Kurt Goldstein and Abraham H. Maslow.

Kurt Goldstein

Kurt Goldstein came to the United States in 1935, at age 57, after achieving considerable status as a neurologist and psychiatrist in Germany. During World War I he had extensive experience working with brain-injured soldiers and this work formed the foundation for his later views. He was impressed with the separation of functions that often occurs in brain-injured patients in contrast with the smooth, coordinated brain functioning of normal individuals. What he observed as differences in brain functioning and disturbances due to brain injury he extended to other aspects of personality functioning. Thus, for example, the healthy human organism is characterized by flexible functioning whereas the disturbed human organism is characterized by rigid functioning. The healthy organism is characterized by planned and organized functioning whereas the disturbed organism is characterized by mechanical functioning. The healthy organism can delay and anticipate the future whereas the disturbed organism is bound by the past and the immediacy of the present. Yet, at the same time, Goldstein was impressed with the

Kurt Goldstein

tremendous adaptive powers of his brain-injured patients, the same powers that he felt were basic to all human functioning.

Like Freud, Goldstein (1939) had an energy view of the organism. However, his views concerning the movement and direction of energy flow differed considerably from that of Freud: "Freud fails to do justice to the positive aspect of life. He fails to recognize that the basic phenomenon of life is an incessant process of coming to terms with the environment; he only sees escape and craving for release. He only knows the lust of release, not the pleasure of tension" (1939, p. 333). Rather than seeking tension reduction, the main motive for the person is self-actualization. All aspects of human functioning are basically expressions of this one motive — to actualize the self. It can be expressed in such simple ways as eating or in such lofty ways as our highest creative productions, but in the final analysis it is this motive that guides our behavior. Each person has inner potentials that are there to be fulfilled in the growth process. It is the recognition of this that ties Goldstein to others in the human potential movement.

The threats to self-actualization come from disturbances inside the person's bodily functioning and from some forms of interaction with the environment. For example, disease, anxiety, or excessive controls from the environment may interfere with healthy functioning and with full expression of the self-actualization drive. However, the motive remains and the growth process can be continued once these internal and environmental disturbances have been eliminated. Thus, the task of the organism always is that of regulating its internal functioning and relating to the environment in such a way that the self-actualization process can be supported.

Goldstein's work with brain-injured patients was of considerable importance for workers in that area. In addition, his views on the general nature of human functioning have had a significant influence on humanist thinkers in the field of psychology.

Abraham H. Maslow

Abraham Maslow (1968, 1971) perhaps has been the major theorist in the human potential movement. It was he who described this psychology as the "third force" in American psychology. He criticized the other forces, psychoanalysis and behaviorism, for their pessimistic, negative, and limited conception of humans. He proposed, instead, that people are basically good or neutral rather than evil, that there is in everyone an impulse toward growth or the fulfillment of potentials, and that psychopathology is the result of twisting and frustration of the essential nature of the human organism. Society often causes such twisting and frustration, and there is a problem when we assume that the result is the essential nature of the organism. Rather, we should recognize what could occur were these obstacles to be removed. Here we see one of the reasons for the popularity of the human potential movement on the part of those

Abraham H. Maslow

who feel excessively restricted and inhibited by their environment. Maslow both speaks to these concerns and offers encouragement for the belief that things can be better if people are free to express themselves and be themselves.

In addition to this overall spirit, Maslow's views have been important in two ways. First, he suggested a view of human motivation that distinguishes between such biological needs as hunger, sleep, and thirst and such psychological needs as self-esteem, affection, and belongingness. We cannot survive as a biological organism without food and water, and likewise we cannot develop fully as a psychological organism without satisfaction of our other needs as well. Far too often, Maslow suggests, psychologists have been concerned with our biological needs and have developed views of motivation that suggest that people respond only to deficiency and only seek tension reduction. While accepting that such motivation exists, Maslow calls for us to recognize as well motivation that is not based on deficiency and that often involves an increase in tension—motivation that is expressed when people are being creative and fulfilling their potential.

Although Maslow's views on human motivation have not received a great deal of research attention, one study did report a relationship between satisfaction of basic needs and psychological well-being (Lester et al., 1983) (Figure 6.1).

A second major contribution by Maslow (1954) was his intensive study of healthy, self-fulfilling, self-actualizing individuals. These were figures from the past as well as some who were living at the time. From

Physiological. I get an adequate amount of rest.

Safety. I think that the world is a pretty safe place these days.

Belongingness. I feet rootless.

Esteem. I feel dissatisfied with myself much of the time.

Self-Actualization. I have a good idea of what I want to do with my life.

FIGURE 6.1 Illustrative Questionnaire Items Measuring Maslow's Hierarchy of Needs (arranged from low to high in the hierarchy). (Lester *et al.*, 1983)

this research Maslow concluded that actualizing people have the following characteristics: they accept themselves and others for what they are; they can be concerned with themselves but also are free to recognize the needs and desires of others; they are capable of responding to the uniqueness of people and situations rather than responding in mechanical or stereotyped ways; they can form profoundly intimate relationships with at least a few special people; they can be spontaneous and creative; and they can resist conformity and assert themselves while responding to the demands of reality. Who are such people? Illustrative figures are Lincoln, Thoreau, Einstein, and Eleanor Roosevelt. Clearly these are very special

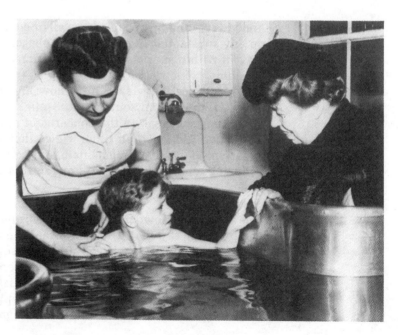

Self-Actualizing Individuals— Abraham Maslow suggested that Eleanor Roosevelt illustrated the self-actualizing person. Here she is speaking to a victim of infantile paralysis during her annual visit to the Children's Hospital.

individuals and few people have all or even most of these characteristics to any substantial degree. What is suggested, however, is that all of us have it within our potential to move increasingly in the direction of these qualities.

At times the views of Maslow and other leaders of the human potential movement sound almost religious and messianic. At the same time, they do speak to the concerns of many people and do serve as a corrective influence on other views that would represent the human organism as passive, fragmented, and completely governed by tension-reducing motives from within or rewards from the environment.

Existentialism

The approach known as existentialism is not new to psychology, but one could hardly say that it has an established or a secure place in mainstream academic psychology. Current personality texts generally contain at least some, and at times a major, reference to existentialism, yet one rarely encounters it in the personality research journals. Existentialism is an approach that many people are deeply moved by, yet there is no single representative figure, nor is there agreement about basic theoretical concepts. There are religious existentialists, atheistic existentialists, and antireligion existentialists. There are those who emphasize hope and optimism, as well as those who emphasize despair and nothingness. There are those who emphasize the philosophical roots of existentialism and those who emphasize the phenomena of clinical cases.

Granted all this diversity, what is there that establishes a common ground among those who would define themselves as existentialists? What is there about this approach that captivates some and leads others to reject it totally? Perhaps the most defining element of existentialism is the concern with *existence*—the person in the human condition. The existentialist is concerned with phenomena that are inherent in the nature of being alive, human, existing. What constitutes the essence of existence varies for different existentialists. However, all agree that certain concerns are fundamental to the very nature of our being and cannot be ignored, dismissed, explained away, or trivialized. Perhaps most of all, for the existentialist, people and experience are to be taken seriously (Pervin, 1960b).

Another major aspect of the existential view is that of the significance of the individual. The existentialist sees the person as singular, unique, and irreplaceable. For the philosopher Kierkegaard, the only existential problem is to exist as an individual. A number of additional emphases are related to this valuing of the individual. First, there is an emphasis on freedom. Freedom, consciousness, and self-reflection are what distinguish humans from other animals. Second, freedom involves responsibility. Each person is responsible for choices, for action, for being authentic, or for acting in "bad faith." Ultimately, each person is responsible for their own existence. Third, there is the existential concern with death, for it is here as nowhere else that the individual is alone and completely irreplaceable. Finally, there is an emphasis on phenomenology and an understanding of the unique experience of each person. Events are looked at in terms of their meaning for the individual rather than in terms of some standardized definition or the confirmation of some hypothesis. Thus, there is an interest in how any intrinsically human phenomenon can be experienced and given meaning—time, space, life, death, the self, or whatever.

We can perhaps better appreciate this approach by considering a few illustrations. For one, we can consider Rogers' (1980) discussion of loneliness. What is it that makes for the existential experience of loneliness? Rogers suggests a number of contributing factors: the impersonality of our culture, its transient quality and anomie, the fear of a close relationship. However, what most defines loneliness is the effort to share something very personal with someone and to find that it is not received or is rejected: "A person is most lonely when he has dropped something of his outer shell or façade—the face with which he has been meeting the world—and feels sure that no one can understand, accept, or care for the part of his inner self that lies revealed" (quoted in Kirschenbaum,

1979, p. 351). On the other hand, there may also be the feeling of being understood (Van Kaam, 1966). Here the person has the sense that another individual can empathize with them in an understanding, accepting way. The feeling of being understood is associated with safety and relief from existential loneliness.

Another illustration involves the search for meaning in human existence (Frankl, 1955, 1958). The existential psychiatrist Viktor Frankl struggled to find meaning while in a concentration camp during the Second World War. He suggests that the will-to-meaning is the most human phenomenon of all since other animals never worry about the meaning of their existence. Existential frustration and existential neurosis involve frustration and lack of fulfillment of the will-to-meaning. Such a "neurosis" does not involve the instincts or biological drives but rather is spiritually rooted in the person's escape from freedom and responsibility. In such cases the person blames destiny, childhood, the environment, or fate for what is. The treatment for such a condition, *logotherapy*, involves helping patients to become what they are capable of being, helping them to realize and accept the challenges of the opportunities that are open to them.

Finally, we can consider Laing's (1959) brilliant effort to give an account, in existential terms, of some forms of madness. Laing describes existential phenomenology as attempting to characterize the nature of a person's experience—of the world and of the self. *The Divided Self* represents a phenomenological account of the experience of schizoid individuals for whom there is a disruption or split in the relation with the world and the self. There is what Laing calls a *basic ontological insecurity* or lack of a firm sense of one's own self or identity. Although everyone may experience some similar feelings, for certain people ontological insecurity is particularly intense and pervasive—going to the very core of their felt existence.

These represent but brief vignettes of representative existential concerns. Can they help us understand why existentialism is such a powerful force among some and so dismissed by others? For many people, existialism speaks in a profound, humane way to issues that are of concern to them. Others are impressed with the importance of understanding the world of meaning and experience—either as independent of scientific pursuits or as integral to them. Such psychologists often experience a freedom from the confining concerns of prediction and control and a freedom to explore the depths of human phenomena. On the other hand, other psychologists are critical of existentialism on philosophical, scientific, and pragmatic grounds. In particular, there is criticism of an approach that abandons hope of predicting behavior in a lawful way and that has yet to establish its utility as a therapeutic effort. In writing about existentialism in 1960, I suggested that "existentialism may have much to offer and psychology considerable to gain" (Pervin,

1960b, p. 309). Such a statement would perhaps be equally appropriate today.

CRITICAL EVALUATION

Except for occasional comments and questions, little has been done in this and the last chapter to assess the strengths and weaknesses of Rogers' theory of personality. Until now, the theory has been presented along with supportive research. It is time, however, to take a more critical look at the theory. Three questions, each related to the other, form the basis for this evaluation: (1) To what extent does Rogers' philosophical view of the person lead to omissions or to minimal consideration of critical causes of behavior? (2) To what extent does Rogers pay a price for defining (for research purposes) the self in terms of conscious perceptions? (3) In the elaboration of his theory, in general, and in his views of the nature of anxiety and defense, in particular, to what extent does Rogers represent a departure from Freud?

Phenomenology

The phenomenological approach has been part of a significant effort by many psychologists to come to terms with human experience as it occurs. The phenomenological approach seeks to consider life as it is experienced by the person, without neglecting that which is most human, without splitting it into unrelated parts, and without reducing it to physiological principles. Two questions may be raised in relation to this approach: What are the limitations of a phenomenological approach to psychology? To what extent does the Rogerian counselor in fact take a phenomenological approach?

Clearly there are potential major limitations to the phenomenological approach in psychology. First, it may exclude from investigation certain critical variables, in particular those that are outside of the consciousness of people. If we restrict ourselves to that which people report, we may ignore important aspects of human functioning. Second, to build a science of psychology, one must go beyond the phenomenal world to develop concepts that are related to objective measures. The study of the phenomenal self is a legitimate part of psychology as long as it is studied empirically, with a boundless curiosity that is tempered by discipline and not with carefree speculation. Empathy is a legitimate mode of observation, but we must make sure that the observations made are reliable and that they can be checked against data from other modes of observation. Rogers was aware of these challenges to the phenomenological approach. His response was that the phenomenological approach is a valuable, perhaps necessary one for psychology, but not the only one to be used (Rogers, 1964).

To turn to our second question, to what extent is the theory based on unbiased phenomenological investigation? In a sense, the question was well put by MacLeod (1964, p. 138) in responding to a presentation by Rogers: "On what basis are you so convinced that you have understood your client better than Mr. Freud has understood his patient?" Rogers' response was that the client-centered therapist brings fewer biases and preconceptions to therapy because of a lighter "baggage of preconceptions." The client-centered therapist is more likely to arrive at an understanding of the phenomenal world of an individual than is the Freudian analyst. In an early paper, Rogers (1947) stated that if one read the transcripts of a client-centered therapist, one would find it impossible to form an estimate of the therapist's views about personality dynamics. But we do not know that this is actually the case. Furthermore, that statement was made at a time when the theory was not very developed and therapists were being nondirective. With the development of the theory and the increased emphasis on client-centered but active involvement by the therapist, is this still true? We know that minor behaviors on the part of the interviewer, including expressions such as m-hm, may exert a profound effect on the verbalizations and behavior of the person being interviewed (Greenspoon, 1962). As one reads the transcripts of the therapy sessions, the comments of the counselor do not appear to be random or inconsequential as far as content is concerned. Counselors appear to be particularly responsive about the self and about feelings, and appear to formulate some of their statements in theory-related terms:

THERAPIST OF MRS. OAK: I'd like to see if I can capture a little of what that means to you. It is as if you've gotten very deeply acquainted with yourself on a kind of a brick-to-brick experiencing basis, and in that sense you have become more self-ish . . . in the discovering of what is the core of you as separate from all the other aspects, you come across the realization, which is a very deep and pretty thrilling realization, that the core of the self is not only without hate but is really something more resembling a saint, something really very pure, is the word I would use.

ROGERS, 1954, p.239

This point (of influence of the interviewer on the client) is quite critical, since so much of Rogers' data comes from clinical interviews.

In summary, the phenomenological approach has distinct merits and potential dangers associated with it. Rogers recognized that it is not the only approach to psychology and that it must be associated with empirical investigation. However, he did not give adequate consideration to the role of unconscious forces in behavior or to the relationship between these forces and the conscious phenomenal field. Furthermore, we are still unclear about the extent to which the behavior of the client in client-centered therapy is, in fact, free of the biases and preconceptions of the counselor.

The Concept of Self

The concept of self is an important area for psychological investigation. A number of questions are relevant to the status of the concept and to its measurement. The concept of self, as developed by Rogers, assumes a constancy over time and across situations; that is, the way people view themselves at one point in time and in one situation is related to their views of themselves at other points in time and in other situations. Furthermore, the Rogerian concept of self assumes a total whole instead of a composite of unrelated parts. Is there evidence to support these assumptions? There is research that supports the view that the self-concept is fairly stable across situations and over time (Coopersmith, 1967). Other studies suggest, however, that individuals may not have a unified view of themselves but, rather, may value themselves in some areas and not others. Stability of the self-concept may itself be a source of individual differences, with some people showing far greater stability in their self-concept than others. Further, one may not have one self but many selves—good and bad, actual and possible (Markus & Nurius, 1986). Finally, concern with the self may vary in importance from person to person. There are people who are very self-conscious and others who are not, some who monitor their every experience and others who are totally unreflective. Indeed, there are cultural differences in the extent to which the self is emphasized, including at least one culture where the term for self does not even exist.

In accepting the concept of the self as important for us as personality psychologists, we must be concerned with the assessment hazards. One problem with many of the tests used to assess the self is that the items are not relevant to certain populations or miss important aspects of particular individuals. Our concepts of self are so varied that it is hard to develop a standard list that will tap the uniqueness of each individual. Beyond this, a second problem concerns the extent to which subjects are willing to give, or are capable of giving, honest self-reports. There is considerable evidence that self-reports are influenced by conscious efforts to present oneself in socially desirable ways as well as by unconscious defensive processes. It is assessment problems such as these that have frustrated so many investigators and left so many questions unanswered (Wylie, 1974).

The concept of self has a long history in psychology, receiving major attention during some periods and virtually disappearing from the literature during other periods (Pervin, 1984). Because of the difficulties in conceptualization and measurement, some psychologists have concluded that the relevant research has led us toward bankruptcy. Still, despite the many conceptual and methodological problems, the concept of self remains one of considerable importance to the layperson and to the field of psychology. Rogers, more than any other theorist, gave the attention it deserves in theory, research, and clinical work.

Conflict, Anxiety, and Defense

Critical attention has been given to Rogers' concepts of congruence, anxiety, and defense, and we have already compared these process concepts with the Freudian model of anxiety and defense. We can recall that, according to the theory, the individual may prevent awareness (through denial or distortion) of experiences that are "subceived" as threatening to the current structure of the self. Anxiety is the response of the organism to the subception that an experience incongruent with the self-structure may enter awareness, thus forcing a change in the self-concept. The incongruence between self and experience remains as a constant source of tension and threat. The constant need to use defensive processes results in a restriction of awareness and freedom to respond.

We have, then, a model in which the essential ingredients are conflict (incongruence), anxiety, and defense. Both the Freudian and Rogerian theories involve conflict, anxiety, and defense. In both theories the defenses are used to reduce anxiety. However, the sources of anxiety and, therefore, the processes through which anxiety is reduced are different in the two theories. For Freud, the conflict leading to anxiety is generally between the drives and some other part of the personality—the ego or the superego as mediated by the ego. For Freud, the defenses are used to deal with the threatening nature of the instincts. The result may be formation of symptoms—symptoms representing partial expressions of the instinct and partial drive reduction. Rogers rejects the assumption that the defenses involve forbidden or socially taboo impulses such as those that Freud describes as coming from the id. Instead, he emphasizes perceptual consistency. Experiences that are incongruent or inconsistent with the self-concept are rejected, whatever their social character. As observed previously, according to Rogers, favorable aspects of the self may be rejected because they are inconsistent or discrepant with the self-concept. Whereas Freud placed an emphasis on instincts and drive reduction, Rogers emphasized experiences and their perceptual inconsistency with the self-concept. The ultimate goal for Freud was the proper channeling of the drives. The ultimate goal for Rogers was a state of congruence between organism and self. The description given by Rogers of possible modes of defense was similar to Freud's and was undoubtedly influenced by psychoanalytic theory. Generally, however, Rogers gave much less attention to differences in types of defense and did not try to relate the type of defense used to other personality variables, as is the case in psychoanalytic theory.

The above distinctions seem fairly clear, until Rogers attempts to account for the development of a rift between organismic experience and self and introduces the concept of the need for positive regard. According to Rogers, if parents make positive regard conditional, their children will not accept certain values or experiences as their own. In other words, children keep out of awareness experiences that, if they were to accept them, might result in the loss of love. According to Rogers, the basic estrangement in humans is between self and experience and this estrangement has come about because humans falsify their values for the sake of preserving the positive regard of others (Rogers, 1959, p. 226). This statement complicates Rogers' position, since it suggests that the individual disregards experiences that formerly were associated with pain (loss of love). This view is not unlike that of Freud's concerning trauma and the development of anxiety. In essence, one can again see a conflict model, in which experiences that were, in the past, associated with pain later become sources of anxiety and defense.

In both the theoretical formulations of Freud and Rogers, the concepts of conflict, anxiety, and defense play a major role in the dynamics of behavior. Both view well-adjusted people as less concerned with these processes and neurotic people as more concerned with them. For Freud, the process aspects of behavior involve the interplay among drives and the efforts on the part of the defenses to reduce anxiety and to achieve drive reduction. For Rogers, the process aspects of behavior involve the efforts of the individual toward actualization and toward self-consistency. Although at times Rogers appears to emphasize the pain associated with the loss of positive regard, his major emphasis appears to be on the maintenance of congruence, which includes disregarding positive characteristics that are inconsistent with a negative self-concept and accepting negative characteristics that are consistent with this self-concept.

Psychopathology and Change

In a study of self–ideal-self discrepancy and social competence, highly competent subjects showed a *greater* self–ideal-self discrepancy than did subjects low in social competence (Achenbach & Zigler, 1963). The Rogerian theory of psychopathology relates to a lack of congruence between experience and self, and the self–ideal-self measure is not critical to the theory. On the other hand, self–ideal-self discrepancies have been used consistently by Rogerians as a measure of adjustment. Thus, the above finding points to some of the problems that emerge in the use of this measure. A variety of studies have found a relationship between the size of the self–ideal-self discrepancy and characteristics such as psychopathology, self-depreciation, anxiety, and insecurity. On the other hand, other studies have found a relationship between high self–ideal-self congruence and defensiveness. For example, Havener and Izard (1962) found a relationship between high congruence and unrealistically high self-esteem in paranoid schizophrenics. These subjects appeared to be defending against a complete loss of positive self-regard. Thus, it appears that the self-ideal-self relationship is far too complex to be an altogether satisfactory measure of adjustment.

The problems associated with using differences between self and ideal-self ratings as a measure of adjustment were recognized by Rogers and many of his followers. The problem is important both in and of itself and also in relation to evaluating the results of therapy. There is considerable evidence to suggest that different methods of therapy may lead to different kinds of change (Garfield & Bergin, 1978). Some changes may be measured by particular personality tests but not by others. For example, a psychological test developed in relation to Rogerian theory may relate well to Q-sort measures of change and to the results of client-centered therapy but not to tests developed in relation to psychoanalytic theory or to the results of psychoanalysis (Grummon & John, 1954; Vargas, 1954). The reverse might be true for tests developed in relation to psychoanalytic theory. The closer the relationship between the test and the theory, the greater the likelihood of the test being sensitive to changes produced by the therapy associated with that theory. Rogers undoubtedly would agree that there are various viewpoints from which to consider the person. Thus, it could be argued that "no single test score, no one rater's rating can be considered adequately representative of the diversity of measured changes accompanying psychotherapy" (Cartwright, Kirtner, & Fiske, 1963, p. 175).

Notice that a conclusion similar to this one was reached during the course of a discussion of a case by Rogers and psychoanalysts (Rogers, 1967). Rogers, Rogerian therapists, and psychoanalysts were concerned with the positive movement that occurred in a case presented for discussion. At one extreme, the analysts could see little or no progress in therapy, whereas at the other extreme, the client-centered therapists tended to see great and consistent movement in therapy. Apparently, psychoanalysts emphasize structure, character, and fixity in human behavior. In their view they go from the twigs of a tree to the trunk of the tree, from the superficial to the core of personality. In contrast to this view, the Rogerian emphasizes process and change in human behavior. For the Rogerian, one need not go beyond what is immediately observable to encounter that which is basic to the person.

Summary Evaluation

How, then, may the theory of Rogers be evaluated? Is it comprehensive, parsimonious, and relevant to research? The theory would appear to be reasonably comprehensive, though many areas of neglect remain. The theory says little about the course of growth and development or about the specific factors that determine one or another pattern. In contrast with Freud, one finds strikingly little mention of sex and aggression or of feelings such as guilt and depression. Yet, much of our lives seem to be concerned with these feelings.

The theory would appear to be economical, particularly in relation to the process of change. Out of all the complexities of psychotherapy, Rogers attempted to define the few necessary sufficient conditions for positive personality change.

In terms of research relevance, much of the theory expresses a philosophical, perhaps religious, view of the person. Assumptions most related to this view, such as the drive toward actualization, have remained assumptions and have not provided the basis for research. Also, the system is still without a measure of self-experience congruence. However, it is clear that the theory has provided extremely fertile ground for research. Rogers always kept clinical work, theory, and research in close touch with one another. Most of his work reflected a reluctance to sacrifice the rigors of science for the intuitive aspects of clinical work, and all of his work reflected an unwillingness to sacrifice the rich complexities of behavior for the empirical demands of science. As is properly the case, the development of his system was the result of a constant interplay among gross observations, theoretical formulations, and systematic research efforts.

This chapter on Rogers is concluded by stating three major contributions (Figure 6.2). Extending beyond the discipline of psychology,

STRENGTHS	LIMITATIONS
1. Focuses on important aspects of human existence.	1. May exclude certain phenomena (unconscious processes, defenses, etc.) from research and clinical concern.
2. Attempts to recognize the holistic, integrated aspects of personality.	2. Lacks objective measures of behavior beyond self-report.
3. Tries to integrate humanism and empiricism.	3. Ignores the impossibility of being totally phenomenological —that is, of making observations that are totally free of bias and preconception.
4. Aims at systematic inquiry into the necessary and sufficient conditions for therapeutic change.	

FIGURE 6.2 Summary of Strengths and Limitations of Rogers' Theory and Phenomenology

Rogers developed a point of view and an approach toward counseling that have influenced teachers, members of the clergy, and people in business. Within psychology, Rogers opened up the area of psychotherapy for research. By recording interviews, by making interviews and transcripts available to others, by developing clinically relevant measures of personality, and by demonstrating the potential value of research in the area, Rogers led the way in the legitimization of research on psychotherapy.

Finally, more than any other personality theorist, Rogers focused both theoretical and empirical attention on the nature of the self. The study of the self has always been a part of psychology, but it has, at times, been in danger of being dismissed as "mere philosophy." As MacLeod (1964) notes, you may not find many papers on the self at meetings of experimental psychologists, but clinicians find the problem staring them in the face. More than any other personality theorist, Rogers attempted to be objective about what is otherwise left to the artists:

> Slowly the thinker went on his way and asked himself: What is it that you wanted to learn from teachings and teachers, and although they taught you much, what was it they could not teach you? And he thought: It was the Self, the character and nature of which I wished to learn. I wanted to rid myself of the Self, to conquer it, but I could not conquer it, I could only deceive it, could only fly from it, could only hide from it. Truly, nothing in the world has occupied my thoughts as much as the Self, this riddle, that I live, that I am one and am separate and different from everybody else, that I am Siddartha; and about nothing in the world do I know less than about myself, about Siddartha.
>
> HESSE, 1951, p. 40

Major Concepts and Summary

[Review concepts from Chapter 5]

self-experience discrepancy

defensive behaviors

client-centered therapy

congruence (genuineness)

unconditional positive regard

empathic understanding

human potential movement

existentialism

In this chapter and the last the phenomenological theory of personality of Carl R. Rogers has been discussed. The theory is concerned with individual differences and the entire personality of the individual. The emphasis is on the phenomenal world of individuals—how individuals perceive and experience themselves and the world about them.

The main structural concepts in the theory are the self, representing an organized pattern of perceptions relating to "me," or "I," and the ideal self, representing the self-concept the individual would like to possess. Although structural concepts are important in terms of representing particular parts of the phenomenal field and in representing stability in an individual's functioning over time, the main focus of the theory is on process and change. The basic tendency in the individual is toward self-actualization — toward maintaining, enhancing, and actualizing the experiencing organism. Beyond this the individual is oriented toward self-consistency, interpreted as a congruence between self and experience. A state of incongruence is created when the individual perceives or subceives experiences that are contradictory with his or her self-image. Such experiences have been associated in the past with the loss of positive regard. The subception of such experiences is associated with tension or anxiety and leads to the use of defensive devices to remove the incongruence and reduce the anxiety. The basic defensive processes are distortion and denial, leading to a distorted representation of experience or to an unawareness of experience. This sequence of threat due to incongruence between self and experience and the consequent use of defenses forms the basis for psychopathology. There is research evidence to support the view that individuals attempt to behave in accordance with the self-concept and that experiences inconsistent with the self-concept are often ignored or denied into awareness.

Rogers has not really developed a theory of growth and development. Basically growth is seen as involving increased differentiation, expansion, and autonomy. The critical theoretical and practical questions are the circumstances that maximize the opportunity for growth. According to Rogers, it is critical that parents give their children feelings of self-worth. Presumably the conditions for growth that parents must provide for their children are the same ones that therapists must provide for their clients — congruence (genuineness), unconditional positive regard, and empathic understanding.

Rogers' view of the person and his approach to research are quite different from those of Freud. Rogers' theory emphasizes constructive forces in contrast to the psychoanalytic emphasis on that which is "innately destructive." Also, in contrast to the psychoanalytic emphasis on hidden meanings, Rogers emphasizes the usefulness of self-reports and direct sources of information. In contrast with Freud's emphasis on the past, Rogers prefers to deal with what is present or anticipated. These differences in points of view obviously translate themselves into differences in theory and research. Instead of the use of free association and dream analysis there is the use of verbal self-report and Q-sorts. Instead of an emphasis on studies of the unconscious, there is an emphasis on studies of the conditions that promote positive change (i.e., change toward self-actualization and openness to experience) and studies of the characteristics of the self.

Evaluation of Rogers' theory has brought out certain problems and limitations. (1) There has been inadequate attention given to unconscious forces, particularly given the fact that the theory recognizes the existence of such phenomena. (2) There are problems with the definitions and assessment devices for some concepts. For example, it is not clear how one studies in a systematic way the drive toward self-actualization and there are serious questions about the extent to which the self–ideal-self discrepancy can be considered to be an accurate measure of psychopathology. (3) There is evidence that even in the Rogerian, client-centered therapy situation, the therapist is a source of considerable bias and differentially rewards certain client behaviors (Truax, 1966).

Nevertheless, Rogers, while aware of these problems, went on to make a number of very significant contributions. (1) He developed an approach to counseling that has had a significant impact on the field. (2) He opened up the entire area of psychotherapy for systematic research. (3) He focused both theoretical and empirical attention on the nature of the self. (4) In his emphasis on self-actualization and openness to experience, he provided one source of leadership for the human potential movement and spoke to the concerns of many individuals in our society.

Chapter Seven
A Cognitive Theory of Personality: George A. Kelly and His Personal Construct Theory of Personality

*C*HAPTER FOCUS: In this chapter we discuss Kelly's personal construct theory as illustrative of a clinical, cognitive theory of personality. What distinguishes this theory is its emphasis on how the individual perceives, interprets, and conceptualizes events and the environment. The person is viewed as a scientist who develops a theory (construct system) to predict events. A different test, the Rep test, is presented as one means of assessing construct systems and thereby of understanding an individual's personality.

> To a large degree—though not entirely—the blueprint of human progress has been given the label of "science." Let us, then, instead of occupying ourselves with man-the-biological-organism or man-the-lucky-guy, have a look at man-the-scientist.
>
> KELLY, 1955, p. 4*

> Man looks at his world through transparent patterns or templets which he creates and then attempts to fit over the realities of which the world is composed. . . . Let us give the name constructs to these patterns that are tried on for size. They are ways of construing the world.
>
> KELLY, 1955, pp. 8–9

In the preceding chapters, two clinical theories of personality have been discussed—the psychodynamic theory of Freud and the phenomenological theory of Rogers. Both theories were derived from clinical contacts with patients; both emphasize individual differences; both view individuals as having some consistency across situations and over time; and both view the person as a total system. Freud and Rogers attempted to understand, predict, influence, and conceptualize behavior without fragmenting people into unrelated parts. Although sharing these characteristics in common, the two theories were presented as illustrative of different approaches to theory and research.

In this chapter, we study a third theory, one that also is expressive

---

*Kelly's references to "man-the-scientist" and "man-the-biological-organism" may strike students as sexist. It should be remembered that Kelly was writing in the 1950s, prior to efforts to remove sexism from language.

of the clinical approach toward understanding personality. The **personal construct theory** of George Kelly, like the theories of Freud and Rogers, was developed mostly out of contact with clients in therapy. Like the theories of Freud and Rogers, Kelly's personal construct theory emphasizes the whole person. It emphasizes individual differences and the stability of behavior over time and across situations. As Kelly observed, the first consideration of personal construct theory is the individual person, rather than any part of the person, any group of persons, or any particular process in a person's behavior. The personal construct clinician cannot fragment the client and reduce the client's problem to a single issue. Instead, the clinician must view the client from a number of perspectives at one and the same time.

Although sharing these characteristics with other clinical theories, Kelly's theory is vastly different from the theories of Freud and Rogers. It is an extremely creative effort to interpret behavior in *cognitive* terms; that is, it emphasizes the ways in which we perceive events, the ways we interpret these events in relation to already existing structures, and the ways that we behave in relation to these interpretations. For Kelly a **construct** is a way of perceiving or interpreting events. For example, good–bad is a construct frequently used by people as they consider events. An individual's personal construct system is made up of the constructs, or ways of interpreting events, that are available and the relationships among these constructs. There is a strong emphasis on cognition in the theory, but Kelly insisted that his theory was not merely a theory of cognition. Kelly's theory dares to reconstrue—that is, reinterpret—the field of psychology, and he challenged others to reconstrue it with him. But, for this part of the story, let the theorist speak for himself.

TO WHOM IT MAY CONCERN

It is only fair to warn the reader about what may be in store for him. In the first place, he is likely to find missing most of the familiar landmarks of psychology books. For example, the term learning, so honorably embedded in most psychological texts, scarcely appears at all. That is wholly intentional; we are throwing it overboard altogether. There is no ego, no emotion, no motivation, no reinforcement, no drive, no unconscious, no need. There are some brand-new psychological definitions. . . .

To whom are we speaking? In general, we think the reader who takes us seriously will be an adventuresome soul who is not one bit afraid of thinking unorthodox thoughts about people, who dares peer out at the world through the eyes of strangers, who has not invested beyond his means in either ideas or vocabulary, and who is looking for an ad interim, rather than an ultimate, set of psychological insights.

KELLY, 1955, pp. x–xi

GEORGE A. KELLY (1905–1966):
A VIEW OF THE THEORIST

Less has been written about the life of Kelly than of Freud and Rogers, but we do know something of his background, and the nature of the man comes through in his writing. He appears to be someone who would enjoy reading his books—an adventuresome soul who is unafraid to think unorthodox thoughts about people and who dares to explore the world of the unknown with the tools of tentative hypotheses. In his review of Kelly's theory, Sechrest (1963) observes that Kelly's philosophical and theoretical positions stem, in part, from the diversity of his experience. Kelly grew up in Kansas and obtained his undergraduate education there at Friends University and at Park College in Missouri. He pursued graduate studies at the University of Kansas, the University of Minnesota, and the University of Edinburgh. He received his Ph.D. from the State University of Iowa in 1931. He developed a traveling clinic in Kansas, was an aviation psychologist during World War II, and was a professor of psychology at Ohio State University and at Brandeis University.

Kelly's early clinical experience was in the public schools of Kansas. While there, he found that teachers referred pupils to his traveling psychological clinic with complaints that appeared to say something about the teachers themselves. Instead of verifying a teacher's complaint, Kelly

George A. Kelly

A COGNITIVE THEORY OF PERSONALITY

decided to try to understand it as an expression of the teacher's construction or interpretation of events. For example, if a teacher complained that a student was lazy, Kelly would not look at the pupil to see if the teacher was correct in the diagnosis. Rather he would try to understand the behaviors of the child and the way the teacher perceived these behaviors — that is, the teacher's construction of them — which led to the complaint of laziness. This was a significant reformulation of the problem. In practical terms, it led to an analysis of the teachers as well as the pupils, and to a wider range of solutions to the problems. Furthermore, it led Kelly to the view that there is no objective, absolute truth, and that phenomena are meaningful only in relation to the ways in which they are construed or interpreted by the individual.

George Kelly, then, was a person who refused to accept things as black or white, right or wrong. He was a person who liked to test new experiences; a person who dismissed truth in any absolute sense and, therefore, felt free to reconstrue or reinterpret phenomena; a person who challenged the concept of "objective" reality and felt free to play in the world of "make-believe"; a person who perceived events as occurring to individuals and, therefore, was interested in the interpretations of these events by individuals; a person who viewed his own theory as only a tentative formulation and who, consequently, was free to challenge views that others accepted as fact; a person who experienced the frustration and challenge, the threat and joy, of exploring the unknown.

KELLY'S VIEW OF THE PERSON

Theories of personality have implicit in them assumptions about human nature. Often, they can be uncovered only as we study why a theorist explores one phenomenon instead of another, and as we observe that theorists go beyond the data in ways that are meaningful in relation to their own life experiences. In general, Kelly's view of the person is explicit. In fact, he begins his presentation of the psychology of personal constructs with a section on his perspectives of the person. Kelly's assumption about human nature is that every person is a scientist. The scientist attempts to predict and control phenomena. Kelly believes that psychologists, operating as scientists, try to predict and control behavior, but that they do not assume that their subjects operate on a similar basis. Kelly describes this situation as follows:

> It is as though the psychologist were saying to himself, "I, being a psychologist, and therefore a scientist, am performing this experiment in order to improve the prediction and control of certain human phenomena; but my subject, being merely a

human organism, is obviously propelled by inexorable drives welling up within him, or else he is in gluttonous pursuit of sustenance and shelter."

KELLY, 1955, p. 5

Scientists have theories, test hypotheses, and weigh experimental evidence and Kelly considered this an appropriate view of people. Not every person is a scientist in the sense of limiting attention to some specific area and of using standard techniques to collect and to evaluate data. However, these are matters of detail, whereas the principles of operation are the same. All people experience events, perceive similarities and differences among these events, formulate concepts or constructs to order phenomena, and, on the basis of these constructs, seek to anticipate events. All people are similar in that they use constructs and follow the same psychological processes in the use of these constructs. In this respect, all people are scientists. However, individuals are unique in their use of particular constructs. Differences between individuals in the constructs that they use correspond to the differences among scientists in their theoretical points of view.

The view of the person as a scientist has a number of further consequences for Kelly. First, it leads to the view that we are essentially oriented toward the future. "It is the future which tantalizes man, not the past. Always he reaches out to the future through the window of the present" (Kelly, 1955, p. 49). Second, it suggests that we have the capacity to "represent" the environment, rather than merely to "respond" to it. Just as scientists can develop alternative theoretical formulations, so individuals can interpret and reinterpret, construe and reconstrue, their environments. Life is a representation, or construction, of reality, and this allows us to make and remake ourselves. Some people are capable of viewing life in many different ways whereas others cling rigidly to a set interpretation. However, everyone can only perceive events within the limits of the categories (constructs) that are available to him or her. In Kelly's terms, we are free to construe events but are bound by our constructions. Thus it is that we come to a new understanding of the issue of free will and determinism. According to Kelly, we are both free *and* determined. "This personal construct system provides him [humankind] with both freedom of decision and limitations of action—freedom, because it permits him to deal with the meaning of events rather than forces him to be helplessly pushed about by them, and limitation, because he can never make choices outside the world of alternatives he has erected for himself" (Kelly, 1958a, p. 58). Having "enslaved" ourselves with these constructions, we are able to win freedom again and again by reconstruing the environment and life. Thus, we are not victims of past history or of present circumstances—unless we choose to construe ourselves in that way.

A COGNITIVE THEORY OF PERSONALITY

KELLY'S VIEW OF SCIENCE, THEORY, AND RESEARCH

Much of Kelly's thinking, including his view of science, is based on the philosophical position of **constructive alternativism**. According to this position, there is no objective reality or absolute truth to discover. Instead, there are efforts to construe events—to interpret phenomena in order to make sense of them. There are always alternative constructions available from which to choose. This is true for the scientist as it is for people who behave as scientists. In Kelly's view the scientific enterprise is not the discovery of truth or, as Freud might have suggested, the uncovering of things in the mind previously hidden. Rather, the scientific enterprise is the effort to develop construct systems that are useful in anticipating events.

Kelly was concerned about the tendency toward dogma in psychology. He thought psychologists believed that constructs of inner states and traits actually existed rather than understanding them as "things" in a theoretician's head. If someone is described as an introvert, we tend to check to see whether he *is* an introvert, rather than checking the person who is responsible for the statement. Kelly's position against "truth" and dogma is of considerable significance. It leads, for instance, to the view that subjective thinking is an essential step in the scientific process. Subjective thinking allows one to establish the "invitational mood" in which one is free to invite many alternative interpretations of phenomena, and to entertain propositions that, initially, may seem absurd. The invitational mood is a necessary part of the exploration of the world, for the professional scientist as well as for the patient in therapy. It is the mood established by the creative novelist. But where the novelist publishes his make-believe and may even be unconcerned with the evidence supporting his constructions, the professional scientist tends to minimize the world of make-believe and to focus on objective evidence.

According to Kelly, it is the freedom to make believe and to establish the invitational mood that allows for the development of hypotheses. A hypothesis should not be asserted as a fact, but instead should allow the scientist to pursue its implications *as if* it were true. Kelly viewed a theory as a tentative expression of what has been observed and of what is expected. A theory has a **range of convenience**, indicating the boundaries of phenomena the theory can cover, and a **focus of convenience**, indicating the points within the boundaries where the theory works best. For example, Freud's theory has a broad range of convenience, providing interpretations for almost all aspects of personality, but its focus of convenience was the unconscious and abnormal behavior. Rogers' theory has a narrower range of convenience and its focus of convenience is more on the concept of the self and the process of change. Different theories have different ranges of convenience and different foci of convenience.

For Kelly, theories were modifiable and ultimately expendable. A theory is modified or discarded when it stops leading to new predictions or leads to incorrect predictions. Among scientists, as well as among people in general, how long one holds on to a theory in the face of contradictory information is partly a matter of taste and style.

Kelly's view of science is not unique, but it is important in terms of its clarity of expression and its points of emphasis (Figure 7.1). It also has a number of important ramifications. First, since there are no "facts," and since different theories have different ranges of convenience, we need not argue about whether facts are "psychological" or "physiological," or whether one theory is right and another wrong—they are different constructions. Second, Kelly's approach involved criticism of an extreme emphasis on measurement. Kelly felt that such an approach can lead to viewing concepts as "things" rather than as representations, and to making a psychologist into a technician rather than a scientist. Third, Kelly's view of science leaves room for the clinical as opposed to the experimental method, which he considered useful because it speaks the language of hypothesis, because it leads to the emergence of new variables, and because it focuses on important questions. Here we have a fourth significant aspect of Kelly's view of science—it should focus on important issues. In Kelly's belief, many psychologists are afraid of doing anything that might not be recognized as science, and they have given up struggling with important aspects of human behavior. His suggestion was that they stop trying to be scientific and that they get on with the job of understanding people. Kelly believed that a good scientific theory should encourage the invention of new approaches to the solution of the problems of people and society.

Finally, as noted, Kelly took a firm stand against dogma. It was his contention that many scholars waste time trying to disprove their colleagues' claims to make room for their own explanations. It is a tribute to

1. There is no objective reality and there are no "facts." Different theories have different constructions of phenomena. These theories also have different ranges of convenience and different foci of convenience.
2. Theories should lead to research. However, an extreme emphasis on measurement can be limiting and lead to viewing concepts as "things" rather than as representations.
3. The clinical method is useful because it leads to new ideas and focuses attention on important questions.
4. A good theory of personality should help us to solve the problems of people and society.
5. Theories are designed to be modified and abandoned.

FIGURE 7.1 Some Components of Kelly's View of Science.

A COGNITIVE THEORY OF PERSONALITY

Kelly's sense of perspective, sense of humor, and lack of defensiveness concerning his own work that he could describe one of his own theoretical papers as involving "half-truths" only, and that he could view his theory as contributing to its own downfall. It is this theory—the theory of personal constructs—that we now discuss.

THE PERSONALITY THEORY OF GEORGE A. KELLY

Structure

Kelly's key structural concept for the person as a scientist is that of the **construct**. A construct is a way of **construing**, or interpreting, the world. It is a concept that the individual uses to categorize events and to chart a course of behavior. According to Kelly, a person anticipates events by observing patterns and regularities. A person experiences events, interprets them, and places a structure and a meaning on them. In experiencing events, individuals notice that some events share characteristics that distinguish them from other events. Individuals distinguish similarities and contrasts. They observe that some people are tall and some short, that some are men and some are women, that some things are hard and some are soft. It is this construing of a similarity and a contrast that leads to the formation of a construct. Without constructs, life would be chaotic.

It is important to note that Kelly viewed all constructs as composed of opposite pairs. At least three elements are necessary to form a construct: two of the elements of the construct must be perceived as similar to each other, and the third element must be perceived as different from these two. The way in which two elements are construed to be similar forms the **similarity pole** of the construct; the way in which they are contrasted with the third element forms the **contrast pole** of the construct. For example, observing two people helping someone and a third hurting someone could lead to the construct kind–cruel, with kind forming the similarity pole and cruel the contrast pole. Kelly stressed the importance of recognizing that a construct is composed of a similarity–contrast comparison. This suggests that we do not understand the nature of a construct when it uses only the similarity pole or the contrast pole. We do not know what the construct *respect* means to a person until we know what events the person includes under this construct and what events are viewed as being opposed to it. Interestingly, whatever constructs one applies to others are potentially applicable to the self. "One cannot call another person a bastard without making bastardy a dimension of his own life also" (Kelly, 1955, p. 133).

A construct is not dimensional in the sense of having many points between the similarity and contrast poles. Subtleties or refinements in construction of events are made through the use of other constructs, these being constructs of quantity and quality. For example, the construct *black – white* in combination with a quantity construct leads to the four-scale value of black, slightly black, slightly white, and white (Sechrest, 1963).

A construct is similar to a theory in that it has a range of convenience and a focus of convenience. A construct's range of convenience comprises all those events for which the user would find application of the construct useful. A construct's focus of convenience comprises the particular events for which application of the construct would be maximally useful. Constructs can themselves be categorized in a variety of ways. For example, there are **core constructs** that are basic to a person's functioning and there are **peripheral constructs** that can be altered without serious modification of the core structure.

It is fascinating as well as enlightening to think of the constructs people use. Often they are part of the person's everyday language, though the individual might be surprised to learn that these are only constructs and that alternative ways of viewing the world are possible. Think, for example, of the constructs that are part of your own construct system. What are the terms or characteristics you use to describe people? Does each term include an opposite one to form a similarity – contrast pair, or is one end of the construct missing in some cases? Can you think of constructs that people you know use to say something about themselves as individuals? What constructs are shared by members of one social class or culture and not shared by members of a different social class or culture? It is interesting to consider whether such differences in construct systems are often part of the problem in communications between groups. In fact, consider a specific application of this point: Can you think of constructs that people use and that often result in problems in interpersonal relationships? For example, a frequent problem in marital relationships is one in which both partners emphasize the core construct guilty – innocent. Typically, each then argues that he or she is the "innocent" party and their partner is "to blame" for the difficulties. Both may initially see the counselor as a judge who will render a verdict rather than as someone who may help them to view things in another light or revise their constructs. Another example would be of a friend who once said to me: "Isn't there a winner and a loser in every relationship?" That person was obviously unaware that "winner – loser" is a possible, but not a necessary, construct. Thus, while seemingly abstract, constructs can be seen as readily relating, in fact, to basic aspects of our daily lives.

Do not assume from this discussion that constructs are verbal or that they are always verbally available to a person. Although Kelly emphasized the cognitive aspects of human functioning—the ones that Freudians would call the conscious—he did take into consideration phenomena described by Freudians as being unconscious. The conscious – unconscious construct is not used by Kelly. However, Kelly did use the verbal–preverbal construct to deal with some of the elements that are otherwise interpreted as conscious or unconscious. A **verbal construct** can be expressed in words, whereas a **preverbal construct** is one that is used even though the person has no words to express it. A preverbal construct is learned before the person developed the use of language. Sometimes, one end of a construct is not available for verbalization—it is characterized as being **submerged**. If a person insists that people do only good things, one assumes that the other end of the construct has been submerged since the person must have been aware of contrasting behaviors to have formed the "good" end of the construct. Thus, constructs may not be available for verbalization, and the individual may not be able to report all the elements that are in the construct, but this does not mean that the individual has "an unconscious." In spite of the recognized importance of preverbal and submerged constructs, ways of studying them have not been developed and generally this area has been neglected.

The constructs used by a person in interpreting and in anticipating events are organized as part of a system. There is a hierarchical arrangement of constructs within a system. A **superordinate construct** includes other constructs within its context, and a **subordinate construct** is one that is included in the context of another (superordinate) construct. For example, the constructs bright–dumb and attractive–unattractive might be subordinate to the superordinate construct good–bad. It is important to recognize that the constructs within the person's construct system are interrelated to at least some extent. A person's behavior generally expresses the construct system rather than a single construct, and a change in one aspect of the construct system generally leads to changes in other parts of the system. Generally the constructs are organized to minimize incompatibilities and inconsistency. However, some constructs in the system can be in conflict with other constructs and thus produce strain and difficulties for a person in making choices (Landfield, 1982).

In terms of the preceding, people can be seen to differ both in the content of their constructs and in the organization of their construct systems. Individuals differ in the kinds of constructs they use, in the number of constructs available to them, in the complexity of organization of their construct systems, and in how open they are to changes in these construct systems.

To summarize, according to Kelly's theory of personal constructs, an individual's personality is his or her construct system. A person uses constructs to interpret the world and to anticipate events. The constructs used by a person define his or her world. Two people are similar to the extent that they have similar construct systems. Most important, if you want to understand a person you must know something about the constructs that person uses, the events subsumed under these constructs, the way in which these constructs tend to function, and the way in which they are organized in relation to one another to form a system.

HAVING WORDS FOR WHAT YOU SEE, TASTE, AND SMELL

"Why are we so inarticulate about these things?" said a student in referring to tastes, odors, and touch sensations. What would the implications be if we had a greater vocabulary for experience, that is, if we had more constructs for such phenomena? Can having more taste constructs develop one's sense of taste? More odor constructs one's sense of smell? Is the secret to becoming a wine connoisseur the development of one's construct system?

At one time it was thought that language determines how we perceive and organize the world. Such a view seems, in the light of today's evidence, too extreme. We are capable of sensing and recognizing many things for which we do not have a name or concept. However, having a concept or construct may facilitate experiencing and recalling some phenomena. For example, research on odor identification suggests that having the right words to describe an odor facilitates recognition of the odor: "People can improve their ability to identify odors through practice. More specifically, they can improve it through various cognitive interventions in which words are used to endow odors with perceptual or olfactory identity." A name for a smell helps to transform it from vague to clear. Not just any word will do, since some words seem to capture better the sensory experience than others do. The important fact, however, is that cognition does play an important role in virtually all aspects of sensory experience.

In sum, expanding one's sensory construct system alone may not provide for increased sensitivity to sensory experience but, together with practice, it can go a long way toward doing so. Want to become a wine connoisseur? Practice, but also expand your construct system.

SOURCE: *Psychology Today*, July, 1981.

Utility of Constructs—Having a relevant construct may facilitate sensitivity to tastes and odors.

The Role Construct Repertory Test (Rep test)

Knowing other people, then, is knowing how they construe the world. How does one gain this knowledge of a person's constructs? Kelly's answer is direct—ask them to tell you what their constructs are. "If you don't know what is going on in a person's mind, ask him; he may tell you" (1958b, p. 330). Instead of using tests that had been developed by others in relation to different theoretical systems, Kelly developed his own assessment technique—the **Role Construct Repertory Test** (Rep test). As an assessment technique the Rep test is probably more closely related to a theory of personality than is any other comprehensive personality test. The Rep test was developed out of Kelly's construct theory and was designed to be used as a way of eliciting personal constructs.

Basically the Rep test consists of two procedures—the development of a list of persons based on a *Role Title List* and the development of constructs based on the comparison of triads of persons. In the first procedure, the subject is given a Role Title List or list of roles (figures) believed to be of importance to all people. Illustrative role titles would be: mother, father, a teacher you liked, a neighbor you find hard to understand. Generally, twenty to thirty roles are presented and subjects are asked to name a person they have known who fits each role. Following this the examiner picks three specific figures from the list and asks the subject to indicate the way in which two are alike and different from the third. The way in which two of the figures are seen as alike is called the *similarity pole* of the construct whereas the way in which the third is different is called the *contrast pole* of the construct. For example, a subject might be asked to consider the persons named for Mother, Father, and Liked Teacher. In considering the three, the subject might decide that the people associated with the titles Father and Liked Teacher are similar in being outgoing and different from Mother, who is shy. Thus, the construct outgoing–shy has been formed. The subject is asked to consider other groups of three persons (triads), usually twenty to thirty of them. With each presentation of a triad, the subject generates a construct. The construct given may be the same as a previous one or a new construct.

One can see how the Rep test follows from Kelly's theory since it elicits people's constructs, or ways of perceiving the world, based on their consideration of the way in which two things are similar and different from the third. It is particularly attractive since subjects are completely free to express how they construe the world. At the same time, however, it makes a number of important assumptions. First, it is assumed that the list of roles presented to the subjects is representative of the important figures in their lives. Second, it is assumed that the constructs that are verbalized by the subject are, indeed, the ones used to construe the world. In turn, this assumes that the subjects can verbalize their constructs and that they feel free to report them in the testing situation. Finally, it is assumed that the words the subjects use in naming their constructs are adequate to give the examiner an understanding of how they have organized their past events and how they anticipate the future.

In a clinical interpretation of the Rep test, the examiner considers the number of different constructs, the manner in which various figures

Sort No.	Similar Figures	Similarity Construct	Dissimilar Figure	Contrasting Construct
1	Boss Successful person	Are related to me	Sought person	Unrelated
2	Rejecting person Pitied person	Very unhappy persons	Intelligent person	Contented
3	Father Liked teacher	Are very quiet and easygoing persons	Pitied person	Nervous hypertensive
4	Mother Sister	Look alike Are both hypercritical of people in general	Boyfriend	Friendliness
5	Ex-flame Pitied person	Feel inferior	Boyfriend	Self-confident
6	Brother Intelligent person	Socially better than adequate	Disliked teacher	Unpleasant
7	Mother Boss	Hypertensive	Father	Easygoing
8	Sister Rejecting person	Hypercritical	Brother	Under-standing
9	Rejecting person Ex-flame	Feelings of inferiority	Disliked teacher	Assured of innate worth
10	Liked teacher Sought person	Pleasing personalities	Successful person	High-powered nervous
11	Mother Ex-flame	Socially maladjusted	Boyfriend	Easygoing self-confident
12	Father Boyfriend	Relaxing	Ex-flame	Uncom-fortable to be with
13	Disliked teacher Boss	Emotionally unpredictable	Brother	Even temperament
14	Sister Rejecting person	Look somewhat alike	Liked teacher	Look unalike
15	Intelligent person Successful person	Dynamic personalities	Sought person	Weak personality

SOURCE: G. A. Kelly, The Psychology of Personal Constructs; New York; Norton, 1955, pp. 242–243.

FIGURE 7.2 Role Construct Repertory Test: Raw Protocol of Mildred Beal. (Kelly, 1955, pp. 242–243)

DESCRIPTIONS OF FIGURES
(Note: Constructs which were used as bases of similarity are italicized)

Figure		Constructs Used to Describe Figure
1	Mother	*Looks like sister, Hypercritical of people in general, Hypertensive, Socially maladjusted*
2	Father	*Quiet,* Easygoing, *Relaxing,* Easygoing
3	Brother	*Socially better than adequate,* Even temperament, Understanding
4	Sister	*Looks like mother, Hypercritical of people in general, Hypercritical, Looks like rejecting person*
5	Boyfriend	*Relaxing,* Easygoing, Self-confident, Self-confident, Friendliness
6	Liked teacher	*Quiet, Easygoing, Pleasing personality, Looks unlike sister and rejecting person*
7	Disliked teacher	*Emotionally unpredictable, Assured of innate worth,* Unpleasant
8	Boss	*Related to me, Hypertensive, Emotionally unpredictable*
9	Rejecting person	*Very unhappy, Hypercritical, Looks like sister, Feelings of inferiority*
10	Ex-flame	*Feels very inferior, Feelings of inferiority, Socially maladjusted, Uncomfortable to be with*
11	Sought person	*Pleasing personality,* Weak personality, *Not related to me*
12	Pitied person	*Very unhappy, Feels very inferior,* Nervous, Hypertensive
13	Intelligent person	*Socially better than adequate, Dynamic personality,* Contented
14	*Successful person*	*Related to me, Dynamic personality,* High-powered, Nervous

are related to the constructs and to one another, and the relationships of the constructs to one another. An illustration of the type of record that is produced on a form of the test used in group testing is given in Figure 7.2. The subject, Mildred Beal, took the test as part of a classroom exercise. Since she had also applied for psychological counseling, there was an opportunity to check the interpretation of the test results against the information that was obtained independently during the course of therapy. The interpretation of the test results focused on the limited number of dimensions Mildred used to construe people and on her limited versatility in relating to people. Superficially, many constructs suggest some intellectual striving. However, on closer examination we find that there are really very few dimensions. One important dichotomy is between unhappy striving (hypersensitive, socially maladjusted, feelings of inferiority) and pleasant, comfortable quiescence (easygoing, relaxing, socially better than adequate). A second dominant dichotomy is in the construct friendly and understanding versus hypercritical.

The analysis of the constructs led the examiner to the following hypotheses: (1) The subject can be expected to show little versatility in handling the figures in her interpersonal world. (2) The subject can be expected to vacillate between unhappy agitation and easy self-indulgence. (3) She may be expected to intellectualize, to state insights glibly but not to retain them. (4) The therapist will initially be viewed as either friendly and understanding or hypercritical. These hypotheses tended to be confirmed by the therapist's reports. Mildred was viewed as being quite inflexible in dealing with people. The therapist observed that she perceived all social situations as forms of social pressure, in which she would win praise and social approval or be criticized and rejected. Although generally presenting herself as cheerful, she could at times become quite sad. She showed a need to be dependent on the therapist and to have him take the initiative in the interviews. On the other hand, she tended to resist all suggestions that he made. An important part of her interaction was an attempt to keep things on a superficially friendly, relaxed level, and to avoid criticism.

One of the remarkable features of the Rep test is its tremendous flexibility. By varying the role titles or instructions, one can determine a whole range of constructs and meanings. For example, a modification of the Rep test has been used to determine the constructs consumers use in purchasing cosmetics and perfumes. These constructs are then used by advertisers to develop advertisements that will appeal to consumers (Stewart & Stewart, 1982). In a recent study, a Sex Rep was developed to measure the meanings men and women associate with the concepts masculinity and femininity. Earlier research on sex role stereotypes had found that both men and women perceive personality characteristics associated with the concept of masculinity more positively than they do characteristics associated with the concept of femininity. In contrast with such results, research using the Sex Rep suggested that women could see themselves as feminine and still be high on self-esteem and health. In other words, the cultural image or stereotype of the concepts masculinity and femininity may be quite different from the personal meanings associated with these concepts (Baldwin *et al.*, 1986). At the stereotype level, the personality characteristics associated with the concept of masculinity may be more favorable or desirable for both men and women. At the personal level, however, psychological health may be reflected in men seeing themselves as masculine and women seeing themselves as feminine, with neither being perceived as intrinsically better than the other. The Rep test offers a method for getting at such personal meanings.

Cognitive complexity–simplicity

As noted, one can describe people not only in terms of the content of their constructs but also in terms of the structure of the construct system. Both the Rep test and modifications of it have again proved to be useful in this regard. An early effort to look at structural aspects of the construct system was Bieri's (1955) study of cognitive complexity. Bieri designated the degree to which a construct system is broken down (levels in the hierarchy) or differentiated as reflecting the system's **cognitive complexity–simplicity**. A cognitively complex system contains many constructs and provides for considerable differentiation in perception of phenomena. A cognitively simple system contains few constructs and provides for poor differentiation in perception of phenomena. A cognitively complex person sees people in a differentiated way, as having a variety of qualities, whereas a cognitively simple person sees people in an undifferentiated way, even to the extent of using only one construct (for example, good–bad) in construing others. Using a modified Rep test, Bieri compared cognitively complex and cognitively simple subjects in relation to their accuracy in predicting the behavior of others and in relation to their ability to discriminate between themselves and others. As predicted, it was found that cognitively complex subjects were more accurate in predicting the behavior of others than were cognitively simple subjects. Furthermore, cognitively complex subjects were more able to recognize differences between themselves and others. Presumably the greater number of constructs available to complex subjects allows for both greater accuracy and greater potential for recognition of differences.

Bieri went on to construe cognitive complexity–simplicity as a dimension of personality, defining it as an information-processing variable: "Cognitive complexity may be defined as the capacity to construe social behavior in a multidimensional way" (Bieri *et al.*, 1966). In one study of the way in which individuals process information, it was found that subjects high in complexity differed from subjects low in complexity in the way that they handled inconsistent information about a person. Subjects high in complexity tended to try to make use of the inconsistent information in forming an impression, whereas subjects low in complexity tended to form a consistent impression of the person and to reject all

COGNITIVE COMPLEXITY, LEADERSHIP, AND INTERNATIONAL CRISES

A series of fascinating studies suggests that cognitive style, in particular the dimension of cognitive complexity–simplicity, may have important implications for leadership and international relations. For example, would one suspect that greater or lesser cognitive complexity would be advantageous for a revolutionary leader? In a study of successful and unsuccessful leaders of four revolutions (American, Russian, Chinese, Cuban), it was found that low cognitive complexity was associated with success during the phase of revolutionary struggle but high complexity was associated with success at the post-struggle, consolidation phase. The suggestion made was that a categorical, single-minded approach is desirable during the early phase but a more flexible and integrated view is necessary during the later phase. Cognitive complexity would also appear to be valuable in exercising leadership in a large corporation. Thus successful corporate leaders are able to develop flexible plans, to include a variety of kinds of information in their decisions, and to make connections between decisions.

How could such a characteristic relate to international relations? Evidence suggests that diplomatic communications prior to international crises that result in war are lower in cognitive complexity than are those prior to crises that do not result in war. For example, communications between the United States and Russia were much less complex prior to the outbreak of the Korean War than prior to the Berlin blockade or the Cuban missile crisis. Also, analysis of samples of Israeli and Arab speeches delivered to the United Nations General Assembly found that complexity was significantly reduced prior to each of four wars in the Middle East (1948, 1956, 1967, 1973). Can such measures be used to predict and possibly avoid future wars or would deception be too easy?

SOURCES: SUEDFELD & RANK, 1976; SUEDFELD & TETLOCK, 1977; SUEDFELD, TETLOCK, & RAMIREZ, 1977; *New York Times*, July 31, 1984.

information inconsistent with that impression (Mayo & Crockett, 1964). Later research has also indicated that more complex individuals are more empathic, or better able to take the role of others, than are individuals who are cognitively simple (Adams-Webber, 1979, 1982; Crockett, 1982).

Thus, the Rep test can be used to determine the content and structure of an individual's construct system as well as to compare the effects of different construct system structures. The Rep test has the advantages of arising from a theory and of allowing subjects to generate their own constructs, instead of forcing subjects to use dimensions provided by the tester. In sum, Kelly posits that the structure of personality consists of the construct system of the individual. An individual is what he construes himself and others to be, and the Rep test is a device to ascertain the nature of these constructions.

Process

In his process view of human behavior, Kelly took a radical departure from traditional theories of motivation. As we mentioned already, the psychology of personal constructs does not interpret behavior in terms of motivation, drives, and needs. For personal construct theory, the term "motivation" is redundant. The term motivation assumes that the person is inert and needs something to get started. But, if we assume that the person is basically active, the controversy as to what prods an inert organism into action becomes a dead issue. "Instead, the organism is delivered fresh into the psychological world alive and struggling" (Kelly, 1955, p. 37). Kelly contrasted other theories of motivation with his own position in the following way:

> Motivational theories can be divided into two types, push theories and pull theories. Under push theories we find such terms as drive, motive, or even stimulus. Pull theories use such constructs as purpose, value, or need. In terms of a well-known metaphor, these are the pitchfork theories on the one hand and the carrot theories on the other. But our theory is neither of these. Since we prefer to look to the nature of the animal himself, ours is probably best called a jackass theory.
>
> KELLY, 1958A, p. 50

The concept of motive traditionally has been used to explain why humans are active and why their activity takes a specific direction. Since Kelly did not feel the need for the concept of motive to account for a person's activity, how did he account for the direction of activity? Kelly's position is simply stated in his fundamental postulate: *A person's processes are psychologically channelized by the ways in which he anticipates events.* Kelly offers this postulate as a given and does not question its truth. The postulate implies that we seek prediction, that we anticipate events, that we reach out to the future through the window of the present. In experiencing events, the individual observes similarities and contrasts, thereby developing constructs. On the basis of these constructs, the individual, like a true scientist, anticipates the future. As we see the same events repeated over and over, we modify our constructs so that they will lead to more accurate predictions. Constructs are tested in terms of their predictive efficiency. But what accounts for the direction of behavior? Again, like the scientist, people choose that course of behavior that they believe offers the greatest opportunity for anticipating future events. Scientists try to develop better theories, theories that lead to the efficient prediction of events, and individuals try to develop better construct systems. Thus, according to Kelly, a person chooses that alternative that promises the greatest further development of the construct system.

In making a choice of a particular construct, the individual, in a sense, makes a "bet" by anticipating a particular event or set of events. If there are inconsistencies in the construct system, the bets will not add up—they will cancel each other out. If the system is consistent, a prediction is made that can be tested. If the anticipated event does occur, the prediction has been upheld and the construct validated, at least for the time being. If the anticipated event does not occur, the construct has been invalidated. In the latter case, the individual must develop a new construct or must loosen or expand the old construct to include the prediction of the event that took place. Maher (1966) gives the example of the child who uses the construct of reassuring–punitive in relation to his mother. The child may find that his mother is at times punitive when he had expected her to be reassuring. The child may abandon the reassuring–punitive construct for a just–unjust construct and may interpret his mother's punishment as just.

In essence, then, individuals make a prediction and consider further change in their construct systems on the basis of whether they have led to accurate prediction. Notice that individuals do not seek reinforcement or the avoidance of pain; instead, they seek validation and expansion of their construct system. If a person expects something unpleasant and that event occurs, he or she experiences validation regardless of the fact that it was a negative, unpleasant event that occurred. Indeed, a painful event may even be preferred to a neutral or pleasant event if it confirms the predictive system (Pervin, 1964).

One should understand that Kelly is not suggesting that the individual seeks certainty, such as would be found in the repetitive ticking of a clock. The boredom people feel with repeated events and the fatalism that comes as a result of the inevitable are usually avoided wherever possible. Rather, the individual seeks to anticipate events and to increase the range of convenience or boundaries of his or her construct system. This point leads to a distinction between the views of Kelly and the views of Rogers. According to Kelly, individuals do not seek consistency for consistency's sake or even self-consistency. Instead, individuals seek to anticipate events, and it is a consistent system that allows them to do this.

Thus far, Kelly's system appears to be reasonably simple and straightforward. The process view becomes more complicated with the introduction of the concepts of anxiety, fear, and threat. Kelly defined **anxiety** in the following way: Anxiety is the recognition that the events with which one is confronted lie outside the range of convenience of one's construct system. One is anxious when one is without constructs, when one has "lost his structural grip on events," when one is "caught with his constructs down." People protect themselves from anxiety in various ways. Confronted by events that they cannot construe, that is, that lie outside the range of convenience, individuals may broaden a construct and permit it to apply to a greater variety of events, or they may narrow their constructs and focus on minute details.

In contrast to anxiety, one experiences **fear** when a new construct

　　　　　　　　　　　　　　A COGNITIVE THEORY OF PERSONALITY

appears to be about to enter the construct system. Of even greater significance is the experience of **threat**. Threat is defined as the awareness of imminent comprehensive change in one's core structure. A person feels threatened when a major shake-up in the construct system is about to occur. One feels threatened by death if it is perceived as imminent and if it involves a drastic change in one's core constructs. Death is not threatening when it does not seem imminent or when it is not construed as being fundamental to the meaning of one's life.

Threat, in particular, has a wide range of ramifications. Whenever people undertake some new activity, they expose themselves to confusion and threat. Confusion may lead to something new, but it may also eventuate in a threat to the individual. Individuals experience threat when they realize that their construct system is about to be drastically affected by what has been discovered. "This is the moment of threat. It is the threshold between confusion and certainty, between anxiety and boredom. It is precisely at this moment when we are most tempted to turn back" (Kelly, 1964, p. 141). The response to threat may be to give up the adventure — to regress to old constructs to avoid panic. Threat occurs as we venture into human understanding and when we stand on the brink of a profound change in ourselves.

Threat, the awareness of imminent comprehensive change in one's core structure, can be experienced in relation to many things. Consider, for example, the experience of music majors who are going to perform before a music jury that will determine whether they pass for the semester. To what extent can they be expected to experience threat associated with the possibility of failure? Why should some music majors experience more performance anxiety than others? Following Kelly, two psychologists tested the hypothesis that students would feel threatened by the possibility of failure at a music jury to the extent that such failure implied reorganization of the self-construal component of their construct system. To test this hypothesis, at the beginning of the semester music majors were administered a Threat Index consisting of forty core constructs (e.g., competent–incompetent, productive–unproductive, bad–good) in relation to which they first rated the *self* and then the *self if performed poorly on the jury*. The *threat index score* consisted of the number of core constructs on which the *self* and *self if performed poorly* were rated on opposite poles. Anxiety was measured through the use of a questionnaire at the beginning of the semester and three days before the onset of the music juries. Consistent with personal construct theory, those students who reported that failure on the jury would result in the most comprehensive change in self-construal were also those who reported the greatest increase in anxiety as the date of the jury approached (Tobacyk & Downs, 1986).

Unfortunately, the investigators in this study used the concept of anxiety in a way that was not necessarily consistent with Kelly's views. Even more significant, what was not studied in this case was the experiences of students anticipating the possibility of performing much better on the jury than would be expected on the basis of their self-construal; that is, would comprehensive change as a result of unexpected exceptional performance also be associated with threat? This is important since in Kelly's view it is the awareness of imminent comprehensive change in the construct system that is threatening, not failure per se.

What makes the concepts of anxiety, fear, and threat so significant is that they suggest a new dimension to Kelly's view of human functioning. The dynamics of functioning can now be seen to involve the interplay between the individual's wish to expand the construct system and the desire to avoid the threat of disruption of that system: "If one wished to state negatively Kelly's position on the psychology of personal constructs, as they relate to motivation, one might say that human behavior is directed away from ultimate anxiety" (Kelly, 1955, p. 894). Thus, we have here a model of anxiety and defense. In response to anxiety, individuals may *submerge* one end of a construct in order to keep perceiving events in a familiar, comfortable way, or they may *suspend* elements that do not fit so well into a construct. Submergence and suspension are responses to anxiety. They are viewed as being similar to the psychoanalytic concept of repression. Thus, in the face of anxiety, individuals may act in ways that will make their constructs or parts of their constructs unavailable for verbalization. In the face of threat, individuals have a

Construct Change—Peace Corps volunteers, such as the one illustrated here, had to be prepared to develop new constructs as they were exposed to new values, attitudes, and behaviors in different cultures.

A COGNITIVE THEORY OF PERSONALITY

choice between constricted certainty and broadened understanding. Individuals always seek to maintain and to enhance their predictive systems. However, in the face of anxiety and threat, individuals may rigidly adhere to a constricted system instead of venturing out into the risky realm of expansion of their construct systems.

To summarize, Kelly assumes an active organism, and he does not posit any motivational forces. For Kelly, the person behaves as a scientist in construing events, in making predictions, and in seeking expansion of the construct system. Sometimes, not unlike the scientist, we are made so anxious by the unknowns and so threatened by the unfamiliar that we seek to hold on to absolute truths and become dogmatic. On the other hand, when we are behaving as good scientists, we are able to adopt the invitational mood and to expose our construct systems to the diversity of events that make up life.

Growth and Development

Kelly was never very explicit about the origins of construct systems. He stated that constructs are derived from observing repeated patterns of events. But he did little to elaborate on the kinds of events that lead to differences like the ones between simple and complex construct systems. Kelly's comments relating to growth and development are limited to an emphasis on the development of preverbal constructs in infancy and the interpretation of culture as involving a process of learned expectations. People belong to the same cultural group in that they share certain ways of construing events and have the same kinds of expectations regarding behavior.

Developmental research associated with personal construct theory generally has emphasized two kinds of change. First, there has been exploration of increases in complexity of the construct system associated with age (Crockett, 1982; Hayden, 1982). Second, there has been exploration of qualitative changes in the nature of the constructs formed and in the ability of children to be more empathic or aware of the construct systems of others (Adams-Webber, 1982; Morrison & Cometa, 1982; Sigel, 1981). In terms of construct system complexity, there is evidence that as children develop they increase the number of constructs available to them, make finer differentiations, and also show more hierarchical organization or integration.

Two studies have been reported that are relevant to the question of the determinants of complex cognitive structures. In one study, the subjects' level of cognitive complexity was found to be related to the variety of cultural backgrounds to which they had been exposed in childhood (Sechrest & Jackson, 1961). In another study, parents of cognitively complex children were found to be more likely to grant autonomy and less likely to be authoritarian than were parents of children low in cognitive complexity (Cross, 1966). Presumably, the opportunity to examine many

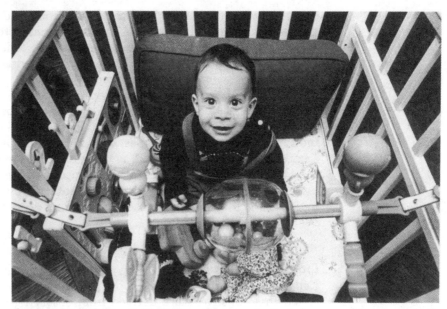

Development of the Construct System—The opportunity to be exposed to many stimuli facilitates development of the construct system. Aware of this, some parents try to develop what *Newsweek* called "superbabies."

different events and to have many different experiences is conducive to the development of a complex structure. One would also expect to find that children who experience long-standing and severe threat from authoritarian parents would develop constricted and inflexible construct systems.

Returning to the question of qualitative change, research indicates that as children develop they become less egocentric; that is, as children develop they become less prone to view everything in terms of themselves and are more able to take the perspective of the other. Younger children (age eight) tend to describe others in the same way that they describe themselves and in terms of concrete, self-relevant activities relative to older children (age thirteen) (Honess, 1979, 1980). For example, younger children frequently describe someone in terms dependent on themselves ("We play together." "We go to the park together."), whereas older children either use descriptions independent of themselves ("He is kind.") or use self-relevant constructs that suggest more of an exchange relationship ("She is nice to me." "We like one another."). Development involves an increase in the ability to take distance on people and events, to see things as not necessarily being related to the self, and to appreciate the construct systems of others as well as one's own (Sigel, 1981).

The question of factors determining the content of constructs and the complexity of construct systems is of critical importance. In particu-

A COGNITIVE THEORY OF PERSONALITY

lar, it is relevant to the field of education, since a part of education appears to be the development of complex, flexible, and adaptive construct systems. Unfortunately, Kelly himself made few statements in this area, and research is only now beginning to elaborate on this part of the theory.

<table>
<tr><td>Major
Concepts
and Summary</td><td>construct
construct system
range of convenience
focus of convenience
similarity and contrast poles
core and peripheral constructs
verbal and preverbal constructs</td><td>submerged part of a construct
superordinate and subordinate
  constructs
Role Construct Repertory Test
  (Rep test)
cognitive complexity – simplicity
anxiety, fear, and threat</td></tr>
</table>

In this chapter we have reviewed an unusual theorist and the basic essentials of his theory of personality. George A. Kelly developed a theory out of a diversity of clinical experiences. His theory of personality avoids many of the standard terms found in the field of psychology and invites the reader to dare to interpret the human organism in a new light — as a scientist who seeks to construe the world in a way that will permit increasingly better prediction of events. The emphasis on the invitational mood is an important part of setting the stage for perceiving phenomena in a different way. The emphasis on the person as a scientist is an important part of his approach — our personality is our theory or construct system as well as the ways in which we act and feel in accordance with our construct system.

For Kelly the essential aspect of personality is the construct — the person's way of looking at, interpreting, or construing events. Constructs are developed as a result of noticing similarities and differences in events as we live our daily lives. The Rep test was developed by Kelly to assess the construct system of a person. Following the logic of personal construct theory, in the Rep test the person is asked to consider triads of persons and to indicate how two are alike and different from the third. This leads to the definition of a similarity pole and a contrast pole. Through the use of the Rep test the psychologist can attempt an analysis of the structure of the person's construct system in terms of core and peripheral constructs, superordinate and subordinate constructs, and the overall level of complexity or simplicity.

Just as the scientist seeks to predict events, so the human organism seeks to anticipate events. The function of the construct system is the anticipation of events—a task that is always before us and that we are always seeking to master. So critical is this to our functioning that we experience anxiety when our constructs do not appear to fit the events we are observing, and experience threat when our construct system itself seems endangered. Under such circumstances one or more parts of the construct system may become submerged, new experiences may be rejected, and the individual may defensively adhere to viewing events in preconceived ways.

As a result of experience we develop a construct system with a variety of kinds of constructs, involving distinct content for each individual, and an organization that reaches varying degrees of complexity or simplicity. Some constructs are learned prior to the development of language (preverbal constructs), but for most people the vast majority of the constructs in their construct system can be expressed in words. Under supportive circumstances the child and the adult feel free to expand their construct systems to include new phenomena and to organize what has been learned in new ways. In other words, increased complexity and integration are aspects of a healthy, developing construct system. Just as scientists attempt to develop theories that will include more phenomena and predict more events, so healthy development involves increasing the range of convenience and focus of convenience of the construct system. On the other hand, if new experiences are not provided or if the person feels too threatened to construe life in a different way, then the construct system may remain fixed, rigid, and unchanged.

In sum, in Kelly's theory we act and move because we are alive, not because of urges from within or pushes from without. Being the scientists we are, we seek to expand our construct systems so as to better anticipate events. The only exceptions are when we are feeling so anxious or threatened that exploration and the invitational mood are impossible. A major part of Kelly's efforts were directed toward understanding people in terms of their own construct systems and toward facilitating their developing more useful ways of construing events. In the next chapter we shall learn about his efforts to develop methods to help people to change their constructions of themselves and events around them.

Chapter Eight
A Cognitive Theory of Personality: Applications and Evaluation of Kelly's Theory

*C*HAPTER FOCUS: In this chapter we consider the clinical applications of Kelly's personal construct theory. Kelly felt that any significant theory of personality has to suggest ways to help people. He saw the area of psychotherapy not only as a major source of interest and concern but also as a major aspect or "focus of convenience" of personal construct theory.

> From the standpoint of the psychology of personal constructs, we may define a disorder as any personal construction which is used repeatedly in spite of consistent invalidation.
>
> KELLY, 1955, p. 831

> Yet we see it as the ultimate objective of the clinical psychology enterprise . . . the psychological reconstruction of life. We even considered using the term reconstruction instead of therapy. If it had not been such a mouth-filling word we might have gone ahead with the idea. Perhaps later we may.
>
> KELLY, 1955, p. 187

CLINICAL APPLICATIONS

Psychopathology

According to Kelly, psychopathology is a disordered response to anxiety. As in the theories discussed previously, the concepts of anxiety, fear, and threat play a major role in Kelly's theory of psychopathology. However, it must be kept in mind that these concepts, although retained, have been redefined in terms relevant to personal construct theory.

For Kelly, psychopathology is defined in terms of disordered functioning of a construct system. A poor scientist is one who retains a theory and makes the same predictions despite repeated research failures. Similarly, abnormal behavior involves efforts to retain the content and structure of the construct system despite repeated incorrect predictions or invalidations. At the root of this rigid adherence to a construct system are anxiety, fear, and threat. Kelly stated that one could construe human behavior as being directed away from ultimate anxiety. Psychological disorders are disorders involving anxiety and faulty efforts to reestablish the sense of being able to anticipate events:

> There is a sense in which all disorders of communication are disorders involving anxiety. A "neurotic" person casts about frantically for new ways of construing the events of his world. Sometimes he works on "little" events, sometimes on "big" events, but he is always fighting off anxiety. A "psychotic" person appears to have found some temporary solution for his anxiety. But it is a precarious solution, at best, and must be sustained in the face of evidence which, for most of us, would be invalidating.
>
> KELLY, 1955, pp. 895–896

What are some of the faulty ways in which people try to hold on to their construct systems? These efforts involve problems in the ways in which constructs are applied to new events, problems in the ways in which constructs are used to make predictions, and problems in the ways in which the overall system is organized. Let us consider an illustration of each. An example of the pathological application of constructs is that of making constructs excessively **permeable** or excessively **impermeable**. An excessively permeable construct allows almost any new content into it whereas an excessively impermeable construct admits no new elements into its context. Excessive permeability can lead to the use of just a few constructs that are very broad and the lack of recognition of important differences among people and events. Too much becomes lumped together, as in stereotypes. Excessive impermeability can lead to pigeonholing each new experience, as if everything is distinctive, and to rejecting events that cannot be pigeonholed. This pattern of response is found in people who are described as being very compulsive.

An illustration of the pathological use of constructs to make predictions is excessive **tightening** and excessive **loosening**. In excessive tightening the person makes the same kinds of predictions regardless of the circumstances. In excessive loosening, the person makes excessively varied predictions with the same construct. In neither case can prediction be very accurate since both involve ignoring circumstances that might call for shifts in the construct system—in the first case through always predicting the same and in the second case through random, chaotic predictions. Tightening may be seen in the compulsive person who rigidly expects life to be the same regardless of changes in circumstances, whereas loosening can be seen in the psychotic person whose construct system is so chaotic that it cannot be used to communicate with others: "They [schizophrenic clients] are not caught short of constructs. But what constructs!" (Kelly, 1955, p. 497).

Personal construct researchers have investigated the extent to which schizophrenics do indeed construe people in unstable and loose ways. For example, in one study subjects were asked to rank eight photographs on six characteristics: kind, stupid, selfish, sincere, mean, and honest. They were then asked to make the ratings a second time without relying on their memory for the previous ratings. Two questions were of particular interest. First, to what extent would people see the concepts as being related? An intensity score was derived as a measure of the extent to which the subject's eight rank orderings were related to one another. A low intensity score suggested that the subject was treating these six characteristics as if they had no relation to one another. Second, to what extent would people maintain their rankings from the first series to the second series? Because the photographs remained the same and there had been no intervening experience, this correlation essentially constituted a measure of the test–retest reliability or consistency of the person's ratings. Here a consistency score was used; a low consistency score indicated that the person applied the concepts in very different ways on the two trials.

A number of patient groups and a normal group of subjects were tested in the above ways. The average intensity scores and consistency scores were then calculated for the members of each group. The hypothesis being tested was that thought-disordered schizophrenics would have particularly low intensity and consistency scores, indicative of loose and unstable construing. Indeed, this was found to be the case (Figure 8.1). Relative both to other patient groups as well as to the normal group, the thought-disordered schizophrenic group showed significantly lower intensity and consistency scores (Bannister & Fransella, 1966). In sum, such patients can be characterized both in terms of the types of constructs formed as well as in terms of how these constructs are employed.

Finally, we come to disordered efforts to maintain the overall organization of the construct system, as illustrated in **constriction** and **dila-**

Group Means (Averages) of Intensity and Consistency Test Scores for Six Groups of Subjects

	Mean Intensity	Mean Consistency
Thought-Disordered Schizophrenics	728	.18
Normals	1253	.80
Nonthought-Disordered Schizophrenics	1183	.73
Depressives	1115	.75
Neurotics	1383	.74
Organics	933	.73

FIGURE 8.1 Personal Construct Theory and Psychopathology. (Bannister & Fransella, 1966)

tion. Constriction involves a narrowing of the construct system to minimize incompatibilities. The range and focus of convenience of the construct system becomes quite small. Constriction tends to be found in people who are depressed and who limit their interests, narrowing their attention to a smaller and smaller area. In contrast to this, in dilation the person attempts to broaden the construct system and to reorganize it at a more comprehensive level. Extreme dilation is observed in the behavior of the manic person who jumps from topic to topic and who makes sweeping generalizations with few ideas. It is as if everything can now be included in the construct system of this person.

These faulty devices to prevent anxiety and avoid the threat of change in the construct system illustrate Kelly's efforts to interpret pathological behavior within the framework of personal construct theory. Another illustration of his interpretation of psychopathology is the case of suicide. According to the psychoanalytic view, every suicide is a potential homicide. Because of anxiety or guilt, the hostility that would otherwise be directed toward some other person becomes directed instead toward the self. Not so, according to the psychology of personal constructs. Kelly (1961) interpreted suicide as an act to validate one's life or as an act of abandonment. In the latter case, suicide occurs because of fatalism or because of total anxiety—because the course of events is so obvious that there is no point in waiting around for the outcome (fatalism), or because everything is so unpredictable that the only definite thing to do is to abandon the scene altogether. As noted, we often must choose between immediate certainty and wider understanding. In suicide, the choice is for the former and represents ultimate constriction. "For the man of constricted outlook whose world begins to crumble, death may appear to provide the only immediate certainty which he can lay his hands on" (Kelly, 1955, p. 64).

Although Kelly did not emphasize the concept of hostility in relation to suicide, he did recognize its importance in human functioning. Again, however, the concept is redefined in terms relevant to personal construct theory. Kelly made an important distinction between aggression and hostility, one that often is absent in other theories. According to Kelly, **aggression** involves the active expansion of the person's construct system. This active expansion of the construct system does not interfere with the functioning of other people. In contrast to this, **hostility** occurs when one tries to make others behave in an expected way. For example, it would be hostile for a person to intimidate someone because they expected them to behave in a submissive way. According to this view, the hostile person does not intend to do harm. Rather, injury is an accidental outcome of the effort to protect the construct system by attempting to make people behave in expected ways—the emphasis is on protection of the construct system. The opposite of hostility is curiosity and respect for the freedom of movement of others.

To summarize Kelly's view of psychopathology, we return to the analogy of the scientist. Scientists attempt to predict events through the use of theories. Scientists develop poor theories when they fear venturing out into the unknown, when they fear testing out hypotheses and making bets, when they rigidly adhere to their theory in the face of contradictory evidence, when they can account only for trivia, and when they try to say that they are accounting for things that, in fact, are outside the range of convenience of their theories. When scientists construe in these ways, we say they are bad scientists. When people construe in these ways, we refer to them as sick people. When people know how to stay loose and also tighten up, we call them creative and reward them for their efforts. When people stay too loose or too "uptight," we say they are ill and consider hospitalization. It all depends on their constructs—and on how others construe the constructs.

Change

The process of positive change is discussed by Kelly in terms of the development of better construct systems. If sickness represents the continued use of constructs in the face of consistent invalidation, psychotherapy is the process whereby clients are assisted in improving their predictions. In psychotherapy, clients are trained to be better scientists. Psychotherapy is a process of reconstruing—a process of reconstruction of the construct system. This means that some constructs need to be replaced, some new ones need to be added; some need to be tightened while others are loosened; and some need to be made more permeable while others are made less permeable. Whatever the details of the process, *psychotherapy is the psychological reconstruction of life*.

According to Kelly's theory, three conditions exist that are favorable to the formation of new constructs. First, and perhaps most important, there must be an *atmosphere of experimentation*. This means that, for example, in therapy "one does not 'play for keeps.' Constructs, in the true scientific tradition, are seen as 'being tried on for size'" (Kelly, 1955, p. 163). In psychotherapy, one creates the invitational mood and accepts the language of hypothesis. Psychotherapy is a form of experimentation. In therapy, constructs (hypotheses) are developed, experiments are performed, and hypotheses are revised on the basis of empirical evidence. By being permissive and responsive, by providing the client with the tools of experimentation, and by encouraging the client to make hypotheses, the therapist assists in the development of the client as a scientist.

The second key condition for change is the *provision of new elements*. Conditions favorable to change include new elements that are relatively unbound by old constructs. The therapy room is a "protected environment" in which new elements can be recognized and confronted. Therapists themselves represent a new element in relation to which their clients can start to develop new constructs. It is here that the question of *transference* emerges, and the therapist must ask: "In what role is the client now casting me?" Clients may attempt to transfer a construct from their repertory that was applicable in the past and to use it in relation to their therapists. They may construe the therapist as a parent, as an absolver of guilt, as an authority figure, as a prestige figure, or as a stooge. Whatever the content of the transference, the therapist tries to provide fresh, new elements in an atmosphere of make-believe and experimentation.

Along with this, therapists provide the third condition for change — they make *validating data available*. We are told that knowledge of results facilitates learning. We know that, given a supportive atmosphere and the permeable aspects of the construct system, invalidation does lead to change (Bieri, 1953; Poch, 1952). The therapist provides new elements in a situation in which the client will at first attempt to use old constructs. It is the therapist's task to share his or her own perceptions of and reactions to the client, against which the client can check his or her own hypotheses: "By providing validating data in the form of responses to a wide variety of constructions on the part of the client, some of them quite loose, fanciful, or naughty, the clinician gives the client an opportunity to validate constructs, an opportunity which is not normally available to him" (Kelly, 1955, p. 165).

We know that there are individual differences in resistance to change, and that rigidity is related to psychopathology (Pervin, 1960). However, given an atmosphere of experimentation, given new elements, and given validating data, people do change. Conversely, the conditions

Fixed-Role Therapy—In Kelly's fixed-role therapy clients are encouraged to behave and represent themselves in new ways. Drawing by Lippman; Copyright © 1972 The New Yorker Magazine, Inc.

Clinical Applications

unfavorable for change include threat, preoccupation with old material, and the lack of a "laboratory" in which to experiment. It is within the context of the former conditions of change that Kelly developed a specific therapeutic technique—**fixed-role therapy**. Fixed-role therapy assumes that, psychologically, people are what they represent themselves to be and that people are what they do. Fixed-role therapy encourages clients to *represent themselves in new ways*, to *behave in new ways*, to *construe themselves in new ways*, and thereby to *become new people*.

In fixed-role therapy, the clients are presented with a new personality sketch that they are asked to act out. On the basis of some understanding of the client, a group of psychologists gets together to write a description of a new person. The task for the clients is to behave "as-if" they were that person. The personality sketch written for each client involves the development of a new personality. Many characteristics are presented in the sketch that are in sharp contrast with the person's actual functioning. In the light of construct theory, Kelly suggested that it might be easier for people to play up what they believe to be the opposite of the way they generally behave than to behave just a little bit differently. Design of the sketch involves setting in motion processes that will have effects throughout the construct system. Fixed-role therapy does not aim at the readjustment of minor parts. Instead, it aims at the reconstruction of a personality. It offers a new role, a new personality for the client in which new hypotheses can be tested out; it offers the client the opportunity to test out new ways of construing events under the full protection of "make-believe."

Just how does the process of fixed-role therapy work? After a personality sketch is drawn up, it is presented to the client. The client decides whether the sketch sounds like someone he would like to know and whether he would feel comfortable with such a person. This is done to make sure that the new personality will not be excessively threatening to the client. In the next phase of fixed-role therapy, the therapist invites the client to act as if he were that person. For a period of about two weeks, the client is asked to forget who he is and to be this other person. If the new person is called Tom Jones, then the client is told the following: "For two weeks, try to forget who you are or that you ever were. You are Tom Jones! You act like him! You think like him. You talk to your friends the way you think he would talk. You do the things you think he would do! You even have his interests and you enjoy the things he would enjoy!" The client may resist, he may feel that this is play-acting and that it is hypocritical, but he is encouraged, in an accepting manner, to try it out and see how it goes. The client is not told that this is what he should eventually be, but he is asked to assume the new person. He is asked to temporarily give up being himself so that he can discover himself.

During the following weeks, the client eats, sleeps, and feels the role. Periodically, he meets with the therapist to discuss problems in acting the role. There may be some rehearsing of the personality sketch in the therapy session so that the therapist and client will have a chance to examine the functioning of the new construct system when it is actually in use. The therapist must himself be prepared to act as if he were various persons and to accept the invitational mood. He must at every moment "play in strong support of an actor—the client—who is continually fumbling his lines and contaminating his role" (Kelly, 1955, p. 399). The purpose of this entire procedure is to reestablish the spirit of exploration, to establish the construction of life as a creative process. Kelly was wary of the emphasis on being oneself—how could one be anything else? He viewed remaining what one is as dull, uninteresting, and unadventuresome. Instead he suggested that people should feel free to make believe, to play, and thereby to become.

Fixed-role therapy was not the only therapeutic technique discussed or used by Kelly (Bieri, 1986). However, it is one that is particularly associated with personal construct theory, and it does exemplify some of the principles of the personal construct theory of change. The goal of therapeutic change is the individual's reconstruction of him- or herself and others. The individual drops some constructs, creates new ones, does some tightening and loosening, and develops a construct system that leads to more accurate predictions. The therapist encourages the client to make believe, to experiment, to spell out alternatives, and to reconstrue the past in the light of new constructs. The process of therapy is very complex. Different clients must be treated differently, and the resistance to change must be overcome. However, positive change is possible in a situation where a good director assists in the playing of the human drama or a good teacher assists in the development of a creative scientist.

Research in the area of psychotherapy has focused on factors in the construct system and factors in the therapeutic relationship that affect change. As one might expect, there is evidence that superordinate constructs are harder to change than subordinate constructs, presumably because they involve more threat of potential disruption of the construct system. It also appears that constructs must undergo some loosening before change can occur. A critical factor in the loosening process is the recognition of new elements. In this regard it is interesting to note that Landfield (1971) has found that a certain amount of similarity in therapist–client construct systems is necessary to facilitate communication but, at the same time, a certain amount of structural difference appears to facilitate the change process. The psychotherapeutic process, then, can be understood as the therapist–client relationship in which there occur experiences that facilitate the reconstruction of the client's construct system.

Personal construct therapists have attempted to explore the potential utility of Kelly's theory in varied ways and in different settings (Epting, 1984). In some cases, this has involved substantial changes in procedure. In one approach, imagery is used to recall past events, leading to a reconstruction of these events (Morrison & Cometa, 1982). For example, a patient construed her father only in negative terms. However, with the use of imagery techniques, the patient was able to recall and imagine scenes in which the father had acted in positive ways, leading to the addition of new constructs or the increased permeability of some constructs. Despite these and related efforts, however, much of Kelly's theory of therapy, what changes and how change occurs, remains unexplored.

A CASE EXAMPLE—RONALD BARRETT

From the phenomenological point of view, and from that of personal construct theory, the client is always right. Although clinicians may choose to construe events differently, they should never ignore the constructions of their clients. Hence, Kelly was led to say: "If you do not know what is wrong with a person, ask him: he may tell you." An approach that is construed as useful in understanding the clients is to have them write a character sketch of themselves. One client who did this was Ronald Barrett, a university student who came to a counseling service with generalized complaints regarding academic, vocational, and social adjustments.

In his self-descriptive character sketch, Ronald Barrett began by indicating that he gives others the impression that he is quiet and calm, and that he dislikes drawing unfavorable attention to himself. Aside from this quiet behavior in public, however, he reported that he was likely to flare up easily. Little anger was shown to others, but he readily became frustrated and worked up about his own errors or those of others. He thought much of his behavior was an effort to impress others and to show that he was considerate and sincere. He considered morals and ethics as guides to behavior, and guilt the result of not being sufficiently kind. Ronald described himself as striving toward being logical, accurate, and aware of minor technicalities. Finally, he described himself as relatively inflexible and as attaching too much importance to kissing a girl.

In his discussion of the sketch, Kelly observed that a conventional approach to it would emphasize its compulsive aspects. However, beyond this view, Kelly suggested an approach in which the effort is made to see the world through the client's own eyes. In his analysis of Ronald's account, Kelly emphasized the need to look at the order in which the material is presented, the way in which it is organized, the terms (inconsiderate, sincerity, conscientiousness, morals, ethics, guilt, kindhearted) that are used, the themes that are repeated, and the similarities and contrasts that are made. In approaching the material in these ways, Kelly made reference to the following:

1. Ronald's vehement assertion that he ought to have the appearance of a quiet and calm personality suggests that he is sensitive to the public. The effort to retain a public mask seems critical.

2. The contrast between external calm and the feeling of sitting on a lid of explosive behavior seems significant. He appears to get upset by behaviors in others which he sees in himself and rejects — the loss of intellectual controls.

3. He reports inconsistencies in his behavior and appears to be aware of breakdowns in his construct system.

4. Sincerity is a key construct and is linked with consideration and kindheartedness. By implication, the characteristics of insincerity, inconsideration, and unkindheartedness are also critical in his construing of events. He appears to vacillate between these poles and to find neither totally satisfactory.

5. He appears to use criticism and correction as an intellectual process through which he can avoid flare-ups. His stress on technicalities is a way of leading a righteous life.

6. Ronald appears to think in terms of "nothing but," preemptive constructs and to think in stereotyped ways. He is concrete in his formulations of events and is not terribly imaginative.

At the time of Ronald's self-description, he had completed a number of therapy sessions. They, however, were not part of a fixed-role therapy program. Such a program was undertaken, and it began with the writing of a fixed-role sketch by a panel of clinicians. The central theme of the sketch was the effort to seek answers in the subtle feelings of others rather than in dispute with them. The sketch, given the name of Kenneth Norton, emphasized attention to feelings. Here is the sketch of "Kenneth Norton" that was presented to Ronald Barrett.

Kenneth Norton

Kenneth Norton is the kind of man who, after a few minutes of conversation, somehow makes you feel that he must have known you intimately for a long time. This comes about, not by any particular questions that he asks, but by the understanding way in which he listens. It is as if he had a knack of seeing the world through your eyes. The things which you have come to see as being important he, too, soon seems to sense as similarly important. Thus he catches not only your words but the punctuations of feeling with which they are formed and the little accents of meaning with which they are chosen.

    Kenneth Norton's complete absorption in the thoughts of the people with whom he holds conversations appears to leave no place for any feelings of self-consciousness regarding himself. If indeed he has such feelings at all, they obviously run a poor second to his eagerness to see the world through other people's eyes. Nor does this mean that he is ashamed of himself, rather it means that he is too much involved with the fascinating worlds of other people with whom he is surrounded to give more than a passing thought to soul-searching criticisms of himself. Some people might, of course, consider this itself to be a kind of fault. Be that as it may, this is the kind of fellow Kenneth Norton is, and this behavior represents the Norton brand of sincerity.

Girls he finds attractive for many reasons, not the least of which is the exciting opportunity they provide for his understanding the feminine point of view. Unlike some men, he does not "throw the ladies a line" but, so skillful a listener is he, soon he has them throwing him one — and he is thoroughly enjoying it.

With his own parents and in his own home he is somewhat more expressive of his own ideas and feelings. Thus his parents are given an opportunity to share and supplement his new enthusiasms and accomplishments.

KELLY, 1955, pp. 374–375

At first, Ronald had trouble in understanding the role he was to play and found that he was not too successful in his role-playing. In the midst of this discouragement, however, he met a former classmate at a movie and found that the role worked better with her than with anyone else. In fact, after a while she was paying him several compliments and indicated that he had changed (presumably for the better) since he had gone away to college. Some role-playing was tried in the therapy sessions. At times, Ronald would lapse back into dominating the conversation. At other times, however, he was able to draw out the therapist, who was now acting the role of various people in Ronald's life. When Ronald performed as Kenneth Norton, the therapist rewarded him with compliments.

Although the early presentations of himself as Kenneth Norton were without spontaneity or warmth, Ronald began to feel more comfortable in the role. He reported to the therapist that he felt less insecure in social situations, that he had fewer quarrels with others, and that he seemed to be more productive in his work efforts. When a difficult situation was described in the session, the therapist asked Ronald how Kenneth Norton would have handled it and then proceeded to engage Ronald in a role-playing rehearsal of the situation. Here, Ronald behaved with greater warmth and spontaneity, and the therapist, congratulated him in an effort to reinforce the new behavior. In general, the therapist tried to reinforce whatever new behavior Ronald exhibited.

The therapy of Ronald Barrett was necessarily incomplete, since after only a few sessions it was time for him to leave school. We are, unfortunately, without data on the exact kinds of changes that did occur and how long they lasted. For example, it would have been interesting to have obtained Ronald's responses to the Rep test before treatment, at the end of treatment, and at some later point in time. This, of course, is the procedure Rogers used in some of his research. In any case, we do have a picture of how a Kellyian might construe an individual and how he might seek to engage a client in a creative process of change.

RELATED POINTS OF VIEW
AND RECENT DEVELOPMENTS

Virtually all personality theorists today attempt to conceptualize cognitive variables, regardless of whether they interpret these variables as only part of the organism or as virtually all of the organism. Kelly's theory was presented at a relatively early stage in the development of this now vigorous trend in the study of personality. In Chapter 1 on theory, it was pointed out that theories are influenced by the Zeitgeist or spirit of the times. It is clear that cognition is part of the current Zeitgeist, although we do not know whether the work of Kelly was merely a forerunner of what was yet to come or itself had an impact on the development. In either case, it is clear that Kelly's theory places great emphasis on the constructions individuals place upon the world, and research associated with the theory has developed within this general orientation.

Although Kelly's theory attracted considerable attention when it was presented in 1955, in the following decade relatively little research was conducted that was tied specifically to the theory. Since then, however, there have been efforts to explore the many leads suggested by personal construct theory. A major focus in this research effort has been the Rep test and the structure of construct systems. There have been studies of the reliability of the Rep test and the evidence to date suggests that the responses of individuals to the role title list and constructs used are reasonably stable over time (Landfield, 1971). Beyond this the Rep test has been used to study a variety of individuals with psychological problems, the construct systems of married couples, and people with varied interpersonal relationships (Duck, 1982). Modifications of the Rep test have been used to study the structural complexity of construct systems, the perception of situations, and, as noted, the use of nonverbal constructs. Indeed, so much research has been conducted on the Rep test that Landfield, a major proponent of personal construct theory, has asked: "'Would we become experimentally paralyzed within Personal Construct Psychology if we accepted a five-year moratorium in the use of the conventional Rep Grids?'" (quoted in Bonarius, Holland, & Rosenberg, 1981, p. 3).

Almost every aspect of Kelly's theory has received at least some research attention (Mancuso & Adams-Webber, 1982). Particularly noteworthy has been the area of investigation of the organization of the construct system and changes in this organization associated with development (Crockett, 1982). The developmental principles emphasized suggest a number of similarities in the developmental theories of both Kelly and Piaget: (1) an emphasis on progression from a global, undifferentiated system to a differentiated, integrated system; (2) increasing use of more abstract structures so as to be able to handle more information more economically; (3) development in response to efforts to accommodate new elements into the cognitive system; (4) development of the cognitive system as a system, as opposed to a simple addition of new parts or elements. At the same time, it is clear that there are differences between the two approaches. For example, Piaget's theory is based on considerable observation of children and is much more advanced than the growth and development views associated with personal construct theory.

Despite the wide variety of research studies and the increasing number of proponents of personal construct theory, certain problems remain. It is to these problems that we now turn as part of our overall critical evaluation of the theory.

CRITICAL EVALUATION

Kelly's theory has been presented as a cognitive theory of personality. Although we discuss it in these terms, it should be recognized that others have construed the theory in different terms and that Kelly himself refused to attach any labels to it. Kelly noted that his theory had been described as humanistic, phenomenological, psychodynamic, existential, and even behavioristic as well as cognitive. Kelly rejected the term cognitive principally because he felt that it was too restrictive and suggested an artificial division between cognition (thinking) and affect (feeling). He rejected phenomenology as being concerned only with subjective reality, and behaviorism as only concerned with objective reality, whereas personal construct theory is concerned with both. If he had to pick a label, Kelly probably would have described himself as a humanist. For Kelly, humanists emphasize what is possible rather than what is inevitable, and are interested in the entire person, in novelty, and in the emancipation of the mind.

Despite these statements, Kelly's theory can be viewed as primarily a cognitive theory in its emphasis on the ways individuals receive and process information about the world and in its use of the Rep test as a way of determining a person's concepts. As such, Kelly's personal construct theory is certainly in the direction of taking (insofar as one can) a cognitive view of behavior. The structural model, with its emphasis on constructs and the construct system, represents a significant contribution to personality theory. The interpretation of behavior in terms of the individual's construing of events is a useful one in theory and in practice. This interpretation allows one to take into consideration the unique aspects of the behavior of individuals and, also, the lawfulness or regularity of much of this behavior. To the extent that Kelly's emphasis on cognitive structures has influenced current research efforts in cognitive style, the theory has made a significant contribution to research. The Rep test, which has the beauty of being derived from the theory, represents an important assessment device. Although it has been criticized by some as so flexible as to be unmanageable (Vernon, 1963), it is also recognized by others as an extremely imaginative technique, quite amenable to quantification (Kleinmuntz, 1967; Mischel, 1968). A remaining, unresolved problem for the Rep test, as well as for the theory as a whole, is that it requires the individual to use words even though it is recognized that preverbal or submerged constructs exist. Given the acknowledged clinical significance of such constructs, the lack of means for assessing them remains a serious limitation.

The process view of Kelly has a number of interesting facets to it. It clearly represents a departure from the drive-reduction or tension-reduction views of Freud and other theorists. In the suggestion that the individual dislikes both the monotony of the ticking of a clock and the threat of the completely unknown, personal construct theory is similar to other views that suggest that the individual experiences small degrees of variety as pleasurable and large degrees of variety or no variety at all as unpleasurable. However, the process view leaves open a number of issues. The basis for action of an individual is not really clear. For example, how does the individual know which construct will be the best predictor? How does one know which end of the construct (similarity or contrast) to use? Also, what determines the individual's response to invalidation (Sechrest, 1963)? Finally, in relation to the process view, what determines whether individuals will choose, in the face of threat, to risk change in their system or to retreat into the conservative strategies of the old system? One would guess that this choice would depend on the external conditions under which a prediction needed to be made, how critical the constructs involved were to the construct system, and the past experiences of the individual with the language of hypothesis. Considerations such as these are involved in Kelly's conceptualization of the process of therapy and construct change, but they are not made as explicit as would be desirable for research purposes.

In his review of Kelly's theory, Bruner (1956) referred to it as the single greatest contribution of the decade between 1945 and 1955 to the theory of personality functioning. There is clearly much to the theory that is new and worthwhile. However, there are some areas of psychology that appear to be more within the range of convenience of the psychology of personal constructs than are other areas. For example, until recently the theory has had little to say about growth and development. The theory offers an interesting analysis of anxiety, but it has almost nothing to say about the important emotion of depression. In fact, for all its worthwhile emphasis on cognition, the theory offers a limited view of the person. Although Kelly denied the charge, the theory is noticeably lacking in emphasis on human feelings and emotions. In his review, Bruner stated that people may not be the pigs that reinforcement theory makes of them, but he wondered also whether people are only the scientists that Kelly suggests. Bruner commented further as follows: "I rather suspect that when some people get angry or inspired or in love, they couldn't care less about their systems as a whole! One gets the impression that the author is, in his personality theory, overreacting against a generation of irrationalism" (Bruner, 1956, p. 356). Despite efforts to come to grips with the area of human emotions (McCoy, 1981), many interpretations within the context of personal construct theory seem strained and, on the whole, human emotions remain an area outside of its range of convenience.

Two additional relevant issues are worthy of consideration. First, although there has been considerable investigation of construct systems, there remains little evidence that measures of these systems are related to overt behavior (Crockett, 1982; Duck, 1982). The theory would certainly suggest that this is the case, but evidence is needed. Second, significant problems remain with Kelly's theory of motivation. As noted, Kelly failed to be specific about the basis for many decisions people make in relation to the functioning of their construct systems. Beyond this, one finds elements of more traditional views of motivation entering into discussion by personal construct theorists. For example, the suggestion is made that people do not like boredom or surprise (Mancuso & Adams-Webber, 1982). However, as noted, emphases on intermediate degrees of novelty or stimulation have typically been associated with pleasure, reinforcement, or hedonic theories of motivation. One may also note how such an emphasis on emotion or pleasure enters into clinical discussion. For example, Landfield (1982) suggests that a person chooses that end of a construct that is positively valued. Furthermore, in his discussion of a case he suggests that the patient stopped having an affair for basically emotional rather than purely cognitive reasons: "After all, she did like her husband better than her lover" (p. 203).

A final note in the evaluation of Kelly's theory concerns its current status as a basis for active research. Clearly there has been activity and growing interest as expressed in the development of an international newsletter, the holding of yearly international meetings devoted to personal construct theory, and the publication of books reporting noteworthy research efforts. However, two recent reviews of these efforts question whether substantial progress is being made as opposed to development being held back by reverence, insularity, and orthodoxy. Thus, Rosenberg suggests that "there is a serious question concerning whether a continuation along the same lines will sustain the aliveness of the theory" (1980, p. 899) and Schneider criticized the papers he reviewed because they "communicated little sense of excitement about major new possibilities or developments. There is almost no criticism of Kelly's original ideas, which tend to be treated as revealed truths" (1982,

p. 712). As noted some time ago by a follower of Kelly, without new ideas no theory of personality can survive (Sechrest, 1977).

It is now over thirty years since the publication of Kelly's theory and twenty years since his death. A recent review of personal construct psychology assessed the impact of Kelly's ideas over this time and suggested that, except for a group of enthusiasts, his ideas are relatively neglected (Jankowicz, 1987). This is less true in England, where Kelly's ideas are widely known and are part of the training of most clinicians. However, in this country, although his ideas are respected by many, they have had relatively little impact on the field in general. Why should this be the case? Two factors appear to be relevant. First, Kelly was a rather reserved and private person. Thus, he did not spread his own word and did not have many graduate student disciples who advanced his view. Second, in attempting a radical departure from traditional views, Kelly set himself and his work apart from that of others: "It was part of Kelly's character that he avoided forging the links of his ideas to those of others" (Bieri, 1986, p. 673). They, in turn, to a great extent ignored his views as well.

In sum, personal construct theory has both strengths and limitations (Figure 8.2). On the positive side, there is the following: (1) The theory makes a significant contribution by bringing to the forefront of personality the importance of cognition and construct systems. (2) It is an approach to personality that attempts to capture both the uniqueness of the individual and the lawfulness of people generally. (3) It has developed a new, interesting, and theoretically relevant assessment technique, the Rep test. On the negative side, there is the following: (1) The theory shows relative neglect of certain important areas such as emotion and

STRENGTHS	LIMITATIONS
1. Places emphasis on cognitive processes as a central aspect of personality.	1. Has not led to research that *extends* the theory.
2. Presents a model of personality that provides both for the lawfulness of general personality functioning and the uniqueness of individual construct systems.	2. Leaves out or makes minimal contributions to our understanding of some significant aspects of personality (growth & development, emotions).
3. Includes a theory-related technique for personality assessment and research (Rep Test).	3. Is not as yet connected with more general research and theory in cognitive psychology.

FIGURE 8.2 Summary of Strengths and Limitations of Personal Construct Theory

motivation. (2) Despite Kelly's view that theories are there to be reformulated and abandoned, no one since 1955 has formulated any significant new theoretical developments in personal construct theory.

With this presentation of Kelly's theory, we have completed our consideration of three personality theories formulated largely on the basis of clinical data. It may be useful now to take stock of the three theories. Following the spirit of personal construct theory, we consider a pair of theories together and finally all three to see the points of comparison and constructs that seem relevant.

Kelly and Freud

Although Kelly was extremely critical of psychoanalytic theory, he appreciated the many important observations and clinical contributions that were made by Freud. The criticisms of Freud are mainly in three areas—Freud's view of the person, the considerable dogmatism in psychoanalytic thinking, and the weaknesses of psychoanalysis as a scientific theory. Kelly was critical of Freud's view of the person-the-biological-organism, and substituted instead the view of person-the-scientist. Kelly was critical of Freud's metaphors and his emphasis on unconscious drives and instincts.

Kelly placed great reliance on understanding the individual's construction of events and on the tentativeness with which theories are put forward. Both of these reflect an open-minded attitude. Against this background, Kelly was critical of Freud's emphasis on understanding what clients mean by examining what they *do not* say. For Kelly, this approach makes psychoanalysis needlessly dogmatic and close-minded. Furthermore, Kelly viewed the followers of Freud as unnecessarily opposed to change.

The third area of major criticism of psychoanalysis was its standing as a scientific enterprise. Kelly observed that Freud's observations of the unconscious were difficult to explore scientifically. As far as Kelly was concerned, the psychoanalytic movement had shunned scientific methodology in favor of impressionist observation. Hypotheses were so elastic that they could not be invalidated. They were what Kelly called "rubber hypotheses"—they could be stretched to fit any kind of evidence. For Kelly, this was the most vulnerable point of psychoanalysis.

Although Kelly was critical of psychoanalysis, he also believed that the psychoanalytic system of dynamics permitted the clinician to determine that something was going on inside the client. According to Kelly, Freud made many astute observations, and his adventurousness helped to open up the field of psychotherapy for exploration. What is particularly striking in reading Kelly is the number of times that he seems to be describing phenomena that were also described by Freud, even though he may interpret them in a different way. For example, Kelly placed great emphasis on the closeness of opposites, a view quite evident in

Freud's thinking. In fact, in dreams, ideas were frequently represented by their opposites. Both Freud and Kelly were sensitive to the fact that the way people view others may also be expressive of views they hold about themselves; both were aware that one is threatened only by something that seems plausible and that one "protests too much" about things one does not want to acknowledge to be true; both viewed people as at times functioning in relation to principles they are unaware of, although in one case the concept of the unconscious was emphasized, whereas in the other the emphasis was on preverbal constructs; both noted that at times an individual may feel uncomfortable with praise, although in one case the concept of guilt was stressed and in the other the emphasis was on the strangeness of new praise and the complex internal reorganization it could imply; both placed emphasis on the concept of transference in therapy; both believed that clients should not get to know their therapists too well and that therapists should avoid social contacts with their clients; both felt that diagnoses could be useful in treatment; both felt that patients are resistant to change; both felt that free associations and dreams could be useful in understanding the person's functioning; and both believed that there was a relationship between the thinking found in some forms of pathology and that found in creative people. In Freud's case, an emphasis on primary process thinking was found in both psychopathology and creativity; for Kelly, there was an emphasis on the process of construct loosening. In addition, Freud, too, saw people as scientists: "Scientific thought is, in its essence, no different from the normal process of thinking, which we all, believers and unbelievers, alike, make use of when we are going about our business in everyday life" (Freud, 1933, p. 232). It is not surprising that the theories of Freud and Kelly share a number of observations, since the foci of convenience of the two theories are somewhat similar.

Kelly and Rogers

There also are a number of similarities in the works of Kelly and Rogers. Both view the person as more active than reactive; both theories emphasize the phenomenological approach, although Kelly believed that personal construct psychology was not just phenomenology. In both, there is an emphasis on consistency, although for Rogers this is on self-consistency per se, and for Kelly it is so that predictions can add up rather than cancel each other out. Both stress the total system functioning of the organism.

Probably, their common emphasis on the phenomenological approach and their common avoidance of a drive model of human functioning lead to the appearance of considerable similarity between Kelly and Rogers. At one point, Kelly asked a question that would be quite characteristic of Rogers: "Is the therapist ever more familiar with the client's construct system than the client is himself?" His answer was clear. "We think not" (Kelly, 1955, p. 1020). Despite these similarities, however, there are major differences between the two theories. Kelly places considerably less emphasis on the self than does Rogers. Also, although Kelly agreed with Rogers that the present is what counts most, he refused to take a completely ahistorical approach toward behavior. Kelly was interested in the past because individuals' perceptions of their past give clues to their construct system and because a reconstruing of the past can be an important element in treatment. In general, Kelly was interested in a whole range of clinical phenomena (e.g., transference, dreams, diagnosis, the importance of preverbal constructs), which brought him closer to Freud than to Rogers in this regard.

Kelly viewed Rogers' position as more of a statement of philosophical convictions about the nature of the person than a true psychological theory. Kelly was critical of the Rogerian principle of growth and contrasted it with personal construct theory. Whereas the former emphasized an unfolding of inner potential, the latter emphasized the continuous development of a changing and everexpanding construct system. Whereas Rogers emphasized the importance of being and becoming, Kelly emphasized the importance of make-believe and doing. The difference has important ramifications for treatment, a point that was made explicit by Kelly:

> The nondirectionist, because of his faith in the emerging being, asks the client to pay attention to himself as he reacts with his everyday world. Somewhere the mature self is waiting to be realized. The nondirective therapist is hesitant to say what the self is, so he prefers to hold a mirror before the client in which can be seen the reflections of those vague stirrings of life which are called feelings. The personal-construct psychologist, because he sees life proceeding by means of a series of hypotheses, and validating experiences, may hold the same mirror, but he sees that mirror, and the image of validating experience which it reflects, as setting up the succession of targets toward which the growth is directed. The personal-construct psychologist is probably more inclined to urge the client to experiment with life and to seek his answers in the succession of events which life unveils than to seek them within himself. . . . He urges the client to see himself in terms of an ever emerging life role rather than in terms of a self which approaches a state of maturity.
>
> KELLY, 1955, pp. 401–402

Kelly greatly emphasized the verbal fluency and acting skill of the therapist. He opposed the view that the therapist must be known as a real person and was critical of phenomenologically oriented therapists who became involved in "lovely personal relationships." The differences between Kelly and Rogers as people are important and translate themselves into views concerning therapy. Rogers (1956), in his review of Kelly's work, expressed the belief that Kelly had found an approach congenial to his personality. However, he was critical of what he thought was Kelly's interpretation of therapy as an intellectual process. Rogers was influenced by Kelly and used the concepts of construct complexity and construct flexibility in his analysis of changes in therapy. However, Rogers was critical of the excessive amount of activity and control assumed in fixed-role therapy. For Rogers, therapy is much more a process of feeling than of thinking, and it is important that therapists be capable of being congruent and not that they be skillful in manipulating the situation. "An overwhelming impression is that, for Kelly, therapy is seen as almost entirely an intellectual function, a view which should be comforting to many psychologists. He is continually thinking about the client, and about his own procedures, in ways so complex, that there seems no time or room for entering into an emotional relationship with the client" (Rogers, 1956, p. 358).

Kelly, Freud, and Rogers

In their study of suicide, Farberow and Schneidman (1961) obtained the ratings by Kelly of a patient, along with the ratings by a Freudian, a Rogerian, and members of other schools of thought. In general, Kelly's ratings of the case, and presumably therefore his interpretation of it, were much more similar to those made by the Rogerian than to those made by the Freudian. In commenting on this study, Kelly (1963) noted that the theories could perhaps be understood in terms of their likenesses and differences. In his own analysis of the ratings, Kelly differentiated the theories according to the attention given to interpersonal relations, with construct psychology giving the most attention, psychoanalytic theory the least, and Rogerian theory something in between. Another dimension of importance was the attention given to aggression and hostility. Here, the psychoanalytic ratings indicated a considerable degree of emphasis, whereas the ratings by Kelly and the Rogerian suggested much less emphasis. A third dimension related to the attention given to the affective dimension of behavior. Here, the psychoanalytic and Rogerian ratings were quite high, whereas Kelly's indicated much less attention to this area.

Although it is not the only approach toward a comparative analysis of theories, the approach emphasized by Kelly does have merit. Thus, because three elements are the necessary number for the formation of a similarity–contrast, we can now use the three theories before us—those of Freud, Rogers, and Kelly—in developing comparative constructs like the ones mentioned in the preceding paragraph. As we examine other theories in successive chapters, we can seek to develop some new constructs, to drop some old ones, to make some more permeable, and to call others so unique that no further elements can be added.

With the completion of this chapter on Kelly, we bring to a close the analysis of three clinical theories of personality. Regardless of their differences, the three theorists have in common the use of clinical material as the original source of data for their hypotheses. The three theories are different, but then each theorist grew out of a different background, was himself a different personality in interacting with his patients, and had a somewhat different patient (subject) population. It may be that, although each theory differs one from the other, the theories are not mutually exclusive—an issue that will be important for us to consider as further theories are assessed; that is, all personality theories may possibly express the same things but in different terms, or it may be that they have different foci of convenience.

These three clinical theories also share an emphasis on individual differences, an emphasis on qualities within the individual that result in relatively stable behavioral characteristics across situations and over time, and an emphasis on the functioning of all parts of the individual within the context of a total system. Later chapters examine other approaches that have quite different views of the person and science, that use different techniques of assessment, and that focus on different problems in research.

Major Concepts and Summary	[Review concepts from Chapter 7]	
	permeable – impermeable constructs	aggression
	tightening – loosening of constructs	hostility
	constriction – dilation	fixed-role therapy

In this chapter and in the preceding one, we have discussed the personal construct theory of George A. Kelly. The theory is distinguished by its clinical approach, its emphasis on the whole person, the use of the Rep test for assessment purposes, and its emphasis on cognition—how the individual perceives, interprets, and conceptualizes events and the environment. This emphasis is further expressed in the view of people as scientists with their own theories (construct systems) and efforts to anticipate events.

The major structural concept for Kelly is that of a construct. A construct is an interpretation placed on the world by the individual. Constructs can be described in terms of their content and in terms of their characteristic mode of functioning. An individual can be described in terms of the constructs used and in terms of the structural aspects of the construct system (e.g., a complex versus a simple construct system).

A COGNITIVE THEORY OF PERSONALITY: KELLY'S THEORY

The emphasis on the system aspects or interrelationships among constructs again points to the holistic properties of the theory, which emphasize the entire person. The Rep test and its modifications represent the principal means for determining how individuals construe their worlds and thereby for describing the personalities of individuals.

In accounting for the activity of people, Kelly assumes that the person is active; he rejects concepts such as motives, drives, and needs. He accounts for behavior in terms of the fundamental postulate—an individual chooses that alternative that offers the greater possibility for expansion and definition of the system. As scientists choose to pursue research along lines that show promise of developing their theories, people choose to act in ways that will facilitate the expansion and development of the construct system. Anxiety, fear, and threat are experienced when individuals find themselves without constructs applicable to a situation or when they face the possibility of change in their construct systems. At the extremes of functioning, we can choose between confusion and certainty, between anxiety and boredom. Individuals can defend against anxiety and threat by processes such as loosening (making variable, unstable predictions) and tightening (making unvarying predictions). Essentially, the dynamics of functioning involve the interplay between the wish to elaborate the construct system and the desire to avoid the threat of disruption of the construct system.

Under favorable circumstances, the developing individual responds to new elements in the environment with the development of new constructs, more abstract constructs, and a more hierarchical construct system. There is a resemblance here to some of the views of Piaget. For growth and expansion of the construct system to occur, there must be the presence of new elements, relative consistency in the environment so that prediction is possible, and sufficient looseness in the construct system so that new predictions can be attempted. Pathological developments occur when anxiety leads to rigid construct system functioning or to chaotic system functioning in the face of repeated invalidations. This may involve making constructs excessively permeable or impermeable to new information, excessive loosening or tightening in making predictions, or excessive construction or dilation of the overall construct system. This may also involve efforts to extort evidence in support of the construct system from others (hostility).

The psychotherapeutic process of change involves the reconstruction of an individual's construct system so that it leads to more accurate predictions. For this to occur conditions are necessary that are similar to those that facilitate growth: an atmosphere of experimentation, the provision of new elements, and the availability of validating data. Fixed-role therapy was developed as one means of encouraging clients to experience new elements and to experiment with new opportunities for obtaining validating data. The aim is the reconstruction of the construct system, that is, of the entire personality and not a minor readjustment of parts of the person. Improvement occurs because behavior change leads to cognitive change and not because of behavior change itself.

Personal construct theory represents a remarkable effort to interpret a broad range of behavior within a cognitive framework. It has led to the development of a significant assessment device (Rep test) that is more closely linked to a specific theory than almost any other assessment device. In its emphasis on cognitive processes, it is part of the current Zeitgeist and, after a period of slow development in research activity, it recently has been associated with a number of serious research efforts. At the same time, the theory has some major weaknesses. It is difficult to test some parts of the theory and it is only with difficulty that emotions such as love, anger, guilt, and depression are incorporated into its range of convenience. Finally, despite Kelly's emphasis on the invitational mood and on the need for constant elaboration and change in a theory or construct system, there have been no new fundamental developments in the theory since its publication in 1955.

A COGNITIVE THEORY OF PERSONALITY: KELLY'S THEORY

Chapter Nine
Trait Approaches to Personality: Allport, Eysenck, and Cattell

*C*HAPTER FOCUS: In this chapter we review theories and research programs that attempt to identify the basic dimensions of personality. The conceptual unit emphasized is the trait, that is, a broad disposition to behave in a particular way. Two of the three trait theorists, Eysenck and Cattell, use a particular statistical procedure, factor analysis, to determine the basic traits that make up the human personality. The trait approach has been popular in American psychology and comes close to the layman's approach to describing someone's personality. Recently it has come under attack from psychologists who suggest that people's behavior varies much more from situation to situation than is suggested by trait theory.

> *Yet something must account for the recurrences and stabilities in personal behavior . . . we do find that personality is relatively stable over time and in different situational fields. . . . The scientific evidence for the existence of a trait always comes from demonstrating by some acceptable method the consistency in a person's behavior.*
>
> ALLPORT, 1961, pp. 312, 343

> *There is a middle ground between treating all humans as if they were exactly alike, and treating them as if they were all entirely different from each other. This intermediate position is the adoption of some type of typological approach, the delineation of certain important dimensions of personality along which individuals can be ranged (extraversion–introversion would be an example of such a dimension).*
>
> EYSENCK, 1982, p. 3

> *The scientific study of personality seeks to understand personality as one would the mechanism of a watch, the chemistry of the life processes in a mammal, or the spectrum of a remote star. That is to say, it aims at objective insights; at the capacity to predict and control what will happen next; and at the establishment of scientific laws of a perfectly general nature. . . . A trait may be defined as that which defines what a person will do when faced with a defined situation.*
>
> CATTELL, 1979, pp. 1, 14

In the preceding chapters attention was given to one major representative of each theoretical point of view. In this chapter on trait theory attention is given to the views of three theorists. Whereas in earlier chapters it was easy to determine the major figure representative of that school of thought, this is not nearly as easy with trait theory. For some time Gordon W. Allport championed trait theory, but he did relatively little empirical research to further its development. Hans J. Eysenck and Raymond B. Cattell both have made important theoretical and research contributions, Eysenck's influence being greater in Great Britain and Cattell's greater in the United States.

Let us put aside the question of who is the leading theorist or representative of trait theory and consider, instead, the essentials of the point of view itself. It is an approach to personality that has been an influential part of personality theory and research. The basic assumption of the trait point of view is that people possess broad predispositions to respond in particular ways. Such predispositions are called **traits**. In other words, people may be described in terms of the likelihood of their behaving in a particular way—for example, the likelihood of their being outgoing and friendly or their being dominant and assertive. People having a strong tendency to behave in these ways may be described as being high on these traits, for example, high on the traits of "extroversion" and "dominance," whereas people with a lesser tendency to behave in these ways would be described as low on these traits. Although various trait theorists differ on how to determine the traits that make up the human personality, they all agree that traits are the fundamental building blocks of the human personality.

Beyond this, trait theorists agree that human behavior and personality can be organized into a hierarchy. An illustration of this hierarchical point of view comes from the work of Eysenck (Figure 9.1). Eysenck suggests that at its simplest level behavior can be considered in terms of specific responses. However, some of these responses generally are linked to one another and form more general habits. Again, we generally find that groups of habits tend to occur together to form what are called traits. For example, people who prefer meeting people to reading also generally enjoy themselves at a lively party, suggesting that these two habits can be grouped together under the trait of sociability. Or, to take another example, people who act without stopping to think things over also tend to shout back at others, suggesting that these two habits can be grouped together under the trait of impulsiveness. Finally, at an even higher level of organization, various traits may tend to be linked together to form what Eysenck calls types. How we find such traits and determine the hierarchical organization of personality will be discussed shortly. What is important to recognize here is the conceptualization of personality as organized at various levels.

In sum, trait theories suggest that people have broad predispositions to respond in certain ways and that there is a hierarchical organization to

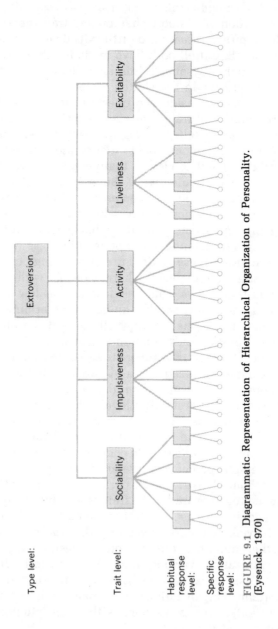

Type level:

Trait level:

Habitual
response
level:

Specific
response
level:

FIGURE 9.1 Diagrammatic Representation of Hierarchical Organization of Personality.
(Eysenck, 1970)

TRAIT APPROACHES TO PERSONALITY

personality. In considering the trait theories of Allport, Eysenck, and Cattell we will see that although differences emerge, these two themes remain constant.

THE TRAIT THEORY OF
GORDON W. ALLPORT (1897–1967)

Gordon W. Allport probably will be remembered more for the issues he raised and the principles he emphasized than for a particular theory. Throughout his long and influential career, he emphasized the human, healthy, and organized aspects of our behavior. This is in contrast with other views that emphasized the animalistic, neurotic, tension-reducing, and mechanistic aspects of behavior. In this regard, he was critical of aspects of psychoanalysis and was fond of telling the following story. At the age of 22, while traveling through Europe, Allport decided that it would be interesting to visit Freud. When he entered Freud's office, he was met with expectant silence as Freud waited to learn of Allport's mission. Finding himself unprepared for silence, Allport decided to start an informal conversation with the description of a four-year-old boy with a dirt phobia, whom he had met on the train. After he completed his description of the boy and his compulsive mother Freud asked, "And was that little boy you?" Allport describes his response as follows:

> Flabbergasted and feeling a bit guilty, I contrived to change the subject. While Freud's misunderstanding of my motivation was

Gordon W. Allport

amusing, it also started a deep train of thought. I realized that he was accustomed to neurotic defenses and that my manifest motivation (a sort of rude curiosity and youthful ambition) escaped him. For therapeutic progress he would have to cut through my defenses, but it so happened that therapeutic progress was not here an issue. This experience taught me that depth psychology, for all its merits, may plunge too deep, and that psychologists would do well to give full recognition to manifest motives before probing the unconscious.

ALLPORT, 1967, p. 8*

Allport's first publication, written with his older brother Floyd, centered on traits as an important aspect of personality theory (Allport & Allport, 1921). Allport believed that traits are the basic units of personality. According to him, traits actually exist and are based in the nervous system. They represent generalized personality dispositions that account for regularities in the functioning of a person across situations and over time. Traits can be defined by three properties—frequency, intensity, and range of situations. For example, a very submissive person would *frequently* be *very* submissive over a *wide range of situations.*

Allport made a distinction among **cardinal traits, central traits,** and **secondary dispositions.** A cardinal trait expresses a disposition that is so pervasive and outstanding in a person's life that virtually every act is traceable to its influence. For example, we speak of the Machiavellian person named after Niccolò Machiavelli's portrayal of the successful Renaissance ruler, of the sadistic person named after the Marquis de Sade, and also of the authoritarian personality who sees virtually everything in black–white, stereotyped ways. Generally people have few, if any, such cardinal traits. Central traits (e.g., honesty, kindness, assertiveness) express dispositions that cover a more limited range of situations than is true for cardinal traits. Secondary traits represent dispositions that are the least conspicuous, generalized, and consistent. In other words, people possess traits of varying degrees of significance and generality.

It is important to recognize that Allport did not say that a trait expresses itself in all situations independent of the characteristics of the situation. Indeed, Allport recognized the importance of the situation in explaining why a person does not behave the same way all the time. Thus, for example, even the most aggressive people can be expected to modify their behavior if the situation calls for nonaggressive behavior, and even the most introverted person may behave in an extroverted

---

*A particularly amusing aspect of this is that Allport was indeed a person who was neat, meticulous, orderly, and punctual—possessing many of the characteristics associated by Freud with the compulsive personality. Freud may not have been as far off in his question as Allport suggested.

TRAIT APPROACHES TO PERSONALITY

fashion in certain situations. A trait expresses what a person *generally* does over many situations, not what will be done in any one situation. According to Allport, both trait and situation concepts are necessary to understand behavior. The trait concept is necessary to explain the consistency of behavior whereas recognition of the importance of the situation is necessary to explain the variability of behavior.

Allport is known not only for his emphasis on traits but also for his emphasis on the concept of **functional autonomy**. The concept of functional autonomy suggests that although the motives of an adult may have their roots in the tension-reducing motives of the child, the adult grows out of them and becomes independent of these earlier tension-reducing efforts. What originally began as an effort to reduce hunger or anxiety can become a source of pleasure and motivation in its own right. What began as an activity designed to earn a living can become pleasurable and an end in itself. Although originally hard work and the pursuit of excellence can be motivated by a desire for approval from parents and other adults, they can become valued ends in themselves—pursued independent of whether they are emphasized by others. Thus, "what was once extrinsic and instrumental becomes intrinsic and impelling. The activity once served a drive or some simple need; it now serves itself, or in a larger sense, serves the self-image (self-ideal) of the person. Childhood is no longer in the saddle; maturity is" (Allport, 1961, p. 229).

Finally, Allport is known for his emphasis on the uniqueness of the individual. Allport emphasized the utility of **idiographic research,** or the in-depth study of individuals, for the purpose of learning more about people generally. One part of such research involves using materials unique to the individual. For example, Allport published 172 letters from a woman that provided the basis for clinical characterization of her

Functional Autonomy—Sometimes a person may select an occupation for one reason, such as job security, and then remain in it for other motives, such as pleasure in the activity itself.

personality as well as quantitative analysis. Another part of such research involves using the same measures for all people, but comparing an individual's scores on one scale with his or her scores on other scales, rather than with the scores of other people on each scale. For example, it may be more important to know whether a person values being with people more or less than acquiring possessions, rather than whether each is valued more or less than it is valued by others. This aspect of the idiographic approach leads to an emphasis on the pattern and organization of traits within a person rather than an emphasis on how a person stands on each trait relative to other people. Finally, Allport's emphasis on the uniqueness of the individual led him to suggest that there are unique traits for each person that cannot be captured by science. Allport's emphasis on the idiographic approach to research was important and is regaining popularity (Pervin, 1983). However, his emphasis on unique traits was interpreted to mean that a science of personality was not possible and resulted in considerable controversy that did not help to advance the field.

Comment on Allport

In 1924 Allport gave the first course on personality ever taught in the United States and in 1937 published a book on personality (*Personality: A Psychological Interpretation*), which for twenty-five years was a basic text in the field. His interests ranged broadly across social psychology as well as personality. He raised many critical issues and discussed the trait concept with such balance and wisdom that he can still be read with profit today. Thus, for example, Allport (1961) suggested that behavior generally expresses the action of many traits, that conflicting dispositions can exist within the person, and that traits are expressed in part by the person's *selection of* situations as opposed to their *response to* situations. Although Allport emphasized the concept of trait and tried to clarify its relation to the situation, he did little research to establish the existence and utility of specific trait concepts. Similarly, although he believed that many traits were hereditary, he did not conduct research to substantiate this. To consider illustrations of such conceptual and research efforts we must turn to the works of the two remaining trait theorists—Hans J. Eysenck and Raymond B. Cattell.

THE TRAIT-TYPE, FACTOR-ANALYTIC THEORY OF HANS J. EYSENCK (1916–   )

Hans J. Eysenck was born in Germany in 1916 and later fled to England to escape Nazi persecution. His work has been influenced by methodological advances in the statistical technique of factor analysis, by the thinking of European typologists such as Jung and Kretschmer, by the research on heredity of Sir Cyril Burt, by the experimental work on classical conditioning by the Russian physiologist Pavlov, and by the American learning theory of Clark Hull. Although his work has included the sampling of both normal and pathological populations, most of it has been done at the Institute of Psychiatry, Maudsley Hospital, England.

Eysenck is strict in his standards for scientific pursuits and places great emphasis on conceptual clarity and measurement. For this reason he consistently has been one of the harshest critics of psychoanalytic theory. Although he supports trait theory, he has emphasized the need to develop adequate measures of traits, the need to develop a theory that can be tested and is open to disproof, and the importance of establishing biological foundations for the existence of each trait. Efforts such as these are emphasized by Eysenck as being important to avoid a meaningless circularity of explanation whereby a trait is used to explain behavior that serves as the basis for the concept of the trait in the first place. For example, Jack talks to others because he is high on the trait of sociability but we know that he is high on this trait because we observe that he spends lots of time talking to others.

The basis for Eysenck's emphasis on measurement and the development of a classification of traits is the statistical technique of **factor analysis**. Factor analysis is a technique in which one starts with a large number of test items that are administered to many people. The question to be answered is: "To which items do groups of people respond in the same way?" Through a number of statistical procedures, clusters or

Hans J. Eysenck

factors are derived, the items within any single factor being highly related to one another and being slightly related, or not at all related, to items in the other factors. According to trait theory, there are natural structures in personality, and factor analysis allows us to detect them. If things (variables, test responses) move together, that is, if they appear and disappear together, then one can infer that they have some common feature behind them, that they belong to the same unity of personality functioning. Factor analysis assumes that behaviors that function with one another are related. It is a statistical device for determining which behaviors are related to one another and thereby for determining the unities or natural elements in personality.

The process described leads to factors, in this case called traits, that are named in terms of the characteristic that seems common to the items or behaviors that have been found to be related to one another. Through some further statistical procedures Eysenck determines the basic dimensions that underlie the factors or traits that have been found. These basic dimensions are called **types**. Thus, for example, the traits of sociability, impulsiveness, activity, liveliness, and excitability can be grouped together under the type concept of extroversion (Figure 9.1). Though the term "type" is used, it is important to recognize that in fact it is a dimension with a low end and a high end that is being considered, such that people may fall along various points between the two extremes.

In his earlier research Eysenck found two basic dimensions to personality that he labeled as **introversion–extroversion** and **neuroticism** (stable–unstable). The relationship of these two basic dimensions of personality to the four major temperamental types distinguished by the Greek physicians Hippocrates and Galen and to a wider range of personality characteristics is presented in Figure 9.2. Since the earlier emphasis on these two dimensions, Eysenck has added a third dimension, which he calls **psychoticism**. People high on this dimension tend to be solitary, insensitive, uncaring about others, and opposed to accepted social custom. Eysenck and Long (1986) note that there is considerable support for the existence of these three dimensions in that they have been found in studies of different cultures and there is evidence of an inherited component to each.

A further appreciation of Eysenck's theoretical system can be gained from a more detailed consideration of one of these three dimensions, that of introversion–extroversion. According to Eysenck, the typical extrovert is sociable, likes parties, has many friends, craves excitement, acts on the spur of the moment, and is impulsive. As can be seen, there appear to be two aspects to this dimension, sociability and impulsiveness, that can be separated out to a certain extent but that have been found to be related sufficiently to be linked under the same concept of extroversion. In contrast to these characteristics, the introverted person tends to be quiet, introspective, reserved, reflective, distrustful of impul-

      TRAIT APPROACHES TO PERSONALITY

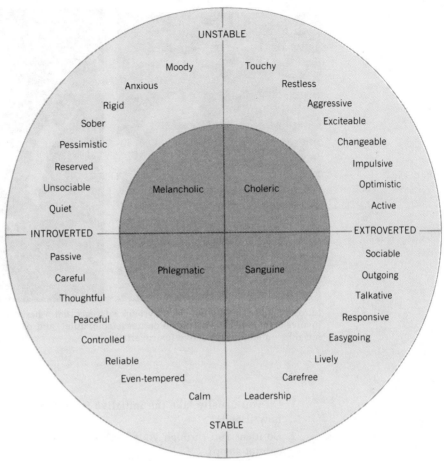

FIGURE 9.2 The Relationship of Two Dimensions of Personality Derived from Factor Analysis to Four Greek Temperamental Types. (Eysenck, 1975)

sive decisions, and to prefer a well-ordered life to one filled with chance and risk.

Eysenck has developed two questionnaires to measure people along the dimension of introversion–extroversion—the Maudsley Personality Inventory and the Eysenck Personality Inventory. The typical extrovert will answer yes to questions such as the following: Do other people think of you as very lively? Would you be unhappy if you could not see lots of people most of the time? Do you often long for excitement? In contrast, the typical introvert will answer yes to these questions: Generally, do you prefer reading to meeting people? Are you mostly quiet when you are with people? Do you stop and think things over before doing anything? Other illustrative items from the Maudsley and Eysenck Personality Inventories are presented in Figure 9.3. These include items relevant

Introversion-Extroversion—Hans Eysenck suggests that a basic dimension of personality involves whether people tend to be unsociable, quiet, and passive (introverts) or sociable, outgoing, and active (extroverts).

	Yes	No
1. Do you usually take the initiative in making new friends?	_____	_____
2. Do ideas run through your head so that you cannot sleep?	_____	_____
3. Are you inclined to keep in the background on social occasions?	_____	_____
4. Do you sometimes laugh at a dirty joke?	_____	_____
5. Are you inclined to be moody?	_____	_____
6. Do you very much like good food?	_____	_____
7. When you get annoyed do you need someone friendly to talk to about it?	_____	_____
8. As a child did you always do as you were told immediately and without grumbling?	_____	_____
9. Do you usually keep "yourself to yourself" except with very close friends?	_____	_____
10. Do you often make up your mind too late?	_____	_____

NOTE: The above items would be scored in the following way: *Extroversion*—1 Yes, 3 No, 6 Yes, 9 No; *Neuroticism*—2 Yes, 5 Yes, 7 Yes, 10 Yes; *Lie Scale*—4 No, 8 Yes.

FIGURE 9.3 Illustrative Items for Extroversion, Neuroticism, and Lie Scale from the Maudsley Personality Inventory and Eysenck Personality Inventory.

TRAIT APPROACHES TO PERSONALITY

to neuroticism and a lie scale to detect individuals faking responses to look good, as well as items relevant to extroversion–introversion. Although the content and direction of scored responses may be obvious in some cases, in other cases this is not true. In addition to such questionnaires, other, more objective, measures have been devised. For example, there is some suggestion that the "lemondrop test" may be used to distinguish between introverts and extroverts. In this test a standard amount of lemon juice is placed on the subject's tongue. Introverts and extroverts differ in the amount of saliva produced when this is done.

Are there other significant and theoretically meaningful differences in behavior associated with varying scores on the extroversion–introversion dimension? A recent review of the dimension presents us with an impressive array of findings. For example, introverts are more sensitive to pain than are extroverts, they become fatigued more easily than do extroverts, excitement interferes with their performance whereas it enhances performance for extroverts, and they tend to be more careful but less fast than extroverts (Wilson, 1978). The following are some additional differences that have been found:

1. Introverts do better in school than extroverts, particularly in more advanced subjects. Also, students withdrawing from college for academic reasons tend to be extroverts whereas those who withdraw for psychiatric reasons tend to be introverts.

2. Extroverts prefer vocations involving interactions with other people whereas introverts tend to prefer more solitary vocations. Extroverts seek diversion from job routine whereas introverts have a lesser need for novelty.

3. Extroverts enjoy explicit sexual and aggressive humor whereas introverts prefer more intellectual forms of humor such as puns and subtle jokes.

4. Extroverts are more active sexually, in terms of frequency and different partners, than introverts are.

5. Extroverts are more suggestible than introverts.

The last finding is interesting in relation to a study of an overbreathing epidemic in England (Moss & McEvedy, 1966). An initial report by some girls of fainting and dizziness was followed by an outbreak of similar complaints, with 85 girls needing to be taken to the hospital by ambulance—"they were going down like ninepins." A comparison of the girls who were affected with those who were not demonstrated, as expected, that the affected girls were higher in both neuroticism and extroversion. In other words, those individuals with a predisposing personality proved most susceptible to influence by suggestions of a real epidemic.

Finally, the results of a recent research investigation of study habits among introverts and extroverts may be of particular interest to college students. The research examined whether such personality differences are associated with differing preferences for where to study and how to study, as would be predicted by Eysenck's theory. In accord with Eysenck's theory of individual differences, the following was found: (1) Extroverts more often chose to study in library locations that provided external stimulation than did introverts. (2) Extroverts took more study breaks than did introverts. (3) Extroverts reported a preference for a higher level of noise and for more socializing opportunities while studying than did introverts (Campbell & Hawley, 1982). Extroverts and introverts differ in their physiological responses to the same noise level (introverts show a greater level of response) and each functions best at their preferred noise level (Geen, 1984). An important implication of such research is that different environmental designs for libraries and residence units might best fit the needs of introverts and extroverts.

What is the theoretical underpinning of this dimension? Eysenck suggests that individual variations in introversion–extroversion reflect differences in neurophysiological functioning. Basically introverts are more easily aroused by events and more easily learn social prohibitions than extroverts. As a result, introverts are more restrained and inhibited. There also is some evidence that introverts are more influenced by punishments in learning whereas extroverts are more influenced by rewards. It is hypothesized that individual differences along this dimension have both hereditary and environmental origins. Indeed, several studies of identical and fraternal twins suggest that heredity plays a major part in accounting for differences between individuals in their scores on this dimension (Shields, 1976).

In sum, the introversion–extroversion dimension represents an important organization of individual differences in behavioral functioning that is rooted in inherited differences in biological functioning. These differences can be discovered through the use of factor analysis and measured through the use of questionnaires as well as in laboratory procedures. Let us now turn to the other two dimensions and at least briefly consider how the theory is extended into other realms, though generally less is known about the psychoticism dimension than is known for the neuroticism dimension. According to Eysenck, people high on neuroticism tend to be emotionally labile and frequently complain of worry and anxiety as well as of bodily aches (e.g., headaches, stomach difficulties, dizzy spells, etc.). Here too an inherited biological difference in nervous system functioning is suggested as the basis for individual differences on this dimension. In this case, the underlying principle is that individuals high on neuroticism respond quickly to stress and show a slower decrease in the stress response once the danger has disappeared than is true for more stable (low neuroticism) individuals. Although less is known about the basis for the psychoticism dimension, here too a genetic association is suggested, in particular one linked with maleness. In general, then, genetic factors play a major role in determining personality and social behavior. Indeed, according to Eysenck, "genetic factors contribute something like two-thirds of the variance in major personality dimensions" (1982, p. 28).

Eysenck's theory of personality is closely linked to his theory of abnormal psychology and behavior change. The kind of symptoms or psychological difficulties one is likely to develop are related to basic personality characteristics and principles of nervous system functioning. For example, according to Eysenck a person develops neurotic symptoms because of the joint action of a biological system and of experiences that contribute to the learning of strong emotional reactions to fear-producing stimuli. Thus, the vast majority of neurotic patients tend to have high neuroticism and low extroversion scores (Eysenck, 1982, p. 25). In contrast, criminals and antisocial persons tend to have high neuroticism, high extroversion, and high psychoticism scores. Such individuals show a weak learning of societal norms.

Despite the strong genetic component in the development and maintenance of such disorders, Eysenck claims that one need not be pessimistic concerning the potential for treatment: "The fact that genetic factors play a large part in the initiation and maintenance of neurotic disorders and also of criminal activities, is very unwelcome to many people who believe that such a state of affairs must lead to therapeutic nihilism. If heredity is so important, they say, then clearly behavior modification of any kind must be impossible. This is a completely erroneous interpretation of the facts. What is genetically determined are predispositions for a person to act and behave in a certain manner, when put in certain situations" (1982, p. 29). Accordingly, it is possible for a person to avoid certain potentially traumatic situations, to unlearn certain learned fear responses, or to learn (acquire) certain codes of social conduct. Thus, while emphasizing the importance of genetic factors, Eysenck has been a major proponent of behavior therapy or the systematic treatment of abnormal behavior according to the principles of learning theory. We will not extend Eysenck's discussion of behavior therapy here since the basic principles will be covered in the chapter on learning foundations of personality (Chapter 10). However, we may conclude our discussion by noting that Eysenck has been a frequent, outspoken critic of psychoanalytic theory and therapy. In particular, his criticism has emphasized the following points: (1) Psychoanalysis is not a scientific theory since it is not falsifiable. (2) Neurotic and psychotic disorders constitute separate dimensions rather than points on a continuum of regression. (3) Abnormal behavior represents learned maladaptive responses rather than disguised expressions of underlying, unconscious conflicts. (4) All therapy involves the application, intended or otherwise, of learning principles. In particular, therapy with neurotic behaviors involves the unlearning or extinction of learned responses (Eysenck, 1979). According to Eysenck, psychoanalysis is not generally an effective method of treatment and succeeds only to the extent that the principles of behavior therapy are unwittingly or accidentally brought into play by the analyst.

Comment on Eysenck

Befitting a trait theorist, Eysenck's scientific record has been consistent in a number of ways. Noteworthy among the positive aspects of this record are the following: (1) Eysenck has been a prolific contributor to diverse areas. In addition to his continuing focus on individual differences and principles of behavior change, he has contributed to the study of criminology, education, aesthetics, genetics, psychopathology, and political ideology. His personality tests have been translated into many foreign languages and used in research around the world. (2) Eysenck has consistently emphasized the value of both correlational and experimental research. Referring to Cronbach's discussion of the two disciplines of scientific psychology (Chapter 2), Eysenck suggests that he has "always looked upon these two disciplines not as in any sense rivals, but as complementary to each other, and indeed each one essential for the success of the other" (1982, p. 4). (3) Eysenck has tied his personality variables to methods of measurement, a theory of nervous system functioning and learning, and an associated theory of psychopathology and behavior change. Significant here is the fact that the theory goes beyond description and can be tested. (4) Historically, Eysenck has been prepared to swim against the tide and argue in favor of unpopular views: "I have usually been against the establishment and in favor of the rebels. Readers who wish to interpret this in terms of some inherited oppositional tendency, some acquired Freudian hatred of father substitutes, or in any other way are of course welcome. I prefer to think that on these issues the majority were wrong, and I was right. But then of course I would think that; only the future will tell" (1982, p. 298).

Given these noteworthy contributions one might wonder, as was done by one recent reviewer of Eysenck's work, why Eysenck has not been "universally celebrated by psychologists everywhere" (Loehlin, 1982, p. 623). Prominent among the reasons for this is Eysenck's tendency to dismiss the contributions of others and exaggerate the empirical support for his own point of view (Buss, 1982, Loehlin, 1982). Most psychologists familiar with Eysenck's work feel that it is significant but that frequently he ignores contradictory findings and overstates the strength of positive results. In relation to this, two additional points can be made. First, alternative models have been proposed that are viewed as better fitting the findings to date. In one such model, it is suggested that individual differences on the dimensions of impulsivity and anxiety are critical (Gray, 1981). Here there is acceptance of the data emphasized by Eysenck and of the import of trying personality variables to biological functions, but different personality dimensions are emphasized. Second, many psychologists feel that it is impossible to account for individual differences with but two or three dimensions. As we shall see in the next section, the trait theorist Cattell suggests that we consider more traits and stay at the trait rather than the type level of personality description. Finally, there are psychologists who oppose the entire trait point of view, an issue that we will address in some detail at the end of this chapter.

THE TRAIT, FACTOR-ANALYTIC APPROACH OF RAYMOND B. CATTELL (1905–   )

Raymond B. Cattell was born in 1905 in Devonshire, England. He obtained a B.Sc. degree in chemistry from the University of London in 1924. Cattell then turned to psychology and obtained a Ph.D. degree at the same university in 1929. Before coming to the United States in 1937, Cattell did a number of studies in personality and acquired clinical experience while directing a child guidance clinic. Since coming to the United States he has held positions at Columbia, Harvard, Clark, and Duke universities. For twenty years he was Research Professor of Psychology and Director of the Laboratory of Personality Assessment at the University of Illinois. During his professional career, he has written more than 200 articles and 15 books.

Although relatively little is known of the experiences that shaped

Raymond B. Cattell

Cattell's life and work, a number of influences seem apparent. First, Cattell's interest in the use of factor-analytic methods in personality research and his attempt to develop a hierarchical theory of personality organization can be related to his associations with two of the same British psychologists who influenced Eysenck: Spearman and Burt. Second, Cattell's views on motivation were influenced by another British psychologist, William McDougall.

His years spent jointly in personality research and clinical experience were a third influence on Cattell. These years sensitized him to the assets and limitations of clinical and experimental research. Finally, Cattell's earlier experience in chemistry influenced much of his later thinking in psychology. In chemistry, the development of the periodic table by Mendeleef in 1869 led to renewed experimental activity. Just as Mendeleef developed a classification of the elements in chemistry, much of Cattell's work can be viewed as an attempt to develop a classification of variables for experimental research in personality. It is factor analysis that will lead psychology to its own periodic table of the elements.

In reading Cattell one gets, at times, the sense of his being unfair in underestimating the contributions of others and in overestimating the conclusiveness of his own findings. However, there is also the wonderful sense of a person who feels that he is on the path of progress and at the brink of discovery. His views are presented in some detail both because of his influence on trait research and because they highlight many important aspects of the trait approach to personality.

Cattell's View of Science, Theory, and Research

An understanding of Cattell's view of science, theory, and research is critical for an understanding of his theory. Cattell ties his research method to his theory of personality more closely than perhaps any other personality theorist. For all his exuberance, Cattell in no way minimizes the difficulties of understanding personality. Research in psychology is difficult because of the intangible and fluid quality of behavior, because of the problem of separating psychology as a science from the daily preoccupation of all humankind, and because of the unique situation in science of scientists studying themselves (Cattell, 1966b). In the face of the complexities of human behavior, Cattell argues that we must have methodological self-awareness instead of unsystematic investigation or compulsive methodology. Furthermore, he contends that we must have a close relationship between research methods and theory. Theory must be based on measurement, but measurement must be meaningful.

Cattell distinguishes among three methods in the study of personality: **bivariate, multivariate,** and **clinical**. The typical *bivariate* experiment, which follows the classical experimental design of the physical sciences, contains two variables, an independent variable that is manipu-

TRAIT APPROACHES TO PERSONALITY

lated by the experimenter and a dependent variable that is measured to observe the effects of the experimental manipulations. In contrast to the bivariate method, the *multivariate* method studies the interrelationships among many variables at once. Furthermore, in the multivariate experiment the investigator does not manipulate the variables. Instead, in multivariate research the experimenter allows life to make the experiments and then uses statistical methods to extract meaningful dimensions and causal connections. The method of factor analysis is illustrative of the multivariate method. Both the bivariate method and the multivariate method express a concern for scientific rigor. The difference between them is that, in the bivariate method, experimenters limit their attention to a few variables that they can manipulate in some way, whereas in the multivariate methods, experimenters consider many variables as they exist in a natural situation.

Cattell is quite critical of the bivariate method. Many of his criticisms are similar to those discussed in Chapter 2 in relation to laboratory research. Thus, he argues that attention to the relationship between two variables represents a simplistic and piecemeal approach to personality. Human behavior is complex and expresses the interactions among many variables. Having understood the relationship between two variables, one is left with the problem of understanding how these relate to the many other variables that are important in determining behavior. Second, the fact that bivariate experimenters attempt to manipulate the independent variable means that they must neglect many matters that are of real importance in psychology. Since the more important emotional situations cannot be manipulated and therefore cannot be used in controlled experiments in humans, the bivariate researcher has been forced to attend to trivia, to look for answers in the behavior of rats, or to look for answers in physiology.

In contrast to the bivariate method, the *clinical* method has the virtues of studying important behaviors as they occur and looking for lawfulness in the functioning of the total organism. Thus, in scientific aims and in philosophical assumptions the clinical method and multivariate method are close to one another and separate from the bivariate method. Both the clinician and the multivariate researcher are interested in global events; both are interested in complex patterns of behavior as they occur in life; both allow life itself to be the source of experimental manipulation; and both are interested in an understanding of the total personality instead of in isolated processes or fragmented pieces of knowledge. The difference between the clinician and the multivariate researcher is that whereas the former uses intuition to assess variables and memory to keep track of events, the latter uses systematic research procedures and statistical analyses. Thus, according to Cattell, "the clinician has his heart in the right place, but perhaps we may say that he remains a little fuzzy in the head" (1959c, p. 45). In the light of these similarities and differences, Cattell concludes that the clinical method is the multivariate method but without the latter's concern for scientific rigor. In sum, Cattell thinks the multivariate method has the desirable qualities of the bivariate and clinical methods (Figure 9.4). The statistical method Cattell associates with multivariate research is *factor analysis*, previously described in relation to the theory of Hans Eysenck. The major difference between the two theorists is that Cattell prefers to work at the trait level whereas Eysenck further factors his data to work at the type level (Figure 9.1).

Cattell's Theory of Personality

Some background factors relating to Cattell's theory of personality now have been examined. The observation has been made that Cattell views behavior as complex and is committed to a multivariate, factor-analytic approach toward description and measurement. It is time now to look at the theory as it stands after thirty years of research.

Structure

Given Cattell's emphasis, one expects him to give considerable attention to the structure of personality. Indeed, in Kelly's terms, we may expect to find the structural aspects of personality to be the focus of convenience of Cattell's theory of personality.

Kinds of traits The basic structural element for Cattell is the **trait,** which was defined earlier as a predisposition. The concept of trait assumes some pattern and regularity to behavior over time and across situations. Among the many possible distinctions between traits, two are of particular importance. The first is that among **ability traits, temperament traits,**

Bivariate	Clinical	Multivariate
Scientific rigor, controlled experiments	Intuition	Scientific rigor, objective and quantitative analysis
Attention to few variables	Consideration of many variables	Consideration of many variables
Neglect of important phenomena	Study of important phenomena	Study of important phenomena
Simplistic, piecemeal	Interest in global events and complex patterns of behavior (total personality)	Interest in global events and complex patterns of behavior (total personality)

FIGURE 9.4 Cattell's Description of Bivariate, Clinical, and Multivariate Research Methods.

TRAIT APPROACHES TO PERSONALITY

and **dynamic traits,** and the second is that between **surface traits** and **source traits.**

Ability traits relate to skills and abilities that allow the individual to function effectively. Intelligence would be an example of an ability trait. Temperament traits relate to the emotional life of the person and the stylistic quality of behavior. Whether one tends to work quickly or slowly, be generally calm or very emotional, or act after deliberation or impulsively have to do with qualities of temperament that vary from individual to individual. Dynamic traits relate to the striving, motivational life of the individual, the kinds of goals that are important to the person. Ability, temperament, and dynamic traits are seen as capturing the major stable elements of personality. Undoubtedly we have said some very fundamental things about an individual's personality if we are able to describe them in terms of their abilities, characteristic style, and important goals.

The distinction between surface traits and source traits relates to the level at which we observe behavior. Surface traits are expressive of behaviors that on a superficial level may appear to go together but in fact do not always move up and down (vary) together and do not necessarily have a common cause. A source trait, on the other hand, expresses an association among behaviors that do vary together to form a unitary, independent dimension of personality. Whereas surface traits can be discovered through subjective methods such as asking people which personality characteristics they think go together, the refined statistical procedures of factor analysis are necessary for the discovery of source traits. These source traits represent the building blocks of personality.

Sources of data: L-data, Q-data, OT-data How do we discover source traits that cover a variety of responses across many situations? Where do we find our building blocks? According to Cattell, there are three sources of data: life record data **(L-data),** questionnaire data **(Q-data),** and objective test data **(OT-data).** The first, L-data, relates to behavior in actual, everyday situations such as school performance or interactions with peers. These may be actual counts of behaviors or ratings made on the basis of such observations. The third, OT-data, involves behavioral miniature situations in which the subject is unaware of the relationship between their response and the personality characteristic being measured. According to Cattell, if multivariate, factor-analytic research is indeed able to determine the basic structures of personality, then the same factors or traits should be obtained from the three kinds of data. This is an important, logical, and challenging commitment.

Originally Cattell began with the factor analysis of L-data and found fifteen factors that appeared to account for most of personality. He then set out to determine whether comparable factors could be found in Q-data. Thousands of questionnaire items were written and administered to large numbers of normal people. Factor analyses were run to see which items went together. The main result of this research is a questionnaire known as the *Sixteen Personality Factor* (16 P.F.) *Inventory*. Although Cattell did not label his personality factors (traits) in standard terms, so as to avoid misinterpretation of them, the terms associated with these traits are presented in Figure 9.5. As can be seen, they cover a wide variety of aspects of personality, particularly in terms of abilities and temperament. In general, the factors found with Q-data appeared to be similar to those found with L-data, but some were unique to each kind of data. Illustrative L-data ratings and Q-data items for one trait are presented in Figure 9.6.

Cattell is committed to the use of questionnaires, in particular, factor analytically derived questionnaires such as the 16 P.F. On the other hand, he also has expressed concern about the problems of motivated distortion and self-deception in relation to questionnaire responses. Also, he feels that the questionnaire is of particularly questionable utility with mental patients. Because of problems with L-data and Q-data, and because the original research strategy itself called for investigations with objective test (OT) data, Cattell's efforts have been concerned more recently with personality structure as derived from OT-data. It is the source traits as expressed in objective tests that are the "real coin" for personality research.

The results from L-data and Q-data research were important in guiding the development of miniature test situations; that is, the effort was to develop objective tests that would measure the source traits

Reserved	Outgoing
Less intelligent	More intelligent
Stable, Ego Strength	Emotionality/Neuroticism
Humble	Assertive
Sober	Happy-go-lucky
Expedient	Conscientious
Shy	Venturesome
Tough-minded	Tender-minded
Trusting	Suspicious
Practical	Imaginative
Forthright	Shrewd
Placid	Apprehensive
Conservative	Experimenting
Group-dependent	Self-sufficient
Undisciplined	Controlled
Relaxed	Tense

FIGURE 9.5 Cattell's Sixteen Personality Factors Derived from Questionnaire Data.

TRAIT APPROACHES TO PERSONALITY

SOURCE TRAIT EGO STRENGTH VS. EMOTIONALITY/
NEUROTICISM (L- AND Q-DATA)

Behavior ratings by observer

Ego Strength		Emotionality/Neuroticism
Mature	vs	Unable to tolerate frustration
Steady, persistent	vs	Changeable
Emotionally calm	vs	Impulsively emotional
Realistic about problems	vs	Evasive, avoids necessary decisions
Absence of neurotic fatigue	vs	Neurotically fatigued (with no real effort)

Questionnaire responses

Do you find it difficult to take no for an answer even when what you want to do is obviously impossible?
  (a) yes   (b) *no*

If you had your life to live over again, would you
  (a) *want it to be essentially the same?*   (b) Plan it very differently?

Do you often have really disturbing dreams?
  (a) yes   (b) *no*

Do your moods sometimes make you seem unreasonable even to yourself?
  (a) yes   (b) *no*

Do you feel tired when you've done nothing to justify it?
  (a) *rarely*   (b) often

Can you change old habits, without relapse, when you decide to?
  (a) *yes*   (b) no

*Answer in italic type indicates high ego strength.

FIGURE 9.6 Correspondence between Data from Two Different Test Domains: L-Data Ratings and Q-Data Responses. (Cattell, 1965)

already discovered. Thus, for example, tendencies to be assertive might be expressed in behaviors such as long exploratory distance on a finger maze test, fast tempo in arm-shoulder movement, and fast speed of letter comparisons. More than 500 tests were constructed to cover the hypothesized personality dimensions. The result of administering these tests to large groups of subjects and repeated factoring of data from different research situations has been the establishment of twenty-one OT-data source traits.

As mentioned before, the source traits or factors found in L-data and Q-data could, for the most part, be matched to one another. How, then, do the OT-data factors match up with those derived from L-data and Q-data? Several relationships have been found between L-data and Q-data

"THE RIGHT STUFF"—CHARACTERISTICS
OF SUCCESSFUL BUSINESS EXECUTIVES

Some time ago Tom Wolfe wrote a book about the United States' first team of astronauts. At the time an all male group, these were men who felt that they had the right stuff—the manly courage it took to make it as a test pilot and astronaut. Others had the necessary skill, but if they didn't have the right stuff they just didn't make it.

Most demanding occupations have their own kind of right stuff—the personality characteristics or traits that, in addition to skill, make for success. For example, what makes for a top business executive? According to some recent research, the difference between those senior executives who make it to chief executive officer and those who do not often is subtle. Members of both groups show considerable talent and have remarkable strengths as well as a few significant weaknesses. Although no one

trait discriminates between the two groups, those who fall short of their ultimate goal frequently are found to have the following characteristics: insensitivity to others, untrustworthy, cold–aloof–arrogant, overly ambitious, moody, volatile under pressure, and defensive. In contrast, the successful executives are most characterized by the traits of integrity and understanding others.

Actually, there is a long history of efforts to define the abilities and personal qualities of leaders. At one point, researchers began to give up on the hope of finding general leadership qualities. Leadership was seen as entirely situational in origin, with different skills and personal qualities being required in different situations. However, a recent review of the literature suggests that sounding the death bell of a trait approach to leadership probably was premature. Certain general qualities such as courage, fortitude, and conviction do stand out. In addition, the following traits seem to be generally characteristic of leaders: energetic, decisive, adaptive, assertive, sociable, achieving, and tolerant of stress.

Trait researchers, particularly those in industrial psychology, continue to try to define those personality characteristics that are essential for success in various fields. A variety of personality tests, including the 16 P.F., are then used in many important aspects of personnel selection.

SOURCES: *Psychology Today*, February, 1983; Bass, 1981.

"The Right Stuff"—Success in different occupations requires possessing certain traits. Sally Ride is America's first female astronaut to be a member of the crew aboard the space shuttle.

factors on the one hand and OT-data factors on the other. However, no simple "point-to-point" relationship has been found.

The issue of the matching of factors in the three kinds of observation—ratings, questionnaires, and objective tests—is highly complex. It will be returned to in the critique and evaluation section. For now, what has been said in this section can be summarized by stating the following: (1) Cattell set out to define the structure of personality in three areas of observation, called L-data, Q-data, and OT-data. (2) He started his research with L-data and through the factor analysis of ratings came up with fifteen source traits. (3) Guided in his research on Q-data by the L-data findings, Cattell developed the 16 P.F. Inventory, which contains twelve traits that match traits found in the L-data research and four traits that appear to be unique to questionnaire methods. (4) By using these results to guide his research in the development of objective tests, Cattell found twenty-one source traits in OT-data that appear to have a complex relationship to the traits previously found in the other data.

The source traits found in the three types of observation do not complete Cattell's formulation of the structure of personality. However, the traits presented in this section do describe the general nature of the structure of personality as formulated by Cattell. In other words, here we have the foundation for psychology's table of the elements—its classification scheme. But what is the evidence for the existence of these traits? Cattell (1979) cites the following: (1) The results of factor analyses of different kinds of data. (2) Similar results across cultures. (3) Similar results across age groups. (4) Utility in the prediction of behavior in the natural environment. (5) Evidence of significant genetic contributions to many traits.

Process

Although Cattell has been concerned with the consistency of behavior and the structure of personality, he has also been concerned with process and motivation. As with the earlier traits, his efforts to determine dynamic traits, the motivational sources of behavior, continue to involve an emphasis on factor analysis (Cattell, 1984). His analysis of the courses of action people take in specific situations, and the patterns of behaviors that go together, has led him to conclude that human motivation consists of innate tendencies, called **ergs,** and environmentally determined motives, called **sentiments**. Illustrative ergs are security, sex, and self-assertion. Illustrative sentiments are religious ("I want to worship God."), career ("I want to learn skills required for a job."), and the self-sentiment ("I want never to damage my self-respect."). Generally our activities involve the effort to satisfy many motives and efforts to satisfy sentiments are made in the service of the more basic ergs or biological goals.

Clearly Cattell does not view the person as a static entity or as behaving the same way in all situations. How a person behaves at any one time depends on the traits and motivational variables relevant to the situation. In addition, two other concepts are of particular importance in relation to accounting for variability in behavior—states and roles. The concept of **state** relates to emotional and mood changes that are partly determined by the provocative power of specific situations. Illustrative states are anxiety, depression, fatigue, arousal, and curiosity. Whereas traits describe *general* action patterns, Cattell emphasizes that the *exact* description of an individual at a given moment requires measurement of both traits and states: "Every practicing psychologist—indeed every intelligent observer of human nature and human history—realizes that the state of a person at a given moment determines his or her behavior as much as do his or her traits" (1979, p. 169). In other words, behavior in a particular situation cannot be predicted from traits alone without regard for whether the person is angry, tired, fearful, and so on.

The second important transient influence relates to the concept of **role**. According to Cattell, certain behaviors are more tied up with environmental situations than with the general run of personality factors. Thus, customs and mores may modify the influence of personality traits so that "everyone may shout lustily at a football match, less lustily at dinner, and not at all in church" (1979, p. 250). In addition, the concept of role gives expression to the fact that the very same stimulus is perceived in a different way by an individual according to his or her role in the situation. For example, a teacher may respond differently to a child's behavior in the classroom than when no longer in the role of teacher.

In sum, although Cattell believes that personality factors lead to a certain degree of stability to behavior across situations, he also believes that a person's mood (state) and the way he is presenting himself in a given situation (role) will influence his behavior: "How vigorously Smith attacks his meal depends not only on how hungry he happens to be, but also on his temperament and whether he is having dinner with his employer or is eating alone at home" (Nesselroade & Delhees, 1966, p. 583). Cattell's theory suggests that behavior expresses the individual's traits that operate in a situation, the ergs and sentiments associated with attitudes relevant to a situation, and the state and role components that may vary from time to time or situation to situation.

Growth and development

Cattell has been concerned with two major issues relevant to the growth and development of personality—the determinants of personality and the pattern of development of the structural traits. Like most personality theorists, Cattell emphasizes the importance of both heredity and learning—of nature and nurture—in the development of personality. However, he is virtually unique among major personality theorists in that he has tried to determine the specific environment and hereditary contributions to each trait. He has done this by administering a number of personality tests to the members of many families and then analyzing patterns of scores within and between families. Cattell suggests from such analyses that the importance of genetic and environmental influences varies from trait to trait. For example, heredity is thought to account for from 80 to 90 percent of the variation found in scores on a measure of the intelligence ability trait, whereas the genetic influence on neuroticism is perhaps half that. Overall an estimate has been made that personality is about two-thirds determined by environment and one-third by heredity (Hundleby, Pawlik, & Cattell, 1965).

In terms of developmental patterns, Cattell has conducted research on age trends, that is, the kinds of traits and general levels of traits associated with each stage of development. Age-trends research also involves the study over time of the development of each trait. Much of the age-trends research suggests that the same underlying factors can be found, both in number and in kind, in subjects from age four through adulthood (Coan, 1966). On the other hand, a study of nursery school children indicated that only about one-third of the traits found in adults are found in children (Damarin & Cattell, 1968).

Clinical Applications of Cattell's Theory

Basic to Cattell's approach to psychopathology is his effort to find concrete differences between normal people and members of various patient groups (Cattell & Rickels, 1964; Cattell & Tatro, 1966; Rickels & Cattell, 1965). In an important study of neuroticism and anxiety, it was found that neurotics differ from normals on several factors. Furthermore, it was found that anxiety is only one of many factors contributing to neurosis, that is, anxiety is a part, but not all, of neurosis (Cattell & Scheier, 1961). Some factors, such as anxiety, appear to be important for all forms of neurosis whereas other factors are important only to some forms of neurosis. For example, low scores on surgency, indicative of restraint and reticence, are characteristic only of depressives. Psychotics have been found to differ from normals in personality source traits, but in ways different from that of neurotics. Psychotics share with neurotics low scores on ego strength but do not deviate on anxiety in the striking way neurotics do (Cattell & Tatro, 1966).

These are some of the results from Cattell's research into psychopathology. The major aspects of this approach are the effort to define factors experimentally for the general population and, then, the effort to define various types of psychopathology in terms of their unique patterns of scores on these factors. In this sense they are similar to Eysenck's efforts. However, in Eysenck's case there is an underlying theory of learning that enters into his explanation for the development of pathological behavior. Although Cattell has been working on a theory of learning (Cattell, 1980), no comparable explanation is available. Another difference is that whereas Eysenck views psychopathology in terms of specific behaviors, Cattell views pathology in terms of patterns of traits—a more holistic view. Similarly, whereas Eysenck emphasizes changes in specific behaviors in the course of behavior therapy, Cattell emphasizes changes in the overall pattern of personality organization. Finally, Eysenck has specifically been involved with the application of behavior therapy to abnormal behavior, whereas Cattell has not been associated with any particular form of psychotherapy. In sum, an emphasis on traits and the utilization of factor analysis can lead to both similarities and differences among theorists.

Comment on Cattell

One cannot help but be impressed with the scope of Cattell's efforts. His research has touched on almost every dimension we have outlined as relevant to personality theory—structure, process, growth and development, psychopathology, and change. Cattell has been a major force in the development of new factor-analytic techniques and in the development of new techniques for determining the genetic contribution to personality. His work covers almost all age ranges and the use of a wide variety of measurement techniques. Furthermore, he has endeavored to put his work in a cross-cultural perspective. In the words of one supporter: "Cattell's theory turns out to be a much more impressive achievement than has been generally recognized. . . . It seems fair to say that Cattell's original blueprint for personality study has resulted in an extraordinarily rich theoretical structure that has generated more empirical research than any other theory of personality" (Wiggins, 1984, pp. 177, 190).

At the same time, many personality psychologists ignore the work of Cattell and others question the validity of the tests used, the reliance on factor analysis, and the theoretical speculation that at times goes far beyond the data. Also, as was true for Eysenck, overstatement often is characteristic of Cattell. Unfortunately, in being so committed to his point of view he is at times unduly accepting of his own efforts and disparaging of the works of others. For example, the gains of clinical and bivariate approaches are minimized and those of the multivariate approach are overstated.

ALLPORT, EYSENCK, AND CATTELL

We have now considered three trait theorists. Before going on to consider recent trait research and the controversy that has surrounded this point of view, let us take note of the similarities and differences among the three theorists. The basis for presenting these theorists together is that they all have emphasized the trait concept, that is, the view that there are broad dispositions to respond in particular ways. Individuals differ in their characteristic responses to situations and in the situations they seek and create. It is these broad dispositional patterns characteristic of indi-

TRAIT APPROACHES TO PERSONALITY

viduals that form the essence of trait theory. Beyond this, all three theorists suggest a physiological basis for many important traits, as well as an inherited component for many traits.

At the same time, it is clear that there are differences among the three theorists. Whereas Eysenck and Cattell are committed to factor analysis, Allport was highly critical of this approach to personality. On the other hand, Eysenck was highly critical of Allport's emphasis on the uniqueness of personality, in particular of the suggestion of unique traits. How could one have a science of unique traits? Whereas Allport and Cattell focused on the organization of personality, Eysenck has focused much more on specific behaviors. And, whereas Allport and Eysenck have been highly critical of psychoanalysis, Cattell has found himself sympathetic to at least some aspects of the theory. Thus, beyond the basic commitment to what has been called the dispositional point of view, important differences can be found among these and other trait theorists.

CURRENT TRAIT RESEARCH AND THE PERSON–SITUATION CONTROVERSY

Over the past two decades trait theory has come in for considerable criticism because of the emphasis it gives to stable and enduring properties of the person. In particular, critics of trait theory argue that behavior is much more variable from situation to situation than trait theorists suggest (Mischel, 1968). Furthermore, the critics claim that trait theory has proven to be ineffective in predicting behavior. Instead of an emphasis on broad predispositions in the *person* to respond in a certain way, many of these critics emphasize the importance of *situations*, or rewards in the environment, in the control of human behavior. Thus, for some time debate raged over whether regularities in behavior could be accounted for by aspects of the person, such as traits, or by aspects of the situation—the person–situation controversy.

Criticism of the trait conception of personality has focused on two points. First, critics of trait theory suggest that there is a lack of evidence of cross-situational consistency to behavior (Mischel, 1968; Mischel & Peake, 1982). An incredible amount of recent personality research has centered on the question of whether people are or are not consistent over time and, more significantly, across situations. Second, critics of trait theory suggest that traits reflect our conceptions of personality characteristics that we assume go together. In other words, rather than representing *actual* behavioral co-occurrences, traits represent labels for behaviors we *believe* go together (Shweder, 1982). In a sense, the suggestion here is that traits represent constructs or stereotypes rather than actual regularities in behavior. This is particularly possible, it is claimed, where the existence of traits is based on Q-data in which subjects may respond in terms of their systematic distortions of which behaviors they think go with which behaviors. Although the question of the extent of consistency in individual behavioral functioning is an old issue that concerned psychologists in the 1930s, it has lately retaken center stage in personality research.

Before reviewing the defense of trait theorists against the situationist criticism, let us consider three more general aspects of recent trait research. This literature may be considered in the light of three questions: Which traits? Is there evidence of a genetic (inherited) contribution? Is there evidence of trait stability?

Which Traits?

If traits represent the fundamental building blocks of personality, then we need to be concerned with how many and which traits exist. We have already seen that this may not be a straightforward question, since the number of traits emphasized by Eysenck and Cattell is quite different and the same traits may vary, at least to some extent, depending on the data used and the age group studied.

In 1963 a factor-analytic study was reported that has served as a focal point for subsequent investigations (Norman, 1963). Based on earlier research by Allport, Cattell, and others, peer ratings were used and five basic factors were found (Figure 9.7). These have come to be known as **The Big Five** and, as noted, have served as a benchmark in trait research. Subsequent investigations with children and other populations, using ratings and questionnaire data, have found similar factors (Digman & Innouye, 1986; McCrae & Costa, 1987). The one exception here is the suggestion that the last factor trait, culture, might better be described as *openness to experience*, with a person high on this trait being described as original, creative, and daring and a person low on this trait being described as conventional, uncreative, and unadventurous.

Can one then be satisfied that these are the basic building blocks of personality? They have been found in a number of studies, are somewhat similar to factors emphasized by Eysenck and Cattell, and have fairly broad acceptance. At the same time, there is not complete agreement within the field. For example, another group of investigators emphasizes three temperament factors that are found early, for which there is evidence of a strong inherited component, and for which there is evidence of stability over time (Buss & Plomin, 1984). These three temperament traits are **emotionality**, involving the tendency to become easily upset, **sociability**, involving the tendency to prefer to be with others, and **activity**, involving the tendency to be restless and have a high energy level. These temperament traits appear to be somewhat similar, but not identical, to some of the big five.

Various trait theorists emphasize fewer or more than five factors, with many being similar to those in the big five but some also being

Factor Name	Illustrative Scales
I. Extroversion or Surgency	Talkative-Silent Frank, Open-Secretive Adventurous-Cautious Sociable-Reclusive
II. Agreeableness	Goodnatured-Irritable Not Jealous-Jealous Mild, Gentle-Headstrong Cooperative-Negativistic
III. Conscientiousness	Fussy, Tidy-Careless Responsible-Undependable Scrupulous-Unscrupulous Persevering-Quitting, Fickle
IV. Emotional Stability	Poised-Nervous, Tense Calm-Anxious Composed-Excitable Not Hypochondriacal-Hypochondriacal
V. Culture	Artistically Sensitive-Artistically Insensitive Intellectual-Unreflective, Narrow Polished, Refined-Crude, Boorish Imaginative-Simple, Direct

FIGURE 9.7 The Big Five Trait Factors and Illustrative Scales. (Norman, 1963)

different. And, whereas some trait theorists consider the factor traits found as the ultimate building blocks, others suggest that they are best considered as useful ways of organizing information about people (Hogan, 1983).

Are Traits Inherited?

We have already seen that Eysenck and Cattell emphasized the genetic, inherited aspect of traits. Over the past decade an impressive amount of evidence has been gathered supporting the view that many important personality traits have a strong inherited component to them (Rushton, Russell, & Wells, 1985; Tellegen, 1986). As suggested by Cattell, the degree to which a trait is inherited varies from trait to trait (Figure 9.8). Thus, the suggestion of some newspapers that "Personality Traits Are Mostly Inherited" or that "People Are Born, Not Made" has some validity to it, but at the same time represents an oversimplification of the issue. For a long time psychologists, as well as people generally, have been reluctant to accept a view of personality as largely inherited. Such a view is seen as going against certain values. At this point a fair amount of data clearly suggests that important components of personality, in particular

Trait	Description	Percentage
Extroversion	Mixes easily, affable, center of attention	61
Conformity	Follows rules, respects tradition & authority	60
Worry, Stress	Easily distressed, feels vulnerable	55
Creativity	Vivid imagination, becomes lost in thought	55
Alienation	Keeps to oneself, feels exploited	55
Optimism	Confident, cheerful, optimistic	54
Cautiousness	Avoids risks & dangers, prefers safe route	51
Aggression	Aggressive, vengeful, physically violent	48
Ambition	Works hard, strives for goals	46
Control	Rational, cautious, plans carefully	43
Intimacy	Prefers emotional closeness	33

FIGURE 9.8 Estimated Contribution of Heredity to Personality Traits. (Tellegen, 1986)

CURRENT APPLICATIONS   ARE CRIMINALS BORN OR MADE?

The extent to which personality characteristics are inherited is an important question for psychologists and one with potential social implications. Some people suggest that there is an "aggressive personality" and that criminals are born, not made. Others suggest otherwise.

A fair amount of evidence, based on twin studies and adoption studies, suggests that perhaps heredity accounts for as much as 50 percent of individual differences in the trait of aggressiveness. Further, there is growing evidence of a genetic contribution to criminality. For example, identical twins are twice as likely as fraternal twins to be similar in their criminal activity. Also, a close relationship has been found between antisocial behavior in adopted children and such behavior in their biological parents. Sarnoff Mednick, one major investigator

concludes: "These studies all suggest that we should take seriously the idea that some biological characteristics that can be genetically transmitted may be involved in causing a person to become involved in criminal activity."

Does this mean that criminal behavior is inevitable in some people? Not necessarily. When a biological parent but not an adoptive parent had a record of conviction, only a minority of the children later had a record of court convictions. Thus, although genetic influences can lead to the development of criminal behavior, improved social conditions can also reduce the likelihood of such a development.

SOURCES: *Psychology Today*, March, 1985; Rushton & Erdle, 1987.

TRAIT APPROACHES TO PERSONALITY

Inherited Traits—Differences in temperament, such as whether high or low levels of arousal are desired, are thought to be largely inherited.

those relating to temperament, have a strong genetic contribution to them. At the same time, environment contributes to the unfolding and development of all personality characteristics.

Trait Stability?

In considering whether people are stable in their personality traits, we may consider two aspects of such stability: longitudinal and cross-situational. The first, longitudinal, asks whether people high on a trait at one point in time are also high on that trait at another point in time. The second, cross-situational, asks whether people high on that trait in some situations are also high on that trait in other situations. Trait theorists suggest that both are true, that is, that people are stable over time and across situations in their trait personality characteristics. Of course, it is this view, particularly the aspect of cross-situational stability, that is attacked by proponents of a more situationist position.

At this time there is fairly good evidence of the longitudinal stability of traits, even over extended periods of time (Conley, 1985; Rowe, 1987). Undoubtedly this is partly because of the direct genetic contribution to many traits. However, some of the stability may also be due to people with certain traits selecting and molding their environments so as to reinforce their traits. Also, once perceived in a certain way, others may behave toward a person in a way that perpetuates certain personality characteristics. This is not to say that personality is fixed. However, because of the person's own actions and because of stereotypes formed by others, the environment may contribute to the stability of personality.

The issue is more complex in relation to cross-situational consistency, in part because of the complexity in defining evidence of such consistency (Epstein & O'Brien, 1985). It would not make sense for a person to behave the identical way in all situations, nor would trait theorists expect this to be the case. Rather, trait theorists would expect a person to behave *consistently* over a *range of situations*, that is, that various behaviors would be expressive of the same trait and that in most situations a person will behave in a way expressive of that trait. Can a conclusion based on the evidence be reached at this time? A fair judgment might suggest that there is evidence of trait consistency, but this appears to be more within certain domains of situations (e.g., home, school, work, friends, recreation) than across domains of situations. Since people tend to be observed over a limited range of situations, there may appear to be greater consistency than is actually the case. Beyond this, the conclusions drawn vary with the psychologist's point of view. There is evidence both for cross-situational consistency and for cross-situational variability. To a certain extent people are the same regardless of context, and to a certain extent they also are different depending on the context. Trait theorists are impressed with the former and use such evidence to support their position, whereas situationist theorists are impressed with the latter and use such evidence to support their position (Pervin, 1984, 1985). The issue of consistency brings us once more to the heart of the person–situation controversy, so perhaps it is time to return to this issue.

Trait Defense and Summation

During the early years of the person–situation controversy, the situationist, antitrait point of view predominated; of late, proponents of trait theory have rallied to the defense. Their arguments have taken varied forms, which have focused on the following topics and claims:

TRAIT APPROACHES TO PERSONALITY

1. *Quality of research* Most studies fail to find evidence of consistency and stability because they are poorly conducted. When relevant research is properly conducted, supportive evidence is found (Block, 1977; Olweus, 1981).

2. *Adequacy of sample* One cannot consider single acts or measures of behavior on single occasions as evidence for or against the existence of a trait. Too much error is involved in the measurement of single acts on single occasions. With an adequate sampling of many behaviors over many occasions, one increases reliability of observation and finds evidence of consistency (Epstein, 1982, 1983).

3. *Phenotype–Genotype* Many behaviors that appear to be different (phenotype) may in fact have the same underlying basis (genotype). Thus, what antitrait theorists take to be indicative of lack of consistency may at another level, in fact, be expressive of consistency (Loevinger & Knoll, 1983). If multiple acts are considered to be expressive of the same trait, greater consistency is observed (Buss & Craik, 1983).

4. *Some people more than others.* Some people are more consistent than others. Therefore, one will only find evidence of consistency if one studies people who are consistent on that trait (Bem & Allen, 1974).

5. *Some situations more than others* People will be more consistent in some situations than in others. One consideration here is that people will be more consistent in situations that are low in constraint or weak in pressure to conform (Monson, Hesley, & Chernick, 1982). This point is particularly interesting since the phenomena that impress the clinician concerning evidence of consistency generally show up in those situations that are less structured and more ambiguous or anxiety arousing. Another consideration here is that people may behave similarly in situations perceived by them to be similar (Champagne & Pervin, 1987; Lord, 1982).

6. *Real world versus laboratory* The evidence in support of consistency is better when self-report data and observations in the natural environment are used as opposed to laboratory test data (Block, 1977). Why should this be so? One reason is that laboratory situations tend to be high in situational constraint and thereby minimize individual differences in response. Another reason is that the laboratory situation removes from the individual the possibility of selecting and creating situations. In other words, in the real world people behave consistently in part because they select and shape the very situations that influence their behavior (Allport, 1961; Snyder, 1981; Wachtel, 1973).

7. *Trait judgments reflect reality* Situationist critics suggest that when people make trait judgments they are doing so on the basis of

assumptions about which personality characteristics go together. These critics suggest that the assumptions people make are without basis in reality. On the other hand, trait theorists suggest that language and trait judgments mirror the real world; that is, people think that certain acts go together, and make ratings accordingly, because they in fact do go together, (Borkenau, 1986; Borkenau & Ostendorf, 1987). Language has evolved, and trait assumptions have evolved, because they are based on observations of how people behave and of which behaviors tend to go together. Traits exist in the eye of the beholder because they exist in reality.

Obviously these arguments in support of trait theory are in addition to the factor-analytic and genetic evidence presented by Eysenck and Cattell in support of the existence of traits. Beyond this, it is clear that often situationist criticism presents a distorted picture of trait theory, as if it is suggested that the person or trait alone accounts for behavior, and that the situation has nothing to do with behavior. It is clear, however, that trait theorists recognize the importance of situations. Traits represent predispositions to respond in specific ways that become manifest when behavior is considered over a wide range of situations. Perhaps the trait position in this regard is best summarized by Eysenck as follows:

> Altogether I feel the debate is an unreal one. You cannot contrast persons and situations in any meaningful sense, or ask which is more important, because clearly you will always have person-in-situations, and the relative importance of personality and situational factors depends on the nature of the situation, the selection of people, and in particular the selection of traits measured. No physicist would put such a silly question as: Which is more important in melting a substance—the situation (heat of the flame) or the nature of the substance!
>
> EYSENCK [PERSONAL COMMUNICATION], AUGUST 7, 1978

The person–situation debate and argument concerning evidence for and against the consistency of behavior go on. Actually most personality psychologists agree that there is evidence for both consistency or stability and for inconsistency or variability. They disagree about how much of each and, perhaps more significantly, the utility of a trait concept in accounting for regularities that do exist. Thus, to a certain extent, we are left with differing views of how much variability in behavior one considers damaging to a trait concept (or, conversely, how much stability is supportive) and how much faith one has that further gains can be made through exploration of trait concepts. At this time, neither trait nor situationist theories do a terribly good job of predicting wide ranges of individual behaviors over varied situations, or of helping us to understand *both* stability and change in personality functioning (Funder & Ozer, 1983; Pervin, 1983).

OVERALL EVALUATION OF TRAIT THEORY

We have now considered three approaches to a trait conceptualization of personality. It is clear that major differences exist among trait theorists. At the same time, it is the common emphasis on characteristic patterns of behaving that provides a unifying base. Previously we have considered the contributions of each theorist. Here we shall consider some issues relevant to trait theory generally.

The Method: Factor Analysis

Central to much of trait theory is the utilization of factor analysis. The utility of this procedure is not, however, something about which there is agreement among psychologists. A number of specific questions come into play. For example, how do we know how many factors or traits exist? Factor analysis is an objective, mathematical procedure. However, there are variations in some details that leave room for investigator judgment. Thus, although both Eysenck and Cattell use factor analysis to gain insight into the structure of personality, the factor-analytic procedure used by Eysenck results in the identification of few factors; that used by Cattell results in the identification of many.

Another issue: Are the same factors being identified in different studies? The answer should be yes if we are really discovering the basic structure of personality. It must be yes if we are to consider the results reliable and replicable. Although Cattell argues that his factors have been identified in numerous studies, others report that they have not been able to replicate them. In reviewing the evidence, one psychologist asks whether these personality factors are "sensitive plants" that can be bred under certain conditions or are "hardy perennials" and concludes that they are the former (Howarth, 1972).

A third issue concerns some questionable assumptions of factor analysis. For example, factor analysis considers the joint rise and decline of behaviors. But suppose that two behaviors are related in a complex fashion such that they sometimes move in the same direction and sometimes in the opposite direction. In this case, the factor-analytic procedure will not discern the relationship between the variables. The general point that can be made is that factor analysis considers simple, linear relationships whereas personality functioning may often involve more complex relationships among variables.

Given these and other questions, we may ask whether we can rely on factor analysis to discover the basic dimensions or underlying structure of personality. It is clear that Cattell remains convinced that factor analysis is an adequate, in fact, necessary tool for the job. Eysenck, though supportive of its utilization as an investigative tool, recognizes the subjective aspects involved and is critical of the value and importance attached to it by Cattell. Others have even more serious reservations. Allport, although committed to trait theory, expressed the feeling that the factors identified through this procedure "resemble sausage meat that has failed to pass the pure food and health inspection" (1958, p. 251). Another psychologist suggests that there is "less there than meets the eye" (Lykken, 1971) and a third suggests that "factor analysis is as appropriate for the unraveling of a dynamic system as complex as man as a centrifuge might be, though the latter rotation would also yield some real and independent components of man's basic stuff" (Tomkins, 1962, p. 287). In sum, the factor-analytic procedure has its problems, and researchers in the field are far from agreeing on its place in personality research.

Genetic Determinants

Both Eysenck and Cattell place considerable emphasis on the inherited, biological component of individual traits and traits generally. Although one can be a trait theorist without emphasizing genetic determinants, most major trait theorists subscribe to such a point of view. The issue here is complex and goes far beyond trait theory. That is, the extent to which and the way in which personality characteristics are influenced by genetic factors raise issues that transcend trait theory. Research in this area has become quite sophisticated while remaining controversial. Historically, the waxing and waning of interest in and emphasis on genetic factors have often provided focal points for political controversy (Pervin, 1984, Chapter 2).

In general, evidence does appear to be accumulating to suggest that many important personality characteristics do have a genetic component to them. Recently, the interesting suggestion was made that some personality traits may be determined by the interaction of a number of genetic influences rather than by a single or additive genetic influence (Lykken, 1982). Under such circumstances, the trait will only appear where the necessary interactions have occurred and will not necessarily run in families in any consistent way. In other words, just as the contributions to behavior can be configural rather than additive, so this may be true for the influence of genes on personality trait formation.

Before leaving this issue, it is important to keep in mind that because a trait is genetically influenced does not mean that it is genetically determined or fixed. What is determined by genes is how the organism initially responds to the environment and not the trait or personality characteristic itself. In addition, as Eysenck emphasized, because a personality characteristic is inherited does not mean that it cannot be altered through chemical or psychological means.

The Trait Concept

Until now we have considered the evidence concerning consistency and factor analysis as a method of discovery. But what of the essence of the trait concept itself? Is this the best concept for us to bank on and, if not, why not?

To a certain extent, this is a hard issue to address since different trait theorists include different things in the trait concept. Some emphasize consistency more than do others. Some tie traits to observable behaviors whereas others, such as Eysenck, emphasize underlying regularities and thereby seek to avoid the circularity of some trait concepts (i.e., the trait being defined in terms of observed behaviors are then used to explain the very same behaviors). However, what is essential to trait theory is the emphasis on observed consistency in *behavior*, and it is with this that some personality psychologists most wish to take issue. The argument here would be that even though personality structure exists, and there is consistency, trait concepts place too much emphasis on overt behavior and present a too static picture of human functioning (Pervin, 1983). Such arguments, for example, would be made by proponents of psychoanalytic theory or by proponents of other dynamic points of view. In other words, the issue here is not consistency and person versus situation, but rather that of the best way of conceptualizing the structure and consistency that do exist.

Some time ago, the personality psychologist Henry Murray explained his rejection of the trait concept in the following way: "According to my prejudice, trait psychology is over-concerned with recurrences, with consistency, with what is clearly manifested (the surface of personality), with what is conscious, ordered, and rational" (1938, p. 715). Murray's preference was for the concept of need. "Need" may be a momentary process, one that may be present within the organism without becoming manifest directly or overtly in behavior. Theories based on "needs" and "drives" have lost popularity in psychology. These concepts may or may not yet prove to be useful. Murray's criticism would appear, however, to still have merit. In other words, the problem with the trait concept may not be that it exaggerates the consistency of personality but rather that it fails to do justice to the complex interplay among the determinants of behavior (Figure 9.9). To their credit Allport, Eysenck, and Cattell have attempted to recognize and do justice to this complexity. Whether the trait concept itself is adequate to the task remains to be seen.

STRENGTHS	LIMITATIONS
1. Investigates relationships among many variables or characteristics.	1. Neglects systematic inquiry into the relation of situations to traits and behaviors.
2. Emphasizes different kinds of research and data: laboratory, naturalistic observation, questionnaire.	2. Relies excessively at times on factor analysis and questionnaires.
3. Develops personality questionnaires.	3. Uses static concepts to the neglect of dynamic processes.

FIGURE 9.9 Summary of Strengths and Limitations of Trait Theory.

Major Concepts and Summary

Allport
cardinal traits, central traits, secondary dispositions

functional autonomy

idiographic research

Eysenck
factor analysis

types

introversion – extroversion, neuroticism, psychoticism

Cattell
bivariate, multivariate, clinical methods

ability, temperament, dynamic traits

surface traits and source traits

L-data, Q-data, OT-data

Sixteen Personality Factor Inventory (16 P.F.)

ergs and sentiments

state

role

General
person – situation controversy

the big five

emotionality, sociability, activity

In this chapter we have explored theories of personality that emphasize the concept of trait, or a predisposition to respond to situations in a particular way. In addition, there is the view of personality structure as hierarchically organized (e.g., habits, traits, types). One of the early proponents of trait theory was Gordon W. Allport. He viewed traits as the basic units of personality, characterized by the properties of frequency, intensity, and range of situations. He also distinguished among cardinal traits, central traits, and secondary dispositions. Allport suggested that most people can be described in terms of traits that represent ranges of possible behaviors or aggregate descriptions of their behavior over a wide range of situations.

Whereas Allport conducted little research on traits and the structure of personality, the personality theorist Hans J. Eysenck has been quite active in research. Although Eysenck finds utility in the concept of trait, and in the even more abstract concept of type, he holds to four criteria for the utility of any such personality concept: (1) It must find support in factor-analytic studies. (2) One must be able to demonstrate a biological-genetic basis for the predictions based on the theory. (3) The concept must be related to theory and to specific predictions based on the theory. (4) The concept must be related to important social events and groups. With such criteria in mind and through the factor analysis of a wide variety of data on many different subject populations, Eysenck has been led to emphasize three basic dimensions of personality: extroversion–introversion, neuroticism, and psychoticism. Major attention was given to the extroversion–introversion dimension. The biological-genetic basis for associated individual differences and the relationship of such individual differences to functioning in a wide variety of areas was discussed in relation to Eysenck's criteria for an adequate concept of personality.

The trait theory of Raymond B. Cattell has been given extended discussion. Cattell's goal is the identification of the basic dimensions of personality and the development of a set of instruments to measure these dimensions. Multivariate research and factor analysis are viewed as providing the tools for defining the basic structural elements of personality. These basic structural elements are called traits and represent broad dispositional tendencies. Of particular interest are source traits that represent associations among behaviors that vary (increase and decrease) together. Three categories of traits are viewed as capturing the major aspects of personality—ability, temperament, and dynamic traits. The argument has been made that, with few exceptions, the same source traits can be found from the analysis of life record data (L-data), questionnaire data (Q-data), and objective test data (OT-data). The Sixteen Personality Factor Inventory has been developed to measure personality using questionnaire data. However, there is a preference for the use of objective test data. Using a variety of tests and subject populations, work goes on to discover the exact number of traits necessary to describe personality and to define the nature of these traits.

Dynamic traits, relating to the why of behavior, are of particular interest in relation to the process aspects of behavior. Some dynamic traits are tied to biological drives and are called ergs. Other dynamic traits are related to the socialization process and are called sentiments. Predicting behavior means that one must take into consideration both the various traits of the individual and such situational, transient variables as states (mood) and role. Behavior, then, is a function of both personality and situational determinants.

Cattell is interested in the relative influence of heredity and environment in determining traits. He has studied the development of traits by age at every stage of development. This research suggests that the same underlying factors can be found, both in number and in kind, in subjects from age four through adulthood.

Cattell's research in the area of psychopathology has involved the analysis of factors on which normal and patient populations differ; that is, psychopathology is defined by differences observed between groups on the same factor tests. High scores on some factors are common to all forms of psychopathology (e.g., high anxiety scores for all neurotics) whereas some are specific to each form of pathology. Psychotherapy, where effective, involves a change in the pattern of traits as opposed to the change of specific behaviors.

There are strengths and limitations to the contributions of each of the trait theorists as well as to trait theory as a whole. Although they are unified by an emphasis on individual differences and the concept of trait, there is diversity among trait theorists. Allport rejects factor analysis as a major tool in research whereas both Eysenck and Cattell make major use of it. Eysenck emphasizes the type level of analysis whereas both Allport and Cattell prefer to stay at the trait level, with Allport even questioning whether this level of analysis gives adequate attention to the uniqueness of the individual. The appeal of trait theory generally is that it focuses attention on individual differences and personality as a central part of psychological investigation. However, trait theory has come under attack for what is seen as a neglect of concern with situation variables and an excessive emphasis on consistency—the person–situation controversy. In addition, critics of trait theory emphasize the limitations of factor analysis as a method for discovering the structure of personality and the limitations of what is essentially a static conceptualization. Trait theorists have not been slow to respond to the critics. In support of the trait position they point to converging lines of evidence supporting the existence of approximately five major traits, evidence of important genetic contributions to many traits, and evidence of longitudinal and cross-situational consistency.

In many ways trait theory serves as a useful bridge between the more clinical theories covered earlier and the learning, behavioral theories yet to be covered. In part, this is because Cattell emphasizes the strengths, as well as the limitations, of both clinical and bivariate research, the latter being typical of learning or behavioral research. In addition, Eysenck emphasizes the importance of many traditional learning principles in the development of personality as well as in the application of behavior therapy. Thus, although some of the theorists yet to be covered are among the harshest critics of trait theory, they would agree with at least some points of emphasis.

Chapter Ten
Behavioral
Approaches to
Personality

*C*HAPTER FOCUS: In this chapter, we study approaches to personality based on principles of learning. The chapter begins by noting that there are many different theories of learning. These theories share a focus on learned behavior and a commitment to the experimental testing of clearly defined hypotheses. This chapter focuses on Watson's behaviorist point of view and on three processes of learning—Pavlov's classical conditioning, Skinner's operant conditioning, and stimulus–response (S–R) theory. Learning, behavioral approaches to assessment and change are then considered along with an overall critical evaluation of these approaches to personality.

> *Psychology as the behaviorist views it is a purely objective, experimental branch of natural science. Its theoretical goal is the prediction and control of behavior. Introspection forms no essential part of its methods. . . . The time seems to have come when psychology must discard all references to consciousness.*
>
> WATSON, 1914, p. 31

> *The practice of looking inside the organism for an explanation of behavior has tended to obscure the variables which are immediately available for scientific analysis. These variables lie outside the organism, in its immediate environment and in its environmental history.*
>
> SKINNER, 1953, p. 31

The concern in this chapter is with approaches to personality that in many ways are radically different from the clinical point of view. Although they share with the trait, factory-analytic approaches an emphasis on empirical investigation, they involve assumptions that lead to considerable criticism of the trait approach to personality.

This chapter, like the one on trait theory, is concerned with the efforts of many individuals. There is a learning theory and behavioral point of view, but there is no one theory of learning or one behavioral theory of personality. In this chapter attention will be directed toward three approaches to learning: Pavlov's classical conditioning, Skinner's operant conditioning, and Hull's stimulus–response learning. As shall be seen, they share certain common features, in particular an emphasis on the importance of learning and a commitment to rigorous methodology.

BEHAVIORAL APPROACHES TO PERSONALITY

Beyond this, there are many important differences in how they interpret the principles of learning and understand behavior.

During the period between the 1950s and the 1970s these approaches greatly influenced thinking in the area of personality and clinical psychology. As we shall see in the chapters that follow, subsequently their influence was replaced by other approaches. However, they continue to have an influence on theory and research and are important to understand in terms of the history of developments in the field.

THE BEHAVIORAL VIEW OF THE PERSON AND SCIENCE

In an effort to understand the learning theory approach to personality, one must be prepared to make new assumptions and to consider new strategies for research. The learning theory approach to personality has two basic assumptions from which a number of critical points follow. The first assumption is that nearly all behavior is learned, and the second that objectivity and rigor in the testing of clearly formulated hypotheses are crucial (Figure 10.1).

Whereas Eysenck and Cattell viewed learning as part of the broader area of personality, the theoretical approaches discussed in this chapter suggest that the study of personality is a branch of the general field of learning (Lundin, 1963). The emphasis is on the laws of learning that hold for all individuals. The focus on individual differences is viewed as a detour from the path of discovery of these general laws. Psychopathology is understood in terms of the learning of maladaptive behaviors or the failure to learn adaptive behaviors. Thus, the medical symptom–disease model of psychopathology is rejected. Therapy involves the application of basic principles of learning to the area of behavior change. Rather than speaking of psychotherapy, followers of the learning–behavioral view speak of **behavior modification** and **behavior therapy.** It is specific behaviors that are to be modified or changed, rather than underlying con-

---

1. Empirical research is the cornerstone of theory and practice.
2. Personality theory and applied practice should be based on principles of learning.
3. Behavior is responsive to reinforcement variables in the environment and is more situation specific than suggested by other personality theories (e.g., trait, psychoanalytic).
4. Rejection of the medical symptom-disease view of psychopathology and emphasis instead on basic principles of learning and behavior change.

FIGURE 10.1 Basic Point of Emphasis of Learning, Behavioral Approaches to Personality.

flicts that must be resolved or a personality that needs to be reorganized. Since most problematic behaviors have been learned, they can be unlearned or otherwise changed through the application of learning-based procedures.

The emphasis on objectivity and rigor, on testable hypotheses and the experimental control of variables, is perhaps of even greater significance. It has led to an emphasis on the laboratory as the place for studying behavior, to an emphasis on simple, rather than complex, behavior, and to the use of animals, such as rats and pigeons, as subjects. Further, the emphasis on the careful manipulation of objectively defined variables has led to an emphasis on forces *external* to the organism as opposed to ones *internal* to it. According to the learning–behavioral approach, one manipulates variables in the environment and observes the consequences of these manipulations in behavior. Whereas psychodynamic theories emphasize causes of behavior that are inside the organism (e.g., instincts, defenses, self-concept, constructs), learning theories emphasize causes that are in the external environment. Stimuli in the environment that can be experimentally manipulated, such as food rewards, are emphasized instead of concepts that cannot be manipulated, such as the self, the ego, and the unconscious. As Skinner argued, when we can control behavior through the manipulation of variables outside the organism, there is no need to be concerned with what goes on inside the organism.

The behavioral emphasis on external, environmental determinants has been associated with an emphasis on **situational specificity** in behavior and a de-emphasis on individual predispositions to behave in particular ways. In contrast with the emphasis in psychodynamic and trait theories on characteristics or traits that express themselves in a range of situations, behavior theory suggests that whatever consistency is found in behavior is the result of the similarity of environmental conditions that evoke these behaviors. "With the possible exception of intelligence, highly generalized behavioral consistencies have not been demonstrated, and the concept of personality traits as broad response predispositions is thus untenable" (Mischel, 1968, p. 146). In summary, the view that is presented here is that behavior is situation specific; that is, that behavior tends to change unless there is a similarity of environmental conditions.

Before turning to consideration of the three approaches to learning, a word should be said about the psychologist Watson, whose views so much influenced the course of American psychology and developments in parts of the field of personality.

Watson's Behaviorism

John B. Watson (1878–1958) was the founder of the approach to psychology known as **behaviorism.** He began his graduate study at the University of Chicago in philosophy, and then switched to psychology. During these years he took courses in neurology and physiology and began to do a considerable amount of animal research. Some of this research consisted of study of the increased complexity of behavior in the rat and the associated development of the central nervous system. During the year before he received his doctorate, he had an emotional breakdown and had sleepless nights for many weeks. Watson described this period as useful in preparing him to accept a large part of Freud (Watson, 1936, p. 274). The graduate work at Chicago culminated in a dissertation on animal education and was associated with the development of an important attitude regarding the use of human subjects.

> At Chicago, I first began a tentative formulation of my later point of view. I never wanted to use human subjects. I hated to serve as a subject. I didn't like the stuffy, artificial instructions given to subjects. I always was uncomfortable and acted unnaturally. With animals I was at home. I felt that, in studying them, I was keeping close to biology with my feet on the ground.
>
> More and more the thought presented itself: Can't I find out by watching their behavior everything that the other students are finding by using O's (human subjects)?
>
> WATSON, 1936, p. 276

Watson left Chicago to become a professor at Johns Hopkins University in 1908, where he served on the faculty until 1919. During his stay there, which was interrupted by a period of service during the First World War, Watson developed his views on behaviorism as an approach to psychol-

John B. Watson

ogy. These views, which emphasized the study of behavior that is observable and which excluded the study of self-observation or introspection, were presented in public lectures in 1912 and were published in 1914 in Watson's book, *Behavior*. Watson's call for the use of objective methods and the end of speculation about what goes on inside the person was greeted enthusiastically, and he was elected president of the American Psychological Association for the year 1915. His views were further developed to include the work of the Russian physiologist Pavlov, and can be found in his most significant work, *Psychology From the Standpoint of a Behaviorist* (1919).

Watson was divorced in 1919, immediately married his student Rosalie Rayner, and was forced to resign from Hopkins. The circumstances of this departure from Hopkins led him to make his livelihood in the business world. Although he had already established a considerable reputation as a psychologist, he now was forced to do studies of potential sales markets. He found, however, "that it can be just as thrilling to watch the growth of a sales curve of a new product as to watch the learning curve of animals or men" (Watson, 1936, p. 280) and became successful in business. After 1920, Watson did write some popular articles and published his book *Behaviorism* (1924), but his career as a productive theorist and experimenter closed with his departure from Hopkins. However, his hope that instructors would begin to teach objective psychology instead of what he termed "mythology" was to be realized in the years ahead.

PAVLOV'S THEORY OF CLASSICAL CONDITIONING

Ivan Petrovitch Pavlov (1849–1936) was a Russian physiologist who, in the course of his work on the digestive process, developed a procedure for studying behavior and a principle of learning that had a profound effect on the field of psychology. Around the beginning of the twentieth century Pavlov was involved in the study of gastric secretions in dogs. As part of his research he would place some food powder inside the mouth of a dog and measure the resulting amount of salivation. Coincidentally he noticed that after a number of such trials a dog would begin to salivate to certain stimuli before the food was placed in its mouth. This salivation would occur in response to cues such as the sight of the food dish or the approach of a person who generally brought the food. In other words, stimuli that previously did not lead to this response (called neutral stimuli) could now elicit the salivation response because of their association with the food powder that automatically caused the dog to salivate. To animal owners this may not seem like a startling observation. However, it

BEHAVIORAL APPROACHES TO PERSONALITY

Ivan Petrovich Pavlov

led Pavlov to conduct some very significant research on the process known as **classical conditioning.**

The essential characteristic of classical conditioning is that a previously neutral stimulus becomes capable of eliciting a response because of its association with a stimulus that automatically produces the same or a similar response. In other words, the dog salivates to the first presentation of the food powder. One need not speak of a conditioning or learning process at this point. The food can be considered to be an **unconditioned stimulus** (US) and the salivation an **unconditioned response** (UR). This is because the salivation is an automatic, reflex response to the food. A neutral stimulus, such as a bell, will not lead to salivation. However, if on a number of trials the bell is sounded *just before* the presentation of the food powder, the sounding of the bell itself without the subsequent appearance of food may take on the potential for eliciting the salivation response. In this case, conditioning has occurred since the presentation of the bell alone is followed by salivation. At this point, the bell may be referred to as a **conditioned stimulus** (CS), and the salivation may be considered a **conditioned response** (CR).

In a similar way, it is possible to condition withdrawal responses to previously neutral stimuli. In the early research on conditioned withdrawal, a dog was strapped in a harness and electrodes were attached to his paw. The delivery of an electric shock (US) to the paw led to the withdrawal of the paw (UR), which was a reflex response on the part of the animal. If a bell was repeatedly presented just before the shock, eventually the bell alone (CS) would be able to elicit the withdrawal response (CR).

The experimental arrangement designed by Pavlov to study classical conditioning allowed him to investigate a number of important phenomena. For example, would the conditioned response become associated with the specific neutral stimulus alone or would it become associated with other similar stimuli? Pavlov found that the response that had become conditioned to a previously neutral stimulus would also become associated with similar stimuli, a process called **generalization.** In other words, the salivation response to the bell would generalize to other sounds. Similarly, the withdrawal response to the bell would generalize to sounds similar to the bell. What are the limits of such generalization? If repeated trials indicate that only some stimuli are followed by the unconditioned stimulus, the animal recognizes differences among stimuli, a process called **discrimination.** For example, if only certain sounds but not others are followed by shock and reflexive paw withdrawal, the dog will learn to discriminate among sounds. Thus, whereas the process of generalization leads to consistency of response across similar stimuli, the process of discrimination leads to increased specificity of response. Finally, if the originally neutral stimulus is presented repeatedly without at least occasionally being followed by the unconditioned stimulus, there is an undoing or progressive weakening of the conditioning or association, a process known as **extinction.** Whereas the association of the neutral stimulus with the unconditioned stimulus leads to the conditioned response, the repeated presentation of the conditioned stimulus without the unconditioned stimulus leads to extinction. For example, for the dog to continue to salivate to the bell, there must be at least occasional presentations of the food powder with the bell.

Psychopathology and Change

The phenomena of generalization, discrimination, and extinction are important to classical conditioning theory as well as other theories of learning. In addition to his work on these phenomena, research by Pavlov was significant in terms of a possible explanation for other phenomena such as conflict and the development of neuroses. An early demonstration of what came to be known as experimental neuroses in animals was completed in Pavlov's laboratory. A dog was conditioned to salivate to the signal of a circle. A differentiation between a circle and an ellipse was then conditioned by not reinforcing the response to the ellipse. When the ellipse was gradually changed in shape to approximate the shape of a circle, the dog first developed fine discriminations but then, as it became impossible to discriminate between the circle and the ellipse, its behavior became disorganized. Pavlov described the events as follows:

> After three weeks of work upon this discrimination not only did the discrimination fail to improve, but it became considerably worse, and finally disappeared altogether. The hitherto quiet dog

began to squeal in its stand, kept wriggling about, tore off with its teeth the apparatus for mechanical stimulation of the skin, and bit through the tubes connecting the animal's room with the observer, a behavior which never happened before. On being taken into the experimental room the dog now barked violently, which was also contrary to its usual custom; in short, it presented all the symptoms of a condition of acute necrosis.

PAVLOV, 1927, p. 291

Pavlov's work on the conditioning process clearly defined stimuli and responses and provided an objective method for the study of learning phenomena. It therefore played an influential role in the thinking of later behaviorists such as Watson. For example, shortly after the publication of *Psychology From the Standpoint of a Behaviorist* (1919), Watson reported on the conditioning of emotional reactions in an infant. The research on Albert, an eleven-month-old child, has become a classic in psychology. In this research, the experimenters, Watson and Rayner (1920), trained the infant to fear animals and objects that previously were not feared. Watson and Rayner found that striking a hammer on a suspended steel bar produced a startle and fear response in the infant Albert. They then found that if the bar was struck immediately behind Albert's head just as he began to reach for a rat, he would begin to fear the rat whereas previously he had not shown this response. After doing this a number of times the experimenters found that the instant the rat alone (without the sound) was shown to Albert, he began to cry. He had developed what is called a **conditioned emotional reaction**. Albert now feared the rat because of its emotional association with the frightening sound. Furthermore, there was evidence that Albert began to fear other objects that somewhat resembled the rat. Despite some evidence that Albert's emotional reaction was not as strong or as general as expected (Harris, 1979), Watson and Rayner concluded that many fears are conditioned emotional reactions. On this basis they criticized the more complex psychoanalytic interpretations.

The Freudians twenty years from now, unless their hypotheses change, when they come to analyze Albert's fear of a seal skin coat . . . will probably tease from him the recital of a dream upon which their analysis will show that Albert at three years of age attempted to play with the pubic hair of the mother and was scolded violently for it. . . . If the analyst has sufficiently prepared Albert to accept such a dream when found as an explanation of his avoiding tendencies, and if the analyst has the authority and personality to put it over, Albert may be fully convinced that the dream was a true revealer of the factors which brought about the fear.

WATSON AND RAYNER, 1920, p. 14

WHAT MAKES SOME FOODS A TREAT AND OTHERS DISGUSTING?

Most people have some odors and food tastes that they love and others by which they are disgusted. Often these responses date back to childhood and seem nearly impossible to change. Can classical conditioning help us to understand them and their power?

Consider some research on food tastes. What makes some foods so unpleasant, even disgusting, that we have emotional reactions to just the thought of them? Eating worms for example, or drinking milk that has a dead fly or dead cockroach in it. The interesting thing about some of these reactions is that a food that evokes a disgust reaction in one culture can be considered a delicacy in another, and a disgust reaction might be evoked by a dead fly or cockroach in the milk even if one is told that the insect was sterilized before it was put in the milk. Having seen the dead insect in the milk, one might not even be prepared to drink a different glass of milk—the disgust reaction now having generalized to the milk itself.

According to the researchers of such reactions, a possible explanation lies in the strong emotional reaction that becomes associated with a previously neutral object. In classical conditioning terms, the disgust response becomes associated with, or conditioned to, a previously neutral object such as milk or another food: "We believe that Pavlovian conditioning is alive and well, in the flavor associations of the billions of meals eaten each day, in the expressions of affects of billions of eaters as they eat away, in the association of foods and offensive objects, and in the association of foods with some of their consequences."

If this is the case, then it suggests that many things that we like, perhaps even feel addicted to, are the result of classical conditioning. This being the case, it may be possible to change our emotional reactions to certain objects through the process of classical conditioning.

(Copyright © 1985 American Psychological Association. Reprinted by permission from *Psychology Today.*)

SOURCES: Rozin & Zellner, 1985; *Psychology Today*, July 1985.

Conditioned food responses—Many strong and persisting emotional responses to foods, such as a disgust response to worms, are acquired through the process of classical conditioning. Copyright © 1985 American Psychological Association. Reprinted by permission from *Psychology Today.*

The classical conditioning of emotional reactions is now seen by many psychologists as playing a critical role in the development of psychopathology and a potentially important role in behavioral change. Behavior therapy based on the classical conditioning model emphasizes the extinction of problematic responses, such as conditioned fears, or the conditioning of new responses to stimuli that elicit such undesired responses as anxiety. An early utilization of this approach, one that followed Watson and Rayner's (1920) study of the conditioning of the fear emotional response in Albert, was the effort of Jones (1924) to remove a fear under laboratory conditions. In this study, described as one of the earliest if not the first systematic utilization of behavior therapy, Jones attempted to treat the exaggerated fear reaction in a boy, Peter, who then was two years and ten months old. Peter was described as a generally healthy, well-adjusted child with a fear of a white rat that also extended to a rabbit, fur coat, feather, and cotton wool. Jones carefully documented the nature of the child's fear response and the conditions that elicited the greatest fear. She then set out to determine whether she could "uncondition" the fear response to one stimulus and whether such "unconditioning" would then generalize to other stimuli. Jones chose to focus on Peter's fear of the rabbit since this seemed even greater than his fear of the rat. She proceeded by bringing Peter to play at a time when the rabbit was present as well as three other children who were selected because they were fearless toward the rabbit. Gradually Peter moved from almost complete terror at the sight of the rabbit to a completely positive response. The steps noted along the way to this progress are represented in Figure 10.2.

1. Rabbit anywhere in the room in a cage causes fear reactions.
2. Rabbit 12 feet away in cage tolerated.
3. Rabbit 4 feet away in cage tolerated.
4. Rabbit 3 feet away in cage tolerated.
5. Rabbit close in cage tolerated.
6. Rabbit free in room tolerated.
7. Rabbit touched when experimenter holds it.
8. Rabbit touched when free in room.
9. Rabbit defied by spitting at it, throwing things at it, imitating it.
10. Rabbit allowed on tray of high chair.
11. Squats in defenseless position beside rabbit.
12. Helps experimenter to carry rabbit to its cage.
13. Holds rabbit on lap.
14. Stays alone in room with rabbit.
15. Allows rabbit in play pen with him.
16. Fondles rabbit affectionately.
17. Lets rabbit nibble his fingers.

FIGURE 10.2 Steps in the "Unconditioning" of Peter's Fear of a Rabbit. (M.C. Jones, 1924)

Actually, Peter's progression through these steps was not even or unbroken, and fortunately Jones gives us a careful, explicit accounting of a fascinating chain of events. Peter had progressed through the first nine steps listed in Figure 10.2 when he was taken to the hospital with scarlet fever. After a delay of two months, Peter returned to the laboratory with his fear response at the original level. Jones describes the cause of this relapse as follows:

> This was easily explained by the nurse who brought Peter from the hospital. As they were entering a taxi at the door of the hospital, a large dog, running past, jumped at them. Both Peter and the nurse were very much frightened. . . . This seemed reason enough for this precipitate descent back to the original fear level. Being threatened by a large dog when ill, and in a strange place and being with an adult who also showed fear, was a terrifying situation against which our training could not have fortified him.

Thus, at this point Jones began anew with "another" method of treatment, that of "direct conditioning." Here Peter was seated in a chair and given food he liked as the experimenter gradually brought the rabbit in a wire cage closer to him: "Through the presence of pleasant stimulus (food) whenever the rabbit was shown, the fear was eliminated gradually in favor of a positive response." In other words, the positive feelings associated with food were counterconditioned to the previously feared rabbit. However, even in the later sessions the influence of other children who were not afraid of the rabbit seemed to be of considerable significance. And what of the other fears? Jones notes that after the "unconditioning" of Peter's fear of the rabbit, he completely lost his fear of the fur coat, feathers, and cotton wool as well. Despite the lack of any knowledge concerning the origins of Peter's fears, the "unconditioning" procedure was found to work successfully and to generalize to other stimuli as well.

Another early procedure that gained considerable attention was one developed by Mowrer and Mowrer (1928) for the treatment of bed-wetting. In general, bed-wetting in children occurs because the child does not respond to stimuli from the bladder so as to awaken and urinate in the bathroom. To deal with this condition, Mowrer and Mowrer developed a device based on the classical conditioning model. This consisted of an electrical device in the bed of the child. If the child urinated, the device activated a bell which awakened the child. Gradually stimuli from the bladder became associated with the awakening response. Eventually, the response was anticipated so that bed-wetting no longer took place.

The classical conditioning procedure also has been used in the treatment of alcoholics. For example, an aversive stimulus such as shock

"Leave us alone! I am a behavior therapist! I am helping my patient overcome a fear of heights!"

Behavior Therapy—One aspect of behavior therapy involves the extinction of learned fears or phobias. © copyright Sidney Harris.

or a nausea-inducing agent is applied immediately after the alcoholic takes a drink. The aversive stimulus acts as an unconditioned stimulus, and the avoidance response is conditioned to the alcohol (Nathan, 1985).

By far the most influential development in this area has been that of Joseph Wolpe's method of **systematic desensitization**. Interestingly, this method of therapy was developed by a psychiatrist rather than a psychologist, and by someone who originally practiced within a psychoanalytic framework. After a number of years of practice, however, Wolpe read and was impressed by the writings of Pavlov and Hull. He came to hold the view that a neurosis is a persistent, maladaptive learned response that is almost always associated with anxiety. Therapy, then, involves the inhibition of anxiety through the counterconditioning of a competing response. In other words, therapy involves the conditioning of responses that are antagonistic to or inhibitory of anxiety. A variety of anxiety-inhibiting responses can be used for counterconditioning purposes. However, the one that has received most attention is that of deep muscle relaxation. Through a process called systematic desensitization, the patient learns to respond to certain previously anxiety-arousing stimuli with the newly conditioned response of relaxation.

The therapeutic technique of systematic desensitization involves a number of phases (Wolpe, 1968). First, there is a careful assessment of the therapeutic needs of the patient. A detailed history is taken of every symptom and of every aspect of life in which the patient experiences

Systematic Desensitization —
Relaxation training forms a part of
the behavior therapy technique
called systematic desensitization.
Here an early leader in the field,
Dr. Arnold Lazarus, conducts a
group session in relaxation training.

undue difficulty. A systematic account of the patient's life history is also
obtained. After having determined that the patient's problems lend
themselves to systematic desensitization, the therapist trains the patient
to relax. A detailed procedure is described for helping the patient to first
relax one part of the body and then all parts of the body. Whereas, at first,
patients have limited success in their ability to feel free of muscle tension, by the end of about six sessions most are able to relax the entire
body in seconds. The next phase of treatment involves the construction
of an anxiety hierarchy. This is a difficult and complex procedure in
which the therapist tries to obtain from the patient a list of stimuli that
arouse anxiety. These anxiety-arousing stimuli are grouped into themes
such as fear of heights or fear of rejection. Within each group or theme,
the anxiety-arousing stimuli are then ordered from the most disturbing
to the least disturbing. For example, a theme of claustrophobia (fear of
closed spaces) might involve placing the fear of being stuck in an elevator
at the top of the list, an anxiety about being on a train in the middle of the
list, and an anxiety in response to reading of miners trapped underground at the bottom of the list. A theme of death might involve being at
a burial as the most anxiety-arousing stimulus, the word death as somewhat anxiety-arousing, and driving past a cemetery as only slightly anxiety-arousing. Patients can have many or few themes, and many or few
items within each anxiety hierarchy.

With the construction of the anxiety hierarchies completed, the
patient is ready for the desensitization procedure itself. The patient has
attained the capacity to calm him- or herself by relaxation, and the

therapist has established the anxiety hierarchies. Now the therapist encourages the patient to achieve a deep state of relaxation and then to imagine the least anxiety-arousing stimulus in the anxiety hierarchy. If the patient can imagine the stimulus without anxiety, then he is encouraged to imagine the next stimulus in the hierarchy while remaining relaxed. Periods of pure relaxation are interspersed with periods of relaxation and imagination of anxiety-arousing stimuli. If the patient feels anxious while imagining a stimulus, he is encouraged to relax and return to imagining a less anxiety-arousing stimulus. Ultimately the patient is able to relax while imagining all stimuli in the anxiety hierarchies. Relaxation in relation to the imagined stimuli generalizes to relaxation in relation to these stimuli in everyday life. "It has consistently been found that at every stage a stimulus that evokes no anxiety when imagined in a state of relaxation will also evoke no anxiety when encountered in reality" (Wolpe, 1961a, p. 191).

A number of clinical and laboratory studies have indicated that systematic desensitization can be a useful treatment procedure. These successful results led Wolpe and others to question the psychoanalytic view that, as long as the underlying conflicts remain untouched, the patient is prone to develop a new symptom in place of the one removed (symptom substitution) (Lazarus, 1965). According to the behavior therapy point of view, there is no symptom that is caused by unconscious conflicts. There is only a maladaptive learned response, and once this response has been eliminated there is no reason to believe that another maladaptive response will be substituted for it.

A Reinterpretation of the Case of Little Hans

In this section the application of the learning theory approach will be observed in a case presented by Wolpe and Rachman (1960) that gives us the excellent opportunity to compare the behavioral approach with that of psychoanalysis. In fact, it is not a case in the same sense as other cases that have been presented. Rather, it is a critique and reformulation of Freud's case of Little Hans.

As we learned in Chapter 4, the case of Little Hans is a classic in psychoanalysis. In this case, Freud emphasized the importance of infantile sexuality and oedipal conflicts in the development of a horse phobia, or fear. Wolpe and Rachman are extremely critical of Freud's approach to obtaining data and of his conclusions. They make the following points. (1) Nowhere is there evidence of Hans' wish to make love to his mother. (2) Hans never expressed fear or hatred of his father. (3) Hans consistently denied any relationship between the horse and his father. (4) Phobias can be induced in children by a simple conditioning process and need not be related to a theory of conflicts or anxiety and defense. The view that neuroses occur for a purpose is highly questionable. (5) There is no evidence that the phobia disappeared as a result of his resolution of his oedipal conflicts. Similarly, there is no evidence of "insight" or that information was of therapeutic value.

Wolpe and Rachman feel handicapped in their own interpretation of the phobia because the data were gathered within a psychoanalytic framework. They do, however, attempt an explanation. A phobia is regarded as a *conditioned anxiety reaction*. As a child, Hans heard and saw a playmate being warned by her father that she should avoid a white horse lest it bite her: "Don't put your finger to the white horse." This incident sensitized Hans to a fear of horses. Also, there was the time when one of Hans' friends injured himself and bled while playing horses. Finally, Hans was a sensitive child who felt uneasy about seeing horses on the merry-go-round being beaten. These factors set the condition for the later development of the phobia. The phobia itself occurred as a consequence of the fright Hans experienced while watching a horse fall down. Whereas Freud suggested that this incident was an exciting cause that allowed the underlying conflicts to be expressed in terms of a phobia, Wolpe and Rachman suggest that this incident was *the* cause.

Wolpe and Rachman see a similarity here to Watson's conditioning of a fear of rabbits in Albert. Hans was frightened by the event with a horse and then generalized his fear to all things that were similar to or related to horses. The recovery from the phobia did not occur through the process of insight, but probably through a process of extinction or through a process of counterconditioning. As Hans developed, he experienced other emotional responses that inhibited the fear response. Or, it is suggested that, perhaps, the father's constant reference to the horse within a nonthreatening context helped to extinguish the fear response. Whatever the details, it appears that the phobia disappeared gradually, as would be expected by this kind of learning interpretation, instead of dramatically, as might be suggested by psychoanalytic, insight interpretation. The evidence in support of Freud is not clear, and the data, as opposed to the interpretations, can be accounted for in a more straightforward way through the use of a learning theory interpretation.

Further Developments

Most of the work on classical conditioning has focused on relatively simple reflex mechanisms that humans share with other animals. However, Pavlov also recognized the importance of speech and thought in what he called the *second signal system*. The concept of the second signal system provides for an understanding of much more complex organizations of stimuli and responses. An illustration of the importance of this concept is provided by Razran's (1939) research on *semantic conditioning*. In this research with human subjects, Razran paired the visual presentation of the words *style, urn, freeze,* and *surf* with food reinforcement, leading to the development of a salivary response to the words. He then tested whether the conditioned response would generalize to words that sounded similar (stile, earn, frieze, and serf) or to the words that sounded different but were similar in meaning (fashion, vase, chill, and wave). What would one expect to find—generalization to sound or to meaning? Razran found a significant difference in terms of the latter, suggesting that conditioning processes can be influenced by meaning or semantics. Pavlov himself did relatively little research on the second signal system, but it has continued to be a major area of investigation in Russian psychology, including developmental studies of changes in the factors controlling conditioning processes.

The concepts of conditioned emotional responses and a second signal system provide for a considerably expanded interpretation of the importance of classical conditioning in human behavior. For example, it has been suggested that people acquire motives or goals on the basis of an association of positive and negative affect with stimuli, including symbols (Pervin, 1983; Staats & Burns, 1982). With the exception of some work in Eastern Europe (Strelau, 1983), however, relevant research has tended to focus on experimental work on learning rather than on extension of the theory as a basis for understanding personality.

SKINNER'S THEORY OF OPERANT CONDITIONING

B. F. Skinner (1904–   ) is the most influential supporter of an extreme behaviorist point of view. He is perhaps the best known American psychologist and his views about psychology and society have been the source of considerable controversy.

A View of the Theorist

The scientist, like any organism, is the product of a unique history. The practices which he finds most appropriate will depend in part upon his history. . . . When we have at last an adequate empirical account of the behavior of Man Thinking, we shall understand all this. Until then, it may be best not to try to fit all scientists into any single mold.

SKINNER, 1959, p. 379

In this passage, Skinner takes the point of view that has been argued in each of the theory chapters in this book; that is, that psychologists' orientations and research strategies are, in part, consequences of their own life history and expressions of their own personalities.

B.F. Skinner was born in New York, the son of a lawyer who was described by his son as having been desperately hungry for praise and a mother who had rigid standards of right and wrong. Skinner (1967)

B. F. Skinner

described his home during his early years as a warm and stable environment. He reported a love for school, and showed an early interest in building things. This interest in building things is particularly interesting in relation to the behavioral emphasis on laboratory equipment in the experimental setting, and because it contrasts with the absence of such as interest in the lives and research of the clinical personality theorists.

At about the time that Skinner entered college, his younger brother died. Skinner commented that he was not much moved by his brother's death and that he probably felt guilty for not being moved. Skinner went to Hamilton College and majored in English literature. At that time, his goal was to become a writer, and at one point he sent three short stories to Robert Frost, from whom he received an encouraging reply. After college, Skinner spent a year trying to write, but concluded that at that point in his life he had nothing to say. He then spent six months living in Greenwich Village in New York. During this time he read Pavlov's *Conditioned Reflexes* and came across a series of articles by Bertrand Russell on Watson's behaviorism. Russell thought that he had demolished Watson in these articles, but they aroused Skinner's interest in behaviorism.

Although Skinner had not taken any college psychology courses, he had begun to develop an interest in the field and was accepted for graduate work in psychology at Harvard. He justified his change in goals as follows. "A writer might portray human behavior accurately, but he did not therefore understand it. I was to remain interested in human behavior, but the literary method had failed me; I would turn to the scientific" (Skinner, 1967, p. 395). Psychology appeared to be the relevant science. Besides, he had long been interested in animal behavior (being able to recall his fascination with the complex behaviors of a troupe of performing pigeons). Furthermore, there would now be many opportunities to make use of his interest in building gadgets.

During his graduate school years at Harvard, Skinner developed his interest in animal behavior and in explaining this behavior without reference to the functioning of the nervous system. After reading Pavlov, he did not agree with him that, in explaining behavior, one could go "from the salivary reflexes to the important business of the organism in everyday life." However, Skinner believed that Pavlov had given him the key to understanding behavior. "Control your conditions (the environment) and you shall see order!" During these and the following years, Skinner (1959) developed some of his principles of scientific methodology: (1) When you run into something interesting, drop everything else and study it. (2) Some ways of doing research are easier than others. A mechanical apparatus often makes doing research easier. (3) Some people are lucky. (4) A piece of apparatus breaks down. This presents problems, but it can also lead to (5) serendipity—the art of finding one thing while looking for something else.

After Harvard, Skinner moved first to Minnesota, then to Indiana, and then returned to Harvard, in 1948. During this time he became, in a sense, a sophisticated animal trainer—he was able to make organisms engage in specific behaviors at specific times. He turned from work with rats to work with pigeons. Finding that the behavior of any single animal did not necessarily reflect the average picture of learning based on many animals, he became interested in the manipulation and control of individual animal behavior. Special theories of learning and circuitous explanations of behavior were not necessary if one could manipulate the environment so as to produce orderly change in the individual case. In the meantime, as Skinner notes, his own behavior was becoming controlled by the positive results being given to him by the animals "under his control" (Figure 10.3).

The basis of Skinner's operant conditioning procedure is the control of behavior through the manipulation of rewards and punishments in the environment, particularly the laboratory environment. However, his conviction concerning the importance of the laws of behavior and his

FIGURE 10.3 "Boy, have I got this guy conditioned! Everytime I press the bar down he drops in a piece of food." (Skinner, 1956)

interest in building things have led Skinner to take his thinking and research far beyond the confines of the laboratory environment. He built a baby box to mechanize the care of a baby, developed teaching machines that used rewards in the teaching of school subjects, and developed a procedure whereby pigeons would be used militarily to land a missile on target. He has written a novel, *Walden Two*, describing a utopia based on the control of human behavior through positive reinforcement (reward). He has committed himself to the view that a science of human behavior and the technology to be derived from it must be developed in the service of humankind.

Before turning to Skinner's theory as it relates to personality, it may be useful to contrast its general qualities with those of theories considered in earlier chapters. Each of the theories covered in these earlier chapters has placed considerable emphasis on structural concepts. Freud used structural concepts such as id, ego, and superego; Rogers used concepts such as self and ideal self; Kelly used the concept of constructs;

CURRENT APPLICATIONS   WHAT IS WRONG WITH DAILY LIFE IN THE WESTERN WORLD?

B.F. Skinner has not been one to shy away from practical issues or big questions. In 1971 his book *Beyond Freedom and Dignity* became a best seller as he spelled out his view of a society in which environmental conditions are manipulated to shape human behaviors. Shades of *1984*, Big Brother, and the loss of individual freedom? Not so according to Skinner. Rather the use of a technology of behavior to make life more rewarding (reinforcing) for people. Thus, Skinner consistently has argued for the use of positive reinforcement and against the use of punishment to shape behavior.

And what of current life? Skinner suggests that current practices in the Western world have eroded the contingencies of reinforcement associated with work. How has this occurred? People in the West have become estranged from their work because they are separated from the final product; people in the West avoid labor through the use of machines but thereby deprive themselves of the reinforcing consequences of labor; and people in the West have become more focused on immediate reinforcement, making daily life more pleasurable but reinforcing little more than the behavior that is associated with such immediate reinforcement. The result, according to Skinner, is that "where thousand of millions of people in other parts of the world cannot do many of the things they want to do, hundreds of millions in the West do not want to do many of the things they can do. In winning the struggle for freedom and the pursuit of happiness, the West has lost its inclination to act."

Is there any hope? Skinner suggests that human behavior in the West has grown weak, but it can be improved by strengthening the contingencies of behavior, that is, by the use of applied behavior analysis.

SOURCE: Skinner, 1986.

---

and Allport, Eysenck, and Cattell used the concept of traits. The concept of structure relates to relatively enduring qualities of organization and tends to be an important element in accounting for individual differences. But the behavioral approach to personality emphasizes situational specificity and minimizes the importance of broad response predispositions relative to the importance of stimuli in the external environment. Therefore, it is not surprising to find few structural concepts. Corresponding to a lack of emphasis on structure, the behavioral approach places considerable emphasis on the concepts of process and, in particular, on processes that hold true for all individuals. In summary, because the theory is based on assumptions that are different from those of other theories, the formal properties of the theory are different from those already studied.

Skinner's Theory of Personality

Structure

The key structural unit for the behavioral approach in, general, and Skinner's approach in particular, is the **response**. The nature of a response may range from a simple reflex response (e.g., salivation to food, startle to a loud noise) to a complex piece of behavior (e.g., solution to a math problem, subtle forms of aggression). What is critical to the definition of a response is that it represents an external, observable piece of behavior (response) that can be related to environmental events. The learning process essentially involves the association or connection of responses to events in the environment.

In his approach to learning, Skinner distinguishes between responses elicited by known stimuli, such as an eyeblink reflex to a puff of air, and responses that cannot be associated with any stimuli. These responses are emitted by the organism and are called **operants**. Skinner's view is that stimuli in the environment do not force the organism to behave or incite it into action. The initial cause of behavior is in the organism itself. "There is no environmental eliciting stimulus for operant behavior; it simply occurs. In the terminology of operant conditioning, operants are emitted by the organism. The dog walks, runs, and romps; the bird flies; the monkey swings from tree to tree; the human infant babbles vocally. In each case, the behavior occurs without any specific eliciting stimulus. . . . It is in the biological nature of organisms to emit operant behavior" (Reynolds, 1968, p. 8).

Process—Operant conditioning

If structural units are of such minor significance to the theory, it is critical that there be considerable sophistication about the process aspects of behavior. Indeed, in the sense that a learning theory approach to personality is being considered, a process orientation is being dealt with. Before discussing some of the processes that this theory views as underlying behavior, it is important to consider the concept of reinforcer. The Skinnerians define a **reinforcer** as an event (stimulus) that follows a response and increases the probability of its occurrence. If a pigeon's pecking at a disk, which is a piece of operant behavior, is followed by a reinforcer such as food, the probability of it pecking at the disk is increased. According to this view, a reinforcer strengthens the behavior it follows and there is no need to turn to biological explanations to determine why a stimulus reinforces behavior. Skinnerians postulate that some stimuli appear to be reinforcing for all animals and appear to be innate, whereas other stimuli only serve as reinforcers for some animals and appear to be based on their past association with innate reinforcers, that is, stimuli that originally do not serve as reinforcers can come to do so through their association with other reinforcers. Some stimuli, such as money, become **generalized reinforcers** because they provide access to many other kinds of reinforcers.

It is important to observe here that a reinforcer is defined by its effect on behavior, an increase in the probability of a response, and is not defined in a theoretical way. Often it is difficult to know precisely what will serve as a reinforcer for behavior, as it may vary from individual to individual or from organism to organism. Finding a reinforcer may turn out to be a trial-and-error operation. One keeps trying stimuli until one finds a stimulus that can reliably increase the probability of a certain response.

The focus of the Skinnerian approach is on the qualities of responses and their relationships to rates and intervals at which they are reinforced or **schedules of reinforcements**. A simple experimental device, the Skinner box, is used to study these relationships. In this kind of box there are few stimuli, and behaviors such as a rat's pressing of a bar or a pigeon's pecking of a key are observed. It is here, according to Skinner, that one can best observe the elementary laws of behavior. These laws are discovered through the control of behavior, in this case the bar-pressing activity of the rat or the key-pecking activity of the pigeon. Behavior is understood when it can be controlled by specific changes in the environment. To understand behavior is to control it. Behavior is controlled through the choice of responses that are reinforced and the rates at which they are reinforced. Schedules of reinforcement can be based on a particular *time interval* or a particular *response interval*. In a time interval schedule, the reinforcement appears after a certain period, say every minute, regardless of the number of responses made by the organism. In response interval, or a response ratio schedule, reinforcements appear after a certain number of responses (e.g., presses of a bar, pecks of a key) have been made.

Thus, reinforcements need not be given after every response, but can instead be given only sometimes. Furthermore, reinforcements can be given on a regular or a *fixed* basis, always a certain period of time or after a certain number of responses, or they can be given on a *variable* basis, sometimes after a minute and sometimes after two minutes, or sometimes after a few responses and sometimes after many responses. Each schedule of reinforcement tends to stabilize behavior in a different way.

In a sense, operant learning represents a sophisticated formulation of the principles of animal training. Complex behavior is *shaped* through a process of **successive approximation**; that is, complex behaviors are developed by reinforcing pieces of behavior that resemble the final form of behavior one wants to produce.

> Operant conditioning shapes behavior as a sculptor shapes a lump of clay. Although at some point the sculptor seems to have produced an entirely novel object, we can always follow the process back to the original undifferentiated lump, and we can make the successive stages by which we return to this condition as small as we wish. At no point does anything emerge which is very different from what preceded it. . . . An operant is not something which appears full grown in the behavior of the organism. It is the result of a continuous shaping process.
>
> SKINNER, 1953, p. 91

The process of shaping or successive approximation is seen most clearly in the work of animal trainers. The difficult tricks performed by circus animals are not learned as complete wholes. Rather, the trainer gradually builds up sequences of learned responses through the reinforcement of particular behaviors that are then linked to or chained to one another. What started off as the learning of individual behaviors ends up as the display of a complex series of acts before a circus audience. The animal ultimately is rewarded for its behavior, but the final reward is made dependent, or contingent, on the performance of the series of previously learned behaviors. In a similar way, complex behaviors in humans may be developed through the process of successive approximation.

Although most of the emphasis in operant conditioning is on the use of positive reinforcers such as food, money, or praise, Skinnerians also emphasize the importance of reinforcers based on the organism's *escape* from, or *avoidance* of, aversive (unpleasant) stimuli. In such cases responses are reinforced by the removal or avoidance of an unpleasant stimulus rather than by the appearance of a pleasant stimulus. In all these cases the effect is to reinforce or increase the strength of the response. Such response–outcome contingencies can be contrasted with the case of *punishment*. In punishment, an aversive stimulus follows a response, decreasing the probability of that response occurring again. However, the effect of punishment is temporary and it appears to be of little value in eliminating behavior. For this reason, Skinner has emphasized the use of positive reinforcement in the shaping of behavior.

Growth and development

The Skinnerian view of growth and development continues to emphasize the importance of schedules of reinforcement in the acquisition and performance of behavior. As the child develops, responses are conditioned and remain under the control of reinforcement contingencies in the environment. The emphasis is on specific response patterns as they are influenced by specific environmental reinforcers. Children become self-reliant through the reinforcement of acts in which they take care of themselves, for instance, in eating and dressing. The child is reinforced immediately on the completion of those acts, both by material rewards such as food and by social rewards such as praise. The child becomes emotionally independent through the development of a stable rate of response (one that occurs at regular intervals) that requires only occasional reinforcement. In learning to tolerate delay of gratification (reinforcement), the child may first be gratified after a brief period of delay and then gradually may be reinforced for longer periods of delay between request and gratification. After a while, delay behavior becomes stabilized, and one can say that the child has developed an ability to tolerate delays in gratification.

What of children who imitate the behavior of parents, siblings, and others? Are such behaviors tied to the same principles of reinforcement? Skinnerians accept the view that behaviors can be imitated without being directly reinforced. However, this only occurs where imitation has been reinforced many times and thus, through generalization, imitation itself takes on the qualities of a reinforcer. Whereas initially the child is reinforced for imitating specific responses, it is now reinforcing to be generally imitative and a generalized imitative response tendency has developed. Thus, from the Skinnerian point of view, new behaviors may be acquired through the process of successive approximations or through the development of a generalized imitative repertoire. In either case, the behaviors are under the control of reinforcement contingencies in the environment.

Psychopathology

The general learning theory position on psychopathology may be stated as follows: the basic principles of learning provide a completely adequate interpretation of psychopathology. Explanations in terms of symptoms with underlying causes are superfluous. According to the behavioral point of view, behavioral pathology is not a disease. Instead, it is a response pattern learned according to the same principles of behavior as are all response patterns. "The specific behavior termed abnormal is learned, maintained, and altered in the same manner as is normal behavior, and normal behavior itself may be viewed as an adjustment resulting from a particular history of reinforcement" (Ullmann & Krasner, 1969, p. 105).

The proponents of the Skinnerian view argue against any concept of the unconscious or a "sick personality." Individuals are not sick, they merely do not respond appropriately to stimuli. Either they fail to learn a response or they learn a maladaptive response. In the former case, there is a **behavioral deficit,** For example, individuals who are socially inadequate may have had faulty reinforcement histories in which social skills were not developed. Having failed to be reinforced for social skills during socialization, as adults they have an inadequate response repertoire with which to respond to social situations. Reinforcement is important not only for the learning of responses but also for the maintenance of behavior. Thus, one possible result of an absence of reinforcement in the environment is depression. According to this view, depression represents a lessening of behavior or a lowered response rate. The depressed person is not responsive because positive reinforcement has been withdrawn (Ferster, 1973).

In the case of learning of a **maladaptive response,** the problem is that a response has been learned that is not considered acceptable by society or others in the person's environment. This may be because the response itself is considered unacceptable (e.g., hostile behavior) or because the response occurs under unacceptable circumstances (e.g., joking at a formal business meeting). Schizophrenia, a serious thought disorder, may be viewed as an extreme example of a situation where a response pattern is "out of whack" with schedules of reinforcement in the environment. According to Ullmann and Krasner (1975), schizophrenia is the result of the failure of the environment to reinforce certain sequences of behavior. Schizophrenics attend to unusual cues in the environment because they have not been reinforced for attending to the social stimuli to which "normal" people respond. What is interpreted by the ordinary observer as a lack of attention is really an attention to unusual cues. Related to this situation is the development of **superstitious behavior** (Skinner, 1948). Superstitious behavior develops because of an accidental relationship between a response and reinforcement. Thus, Skinner found that if he gave pigeons small amounts of food at regular intervals regardless of what they were doing, many birds would come to associate the response that was coincidentally rewarded with systematic reinforcement. For example, if a pigeon was coincidentally rewarded while walking around in a counterclockwise direction, this response might become conditioned even though it had no cause–effect relationship with the reinforcement. The continuous performance of the behavior would result in occasional, again coincidental, reinforcement. Thus, the behavior could be maintained over long periods of time. An observer looking in on this situation might be tempted to say: "Look at that crazy pigeon."

In sum, people develop faulty behavior repertoires, what others call "sick" behavior or psychopathology, because of the following: they were not reinforced for adaptive behaviors, they were punished for behaviors that later would be considered adaptive, they were reinforced for maladaptive behaviors, or they were reinforced under inappropriate circumstances for what would otherwise be adaptive behavior. In all cases there is an emphasis on observable responses and schedules of reinforcement rather than on concepts such as drive, conflict, unconscious, self-esteem, or a construct system.

Behavioral assessment and behavior change

The emphasis on specific behaviors tied to defined situational characteristics forms the basis for what has come to be known as **behavioral assessment.** Heavily influenced by the thinking of Skinner, the behavioral approach to assessment emphasizes three things: (1) identification of specific behaviors, often called **target behaviors** or **target responses;** (2) identification of specific environmental factors that elicit, cue, or reinforce the target behaviors; and (3) identification of specific environmental factors that can be manipulated to alter the behavior. Thus a behavioral assessment of a child's temper tantrums would include a clear, objective definition of temper tantrum behavior in the child, a complete description of the situation that sets off the tantrum behavior, a complete description of the reactions of parents and others that may be reinforcing the behavior, and an analysis of the potential for eliciting and reinforcing other nontantrum behaviors (Kanfer & Saslow, 1965; O'Leary, 1972). This **functional analysis of behavior,** involving the effort to identify the environmental conditions that control behavior, sees behavior as a function of specific events in the environment. The approach has also been called the **ABC assessment**—one assesses the Antecedent conditions of the behavior, the Behavior itself, and the Consequences of the behavior.

Behavioral assessment generally is closely tied to treatment objectives in accordance with the pragmatic emphasis characteristic of this approach. For example, consider the task of assisting a mother who comes to a clinic because she feels helpless in dealing with her four-year-old son's temper tantrums and general disobedience (Hawkins et al., 1966). The psychologists involved in this case followed a fairly typical behavioral procedure to assessment and treatment. First, the mother and child were observed in the home to determine the nature of the undesirable behaviors, when they occurred, and which reinforcers seemed to maintain them. The following nine behaviors were determined to constitute the major portion of the boy's objectionable behavior: (1) biting his shirt or arm; (2) sticking out his tongue; (3) kicking or biting himself, other, or objects; (4) calling someone or something a derogatory name; (5) removing or threatening to remove his clothing; (6) saying "NO!" loudly and vigorously; (7) threatening to damage objects or persons; (8) throwing objects; (9) pushing his sister. Observation of the mother–child interaction suggested that the objectionable behavior was being maintained by attention from the mother. For example, often she would try to distract him by offering him toys or food.

The treatment program began with a behavioral analysis of the frequency with which the son expressed one of the objectionable behaviors during one-hour sessions, conducted in the home two to three times a week. Two psychologists acted as observers to ensure that there was high reliability or good agreement concerning recording of the objectionable behavior. This first phase, known as a baseline period, lasted for sixteen sessions. During this time, mother and child interacted in their usual way. Following this careful assessment of the objectionable behavior during the baseline period, the psychologists initiated their intervention or treatment program. Now the mother was instructed to tell her son to stop or to put him in his room by himself without toys each time that he emitted an objectionable behavior. In other words, there was a withdrawal of the positive reinforcer for objectionable behavior. At the same time, the mother was instructed to give her son attention and approval when he behaved in a desirable way. In other words, the positive reinforcers were made contingent on desirable behavior. During this time, known as the first experimental period, the frequency of objectionable behaviors was again counted. As can be seen in Figure 10.4, there was a marked decline in the frequency of objectionable behavior from between 18 and 113 such responses during a one-hour period (preexperimental baseline) to between 1 and 8 such responses per session (first experimental period).

Following the first experimental treatment period, the mother was instructed to return to her former behavior to determine whether it was the shift in her reinforcement behavior that was determining the change in her son's behavior. During this second baseline period, her son's

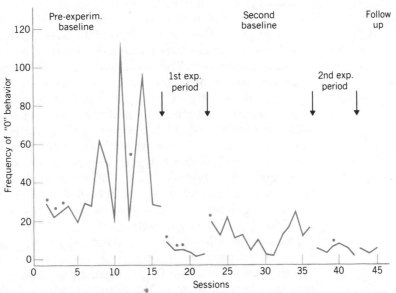

FIGURE 10.4 Number of 10-second Intervals per 1-hour Session, in Which Objectionable Behavior Occurred. Dots indicate sessions in which reliability was tested. (Hawkins *et al.*, 1966)

objectionable behavior ranged between 2 and 24 per session (Figure 10.4). There was an increase in this behavior, though not a return to the former baseline level. However, the mother reported she had trouble responding in her previous way because she now felt more "sure of herself." Thus, even during this period she gave her son more firm commands, gave in less after denying a request, and gave more affection in response to positive behaviors in her son than was previously the case. Following this there was a return to a full emphasis on the treatment program, resulting in a decline in objectionable behavior (second experimental period). The rate of objectionable behavior was found to remain low after a 24-day interval (follow-up period) and the mother reported a continuing positive change in the relationship.

In sum, in this case it was possible to assess the target responses in the home environment as well as their reinforcers, and then to specify a treatment regimen that would result in measurable changes in the frequency of these behaviors. As well as illustrating behavioral assessment, this study illustrates an interesting variant of the experimental method —the Skinnerian **own-control** or **ABA research design** (Krasner, 1976). Basically the ABA, own-control research design involves the experimental manipulation of a specific behavior and the demonstration that changes in behavior can be attributed directly to specific changes in environmental events. One subject is used and serves as his or her own control relating to variations in experimental conditions. In the first or baseline phase (A) of this design, the current rate of occurrence of the behavior of interest is recorded. In the second or reinforcement phase (B), a reinforcer following the behavior of interest is introduced in an effort to increase the frequency of that behavior. Once the behavioral response has been established at the desired frequency, the reinforcer may be withdrawn (A phase) to see whether the behavior returns to the original (baseline period) rate. This is called the nonreinforcement period. Instead of comparing a subject who is reinforced with one who is not, the subject is treated differently in the various phases—he is his own control. In some research, a fourth phase is also included in which the reinforcer is reintroduced to reestablish the desired behavior (see Figure 10.4). Also, some experiments may begin with the reinforcement phase and then move to nonreinforcement and then reintroduction of reinforcement. This approach is typical when it does not make sense to begin with a baseline period, as when a new behavior is being taught.

As can be seen, in behavioral assessment there is emphasis on single variables (specific target behaviors) and the gathering of reliable and objective data. What is different about behavioral assessment in comparison to some other personality measures is that the behavior itself is of interest, not some theoretical construct (ego strength, extroversion) presumed to be expressed in the behavior. Mischel (1968, 1971) has contrasted these differences in terms of **sign and sample approaches to assessment.** In the *sign* approach, traits are inferred from test behavior.

Test items are assumed adequate to reflect personality characteristics and interpretations are made of test behavior relative to assumed underlying traits. There is, in other words, a high level of inference from test behavior to interpretations concerning personality characteristics. In the *sample* approach, interest is in the behavior itself and how it is affected by alterations in environmental conditions. Interest is in overt behavior and it is assumed that one must understand the surrounding stimulus conditions to understand the relevant behavior. There is, in other words, a low level of inference from test behavior to other similar behaviors in the individual. The sign approach asks about motives and traits that act together to result in observed behavior; the sample approach asks about environmental variables that affect behaviors in terms of their frequency, intensity, and duration. A summary of many of these differences is given in Figure 10.5.

The use of behavioral technicians and the principles of operant conditioning to regulate behavior can be seen in a **token economy** (Ayllon & Azrin, 1965). Under a token economy, the behavioral technician rewards, with tokens, the various patient behaviors that are considered desirable. The tokens in turn can be exchanged by the patient for desirable products, such as candy and cigarettes. Thus, for example, patients could be reinforced for activities such as serving meals or cleaning floors. In a tightly controlled environmental setting, possibly in a state hospital

	BEHAVIORAL ASSESSMENT	TRADITIONAL ASSESSMENT
Assumptions		
1 Personality concept	Behavior as a function of the environment	Behavior as a function of underlying-causes
2 "Test" interpretation	Behavior as sample	Behavior as sign
3 Situations sampled	Varied and specific	Limited and ambiguous
Primary Functions	Description in behavioral-analytic terms	Description in psychodynamic terms
	Treatment selection	Diagnostic labeling
	Treatment evaluation	
Practical aspects		
1 Relation to treatment	Direct	Indirect
2 Time of assessment	Continuous with treatment	Prior to treatment

FIGURE 10.5 A Comparison of Traditional and Behavioral Assessment Strategies. (Cimenero, 1977)

for long-term psychiatric patients, it is feasible to make almost anything that a patient wants contingent on the desired behaviors.

According to a 1970 report, there are over 100 token economies in existence in over 50 different institutions (Krasner, 1970). By now there may be two or three times that number. There is evidence in support of the effectiveness of token economies in increasing such behaviors as social interaction, self-care, and job performance in severely disturbed patients and mentally retarded individuals. They also have been used effectively to decrease aggressive behavior in children and to decrease marital discord (Kazdin, 1977).

In sum, the Skinnerian behavioral technician seeks a straightforward application of the operant conditioning method to the problem of behavior change. Target behaviors are selected, and reinforcement is made contingent on performance of the desired responses. We have here, then, a view that emphasizes how the environment acts upon people, as opposed to how people act upon the environment. This view has resulted in a group of social engineers who are committed to acting on the environment. Watson suggested that through control of the environment he could train an infant to become any type of specialist he might select. Skinnerian social engineers take this principle one step further. As seen in the development of token economies, as well as in the development of communes based on Skinnerian principles, there is an interest in the design of environments that will control broad aspects of human behavior.

STIMULUS–RESPONSE THEORY: HULL, DOLLARD, AND MILLER

Stimulus–response (S–R) theory was being developed by people such as Hull and Dollard and Miller while Skinner was developing his operant conditioning view. However, S–R theory probably reached its peak of systematization and influence earlier than did Skinner's approach. For some time the operant and S–R approaches represented competitive points of view and considerable controversy and debate existed over their relative merits. This is not quite so true today, although differences remain and often these differences do become controversial.

A View of the Theorists

Several theorists have made significant contributions to the development of stimulus–response learning theory. Among these, however, three figures are of particular significance. The first, Clark L. Hull, made a major effort to develop a systematic, comprehensive theory of learning. The second two, John Dollard and Neal E. Miller, are particularly well known for their efforts to bring together the remarkable accomplishments of Freud and Hull.

Clark L. Hull (1884–1952)

Clark Hull was born in New York, but early in his life he and his family moved to a farm in Michigan. There was a considerable emphasis on religion in his family. Although at one point he had a religious conversion experience at an evangelist revival meeting, Hull began to have considerable doubt about religion and abandoned his beliefs in it.

During his early school years, Hull was very interested in mathematics and described the study of geometry as the most important event of his intellectual life. At college, he began studying math, physics, and chemistry with the goal of becoming a mining engineer. However, after two years at school, he became ill with polio and was forced to consider a new life occupation. His interest in theory and in the design of automatic equipment led him to the study of psychology. After a difficult and incomplete recovery from polio, Hull returned to college to concentrate in psychology at the University of Michigan.

After a brief stint as a teacher in Kentucky, Hull went on to graduate work in psychology at the University of Wisconsin. He first developed an interest in finding a scientific basis for aptitude testing and then systematically studied what takes place during hypnosis. During the time that he was at the University of Wisconsin, word was spreading of Watson's

Clark L. Hull

views of behaviorism and Hull found himself sympathetic to this new emphasis on objectivity.

In 1929, Hull went to Yale as a professor of psychology. He had just read a translation of Pavlov's *Conditioned Reflexes* and was interested in comparisons between Pavlov's research and the experiments that were being conducted in this country. Also, he was forced to end his research on hypnosis because of an attitude of fear of hypnosis. The following years witnessed a coming together of his interests in math, geometry, theory, apparatus construction, and psychology as a natural science. In 1940, he published his *Mathematico-Deductive Theory of Rote Learning*, and, in 1943, his *Principles of Behavior*. Of particular importance was Hull's emphasis on a systematic theory of the process of instrumental learning.

Hull's emphasis on a systematic theory of learning, careful experimentation, and the development of habits (stimulus–response associations) as a result of reward laid much of the groundwork for a learning theory approach to social psychology and to the study of personality.

John Dollard (1900–1980) and Neal E. Miller (1909–)

John Dollard was born in Wisconsin and received his undergraduate degree from the University of Wisconsin in 1922. He obtained his graduate degree (Ph.D., 1931) in sociology from the University of Chicago. Following this he taught sociology, anthropology, and psychology at Yale University. An unusual aspect of Dollard's professional development, and one that significantly influenced his later thinking, was his training in psychoanalysis at the Berlin Psychoanalytic Institute. His interest in psychoanalysis, clinical work, and the social sciences continued throughout his professional career.

Neal E. Miller also was born in Wisconsin. He received his undergraduate degree from the University of Washington and his Ph.D. from Yale University in 1935. During this time he came into contact with Hull and Dollard, and also obtained training in psychoanalysis at the Vienna Institute of Psychoanalysis. He continued to spend the major part of his professional career at Yale until 1966 when he joined the faculty at Rockefeller University. During his time at Yale, Miller made many significant experimental and theoretical contributions to stimulus–response theory, particularly in the area of motivation and learned drives. Subsequently he has become a major figure in the area of biofeedback or the learning of voluntary control over bodily processes such as heart rate and blood pressure (Miller, 1978, 1983). In 1951 Miller was elected president of the American Psychological Association.

The collaborative work of Dollard and Miller is expressed in three major books. In the first, *Frustration and Aggression* (1939), completed with colleagues at Yale's Institute of Human Relations, there was an attempt to develop a scientific theory of aggressive behavior based on the

John Dollard

assumption that aggression is a response to frustration. In the second, *Social Learning and Imitation* (1941), Miller and Dollard attempted to apply Hull's theory to personality and social psychology. Finally, in the third book, *Personality and Psychotherapy* (1950), Dollard and Miller attempted to integrate the achievements of learning theory, as expressed in the works of Pavlov, Hull, and others, with the achievements of psychoanalysis, as expressed in the works of Freud, and with the achievements of other figures in the social sciences. In this book they attempted to apply the basic principles of learning to complex personality functioning, neurotic phenomena, and psychotherapy. This was significant in that it directed attention to the application of learning theory to clinical phenomena. However, in contrast with the approaches of current behavior modificationists and behavior therapists, the use of learning theory did not itself lead to the development of new therapeutic techniques.

The S–R Theory of Personality

The helpless, naked, human infant is born with primary drives such as hunger, thirst, and reactions to pain and cold. He does not have, however, many of the motives that distinguish the adult as a member of a particular tribe, nation, social class, occupation, or profession. Many extremely important drives, such as the desire for money, the ambition to become an artist

Neal E. Miller

or a scholar, and particular fears and guilts are learned during socialization.

DOLLARD AND MILLER, 1950, p. 62

Structure

As in Skinner's operant theory, the key structural concept for S–R theory is the *response*. However, whereas Skinner places little importance on the stimulus that leads to and becomes associated with the response, the S–R view is that stimuli become connected to responses to form stimulus–response bonds. According to Hullian theory, an association between a stimulus and a response is called a **habit**; personality structure is largely composed of the habits, or S–R bonds, that are learned by the organism and of the relationships among these habits.

Another structural concept used by the followers of Hull is that of **drive**. A drive is broadly defined as a stimulus strong enough to activate behavior. Using the Hullian model, it is drives that make the individual respond. A distinction is made between *innate, primary drives* and *learned, secondary drives*. The primary drives, such as pain and hunger, are generally associated with physiological conditions within the organism. "One of these is pain. Pain can reach stabbing heights of greater strength than probably any other single drive. The parching sensation of thirst, the pangs of extreme hunger, and the sore weight of fatigue are other examples of powerful innate drives. The bitter sting of cold and the

BEHAVIORAL APPROACHES TO PERSONALITY

insistent goading of sex are further examples" (Dollard & Miller, 1950, p. 30).

Secondary drives are drives that have been acquired on the basis of their association with the satisfaction of the primary drives. "These learned drives are acquired on the basis of the primary drives, represent elaborations of them, and serve as a façade behind which the functions of the underlying innate drives are hidden. These learned drives are exceedingly important in human behavior" (Dollard & Miller, 1950, pp. 31–32). An acquired drive of considerable importance is that of anxiety or fear. Based on the primary drive of pain, the secondary drive of anxiety is important because it can be learned quickly and become strong. Anxiety can lead the organism toward a variety of behaviors and is of particular importance in relation to abnormal behavior.

Process

According to S–R theory, learning consists of the association of stimuli with responses as a result of the reinforcement that follows these connections. In **instrumental learning** there is an emphasis on learned responses being instrumental in bringing about a desirable situation (e.g., reward, escape from pain, avoidance of pain). The Hullian model of instrumental conditioning is derived from an interest in more complex forms of learning (e.g., problem solving, motivation, goal-directed activity) than is classical or operant conditioning. In the Hullian model, there is an emphasis on drives that lead to internal stimuli, these stimuli then leading to responses that result in rewards. The rewards represent a reduction of the drive stimuli.

The typical experiment in instrumental learning might involve the variables affecting a rat's learning to run a maze. The experimenter changes the number of hours of food deprivation, assumes that this is related to the strength of internal drive (hunger) stimuli, and then observes the behavioral consequences of the rat's having been rewarded for making certain turns in the maze. If a hungry rat receives food for making a response or series of responses in the maze, then the probability is increased that it will make the same responses on further trials in the maze. The responses are reinforced through the reduced strength of hunger drive stimuli.

Another type of experiment is conducted in relation to instrumental escape learning. In this type of experiment (Miller, 1951), a rat is put into a box with two compartments: a white compartment with a grid as a floor and a black compartment with a solid floor. The compartments are separated by a door. At the beginning of the experiment, the rats are given electric shocks while in the white compartment and are allowed to escape into the black compartment. Thus, a fear response is conditioned to the white compartment. A test is then made as to whether the fear of the white compartment can lead to the learning of a new response. Now, in order for the rat to escape to the black compartment, it must turn a wheel placed in the white compartment. The turning of the wheel opens the door to the black compartment and allows the rat to escape. After a number of trials, the rat begins to rotate the wheel with considerable speed. The interpretation is that the rat has acquired a fear drive in relation to the white compartment. This drive operates to activate the organism and to set the stage for reinforcement, just as the hunger drive did in the maze experiment. Escape from the white into the black compartment involves the learning of a new response—the turning of a wheel. This instrumental learning is based on the consequences of the response, escape from the white compartment, and on the associated reduction in the strength of the fear drive stimuli.

Growth and development

In general, S–R theory interprets growth and development as consisting of the accumulation of habits, which are then related to one another in a hierarchical arrangement or order of importance. Initially the behavior of the infant is largely a reflexive response to external stimuli and internal drives. In the course of development, however, behavior reflects the central role of thought or **higher mental processes**. Language is of particular importance in the functioning of our higher mental processes and in enabling us to go beyond simple, reflexive responses to stimuli. Language helps us to make important discriminations and generalizations. Words can be attached to drives and, through their symbolic function, themselves lead to drives being aroused. Language enables us to anticipate the future, and thus to go beyond reinforcers in the immediate situation.

Miller and Dollard's social learning interpretation of development included an emphasis on the role of **imitation**. According to them the imitative process develops out of trial and error or random behavior and is based on the positive reinforcement of matching behavior. For example, a boy might hear his father approach and run to greet him, following which he receives some candy. His younger sister might on one occasion run when she saw her older brother run. She too receives candy, resulting in a reward for matching the behavior of the older brother. Subsequently, through the process of generalization, the younger girl might imitate other behaviors of the older brother. In an experimental analysis of such a situation, Miller and Dollard rewarded rats for going in the same direction in a maze as the leader. Whereas the leader was trained to make use of a cue for finding food, the other rats were not. Put in other situations, the rats continued to imitate the behavior of the leader rather than independently making use of the available cues. In sum, rats reinforced for following the behavior of a leader learned the response of imitating, and this learned response generalized from the original situation to other situations.

Other efforts have been made to translate Hullian theory into principles of growth and development. Such efforts generally have emphasized the importance of rewards in parental child-rearing practices. For

BEHAVIORAL APPROACHES TO PERSONALITY

example, in one research program the pattern of child rearing found to be most likely to result in "high conscience" development in children was one in which the mother is generally warm and loving but also uses the threat of withdrawal of affection as a method of control (Sears, Rau, & Alpert, 1965). Later research has suggested that the concept of "conscience" is complex and involves many possible behaviors. Furthermore, the relationship of child-rearing practices to personality development is very complicated. As a result, there have tended to be fewer such studies relating early patterns of parenteral reward to the later development of broad personality characteristics.

Psychopathology

If a neurosis is functional (i.e., a product of experience rather than of organic damage or instinct), it must be learned. . . .

The dynamics of conflict behavior are systematically deduced from more basic principles. Thus, a fundamental fact of neurosis—that of conflict—is tied in with general learning theory.

DOLLARD AND MILLER, 1950, pp. 8, 10

The Hullian theory of learning emphasizes the importance of drives and the reinforcement that comes from the reduction of drive stimuli. One drive that is critical in the learning of abnormal behaviors is that of

Conflict—This man is facing an approach-approach conflict in terms of what to choose to eat. If he were concerned about gaining weight, he would face an approach-avoidance conflict (i.e., the desire to enjoy the cake and the wish to avoid gaining weight).

anxiety. Although the details of various Hullian explanations of abnormal behavior differ, and some are supportive of psychoanalytic theory whereas others are not, they all state that abnormal behaviors are learned because they result in the reduction of anxiety drive stimuli.

Dollard and Miller (1950) were among the first to relate the principles of learning theory to personality phenomena, in general, and to abnormal behavior, in particular. In this effort they emphasized the concepts of drive, drive conflict, anxiety, and reinforcement through the reduction of anxiety.

According to Dollard and Miller, a neurosis represents the expression of learned conflicts that are inaccessible to verbal awareness. Neuroses are caused by conflict. In the course of development, children must learn socially accepted outlets for their drives. Particularly critical learning situations are the ones involving feeding, toilet training, and sexual and aggressive behavior. As children grow, they may wish to express certain drives but be punished for doing so by their parents. Or, children may wish to express aggression toward the parents, but be punished for this. The result of punishment is the development of an acquired fear drive in relation to certain stimuli. As described earlier, Miller demonstrated that the response of fear could be conditioned to a previously neutral stimulus (white compartment) and then, itself, take on the properties of a drive stimulus. In some cases, the same stimulus may come to elicit both an approach response and an avoidance response associated with the same drive. At this point, the individual experiences an **approach–avoidance conflict**. Thus a boy may be torn between making sexual advances toward a girl (approach) and the fear of doing so (avoidance). Another example would be of an individual who wishes to express anger (approach) but is afraid of doing so (avoidance).

Thus, the approach–avoidance conflict between two drives is the basic ingredient for the development of neurotic behavior. As a result of the conflict and the anxiety involved, the individual develops a symptom. The symptom reduces the anxiety and relieves the pressure of the conflict. For example, Dollard and Miller described the case of a twenty-three-year-old married woman who had developed a number of fears, one of which was that her heart would stop beating if she did not concentrate on counting the beats. The difficulties started with her feeling faint in a store, then developed into a fear of going out alone, and then into a fear of heart trouble. Dollard and Miller interpreted the symptom as involving a sex–fear conflict. When on the streets alone, the woman was afraid of sexual temptation. She felt that someone might try to seduce her and that she would be vulnerable to the seduction. The increased sex desire accompanying the fantasied seduction touched off anxiety and guilt, leading to the sex–anxiety conflict. Going home and avoiding being alone on the streets were reinforced because they reduced the anxiety and relieved the conflict. The counting of heartbeats was similarly reinforcing because it preoccupied her and did not allow her to think of possible seductions. The counting habit was reinforced by the drop in anxiety.

The case illustrates how Dollard and Miller made use of the concepts of drive, drive conflict, anxiety, and reinforcement through drive reduction to account for the development of a neurosis. Although the details are only sketchy, the case also illustrates how Dollard and Miller attempted to use Hullian theory in a way that was consistent with psychoanalytic theory.

Although most attention has been given to approach–avoidance conflicts in the development of neuroses, Dollard and Miller also emphasized the importance of approach–approach and avoidance–avoidance conflicts. In an **approach–approach conflict** the person is torn between two desirable alternatives. Should the person date one or another attractive individual, watch this great movie or the other great movie, buy this car or that car? In an **avoidance–avoidance conflict** the person is torn between undesirable, unpleasant alternatives. Should the person pay the bill now and be without money or pay a larger bill later, is divorce or living in an unpleasant situation worse, should the child tell the parent and risk punishment or stay silent and feel guilty?

There have been other efforts to use Hullian theory to explain abnormal behavior. Although they have emphasized the concepts of anxiety as a drive, and symptoms as responses that are drive reducing, they have used neither the conflict model nor psychoanalytic theory. In fact, other efforts along Hullian lines have been hostile to psychoanalytic interpretations. Whereas Dollard and Miller, in their application of learning theory to psychoanalytic concepts, continued to use a term such as symptom, current learning approaches reject such concepts. As noted earlier, they are viewed as part of a medical symptom–disease model that is rejected in favor of a behavioral-psychological model. S–R theory has not been as influential as classical conditioning theory and operant conditioning theory in the development of new approaches to behavior change. In part, this is probably due to the S–R emphasis on the concept of drive, an internal variable that grew out of favor after the 1940s. In part, it also is probably due to the early efforts of Dollard and Miller to relate S–R theory to psychoanalysis rather than focusing on the application of the theory to new methods of behavior change.

A COMPARISON OF BEHAVIORAL APPROACHES WITH EARLIER VIEWS

This chapter has considered learning, behavioral approaches, in particular those based on principles of classical conditioning, operant conditioning, and stimulus–response learning. To an even greater extent than any of the approaches considered previously, there is a diversity of views and even hostility among alternative camps. Such diversity makes comparison with earlier views difficult. At the same time, the approaches considered in this chapter hold enough in common for them to be considered together, and enough that generally distinguishes them from the views presented earlier for some comparison to be made (Figure 10.6).

Perhaps the most significant comparison that can be drawn between the theories presented in this chapter and those considered previously is the emphasis on *processes* of learning rather than on *structures* such as motives, traits, the self-concept, or constructs. In part following from this, learning–behavioral approaches tend to emphasize the importance of specific behaviors rather than general personality characteristics. In addition, there is an interest in general laws of learning rather than in individual differences. Also, in terms of method of research, there is an emphasis on experiments in the laboratory rather than clinical investigation or the use of questionnaires. To return to the distinction considered in Chapter 2, there is a contrast between two disciplines, the one (behavioral) interested in general laws and the experimental control of variables, the other (traditional personality theory) interested in individual differences and correlations among variables that cannot necessarily be studied in the laboratory.

Finally, there tends to be a difference in the extent to which the focus is on variables internal to the organism as opposed to those external to it. As noted in the first chapter, the internal–external issue is one that has existed in the field for some time. It is perhaps seen most clearly in the contrast between Freud and Skinner, the former emphasizing the extent to which we are "lived" by unknown, internal forces and the latter emphasizing that "a person does not act upon the world, the world acts upon him" (Skinner, 1971, p. 211). Beyond these two theorists, however, differences tend to remain in the extent to which internal and external variables are emphasized. Relative to the views presented earlier, the theories considered in this chapter emphasize the importance of variables in the environment in the regulation and control of behavior.

Having made these comparisons, we are now at a point at which a

Learning-Behavioral Views	Traditional Personality Theory
Processes of learning	Personality structures
Specific behaviors	General characteristics
General laws	Individual differences
Laboratory data	Clinical data & questionnaires
Environmental variables	Internal variables

FIGURE 10.6 Contrasting General Points of Emphasis of Learning–Behavioral Views and Traditional Theories of Personality.

BEHAVIORAL APPROACHES TO PERSONALITY

critical evaluation of learning, behavioral approaches to personality can be undertaken.

CRITICAL EVALUATION

We have now covered considerable ground, including a variety of theoretical and applied approaches. It is time to take stock of learning, behavioral approaches to personality.

Strengths of Behavioral Approaches

Three major contributions may be noted in relation to behavioral approaches: a commitment to systematic research and theory development; a recognition and exploration of the role of situational, environmental variables in influencing behavior; and a pragmatic approach to treatment leading to important new developments.

Behavioral psychologists share a commitment to empiricism or systematic research. Whatever the differences in theory, the various approaches tend to be characterized by a respect for scientific methodology and a respect for evidence in support for a new point of view. In contrast with the development of psychoanalysis, and to a certain extent with that of phenomenology and humanistic approaches, behavioral psychology has been largely tied to academic departments. There the emphasis is on clarity in defining constructs and on replicability in verifying data. Although at times these constraints may impose limitations on what is studied and how phenomena are conceptualized, they also set some useful boundaries on armchair speculation and quasi-religious debate. Thus, to a greater extent than most other approaches considered to this point, the behavioral approach emphasizes laboratory research which leads to the establishing of causal relationships.

Because behavioral psychologists have emphasized research and because they have been based in academic departments, there has been an openness to new developments in other areas of psychology. This is not to say that theoretical biases are given up easily, but rather that there is a commitment to discovery as opposed to dogma. Thus, not only are experiments designed to test competing theories but new data can provide the basis for theoretical development.

The second contribution and strength of learning, behavioral theory is a recognition of the role of environmental and situational variables in behavior. Most behavioral approaches emphasize the importance of regulating or maintaining conditions in the environment; all emphasize the importance of situational analysis. For some time traditional personality theory and assessment gave minimal attention to such variables. The importance of the situation or environment was noted by psychoanalytic and trait theorists, but there was not active exploration or conceptual development. In many ways, it has been unfortunate that the emphasis on situational variables and situation-specific aspects of performance became associated with the person–situation controversy. As most personality psychologists now recognize, both personal and situation variables enter into behavior and our effort must be to understand how they relate to one another. The particular contribution of the behavioral approach has been to call attention to the variability and flexibility that is characteristic of much of human behavior and to call attention to the diversity of skills that are relevant to specific tasks.

Related to this has been a pragmatism characteristic of behavior therapists, a pragmatism that has led to the development of many important procedures for behavior change. In contrast with the focus of many traditional treatment programs on young, verbal, intelligent, and successful patients, many behavior modification programs started by treating individuals on whom almost everyone else gave up—the chronic schizophrenic, the autistic child, the retarded, the addicted, and so on. Traditional therapy programs were not working and new approaches were required. Behavior therapists filled the void, in particular with the application of Skinnerian principles in behavior modification programs. These programs have raised moral and ethical issues concerning the control of human behavior, but on the whole significant gains have been made in assisting people who otherwise would have been left untouched.

Limitations of Behavioral Approaches

If the strengths outlined above seem significant, the limitations to be detailed are no less noteworthy. In some cases they speak to the same issues already covered, suggesting that the reality is not always as pretty as the picture presented. For example, with its concern for objectivity and rigor there has been an oversimplification of personality and the neglect of important phenomena. Human behavior is complex. Measurement of one response or one component of the personality system may give a very incomplete picture of what is occurring, and an exclusive emphasis on one mechanism of change may give a very inaccurate representation of the multiple processes leading to multiple effects (Schwartz, 1982). Human personality involves structure and organization as well as discrete responses, and it involves motivation and emotion as well as overt behavior.

There are many components to the criticism that learning theorists oversimplify behavior. One component is the claim that the principles of learning used are derived from research on rats and other subhuman animals, and there is a question of whether the same principles are involved in human learning. In other words, can rat laws be applied to human behavior? A second component of this criticism is the claim that the behaviors studied by the learning theorists are superficial. In their effort to gain experimental rigor and control over relevant variables, learning theorists have limited themselves to simple, specific responses and have avoided complex behaviors. We may recall here Cattell's argument that the bivariate method limits investigators to the study of a few variables, and this means that they must ignore behaviors that cannot be produced in the laboratory.

A third and critical component of the criticism regarding oversimplification is concerned with cognitive behavior. Cognitive behavior involves the way in which the individual receives, organizes, and transmits information. The work of many psychologists gives clear evidence of the importance of an understanding of cognitive behavior. Yet, for a long time behaviorists avoided considering these phenomena. Whether because of a reluctance to look at internal processes or because of a reluctance to consider complex processes, learning theorists stuck fast in their attempts to understand all behavior in terms of stimulus–response bonds or in terms of operants and successive approximation.

Critics of the approaches considered in this chapter also emphasize that there is no agreed-on theory of learning and that a large gap exists between theory and practice. Some time ago a supporter of behavior therapy suggested that it is a group of techniques rather than a theory-based scientific procedure: "When you eliminate the polemics and politics and gratuities, however, what remains of the theory to define the field and to tell you what it is about? Not a whole lot" (London, 1972, p. 916). Further, where there is evidence that procedures can be effective, such as with systematic desensitization, there is question concerning the effective processes involved, that is, such a procedure may be working for reasons other than those suggested by behavior therapists (Kazdin & Wilson, 1978; Levis & Malloy, 1982).

Finally, let us consider the effectiveness of behavioral approaches to treatment. There is a need for evidence concerning the effectiveness of most behavioral treatment procedures, particularly where they are used with actual clinical populations and in relation to significant effects that are maintained over time. Initially, there was a burst of enthusiasm for the successes of behavior therapy, as is often the case with a new development. Following this, some sobering questions were raised, including the following: To what extent is there, in behavior therapy, successful generalization from one situation to another and from one response to another? To what extent are the results durable or stable over time? Are the originally published success rates accurate and are behavioral techniques equally successful with all patients?

Historically, a problem with behavior therapy has been that often the results do not generalize and/or they do not remain stable over time. Questions have been raised, for example, as to whether results obtained in the laboratory or clinic are maintained in the natural environment (Bandura, 1972; Kazdin & Bootzin, 1972). In addition, some studies suggest that in many patients gains are eventually lost (Eysenck & Beech, 1971). Finally, techniques found to be useful with mild problems in the laboratory may be found to be of far lesser significance when applied to clients with more serious difficulties. Although there are many reports of success, a recent review of the literature concluded that "research in which the effectiveness of behavior therapy has been compared to other treatment approaches has failed to provide convincing support for the superiority of behavior therapy" (Turkat & Forehand, 1980, p. 17).

Summary Evaluation

It is, of course, hard to evaluate in an overall way approaches that often are so diverse. However, the strengths and limitations noted do have general relevance (Figure 10.7). It should be noted that the criticism of learning, behavioral approaches to personality have not gone unchallenged. To the charge of oversimplification, the suggestion is that one must start somewhere and that it makes sense to start with simple events. Similarly, it is suggested that as understanding progresses, there is movement from the simple to the complex. To questions concerning theory, the suggestion is that many learning processes may exist and that the development of techniques of behavior change can themselves facilitate the further development of theory. In other words, not only does treatment success not always depend on theoretical understanding but in some cases it can lead to such understanding. Finally, to questions concerning effectiveness the suggestion is made that there is sufficient empirical basis for encouragement. Generally, behavior therapists receive enough intermittent reinforcement to maintain them in the belief that they are on the right track and that further success lies ahead.

In sum, the qualities of rigor, objectivity, and measurability of concepts have appeal for those who have accepted the values of the scientist and work in academic settings. In addition, successes in applied efforts

STRENGTHS	LIMITATIONS
1. Committed to systematic research and theory development.	1. Oversimplifies personality and neglects important phenomena.
2. Recognize the role of situational and environmental variables in influencing behavior.	2. Lacks a single, unified theory; gap between theory and practice.
3. Take a pragmatic approach to treatment which can lead to important new developments.	3. Requires further evidence to support claims of treatment's effectiveness.

FIGURE 10.7 Summary of Strengths and Limitations of Learning, Behavioral Approaches.

BEHAVIORAL APPROACHES TO PERSONALITY

have buoyed hopes and created a sense of optimism about the future. Although considerable controversy and soul searching go on, generally there is the hope that eventually there will evolve a single, integrated framework that retains the values of scientific objectivity and provides for an understanding of complex behavior.

Major Concepts and Summary	
situational specificity	target behaviors, responses
behaviorism	functional analysis of behavior
classical conditioning	ABC assessment
generalization	own-control, ABA design
discrimination	sign and sample approaches to assessment
extinction	
conditioned emotional reaction	behavior modification
systematic desensitization	behavior therapy
second signal system	token economy
semantic conditioning	habit
operant conditioning	imitation
positive and negative reinforcers	approach–avoidance conflict
generalized reinforcers	drives (primary and secondary)
schedules of reinforcement	instrumental learning
shaping—successive approximation	higher mental processes

This chapter has focused on approaches to personality that are strikingly different from those previously covered. First, in contrast to the theories of Freud, Rogers, and Kelly, the learning approach comes from the laboratory rather than from the clinic. Second, in contrast to the approach of trait theorists, the learning approach emphasizes specific connections between behavior and environmental events (reinforcers) rather than broad personality dispositions. Third, in this approach, there is a much greater tendency to look for controlling conditions in the environment rather than for forces within the organism.

Watson spelled out the rationale for a behaviorist approach to psychology and laid the foundation for the learning theory, behavioral approach to personality. Pavlov's work on classical conditioning illustrates how a previously neutral stimulus can become capable of eliciting a response because of its association with a stimulus that automatically produces the same or similar response (e.g., the dog salivates to the bell stimulus associated with the food powder). Generalization, discrimination, and extinction represent three important processes studied by Pavlov. The classical conditioning procedure suggests that many abnormal behaviors are the result of conditioning responses to inappropriate stimuli. Watson and Rayner's case of little Albert illustrated such a conditioned emotional reaction.

The application of principles of classical conditioning is seen in the classic case of Peter's fear of a white rabbit, in the treatment of bedwetting in children, and in Wolpe's method of systematic desensitization. In systematic desensitization, the relaxation response is counterconditioned to a graded, imagined hierarchy of stimuli that formerly were associated with anxiety.

Although Pavlov primarily emphasized reflexlike behaviors shared by humans with other animals, he also emphasized the importance of speech and thought in the second signal systems. Research on semantic conditioning illustrates the importance of this system as well as the role of classical conditioning in more complex human phenomena.

In Skinner's operant conditioning, there is an interest in responses (operants) that cannot be linked with known stimuli but that are learned because they are followed by reinforcement. A reinforcer increases the probability of the responses it follows. Behavior is brought under the control of the experimenter through the manipulation of schedules of reinforcement. Complex behaviors are shaped by reinforcing successive approximations to the desired, final behavior. Imitation of behaviors occurs where the person has been reinforced for specific imitative responses and thus developed a generalized imitative response tendency. The Skinnerian interpretation of psychopathology- emphasizes behavioral deficits (e.g., lack of speech, lack of social skills) and the development of maladaptive responses that are maintained by reinforcers in the environment.

Behavioral assessment procedures follow from the basic assumptions of learning, behavioral theory. Thus, there is an emphasis on target behaviors or target responses and their relation to stimuli and reinforcers in specific situations. A functional analysis of behavior includes an analysis of the Antecedent conditions of the behavior of interest, the Behavior itself, and the Consequences of the behavior—the ABCs of behavioral assessment. A distinction has been drawn between sign and sample approaches to assessment. Whereas in sign approaches personality and behavior are inferred from test responses, in sample approaches interest is in the behavior itself and how it is affected by environmental conditions. Those who emphasize behavioral assessment support the utility of sample approaches and are critical of sign approaches to personality assessment. When questionnaires rather than direct observation of behavior are used, test items generally relate to specific behaviors or reinforcers rather than to traits or general personality characteristics.

Although there is no single method of behavior therapy or behavior modification, the procedures included in this category emphasize principles of learning theory. In behavior modification involving the use of

Skinnerian principles of operant conditioning, desired behaviors are shaped through stages of successive approximation. The ABA or own-control design can be used to demonstrate that the reinforcers being manipulated are indeed the causal agents in the change process. The application of these principles to the regulation of behavior in an institutional setting is seen in a token economy. Under such circumstances, desired behaviors are rewarded with tokens that can then be exchanged for desired articles.

In the S–R, instrumental learning approach of Hull and Dollard and Miller, habits are learned through the reinforcement of stimulus–response connections. Reinforcement consists of the reduction of drive stimuli, either of primary, innate drives or of secondary, learned drives, such as anxiety. The emphasis in growth and development is on the development of higher mental processes and imitation. The S–R interpretation of psychopathology places major emphasis on the role of approach–avoidance conflicts and the role of anxiety drive stimuli. As with other learning approaches, the basic principles of learning are seen as adequate for an understanding of the development of abnormal behavior. Psychopathology is viewed in terms of learned maladaptive responses and adaptive responses that have not been learned adequately. In other words, a behavioral-psychological model is used rather than a medical symptom–disease model.

Because there is considerable diversity to learning, behavioral approaches, any overall evaluation will be more relevant to some approaches than to others; however, some strengths and limitations generally apply to all such approaches. Behavioral psychologists share a positive commitment to research and generally are open to theoretical developments that better account for empirical data. Also, the pragmatic approach to treatment has encouraged innovation and the development of important procedures of behavior change. Often the application of these treatment procedures has involved populations previously neglected by psychotherapists. Finally, the emphasis on situational and environmental variables that influence behavior has been a useful correction to procedures of assessment and change that tended toward exclusive emphasis on global personality characteristics. At the same time, behavioral theory and behavioral psychologists appear to be limited in their oversimplification of personality and neglect of important phenomena. People are complex, with many factors, including motivational and emotional variables, entering into behavior. A second limitation involves the lack of a unified, systematic theory of learning and a clear connection between theory and therapeutic procedures. At present, there are competing theories and often at best a vague relation between a therapeutic technique and a theory of learning. Finally, despite the admirable respect for research and the commitment to experimental investigation of therapeutic procedures, there is a need for demonstration of the effectiveness of behavioral treatment procedures on a wide range of cases, in a wide range of settings, and in the hands of diverse practitioners. Efforts that are successful in studies with a select group of clients are not always found to be equally successful under the more demanding conditions of general practice.

In concluding our consideration of learning, behavioral approaches to personality, we have paved the way for consideration of social cognitive theory. Social cognitive theory represents a very recent effort at systematic conceptualization that attempts to build on the strengths of past theories of learning while, at the same time, avoiding their pitfalls. It is to this approach to personality that we now turn.

Chapter Eleven
Social Cognitive Theory: Bandura and Mischel

*C*HAPTER FOCUS: In this chapter we consider a personality theory that shares some features with earlier learning approaches but is distinctive in its emphasis on the *social* origins of behavior and the importance of *cognitive* (thought) processes in all aspects of human functioning. Particular attention is given to how people learn complex patterns of behavior independent of reward (observational learning or modeling), to people's perceptions of their ability to perform tasks vital to achieving goals (perceived self-efficacy), and to people as active agents in influencing events in their lives. While evolving from earlier learning traditions, social cognitive theory has taken on new dimensions and today is an important new force in the field of personality.

> *In the social cognitive view people are neither driven by inner forces nor automatically shaped and controlled by external stimuli. . . . In the social cognitive view persons are active agents who exercise some influence over their own motivation and actions.*
>
> BANDURA, 1986, pp. 18, 255

Social cognitive theory has its roots in learning theory. Originally it was known as social learning theory and was presented in previous editions of this text as part of the section on learning approaches to personality. Over time the theory has evolved—it increasingly has emphasized cognitive (thought) processes in human functioning and has become more systematic. Today it is known as social cognitive theory, or social cognitive learning theory, and warrants consideration separate from other learning approaches to personality.

Social cognitive theory emphasizes the *social* origins of behavior and the importance of *cognitive* thought processes in all aspects of human functioning—motivation, emotion, and action. In defining their position, social cognitive theorists have been critical of many aspects of the theories already presented. For example, Bandura (1986) is critical of the psychoanalytic emphasis on internal instincts and unconscious forces that cannot be studied systematically. As noted in Chapter 9, Mischel (1968) has been critical of traditional trait and psychoanalytic theory for their emphasis on internal dispositions that are seen as leading to consistency in behavior across situations. Instead, there is an emphasis on the variability of behavior as the person responds to changing circumstances in the environment. In attempting to go beyond traditional debate in the

SOCIAL COGNITIVE THEORY: BANDURA AND MISCHEL

field concerning the relative importance of internal and external determinants of behavior, social cognitive theorists suggest that there is always a process of interaction between the organism and its environment.

In addition, social cognitive theorists attempt to go beyond the traditional division of the field into behavioral "as opposed to" humanistic views of the person. These psychologists are behavioral in their emphasis on the systematic study of specific aspects of human behavior, but they are humanists in their emphasis on the potential for people to influence their destinies and develop themselves within their biological limits.

Finally, although emphasizing the importance of learning in understanding human behavior, there is a break from traditional reinforcement learning theory in an emphasis on cognitive processes and the suggestion that learning occurs in the absence of rewards. Whereas both Hullian and Skinnerian theories of learning emphasize the importance of reward, Bandura suggests that rewards are far more important in the *performance* of learned behaviors than in their *acquisition*.

Within the academic community, cognitive social theory is probably the most popular personality theory, and it is gaining increasing numbers of adherents in the clinical community as well. It is most clearly represented in the works of two psychologists, Albert Bandura and Walter Mischel. Bandura has been particularly important in systematizing the theory and Mischel in defining critical issues in the field. Let us turn now to the theorists and to consideration of a social cognitive theory of personality.

A VIEW OF THE THEORISTS

Albert Bandura (1925 –   )

Little is known about the early life of Albert Bandura other than that he grew up in northern Alberta, Canada. He went to college at the University of British Columbia. On graduation he chose to do graduate work in clinical psychology at the University of Iowa because it was known for the excellence of its research on learning processes. Even then Bandura was interested in the application of learning theory to clinical phenomena. In an interview Bandura indicated that he "had a strong interest in conceptualizing clinical phenomena in ways that would make them amenable to experimental test, with the view that as practitioners we have a responsibility for assessing the efficacy of a procedure, so that people are not subjected to treatments before we know their effects" (quoted in Evans, 1976, p. 243). At Iowa he was influenced by Kenneth Spence, a follower of Clark Hull, and by the general emphasis on careful conceptual analysis and rigorous experimental investigation. During that

Albert Bandura

time he was also influenced by the writings of Neal Miller and John Dollard.

After obtaining his Ph.D. at Iowa in 1952, Bandura went to Stanford and began to work on interactive processes in psychotherapy and on family patterns that lead to aggressiveness in children. The work on familial causes of aggression, with Richard Walters, his first graduate student, gave rise to the emphasis on the central role of modeling influences (learning through observation of others) in personality development. These findings and consequent laboratory investigations of modeling processes resulted in the books *Adolescent Aggression* (1959) and *Social Learning and Personality Development* (1963). Since then he continued with research on aggression, modeling and observational learning, and the processes of behavior change. Bandura describes himself as conducting a multifaceted research program aimed at clarifying aspects of human capability that should be emphasized in a comprehensive theory of human behavior. His 1986 book, *Social Foundations of Thought and Action*, represents an effort to develop such a comprehensive theory. An emphasis on human capabilities is an important aspect of Bandura's recent thinking and research. It is related to his interest in processes of development and therapeutic change and is associated with what some perceive as a humanist emphasis in his work. Professor Bandura has received a number of distinguished scientific achievement awards. In 1974 he was elected president of the American Psychological Association and in 1980 he received the Association's Distinguished Scientific Con-

SOCIAL COGNITIVE THEORY: BANDURA AND MISCHEL

tribution Award "for masterful modeling as researcher, teacher, and theoretician."

Walter Mischel (1930–)

Mischel's early life and roots in psychology, like Bandura's, are known only sketchily. Mischel was born in Vienna and lived his first nine years "in easy playing distance of Freud's house." He describes the possible influence of this period as follows:

> When I began to read psychology Freud fascinated me most. As a student at City College (in New York, where my family settled after the Hitler-caused forced exodus from Europe in 1939), psychoanalysis seemed to provide a comprehensive view of man. But my excitement fizzled when I tried to apply ideas as a social worker with "juvenile delinquents" in New York's Lower East Side: somehow trying to give those youngsters "insight" didn't help either them or me. The concepts did not fit what I saw, and I went looking for more useful ones.
>
> MISCHEL, 1978, PERSONAL COMMUNICATION

The experience with "juvenile delinquents" is of particular interest for two reasons. First, it probably relates to Mischel's long-standing interest in the psychological mechanisms underlying delay of gratification and

Walter Mischel

self-control. Second, there is a similarity to Bandura in that both did their early clinical work with aggressive youngsters.

Mischel did his graduate work at Ohio State University, where he came under the influence of two significant figures: "George Kelly and Julian Rotter were my dual mentors and each has enduringly influenced my thinking" (Mischel, 1978, personal communication). The work of George Kelly has already been discussed. The thinking of Julian Rotter (1954) has only lately become popular in the field of personality, primarily because of his concept of internal–external locus of control (Chapter 2). However, Rotter's views were developed much earlier and had a number of distinguishing elements. First, Rotter emphasized learning theory in relation to important human social (interpersonal) phenomena; second, he emphasized the importance of situational factors as well as person factors in behavior. Rotter was critical of personality theories and measurement devices that ignored the contribution of situational factors to the variability in any person's behavior. Third, Rotter emphasized the importance of cognitive processes in learning as opposed to mechanical stimulus–response connections. In particular, he emphasized the importance of individual *expectancies* concerning reinforcements for various behaviors in particular situations. These concepts, together with those emphasized by Kelly, have increasingly played a major role in Mischel's thinking in particular and in social cognitive theory in general. Mischel describes his work in relation to that of his dual mentors as follows: "I see my own work both with cognition and with social learning as clearly rooted in their contributions, a focus on the person both as construer and actor, interacting with the vicissitudes of the environment, and trying to make life coherent even in the face of all its inconsistencies" (Mischel, 1978, personal communication).

After completing his graduate work at Ohio State, Mischel spent a number of years at Harvard University and then joined Bandura at Stanford. In 1978 he received the Distinguished Scientist Award from the Clinical Psychology Division of the American Psychological Association. Since 1984 he has been a professor of psychology at Columbia University.

VIEW OF THE PERSON

Both Bandura and Mischel recognize the relationship of a general view of the person to a theory of personality and have attempted to be explicit concerning this view. In a statement very much in tune with a point made throughout this book, Bandura notes that "views about human nature influence which aspects of psychological functioning are studied most thoroughly and which remain unexamined. Theoretical conceptions similarly determine the paradigms used to collect evidence which, in turn, shape the particular theory" (1977a, p. vi). In other words, there is a back-and-forth or reciprocal relationship between a view of the person, a program of research, and a theory of personality.

Current social cognitive theory emphasizes a view of the person as active and using cognitive processes to represent events, anticipate the future, choose among courses of action, and communicate with others. Alternative views of the person as a passive victim of unconscious impulses and past history or a passive respondent to environmental events are rejected. Theories of personality that emphasize internal factors to the exclusion of environmental events are rejected because of their disregard for the individual's responsiveness to varying situations. At the same time, theories that emphasize external factors to the exclusion of internal factors are rejected because of their failure to consider the role of cognitive functioning in behavior.

Rejecting both the view that people are driven by inner forces and the view that they are buffeted by environmental stimuli, social cognitive theory suggests that behavior can be explained in terms of an interaction between the person and the environment, a process Bandura calls **reciprocal determinism**. People are influenced by environmental forces but they also choose how to behave. The person is both responsive to situations and actively constructs and influences situations. People select situations as well as are shaped by them, and they influence the behavior of others as well as are shaped by the behavior of others.

Basically, social cognitive theory sees the person, when functioning properly, as a well-tuned organism capable of adapting to changing conditions in the environment. The ongoing process of reciprocal determinism involves the person actively choosing among goals and discriminating among situations in terms of their task requirements and potential for different outcomes. People make judgments of their ability to meet various task requirements and, once having acted, assess the outcome in terms of the responses of others and their own internal standards. In a sense, the person is a problem-solving organism seeking to behave in ways that will maximize both rewards in the environment and internal rewards in the form of self-praise. Mischel describes the emerging image of the human being as follows:

> The image is one of the human being as an active, aware problem-solver, capable of profiting from an enormous range of experiences and cognitive capacities, possessing great potential for good or ill, actively constructing his or her psychological world, and influencing the environment but also being influenced by it in lawful ways—even if the laws are difficult to discover and hard to generalize. . . . It is an image that has moved a long way from the instinctual drive-reduction models, the static global traits, and the automatic stimulus–response bonds of

traditional personality theories. It is an image that highlights the shortcoming of all simplistic theories that view behavior as the exclusive result of any narrow set of determinants, whether these are habits, traits, drives, reinforcers, constructs, instincts, or genes and whether they are exclusively inside or outside the person.

MISCHEL, 1977, p. 253

VIEW OF SCIENCE, THEORY, AND RESEARCH

Both Bandura and Mischel are committed to the use of theory and empirical research. There is a strong commitment to concepts that are clear and based on systematic observations. Theories that emphasize motivational forces in the form of needs, drives, and impulses are criticized for being vague and inferred from the behavior they supposedly caused. In other words, too often it is said that a person has an aggressive impulse or trait because they behave aggressively and that they behave aggressively because of their instinct or motive for aggression.

Whereas extreme behaviorism rejects the study of cognitive processes because of a distrust for introspective data, Bandura and Mischel feel that such inner processes must be studied and that the use of some types of self-report is both legitimate and desirable. They suggest that self-reports that are general, based on long-term recall, and involve anxiety that can lead to defensiveness are *not* likely sources of reliable information. However, self-reports that are specific and given as events occur and under conditions that do not arouse evaluative apprehensions can be valuable aids in understanding cognitive processes. In defense of the use of verbal self-reports, Bandura notes that "vast numbers of people are outfitted by ophthalmologists with suitable corrective eyeglasses on the basis of verbalized discriminations of printed and pictorial stimuli. They can be easily outfitted with defective eyeglasses by reporting that the blurred stimuli are the clearer ones. However, this would hardly constitute justification for renouncing the optometric enterprise. Rather than decrying the limitations of verbal probes of thought, we should be improving the tools for measuring it" (Bandura, 1978a, p. 15).

In sum, social cognitive theory is concerned with both a broad variety of aspects of human behavior and scientific rigor. There is a concern with both important inner processes and systematic observations. In all likelihood it is this blend of concern with important human events and scientific respectability that most accounts for the theory's current popularity.

SOCIAL COGNITIVE
THEORY OF PERSONALITY

The stage has been set for considering the details of the social cognitive theory of personality. Central to appreciating these details will be keeping in mind the importance of cognitive processes in human motivation, emotion, and action as well as the social origins of human behavior.

Structure

Personality structures, to the extent that social cognitive theory emphasizes them, involve an emphasis on cognitive processes. Two structural concepts are particularly noteworthy, the concept of *self* and that of *goals*.

In the context of social cognitive theory, the *self* is not a fixed structure but rather a set of cognitive processes. An understanding of people's self-conceptions and responses to their own behavior, such as self-praise or self-criticism, is seen as being essential to understanding what goes on between environmental events and behavior. At the same time, it should be clear that the social cognitive concept of self does not suggest "an extra causal agent that dwells in the person and somehow generates or causes behavior in ways that are separable from the organism in which 'it' resides" (Mischel, 1977, pp. 49–50). The social cognitive concept of self refers to processes that are part of the person's psychological functioning. In a sense, the person does not have a structure called "the self," but rather self-processes that are part of the person. In addition, earlier concepts of the self are criticized for being too global. Rather than having a self-concept, social cognitive theory suggests that a person has self-conceptions and self-control processes that may vary from time to time and from situation to situation.

A particular aspect of the perception of self has become central to Bandura's thinking, that concerning **self-efficacy** or the perceived ability to cope with specific situations. The concept of self-efficacy relates to judgments people make concerning their ability to perform behaviors relevant to a specific task or situation. According to Bandura, the influence of self-percepts of efficacy is widespread, including the following: (1) *which activities* people engage in ("People avoid activities that they believe exceed their coping capabilities, but they undertake and perform assuredly those that they judge themselves capable of managing." 1982, p. 123); (2) *how much effort* will be expended in a situation; (3) *how long* people will persist in the face of obstacles; (4) *thought patterns* while engaged in a task; and (5) *emotional reactions* while anticipating a situation or while involved in it. Clearly, we think, feel, and behave differently in situations in which we feel confident of our ability than in situations in which we are insecure or feel incompetent. In sum, self-percepts of efficacy influence thought patterns, motivation, performance, and emotional arousal.

These influences of self-efficacy are spelled out further throughout this chapter. For now, however, it is important to consider how Bandura assesses self-efficacy and how he distinguishes it from what might appear to be related concepts. In terms of assessment, Bandura emphasizes what he calls a **microanalytic research strategy**. According to this strategy, detailed measures of perceived self-efficacy are taken before performance of behaviors in specific situations. Thus, subjects are asked to designate in a specific situation those tasks they can do and their degree of certainty about doing them successfully. This strategy reflects the view that self-efficacy judgments are situation specific and do not represent global dispositions that can be measured by comprehensive personality inventories. As noted before, a global self-concept is criticized because it "does not do justice to the complexity of self-efficacy perceptions, which vary across different activities, different levels of the same activity, and different situational circumstances" (Bandura, 1986, p. 41). Finally, the concept is distinguished from Rotter's concept of locus of control and Seligman's concept of learned helplessness. Self-efficacy judgments relate to perceptions of one's ability to perform certain activities and not to one's ability to control outcomes or reinforcers. Generally, there is a relationship between task requirements and outcomes. However, this is not always the case in that sometimes one may be able to perform certain critical tasks but reinforcement for performance may be beyond one's control. What is important here is Bandura's suggestion that it is self-efficacy judgments that operate as the critical cognitive mediators of action: "Among the different aspects of self-knowledge, perhaps none is more influential in people's everyday lives than conceptions of their personal efficacy. . . . Research shows that people who regard themselves as highly efficacious act, think, and feel differently from those who perceive themselves as inefficacious. They produce their own future, rather than simply foretell it" (1986, pp. 390, 395).

The concept of *goals* relates to the ability of people to anticipate the future, to be self-motivated, and to undertake purposive action directed toward achieving certain standards or other outcomes. It is goals that guide us in establishing priorities among rewards and in selecting among situations. It is goals that enable us to go beyond momentary influences and to organize our behavior over extended periods of time. A person's goals are organized in a system, so that some are more central or important than others. However, generally this is not a rigid or fixed system. Rather the person may flexibly select among goals depending on what seems most important to them at the time, what the opportunities in the environment appear to be, and their judgments of their self-efficacy relative to the demands of the environment.

The relation of goals and conceptions of self-efficacy to behavior will become clearer as we consider process aspects of the theory in the next section.

Process

It can be seen that the emphasis on cognitive processes and the interplay between external and internal sources of influence is critical to the understanding of social cognitive theory. It is these processes that increasingly have been emphasized and have set it apart from other theories of learning.

Social cognitive theory emphasizes two processes distinct from other learning theories of personality—observational learning and self-regulation. Observational learning involves the ability to learn complex behaviors by watching others. "Because people can learn from example what to do, at least in approximate form, before performing any behavior, they are spared needless errors" (Bandura, 1977b, p. 22). Self-regulation involves the ability of individuals to exercise influence over their own behavior rather than reacting mechanically to external influences. Both observational learning and self-regulation involve considerable use of thought (cognitive) processes. Both are influenced by rewards and punishments, but they are not determined by them.

Observational learning

The theory of **observational learning** suggests that people can learn merely by observing the behaviors of others. The person being observed is called a model. There is evidence to suggest that an individual can

Modeling—Social learning theorists emphasize the importance of observing others in the acquisition of behavior. Drawing by Opie; © 1978 The New Yorker Magazine, Inc.

Social Cognitive Theory of Personality

learn behaviors by observing a model perform these behaviors. Thus, for example, the child may learn language by observing parents and other people speaking, a process called **modeling**. The type of behaviors under consideration are often included under the terms *imitation* and *identification*. However, imitation has the very narrow connotation of response mimicry and, at the other extreme, identification implies an incorporation of entire patterns of behavior. Modeling involves something broader than imitation but less diffuse than identification. In addition, these terms are rejected because they have been associated with stimulus – response reinforcement theories and with psychoanalytic theory. These theories are considered inadequate in accounting for the observed data.

The theories of Hull and Skinner are viewed as inadequate in the following ways: (1) They do not account for the appearance of new, or novel behaviors. (2) In particular, they do not account for the appearance of new, large segments of behavior in their entirety; that is, they do not account for the fact that, with a model, full patterns of behavior can be acquired that would be difficult to account for in terms of a slow, gradual conditioning process. (3) The acquisition of these response patterns appears to occur independent of reinforcement variables. (4) The first appearance of the behaviors learned may not occur for days, weeks, or months after the model has been observed. The importance of the process of observational learning is well described by Bandura (1969a, p. 213). He states that "the provision of social models is also an indispensable means of transmitting and modifying behavior in situations where errors are likely to produce costly or fatal consequences. Indeed, if social learning proceeded exclusively on the basis of rewarding and punishing consequences, most people would never survive the socialization process." Observational learning, then, accounts for the learning of new, complex patterns of behavior independent of reinforcements.

An important part of the theory of modeling is the distinction made between **acquisition** and **performance**. The early research suggested that children who observed a model rewarded for aggressive behavior would reproduce these behaviors, and those who observed the model punished would not. Since learning is expressed in performance, this might suggest that reinforcements to the model are critical for the learning process. However, many of the children who did not reproduce the model's aggressive behavior in the test situation were able to describe it with considerable accuracy. This led to an experiment in which children observed a model express aggressive behavior with either rewarding consequences, punishing consequences, or no consequences. Although in the initial test situation (No Incentive) the children who observed the punished model performed fewer imitative acts than the children observing other models, this difference could be wiped out by offering the children attractive incentives for reproducing the model's behavior (Positive Incentive, see Figure 11.1) (Bandura, Ross, & Ross, 1963a). In other words, the consequences to the model for the aggressive acts had an

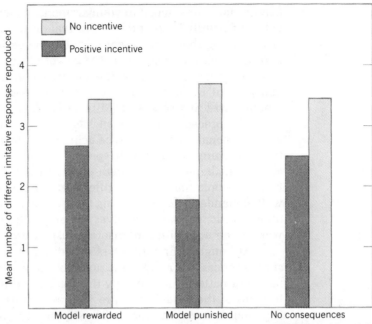

FIGURE 11.1 Mean Number of Different Imitative Responses Reproduced by Children as a Function of Response Consequences to the Model and Positive Incentives. (Bandura, 1965)

effect on the children's performance of these acts but not on the learning of the aggressive behaviors.

A number of other studies have since demonstrated that the observation of consequences to a model affects performance but not acquisition. The difference between acquisition and performance suggests, however, that in some way the children were being affected by what happened to the model; that is, either on a cognitive basis or on an emotional basis, or both, the children were responding to the consequences to the model. The suggestion here is that the children learned certain emotional responses by sympathizing with the model, that is, vicariously by observing the model. Not only can behavior be learned through observation, but emotional reactions such as fear and joy can also be conditioned on a vicarious basis: "It is not uncommon for individuals to develop strong emotional reactions toward places, persons, and things without having had any personal contact with them" (Bandura, 1986, p. 185). The process of learning emotional reactions through observing others, known as **vicarious conditioning**, has been demonstrated in both humans and animals. Thus, for example, human subjects who observed a model express a conditioned fear response were found to develop a vicariously conditioned emotional response to a previously neutral stimulus (Bandura & Rosenthal, 1966; Berger, 1962). Similarly, in an experiment with animals it was found that an intense and persistent fear of snakes developed in younger monkeys who observed their parents behave fearfully in the presence of real or toy snakes. What was particularly striking about this research is that the period of observation of their parents' emotional reaction could be very brief. Further, once the vicarious conditioning took place, the fear was found to be intense, longlasting, and present in situations different from those in which the emotional reaction was first observed (Mineka et al., 1984).

The preceding discussion has indicated that behavioral responses and emotional reactions can be acquired through the process of observational learning. In addition to specific responses, rules or general plans for action can be learned through observation. For example, by observing models people may acquire rules concerning language and grammer as well as standards for evaluating their own behavior and that of others. In other words, modeling involves the acquisition of abstract principles as well as the acquisition of discrete responses.

Although at first glance observational learning may appear to be a simple process, in reality it is not. Not all observers acquire the model's behavior patterns. Apparently this has something to do with the characteristics of the model (e.g., prestige) and characteristics of the observer (e.g., dependence on others). Thus, although observational learning can be a powerful process, one should not think that it is automatic or that one is bound to follow in the footsteps of others. Children, for example, have multiple models and can learn from parents, siblings, teachers, peers, and television. In addition, they learn from their own direct experience. Beyond this, as children get older they may actively select which models they will observe and attempt to emulate.

Self-regulation

Bandura distinguishes between the acquisition of responses and the maintenance, regulation, or performance of responses. Learning or response acquisitions occur through observation and through the positive and negative effects that actions produce (response consequences). Among the responses learned are **standards** for expecting reinforcement from others and standards for reinforcing oneself. We learn to set appropriate goals for ourselves and to reward ourselves with self-praise or punish ourselves with self-criticism by observing models engaged in such behavior and by being reinforced directly for such behavior. Thus, behavior is maintained by its consequences, but these consequences include not just external rewards but also internal self-evaluative responses such as praise and guilt.

It should be clear that the processes being described here differ from those emphasized by reinforcement learning theorists. The emphasis is on information rather than the development of mechanical stimulus–response connections. In social cognitive theory the emphasis is on the cognitive development of expectations concerning the results of various actions and the development of rules and standards for action. Rather than being maintained by its immediate consequences, behavior is maintained by **expectancies** or anticipated consequences. In addition, rather than behavior being regulated exclusively by external reinforcers there is the process of **self-reinforcement** through which individuals reward themselves for attaining standards they set for themselves. These performance standards serve as motivators for behavior. It is the anticipation of satisfactions for desired accomplishments and dissatisfactions with insufficient accomplishments that provides the incentive for our efforts. Performance standards and anticipated consequences thus explain goal-directed behavior.

The emphasis on the development of standards for self-reinforcement and on cognitive processes is of critical importance for social learning theory. Through them the emphasis is shifted from a purely external, environmental locus of control to an emphasis on both internal and external factors. Through the development of such cognitive mechanisms people not only are able to exercise some control over their lives but also are able to establish plans or goals for the future. In other words, people can change the environmental contingencies that eventually will affect their behavior. The capacities to anticipate the future, to set standards, and to experience self-satisfaction and self-criticism are critical in permitting us to engage in endeavors over long periods of time. Human behavior is regulated by cognitive processes that integrate information coming from external and from self-generated consequences. Expectancies of reward from external and internal sources serve as incentives and guides for action.

Self-efficacy and performance

As previously noted, Bandura increasingly has emphasized the importance of self-perceptions of efficacy as cognitive mediators of action. While considering action and once engaged in it, people make judgments concerning their ability to perform various task requirements. These self-efficacy judgments influence thought ("This is what I need to do and I can make it." versus "I'll never manage this. What will people think of me?"), emotion (excitement, joy versus anxiety, depression), and action (greater commitment versus inhibition, immobilization). A person sets standards and goals, both distant (long-term) and proximal (immediate), and makes judgments concerning the ability to perform the tasks necessary for goal achievement. Although influenced by situations, people are active in terms of establishing goals, making self-efficacy judgments, and making self-evaluative judgments.

An earlier edition of this text criticized social cognitive theory for its relative lack of concern with human motivation. More recently this has been an important area of concern and Bandura (1988) has increasingly emphasized a purposive view of human action. In a relevant piece of research, Bandura and Cervone (1983) studied the effects of goals and performance feedback on motivation. The hypothesis tested was that performance motivation reflects both the presence of goals and the awareness of how one is doing relative to standards: "Simply adopting goals, whether easy or personally challenging ones, without knowing how one is doing seems to have no appreciable motivational effects" (1983, p. 123). The assumption was that greater discrepancies between standards and performances would generally lead to greater self-dissatisfaction and efforts to improve performance. However, a critical ingredient of such efforts is self-efficacy judgments, and thus the research tested the hypothesis that self-efficacy judgments, as well as self-evaluative judgments, mediate between goals and goal-directed effort.

In this research, subjects performed a strenuous activity under one of four conditions: goals with feedback on their performance, goals alone, feedback alone, and absence of goals and feedback. Following this activity, described as part of a project to plan and evaluate exercise programs for postcoronary rehabilitation, subjects rated how self-satisfied or self-dissatisfied they would be with the same level of performance in a following session. In addition, they recorded their perceived self-efficacy for various possible performance levels. Their effortful performance was then again measured. In accord with the hypothesis, the condition combining both goals and performance feedback had a strong motivational impact, whereas neither goals alone nor feedback alone was of comparable motivational significance (Figure 11.2). Also, subsequent effort was most intense when subjects were both dissatisfied with substandard performance and were high on self-efficacy judgments for good attain-

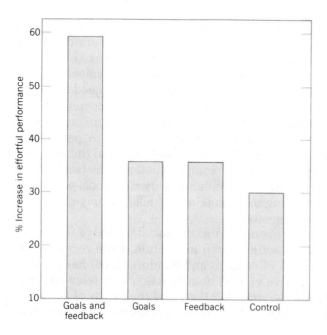

FIGURE 11.2 Mean Percentage Increase in Effortful Performance under Conditions Varying in Goals and Performance Feedback. (Bandura & Cervone, 1983)

SOCIAL COGNITIVE THEORY: BANDURA AND MISCHEL

ment. Neither dissatisfaction alone nor positive self-efficacy judgments alone had a comparable effect. Often there was a reduction in effort where there were both low dissatisfaction with performance and low perceived self-efficacy. The authors concluded that there was clear evidence in support of the theory that goals have motivating power through self-evaluative and self-efficacy judgments.

Performance feedback and self-efficacy judgments have been found to be particularly important in the development of intrinsic interest. Thus, for example, psychologists have been able to enhance the interest of students in learning and their level of performance by helping them to break down tasks into subgoals, helping them to monitor their own performance, and providing them with feedback that increased their sense of self-efficacy (Bandura & Schunk, 1981; Morgan, 1985; Schunk & Cox, 1986). Intrinsic interest thus develops when the person has challenging standards that provide for positive self-evaluation when met, and the sense of self-efficacy in the potential for meeting those standards. It is such intrinsic interest that facilitates effort over extended periods of time in the absence of external rewards. Conversely, it is difficult to sustain motivation where one feels that the external or internal, self-evaluative rewards are insufficient or where one's sense of efficacy is so low that a positive outcome seems impossible. Self-perceived inefficacy can nullify the motivating potential of even the most desirable outcomes. For example, no matter how attractive it might seem to become a movie star, a person will not be motivated in that direction unless they feel that they have the ability to perform the tasks necessary for stardom. In the absence of such a sense of self-efficacy, becoming a movie star remains a fantasy rather than a goal that is pursued in action.

To summarize the social cognitive view of motivation, the person develops goals or standards that serve as the basis for action. The person considers alternative courses of action and makes a decision on the basis of the anticipated outcomes (external and internal) and the perceived self-efficacy for performing the necessary behaviors. Once action has been taken, the outcome is assessed in terms of the external rewards from others and one's own internal self-evaluations. Successful performance may lead to enhanced self-efficacy and either a relaxation of effort or the setting of higher standards for further effort. Unsuccessful performance, or failure, may lead to giving up or continued striving, depending on the value of the outcome to the person and their sense of self-efficacy in relation to further effort.

Although cognitive in nature, the foregoing processes need not be conscious or completely "rational." Thus, one may have beliefs and expectancies of which one is unaware and may value certain outcomes in a personally idiosyncratic way. One can think of all these processes in relation to maintaining effort in college courses or other areas. The critical concepts are goals or standards, anticipated outcomes, self-evaluative responses, and perceived self-efficacy. For example, it is possible to remain motivated in one's academic studies when there are high standards, positive outcomes, feelings of pride associated with meeting those standards, and the sense that one is capable of meeting them. On the other hand, boredom and low motivation are likely when standards are low and few external or internal rewards are expected for accomplishment, or when one perceives successful performance as impossible.

Growth and Development

The social cognitive theory of growth and development follows from the principles already established. A behavioral repertoire and skills in processing information, or **cognitive competencies**, are developed through observational learning and direct experience. In addition, the development of expectancies, plans, and self-regulatory functions are important. These developing competencies are greatly influenced by experience, but biological factors set constraints on behavioral development.

Although social cognitive theory recognizes the importance of biological factors, it does not emphasize maturational factors as do stage theorists such as Piaget and Freud. Stage theorists assume that a structure emerges in the course of maturation and that the acquisition of cognitive skills and rules at one stage is dependent on the person having passed through previous stages. Social cognitive theory emphasizes social influence variables and suggests that individuals need not learn various skills in a fixed, sequential fashion. Furthermore, the suggestion is made that the person's cognitive functioning is not uniform at a particular level but may vary from issue to issue and from situation to situation. Bandura suggests that a major problem with stage theories is that it is hard to find people who fit them well. Most people exhibit a mixture of thought patterns that span several "stages." Rather than viewing people in terms of stages or categories, it is suggested that we view them in terms of the individuality of their thought and action.

Finally, the suggestion is made that stage doctrines underestimate human capabilities and accept as unchangeable certain limitations that otherwise might be modified. In contrast, social cognitive theory suggests that earnest teaching efforts may eradicate deficiencies formerly attributed to shortcomings in children.

In terms of the development of capabilities and competencies, Bandura places particular emphasis on the development of self-efficacy. One's sense of self-efficacy comes from many sources—actual accomplishments, vicarious experiences through observing others, and verbal persuasion. Direct personal experiences of accomplishment in relation to specific goals are of importance generally and specifically in relation to the development of intrinsic interest.

The social cognitive theory view of growth and development can be illustrated further by consideration of three areas: aggression, moral judgments, and delay of gratification. In terms of the development of aggressive behavior, a distinction is made among the acquisition of aggressive responses, the events that instigate these behaviors, and the processes that regulate and maintain aggression (Bandura, 1977a). In other words, social cognitive theory seeks to explain how aggressive patterns are developed, what provokes people to behave aggressively, and what sustains such actions once they have begun.

In general, aggression is learned through observation of aggressive models and learning by direct experience. Aggressive styles of behavior are learned from observation of family models ("Familial violence breeds violent styles of conduct."), from observation of peer behavior ("The highest incidence of aggression is found in communities in which aggressive models abound."), and from observation of models through mass media such as television ("Both children and adults today have unlimited opportunities to learn the whole gamut of violent conduct from televised modeling within the comfort of their homes.").

In terms of the activation of aggression, social cognitive theory emphasizes how aggressive behaviors can be provoked by painful stimulation, by expectations of reward for such behavior, or by both. What is emphasized is that when a person is aroused by painful or aversive events it may or may not lead to an aggressive response. Whether or not the person responds aggressively depends on both the interpretation of the conditions of arousal and the expectations of consequences for aggressive behavior. Such a view is distinct from an instinct view, which focuses on an automatic buildup of aggressive energy, and from other learning theories that view aggressive behavior as a response to frustration (Figure 11.3). According to social cognitive theory, frustration may or may not lead to aggression, and aggression can occur in the absence of frustration. Thus, whether or not frustration leads to aggression depends

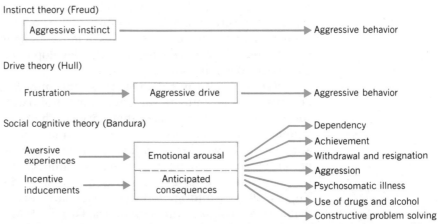

FIGURE 11.3 Comparison of Social Learning Theory of Aggression with Instinct and Drive Theories of Aggression.

on how the person interprets the arousal, the alternative modes available for response, and the expectations of consequences for these various responses given the particular situation.

Finally, aggressive behavior is sustained or ended depending on its consequences. As with other behaviors, aggressive behavior is regulated by its consequences, which can come from three sources — **direct external consequences**, **vicarious experiencing of consequences to others**, and **self-produced consequences**. The first two are social consequences and the third is personal consequences. Aggressive behavior may be stopped through threats of external punishment or through expectations of self-condemnation, otherwise known as control through fear and guilt, respectively. Guilt involves the learning of ethical and moral standards of behavior.

The observation of models and the development of standards and self-control mechanisms are important not only in aggression but in moral judgments and in toleration of delays in gratification as well. Social cognitive theory views moral judgments as complex, multidetermined social decisions. General rules are formed from a wide range of experience. At the same time, considerable **discrimination** may be involved in invoking different moral judgments in different circumstances. Since people vary their judgments depending on circumstances, it is hard to fit them into moral judgment types. Also, because many more factors begin to be considered in moral judgments and greater discrimination is used in the application of various moral criteria to specific situations, moral judgment processes do become more complex with age. In addition, as children mature there is a shift from external to internal control. Initially, parents use punishment and the threat of punishment to discourage certain behaviors. In successful socialization, however, there is a "gradual substitution of symbolic and internal controls for external sanctions and demands. After moral standards of conduct are established by instruction and modeling, self-evaluative consequences serve as deterrents to transgressive acts" (Bandura, 1977a, p. 43). Obviously, both the development of more complex rules of moral judgment and the increased use of internal controls depend on the development of increasingly complex cognitive skills and abilities.

Research also has demonstrated the importance of modeling and observational learning in the development of performance standards for success and reward that may then serve as the basis for **delays in gratification**. Children exposed to models setting high standards of performance for self-reward tend to limit their own self-rewards to exceptional performance to a greater degree than do children who have been exposed to models setting lower standards or to no models at all (Bandura & Kupers, 1964). Children will model standards even if they result in self-denial of available rewards (Bandura, Grusec, & Menlove, 1967) and will also impose learned standards on other children (Mischel & Liebert,

Delay of Gratification—Children must learn to postpone pleasure until the proper time. Here a child considers how much he will have to save to get a desired toy.

1966). Children can be made to tolerate greater delays in receiving gratification if they are exposed to models exhibiting such delay behavior.

The effects of a model on delay behavior in children are well illustrated in research by Bandura and Mischel (1965). Children found to be high and low in delay of gratification were exposed to models of the opposite behavior. In a live-model condition, each child individually observed a testing situation in which an adult model was asked to choose between an immediate reward and a more valued object at a later date. The high-delay children observed a model who selected the immediately available reward and commented on its benefits, whereas the low-delay children observed a model who selected the delayed reward and commented on the virtues of delay. In a symbolic-model condition, children read verbal accounts of these behaviors, the verbal account again being the opposite of the child's pattern of response. Finally, in a no-model condition children were just appraised of the choices given the adults. Following exposure to one of these three procedures, the children were again given a choice between an immediate reward and a more valuable reward. The results were that the high-delay children in all three conditions significantly altered their delay-of-reward behavior in favor of immediate gratification. The live-model condition produced the greatest effect (Figure 11.4). The low-delay children exposed to a delay model

Social Cognitive Theory of Personality

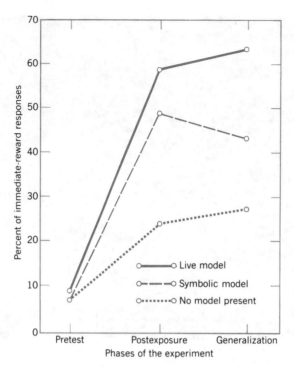

FIGURE 11.4 Mean Percentage of Immediate-Reward Responses by High-Delay Children on Each of Three Test Periods for Each of Three Experimental Conditions. (Bandura & Mischel, 1965)

significantly altered their behavior in terms of greater delay, but there was no significant difference between the effects of live and symbolic models. Finally, for both groups of children, the effects were found to be stable when the tests were readministered four to five weeks later.

As mentioned previously, the performance of observed behaviors clearly is influenced by the observed consequences to the model. For example, children who watch a film in which a child is not punished for playing with toys that were prohibited by the mother are more likely to play with prohibited toys than are children who see no film or see a film in which the child is punished (Walters & Parke, 1964). The old saying "Monkey see, monkey do" is not completely true. It would be more appropriate to say "Monkey sees rewarded or not punished, monkey does." After all, the monkey is no fool.

The ability to delay gratification involves the development of **cognitive and behavioral competencies**. Relevant behaviors are acquired through the observation of others and through direct experience. The ability to delay gratification is determined by the outcomes expected, as influenced by past direct personal experience, observation of consequences to models such as parents and peers, and self-reactions. Delay decisions are influenced by context and circumstances. Thus, people who exhibit control in some circumstances may act impulsively in others. Gratification may not be delayed because the person lacks the

SOCIAL COGNITIVE THEORY: BANDURA AND MISCHEL

necessary skills for delay or because the rewards expected for delay do not outweigh those expected for nondelay. The discriminations people make among situations and the variability found in their behavior are such as to reject stage theories as well as trait and psychoanalytic theories of conscience or superego: "Rather than acquiring a homogeneous conscience that determines uniformly all aspects of their self-control, people develop subtler discriminations that depend on many moderating variables and involve complex interactions" (Mischel, 1977, p. 39).

Major Concepts and Summary	reciprocal determinism	self-regulation
	self	expectancies
	goals	direct, vicarious, and self-produced consequences
	self-efficacy	discrimination among situations
	microanalytic research	delay of gratification
	observational learning	cognitive and behavioral competencies
	modeling	
	acquisition, performance, and maintenance of behaviors	
	vicarious conditioning	
	internal standards	

Social cognitive theory is an evolving, influential, and popular theory of personality. It shares with the Hullian and Skinnerian positions an emphasis on the central importance of learned patterns of behavior. However, its emphasis on learning independent of reinforcement and the importance of cognitive processes results in a different view of the human organism. The human organism is one that affects the environment as well as is affected by it, one that responds to information from the environment in an organized and selective way rather than in a mechanical way, and one that is capable of responding to self-reward and self-punishment as well as to external forms of reinforcement. Instead of emphasizing internal (person) factors or external (environment) factors, social cognitive theory stresses the process of reciprocal determinism between person and environment.

Social cognitive theory distinguishes between response acquisition and response performance. As is evident in observational learning, reinforcement is not necessary for response acquisition; people can learn complex behaviors through the observation of others performing such behaviors. Emotional reactions as well can be conditioned vicariously through the observation of others. Such learning processes have functional, adaptive value since we are thereby spared the inefficiency and hazards of trial-and-error learning. Learning from observing others, modeling, involves something broader than imitation but less diffuse and global than identification. Considerable attention has been directed to the factors that influence the modeling process (e.g., consequences to the model) and to the components of this process.

Although reinforcement is not critical for the acquisition of responses, it is critical for the performance and maintenance or regulation of behavior. According to social cognitive theory, behavior is regulated by its consequences—which can come from the person (self-praise and self-criticism) as well as from the environment. Among the responses an individual learns are standards of goal attainment and standards for self-reinforcement. These standards permit the person to continue working toward a goal in the absence of outside reward or despite outside interference and punishment. They form the basis for self-regulation and self-control. Although behavior is regulated by internal and external consequences, it is the expectation of these consequences that is important rather than the mechanical linking of behavior with reinforcement. Here, too, there is an emphasis on cognitive processes and reinforcement as representing information from the environment.

Although the main focus remains on processes explaining the acquisition and maintenance of behavior, social cognitive theory has recently also emphasized structural concepts such as goals–plans and the self. Goals are derived from learned standards for reinforcement and help to establish priorities among alternative patterns of behavior, particularly over long periods of time. The concept of self does not represent a little person inside the organism controlling behavior but rather a set of cognitive processes involved in self-conception, self-reinforcement, and self-regulation. Self-concepts and self-control processes are viewed as relatively specific and as varying from situation to situation and from time to time.

Particularly important here is the concept of self-efficacy or the person's judgment of his or her ability to perform the tasks relevant to a particular situation. Self-efficacy judgments are viewed as cognitive mediators of action, functioning together with self-evaluative judgments to mediate between goals and actual performance. In other words, goals and external reinforcement expectancies are important in behavior, but feedback information that is utilized to make self-efficacy and self-evaluative judgments also is crucial. Self-efficacy judgments influence thought patterns, motivation, performance, and emotional arousal. In tune with the general social cognitive rejection of broad dispositional personality characteristics, such as traits, self-efficacy judgments are viewed as changing and relatively situation specific, and as best assessed through a microanalytic research strategy.

Social cognitive theory views growth and development as resulting from the interplay of biological and experiential factors. It is critical of stage theories that suggest a fixed order of development and a single level for a person's cognitive processes. Instead, social cognitive theory emphasizes the potential for cognitive development and the processes through which cognitive functioning varies from issue to issue and situation to situation. As noted, this is true of developing self-efficacy judgments that are based on direct experience (performance accomplishments), vicarious experience, and communications from significant others. Considerable research attention has been directed toward an understanding of the development of aggressive behavior, moral judgments, and tolerance for delay of gratification. Similar principles are stressed throughout. For example, a distinction is made between the factors that determine the acquisition of responses, those that instigate these responses, and those that regulate and maintain the responses. Behavioral responses are acquired through observational learning or direct experience. Behavior is activated by internal or external stimuli and/or expectations of reward. Behavior is then sustained or terminated, depending on its consequences. Expectancies concerning consequences arise from three sources — direct external consequences, vicarious experiencing of consequences to others, and self-produced consequences. Information from these three sources is combined to lead both to discriminations among situations in terms of their potential for various consequences and to the formation of general rules of behavior.

Because of its emphasis on cognitive and social processes, social cognitive theory has different implications for an understanding of abnormal behavior and change than was true for the theories previously considered. It is to these implications that we now turn.

Chapter Twelve
Social Cognitive Theory: Applications and Evaluation

*C*HAPTER FOCUS: In this chapter we consider the clinical applications of social cognitive theory. Attention is given to dysfunctional cognitive processes that play a role in abnormal behavior and to procedures for producing change in these processes. In particular, attention is given to the role of self-efficacy beliefs and to procedures for enhancing individual beliefs concerning their ability to cope with specific situations. The chapter concludes with a comparison of social cognitive theory with the approaches to personality previously considered in the text.

The value of a theory is ultimately judged by its usefulness as evidenced by the power of the methods it yields to effect psychological changes.

BANDURA, 1986, p. 4

In the social learning view, psychological changes, regardless of the method used to achieve them, derive from a common mechanism. . . . Psychological procedures, whatever their form, alter expectations of personal efficacy.

BANDURA, 1977a, p. 79

CLINICAL APPLICATIONS

Psychopathology

To a certain extent the social cognitive view of psychopathology is in accord with the view presented in Chapter 10. For example, the earlier views and social cognitive theory share these points of emphasis: (1) Rejection of the medical symptoms–disease model in favor of a model emphasizing the learning of maladaptive behaviors. (2) An emphasis on the present as opposed to the past: "Instead of asking 'why did he become this kind of person?' behavioral approaches ask 'what is *now* causing him to behave as he does?'" (Mischel, 1976, p. 252). (3) An emphasis on overt behavior rather than underlying dynamics. (4) An emphasis on therapy as the learning of new patterns of thinking and behaving rather than therapy as cure to some underlying cause. What differentiates social cognitive theory from the Hullian and Skinnerian views is the emphasis on cognitive variables, particularly as they enter into self-evaluative processes and judgments concerning self-efficacy.

According to social cognitive theory, maladaptive behavior is the result of dysfunctional learning. As with all learning, maladaptive responses can be learned as a result of direct experience or as the result of exposure to inadequate or "sick" models. Thus, Bandura (1968) suggests that the degree to which parents themselves model forms of aberrant behavior is often a significant causal factor in the development of psychopathology. Again, there is no need to look for traumatic incidents in the early history of the individual or for the underlying conflicts. Nor is there necessarily the need to find a history of reinforcement for the initial acquisition of the pathological behavior. On the other hand, once the behaviors have been learned through observational learning, it is quite likely that they have become manifest and that they have been maintained because of direct and vicarious reinforcement. One can again think here of research on the vicarious conditioning of emotional responses. Remember that monkeys who observed their parents express a fear of snakes developed a conditioned emotional response that was intense, longlasting, and generalized beyond the context in which it was first learned. Thus, there is the suggestion that observational learning and vicarious conditioning may account for a great proportion of human fears and phobias.

Although the learning of specific overt behaviors is important in psychopathology, increasingly social cognitive theory has come to emphasize the role of **dysfunctional expectancies** and **self-conceptions**. People may erroneously expect painful events to follow some events or pain to be associated with specific situations. They then may act so as to avoid certain situations or in a way that creates the very situation they were trying to avoid. An example would be the person who fears that closeness will bring pain and then acts in a hostile way, resulting in rejection by others and presumed confirmation of the expectancy that closeness leads to disappointment and rejection. Cognitive processes enter not only into such dysfunctional expectancies but also into **dysfunctional self-evaluations**. One example would be the person who fails to develop standards for self-reward and thus experiences boredom or almost complete dependence on momentary, external pleasures. Even more common are the problems associated with the development of overly severe standards. Such developments lead to excessive self-punishment and depression: "In more extreme forms, harsh standards for self-evaluation give rise to depressive reactions, chronic discouragement, feelings of worthlessness, and lack of purposefulness. Excessive self-disparagement, in fact, is one of the defining characteristics of depression" (Bandura, 1977a, p. 141).

In addition to emphasizing the role of stringent internal standards of self-evaluation in depression, Bandura suggests that feelings of inefficacy play a major role: "The greater the perceived self-inefficacy, the higher the depression" (Bandura, 1988). The problem with depressives is that they rigidly maintain strict standards and devalue themselves when they

CURRENT APPLICATIONS   SELF-EFFICACY AND HEALTH

According to social cognitive theory, perceptions of self-efficacy have important implications for emotional reactions to situations and motivation to undertake various behaviors. Such a concept would appear to have important implications for health in terms of understanding people's emotional and behavioral responses to stressful conditions and health-related programs.

Recent research by Bandura and others suggests that this is indeed the case. A variety of studies indicate that feelings of low self-efficacy are associated with increased stress responses, poorer responses to pain, and low motivation to pursue health-related programs. Conversely, increased feelings of self-efficacy are associated with lower self-reported stress, decreased physiological responses indicative of stress, increased coping, and increased involvement in programs prescribed by health-care workers. In one treatment program, arthritic patients were given a treatment program to enhance their perceived self-efficacy in coping with their difficulty. The treatment

not only accomplished this but also resulted in reduced pain and joint inflammation as well as improved psychosocial functioning. In another treatment program with bulimics, or individuals who binge eat and then vomit to purge themselves of the food, increases in self-efficacy were found to be associated with greater self-control in eating and decreases in vomiting frequency. Finally, in a third program, changes in perceived self-efficacy for walking were found to be associated with increased exercise in an activity program prescribed for patients at risk for heart disease.

Research to date suggests that self-efficacy theory has important implications for such diverse health-related behaviors as smoking cessation, pain experience and management, control of eating and weight, and adherence to preventive health programs.

SOURCES: O'Leary, 1985; O'Leary *et al.*, 1988; *Psychology Today*, October 1980; Schneider *et al.*, 1987.

Programs that increase self-efficacy help arthritic patients to overcome their fears of pain and disability. Copyright © American Psychological Association. Reprinted by permission.

do not meet them. In contrast to this, normal people adopt more flexible standards and are capable of abandoning goals that are impossible to attain rather than berating themselves for not achieving them (Bandura & Abrams, 1986). The interesting thing, however, is that this does not mean that depressives are less realistic than normals. Indeed, there is evidence that depressed people are more realistic in their self-appraisals of their competencies than are normals: "The depressed appear as realists, the nondepressed as confident distortionists" (Bandura, 1988). The terrible thing about feelings of inefficacy leading to depression is that a cyclical process can be set in motion. Thus, a depressed mood triggered by feelings of inefficacy can lead to memories of past failures and further feelings of inefficacy (Kavanagh & Bower, 1985).

Although it is not the only element in psychopathology, low self-efficacy is considered to be an ingredient of all psychological disturbance. For example, in a study of depressed and paranoid patients, it was found that both suffered from perceptions of low self-efficacy but, whereas depressives viewed events as caused by chance, paranoids viewed events as under the control of others (Rosenbaum & Hadari, 1985). Thus, the specific nature of the outcome expectancies and beliefs may play a major role in determining each particular form of disturbance.

The social cognitive view of psychopathology may be contrasted with the psychoanalytic and other views of anxiety and defense. According to Bandura, the social cognitive view differs on two counts. First, there is a different view of anxiety. In social cognitive theory, anxiety results from **perceived inefficacy** in coping with potentially aversive events rather than from the threat of unconscious impulses. Second, anxiety is not seen as leading to **defensive** (avoidance) **behaviors**. Rather, anxiety *and* defensive, avoidance behavior both are seen as resulting from expectancies of injury. It is this expectation and the perceived inability to cope that leads to both anxiety and defensive behaviors.

Defensive behaviors, as responses to threat or the signal of the potential for a painful outcome, are difficult to unlearn because they remove the person from the circumstances. This is a phenomenon that in the past has been called the "neurotic paradox" and which Bandura describes as the problem of "subjective confirmation" of the utility of defensive behavior.

> Avoidance prevents the organism from learning that the real circumstances have changed. The failure of anticipated hazards to materialize reinforces the expectation that the defensive maneuvers forestalled them. This process of subjective confirmation is captured in the apocryphal case of a compulsive who, when asked by his therapist why he snapped his fingers ritualistically, replied that it kept ferocious lions away. When informed that obviously there were no lions in the vicinity to ward off, the compulsive replied 'See, it works!'
>
> BANDURA, 1977a, p. 62

The social cognitive theory of psychopathology emphasizes the acquisition of maladaptive, dysfunctional behaviors and expectancies as the result of direct experience and observational learning. Such behaviors and expectancies are then maintained by their consequences, either external or internal. Particularly important is the role of learned expectancies of harm or injury and the sense of inefficacy or inability to cope with a perceived threat. Such expectancies and self-evaluations lead to defensive behaviors that are difficult to unlearn because their value is subjectively confirmed when harm does not occur.

Change

Therapeutic work within the social learning framework is relatively recent, though it has become an important area of theory and research. Bandura's efforts increasingly have been directed toward developing methods of therapeutic change and toward working out a unifying theory of behavioral change. In many ways the emphasis given to developments in this area is quite remarkable. Indeed, Bandura goes so far as to suggest that "the value of a theory is ultimately judged by its usefulness as evidenced by the power of the methods it yields to effect psychological changes" (1986, p. 4). Although Bandura emphasizes the importance of the development of such procedures, he is extremely cautious in his approach. He suggests that therapeutic procedures should be applied clinically only after there is understanding of the basic mechanisms involved and adequate tests of the effects of the methods.

According to Bandura, the change process involves not only the acquisition of new patterns of thought and behavior, but also their generalization and maintenance. The social cognitive view of therapy consequently emphasizes the importance of changes in the sense of efficacy. Throughout, the emphasis is on specific learned expectancies and behaviors rather than on "underlying dynamics" or generalized defensive styles.

The treatment approach most emphasized by social cognitive theory is the acquisition of cognitive and behavioral competencies through **modeling** and **guided participation**. In the former, desired activities are demonstrated by various models who experience positive consequences or at least no adverse consequences. Generally, the complex patterns of behavior that are to be learned are broken down into subskills and increasingly difficult subtasks so as to ensure optimal progress. In guided participation the individual is assisted in performing the modeled behaviors.

Much of the research on therapeutic modeling and guided participation has been carried out in the laboratory using severe snake phobias and children's avoidance of dogs as targets of behavior change. In one early study the modeling technique was compared with systematic desensitization and with a no-treatment control condition (Bandura, Blanchard, & Ritter, 1967). The subjects were people who answered a newspaper advertisement offering help to people with a snake phobia. Subjects were tested for how much contact they could stand to have with a snake both before and after they participated in one of the following four conditions: (1) *live modeling with participation* (a model demonstrated the desired behavior and then assisted the subject to learn increasingly more difficult responses); (2) *symbolic modeling* (subjects observed a film that showed children and adults engaged in progressively more threatening interactions with a large king snake; subjects were also trained to relax while watching the film); (3) *systematic desensitization;* (4) control–no treatment. The results were that the control subjects remained unchanged in their avoidance behavior, the symbolic modeling and systematic desensitization subjects showed substantial reductions in phobic behavior, and the live modeling combined with guided participation subjects showed the most substantial improvement. Live modeling with guided participation proved to be a superior and unusually powerful treatment that eliminated the snake phobia in virtually all subjects. As an illustration, all the subjects in this group progressed to the point where they were able to sit in a chair with a snake in their laps for 30 seconds.

A study of nursery school children who were afraid of dogs found that observation of another child playing with a dog helped to remove much of the fear and avoidance behavior (Bandura, Grusec, & Menlove, 1967). Of particular importance is the fact that these gains were main-

Guided Participation—Bandura emphasizes the role of modeling and guided participation in behavior change. Here a woman who is afraid of snakes is being helped to overcome her fear by a woman who models the desired behavior.

tained at a follow-up test one month later. In another study, Bandura and Menlove (1968) demonstrated that watching films of models playing with dogs could be helpful in reducing children's avoidance behavior. A particularly interesting finding was the possibility that the real-life models themselves were afraid of dogs. Whereas only one parent in a group of bold children reported any fear of dogs, in the group of avoidant children many of the parents were found to have such a fear.

These studies relate to the reduction of fear and avoidance behavior through the observation of models. What is the process that underlies such changes? Bandura's most recent explanation of the change process is a marked shift from his earlier views but is in accordance with his current emphasis on cognitive processes. In his earlier interpretations of psychotherapy as a learning process, Bandura (1961) emphasized such therapeutic processes as extinction, discrimination learning, counterconditioning, and reinforcement. However, his most recent statement suggests that psychological procedures, whatever their form, alter the level and strength of **self-efficacy** or the perceived ability to cope with specific situations (Bandura, 1982). Cognitive processes are part of psychopathology in that these processes involve dysfunctional expectancies and perceptions of self-inefficacy. Such expectancies and self-perceptions lead to anxiety and the defensive avoidance of threatening situations. Therefore, it makes sense that an effective therapeutic procedure would alter such expectancies and self-perceptions. Procedures such as modeling and guided participation help to effect such changes and thereby enable the person to reduce anticipatory fears and avoidance behaviors. At the root of such procedures, as well as other diverse therapeutic procedures, is a cognitive process involving changed expectations of personal efficacy.

Is there evidence to support this theory of psychological change? A number of studies have been conducted in which individuals with phobias have received treatment while their efficacy expectations and behaviors were measured (Bandura & Adams, 1977; Bandura, Adams, & Beyer, 1977; Bandura, Reese, and Adams, 1982). As predicted, subject statements of self-efficacy consistently predicted performance on tasks of varying levels of difficulty or threat. In other words, as therapeutic procedures led to improvement in perceived self-efficacy, individuals were increasingly able to confront previously feared objects.

For example, in one such illustrative research effort, subjects who suffered from chronic snake phobia were assigned to one of three conditions: *participant modeling* (therapist models the threatening activities and subjects gradually perform the tasks along with therapist assistance until they can be performed alone); *modeling* (subjects observe the therapist perform the tasks but do not engage in them; and *control condition* (Bandura, Adams, & Beyer, 1977). Both before and after these conditions, the subjects were tested on a Behavioral Avoidance Test (BAT), consisting of twenty-nine performance tasks requiring increasingly more threatening interactions with a red-tailed boa constrictor. The final task involved letting the snake crawl in their lap while their hands were held passively at their sides. To test the generality of change, subjects were also tested after treatment with a dissimilar threat—a corn snake. In addition, efficacy expectations were obtained before treatment, after treatment but before the second administration of the BAT, following the second administration of the BAT, and again one month following the completion of treatment. The results indicated that participant modeling and modeling produced significant increases in approach behavior toward both the similar threat and the dissimilar threat as well as significant increases in self-efficacy judgments (Figure 12.1). These gains clearly surpassed those made by subjects in the control condition. In addition, self-efficacy judgments (before the second BAT) were uniformly accurate predictors of performance; that is, strong self-efficacy judgments were associated with higher probabilities of successful task performance. These efficacy expectations in fact had superior predictive power over past performance! Follow-up data indicated that the subjects not only maintained their gains in self-efficacy and approach behavior but

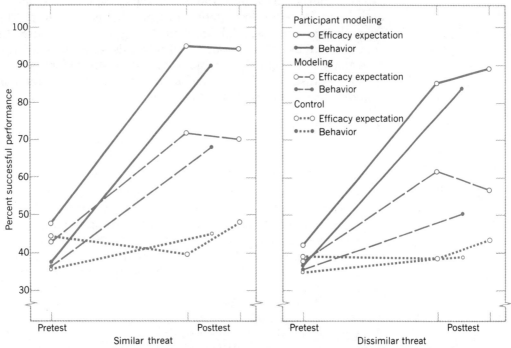

FIGURE 12.1 Level of Self-efficacy and Approach Behavior Displayed by Subjects toward Different Threats after Receiving Vicarious (Modeling) or Performance-Based Participant Modeling Treatments or No Treatment. (In the posttest phase, level of self-efficacy was measured prior to and after the behavioral avoidance tests with the two subjects.) (Bandura, Adams, & Beyer, 1977; Copyright © 1977 American Psychological Association. Reprinted by permission.)

achieved some further improvements. In sum, the data supported the utility of guided participation and the social learning view that treatments improve performance because they raise expectations of personal efficacy.

The preceding discussion has focused on the treatment of phobias and other fears. However, as indicated in the discussion of self-efficacy and health, the social cognitive approach has been used in the treatment of a wide variety of difficulties. At times cognitive methods of change, discussed more fully later in the text, are used to produce changes in beliefs. For example, there may be efforts to help depressives alter their performance standards, become more positive in their self-appraisals, and become less self-devaluing when performance does not meet the standard. However, at all times the emphasis is on change in self-efficacy as the basic process underlying therapeutic change.

Further, Bandura suggests that efforts to modify faulty cognitions solely by cognitive means may have weak results — behavior and powerful experiences that produce the sense of mastery may be essential: "Clinical applications that prescribe actions as well as dispute misbeliefs doubtless produce better results. The benefits of the combined procedure probably derive more from the corrective assignments to behave differently than from the exhortation to think better" (1986, p. 515). Thus, even though the essential problem is cognitive in nature, treatment should make use of action-oriented methods to produce change. In the final analysis, imagined attainments are no substitute for masterly action. This is because actual accomplishments are a critical component of perception of self-efficacy (Figure 12.2).

A CASE EXAMPLE

It is interesting and perhaps significant that few, if any, in-depth individual cases have been reported by proponents of social cognitive theory.

Mischel (1968, 1976) has taken a case previously reported in the literature and interpreted it from a social learning standpoint. Originally reported by two psychiatrists–psychoanalysts in a book on the psychological trauma experienced by servicemen during the Second World War (Grinker & Spiegel, 1945), the case involved a bombardier who, during one of his missions, experienced psychological and physical trauma. His plane was damaged by flak and although it began to dive, it was pulled out of the dive just before crashing. However, the bombardier was hurled against the bombsight. Upon return to flight duty, he found that he would become faint whenever the plane reached an altitude of about 10,000 feet. This, of course, interfered with his continuation on active duty.

Mischel notes that the analysts concluded that the bombardier's fainting was related to deep, underlying anxieties rooted in his childhood experiences. Instead of such a dynamic explanation Mischel suggests a

GENERAL VIEW Psychological procedures, whatever their format, serve as ways of creating and strengthening expectations of personal effectiveness. Social cognitive therapy emphasizes the acquisition of cognitive and behavioral competencies through modeling and guided participation.

ATTRIBUTES OF GOOD MODELS: RELEVANCE AND CREDIBILITY Models who compel attention, who instill trust, who appear to be realistic figures for self-comparison, and whose standards seem reasonable to the learner will be good sources for therapeutic modeling effects. These attributes may be summarized in terms of the positive functions of relevance and credibility.

SOME ILLUSTRATIVE RULES FOR INDUCING AND MAINTAINING DESIRED CHANGES

1. Structure the tasks to be learned in an orderly, stepwise sequence.

2. Explain and demonstrate general rules or principles. Check client's understanding and provide opportunities for clarification.

3. Provide guided simulated practice with feedback concerning success and error.

4. Once the desired behavior is established, increase opportunities for self-directed accomplishment.

5. Test newly acquired skills in the natural environment under conditions likely to produce favorable results.

6. Test skills in increasingly more demanding situations until a satisfactory level of competence and self-efficacy has been obtained.

7. Provide opportunity for therapist consultation and feedback during periods of increased independent mastery.

THERAPEUTIC EFFECTS OF MODELING

1. *Development of New Skills.* Through observing models and through guided participation people acquire new patterns of behavior and new coping strategies. For example, submissive clients learn to model assertive behavior.

2. *Changes in inhibitions about Self-expression.* As a result of modeling, responses already available to the person may be weakened or strengthened. For example, inhibitory effects can occur as a result of observing models receive negative consequences for certain behaviors. Disinhibitory effects, which are more common in therapy, result from observing models perform behaviors without adverse consequences or with positive consequences. Fears may be overcome in this way.

3. *Facilitation of Preexisting Patterns of Behavior.* Behaviors already available to the person and that are not associated with anxiety may occur more often as a result of modeling influences. For example, learners may be aided to become more skillful conversationalists.

4. *Adoption of More Realistic Standards for Judging One's Own Performance.* Observing models reward themselves for varying levels of performance can affect the learner's self-standards. For example, rigid self-demands characteristic of depressed people can be relaxed as a result of modeling.

CONCLUSION "A burgeoning literature confirms the value of modeling treatments for redressing deficits in social and cognitive skills, and for helping to remove defensive avoidance behavior" (Rosenthal and Bandura, 1978, p. 622).

FIGURE 12.2 Summary of Social Cognitive Therapy

GIVING UP ADDICTIONS AND AVOIDING RELAPSE

An incredible number of people suffer from compulsive patterns of behavior that have an addictive quality to them—smoking, overeating, gambling, drinking, drugs. Often they give up the troublesome pattern of behavior for a period of time, only to find that it returns. What is it that accounts for relapse and how can its risks be minimized?

Although many people claim a physiological basis for addictive behavior, two points are noteworthy: (1) In some of these compulsive patterns it is clear that no true physiological addiction exists. Yet, a psychological craving remains. Generally, periods of intense craving are associated with feelings of threat and inability to cope with events. (2) Many people are able to go through an extended period of abstinence only to experience a relapse—overeating after weight loss, habitual smoking after abstinence, and so on. Researchers in this area have identified a common element in the relapse process. Those who are able to maintain abstinence perceive themselves as

more able to cope with and affect events than do those who relapse. They have better self-efficacy judgments. Many people show occasional lapses from total abstinence. Those who relapse, however, treat the event as a statement about themselves and their efficacy. Thus, they make statements such as "I'm a failure" or "I just can't do it" or "I have no willpower." Already feeling vulnerable in relation to the task at hand, they treat occasional lapses in a way that only serves to damage further their beliefs in themselves.

In treating addictions and compulsive patterns of behavior, getting people to abstain is only part of the job. In many cases this turns out to be easier than helping them to remain abstinent. Evidently changing the way they interpret occasional lapses and enhancing their feelings of self-efficacy concerning abstinence are an important part of the work that needs to be done.

SOURCE: Marlatt & Gordon, 1980; *New York Times*, February 23, 1983, C1.

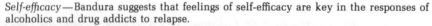

Self-efficacy—Bandura suggests that feelings of self-efficacy are key in the responses of alcoholics and drug addicts to relapse.

social behavior analysis according to which the emotional trauma probably was conditioned to the altitude the plane reached at about the time of the mishap. When he went on a flight and reached that altitude he would reexperience the cues connected with the accident and become emotionally helpless. Therefore, the causes of the problem lie in the current conditions rather than in early childhood antecedents. Rather than needing insight therapy Mischel suggests that "the treatment implications seem clear for social behavior theory: render the traumatic cues neutral by desensitizing him to them through slow, graded exposure under conditions that prevent arousal and that, instead, insure incompatible responses such as relaxation" (1968, p. 267). Mischel is critical of the approach that emphasizes events in childhood, defenses against feelings, dynamic explanations, and the value of insight. Instead, he argues for an emphasis on the conditions precipitating the difficulty, the situational factors maintaining the problem, and the kinds of structured tasks or situations that will facilitate new kinds of learning.

COMPARATIVE ANALYSIS

It may be of interest at this point to consider social cognitive theory in relation to the theories previously considered in the text. In part we will be helped in this endeavor by Bandura himself, since he begins his 1986 book with a critique of psychoanalytic theory, trait theory, and radical behaviorism. Our analysis may be simplified by keeping in mind four points emphasized by social cognitive theory: (1) Cognitive processes are important in motivation, emotion, and action. (2) People discriminate among situations and behavior tends to be specific to contexts or domains. (3) There is an interactive, reciprocal relationship between persons and situations as well as among thought, feeling, and behavior (i.e., people influence situations as well as are influenced by them and thoughts, feelings, and overt behavior can influence one another). (4) Experimental research is important in defining concepts and providing support for the effectiveness of therapeutic methods.

Social Cognitive Theory and Psychoanalysis
Bandura is critical of psychoanalysis for its reliance on concepts that cannot be studied experimentally and on therapeutic procedures that have not demonstrated their effectiveness in changing actual psychosocial functioning. In particular, Bandura suggests that laboratory investigations have "failed to unearth an unconcscious agency of the type assumed by psychodynamic theory" (1986, p. 3) and that "insight into dubious unconscious psychodynamics has little effect on behavior" (p. 5).

It is clear that Bandura's emphasis on experimental, laboratory data represents a contrast with the roots of psychoanalytic theory in the clinical, therapeutic setting. Beyond this, however, there is a very different view of the functioning of the organism. Social cognitive theorists are critical of the psychoanalytic emphasis on broad personality dispositions (character types) and the relative fixity of behavior established during the early years. Instead, social cognitive theory suggests that behavior is situation or context specific and that behavior is governed by what is occurring in the present. Rather than broad stages of development, development in particular areas is emphasized; rather than generalized dynamics and defenses, specific expectancies and self-evaluations are emphasized; rather than early traumatic experiences, observational learning and vicarious conditioning are emphasized; rather than insight into unconscious dynamics, changes in conscious cognitive functioning are emphasized.

Social Cognitive Theory and Phenomenology

Social cognitive theory shares with Rogers and proponents of the human potential movement an emphasis on the vast potential of humans as well as an emphasis on the concept of self. However, such points of agreement are overshadowed by more important fundamental differences. According to social cognitive theory, people have self-conceptualizations and self-evaluations, but they do not have selves or generalized self-concepts: "A global self-conception does not do justice to the complexity of self-efficacy percepts, which vary across different activities, different levels of the same activity, and different circumstances" (Bandura, 1986, p. 410).

Other differences between the two theoretical approaches can be considered. First, although Rogers emphasized the importance of research, he also valued clinical observations and other members of the human potential movement have tended to ignore research, in particular laboratory research. Clearly this is not the case for Bandura and followers of social cognitive theory. Second, whereas Rogers was interested in the therapeutic climate as the primary ingredient of change, social cognitive theory emphasizes the importance of experiences in changing self-efficacy percepts. Finally, although both Rogerian theory and social cognitive theory emphasize emotions *and* cognitions, the primary emphasis for Rogers was on feelings (positive regard, empathic understanding, congruence), whereas for Bandura it is on cognitions.

Social Cognitive Theory and Personal Construct Theory

Social cognitive theory and personal construct theory share a common emphasis on cognitive processes in human behavior. They also share an emphasis on the utility of behavioral experiences in changing constructs or cognitions. Despite this, and Kelly's acknowledged influence on Mischel, followers of the two approaches tend to go their own ways and Bandura gives virtually no recognition to the work of Kelly.

Why should this be the case? In part this reflects the differing roots of the two approaches and in part it reflects their different groundings. Whereas Kelly set his views apart from traditional psychology, social cognitive theory had its roots in learning theory and continues to be rooted in developments in traditional psychology. Whereas personal construct theorists have tended to limit themselves to the study of constructs, and to the use of the Rep test as a measuring device, the social cognitive theoretical framework and approach to research have been much broader. In addition, to a certain extent personal construct theorists have been interested in what people think, whereas social cognitive theorists have been interested in the relation of what people think to what they feel and do. Whereas Kelly could dismiss the concept of motivation and "carrot and stick" theories of motivation, social cognitive theory emphasizes the importance of rewards in influencing outcome expectancies and performance.

Social Cognitive Theory and Trait Theory

Social cognitive theorists are critical of trait theorists for their emphasis on broad dispositions and trait questionnaires as opposed to the study of processes that account for how behavior is acquired, maintained, and changed. As noted in Chapter 9, the differing views were crystallized, and polarized, in terms of the person–situation debate.

Although trait and social cognitive theorists share an emphasis on research, their basic assumptions and focus of investigation are different. Whereas trait theorists suggest that behavior is largely the product of dispositions, and is fairly consistent across situations and over time, social cognitive theorists emphasize the role of people's cognitive competencies in discriminating among situations, in terms of both their self-efficacy percepts and outcome expectancies. At this point, both trait and social cognitive theorists would agree that there is evidence of both consistency and variability in behavior. However, they disagree about how much of each there is, how to account for behavior, and what should be studied. Trait theorists emphasize stability and consistency, social cognitive theorists variability and change; trait theorists emphasize broad dispositions, often genetically based, social cognitive theorists learned cognitive expectancies and competencies; trait theorists focus on factor structures, social cognitive theorists on person processes that provide for adaptation to changing circumstances.

Social Cognitive Theory and Learning Theory

Social cognitive theory has its roots in learning theory. As noted, originally it was called social learning theory. It shares with Hullian and Skinnerian learning theories an emphasis on research, an emphasis on the importance of learned behavior in relation to specific situations or contexts, and an emphasis on the importance of rewards in influencing behavior. However, in their emphasis on cognitive processes, social cognitive theorists argue that behavior is regulated not just by consequences but by expectancies and self-regulatory processes: "In reducing the determinants of human behavior to contingency control, proponents of radical behaviorism place the agency of action in environmental forces, and they strip thought and other internal events of any causal efficacy" (Bandura, 1986, p. 12).

Another important difference involves the use of verbal, self-report data. Whereas learning theorists typically avoid the use of such data, and Skinnerians specifically argue against the use of such data to infer internal events, Bandura takes a much different view. According to him, cognitive processes are not publicly observable but self-report data can be useful in learning about such processes. As a minimum, the value of self-reports is seen as an open, empirical question. Beyond this, however, the suggestion is made that such data can be useful when reports are made specific and just prior to action.

CRITICAL EVALUATION

Strengths of the Theory

Social cognitive theory is probably the current favorite among academic personality psychologists, and a good number of clinicians would also label themselves social cognitive psychologists. How can we account for this growth in popularity and influence? Probably the major factors have been the attention given to experimentation and evidence and a parallel consideration of important human phenomena. Beyond this there is an impressive openness to change as well as a continuing concern with other points of view. These strengths will be considered in greater detail.

Concern with experimentation and evidence

Developments in social cognitive theory have been grounded in careful experimental research. Bandura and Mischel have been concerned with defining concepts in ways that leave them open to empirical verification and have always conducted active research programs. The record of phenomena investigated and the ways in which they have been investigated is impressive. For example, the research on modeling indicates that the observation of models can lead to the acquisition of new responses and to changes in the frequency of occurrence of behaviors already learned. The range of behaviors investigated includes aggression, moral judgments, setting of standards, vicarious conditioning of fears, delay of gratification, and helping behavior. Children and adults have been found to be influenced by a wide range of models—live humans, filmed humans, verbally presented models of behavior, and cartoons. The process of modeling has been studied in terms of the influences of model characteristics, observer characteristics, and observed consequences to the model of the demonstrated behavior. The concept of self-efficacy has been studied in terms of its determinants, implications for a wide range of behaviors, and potential for change—an impressive record of research.

Importance of phenomena considered

Most social cognitive research has been conducted with the social behaviors of humans. Thus, in considering the evidence, we are not asked to make large extrapolations from animal research to humans and from simple behaviors to complex human processes. Social cognitive theory investigates and attempts to account for the very phenomena that are of interest to most people—aggression, the effects of parents and mass media on children, the change of dysfunctional behaviors, the development of self-regulatory capacities, and the increase of control over one's life.

A theory open to change

Social cognitive theory has changed and evolved over the years. A comparison of *Social Learning and Personality Development* (1963) by Bandura and Walters with Bandura's *Social Foundations of Thought and Action* (1986) gives ample testimony to the changes that have come about. The emphasis on behavior, observational learning, and the importance of reinforcers in maintaining behavior has been continued. However, with time there has been an increased emphasis on cognitive processes and self-regulation. Not only are external events emphasized, but internal ones are emphasized as well. In the process of reciprocal determinism we not only have environmental contingencies shaping people but also people shaping environmental contingencies. Not only is there an emphasis on behavior but one on cognition and emotion as well. Furthermore, there is an emphasis on the relationships among thought, feeling, and overt behavior. Social cognitive theorists have tried to remain informed about developments in other areas of psychology and to adjust their position so that it remains consistent with these developments. Beyond this, social cognitive theory itself has influenced and contributed to other parts of psychology. While social cognitive theory draws on advances in fields such as cognition and development, it also contributes to these advances.

Focus of attention on important issues

Social cognitive theorists have played a valuable role in criticizing other theoretical positions (psychoanalytic, trait, Skinnerian) and in bringing critical issues to the forefront, among them the role of reinforcement in the acquisition and performance of behavior. Mischel, in particular, has been influential in drawing attention to the problems associated with views that overemphasize trait factors. The person–situation controversy has led in some wasteful directions, such as examining whether persons or situations are more important in determining behavior. Generally, however, it has led to a more realistic assessment of the complex, interacting causes of behavior.

View of the person and social concern

Social cognitive theory offers a view of the person that is more reasonable than a robot or telephone switchboard and suggests possible solutions to problems of genuine social concern. Social cognitive approaches are used to help people with common problems of life. Yet they are also considered in relation to larger problems of social change. Bandura (1977a) considers the soundness of a legal system of deterrence, the potential for creating environments conducive to learning and intellectual development, and the interplay between personal freedom and limits on conduct that must exist in every society. Interestingly enough, he concludes his book: "As a science concerned with the social consequences of its applications, psychology must promote public understanding of psychological issues that bear on social policies to ensure that its findings are used in the service of human betterment" (p. 213).

Limitations of the Theory

Given these significant strengths, what are the limitations of social cognitive theory? Some of these are associated with new developments and the fact that many of the approaches are recent. Social cognitive theory has shown a constructive openness to change but has not followed a path that has led to a carefully integrated network of theoretical assumptions. Many of the concepts, findings, and therapeutic procedures have been challenged by proponents of alternative points of view. Finally, social cognitive theory would appear to continue to ignore phenomena of importance that are recognized by other approaches. Again, these points will be considered in greater detail.

Social cognitive theory is not yet
a systematic, unified theory

Social cognitive theory is not yet a systematic, unified theory in the sense of a network of assumptions tied together in a systematic way leading to specific predictions. Bandura's (1986) recent effort in this direction represents an important development. One recent reviewer suggests, for example, that the outline of a "grand theory" of human behavior is there and "what more can we ask from a single colleague and scholar" (Baron, 1987, p. 415). At the same time, it is important to recognize that social cognitive theory represents a blending together of contributions and concepts, some unique to the theory and others taken from other theories, rather than a unified theory. Occasionally diverse concepts are merely lumped together and sometimes opposing findings would appear to fit equally well into the theory. In attempting to go beyond a simplistic emphasis on internal (person) or external (environment) determinants, and a simplistic emphasis on cognition, affect, or overt behavior as all important, social cognitive theory represents an important contribution. However, what one has is a general view or orientation, rather than a fully worked out statement of relationships.

New problems have arisen
with new developments

Perhaps not unexpectedly, each new development in social cognitive theory creates new criticism and new difficulties. Social cognitive theory's emphasis on the learning of complex acts in the absence of reinforcement has been attacked consistently by Skinnerians, who suggest, for example, that observational learning may, in fact, illustrate a generalized imitative response that is sometimes, but not always, reinforced (Gewirtz, 1971). Skinnerians suggest that although the individual may learn a response performed by a model, without being reinforced, this does not mean that reinforcement was not a necessary part of the overall learning process; one cannot determine this without knowing the reinforcement history of the individual. Other psychologists, working within a strict behaviorist framework, are critical of the recent emphasis on internal variables and verbal self-report. Developments here have occurred with an eye toward past pitfalls of research on the self and the use of verbal reports. It is strange, perhaps welcome, to see social cognitive psychologists emphasizing what people have to report about themselves. However, it remains to be seen whether detailed verbal report procedures and supportive reporting conditions can take care of the fact that people often are unaware of processes in themselves. Years of research on the concept of self have left us with a host of major unresolved problems (Wylie, 1974). Can social cognitive theory find a way to overcome them?

Most recently the concept of self-efficacy has come under attack. Three aspects of this criticism can be considered. First, there is the suggestion that self-efficacy beliefs are tied to outcome expectancies and it is outcome expectancies that govern behavior. Ordinarily, if people believe they can perform the tasks relevant to a situation, wouldn't they expect a positive outcome? Also, if they feel that they cannot perform the necessary tasks, ordinarily wouldn't they expect a negative outcome? Thus, to the extent that one believes performance to be related to outcome, one's self-efficacy beliefs would be expected to relate fairly closely to one's outcome expectancies.

Bandura suggests, however, that self-efficacy beliefs do not always match outcome expectancies, particularly in situations where outcomes are partially or totally beyond the control of the person. Further, research suggests that self-efficacy beliefs predict behavior better than outcome expectancies. Thus, Bandura argues that self-efficacy beliefs are fundamentally different from outcome expectancies—what one believes one can do is different from what one believes will be the outcome of behavior. What remains to be worked out in this controversy are the factors that determine when self-efficacy beliefs and outcome expectancies match one another and when they diverge, as well as the contributions of each to behavior.

A second aspect of the criticism of the concept of self-efficacy is that although Bandura has broadly articulated the factors contributing to the development of self-efficacy beliefs, we do not understand such events as the sudden erosion of a self-efficacy belief or the rapid fluctuation between strong beliefs in efficacy and those in inefficacy. Thus, for example, people may first feel very confident in a situation and then rapidly lose all confidence or fluctuate rapidly in the sense of self-efficacy. Why some self-efficacy beliefs are stable and others unstable, some resistant to change and others open to change, remains to be determined.

Third, there is the question concerning the relationship of self-efficacy beliefs to broad aspects of behavior. Self-efficacy is measured according to Bandura's microanalytic strategy—at specific moments in time and in relation to specific tasks. This allows for considerable precision in measurement but does not provide for broad explanatory power. If self-efficacy percepts are so specific to tasks and contexts, of what value are they in relation to broader aspects of a person's life or new situations? Also, how are we to account for situations where self-efficacy beliefs appear to be unrelated to behavior, such as where a person indicates that they believe they have the ability to do something and it makes sense to do it, yet they still find themselves unable to act?

In sum, self-efficacy appears to be a valuable concept, but one in need of further examination and elaboration.

Social cognitive theory neglects or gives
minimal emphasis to some important areas

It undoubtedly is impossible for a theory of personality to be truly encompassing at this time. Accepting such qualifications, it would still appear that social cognitive theorists ignore or give minimal emphasis to significant aspects of human functioning. Without accepting all of the viewpoint of stage theorists, maturational factors would appear to be important in the feelings people experience and in the way that they process information. Sexual feelings do become increasingly important at particular times in the life cycle and the thinking of a child is fundamentally different from that of an adult in a variety of ways.

Beyond this, although social cognitive theory recognizes the importance of motivational factors and conflict, it only recently has begun to give serious attention to these processes. Recently the concepts of standards and goals have also been emphasized, and related research represents an important development in the social cognitive view of motivation. At the same time, this is an area in need of further development. In particular, there is need for study of the kinds of goals people have and the basis for the acquisition of these goals. Bandura seems to equate goals with standards, as if the only thing that motivates people is standards. But don't people pursue other goals? Similarly, Bandura suggests that people are motivated by the discrepancy between performance and a standard, but are not people also motivated by the desire to achieve the goal itself rather than to close a discrepancy between performance and a standard?

Turning to the concept of conflict, Bandura recognizes that most behavior is determined by multiple goals, yet he strangely ignores the concept of conflict. Most people can readily think of situations where they felt in conflict between goals. For some people conflict is a fundamental part of their lives. Not only is the concept of conflict central to psychoanalytic theory, but it was emphasized by the learning theorists Dollard and Miller. Thus, it seems strange that a concept of such seeming importance would be so neglected.

Many developments are recent and findings should be regarded as preliminary rather than conclusive

Throughout its history, psychology generally, and the field of psychotherapy in particular, has been beset with fads. Therefore one must be cautious in distinguishing between actual progress and overzealous commitment to a new idea. Whereas at one time theories that emphasized cognitive processes were viewed with skepticism, later such theories were adopted readily: "1976 could well be designated the year of cognition for both theoretician and practitioner. Like the activities of Superman and the Scarlet Pimpernel, cognition is in the air, it is here, there, and everywhere" (Franks & Wilson, 1978, p. vii). Without minimizing their importance in human behavior, we should be careful about prematurely accepting cognitive processes as our basic explanatory concepts.

Although the results of guided participation and modeling are significant, these therapeutic processes remain to be tested by other therapists, with different patients and with different problems. Bandura has answered critics who suggest that his results are of limited generalizability. However, the history of psychotherapy is filled with methods that were introduced as solving the problems of those in psychological distress. Most recently, evaluation of efforts in the area of behavior modification and behavior therapy should make us aware of the complexities of the problem and the work that remains to be done.

In sum, there are good grounds both for enthusiasm about social cognitive theory and for caution and even skepticism. Social cognitive theory represents a major development. It is still evolving, and its further efforts are worthy of careful attention.

	STRENGTHS		LIMITATIONS
1.	Has impressive research record.	1.	Is not a systematic, unified theory.
2.	Considers important phenomena.	2.	Contains potential problems associated with the utilization of verbal self-report.
3.	Shows consistent development and elaboration as a theory.	3.	Requires more exploration and development in certain areas (e.g., motivation, affect, system properties of personality organization).
4.	Focuses attention on important theoretical issues.	4.	Provides findings concerning therapy that are tentative rather than conclusive.

FIGURE 12.3 Summary of Strengths and Limitations of Social Cognitive Theory.

Major Concepts and Summary

dysfunctional expectancies defensive behaviors

self-conceptions guided participation

dysfunctional self-evaluation self-efficacy expectations

self-efficacy and inefficacy

Social cognitive theory rejects the medical symptoms–disease model of psychopathology and sees abnormal behavior as being on a continuum with normal behavior. According to social cognitive theory, behavior that is maladaptive or pathological represents the result of dysfunctional learning of behaviors, expectancies, standards for self-reward, and, most significantly, self-efficacy beliefs. Such maladaptive responses are learned, as are other behaviors, either directly or through the observation of inadequate models. A central role in the interpretation of psychopathology is given to the feeling of inefficacy. This is experienced when the person perceives the self as unable to cope with a threat or a situation expected to lead to pain or injury and leads to defensive behaviors. Anxiety, in this view, does not lead to defensive behaviors. Anxiety and defensive behaviors both are seen as resulting from perceived inefficacy in coping with potentially aversive events rather than as causing one another.

Whereas anxiety involves judgments of inefficacy in relation to potentially threatening events, depression involves judgments of inefficacy in relation to gaining desired outcomes. Overly stringent self-evaluative standards are also viewed as playing a role in depression.

Feelings of futility may arise either because the person perceives the self as unable to do what is required (self-inefficacy) or because the environment is viewed as punitive or unresponsive.

Defensive behaviors are difficult to unlearn because they remove the person from the threatening circumstances and prevent one from revising one's expectancies. The task in psychotherapy, then, is to increase the sense of self-efficacy so that previously avoided situations may be confronted and new expectancies learned. According to social cognitive theory, all psychological procedures, whatever their form, alter the level and strength of self-efficacy or the perceived ability to cope with specific situations. Modeling and guided participation have been used in therapeutic efforts. Recent research has suggested that self-efficacy expectations are excellent predictors of performance and are superior in this regard to past performance itself.

Interest in and support for social cognitive theory is probably largely influenced by its dual emphasis on experimentation and important personality and social phenomena. In addition, proponents of the theory have shown a striking willingness to revise the theory as new evidence emerges. At the same time, it has been criticized for not being a truly systematic theory and for ignoring or giving minimal attention to important areas such as maturation, conflict, and the holistic (system) properties of the organism. In addition, although recent developments in social cognitive theory are noteworthy, they have created new conceptual and methodological difficulties. It is too early to evaluate fully the potential of therapeutic efforts based on social cognitive theory. The theory represents a significant effort and has already been associated with noteworthy research accomplishments. How much it can be extended and systematized in the future remains to be seen.

Chapter Thirteen
A Cognitive, Information– Processing Approach to Personality

*C*HAPTER FOCUS: The world about us and within us is filled with many events and a vast array of information. From all that we can observe, what is it that we do observe? From all the ways that we can view people, ourselves, and events, how do we end up selecting certain representations and explanations? Living in a complex and changing world in which it is important to make decisions, how do we go about organizing information in order to make our lives reasonably stable and productive? These are the kinds of questions that are of interest to cognitive personality psychologists and the kinds of questions that concern us in this chapter. Here we turn to a different model of human functioning than we considered previously — the computer. Here we also consider an approach more firmly tied to experimental psychology than to clinical work, an approach more narrowly attuned to concepts and research procedures than to a comprehensive theory of personality. Notwithstanding these facts, this approach is perhaps at present the main exploratory thrust in the field of personality theory.

> *In a normal revolution, and in any biological model, the central energy is information. And in the new process of production, information is the central energy. . . . That's a major industrial revolution of which we're at the very beginning.*
>
> DRUCKER, INTERVIEW, 1982

> *The information processing view of the person takes the computer as its guiding metaphor.*
>
> BOWER, 1978, p. 123

> *We place social intelligence at the center of this personality theory and define it as the concepts, memories, and rules — in short, the knowledge — that individuals bring to bear in solving personal life tasks.*
>
> CANTOR AND KIHLSTROM, 1987, p. IX

Theories of personality tend to be associated with models of human nature. To take two illustrations already noted: in psychoanalytic theory, there is the model of the person as a hydraulic energy system; in personal construct theory, there is the model of the person as a scientist. Since the 1960s, we have witnessed in psychology a revolution — the cognitive revolution. This revolution in psychology has matched the technological revolution in industry. The technological revolution is that of the computer and information processing. The cognitive revolution's model of the person is that of a complex, sophisticated — though error-prone — processor of information.

Like all such models, this one cannot be taken completely literally. No psychologist would suggest that people are the same as computers or that computers can, as yet, perform all the thinking operations of humans. However, such models are viewed as useful in conceptualizing how people think and in defining which issues are particularly important to investigate. Thus, many psychologists have begun to probe ways in which people do function like computers. Computers are information-processing devices in which information is received or encoded, stored or remembered, and retrieved when needed. The key terms here are encoding, memory, and retrieval, and the question of import becomes how people encode, store, and retrieve information.

Given this model, which aspects of human information processing appear to be of particular importance to investigate? And, accepting it only as a model, are there any uniquely human qualities of thought and information processing that need to be kept in mind? As we live our daily lives, we are exposed to a great deal of information concerning ourselves, others, and social behavior. How do we organize and utilize this information to make sense out of the world? How do we go about developing representations of the world about us and of ourselves, and how do we develop causal explanations for events? What categories do we use to classify people, situations, and events? What rules do we follow in interpreting events and do these rules sometimes lead us into trouble? These are some of the questions of interest to the cognitive personality psychologist and represent the kinds of questions that we address in this chapter.

Before turning to these questions, let us consider the history of this approach and place it in its proper context relative to other theories already considered. In relation to the former, cognitive personality psychologists have borrowed heavily from the concepts and research procedures of experimental cognitive psychologists. Whereas the cognitive revolution in experimental psychology dates back to the 1960s, the current wave of interest in personality dates back to the late 1970s and early 1980s. In relation to the latter, we can consider three significant ways in which cognitive personality psychology departs from the views presented earlier in the text. First, until now we have considered theories of personality. In the present case, there is no cognitive or information-processing theory of personality. Rather, there is research that will lead, one hopes, to an understanding of cognitive functioning and thereby eventually to a comprehensive theory of personality. Second, most theories presented in this text take clinical case material as their point of departure. This is seen most clearly in the theories of Freud, Rogers, and Kelly. In other cases, as in trait theory, the focus is on individual differences. In

CURRENT APPLICATIONS

COMPUTER PERSONALITIES?

If we can use computers as a model for personality, can we also use computers to model personality? Many psychologists in the area of artificial intelligence think so, as they go about the task of trying to simulate human thought and behavior on the computer. At this point not only can you play chess with the computer, but you can interact with nine different computer personalities in a variety of social situations.

A recent article in the *Wall Street Journal* asks: Can the computer learn how to be a football coach? Football fans undoubtedly are familiar with the picture of a coach on the sidelines with a list of plays and formations that are believed to work in various situations. Can a computer incorporate the information used by a coach to call plays in a dynamic way? Can it produce a winning coach? Can it help to reduce stress and burnout? Can it enlighten us about how human information processing works? These are some of the questions being asked by Roger Schank at the Yale University Artificial Intelligence Laboratory. According to the article, Professor Schank also believes that a properly programmed computer might even make a good president some day.

Another creative and challenging effort along these lines has been Kenneth Mark Colby's computer modeling of a paranoid mind. Starting from a theory that suggests that paranoia expresses a strategy of blaming others as a protective defense against the painful affect of shame—humiliation ("I am being wronged, harassed, etc." versus "I am inadequate and to blame"), a computer has been programmed to respond to a psychiatric interview as a paranoid person might. Can psychiatrists interacting with a patient or a computer at the other end of a teletype machine tell which is which—paranoid computer or paranoid person? Evidently not. The responses from the "paranoid mind" of the computer seem indistinguishable from those of the paranoid mind of the person.

Can a computer be programmed to "think" and "feel" like a person? Evidently so. Can such computer simulations of human personality enlighten us about how people really function? That remains for the future to tell. Can computers eventually "really" think, feel, and have personalities? That, perhaps, is for philosophers to debate.

SOURCE: Colby, 1981; *Wall Street Journal*, March 30, 1983, p. 1.

"THAT DAMN COMPUTER THINKS IT KNOWS IT ALL!"

Computers and Personality—Cognitive psychologists use the computer as a model for personality and try to model human behavior on computers. © Robert Schochet..

the work to be discussed, the point of departure is experimental cognitive psychology rather than clinical work. The effort is to tie personality psychology to experimental work in cognitive psychology. Third, following from the point just made, the work of cognitive personality psychologists focuses more on general aspects of information processing rather than it does on individual differences.

With the approach to be considered here perhaps just a decade old, clearly it is still in the process of emerging as a theory of personality. Just as computers have become more sophisticated and capable of solving more problems, so information-processing models of personality have become more complex in their attempts to come to grips with a greater variety of human problems. Thus, although originally the focus was on thinking and information-processing, increasingly attention has been paid to how people attempt to solve life's tasks, and thereby to questions of emotion and motivation (Cantor & Kihlstrom, 1987). However, it is knowledge and cognitive processes that remain at the core of this approach to personality.

REPRESENTATION OF THE WORLD ABOUT US

Starting from birth, we are bombarded with information concerning people and events in the world. How do we go about organizing this information? In this section, we will consider research in three relevant areas—the organization of information relevant to *people* in the world, the organization of information relevant to *situations*, and the organization of information relevant to *events*.

Organizing Information Relevant to People

When asked to describe people we know, which terms do we use? In thinking about friends, we find that we use particular terms to describe them and that sometimes we group people into types—we say that a friend has these characteristics or is this type of person. In meeting new people, we also find that we tend to be sensitive to particular characteristics and to perceive them in particular terms. In some cases, these perceived characteristics are more or less neutral; in other cases they are heavily value laden. Thus, for example, one may describe someone in physical terms (e.g., tall, ruddy, angular) that may not express value preferences or in trait terms (e.g., honest, kind, hostile) that are generally associated with considerable emotion. People differ in the terms they use to describe people and in the ways they organize these terms or categories, but everyone seeks to organize the information they have relative to others. Given the diversity of people we encounter, each of whom also behaves somewhat differently according to the situation, such organization is necessary for us to make sense out of and provide stability to the world we encounter. If we were more equipped with innate or programmed responses, such cognitive constructions would not be necessary. In the absence of such responses, however, we must organize and structure our experiences so as to avoid being overwhelmed with information and detail. What kinds of categories do we form to simplify things? What kinds of perceived regularities enable us to make predictions in our interactions with others?

Such questions are addressed in the area known as person perception or **implicit personality theory**. The term implicit personality theory relates to the suggestion that each of us has a theory of personality, defined in terms of the traits we believe go together in people. Such theories are considered implicit in that most people cannot make explicit their trait categories or organize them as part of a formal theory of personality. Research in this area dates back at least to the 1950s. Early research focused on the tendency of people to perceive a person as having one characteristic and to then assume that she or he possesses a related characteristic. For example, if a person is perceived to be intelligent, what is the likelihood that that person will also be perceived as warm, generous, or feminine? Research also focused on the general dimensions people use to perceive others, with three dimensions found to be fairly general: *evaluation* (to what extent are people good or bad?), *activity* (to what extent are people active or passive?), and *potency* (to what extent are people strong or weak?).

A problem with this research was that it required everyone to use the same trait terms and often required subjects to rate abstract people rather than people they actually knew. These problems were solved by Rosenberg (1977; Rosenberg & Sedlak, 1972) in a method that allowed subjects to describe, in their own words, people they knew — including themselves. In addition, they could describe the feelings they associated with each of these people. This resulted in a list of people known to the subject and a list of traits and feelings associated with them. The subject then rated each person on the list in terms of the relevance of each trait and feeling. From this, Rosenberg could determine the traits and feelings that people tend to link with one another in the perception of self and others.

What general categories might one expect to emerge? In Kelly's terms, what constructs do people generally use to perceive and experience the human world? First, Rosenberg found an *evaluative* (good – bad) dimension in the categorization of people. In other words, apparently a major component in our perception of self and others is a like – dislike judgment and a decision about whether or not we feel good about the person being perceived. Rosenberg also found that this evaluative judgment seemed to involve two major concerns — a social concern (being accepted by or intimate with others) and a competence concern (being successful or competent in some area). Some illustrative traits and feelings associated with these categories are presented in Figure 13.1.

Although clearly of general interest, such lists of trait categories fail to do justice to the uniqueness of each individual's implicit theory of personality. Can such a method be utilized to capture a person's unique representation of others in the surrounding world? A demonstration of how this could be done was provided in an analysis of the author Theodore Dreiser's portrayal of women in his book, *A Gallery of Women* (Rosenberg & Jones, 1972). In this book, Dreiser (1929) provided sketches of fifteen women. In the course of describing these women, he applied 100 trait terms to 241 different characters. It was thereby possible to assess the trait categories and personality dimensions that were the basis for Dreiser's perception of people, at least as expressed in this book. Three dimensions were found to be of particular significance and each was associated with specific characteristics: *male* (handsome, great, erratic, sincere)–*female* (attractive, sensual, lovely, understanding); *conform* (serious, nice, ambitious, shrewd)–*does not conform* (fighter, free, lonely, sad); *hard* (critical, indifferent, cold)–*soft* (sensual, kind, sympathetic). In other words, the suggestion was that Dreiser used these three dimensions, and the associated traits, to judge and categorize people.

What was of particular interest in this analysis was that these dimensions could be related to themes in Dreiser's life. For example, a salient feature of Dreiser's life was his involvement with women. His sexual involvement with women is expressed in certain traits he clearly associated with them—attractive, sensual, alluring. Although some traits he associated with women are perhaps part of a more general stereotype of women, it is interesting that Dreiser did not characterize women as more conforming than men. He also associated such traits as

Positive Social	Negative Social	Positive Competence	Negative Competence
friendly	unfriendly	intelligent	unintelligent
warm	cold	reliable	unreliable
witty	dull	skillful	clumsy
humorous	humorless	determined	frivolous
popular	unpopular	cautious	impulsive
happy	unhappy	artistic	unimaginative
generous	unsympathetic	serious	superficial

FIGURE 13.1 Illustrative Trait and Feeling Categories Used in the Perception of Self and Others. (Rosenberg, 1977)

defiant, intelligent, and cold with women, which is of interest since in his personal life he was drawn to women who were unconventional and intellectually strong. The second dimension noted, conform–does not conform, was also of interest because it could be related to the theme of conflict with the forces of convention, which was a part of Dreiser's life. Indeed, one biographer formulated "Dreiser's Law" as follows: "Beliefs held by the multitude, the bourgeois and their leaders, are likely to be wrong per se. Beliefs held by unconventionalists which fly in the face of orthodoxy are in all probability right" (Swanberg, 1965, p. 181).

Rosenberg's research considers the trait categories and dimensions people use to perceive others. However, it does not address the question of how people go about forming categories. Also, it does not indicate how new people or objects are assigned to categories once they have been established. For example, how do I go about establishing a category of competence, and how do I decide whether to associate someone with that category? Or, to take another example, how do I form the categories of dogs and cats and then assign animals accordingly? Furthermore, is there some overall organization to these categories, or are they all of equal importance? These are questions addressed by cognitive psychologists. For example, a group of cognitive psychologists studied such questions by asking subjects to list characteristics they associate with various objects (Rosch, 1978). Illustrative objects were car, eagle, city bus, and bird. Then another group of subjects judged the truth or accuracy of these characteristics to see if there was agreement concerning these characteristics. Additional subjects then were asked to organize the objects into categories, with some categories being more inclusive than others. These and related studies led to the following conclusions:

1. Subjects can reach high levels of agreement concerning characteristics associated with specific categories. For example, subjects agree about characteristics defining a car or dog.

2. Whether or not an object is assigned to membership in a category depends on its sharing characteristics with other members of that category.

3. No one characteristic may be critical or sufficient to define membership in that category. Thus, for example, no one characteristic may be necessary or sufficient to describe a car as a sports car. Rather, membership is defined by a pattern of characteristics. Sports cars can vary considerably in terms of specific details but share a general pattern of characteristics.

4. Different categories possess different patterns of characteristics though there may be some overlap between categories. Thus, for example, sedans and sport cars have different patterns of characteristics though the two car categories also share certain characteristics in common. Animals and furniture represent different object

categories with different patterns of characteristics, though both some animals and some pieces of furniture have four legs.

5. While no member of a category is likely to have all the characteristics included as descriptive of membership in that category, some members best exemplify the category. For example, a Porsche might best exemplify a sports car. Such an object is called a **prototype**.

6. At the other extreme, because of overlapping characteristics between categories, some objects are difficult to classify. There is a fuzziness or ambiguity at the boundaries. For example, is a hatchback a sedan or a sports car? We designate some such cases as hybrids or crosses between categories (Figure 13.2).

7. Good agreement can be found concerning a taxonomy or hierarchical arrangement of categories. Two such hierarchical arrangements are illustrated in Figure 13.3.

8. Categories at different levels in the hierarchy are useful for different purposes. Categories at the lowest level are rich in defining characteristics whereas categories at the top are the most distinctive from one another. Middle-level categories such as car and eagle are particularly valuable because they are sufficiently specific and concrete to be useful in differentiating objects from one another while still being sufficently general to be economical to use.

FIGURE 13.2 The Minivan by Chrysler Motors. A Hybrid or Cross Between the car Categories of Van and Station Wagon. (New York Times, November 15, 1982)

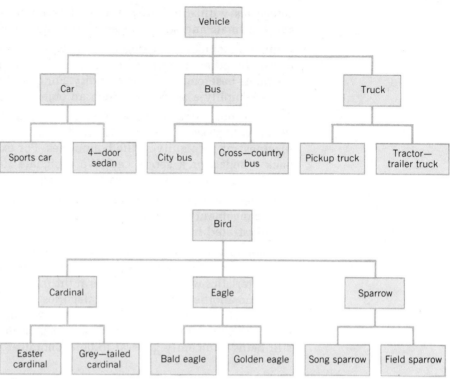

FIGURE 13.3 Illustrative Taxonomies or Hierarchical Category Structures. (Adapted from Rosch, *et al.*, 1976)

9. These middle-level categories tend to be the first ones used in perceiving the environment and the earliest categories named by children.

What are the implications of such research in cognitive psychology for personality? Do we form categories in perceiving people along lines similar to those developed in perceiving nonhuman objects and, if so, what are the implications for personality functioning? Before turning to some relevant research, you might think about the categories you use in perceiving others. Are they similar to those used by Dreiser or otherwise suggested in the Rosenberg research (Figure 13.1)? Can they be hierarchically arranged? What are the personality and physical characteristics that define membership in a category? Let us turn now to a series of studies by Cantor and Mischel (1979; Cantor, Mischel, & Schwartz, 1982) in which the following questions were addressed: (1) Given a list of objects (titles of persons), will people sort them into similar categories? For example, how might the persons listed in Figure 13.4 be categorized? (2) Can the categories formed be arranged hierarchically with good agreement? For example, if one were to form three levels of categories from the above list, as was done in Figure 13.3, what would they look like? (3) Will the objects or titles in each category be clearly identifiable in terms of the characteristics they share with one another? (4) Are there special features and advantages associated with categories at one or another level? That is, does it make a difference whether we use a more or less inclusive category in perceiving others in the world about us?

As in the earlier research, a group of subjects was asked to sort cards containing the titles listed in Figure 13.4 into categories. To start, the subjects were given four titles as high-level categories (emotionally unstable person, person committed to a cause, cultured person, extroverted person) and then asked to sort under them the remaining thirty-two titles into middle- and low-level categories. The resulting hierarchical structures showed good agreement with one another along the lines represented in Figure 13.5.

Having found good agreement concerning the hierarchical categorization of person titles, Cantor and Mischel had additional subjects list the attributes they associated with each title and rate the likelihood that a category member would have each characteristic. This resulted in a picture of which characteristics seemed particularly descriptive and critical for the inclusion of a person in a particular category. In sum, each person or title could be defined in terms of the number and quality of descriptive characteristics associated with it.

These data have two important implications. The first implication of

Phobic	Campaign manager	Claustrophobic	Criminal madman
Social activist		Hasidic Jew (orthodox)	
Gourmet	Antiwar protestor	Press agent for the President	Committed (to belief/cause) person
Extrovert	Cultured person		
Circus clown	Religious devotee	Practical joker in a fraternity	Sophisticated person
Strangler			
Acrophobic	Supporter of community orchestra	Fighter against child abuse	Emotionally unstable person
Nun			
Patron of the arts		"P.R. type"	Donator to museum
Comic joker	Torturer	Hydrophobic	
World traveler	Buddhist monk	Save-the-whale campaigner	Rapist
Donator to repertory theater	Couturier		
	Television comedian		
	Salesman		

FIGURE 13.4 List of Person Titles To Be Categorized. (Based on Cantor & Mischel, 1979)

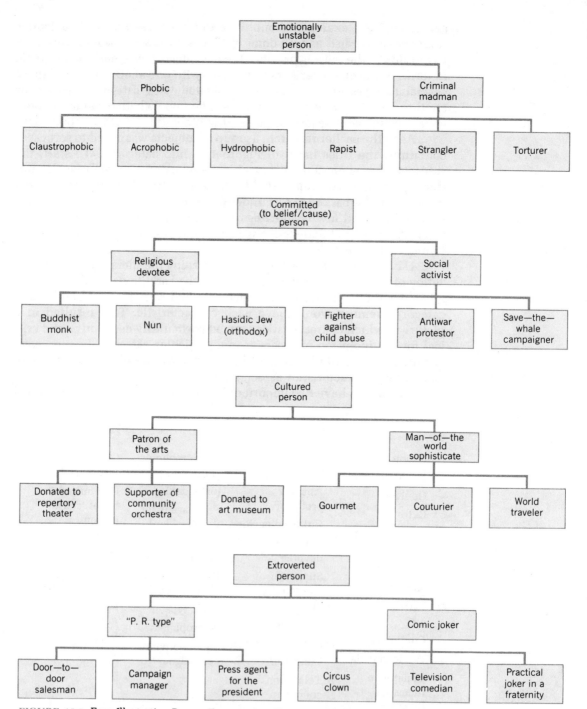

FIGURE 13.5 **Four Illustrative Person Taxonomies.** (Cantor & Mischel, 1979)

the Cantor and Mischel data concerns how we go about assigning people to categories. The suggestion here is that for each category there are characteristics that are taken to most exemplify or be most illustrative of a person in a given category. Generally, no one characteristic is necessary or sufficient to define category membership, but rather it is a pattern of characteristics. It is this pattern of characteristics, which exemplifies membership in the category, that represents a *prototype*. In other words, when asked to describe an extroverted person we think in terms of a prototype or image of someone who best combines the characteristics of extroverted people. No one extrovert may possess all these characteristics, but each may possess some; and that is enough for them to be included in the category. The prototype is thus a kind of ideal type, and each member of the category need not possess either all the characteristics or any single characteristic of the ideal type to be included in the category. As we meet people we tend to match them against prototypes of categories and then assign them membership in a particular category accordingly.

In some cases the boundaries of the categories we use are clear-cut, as in the difference between male and female. In other cases, the boundaries between categories may be fuzzy, as when we classify someone as a child or an adolescent, as an adolescent or a young adult (Lewis, 1982). Also, some objects are more clear-cut in category assignment than are others. We can easily say about some things that they are a car or a truck, or about some people that they are an introvert or an extrovert. On the other hand, in some case we may find it hard to assign a vehicle to membership in a car or truck category (e.g., WV camper) or to say that a person is an introvert or an extrovert. Presumably, what we do here is go along weighing the evidence, seeing the extent to which a person expresses the characteristics associated with one prototype and does not express those associated with a different prototype, and make our judgments accordingly. Apparently, however, there is some push toward making a judgment since assigning someone to a category facilitates prediction of behavior and memory for details about them (Cantor & Mischel, 1979). Although clearly advantageous in these ways, we must also appreciate that assigning someone to a category can make us overlook inconsistencies in behavior or, on the other hand, exaggerate an inconsistency because it departs from a prototype.

The second implication of the data concerns the advantages and disadvantages of using categories at each of the levels illustrated in Figure 13.5. For example, it was found that middle-level and low-level categories are particularly rich in the number of attributes associated with them. Being able to assign people to one of these categories allows one to be more specific about their characteristics than if they are assigned to a high-level category. On the other hand, high-level categories are more differentiated from one another in that they share fewer characteristics. In other words, categories at low levels have lots of characteristics associated with them, but some or many of these might be shared by members of more than one category. Categories at the highest level are less rich in detail but also hold few characteristics in common with one another. Overall, categories at the middle level have the benefits of being relatively rich and distinctive. This is of particular interest since it suggests that overall we may be better off using middle-level categories to perceive people, though for some purposes categories at either higher or lower levels may be more appropriate. We may think here of Eysenck's (Chapter 9) hierarchical organization of personality in terms of types, traits, and responses. The suggestion would be that we naturally are drawn to the trait or middle level in perceiving others, since overall such terms provide for the best combination of richness of detail, differentiation among people, and economy of thought. At other times, however, we are drawn to a higher level of describing people in terms of types or to the lower level of organization in describing people in terms of habits or behaviors.

Before turning to further illustrations of the information-processing approach to personality, we may pause here to consider some of the implications of the preceding work for personality theory and our understanding of people. First, we have some insight into how we perceive and organize information concerning the interpersonal world about us. For example, we may think of how we organize information in terms of categories with shared patterns of characteristics and assign people we meet to membership in a category according to the match of their characteristics with those defining a specific category. Second, we have some insight into the advantages and disadvantages of categories at varying levels of inclusion and abstraction. In particular, we can appreciate why traits are attractive categories for both lay people and psychologists— that is, they are both descriptive and economical to use. Third, we can also appreciate the utility of an approach to personality that is tied to research procedures and findings in cognitive psychology. Finally, we can see in this work certain similarities with the work of George A. Kelly and, at the same time, some distinct differences. In relation to the latter, we can contrast Cantor and Mischel's emphasis on experimental research and processes through which people organize information to Kelly's emphasis on more clinical procedures and the structure of a construct system. We shall return to these and related issues again at the end of the chapter.

Organizing Information Relevant to Situations

Personality psychologists have always recognized that situations play a vital role in how people behave. As was indicated earlier in this text, even trait theorists recognize that situations are important in influencing which traits would come into play at any one time. However, the situationist attack on trait theory and "traditional personality theory" focuses attention on the need for understanding how situations influence behavior. As it turns out, this is not an easy question, in particular since often it is difficult to specify just what the situation is (Pervin, 1978). One of the most difficult issues has been whether to define a situation objectively or in terms of how it is perceived by a person. Some psychologists would suggest that situations have objective properties regulating behavior and that it is to these properties we must attend. For example, driving on a highway is regulated by lanes and speed limits. Skinner's work in the control of behavior through manipulation of situational reinforcers represents such a view. On the other hand, other psychologists suggest that it is the meaning of situations that influences behavior. This being the case, we must understand how people perceive and interpret situations before we can predict the effects of situations on behavior.

If behavior is influenced by the perceived environment, then we must be interested in how people organize information concerning situations and how they go about classifying them. In many ways the issues are similar to those discussed in relation to the perception of people. Which aspects of situations do people attend to? Are they formal characteristics (e.g., home, school, work, recreation, small, large, public, private), or do they have to do with perceived qualities such as reinforcers? Are there situational terms that are comparable to the trait terms used for people? Do people perceive situations in terms of dimensions that are similar to those used for people (e.g., good–bad, interesting–dull, conforming–nonconforming)? Do people categorize situations in a hierarchical fashion similar to the ways in which they categorize people?

Psychologists have almost always been intrigued with the idea of reinforcers as critical elements of situations. There is for us an intuitive appeal to the idea that we behave in situations according to what we expect will follow various behaviors. In other words, without necessarily going through a conscious decision-making process, we process information concerning potential reinforcers in the situation and act accordingly. Thus, for example, the social learning theorist Rotter (1955) suggests that people perceive situations in terms of reinforcers associated with specific behaviors. Each reinforcement has a value for the person and a perceived probability of following that behavior in the situation. A person might expect love or affection to follow as a likely consequence of their being kind and to value love and affection highly. Alternatively, they might expect rejection to follow as an unavoidable result of hostility on their part and to seek to avoid rejection at all costs. Such values and expectancies associated with behaviors can be specific to certain situations or be part of a person's generalized expectancies concerning their relationships with others. In either case, the point is that attention is focused on the reinforcers in the situation and their connections to alternative behaviors. Situations can be viewed, then, in terms of perceived behavior—outcome relationships.

More recently, the social learning theorists Bandura (1977a) and

Mischel (1977) have extended this view to suggest that people behave similarly in situations perceived to be similar in their reinforcement contingencies. Again, the suggestion is that people attend to reinforcement information in a situation, act in terms of this information, and categorize situations accordingly. There indeed is evidence to suggest that reinforcers are a strong component of how we perceive situations and that we behave similarly in situations perceived to have similar rewards for various behaviors (Champagne & Pervin, 1987). However, although reinforcers clearly are important, other factors also influence our behavior and we process many other kinds of information concerning what is going on in a situation. What are some of the other aspects of situations to which we attend? The British social psychologist Argyle (1981) suggests that people attend to features of situations such as the goals of the participants and the rules of behavior. The goals and rules associated with a cocktail party are different than those for a lecture, and those for soccer or rugby are different than those for cricket. Although one could argue that reinforcers may still be involved, a third alternative takes us even further away from such a view. Here the suggestion is that we perceive situations in terms of the same three dimensions that we use to perceive people—*evaluation* (good–bad), *activity* (fast–slow), and *potency* (strong–weak). In addition, perception of situations in these ways leads us to associate certain felings with them (Mehrabian & Russell, 1974).

Is one of these necessarily more accurate than the others? Are other constructions and ways of organizing situation information possible? The interesting thing is that one could argue that people do not perceive and classify situations in any fixed way. Rather they are capable of attending first to some aspects of a situation and then to other aspects, and of categorizing a situation first in one way and then in a different way. In other words, people may have multiple ways of construing situations and be capable of shifting among them depending on their own goals and characteristics of the situation itself. One may at one point construe a situation as a social occasion and then rapidly reconstrue it as a business situation. One may think of a situation in terms of its potential reinforcers but then respond to it in terms of feelings associated with it.

Let us consider here two illustrative research efforts in this area. The two are similar in considering how subjcts perceive situations but are quite different in the analyses made of these perceptions. The first approach follows from the preceding analysis of person categories and person prototypes (Cantor, 1981; Cantor, Mischel, & Schwartz, 1982). In this case subjects were asked to sort thirty-six situations into a hierarchical category structure. Two illustrative situation hierarchies are presented in Figure 13.6. Subjects were then asked to describe characteristics common to situations in each category. From this a consensual list of situation characteristics was derived leading to the development of a *situational consensual prototype*. For example, "Being at a Revival Meet-

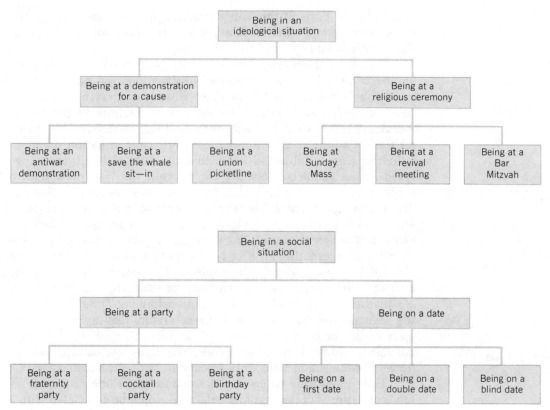

FIGURE 13.6 Two Illustrative Situation Taxonomies. (Cantor, Mischel, & Schwartz, 1982)

ing" was associated with characteristics such as the following: preacher, togetherness, chanting, singing, bibles, emotion, loud shouting. Generally each situation prototype consisted of a combination of physical characteristics of the situation, characteristics (traits) of people in the situation, feelings associated with the situation, and behaviors associated with the situation. The conclusions drawn from the research were similar to those with which we are familiar: (1) People can readily form and agree on a hierarchical taxonomy of situations, (2) People can readily describe and agree on characteristics associated with situations, (3) Situation prototypes generally include physical characteristics of the situation, personality and feeling characteristics of the participants, and expected behaviors, (4) Middle-level situation categories (e.g., Being at a Demonstration, Being at a Party) are particularly rich in detail and well differentiated from characteristics associated with other categories.

In sum, once more there is evidence of the utility of people using a categorical approach and forming behavioral expectations on the basis of these categories. Apparently in entering into a situation, we attend to and encode certain information that leads us to say "this is X kind of situation." On the basis of this categorization, we generate a range of additional feelings and behavioral expectations—both for ourselves and for those with whom we will be interacting.

The second approach to the analysis of situations places greater emphasis on individual perceptions of situations and perceived feelings and behaviors associated with these situations (Pervin, 1976, 1977). In this approach the situations considered are unique to the life of the individual rather than abstract generalizations established by the experimenter. In addition, the situation categories and situation–behavior relationships are established for each individual rather than being analyzed across subjects. Consider for yourself the task presented to the subjects. First, they are asked to form a list of situations in their current life or recent past. The subjects review their daily lives and list representative situations in terms of who is there, what is going on, where it takes place, and when it occurs. For example, a subject might list a specific situation of presenting an idea before a class, being on a date, or being alone with a good friend. The subjects then describe each situation as well as their feelings and behaviors in the situation. This generates a list of situation characteristics, feelings, and behaviors. The subjects then rate the relevance of each situation characteristic, feeling, and behavior to each of the original situations that had been listed. In this way it is possible to study each subject's categorizations of situations and perceptions of feelings and behaviors associated with these categories.

How might one categorize the situations in one's own life? What kinds of patterns of feelings and behaviors might be associated with these situation categories? Let us consider the answers to these questions for two subjects. The data for each subject were factor analyzed to determine which situation characteristics, feelings, and behaviors seemed to go together. The results for two subjects are presented in the figures that follow (Figures 13.7 and 13.8). Considering Figure 13.7, we can see that Jennifer groups some situations into a category titled "Home–Volatile." These situations are emotional; in them she feels angry and insecure and behaves in a caring, concerned fashion—at least in terms of her perceptions. She also perceives a group of situations with friends that, though again emotional, are now associated with caring and concerned feelings. Interestingly enough, she associates some of the same behaviors with these situations that she does with the home–volatile situations, where the feelings are quite different. Considering Figure 13.8 we can see that Ben also has a category of situations associated with friends but the illustrative situations, situation characteristics, feelings, and behaviors associated with this category are different from those reported by Jennifer. One may similarly consider Ben's family category of situations and contrast it with the characteristics Jennifer associates with this category.

Although the specific situations studied through this research procedure are unique to each individual, generally subjects list situations that fall into such categories as home, school, work, and recreation with

Situation Categories	Illustrative Situations	Situation Traits	Feelings	Behaviors
Home—Volatile	mother blows up at me honest with parents about leaving mother refuses gift someone else comes home upset	emotional, angry, volatile, excitable	angry, pressured, involved, insecure, unhappy	sensitive, concerned, caring, suppressed, confused, not compulsive
School, Work— Pressure to Perform	have to participate in class have to perform at work do the job wrong at work in a strange place	demanding, threatening, pressuring, awkward, challenging, embarrassing, unconcerned	self-conscious, challenged, vulnerable, awkward, pressured, anxious	self-conscious, controlled, ambitious, determined, compulsive, cool, responsible, diligent, nonrebellious
Friends, Alone	with friend—no problem with friend—problem alone	emotional, gentle, friendly, generous	caring, concerned, comfortable, melancholy, sad	concerned, caring, emotional, involved, insightful, responsive
Uncertain	come home from Philadelphia in a crowd taking the bus to class want to leave to go to Philadelphia in a strange place	ambiguous, nondefined, uncertain, unconcerned, ignoring	bottled-up, melancholy, sad, lonely, frustrated, confused	preoccupied, detached, quiet, self-conscious, controlled, cool, introverted

FIGURE 13.7 Illustrative Categories—Jennifer. (Pervin, 1976) (Copyright © 1976 by the American Psychological Association. Reprinted by permission.)

Situation Categories	Illustrative Situations	Situation Traits	Feelings	Behaviors
Social-Friends	drinking with Joe talking with Paul harmony in the band with girl friend	unhibited, comfortable, open, flexible, receptive, masculine, talkative, not demanding	humorous, participating, not guilty, happy	uninhibited, receptive, friendly, masculine, humorous, tolerant, attentive
Work-Nonstimulating Situations	in a nonstimulating classroom living with group in Edison loading cartons at work at a boring party	boring, unstimulating, masculine, independent, traditional, affected by mood	eager to leave, aloof, bored, withdrawn	loner, aloof, masculine, intolerant, adamant
Family	visit my parents talk with my mother visit sister and her family	affectionate, loving, traditional, caring	emotional, affectionate, guilty, not free, not relaxed	affectionate, loving, emotional, masculine, bright, sensitive, loyal, not uninhibited, compromising
Army	working at Army headquarters in Army drills short timer in Army	humorous, authoritarian, new, serious, tense, militaristic, traditional, structured	nervous, powerless, scared, learning	nervous, learning, growing, masculine, eager, not uninhibited, sleepy
Band-Conflict	conflict in the band new band performance	challenging, demanding, musically tight, exclusive, frustrating	together, interested, participating, not calm, not secure	responsible, contributing, serious, decisive, demanding, intolerant, controlling, loyal

FIGURE 13.8 Illustrative Situation Categories—Ben. (Pervin, 1976) (Copyright © 1976 by the American Psychological Association. Reprinted by permission.)

peers. The situations can also be characterized as falling within such categories as positive social, negative social, and competence–self-esteem. The dimensions of situations that appear to be most significant for the subjects are friendly–unfriendly, tense–calm, interesting–dull, and constrained–free. What is interesting about these situation dimensions is that they are similar to dimensions often used to categorize people and that they heavily emphasize the emotion-eliciting qualities of situations. These qualities tend to be common to the categorizations of most subjects. However, the situations listed under each category and the patterns of feelings and behaviors associated with each category are unqiue to the individual. Thus, as noted, both Jennifer and Ben have a category for home–family and one for friends, but the nature of the situations listed in them and the associated situation characteristics, feelings, and behaviors differ considerably. Some categories may also be unique to the individual as in Jennifer's "Uncertain" category and Ben's "Band–Conflict" category. Finally, each subject has a reported pattern of feeling and behavior that in some ways is constant across all situations, in some ways is generally present except for some situations, and in some ways is never present except perhaps for a few situations. For example, according to her reports Jennifer is almost always sensitive, vulnerable, and insightful. She also is friendly, warm, and accepting most of the time except when she is in some volatile home situations, at which times she is uniquely irritable, angry, upset, depressed, uncontrolled, and rebellious. She also tends to be involved and caring, except when she is detached, preoccupied, introverted, controlled, and cool. Whereas some individuals may be introverted in all situations and some individuals extroverted in all situations, many individuals are introverted in some situations and extroverted in others. Individuals may differ, then, in the behaviors on which they are stable or varying or in the kinds of situations in relation to which their behavior varies. To summarize this research, we may suggest the following:

1. People appear to form categories of situations and situation–feeling–behavior relationships as well as forming categories of people.
2. There appear to be some common dimensions to the categorization of situations, these dimensions being related to dimensions used in the categorization of people.
3. Each person appears to perceive a unique pattern of stability and change in feelings and behaviors in relation to different categories of situations.

In considering the organization of information concerning situations and situation–behavior relationships, it is important to recognize differences among situations and people. In relation to situations we may consider, for example, the extent to which they are highly structured, constraining, or scripted. The concept of **script** has been used by some proponents of a computer model to define a series or pattern of behaviors considered to be appropriate for that situation (Schank & Abelson, 1977). For example, behavior in a restaurant generally is highly scripted. Not only are specific behaviors well defined but the order or sequence of behaviors is clearly set forth. Generally we act out roles in such situations and our behavior is regulated by norms or sanctions for behaving in an inappropriate way. Violating the script in a restaurant may sometimes be funny, but more often it leads to errors in the meal being served or in being asked to leave, particularly if the restaurant is busy or is formal in atmosphere. Functioning in such cases requires us to recognize that we are in a scripted situation and to call forth images of the required scripts. A breakdown in either cognitive skill or in the skill in performing the requisite behaviors leads to difficulties. On the other hand, other situations are less structured or scripted. For example, an informal meeting among friends generally is associated with fewer prescriptions or well-defined scripts. Under such circumstances often people feel less inhibited or "more able to be themselves."

Just as some situations call for more careful monitoring of what is going on and what is prescribed, so too there are individual differences in the extent to which people monitor or regulate their behavior according to situational cues. Snyder (1974, 1979) has developed a scale to measure such individual differences (Figure 13.9). The *high* **self-monitoring** indi-

Scripts—Some situations, such as eating in a restaurant, require following a clearly defined series of behaviors.

My behavior is usually an expression of my true inner feelings. (F)

At parties and social gatherings, I do not attempt to do or say things that others will like. (F)

When I am uncertain how to act in a social situation, I look to the behavior of others for cues. (T)

I sometimes appear to others to be experiencing deeper emotions than I actually am. (T)

I laugh more when I watch a comedy with others than when alone. (T)

In different situations and with different people, I often act like very different persons. (T)

T = True, F = False

FIGURE 13.9 Illustrative Items and Scoring for the Self-Monitoring Scale. (Snyder, 1974)

vidual is one who is highly sensitive to cues of situational appropriateness and regulates his or her behavior accordingly. In a moderate form, such a person shows competence in handling a great variety of situations; in an extreme form, such a person can be a chameleon, always changing to meet the situation and never being sure of who they are. On the other hand, the *low self-monitoring individual* is less attentive to social information and generally behaves more in accord with internal feelings and attitudes. In a moderate form, such a person can demonstrate independence and fortitude; in an extreme form, such an individual can show an insensitivity to the feelings and wishes of others. A variety of differences have been found to be associated with high self-monitoring (HSM) and low self-monitoring (LSM) scores. Some of these are described by Snyder as follows:

1. HSMs are better able to intentionally express and communicate emotions and expressive behavior than are LSMs.

2. HSMs are better able to deceive others in face-to-face interviews than are LSMs.

3. HSMs are better able to correctly infer the emotional state of others than are LSMs.

4. HSMs are more discriminating about situations and more variable in their behavior across situations than are LSMs.

5. HSMs generally appear to other people to be more friendly, outgoing, extroverted and less worried, anxious, or nervous than LSMs.

6. HSM are less influenced in their self-presentations by changes in mood states than are LSMs.

7. HSMs remember more information about other people and make more inferences concerning the traits of others than do LSMs.

To summarize this section, we have considered the ways in which people organize information concerning situations and situation–behavior scenarios. To a certain extent discussion here has paralleled that concerning the organization of person-relevant information. There is evidence that people categorize situations so as to make manageable relevant information and to make predictable the social world. There also is evidence that such categories are organized into a hierarchical structure with categories higher in the structure being more differentiating and categories lower in the structure being richer in detail. There is evidence of some common categories and dimensions of categories among people but there also is evidence of diversity in classification and uniqueness of categorization of specific situations. Each person appears to perceive a unique pattern of stability and change in his or her behavior in relation to categories of situations and, in all likelihood, also perceives distinctive patterns in the behavior of others. Finally, situations differ in how constraining or scripted they may be and individuals differ in how attentive they are to situational cues concerning appropriate behavior.

Organizing Information Relevant to Events

In the preceding two sections we have been concerned with how people organize information relevant to people and situations. In this section we are concerned with how people organize information relevant to events, in particular with how they go about attributing causes to events. We see someone hit or yell at another and we infer some reason for the action. Is the person generally hostile? Was something malicious done to them? We see someone act in a strange way. Were they not feeling well? Was our previous picture of them inaccurate and now we have to view them in a new way? These are the kinds of inferences and attributions we are constantly making in our daily lives, and it is these processes that have been of considerable interest to social psychologists since the 1960s. For example, it has been found that we tend to attribute the causes of behavior in other people to their traits or personality characteristics, whereas we tend to attribute the causes of our own behavior to situations (Jones & Nisbett, 1971). One reason for this difference may be that we observe others in a limited range of situations and see them acting consistently, whereas we observe our own behavior over a much wider range of situations and see it varying accordingly.

We already are familiar with the fact that individuals may maintain beliefs about their ability to influence or control events in their lives (e.g., learned helplessness and locus of control, Chapter 2). A related area of research has concerned people's explanations for success or failure. Weiner (1985) has suggested that there are three dimensions relevant to causal explanations. The first dimension, related to the work of Rotter on locus of control, concerns whether causes are perceived as coming from within (internal) or from outside (external) the person. This dimension has been named *locus of causality*. A second dimension of causality, *stability*, concerns whether the cause is stable and relatively fixed as opposed to being unstable or variable. The implications for causal attributions from combining these two dimensions can be seen in Figure 13.10. Accordingly, we can attribute success or failure to *ability* ("I am bright."), *effort* ("I tried hard."), *task difficulty* ("The test was easy."), or *chance* or *luck* ("I was lucky in guessing right."). The third dimension, *controllability*, has to do with whether events are subject to control or influence through additional effort. For example, social rejection because of physical unattractiveness might be attributed to internal, stable, and uncontrollable causes, whereas social rejection because of obnoxious behavior might be attributed to internal, stable, and controllable causes. In each case it is the beliefs and causal ascriptions of the person that are important. Thus, for example, one person might see their physical appearance as uncontrollable whereas another sees it as controllable, and one person might see their intellectual performance as due to fixed intelligence whereas another might see it as due to effort and acquired knowledge (Dweck, 1986).

An illustration of the practical implications of differing attributions for performance can be seen in a study of college freshmen (Wilson & Linville, 1985). In this study freshmen whose grades were below the median and who indicated that they were worried about their academic performance were put into one of two groups. In one group students were given information suggesting that the causes of their poor performance were unstable. This information consisted of statistics indicating that grades typically improve after the first year and videotaped interviews of upperclass students who reported improved performance following poor grades during their freshman year. In the second group students were given some general information that did not related to grade improvement and saw videotaped interviews in which there was no mention of grades. The hypothesis tested was that the attribution of poor grades to unstable causes would reduce anxiety about academic performance and increase expectations about future grades, leading to improvement in actual performance. Indeed, it was found that students in the first ("unstable attribution") group improved in their subsequent grade performance to a significantly greater degree than did subjects in the second (control) group. In addition, a smaller proportion of the students in the

Cause	Internal	External
Stable	Ability	Task difficulty
Variable	Effort	Chance or luck

FIGURE 13.10 Possible Causal Attributions for Success and Failure. (Weiner, 1979)

first group left college the following semester than did students in the second group. Thus, the authors of the study concluded that communicating to college freshmen that the causes of low grades are temporary can have substantial beneficial effects on academic performance.

Additional dimensions have been suggested, but the point here is that people make causal attributions, and that such attributions have important psychological implications. For example, such attributions have important implications for motivation. A person is more likely to persist at a task if it is viewed as one involving effort than if success or failure is viewed as being due to chance. Similarly, a person will behave differently if they believe health or illness is due to internal or external causes ("I am a sickly person." versus "The flu bug got me.") and whether they believe in the efficacy of self-care ("Basic health principles prevent illness." versus "One can do little to prevent illness.") (Lau, 1982). Some fascinating and extremely important insights into how women seek to understand and explain the trauma of breast cancer are presented in Figure 13.11 (Taylor, 1982).

Causal attributions also are important aspects of stereotypes. For example, success in males and failure in females tend to be attributed to ability, whereas failure in men and success in women tend to be attributed to effort or luck (Deaux, 1976). Finally, differences in casual attribu-

---

1. An event that is clearly followed by another event may be seen as causing that event (e.g., belief that breast cancer was caused by a recent auto accident).

2. An event that is located close to (spatial proximity) another event may be seen as having been caused by it (e.g., belief that continued pressure to an area near the breast caused breast cancer).

3. Causes resemble effects and big effects are produced by big causes whereas small effects are produced by small causes (e.g., cancer is a large effect and must have been produced by a large cause rather than an accumulation of small events).

4. Unknown causes are associated with similar or representative known causes (e.g., a malignant lump is attributed to a blow to the breast since lumps are usually caused by blows).

5. Frequent co-occurrences of events are seen as having a causal relationship (e.g., a woman attributed a causal quality to her golf club since four of her acquaintances here had also developed breast cancer).

6. Attributions are made to single causes rather than multiple causes (e.g., cancer is caused by stress, a virus, heredity, or an environmental carcinogen rather than by an interaction among many of these).

FIGURE 13.11 Illustrations of Errors of Causal Attribution in Patients with Breast Cancer. (Taylor, 1982)

tion have important implications for emotion. As noted in relation to learned helplessness, depression is seen as resulting from an internal, stable, global attribution. Other illustrations of emotional consequences of causal attributions would be to feel proud following success and a causal attribution to ability and to feel guilty following failure and a causal attribution to effort (Weiner, 1985). It should be clear that what is being suggested here is that attributions cause certain emotions, beliefs, and motivations to follow. However, some research suggests that pleasant and unpleasant events themselves account for emotion and motivation, with attributions only part of the cause of what follows or may themselves be part of that response (Covington & Omelich, 1979; Smith & Kluegel, 1982; Stephan & Gollwitzer, 1981). Basically, the question is that of the relation of attributions to emotion and motivation—causes of them, correlates of them, or even responses to them. It may be recalled here that similar questions were raised in Chapter 2 concerning the relation between attributions for helplessness and depression. This remains an area of continuing investigation.

The categories people form and the causal ascriptions they make lead people to have certain expectations. Knowledge of a script for a situation leads one to expect specific behaviors from others, and attribution of a trait to a person leads one to expect that person to behave in a particular way. Further, as noted, different causal attributions lead one to have varying expectations for oneself and others. The attribution of events to internal, controllable causes may lead one to expect that further effort will pay off, whereas the attribution of events to external, uncontrollable causes may lead one to expect little from further effort. Bandura's self-efficacy expectancies and outcome expectancies, discussed in the previous chapter, represent illustrations of the kinds of expectancies a person can develop depending on their assessment of their own ability and the characteristics of the situation.

In some cases expectancies may be very specific to the situation or person. On the other hand, people may also develop *generalized expectancies*. Thus, for example, Rotter (1971) suggests that people develop generalized expectancies concerning interpersonal trust. People with generalized trust expectancies tend to be more honest, more respectful of the rights of others, and more often are sought as friends than are people with generalized expectancies of interpersonal distrust. Another example of generalized expectancies would be what has been called dispositional optimism as opposed to dispositional pessimism (Scheier & Carver, 1987). Whereas *optimists* have a generalized expectation that good things will happen ("In uncertain times, I usually expect the best."), *pessimists* have a generalized expectancy for negative outcomes ("If anything can go wrong with me, it will."). Although expectancies often are specific to the situation, it is suggested that generalized expectancies are important in new and uncertain situations.

Theory and research in relation to causal attributions view the person as an **intuitive social scientist** trying to gather and organize data that will be useful in predicting and controlling events (Nisbett & Ross, 1980; Ross, 1981). The emphasis here is on people as seeking information and understanding rather than on people seeking instinctual gratification or self-esteem. Explanations of findings are in the form of information-processing strategies rather than in terms of motivation. When errors in judgment and inference are observed they are explained in terms of shortcomings in information-processing strategies rather than in terms of motivation. Thus, for example, internal or external attributions for success and failure are viewed as results of the data available to the person rather than as serving self-protective functions. In the illustrations provided of causal attributions for breast cancer, the emphasis was on information-processing errors rather than on the anxiety generated by uncertainty, the terror of believing there is an internal process of growth that has gradually gone out of control, or the guilt associated with the idea that something was done to cause the illness or not done that could have prevented the illness. Similarly, superstitions are seen as coming from observation of chance relationships among events rather than from underlying wishes and fears. The fact that people maintain certain beliefs despite nonsupportive evidence is explained in terms of a tendency to

1. *Observational Bias.* Our pre-existing theories bias what we see and lead us to see in others what we expect. (Seen in stereotypes about individuals and groups.)

2. *Discounting Error.* We ignore events that do not confirm our beliefs or discount their significance by considering them as exceptions to the rule. (Seen in stereotypes about individuals or groups.)

3. *Categorizing Error.* We may judge things to be similar or people to be alike (i.e., belonging to the same category) on the basis of superficial similarities and ignore fundamental but subtle differences. (Seen in stereotypes about individuals and groups.)

4. *Causal Interpretation Error.* We may view events that follow one another in time to be causally related when they are unrelated or both are caused by something else. (Seen in superstitious behavior.)

5. *Prediction Error.* We may make inaccurate predictions because we follow incorrect principles or overweight evidence that is vivid and salient. (Seen, for example, in people who are sensitive to rejection and who vividly recall each instance of slight or rejection.)

SUM. In ordinary life people look at the wrong data, weigh the data improperly, and make incorrect inferences. The errors of the intuitive, lay, or naive scientist are best understood as cognitive failings rather than as motivational.

FIGURE 13.12 Cognitive Errors in Everyday Life. (Based on Nisbett & Ross, 1980)

weigh confirming evidence more heavily than disconfirming evidence rather than in terms of a motivation for being right. In sum, the argument is made "that many phenomena generally regarded as motivational . . . can be understood better as products of relatively passionless information-processing errors than of deep-seated motivational forces" (Nisbett & Ross, 1980, p. 12). The point here is that all of us necessarily utilize strategies to organize information concerning events and to make inferences concerning the future. However, inherent in our ordinary information-processing activity are cases of incorrect information, memory, and inference (Figure 13.12).

CURRENT APPLICATIONS   HOW RATIONAL ARE WE?

Consider the following problem. The United States is preparing for the outbreak of a disease that is expected to kill 600 people. Choose between the following two programs to combat the disease:

> If Program A is adopted, 200 people will be saved.

> If Program B is adopted, there is a one-third probability that 600 people will be saved and a two-thirds probability that no people will be saved.

Now choose between the following two programs:

> If Program C is adopted, 400 people will die.

> If Program D is adopted, there is a one-third probability that nobody will die and a two-thirds probability that 600 people will die.

Most people prefer Program A to Program B, and Program D to Program C, despite the fact that the options in the second case are indistinguishable in real terms from those in the first case. However, the problem is framed differently in the two cases and in each case people tend to focus on the aspect of people not dying.

Consider another problem. You go to see a play having paid the admission price of $10. Upon entering the theater you discover that you have lost the ticket. Would you pay $10 for another ticket? Now, consider the situation where you go to see a play and, prior to entering the theater, you discover that you have lost $10. Would you still go to see the play if the admission price was $10? Most people will reject spending $10 after having lost a ticket, yet they will readily spend that sum after losing an equivalent amount in cash! If the lost ticket is thought of as lost cash, most people feel ready to replace the lost ticket. Thus, once more, the framing of the problem and the outcomes makes an enormous difference in the choices people make.

The conclusion to be drawn? People are influenced in their choices simply by how the problem is formulated, and this is as true for those who are sophisticated as for those who are naive. Also, this is as true for physicians making decisions concerning their patients and presidents making decisions concerning national policy as it is for people concerned with lesser decisions in their daily lives.

SOURCE: Kahneman & Tversky, 1984; *New York Times*, December 6, 1983, C1.

Until now, we have focused on people's efforts to organize information concerning the world around them—people, situations, events. Additional information to be acquired, organized, processed, stored, and retrieved relates to the self. As has been seen in earlier chapters, the concept of self has been significant in many theories of personality. What is the unique contribution offered by a cognitive, information-processing approach to the self?

An important impetus for work in this area was the research by Markus (1977). She suggested that people form cognitive structures about the self just as they do about other phenomena. Such cognitive structures are called **self-schemata**: "Self-schemata are cognitive generalizations about the self, derived from past experience, that organize and guide the processing of the self-related information contained in an individual's social experiences" (p. 63). As is true with other schemata or concepts, self-schemata influence whether information is attended to, how it is structured, and the ease with which it can be remembered. For example, Markus suggested that people with particular self-schemata should be able to process relevant information with ease, retrieve relevant behavioral evidence, and resist evidence counter to the self-schemata. In research investigating these hypotheses, she had subjects rate themselves on several scales relevant to the independent–dependent personality dimension. On the basis of their responses, she formed three groups of subjects: *Independents* (or subjects who tended to rate themselves as independent on the scales); *Dependents* (or individuals who tended to rate themselves as dependent on the scales): and *Aschematics* (or individuals who did not show any clear tendency to rate themselves as independent or dependent). The latter individuals were assumed to lack a self-schema for the independent–dependent personality dimension.

Having formed these three groups, Markus compared their behavior on four tasks. In the first task, subjects observed words being flashed on a screen and responded by indicating whether or not the word was self-descriptive. Some of the words were independent adjectives (e.g., individualistic, adventurous, self-confident), some were dependent adjectives (e.g., conforming, submissive, dependent), and some were unrelated to either. Independents were found to judge more of the independent words as self-descriptive than did Dependents, whereas the reverse was true for dependent words. Aschematics were midway between for both sets of words. In addition, Independents were faster at making *me* or self-descriptive judgments for independent adjectives than for dependent adjectives, whereas the reverse was true for Dependents. Aschematics did not differ in response speed to the two sets of adjectives.

In the second task subjects were given some of the words from the independent and dependent word lists and asked to give evidence from their past behavior of the relvance of each trait or characteristic. The data here supported the hypothesis that since a schema reflects past behavior, schematic subjects should be able to provide relevant behavioral evidence. Independent subjects wrote more behavioral descriptions for independent words than did subjects in the other groups. Dependent subjects wrote more behavioral illustrations for dependent words than did members of the other two groups. In the third task, subjects rated the likelihood of their behaving in various ways. The behaviors rated had previously been determined to be expressive of independent or dependent personalities. In accord with the hypothesis, Independent subjects rated the independent behaviors as more likely to be expressed by them than the dependent behaviors, whereas the reverse was true for the Dependents. Aschematics did not differ in their probability ratings for the two sets of behaviors. In responses to a final task, Markus found evidence that Independents and Dependents resisted information contrary to the ways in which they thought of themselves. In both cases subjects showed evidence of rejecting the accuracy of test information that was incongruent with their self-schemata. In sum, data from the four tasks supported the utility of the concept of self-schemata or cognitive generalizations about the self that organize, summarize, and explain behavior.

More recently Markus and her colleagues have followed a similar strategy in the investigation of self-schemata related to gender. All people are aware of sex differences. Individuals differ, however, in the meanings they associate with sex differences and in the extent to which they represent themselves as masculine, feminine, and androgynous (possessing both masculine and feminine attributes). Do people who have masculine self-schemata (give themselves high self-ratings on traits such as aggressive, dominant, acting as leader), feminine self-schemata (high self-ratings on traits such as gentle, emotional, sensitive), and androgynous self-schemata (high self-ratings on both sets of traits) differ from one another as well as from gender aschematics (people who rate themselves low on both masculine and feminine sets of traits) in their processing of gender-related information? Evidently this is the case. Consistent with earlier studies, it was found that people for whom masculine schemata are an important part of their identity remember more masculine than feminine attributes, require shorter processing time for "me" judgments to these attributes, are more confident of these judgments, and are able to provide more examples of past masculine behavior than feminine behavior. Individuals with feminine self-schemata demonstrate the reverse pattern of information processing. On the other hand, subjects identified as high on androgyny are able to process masculine and feminine information with equal efficiency. Finally, individuals who rate themselves as low on both masculine and feminine characteristics give low confidence ratings for gender-related self-judgments and are relatively poor in supplying behavioral evidence in support of gender-related self-descriptions (Markus *et al.*, 1982). In sum, people differ in the extent to which they incorporate masculine and feminine concepts into their self-concepts. The extent to which people define themselves as masculine, feminine, or androgynous then plays a significant role in how they process gender-relevant information in the world about them. What makes this of particular significance is that these schemata are not only used in relation to the self, but are used in relation to the perception of others as well (Fong & Markus, 1982).

Markus' research involved already formed schemata. Additional research has involved investigation of the development of self-schemata, research on how self-schemata affect attention and memory, and how self-schemata are maintained in social interaction. In relation to the development of the concept of self, one question asked is: What leads people to infer that they have particular traits (Locksley & Lenauer, 1981)? Research suggests that people infer they have a trait or personality characteristic when they observe themselves behaving in a particular way. In other words, just as we infer personality characteristics from the behavior of others. so we observe our own behavior and accordingly infer our own personality characteristics. Associated with this will be typical errors in concept formation. Thus, in forming a self-schema we may exaggerate the stability of certain behaviors relative to situational influences and occurrences of other behaviors. Similarly, we may see superficially similar behaviors as related while in fact they are different. Since people generally have a bias for confirming evidence over disconfirming evidence, they may observe and recall confirming evidence more readily. What is particularly interesting about such an accounting of the development and maintenance of self-schemata is that it again emphasizes "informational gains" over "motivational or emotional gains"; that is, the emphasis is on everyday problems of inference error and bias rather than on ego-enhancing or self-esteem biases. In this way, cognitive processes relevant to the concept of self are seen as following the same rules as cognitive processes relevant to other concepts rather than following a process of their own.

Evidence has been accumulating that once we establish self-schemata these cognitive structures influence what we attend to. For example, the evidence suggests that attention to the self greatly restricts our ability to attend to information that is not self-relevant (Bargh, 1982). Also, because people experience events with themselves as the central focus, self-relevant information is more easily and quickly accessed than other information. Again, the emphasis is on the *informational relevance* of self-schemata rather than on their *emotional significance*. Extending this role of self-schemata, the suggestion has been made that such schemata or cognitive generalizations about the self form the basis for *all* of our perceptions of others: "All incoming stimuli are evaluated according to the relevance to the self" (Markus & Smith, 1981, p. 245). Does this mean that we evaluate others in the same way that we evaluate ourselves? Not necessarily. Although similar categories and category characteristics may be used, it also is possible for us to use different categories or category criteria in our self-judgment than in our judgment of others. The self provides a framework against which we can judge others, highlighting their similarities to us or their differences from us, but we are not totally bound by the framework.

Research also suggests the power of self-schemata in recall. Attending to words in terms of whether they are self-relevant increases our ability to remember them. This supports our intuitive sense that often we learn material better when we can see how it relates to us (Rogers, Kuiper, & Kirker, 1977). We can return here to the concept of prototype. Do we have a prototype concept of ourselves and, if so, what are the memory implications of such a prototype? If the self is a cognitive category like other categories, we should have a prototypical self-concept ("This is what I am *really* like.") and we should most easily remember material relevant to this concept. A recent study indeed found that people best remember photographs of themselves that are rated as most exemplary of their "real self" (Yarmey & Johnson, 1982). Note that the prototype concept of real self is different from the concept of ideal self. The concept of what one is really like or most like is different from the prototype concept of what one would most want to be like, and the two prototypes can be very similar to or very different from one another.

Finally, we can consider how self-schemata are confirmed and may prove to be resistant to change. One relevant component has already been suggested earlier in terms of our bias toward confirming evidence over disconfirming evidence. There is clear evidence that people prefer self-confirmatory social feedback over self-disconfirmatory feedback (Swann & Read, 1981). There also is evidence to suggest that people solicit self-confirming evidence from others and present themselves in ways that will elicit confirming evidence from others (Baumeister, 1982; Swann & Hill, 1982). In other words, people not only extrapolate supportive evidence from an unfolding reality but actively manage and maintain that reality. As described by Snyder (1981), high self-monitors choose to live in worlds that allow them to bring out their various selves, whereas low self-monitors choose worlds that allow them to "be themselves." Of course, people often are unaware of the extent to which they maintain certain patterns of social interaction. Processes such as these may help to appreciate why changes in the self-concept are so often difficult to produce. Also, this may explain the beneficial effects of therapies that encourage people to behave differently to elicit different responses from others.

One unique contribution offered by this approach to the self clearly is a model that facilitates systematic research. There is a second aspect that also is noteworthy, namely, an emphasis on many selves or a "family of selves" rather than a single self (Cantor & Kihlstrom, 1987). According to this view, you are many things, in many places, with many people. Thus, you have many contextualized selves, each with a set of features. The features of these contextualized selves, this family of selves, will overlap in some ways and be distinctive in others. Returning to Jennifer in Figure 13.7, we can see that there is a Home Self, a School–Work Self, a Friends Self, and an Uncertain Self. Associated with each contextual self is a group of situations, feelings, and behaviors. Her various selves contain some overlapping features as well as some that are distinctive. Perhaps at a higher level of organization there is a Good Self and a Bad Self, the former characterized in particular by situations in which she is caring with friends and the latter characterized in particular by situations in which she is cool and detached. Each of us, then, has a family of selves, the contents and organization of which are unique.

The information-processing view of the self is leading to the investigation of many selves, perhaps best captured by the concept of **possible selves** (Markus & Nurius, 1986). Possible selves represent what people think they might become, what they would like to become, and what they are afraid of becoming. As we have seen, Carl Rogers emphasized the importance of the Ideal Self. This represents one kind of possible self. The important point, however, is that the person may have many ideal selves, and the ideal self is but one of many possible selves. Although important, the ideal self may be no more important than other possible selves such as the Ought Self (Higgins, 1987) and the Undesired Self (Ogilvie, 1987). Each possible self represents a cognitive construction that acts as a guide for the person in evaluating current behavior and planning future behavior. Thus, possible selves are important in influencing emotion and motivation.

In summarizing this section on the representation of the self we may say that from a cognitive, information-processing point of view the self is an important cognitive structure that influences the encoding, organization, and memory of a great deal of information. Treatment of the self as a cognitive category allows one to study it in the same way as other cognitive categories and to understand its functioning in terms of cognitive processes followed by all conceptual categories. The self is an important conceptual category but it is not some internal homunculus or controlling agent. We may associate specific aspects with the self and may even tie certain motives to the self-concept, but we should not ignore the role of "everday cognitive processes" in accounting for how we treat self-relevant information. In other words, although concepts such as ego-enhancement and self-esteem may have some utility, we should be aware that more straightforward information-processing interpretations may account for the phenomena equally well and in a more parsimonious way.

OVERVIEW

In the next chapter, we will consider some of the clinical implications of the cognitive, information-processing approach to personality. Prior to doing this, let us again recognize some of the key points of this approach. First, and foremost is the emphasis on cognition or information. According to this view the essence of personality is the organization of the person's ideas and beliefs concerning situations, events, people, and the self. Second, generally there is a greater emphasis on cognitive processes than on cognitive structures, and on context-specific functioning rather than on global personality characteristics. The computer has been used as a model for thinking about people and personality but clearly work in the field is progrssing beyond a narrow utilization of the model. We can see in this approach links with approaches already considered, as well as striking contasts with others. We will have more to say about this at the conclusion of the next chapter. For now, however, let us take stock of where we have been.

Major Concepts and Summary

implicit personality theory	generalized expectancies
prototype	intuitive social scientist
script	self-schemata
self-monitoring	possible selves
locus of causality	

In this chapter we considered material from the information-processing revolution in psychology. The analogy has been made to a computer that takes in (encodes), stores, organizes, and retrieves information. By using the concepts and research methods of experimental cognitive psychologists, personality psychologists have attempted to explore how people organize and utilize information concerning their own experiences and behaviors. Three things in particular distinguish this approach to personality from others we have considered. (1) The theory uses a model based on computer functioning. (2) It is not truly a theory of personality but rather an approach to conceptualization and research. (3) It is more clearly tied to other parts of psychology (cognitive and social) than is true for the more clinical theories of personality presented earlier in the text.

Given the diversity of people and behavior about us we are required to organize the relevant information to provide some structure and stability to our interpersonal world. The organization of this information is called our implicit theory of personality or conceptualization of the personality characteristics that people have and how these characteristics are organized. Research in the area of person perception and implicit personality theory has considered the kinds of categories people use in perceiving others, how these categories are formed, and the utility of these categories generally as well as the utility of categories at differing levels of abstraction. In general, it has been found that we organize information concerning both physical objects and people in terms of categories with shared patterns of characteristics and assign people we meet to membership in a category according to the match of their characteristics with those defining a specific category. This assignment process may be facilitated by some representation of a prototype for that category. Difficulties arise because of the fuzziness of boundary categories so that we may meet people who are hybrids or do not easily fit into one or another category. The categories we use are arranged in a hierarchical fashion similar in some ways to the type, trait, and behavior hierarchy suggested by trait theorists. Categories at varying levels have different strengths and limitations, with middle-level categories striking a balance between being economical yet rich in detail.

Discussion of how we organize information relevant to situations followed a similar theme. There is evidence that people categorize situations in a hierarchical fashion so as to make information manageable and to make the world predictable. People differ in the situation categories they form, in the organization of these categories, and in the characteristics they use to define the categories. Each person appears to perceive a unique pattern of stability and change in behavior in relation to different categories of situations. Situations differ in how constraining or scripted they are; individuals differ in how attentive they are to situational cues concerning appropriate behavior. People who are very attentive to such situation cues are called high self-monitors in contrast with low self-monitors who rely more on internal cues and who tend to be consistent in their behavior from situation to situation.

The third area considered was that of the organization of information concerning events, in particular how we go about attributing causes to events. People appear to be concerned with whether events are caused from within or from without (locus of causality), whether causes are stable or unstable, and whether or not they are controllable. Thus, people make such distinctions as between events due to ability, effort, task difficulty, and chance or luck. Such causal attributions are important for understanding a wide range of phenomena including motivation, stereotypes, and superstitions. In addition to causal explanations or attributions, expectancies represent an important aspect of personality functioning. People develop expectancies concerning themselves and outcomes, and most of these tend to be specific to situations or contexts. However, people may also develop generalized expectancies, such as concerning interpersonal trust and optimism–pessimism, which are particularly important in new and uncertain situations.

Inherent in the preceding is the view of the person as an intuitive social scientist trying to gather and organize data that will be useful in making events in the world comprehensible and predictable. Although necessary and useful for daily living, these cognitive organizations and inference processes sometimes lead to erroneous conclusions. It is suggested that many such phenomena otherwise attributed to motivational forces can be better understood as products of information-processing errors.

Finally, we have considered how people organize information concerning the self and the implications of these organizations. Cognitive structures concerning the self have been called self-schemata. There is evidence that people develop such categories or concepts, probably partly through the observation of their own behavior, and that once developed they have a powerful influence on what is observed or encoded and what is remembered. People are particularly sensitive to self-relevant information and memory is facilitated when information is associated with self-schemata. In addition, there appears to be a bias toward accepting information confirmatory of existent self-schemata as opposed to disconfirmatory information. It is again suggested that many errors people make in relation to self-relevant information are better understood in terms of everyday cognitive processes rather than in terms of motivational principles such as the need for self-esteem.

Although other personality theories treat the self as a unitary concept, information-processing psychologists suggest that the self is really a family of contextualized selves. Members of the family of selves share some characteristics in common and retain some features that are distinctive. Particularly important among the family of selves are the possible selves, representing the wishes and fears of people concerning what they may become. Some people have a complex family of selves, others a simple family, some an integrated family structure, and others a family of selves filled with conflict. In the following chapter we shall see that beliefs concerning the self, as well as those concerning the rest of the world, play an important role in the information-processing interpretation of psychopathology and personality change.

The content and concepts emphasized by cognitive personality psychologists are similar in some ways to those emphasized by Kelly and Rogers. However, the latter were more influenced by clinical work and were more concerned with the study of individual differences. In contrast, cognitive personality psychologists have borrowed more from the work of cognitive and social psychologists and focused more on general principles of cognitive functioning established primarily through laboratory research. Such a focus results in certain gains and strengths for the cognitive, information-processing approach to personality. It allows psychologists who follow this approach to investigate important phenomena (i.e., how we organize the world about us and within us) in a systematic fashion that is related to the work being done by psychologists in other fields. It also calls attention to the enormous capacity people have for differentiating among events and for organizing information in varying ways.

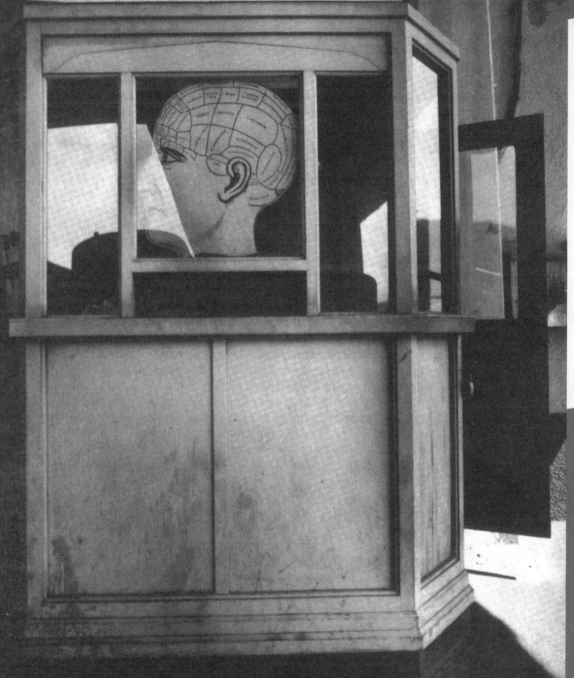

Chapter Fourteen
A Cognitive, Information-Processing Approach to Personality: Applications and Evaluation

C *HAPTER FOCUS:* In this chapter we continue considering the cognitive, information-processing approach to personality, with an emphasis on the clinical implications. In particular, we will focus on how individuals cope with stress and interpretations of psychopathology and change. Consistent with the content of the previous chapter, the focus will be on the cognitive processes in the individual—the thoughts, beliefs, and ways of processing information that play a role in distress and that, when changed, can lead to improved psychological functioning. Finally, we will compare this approach with earlier approaches and consider its own strengths and limitations.

> *Cognitive behavior therapy is designed to help the client identify, reality-test, and correct maladaptive, distorted conceptualizations and dysfunctional beliefs.*
>
> MEICHENBAUM AND GILMORE, 1983, p. 134

> *Cognitive therapy contrasts with behavior therapy in its greater emphasis on the patient's internal (mental) experiences, such as thoughts, feelings, wishes, daydreams, and attitudes. The overall strategy of cognitive therapy may be differentiated from the other schools of therapy by its emphasis on the empirical investigation of the patient's automatic thoughts, inferences, conclusions and assumptions.*
>
> BECK ET AL., 1979, p. 7

The clinical, applied implications of the cognitive, information-processing model have been very significant, influencing vast parts of the health professions. Within a relatively short period of time, perhaps a decade or so, it has become one of the dominant themes among psychologists interested in understanding and treating stress-related disorders and serious psychological difficulties such as depression. Although there is no one theory or mode of therapy, the approaches involved share some common assumptions:

1. Cognitions (attributions, beliefs, expectancies, memories concerning the self and others) are viewed as critical in determining feelings and behaviors. Thus, there is an interest in what people think and say to themselves.

2. The cognitions of interest tend to be specific to situations or categories of situations, though the importance of some generalized expectancies and beliefs is recognized.

3. Psychopathology is viewed as arising from distorted, incorrect, maladaptive cognitions concerning the self, others, and events in the world. Different forms of pathology are viewed as resulting from different cognitions or ways of processing information.

4. Faulty, maladaptive cognitions not only lead to problematic feelings and behaviors but these in turn lead to further problematic cognitions. Thus, a self-fulfilling cycle may set in whereby the person acts so as to confirm and maintain their distorted beliefs.

5. Cognitive behavior therapy, or cognitive therapy, involves a collaborative effort between therapist and patient to determine which distorted, maladaptive cognitions are creating the difficulty and then to replace them with other more realistic, adaptive cognitions. The therapeutic approach tends to be active, structured, and focused on the present.

6. In contrast with other approaches, cognitive therapists do not see the unconscious as important, except insofar as patients may not be aware of their routine, habitual ways of thinking about themselves and life. Further, there is an emphasis on changes in specific problematic cognitions rather than global personality change. Finally, in contrast with early behavior therapists, thoughts that go on inside the person's head are treated as behaviors and as determinants of the overt behaviors of traditional interest to behaviorists.

Given these common assumptions, let us move on to consider the approach in relation to the areas of stress and coping, psychopathology, and change.

STRESS AND COPING

As noted, the work of cognitively oriented psychologists has been very important in the area of stress and health. Lazarus and his associates, whose work has been very influential in this area, suggest that psychological stress depends on cognitions relating to the person and the environment (Lazarus & Folkman, 1984). According to the cognitive theory of psychological stress and coping, **stress** is viewed as occurring when the person views circumstances as taxing or exceeding his or her resources and endangering well-being. Involved in this are two stages of cognitive appraisal. In *primary appraisal*, the person evaluates whether there is anything at stake in the encounter, whether there is a threat or danger. For example, is there potential harm or benefit to self-esteem? Is one's personal health or that of a loved one at risk? In *secondary appraisal*, the person evaluates what, if anything, can be done to overcome harm, prevent harm, or improve the prospects for benefit. In other words, secondary appraisal involves an evaluation of the person's resources to cope with the potential harm or benefit evaluated in the stage of primary appraisal.

In a stressful situation, various means of *coping* are viewed as possible to manage, master, or tolerate the circumstances appraised as taxing or exceeding the person's resources. In particular a distinction is made between problem-focused forms of coping (e.g., efforts to alter the situation) and emotion-focused forms of coping (e.g., emotional distancing, escape–avoidance, seeking social support). Recent research on this model has focused on the development of a questionnaire to assess coping, the *Ways of Coping Scale*, an assessment of whether people are stable or variable in their coping methods, and the implications for somatic and psychological health of varying degrees of stress and the use of differing coping strategies. This research suggests the following conclusions (Folkman, Lazarus, & Gruen, 1986):

1. People are quite variable or differentiating in their appraisals of various situations. In other words, individual appraisals appear to be sensitive to conditions in the environment.
2. There is evidence of both stability and variability in the methods individuals use to cope with stressful situations. Although the use of some coping methods would appear to be influenced by personality factors, the use of many coping methods appears to be strongly influenced by the situational context.

Escape-Avoidance Coping—People sometimes use activities such as shopping as a means of escaping from or avoiding stressful situations.

3. In general, the greater the reported level of stress and efforts to cope, the poorer is the physical health and the greater is the likelihood of psychological symptoms. In contrast, the greater the sense of mastery, the better is the physical and psychological health.

4. Although the value of a particular form of coping depends on the context in which it is used, in general planful problem solving ("I made a plan of action and followed it" or "Just concentrated on the next step") is a more adaptive form of coping than escape–avoidance ("Hoped a miracle would happen" or "Tried to reduce tension by eating, drinking, or using drugs") or confrontative coping ("I let my feelings out somehow" or "I expressed anger to those who caused the problem").

Research by other investigators has similarly focused on the **cognitive strategies** people may use to cope with difficult situations and the implications of the utilization of these strategies. For example, the *self-handicapping strategy* involves giving oneself a handicap (e.g., coming late for an important interview) so as to avoid the threat of a failure that results in a blow to one's self-esteem (Berglas, 1985; Berglas & Jones, 1978). In other words, the person acts in ways that will lead to, but "justify" failure. The advantage of such a strategy is that it leaves one with the illusion of success without risking "real" failure. At times this strategy may be useful in helping the person to deal with anxiety associated with the threat of failure. However, it also may lead to a pattern of avoidance and doubts about one's competence.

An interesting illustration of a possible self-handicapping strategy is the use of hypochondriacal complaints (exaggerated concern with health and bodily functioning) as an explanation for poor performance. The suggestion here is that some individuals use reports of physical illness as a potential explanation for poor performance and thereby protect themselves against subjective failure and blows to their self-esteem — if failure occurs it is due to their not feeling well rather than do something more fundamental about them. In a study of the possible use of such a self-handicapping strategy it was found that hypochondriacal individuals reported more symptoms of physical illness in evaluative settings than did nonhypochondriacal individuals. This, of course, is not surprising or critical to the self-handicapping hypothesis. What was more revealing, however, was the fact that their reports of physical illness were only present in settings where poor health could serve as an excuse for poor performance. This strategic pattern of reporting illness was not found in settings where poor health could not be used as an explanation for poor performance or in nonevaluative settings (Smith, Snyder, & Perkins, 1983). Although suggesting that hypochondriacal complaints may be expressive of a self-handicapping strategy, the data do not mean that such complaints are "nothing but" such a strategy. Nor do they necessarily suggest that self-handicapping strategies are conscious devices or planned manipulations.

Another strategy worthy of note is that of *defensive pessimism* (Norem & Cantor, 1986). In this strategy the person uses low expectations to cope with the anxiety associated with failure. For example, one can

think of the straight-A student who repeatedly expresses concern that they will "bomb" the upcoming exam. What is important about this strategy is that it does not lead to lower motivation or a self-fulfilling prophecy of failure. Rather, it may be quite adaptive in helping the person to cope with their anxiety concerning failure and motivate them to work harder. Of course, at the same time it leaves the person with some ongoing insecurities and anxieties. In addition, there is some evidence that where pessimism becomes part of a generalized coping strategy or style, it may have negative implications for one's health.

PATHOLOGY AND CHANGE

As noted in the introduction to this chapter, the cognitive, information-processing view holds that psychopathology results from unrealistic, maladaptive cognitions. Therapy then involves efforts to change such cognitive distortions and replace them with more realistic, adaptive cognitions. For example, according to Albert Ellis, a former psychoanalyst who developed a system of change known as *Rational–Emotive Therapy* or RET, the causes of psychological difficulties are irrational beliefs or irrational statements we make to ourselves—that we *must* do something, that we *have* to feel some way, that we *should* be some kind of person, that we cannot do anything about our feelings or situation in life. Through the use of logic, argument, persuasion, ridicule, or humor an effort is made to change the irrational beliefs causing the difficulties. Although Ellis' views were long neglected by behavior therapists, with their emphasis on overt motor behavior, they have received greater interest with the development of cognitive behavior therapy.

What kinds of maladaptive cognitions do people have? About as many different kinds as there are cognitive processes. Consider the following possibilities:

Irrational Beliefs "If good things happen bad things must be on the way." "If I express my needs, others will reject me."

Faulty Reasoning "I failed on this effort so I must be incompetent." "They didn't respond the way I wanted them to so they must not think much of me."

Dysfunctional Expectancies "If something can go wrong for me it will." "Catastrophe is just around the corner."

Negative Self-Views "I always tend to feel that others are better than me." "Nothing I do ever turns out right."

Maladaptive Attributions "I'm a poor test taker because I am a nervous person." "When I win, it's luck; when I lose, it's me."

Memory Distortions "Life is horrible now and always has been this way." "I've never succeeded in anything."

Maladaptive Attention "All I can think about is how horrible it will be if I fail." "It's better not to think about things, there's nothing you can do anyway."

Self-Defeating Strategies "I'll put myself down before others do." "I'll reject others before they reject me and see if people still like me."

Obviously there is overlap among the above maladaptive cognitions. Often important maladaptive cognitions have more than one flawed aspect to them. However, they are illustrative of the kinds of cognitions that create problematic feelings and situations for people. For a better feeling for such cognitions and the efforts of cognitive therapists to change them, let us turn to two representative approaches — Meichenbaum's *stress inoculation training* and Beck's *cognitive therapy for depression.*

Stress Inoculation Training

According to Meichenbaum, "cognitive behavior therapy is designed to help the client identify, reality-test, and correct maladaptive, distorted conceptualizations and dysfunctional beliefs. . . . The cognitive behavior therapist works to make the client a better problem solver and a more competent personal scientist" (Meichenbaum & Gilmore, 1982, pp. 134, 148). In accord with the earlier description of stress, he suggests that stress be viewed in cognitive terms; that is, stress involves cognitive appraisals and individuals under stress often have a variety of self-defeating and interfering thoughts. In addition, such self-defeating cogni-

Don Meichenbaum

tions and related behaviors have a built-in self-confirmatory component to them (e.g., people get others to treat them in an overprotective way). Finally events are perceived and recalled in ways that are consistent with a negative bias. The procedure developed by Meichenbaum (1985) to help individuals cope better with stress is called **stress inoculation training**. It is seen as analogous to medical inoculation against biological disease.

Meichenbaum's stress inoculation training involves three phases: Conceptualization Phase, Skill Acquisition and Rehearsal Phase, Application and Follow-Through Phase. In the Conceptualization Phase, clients are taught the cognitive nature of stress and information is collected concerning maladaptive thoughts and images they may be having. This is done through the use of questionnaires or interview procedures. In either case, the effort is to have the client become aware of such negative, stress-engendering, automatic thoughts as "It is such an effort to do anything" and "There is nothing I can do to control these thoughts or change the situation." The important point here is that the person may not be aware of having these automatic thoughts and thus must be taught to be aware of them and their negative effects.

In the Skill Acquisition and Rehearsal Phase, a variety of procedures are used to help the person cope with stress and change their cognitions. First, the client may be taught relaxation as an active coping skill. Second, the client may be taught cognitive strategies such as how to restructure problems so that they appear more manageable. Or the client may be taught problem-solving strategies, such as how to define problems, generate possible alternative courses of action, evaluate the pros and cons of each proposed solution, and implement the most practicable and desirable one. Third, the client may be given self-instructional training in making coping self-statements such as "I can do it," "One step at at time," "Focus on the present; what is it I have to do?" "I can be pleased with the progress I'm making," "Keep trying, don't expect perfection or immediate success."

In the third phase, Application and Follow-Through, the client is taught to apply the skills learned in the second phase to actual situations. First, this may be done through imagery rehearsal. In this case the client imagines various stressful situations and the use of the skills and strategies learned in the second phase. Second, there may be behavioral rehearsal, role playing, and modeling involving the therapist and client. Third, there is the application of these skills to real-world situations. Finally, to prevent relapse, the client is taught to interpret occasional difficulties or slips as understandable occurrences rather than as evidence of failure and personal inadequacy. In addition, follow-up sessions may be scheduled to make sure that the person is not returning to the use of earlier maladaptive cognitions and strategies.

In line with most cognitive behavior therapy, the stress inoculation training procedure is active, focused, structured, and brief. It has been

What is the relation of imagery, an internal cognitive process, to action? Can you do something you can't imagine and, alternatively, does it help to first imagine something you want to do?

Psychologists have begun to be interested in the uses to which imagery processes, both natural and directed, can be put. For example, patients are encouraged by therapists to imagine various scenes, both to determine the nature of their fears as well as to develop positive courses of action. One of the most interesting applications of such efforts is in the world of sports. Take, for example, the efforts of Dan Smith, assistant coach of the University of Illinois basketball team and doctoral candidate in sports psychology. Finding a not terribly bright outlook for the team, Smith undertook a psychological training program that involved relaxation and imagery training: "We went ahead to create vivid, controlled images in the mind's eye. We taught each player to see himself taking a good shot, making it and then feeling a sense of reward, a positive emotion, for doing it. They applied the technique to other things such as playing defense and ball handling." The results? Both players and coaches report striking benefits from utilization of the program.

What are the limits of such programs? Clearly there are physical-talent limits. Beyond this, however, we have just begun to explore the potential role of imagery in facilitating performance as well as how we experience action.

SOURCE: *New York Times*, March 7, 1983, C2.

Cognitive Therapy—Cognitive therapists focus on specific problems and take an active approach toward the goal of behavioral change. © 1983 by The New York Times Company. Cartoon by Gil Eisner.

used with medical patients about to undergo surgery, with athletes to help them deal with the stress of competition, with rape victims to help them deal with the trauma of such assaults, and in the work environment to teach workers more efficient coping strategies and to help worker–management teams consider organizational change.

Beck's Cognitive Therapy for Depression

Like Albert Ellis, Aaron Beck is a former psychoanalyst who became disenchanted with psychoanalytic techniques and gradually developed a cognitive approach to therapy. His therapy is best known for its relevance to the treatment of depression but it has relevance to a wider variety of psychological disorders. According to Beck (1976), psychological difficulties are due to automatic thoughts, dysfunctional assumptions, and negative self-statements. In depression these thoughts generally concern self-worth, whereas in people with anxiety problems they concern danger.

Beck's cognitive model of depression emphasizes that the depressed person systematically misevaluates ongoing and past experiences, leading to a view of the self as a "loser," the view of the world as frustrating, and the view of the future as bleak. These three negative views are known as the **cognitive triad** and include negative views of the self such as "I am inadequate, undesirable, worthless," negatives views of the world such as "The world makes too many demands on me and life represents constant defeat," and negative views of the future such as

Aaron T. Beck

"Life will always involve the suffering and deprivation it has for me now." In addition, the depressed person is prone to faulty information processing such as in magnifying everyday difficulties into disasters and overgeneralizing from a single instance of rejection to the belief that "Nobody likes me." It is these thinking problems, these negative schemata and cognitive errors, that cause depression.

Cognitive therapy of depression is designed to "identify, reality-test, and correct distorted conceptualizations and the dysfunctional beliefs (schemata) underlying these cognitions" (Beck, Rush & Shaw, 1979, p. 4). Therapy generally consists of fifteen to twenty-five sessions at weekly intervals. The approach is described as involving highly specific learning experiences designed to teach the patient to monitor negative, automatic thoughts, to recognize how these thoughts lead to problematic feelings and behaviors, to examine the evidence for and against these thoughts, and to substitute more reality-oriented interpretations for these biased cognitions. The therapist helps the patient to see that interpretations of events lead to depressed feelings. For example, the following exchange between therapist (T) and patient (P) might occur:

P: I get depressed when things go wrong. Like when I fail a test.

T: How can failing a test make you depressed?

P: Well, if I fail I'll never get into law school.

T: So failing the test means a lot to you. But if failing a test could drive people into clinical depression, wouldn't you expect everyone who failed the test to have a depression? . . . . Did everyone who failed get depressed enough to require treatment?

P: No, but it depends on how important the test was to the person.

T: Right, and who decides the importance?

P: I do.

BECK, RUSH, AND SHAW, 1979, p. 146

In addition to the examination of beliefs for their logic, validity, and adaptiveness, behavioral assignments are used to help the patient test certain maladaptive cognitions and assumptions. This may involve the assignment of activities designed to result in success and pleasure. In general, the focus in therapy is on specific target cognitions that are seen as contributing to the depression. Beck contrasts cognitive therapy with traditional analytic therapy in terms of the therapist being continuously active in structuring the therapy, in the focus on the here and now, and in the emphasis on conscious factors. Beck and others have conducted a number of studies evaluating the efficacy of cognitive therapy for depression. A recent review suggests that "cognitive behavior therapy for depressed persons is a highly effective treatment with comparatively few dropouts and essentially no adverse side effects" (O'Leary & Wilson, 1987, p. 227).

THE RELATION OF INFORMATION-PROCESSING THEORY TO TRADITIONAL PERSONALITY THEORY

Now that we have considered the cognitive, information-processing approach to personality, what can be said about it relative to approaches previously considered? Clearly, certain concepts sound familiar. This is most clearly seen in the similarities with social cognitive theory. On the other hand, many aspects are distinctive. The cognitive emphasis in these chapters reminds one of the work of George Kelly. Kelly emphasized the person as a scientist and the importance of constructs and the construct system in psychological functioning. Kelly suggested that constructs are oganized in a hierarchical fashion and that people can be quite flexible in utilizing their constructs — people have constructs but their constructs need not have them. Indeed, Mischel states that "Kelly suggested, long before others, that the same orientation and principles ought to be used in talking about our 'subjects' as about ourselves. He thus foreshadowed much in contemporary psychology and his wisdom has not yet been fully recognized" (1981, p. 16). One can think here of Meichenbaum's description of cognitive therapy as an effort to make the client not only a better problem solver, but also a more competent personal scientist.

In addition, one may be reminded of the work of Carl Rogers in the cognitive emphasis on the concept of self and in the emphasis on how people give meaning to the world about them. Here too Mischel (1981), in reviewing work in the area of personality and cognition, recognizes that Rogers anticipated current developments in emphasizing the importance of the phenomenal world and the concept of self.

While noting these similarities, one can at the same time observe critical differences between personality information-processing theory and the works of Kelly and Rogers. The works of Rogers and Kelly emanated from clinical experience whereas the work in information processing derives from the experimental laboratory. Rogers and Kelly were attempting to develop a theory of personality whereas the work presented here might better be construed as an *approach to* personality rather than a *theory of* personality. Both Rogers and Kelly were interested in the study and understanding of individuals, whereas cognitive personality psychologists have yet to demonstrate the utility of their approach for the understanding of an individual or the utility of studying the individual for learning about people generally. Even though Rogers and Kelly emphasized process and change, they also emphasized the importance of structure and the continuity of personality. Cognitive personality psychologists, though recognizing structure and consistency, tend to give greater emphasis to process and variability in personality functioning. Perhaps this is seen most clearly in the emphasis on the contextualized self and family of selves, in contrast with Rogers' emphasis on the self as a more unitary concept.

If such differences between cognitive personality theory and the theories of Rogers and Kelly are noteworthy, differences between the former and traditional personality theory (psychoanalytic and trait theory) are even more apparent and noteworthy (Figure 14.1). At the heart of this difference lies the emphasis of traditional personality theory on structure and consistency–stability in personality functioning. In contrast with this lies the cognitive personality psychologist's emphasis on processes and the flexibility inherent in people's ability to discriminate among situations and manage their behavior accordingly. In addition, traditional personality theory places much greater emphasis on human motivation than is true for cognitive personality psychologists. As has been noted previously, the latter see people as *information seeking* rather than *pleasure seeking*. Finally, cognitive personality psychologists emphasize experimental observations of behavior and relate concepts of internal processes, such as cognitions, to behaviors that can be measured. In contrast, traditional personality theory puts greater faith in clinical observation (psychoanalytic theory) and in responses to questionnaires (trait theory). Personality questionnaires in particular often are discounted by cognitive personality psychologists because they are viewed as getting at a person's *construction* of personality rather than at a person's *actual* personality (Shweder, 1982). According to cognitive personality psychologists, we should be studying people's category structures and inference processes rather than their needs and dispositions, we should be studying behavior and cognitive representations of behavior

Traditional Personality Theory	Cognitive, Information-Processing Theory
1. Stability and consistency of personality	1. Discriminativeness and flexibility of behavior
2. Generalized predictions of person's behavior	2. Predictions specific to situations
3. Emphasis on structure-stability	3. Emphasis on process-fluidity
4. Dispositions, traits, needs	4. Category structures, belief systems, inferential strategies, cognitive competencies
5. Motivation and dynamics	5. Cognitive economics and everyday cognitive processes
6. Self as unitary concept	6. Self as composed of multiple schema

FIGURE 14.1 Prototypic Characteristics of Two Personality Theories.

rather than responses to questionnaires or projective techniques, and we should ally ourselves with other parts of psychology such as cognitive and social psychology rather than pursuing an entirely independent course of action.

EVALUATING THE STRENGTHS AND LIMITATIONS OF A COGNITIVE, INFORMATION-PROCESSING APPROACH TO PERSONALITY

Earlier the question was asked whether the cognitive, information-processing approach has any distinctive contribution to make to personality. Having considered some of the relevant theory and research, what can be suggested?

It would appear that there are three main contributions and strengths of this approach (Figure 14.2). First, it is tied to an experimental foundation in cognitive psychology and continues with that tradition while investigating issues in personality. Many personality theories have suffered from the problem of vague concepts and difficulty in suggesting relevant experimental efforts. To a certain extent, this has been true of psychoanalysis; to a greater extent, it has been true of humanistic and human growth potential theories. Also, most theories of personality have arisen independently of other ongoing efforts in psychology. Where commonalities with other parts of psychology could be observed this had more to do with a common influence than with the results of one having an impact on the results of another. Thus, when one considers the various theories covered in this book, one often finds it hard to say what aspects that are fundamental to the theory have been learned from other areas of psychology. This is particularly true for the more clinical theories presented earlier in the text and somewhat less true for the theories of learning presented later. With the cognitive, information-processing approach, however, we encounter a radical departure from this tradition. In going social and cognitive, personality psychologists following this approach have attempted to take from social psychology and cognitive psychology concepts and experimental procedures that might be useful in exploring personality.

The second strength of the cognitive, information-processing approach to personality lies in the phenomena investigated. Although it emphasizes an experimental tradition, important aspects of human personality functioning have not altogether been neglected. Consider here the issues covered—how individuals organize their representations of people, situations, events, and themselves. These indeed are topics that strike one as the kinds of issues that should be of concern to personality psychologists. Thus, when parallels are noted between issues explored by cognitive personality psychologists and earlier theories of personality, this may be taken as a strength. The approach is not neglecting long-standing issues that remain of concern to us. Whereas for some time experimental psychologists ignored questions of the self and questions of consciousness and thought, these psychologists are prepared to tackle them. Though they remain committed to the laboratory, for the most part they also remain aware of and concerned about phenomena observed in daily living.

Finally, one can note the importance of the clinical applications associated with this approach. The defining characteristic of cognitive therapy is an interest in what people think and say to themselves. Beyond this, there is an interest in how people process information, in the cognitive distortions that lead to psychological difficulties, and in the procedures that can be used to change these distortions. In the emphasis on an active, structured approach, this is a radical departure from psychoanalysis and Rogerian therapy. At the same time, in the emphasis on what goes on inside the person it is a radical departure from behaviorism and, in this regard, it continues to come under attack from conservative behaviorists. Still, the legions of those who consider themselves cognitive therapists are growing, and the application of the approach to a broad spectrum of difficulties is increasing.

But what of the limitations of the approach? Here we may again consider three relevant points. First, we can examine the underlying model critically. Second, we can consider whether in following in the footsteps of cognitive psychology, major aspects of personality functioning have been neglected. Third, we can consider questions concerning the conceptual basis and effectiveness of cognitive-based therapies.

Turning to the first point, how useful is the computer, information-processing model that underlies this approach to personality? We must recall that a model need not be an accurate reflection of human behavior for it to be useful in the study of that behavior. Thus, when it comes down to it, the question is not whether humans function like computers but whether studying people *as if* they function like computers assists us in understanding their behavior. Relevant to this is the question of whether the model misleads us into thinking about phenomena in ways that are not useful.

To a certain extent, the jury is still out deliberating on this question. We do know that in many ways people do not think like computers, let alone behave like them. George Miller was one of the early leaders in the development of computer models of human thinking. Today he suggests that "how computers work seems to have no real relevance to how the mind works any more than a wheel shows how people walk" (1982, p. C8). Computers are becoming faster and capable of handling increasing amounts of information. We are becoming increasingly sophisticated in writing programs to make the computer think like humans. However, many people believe that the nature of human thinking is fundamentally different from machine thinking. Not only does a machine inevitably require a person to select the information to be stored and write the program for organizing information, two critical processes in information processing, but machines do not make the many economies and irrational connections that are part of human thought. In addition, people make judgments such as attributing intent to the action of others. Although it is possible to make a computer think in an analogous way, there remains a considerable gap between the two. Furthermore, it is possible that thinking about social phenomena in a social context is fundamentally different from the isolated processing of neutral information.

This last point brings us to the second criticism of this approach. This is that in going cognitive, psychology has neglected such important human phenomena as affect and motivation. In following in the footsteps of cognitive psychology, personality psychologists may be in danger of committing the same errors without breaking new ground. In gaining our head, we may be in danger of losing our soul. A short time ago there was a symposium of outstanding social and personality psychologists presenting papers on "social knowing." Consider the following commentary on these papers by Ulric Neisser, one of the founding fathers of the cognitive revolution in psychology: "Information processing concepts are overused in social psychology just as I think they are in cognitive psychology. . . . I am disturbed by the extraordinarily narrow perspective from which scholars in this field approach their work. . . . Freud's observations and insights have affected every institution in western culture, but they receive no recognition here" (1980, pp. 601, 602).

During the 1920s and 1930s behaviorism was particularly strong in this country and the study of cognitive processes was not popular. The learning theorist Tolman was an exception in this regard in emphasizing the importance of cognition and criticizing the popular telephone switchboard model (stimulus–response) of human behavior. One psychologist who was critical of Tolman suggested that he left animals buried in thought and did not consider why they made the choices they did (Guthrie, 1952). Similarly, today a leading cognitive psychologist suggests that "just as cognitive psychology presents the danger of leaving the human subject lost in thought without being able to act, so does the current approach [to cognition and personality] leave unsolved the problem of how action occurs" (Posner, 1981, p. 340).

Sometime ago the distinction was made between "cold cognition" and "hot cognition." Psychologists, including both cognitive psychologists and cognitive personality psychologists, have tended to study cold cognition. Although they study important phenomena, they have tended to study the more emotionally neutral aspects of these phenomena in the relatively cool setting of the laboratory. But true social cognition in important life situations may be fundamentally different from the cool, detached processes that have typically been the focus of investigation. In reviewing the results of research following the information-processing model, a leading cognitive psychologist suggested that there was "sterility over-all, for the organism we are analyzing is conceived as pure intellect. . . . Alas, that description does not fit actual behavior. . . . I conclude that there is more to human intelligence than the pure cognitive system, and that a science of Cognition cannot afford to ignore these other aspects" (Norman, 1980, p. 4). Prominent among these other aspects were emotion and motivation. Here too attention was drawn to Freud's efforts to understand the linkages between emotions or motivation and thought.

In the period since 1980, the situation has changed and there are encouraging signs of an interest in "hot cognition"—emotion and motivation. The work on possible selves represents one move in this direction, work on stress and cognitive coping strategies represents another, and work on the effects of emotions such as depression on cognitive processes represents a third. However, such efforts are in the early stages of development and how far they will take us in understanding such areas remains to be seen.

Finally, let us consider some questions regarding cognitive therapy or, more accurately, cognitively based therapies. First, although many of these approaches share a common cognitive emphasis, there is no one theoretical model. Further, often there may be little direct tie to work in cognitive psychology itself (Power & Champion, 1986). Second, although these approaches suggest that cognitive distortions are causal of disturbances in emotion such as anxiety and depression, it is not yet clear that they determine negative affects rather than being associated with negative affect or a result of negative affect (Cochran & Hammen, 1985). As one authority in the field of behavior therapy suggests, "on the causal side, is it possible that the irrational cognitions characteristic of depression are the *result* of disturbed affect rather than cause?" (Rachman, 1983, p. 83). Third, it is not clear whether cognitive therapy emphasizes the change from irrational, unrealistic cognitions to rational, realistic cognitions or the change from maladaptive to adaptive cognitions. Both are mentioned, often being used interchangeably. Yet, there is evidence that depressives, for example, suffer *less* cognitive distortion than do normals (Layne, 1983; Power & Champion, 1986). Is the goal of therapy then to be helping people learn how to distort better so as to feel better? If so, what kind of scientist are we training them to be? Finally, although there is *some* evidence of the efficacy of *some* forms of cognitive therapy with *some* patients, the jury is still out in this regard (Miller & Berman, 1983). In the words of one authority: "Notwithstanding some recent and encouraging advances in developing effective forms of cognitive therapy, few people will contest the view that attempts at overcoming psychological problems by cognitive methods have fallen short of hopes and expectations" (Rachman, 1981, p. 287). Thus questions can be raised concerning the conceptual status and clinical efficacy of cognitive therapies.

In sum, cognitive approaches to personality and therapy represent promising leads. At this time we can recognize their contributions while remaining guarded in our optimism concerning the future.

STRENGTHS	LIMITATIONS
1. Ties its approach to work in experimental cognitive psychology. Defines concepts clearly and makes them accessible to experimental investigation.	1. Has yet to achieve an integrated theory of personality.
2. Considers some important aspects of human personality functioning (e.g., how people represent other people, situations, events, and themselves).	2. Neglects affect and motivation as important correlates and determinants of cognition.
3. Important contributions to health management and psychotherapy.	3. Questions concerning the conceptual status and clinical efficacy of cognitive therapies.

FIGURE 14.2 Summary of Strengths and Limitations of a Cognitive, Information-Processing Approach to Personality.

Major Concepts and Summary

stress

cognitive strategies (self-handicapping, defensive pessimism)

stress inoculation training

cognitive triad (negative views of self, world, and future)

In this chapter we have considered some of the clinical implications of a model of personality that emphasizes the person's organization of ideas and beliefs concerning situations, events, people, and the self. According to the cognitive view of stress and coping, stress occurs when the person views circumstances as taxing or exceeding the available resources and endangering well-being. In primary appraisal the person evaluates what is at stake in the encounter, and in secondary appraisal the personal resources available to meet the threat. Coping devices, such as planful problem-solving, escape–avoidance, and confrontation, are used to deal with stress. There is evidence of broad individual differences in the kinds of coping devices used to deal with stress but each individual also tends to use different coping devices in accord with the perceived situational context. In general, higher levels of stress and efforts to cope are associated with poorer levels of physical and psychological health.

Other cognitive strategies considered were self-handicapping and defensive pessimism, the former involving giving oneself a handicap so as to protect one's self-esteem against the threat of a failure, and the latter involving the use of low expectations to cope with anxiety associated with failure. Both cognitive strategies have value in helping the individual to cope with the stress associated with failure but also may. have negative implications for the development of one's competence and self-esteem.

The cognitive, information-processing model holds that psychopathology results from unrealistic, maladaptive cognitions or ways of processing information. Therapy then involves ways of changing the distorted, maladaptive cognitions and processes. Meichenbaum's stress inoculation training and Beck's cognitive therapy for depression were considered as illustrative of such approaches to psychopathology and change. Stress inoculation training involves the phases of Conceptualization, Skill Acquisition and Rehearsal, and Application and Follow-Through. Beck's cognitive therapy for depression emphasizes the importance of the negative triad in depression—negative views of the self, world, and future. Both of these procedures are structured and focused on current and specific cognitions (automatic thoughts, irrational beliefs, dysfunctional expectancies) that contribute to problematic functioning. In contrast with psychoanalytic therapy, the therapist is active, the unconscious is not emphasized, there is a focus on the here and now, and the emphasis is on changes in specific cognitions rather than broad personality change.

There is no one cognitive, information-processing model of personality or cognitive form of therapy. Rather there is a model that leads to characteristic forms of research and treatment. The strengths of this model are that it is tied to work in experimental cognitive psychology, that it emphasizes concepts that relate to important aspects of human functioning that can still be studied systematically, and that it is associated with important procedures designed to improve health and psychological well-being. At the same time, we must be aware that this is not an integrated theory of personality, that further attention remains to be given to such important areas as affect and motivation, and that questions remain concerning the conceptual status and clinical efficacy of cognitive therapies. Much has been done with this model over the past decade and a more complete evaluation of it must await further developments over the next decade.

Chapter Fifteen
Theory and Assessment in the Study of the Individual: The Case of Jim

CHAPTER FOCUS: In this chapter, we study the personality of an individual from the perspective of the preceding theories and methods of personality assessment.

Rorschach: Card 5

16 P. F.—partial profile

Reserved	1	2	3	4	5	6	7	8	⑨	10		Outgoing
Less intelligent	1	2	3	4	5	6	7	8	9	⑩		More intelligent
Easily upset	1	②	3	4	5	6	7	8	9	10		Emotionally calm
Humble	1	2	3	4	5	6	⑦	8	9	10		Assertive
Conservative	1	2	3	4	5	6	⑦	8	9	10		Experimenting
Group dependent	1	2	3	④	5	6	7	8	9	10		Self-sufficient
Low integration	①	2	3	4	5	6	7	8	9	10		High self-concept control
Relaxed	1	2	3	4	5	6	7	⑧	9	10		Tense

"Sort of brings to mind a dancing girl, sort of a stripper. Could almost be a ballet dancer on toes. Gypsy Rose Lee. Type that comes out with a magnificent gown. Sort of bowlegged. Body hidden by stuff to be discarded. A stripper (Stripper?). Nobody wears this unless it is to be taken off subsequently. Arms outstretched."

Jim: Age 40
Self-efficacy Belief: "I can pull off anything and have a lot of confidence in myself socially."
Dysfunctional Thought: "I wish I were a better person."

A variety of approaches to personality have now been examined: Freud's psychoanalytic theory, Rogers' self-concept theory, Kelly's construct theory, trait theory, social cognitive theory, and information-processing approaches. Each has been studied as an outgrowth of certain kinds of theorists as well as in relation to the data available to them. In particular, it has been emphasized that each theory tends to be associated with a different technique of *assessment* and with a different emphasis in research. *Beginning with different assumptions and styles of investigation, the theorists were led to use different tools to unravel the secrets of personality functioning. These different tools in turn led to the different observations that served as the basis for the theories examined here.*

In Chapter 1 it was suggested that theories of personality can be compared in terms of such criteria as comprehensiveness, parsimony or economy, logical consistency, and productivity in research. In this chapter we deal with another question: Are the observations obtained similar when assessment techniques associated with the different theories are applied to the same individual? Recall here the story of the wise blind men and the elephant. Each wise man examined a part of the elephant and assumed that he knew what it was. None knew that it was an elephant and each came to a different conclusion on the basis of his observations. One felt the tail and thought it was a snake, another a leg and thought it was a tree, another a trunk and thought it was a hose, and another a body and thought it was a wall. The study of one individual through the use of different techniques of assessment may provide us with a useful analogy: Do the theories refer to different parts of the same person, each representing an incomplete picture of the whole and each describing some of the same qualities in different terms, or do the theories refer to different people? When applied to an individual, are the theories talking about different parts of the individual, about the same parts but in different terms, or are they basically in conflict with one another?

THE CASE OF JIM

Jim was a student at Harvard when he agreed to serve as a subject for a project involving the intensive study of college students. He participated in the project mainly because of his interest in psychology. He also hoped that the tests would give him a better understanding of himself. His autobiography reveals some of the essentials of his life. Jim was born in New York City after the end of the Second World War, the first child in a Jewish family, and received considerable attention and affection. Jim's father is a college graduate who owns an automobile sales business; his mother is a housewife who also does volunteer reading for the blind. He has a sister four years younger and two brothers, one five years younger and one seven years younger. The main themes in his autobiography concerned his inability to become involved with women in a satisfying way, his need for success and his relative failure since high school, and his uncertainty about whether to go on to graduate school in business administration or in clinical psychology.

Rorschach and TAT: Psychoanalytic Theory

The Rorschach Inkblot Test and Thematic Apperception Test, both projective, were administered to Jim by a professional clinical psychologist. On the Rorschach, which was first, Jim gave relatively few responses— 22 in all. This is surprising in the light of other evidence of his intelligence and creative potential. It may be of interest here to follow his responses to the first two cards and to consider the hypotheses formulated by the psychologist, who also is a practicing psychoanalyst.

CARD 1

JIM: The first thing that comes to mind is a butterfly.

COMMENT: Initially cautious and acts conventionally in a novel situation.

JIM: This reminds me of a frog. Not a whole frog, like a frog's eyes. Really just reminds me of a frog.

COMMENT: He becomes more circumspect, almost picky, and yet tends to overgeneralize while feeling inadequate about it.

JIM: Could be a bat. More spooky than the butterfly because there is no color. Dark and ominous.

COMMENT: Phobic, worried, depressed, and pessimistic.

CARD 2

JIM: Could be two headless people with their arms touching. Looks like they are wearing heavy dresses. Could be one touching her hand against a mirror. If they're women, their figures are not good. Look heavy.

COMMENT: Alert to people. Concern or confusion about sexual role. Anal-compulsive features. Disparaging of women and hostile to them—headless and figures not good. Narcissism expressed in mirror image.

JIM: This looks like two faces facing each other. Masks, profiles— more masks that faces—not full, more of a façade, like one with a smile and one with a frown.

COMMENT: He presents a façade, can smile or frown, but doesn't feel genuine. Despite façade of poise, feels tense with people. Repeated several times that he was not imaginative. Is he worried about his productivity and importance?

A number of interesting responses occurred on other cards. On the third card he perceived women trying to lift weights. Here again was a suggestion of conflict about his sexual role and about a passive as opposed to an active orientation. On the following card he commented that "somehow they all have an Alfred Hitchcock look of spooky animals," again suggesting a possible phobic quality to his behavior and a tendency to project dangers into the environment. His occasional references to symmetry and details suggested the use of compulsive defenses and intellectualization while experiencing threat. Disturbed and conflicted references to women come up in a number of places. At the beginning of this chapter we quoted his response to Card 5, involving a stripper. On Card 7, he perceived two women from mythology who would be good if they were mythological but bad if they were fat. On the next-to-last card he perceived "some sort of a Count, Count Dracula. Eyes, ears, cape. Ready to grab, suck blood. Ready to go out and strangle some woman." The reference to sucking blood suggested tendencies toward oral sadism, something which also appeared in another percept of vampires that suck blood. Jim followed the percept of Count Dracula with one of pink cotton candy. The tester interpreted this response as suggesting a yearning for nurturance and contact behind the oral sadism; that is, the subject uses his oral aggressive tendencies (e.g., sarcasm, verbal attacks) to defend against more passive oral wishes (e.g., to be fed, taken care of, and to be dependent).

The examiner concluded that the Rorschach suggested a neurotic structure in which intellectualization, compulsivity, and hysterical operations (irrational fears, preoccupation with his body) are used to defend against anxiety. However, it was suggested that Jim continues to feel anxious and uncomfortable with others, particularly authority figures. The report from the Rorschach concluded as follows. "He is conflicted about his sexual role. While he yearns for nurturance and contact from the motherly female, he feels very guilty about the cravings and his intense hostility toward women. He assumes a passive orientation, a continual role playing and, behind a façade of tact, he continues his rage, sorrow, and ambition."

What kinds of stories did Jim tell on the Thematic Apperception Test? Most striking about these stories were the sadness and hostility involved in all interpersonal relationships. In one story a boy is dominated by his mother, in another an insensitive gangster is capable of gross inhumanity, and in a third a husband is upset to learn that his wife is not a virgin. In particular, the relationships between men and women constantly involve one putting down the other. Consider this story.

> Looks like two older people. The woman is sincere, sensitive, and dependent on the man. There is something about the man's expression that bespeaks of insensitivity—the way he looks at her, as if he conquered her. There is not the same compassion and security in her presence that she feels in his. In the end, the woman gets very hurt and is left to fend for herself. Normally I would think that they were married but in this case I don't because two older people who are married would be happy with one another.

In this story we have a man being sadistic to a woman. We also see the use of the defensive mechanism of denial in Jim's suggestion that these two people cannot be married since older married people are always happy with one another. In the story that came after the one above again there is the theme of hostile mistreatment of a woman. In this story there is a more open expression of the sexual theme along with evidence of some sexual-role confusion.

> This picture brings up a gross thought. I think of Candy. The same guy who took advantage of Candy. He's praying over her. Not the last rites, but he has convinced her that he is some powerful person and she's looking for him to bestow his good graces upon her. His knee is on the bed, he's unsuccessful, she's naive. He goes to bed with her for mystical purposes. [*Blushes*] She goes on being naive and continues to be susceptible to that kind of thing. She has a very, very sweet compassionate look. Could it possibly be that this is supposed to be a guy wearing a tie? I'll stick with the former.

The psychologist interpreting these stories observed that Jim appeared to be immature, naive, and characterized by a gross denial of all that is unpleasant or dirty, the latter for him including both sexuality and marital strife. The report continued: "He is vacillating between expressing sadistic urges and experiencing a sense of victimization. Probably he combines both, often in indirect expressions of hostility while feeling unjustly treated or accused. He is confused about what meaningful relationships two people can have. He is ambivalently idealistic and pessimistic about his own chances for a stable relationship. Since he sees sex as dirty and as a mode for using or being used by his partner, he fears involvement. At the same time he craves attention, needs to be recognized, and is often preoccupied with sexual urges."

Between the Rorschach and the Thematic Apperception Test a number of important themes come out. One theme involves a general lack of warmth in interpersonal relationships, in particular a disparaging and at times sadistic orientation toward women. In relation to women, there is conflict between sexual preoccupation and the feeling that sex is dirty and involves hostility. The second theme involves experiencing tension and anxiety behind a façade of poise. A third theme involves conflict and confusion about his sexual identity. Although there is evidence of intelligence and creative potential, there also is evidence of rigidity and inhibition in relation to the unstructured nature of the projective tests. Compulsive defenses, intellectualization, and denial are only partially successful in helping him deal with his anxieties.

What can be said about the data from the projective tests, particularly since these tests relate to psychoanalytic theory? The unstructured quality of these tests led to many personal responses that relate to unique aspects of Jim's personality. Furthermore, the unstructured quality of these tests allows for the development of a rich and varied response pattern that allows for some understanding of many different aspects of Jim's personality. Finally, the disguised quality of the tests allows us to penetrate the façade of his personality (in psychoanalytic terms his defenses) to be able to view his underlying needs, motives, or drives. We have a test that allows for considerable uniqueness of response and a theory of personality that is clinical in its emphasis on the individual. We have a test that disguises its true purpose and a theory of personality that is dynamic in its emphasis on behavior as a result of the interplay among forces, drives, conflicts, and layers of personality.

The picture of Jim given in the Rorschach and Thematic Apperception tests is quite different from that presented in the autobiography. In his autobiography Jim indicated that he received unlimited affection from his parents and was quite popular and successful through high school. He described himself as having a good relationship with his father. He described his mother as having "great feelings for other people—she is a totally 'loving' woman." At the same time, we know that Jim feels he is troubled. In his autobiography he wrote that people had a high estimate of him because they could use only superficial criteria and that inwardly he was troubled. We thus have support for the interpretation in the Rorschach that he hides his tension and anxiety behind a façade of poise. There also is evidence in his autobiography of a conflicted relationship with women.

> My relationships with women were somewhat better in high school than they are now, but they weren't really satisfying then either. I was operating in a small subculture then, and I was very respected by everyone, so that probably made me more popular than I would have been otherwise. I have never had a really long-term, intimate relationship with a girl and I think those are the only kind that are meaningful. I had a number of superficial relationships, but there was always a barrier set up against my really becoming involved, and that barrier has been reinforced and made stronger over the last four years. Once a girl starts liking me a great deal I start liking her less—this has obvious implications about my lack of feelings of self-worth. It's a vicious and self-defeating circle: I like a girl only until she starts to like me. Thus in high school I was much sought after, but I managed to remain safely uninvolved.

Jim did not like the Rorschach. He felt that he had to see something and that whatever he perceived would be interpreted as evidence that he was neurotic. He suggested that he didn't feel defensive about his troubles since he was willing to accept having them but he didn't want them overstated. When he read over some of the comments made by the psychologist, he observed that he himself believed that there was a sexual problem and that this would be the major issue if he went into therapy. Jim said that he had fears about ejaculating too quickly, his potency, and his ability to satisfy the female. It is interesting that the fear of losing control, or premature ejaculation, occurs in an individual who uses compulsive defenses and who strives to be in complete control of most situations.

What can be said about the relationship between the projective data and psychoanalytic theory? Clearly some of the importance of the data from the Rorschach and the TAT lies in the theoretical interpretations given to the responses, in particular the use of psychoanalytic symbolism. However, aside from this, it is difficult to determine how other theories of personality could make as much use of the data as psychoanalytic theory can. As we shall see, the data from the projectives are of a qualitatively different sort than those found in the other tests. It is only on the Rorschach that we obtain content such as "a stripper," "women trying to lift weights," "Count Dracula . . . ready to grab, suck blood. Ready to go out and strangle some woman," and "pink cotton candy." And only on the TAT are there repeated references to themes of sadness and hostility in interpersonal relationships. It is the content of the responses and the way in which the tests are handled that allows for the psychodynamic interpretations.

Obviously, Jim is not a Count Dracula and there is little overtly to suggest that he is a sadist. But the content of the projectives allows for the interpretation that an important part of his personality functioning involves a defense against sadistic urges. Obviously Jim does not still drink out of a milk bottle, but the references to sucking blood and to cotton candy, together with the rest of his responses, allow for the interpretation that he is partially fixated at the oral stage. It is interesting to observe in relation to this that Jim has an ulcer, which involves the digestive tract, and that he must drink milk to manage this condition.

Perhaps the point here is that if you let people's imaginations wander, you will be led to the world of the irrational. Freud not only allowed this but, indeed, encouraged it. He encouraged his patients to dream, to fantasize, to associate freely. He studied his subjects intensively and was exposed to the world of the individual and to the world of drives, conflicts, guilt, sex, and aggression. Encouraged to do so, Freud's patients reported feelings and memories that they were previously unaware of. Similarly, in Jim's Rorschach and TAT we have content and themes that seem out of character with the rest of his responses to other personality tests. Having access to these feelings and memories, Freud was able to draw certain relationships between them and the problems that first brought his patients to treatment. In Jim's case we can guess in the same way that it is his sexual confusion and latent hostility that make him feel anxious or insecure and that prevent him from becoming involved with women. Finding himself making discoveries in the world of the irrational and basing his theory on observations with patients, Freud was led to overemphasize the importance of the unconscious and to overemphasize the pathological in individuals. Similarly, Jim's performance on the projectives gives little indication of the skills, talents, and resources he has used to make some significant achievements.

Semantic Differential: Phenomenological Theory

How do these observations compare with those obtained from other assessment techniques? Jim filled out the semantic differential, rating the concepts self, ideal self, father, and mother on 104 scales. Typical scales were authoritarian–democratic, conservative–liberal, affectionate–reserved, warm–cold, and strong–weak. Each of the four concepts was rated on the same scales so that comparisons could be made of the meaning of these concepts for Jim. The test is clearly different from the Rorschach in being undisguised rather than disguised. The semantic differential test does not immediately follow from Rogerian theory. However, we can interpret data from the test in relation to Rogerian theory, since there is a phenomenological quality to the data and we are assessing the individual's perception of his self and his ideal self.

First, we look at the ways in which Jim perceives his self. Jim perceives himself as intelligent, friendly, sincere, kind, and basically good. The ratings suggest that he sees himself as a wise person who is humane and interested in people. At the same time, other ratings suggest that he does not feel free to be expressive and uninhibited. Thus he rates himself as reserved, introverted, inhibited, tense, moral, and conforming. There is a curious mixture of perceptions of being involved, deep, sensitive, and kind while also being competitive, selfish, and disapproving. There is also the interesting combination of perceiving himself as being good and masculine while at the same time he perceives himself to be weak and insecure. One gets the impression of an individual who would like to believe that he is basically good and capable of genuine interpersonal relationships at the same time that he is bothered by serious inhibitions and high standards for himself and others.

This impression comes into sharper focus when we consider the self ratings in relation to those for the ideal self. In general, Jim did not see an extremely large gap between his self and his ideal self. However, large gaps did occur on a number of important scales. In an arbitrary way, we can define a gap of three or more positions on a seven-point scale as considerable and important. Thus, for example, Jim rated his self as 2 on the weak–strong scale and his ideal self as 7 on the same scale—a difference of five positions. In other words, Jim would like to be much stronger than he feels he is. Assessing his ratings on the other scales in a similar way, we find that Jim would like to be more of each of the following than he currently perceives himself to be: warm, active, equalitarian, flexible, lustful, approving, industrious, relaxed, friendly, and bold. Basically two themes appear. One has to do with *warmth*. Jim is not as warm, relaxed, and friendly as he would like to be. The other theme has to do with *strength*. Jim is not as strong, active, and industrious as he would like to be.

Jim's ratings of his mother and father give some indication of where he sees them in relation to himself in general and these qualities in particular. First, if we compare the way Jim perceives his self with his perception of his mother and father, clearly he perceives himself to be much more like his father than his mother. Also, he perceives his father to be closer to his ideal self than his mother, although he perceives himself to be closer to his ideal self than either his mother or his father. However, in the critical areas of warmth and strength, the parents tend to be closer to the ideal self than Jim is. Thus, his mother is perceived to be more warm, approving, relaxed, and friendly than Jim and his father is perceived to be stronger, more industrious, and more active than Jim. The mother is perceived as having an interesting combination of personality characteristics. On one hand, she is perceived as affectionate, friendly, spontaneous, sensitive, and good. On the other she is perceived as authoritarian, superficial, selfish, unintelligent, intolerant, and uncreative.

With the autobiography and the semantic differential we begin to get another picture of Jim. We learn of his popularity and success through high school and of his good relationship with his father. We find support for the suggestions from the projective tests of anxiety and difficulties with women. Indeed, we learn of Jim's fears of ejaculating too quickly and not being able to satisfy the female. However, we also find an individual who believes himself to be basically good and is interested in doing humane things. We become aware of an individual who has a view of his self and a view of his ideal self, and of an individual who is frustrated because of the feelings that leave a gap between the two.

Given the opportunity to talk about himself and what he would like to be, Jim talks about his desire to be warmer, more relaxed, and stronger. We feel no need here to disguise our purposes, for we are interested in Jim's perceptions, meanings, and experiences as he reports them. We are interested in what is real for Jim—in how he interprets phenomena within his own frame of reference. We want to know all about Jim, but all about Jim as he perceives himself and the world about him.

When using the data from the semantic differential, we are not tempted to focus on drives, and we do not need to come to grips with the world of the irrational. In Rogers' terms, we see an individual who is struggling to move toward self-actualization, from dependence toward independence, from fixity and rigidity to freedom and spontaneity. We find an individual who has a gap between his intellectual and emotional estimates of himself. In Rogers' terms, we observe an individual who is without self-consistency, who lacks a sense of congruence between self and experience.

Rep Test: Personal Construct Theory

Jim took the group form of Kelly's Role Construct Repertory Test (Rep test) on an occasion separate from the other tests (Figure 15.1). Here we have a test that is structured in terms of the roles that are given to the subject and in terms of the task of formulating a similarity–contrast construct. However, the subject is given total freedom in the content of the construct formed. As we noted in Chapter 7, the Rep test is derived quite logically from Kelly's theory of personal constructs. Two major themes appear in these constructs. The first theme has to do with that of the *quality of interpersonal relationships.* Basically this involves whether people are warm and giving or cold and narcissistic. This theme is expressed in constructs such as Gives Love–Is Self-oriented, Sensitive–Insensitive, and Communicates With Others as People–Is Uninterested in Others. A second major theme concerns *security* and is expressed in constructs such as Hung up–Healthy, Unsure–Self-confident, and Satisfied with Life–Unhappy. The frequency with which constructs relevant to these two themes appear suggests that Jim has a relatively constricted view of the world, that is, much of Jim's understanding of events is in terms of the Warm–Cold and Secure–Insecure dimensions. Although not evident in the data, there may be a relationship between the two dimensions. The Warm–Cold theme has a dependency quality, and it may be that he feels more secure when he is receiving love from others. Notice here that Jim did rate himself as slightly dependent on the semantic differential and on the Rorschach gave responses that suggested passivity and oral dependency.

How do the constructs given relate to specific people? On the sorts that involved himself, Jim used constructs expressing insecurity. Thus, Jim views himself as being like his sister (so hung up that their psychological health is questionable) in contrast to his brother, who is basically healthy and stable. In two other sorts, he sees himself as lacking self-confidence and lacking genuine social poise. These ways of construing himself are in contrast with the constructs used in relation to the father. The father is construed as being introverted and retiring, but he also is construed as being self-sufficient, open-minded, outstanding, and successful.

The constructs used in relation to the mother are interesting and again suggest conflict. On one hand, the mother is construed to be outgoing, gregarious, and giving of great love, whereas on the other she is construed to be mundane, predictable, close-minded, and conservative. The close-minded, conservative construct is particularly interesting since, in that sort, mother is paired with the person with whom he, Jim, feels most uncomfortable. Thus mother and the person with whom he feels most uncomfortable are contrasted with father, who is construed to be open-minded and liberal. The combination of sorts for all persons suggests that Jim's ideal person is someone who is warm, sensitive, secure, intelligent, open-minded, and successful. The women in his life —

The constructs formed by Jim are:

CONSTRUCT	CONTRAST
Self-satisfied	Self-doubting
Uninterested in communicating with students as people	Interested in communicating with students as people
Nice	Obnoxious
Sensitive to cues from other people	Insensitive to cues
Outgoing-gregarious	Introverted-retiring
Introspective-hung up	Self-satisfied
Intellectually dynamic	Mundane and predictable
Outstanding, successful	Mediocre
Obnoxious	Very likeable
Satisfied with life	Unhappy

CONSTRUCT	CONTRAST
Shy, unsure of self	Self-confident
Worldly, open-minded	Parochial, close-minded
Open, simple to understand	Complex, hard to get to know
Capable of giving great love	Somewhat self-oriented
Self-sufficient	Needs other people
Concerned with others	Oblivious to all but his own interests
So hung up that psychological health is questionable	Basically healthy and stable
Willing to hurt people in order to be "objective"	Unwilling to hurt people if he can help it
Close-minded, conservative	Open-minded, liberal
Lacking in self-confidence	Self-confident
Sensitive	Insensitive, self-centered
Lacking social poise	Secure and socially poised
Bright, articulate	Average intelligence

FIGURE 15.1 Rep Test Data.

mother, sister, girlfriend, and previous girlfriend—are construed as having some of these characteristics but also as missing others.

The Rep test gives us valuable data about how Jim construes his environment. With it we continue the phenomenological approach discussed in relation to Rogers, and again find that Jim's world tends to be perceived in terms of two major constructs: warm interpersonal relationships–cold interpersonal relationships and secure, confident people – insecure, unhappy people. Through the Rep test we gain an understanding of why Jim is so limited in his relationships to others and why he has so much difficulty in being creative. His being restricted to only two constructs hardly leaves him free to relate to people as individuals and instead forces him to perceive people and problems in stereotyped or conventional ways. A world filled with so little perceived diversity can hardly be exciting, and the constant threat of insensitivity and rejection can be expected to fill Jim with a sense of gloom.

The data from the Rep test are tantalizing, much like Kelly's theory. What is there seems so clear and valuable, but one is left wondering about what is missing. Both figuratively and literally, there is the sense of the skeleton for the structure of personality, but one is left with only the bones. Jim's ways of construing himself and his environment are an important part of his personality. Assessing his constructs and his construct system helps us to understand just how he interprets events and how he is led to predict the future. But where is the flesh to go along with the bones — the sense of an individual who cannot be what he feels, the sense of an individual struggling to be warm amid feelings of hostility and struggling to relate to women although confused about his feelings toward them and confused about his own sexual identity?

Sixteen Personality Factor Inventory: Trait, Factor-Analytic Theory

Let us now move to the data from structured tests, in particular the 16 Personality Factor Inventory (16 P.F.) developed by Cattell. Jim completed both forms (A and B) of the 16 P.F. His profiles for each of these forms and for the composite of the two forms are given in Figure 15.2. First, notice that although in most cases the scores on Form A and Form B are quite close, in a number of cases they are quite different (e.g., A,B,C,N,Q_2). The following brief descriptions of Jim's personality were written by a psychologist who assessed the results of the 16 P.F. but was unaware of any of the other data on Jim.

Form A

Jim appears as a very bright yet conflicted young man who is easily upset and quite insecure. His profile indicates he is somewhat cynical and introspective. His identity confusion is shown by the fact that he appears to be outgoing while he feels shy and restrained, and he evades responsibilities and obligations and then experiences the consequent guilt, anxiety, and depression.

Form B

Jim presents himself as a very outgoing young man who is really quite shy, approval-seeking, dependent, and tense. Brighter than average, he is quite confused about who he is and where he is

16 P. F. test profile

A + B =
A =
B =

Standard ten score (Sten)

Factor	Raw score Form A	Raw score Form B	Raw score Total	Standard score	Low score description	Sten (1–10)	High score description
A	12	15	30	9	Reserved, detached, critical, cool (sizothymia)		Outgoing, warmhearted, easy-going, participating (affectothymia, formerly cyclothymia)
B	13	10	23	10	Less intelligent, concrete-thinking (lower scholastic mental capacity)		More intelligent, abstract-thinking, bright (higher scholastic mental capacity)
C	7	12	19	2	Affected by feelings, emotionally less stable, easily upset (lower ego strength)		Emotionally stable, faces reality, calm, mature (higher ego strength)
E	18	11	29	7	Humble, mild, accommodating, conforming (submissiveness)		Assertive, independent, aggressive, stubborn (dominance)
F	15	15	30	5	Sober, prudent, serious, taciturn (desurgency)		Happy-go-lucky, impulsively lively, gay, enthusiastic (surgency)
G	11	14	25	5	Expedient, evades rules, feels few obligations (weaker superego strength)		Conscientious, persevering, staid, rule-bound (stronger superego strength)
H	10	7	17	4	Shy, restrained, diffident, timid (threctia)		Venturesome, socially bold, uninhibited, spontaneous (parmia)
I	12	14	26	8	Tough-minded, self-reliant, realistic, no-nonsense (harria)		Tender-minded, dependent, over-protected, sensitive (premsia)

				Left pole	Right pole
L	13	9	22	7	Trusting, adaptable, free of jealousy, easy to get on with (alaxia)	Suspicious, self-opinionated, hard to fool (protension)
M	16	14	30	8	Practical, careful, conventional, regulated by external realities, proper (praxernia)	Imaginative, wrapped up in inner urgencies, careless of practical matters, bohemian (autia)
N	10	14	24	7	Forthright, natural, artless, sentimental (artlessness)	Shrewd, calculating, worldly, penetrating (shrewdness)
O	14	18	32	8	Placid, self-assured, confident, serene (untroubled adequacy)	Apprehensive, worrying, depressive, troubled (guilt proneness)
Q_1	12	10	22	7	Conservative, respecting established ideas, tolerant of traditional difficulties (conservatism)	Experimenting, critical, liberal, analytical, free-thinking (radicalism)
Q_2	12	5	17	4	Group-dependent, a "joiner" and sound follower (group adherence)	Self-sufficient, prefers own decisions, resourceful (self-sufficiency)
Q_3	0	7	7	1	Undisciplined, self-conflict, follows own urges, careless of protocol (low integration)	Controlled, socially-precise, following self-image (high self-concept control)
Q_4	15	19	34	8	Relaxed, tranquil, torpid, unfrustrated (low ergic tension)	Tense, frustrated, driven, overwrought (high ergic tension)

A sten of 1 2 3 4 5 6 7 8 9 10 is obtained
by about 2.3% 4.4% 9.2% 15.0% 19.1% 19.1% 15.0% 9.2% 4.4% 2.3% of adults

FIGURE 15.2 16 P.F. Test Profile of Jim. (16 P.F., Forms A and B. Copyright © 1956, 1957, 1961, 1962, Institute for Personality and Ability Testing. 1602–04 Coronado Drive, Champaign, Illinois, U.S.A. All property rights reserved. Printed in U.S.A.)

going. His profile indicates that Jim is shrewd, introspective, tends to be overly sensitive, and pays for his impulsivity with guilt and depression.

Composite forms A and B
Jim presents himself as a very bright and outgoing young man although he is insecure, easily upset, and somewhat dependent. Less assertive, conscientious, and venturesome than he may initially appear, Jim is confused and conflicted about who he is and where he is going, tends toward introspection, and is quite anxious. His profile suggests that he may experience periodic mood swings and may also have a history of psychosomatic complaints.

Since the 16 P.F. has been administered to college students throughout the country, we can compare Jim with the average college student. Compared to other students, Jim is higher on the following traits: outgoing, intelligent, affected by feelings – easily upset, sensitivity, depression, poor self-sentiment, anxiety.

Let us turn to the factor-analytic method in an effort to reduce the number of traits necessary to describe Jim's personality. Four second-order factors have been derived from the sixteen first-order factors: Low Anxiety–High Anxiety, Introversion–Extroversion, Tenderminded Emotionality–Alert Poise, and Subduedness (group-dependent, passive)–Independence. Jim's scores are extreme on two of these factors. First, Jim is extremely high on anxiety. This suggests that he is dissatisfied with the degree to which he is able to meet the demands of life and to achieve what he desires. The high level of anxiety also suggests the possibility of physical disturbances. Second, Jim is very low on alert poise or, conversely, he is high on tenderminded emotionality. This suggests that he is not an enterprising and decisive personality. Instead, it is suggested that Jim is troubled by emotionality and often becomes discouraged and frustrated. Although sensitive to the subtleties of life, this sensitivity sometimes leads to preoccupation and to too much thought before he takes action. Jim's other two scores indicate that he is neither introverted nor extroverted and is neither excessively dependent nor independent. The outstanding characteristics are the anxiety, the sensitivity, and the emotionality.

Before we leave the 16 P.F., it should be noted that two important features came out in sharper focus on this test than on any of the other assessment devices. The first is the frequency of mood swings in Jim. In reading over the results on the 16 P.F. Jim stated that he has frequent and extreme mood swings, ranging from feeling very happy to feeling very depressed. During the latter periods, he tends to take his feelings out on others and becomes hostile to them in a sarcastic, "biting," or "cutting" way. The second feature of importance concerns psychosomatic complaints. As we mentioned previously, Jim has had considerable difficulty with an ulcer and frequently must drink milk for the condition. Notice that, although this is a serious condition that gives him considerable trouble, Jim did not mention it at all in his autobiography.

From the data on the 16 P.F. we can discern many important parts of Jim's personality. The concept of trait, expressing a broad reaction tendency and relatively permanent features of behavior, appears to be a useful one for the description of personality. We learn from the 16 P.F. that, although Jim is outgoing, he is basically shy and inhibited. Again, the characteristic of being anxious, frustrated, and conflicted comes through. But one is left wondering whether sixteen dimensions are adequate for the description of personality, particularly when these can be reduced further to four dimensions. One also wonders whether a score in the middle of the scale means that the trait is not an important one for the individual or simply that he is not extreme on that characteristic. The latter appears to be the case. Yet, when one writes up a personality description based on the results of the 16 P.F., the major emphasis tends to fall on scales with extreme scores.

Perhaps most serious, however, is the fact that Cattell has failed to retain the virtues of the clinician in spite of his efforts to do so. The results of the 16 P.F. have the strengths and limitations of being a trait description of personality. The results are descriptive, but they are not interpretive or dynamic. Although Cattell has attempted to deal with the individual as a whole, the results of the 16 P.F. leave one with only a pattern of scores—not a whole individual. Although the theory takes into consideration the dynamic interplay among motives, the results of the 16 P.F. appear unrelated to this portion of the theory. Jim is described as being anxious and frustrated, but anxious about what and why frustrated? Why is Jim outgoing and shy? Why does he find it so hard to be decisive and enterprising? The theory recognizes the importance of conflict in the functioning of the individual, but the results of the 16 P.F. tell us nothing about the nature of Jim's conflicts and how he tries to handle them. As pointed out in Chapter 9, the factor traits appear to have some degree of validity, but they also tend to be abstract and to leave out the richness of personality found in data from other assessment devices.

JIM: FIVE YEARS LATER

The material on Jim presented so far was written at approximately the time of his graduation from college. Since this book was first published and then republished in a second edition, sufficient time had elapsed to bring discernible changes to Jim's life—to say nothing of the personality theories themselves. Here let us try to follow trends established on the basis of Jim's earlier test results and see whether current patterns of behavior follow from earlier patterns. In other words, let us attempt to assess how stable and consistent Jim had been in his personality functioning. In noting and attempting to account for significant changes, we can ask about earlier hints of potential change and about the role of changes in environmental events. We can also ask about which theories facilitated our understanding of Jim at the time of graduation and which facilitate our understanding of his functioning during the period of time since then.

Five years after graduation Jim was contacted and asked to (1) indicate whether there had been significant life experiences for him since graduation and, if so, to describe how they had affected him and (2) give a brief description of his personality and to describe the ways, if any, in which he had changed since graduation. His response in each of these two areas should help us answer some of the questions raised above.

LIFE EXPERIENCES — AS TOLD BY JIM

After leaving Harvard, I entered business school. I only got into one graduate school in psychology; it was not particularly prestigious, whereas I got into a number of excellent business schools, and so on that basis I chose to go to business school. I did not really enjoy business school, though it was not terribly noxious either, but it was clear to me that my interest really was in the field of psychology, so I applied to a couple of schools during the academic year, but did not get in. I had a job in a New York import–export firm over the summer, and disliked it intensely enough to once more write to graduate schools over the summer. I was accepted at two, and then went into a very difficult decision-making process. My parents explicitly wanted me to return to business school, but I eventually decided to try graduate school. My ability to make that decision in the face of parental opposition was very significant for me; it asserted my strength and independence as nothing else in my life ever had.

Going through graduate school in the Midwest in clinical psychology was extremely significant for me. I have a keen professional identification as a clinician which is quite central to my self-concept. I have a system of thinking which is well-grounded and very central to the way I deal with my environment. I am entirely pleased with the decision I made, even though I still toy with the idea of returning to business school. Even if I do it, it would be to attain an adjunct degree; it would not change the fact that my primary identification is with psychology. I also fell in love during my first year in graduate school, for the first and only time in my life. The relationship did not work out, which was devastating to me, and I've not gotten completely over it yet. Despite the pain, however, it was a life-infusing experience.

Last year I lived in a communal setting and it was a watershed experience for me. We worked a lot on ourselves and each other during the year, in our formal once-a-week groups and informally at any time, and it was a frequently painful, frequently joyful, and always a growth-producing experience. I am convinced that I would like to live communally as my basic style of life, though I need a very special group of people to do it with and would rather live alone or with one or two other people than with just any group. Our group is thinking about getting together again in a more permanent arrangement, and I may very well decide to live with them again beginning next year. Whether or not this happens, last year's experience was very significant for me, and therapeutic in every respect.

Toward the end of last year, I began a relationship which has now become primary for me. I am living with a woman, Kathy, who is in a master's program in social work. She has been married twice. It is a sober relationship with problems involved; basically, there are some things about her that I am not comfortable with. I do not feel "in love" at this point, but there are a great many things about her that I like and appreciate, and so I am remaining in the relationship to see what develops, and how I feel about continuing to be with her. I have no plans to get married, nor much immediate interest in doing so. The relationship does not have the passionate feeling that my other significant relationship had, and I am presently trying to work through how much of my feeling at that time was idealization and how much real, and whether my more sober feelings for Kathy indicate that she's not the right woman for me or whether I need to come to grips with the fact that no woman is going to be "perfect" for me. In any event, my relationship with Kathy also feels like a wonderful growth-producing experience, and is the most significant life experience I am currently involved in.

I think these constitute my significant life experiences since leaving Harvard.

BRIEF PERSONALITY DESCRIPTION AND CHANGES—AS TOLD BY JIM

I do not think I've changed in very basic ways since leaving college. As a result of going into psychology, I think of myself as somewhat more self-aware these days, which I think is helpful. As I remember your interpretation of the tests I took back then, you saw me as primarily depressive. At this point, however, I think of myself as being primarily obsessive. I think I am prone to depression, but on balance see myself as happier these days—less frequently depressed. I see my obsessiveness as a deeply engrained characterological pattern, and have been thinking for some time now about going into analysis to work on it (amongst other things, of course). Though I consider my thinking about this serious, I am not yet very close to actually doing it. This is at least in part because I expect to be leaving Michigan at the end of this academic year, and so entering analysis at this point obviously makes no sense. On the other hand, it's a frightening proposition requiring a serious commitment, so there is some resistance to overcome over and above the geographic issue. Nevertheless, I see it as a definite possibility for myself in the next couple of years.

Let me say a word about my history with psychotherapy as a patient. I have made a number of abortive efforts to become involved, only one of which was even moderately successful. I saw someone at college a handful of times, but as I remember it, it was very superficial in every sense. I did nothing my year at business school. During my first year in graduate school, I saw an analytically oriented psychiatrist for three "evaluative sessions," after which he recommended: (1) analysis; (2) group therapy; (3) analytically oriented individual therapy. I was not ready to enter either analysis or a group, and did not want to continue with what he considered a third alternative, so I stopped. My second year in graduate school, I saw an analytically oriented psychiatrist for between six and eight sessions, but became very frustrated with his giving me so little, so that when he recommended increasing the frequency of visits from once to twice a week, I terminated. A big issue for me was how good a therapist he was: I saw him as pretty average, and felt I wanted someone special. This is clearly a form of resistance, I know, though I still feel there was some reality to my impressions of him. During my third year in graduate school, I saw a non-traditional psychiatrist about ten times. He used a mixed bag of techniques: cathartic, gestalt, behavioral, and generally folksy and friendly (very anti-analytic). At the end of our relationship, which I thought was somewhat useful at the time, we both felt I'd had enough therapy, and that what I needed were "therapeutic" life experiences: e.g., a relationship with a woman, some time to play, etc. Since then I have had some important therapeutic life experiences, the most significant of which was living in the house I lived in last year. As a result, I feel less immediate pressure to get help, and think of going into analysis to work through basis characterological issues (like my obsessiveness). In other words, I feel in less acute pain these days.

As I said previously, I see myself as more similar to, than different from, the way I was five years ago. I think of myself as a witty, aware, interesting and fun-loving person. I continue to be quite moody, so sometimes none of these characteristics is in evidence at all. My sexual relationship with my girlfriend has put to rest my concern about my sexual adequacy (especially about premature ejaculation).

I still see myself as having an "authority" issue — i.e., being quite sensitive and vulnerable to the way in which those who have authority over me treat me. However, I see myself as having a number of important professional skills, and as being in the field I want to be in. I still have money issues — i.e., I am concerned about being paid fairly for what I do, I resent psychiatrists making more than me, I am vigilant around making sure I am not "ripped off," etc. I still have not fully come to grips with my father having money, and the fact that I will be getting some of that, but on the other hand I'm not terribly concerned about it, and it feels more like an intellectualized concern about the future than an emotional concern in the present. I am extremely compulsive, I very efficiently get done what needs to be done, and experience considerable anxiety when I am not on top of things. My life must be very well ordered for it to be possible for me to relax and enjoy myself. Unfortunately, the compulsiveness spills over into my personal life, so that my room must be orderly, my books stacked appropriately, etc., or else I experience anxiety. Again, this feels like a deeply engrained pattern which would not be easy to overcome.

JIM: TWENTY YEARS LATER

Jim is now nearing forty, practicing as a consulting psychologist in a medium-sized city on the west coast, and has just become the father of a baby boy. At this time he agreed to be assessed from a social-cognitive, information-processing point of view and to share his reflections on the assessment of twenty years ago and life changes since then.

Social Cognitive and Information-Processing Approaches

Twenty years ago Jim was assessed from a variety of theoretical points of view — psychoanalytic, phenomenological, personal construct, and trait. At the time, current cognitive approaches to theory and assessment had not yet emerged and thus he was not considered from this standpoint. It is possible now, however, to consider him from this standpoint as well, though of course comparisons with earlier data may be problematic because of the time lapse. In the last four chapters we have considered a variety of personality variables emphasized by cognitive personality psychologists — cognitive skills and competencies, self-efficacy beliefs, subjective values (reinforcers), attributions and dysfunctional thoughts, coping methods, and goals. An effort was made to assess Jim within each of these areas of personality functioning. Both interview procedures and questionnaires developed within this framework were used.

Competencies and self-efficacy beliefs

Jim was asked about his competencies or skills, both intellectual and social. In the intellectual area he reported that he considered himself to be very bright and functioned at a very high intellectual level. He felt that he didn't have any real intellectual deficiencies though he distinguished between tight, logical thinking and loose, creative thinking, and felt that he was somewhat weak in the latter. Similarly, he felt that he writes well from the standpoint of a clear, organized presentation but he had not written anything that was innovative or creative.

In the social area, Jim felt that he was very skilled: "I do it naturally, easily, well. I can pull off anything and have a lot of confidence in myself socially. If I was meeting with President Reagan tomorrow I could do it easily. I am at ease with both men and women, in both professional and social contexts." The one social concern noted was his constant struggle with "how egocentric I should be, how personally to take things." He felt that sometimes he took things too personally. For example, he often feels hurt, offended, and disappointed if someone doesn't call him, wondering why they don't care about him and whether he's done something to offend them. He related this to the time he lived in a commune when he would nightly go over a checklist of people in the commune and how he was doing with each of them: "My security is based on how I'm doing with others. I put a lot of energy into friendships and when I'm relating well I feel good."

In terms of self-efficacy beliefs, it is clear that Jim has many positive views of himself. He believes that he does most things well—he is a good athlete, a competent consultant, bright, and socially skilled. Are there areas of low self-efficacy? Jim mentioned three such areas. First, he feels that he is not genuinely accepting of his love partner. He tends to be critical of others generally and of his primary partner in particular. Related to this is the second area mentioned, a difficulty in "getting out of myself so that I can be genuinely devoted to others." He is particularly concerned about this in relation to whether he will be able to maintain the kind of parental interest and commitment that he would like. This is a high priority for him but he is concerned that he will not want to be inconvenienced or put out by the new addition to the household. Finally, the third area of low self-efficacy concerned creativity: "I know I'm not good at being creative so I don't try it."

Whereas Bandura emphasizes the situation-specific aspects of self-efficacy beliefs, Jim felt that these represented fairly broad, consistent areas of high and low self-efficacy and could not pick out more specific situations expressive of his beliefs in this area.

Subjective values—Reinforcers

Jim was asked about the positive and aversive reinforcers, things he found rewarding and things he found unpleasant, that were important to him. Concerning positive reinforcers, he reported that money was "a biggie." In addition he emphasized time with loved ones, the glamor of going to an opening night, and generally going to the theater or movies. He had a difficult time thinking of negative reinforcers. He described writing as a struggle and then noted "I'm having trouble with this." I mentioned his concerns about rejection and he responded: "Oh, to be sure. I agree. Somehow I'm blanking. I think there's more there but I don't know."

Jim was asked about specific or general beliefs he held. He noted that he believed in hard work, earning things, and being responsible for what one does. He believes that some people are natural winners and others are losers, the former making life easy for themselves and the latter making life difficult for themselves. Generally he feels that he likes life the easy way and enjoys being a winner. Other beliefs about himself are that he is intelligent, hard-working, personable, humorous, needy of approval, and possessive of a depressive streak. Ideally he would like to be more selfless and generous, take setbacks more easily, and able to relax more. In terms of generalized expectancies, the *Life Orientation Test* (Scheier & Carver, 1985) was given to Jim as a measure of generalized optimism–pessimism. His responses indicated a strong pessimistic orientation that fits with his depressive streak. For example, he strongly disagreed with the statements "I'm a believer in the idea that 'every cloud has a silver lining'" and "I'm always optimistic about my future." In contrast to these statements, he strongly disagreed with the statement "I hardly ever expect things to go my way," which probably reflects his strong belief that control is possible and desirable. Thus, he had an extremely high score on the *Desirability of Control Scale* (Burger & Cooper, 1979).

Jim gave the following as categories he used to view the world: successful–not successful, wealthy–not wealthy, attractive–not attractive, bright–not bright, interesting–not interesting, kind and loving–unloving, patient–impatient, generous–not generous, deep–shallow. In terms of attributions, he again emphasized his belief in control and responsibility as opposed to belief in luck, chance, or fate. Jim filled out the *Attributional Style Questionnaire* and his responses reflected a general tendency toward internal, stable, and global attributions. Such an attributional style would fit with his tendency toward depressive streaks and belief in the desirability of control. However, an analysis of the subsections of this questionnaire reveals that this pattern holds more for positive events than for negative events. In particular, his internal and stable attributions tend to be much more true for positive events than for negative events. Thus, his belief that positive events can be controlled by his own efforts and can remain stable, reflected in the generalized expectancy that things can work out the way he wants them to, probably helps him to be less depressed than might otherwise be the case. In addition, his responses indicate a greater internal attribution for interpersonal events than for events having to do with professional achievement.

Finally, let us consider the area of irrational beliefs, dysfunctional thoughts, and cognitive distortions. One important point here is what Jim describes as his tendency to overpersonalize: "This is a problem of mine. If someone doesn't call I attribute it to a feeling state in relation to me. I can feel terribly injured at times." Although he could not come up with any irrational beliefs or dysfunctional thoughts in the interview, his responses to the *Automatic Thoughts Questionnaire* (Hollon & Kendall, 1980) shed some light on this area of his functioning. He reported having the following thoughts frequently: "I've let people down," "I wish I were a better person," "I'm disappointed in myself," and "I can't stand this." These frequent thoughts have to do with his not being as loving or generous as he would like, his being very demanding of himself professionally and in athletics, his obsession about things that might go wrong, and his intolerance of things not going his way. For example, he cannot stand to be in traffic and will say: "I can't stand this. This is intolerable." Although Jim does not think much of Ellis' work and in the interview suggested that he didn't have many irrational beliefs, on the questionnaire he checked four out of nine items as frequent thoughts of his: "I must have love or approval," "When people act badly, I blame them," "I tend to view it as a catastrophe when I get seriously frustrated or feel rejected," and "I tend to get preoccupied with things that seem fearsome." He also described his tendency to make it a catastrophe if he is going to be late for a movie: "It's a calamity if I'm going to be one minute late. It becomes a life and death emergency. I go through red lights, honk the horn, and pound on the wheel." This is in contrast to his own tendency to be at least a few minutes late for virtually all appointments, though rarely is he more than a few minutes late.

Coping methods

When asked about his coping methods, Jim responded: "Heavy duty compulsivity. It's part of my character, in everything—clean ash trays in the car, the bed made in the morning, everything in the apartment in place. Order is very important. It's pervasive. Also intellectualization and humor." Jim also filled out the *Ways of Coping Scale* (Folkman, Lazarus, & Gruen, 1986). His responses to this scale indicate that his primary modes of coping with stressful events are to accept responsibility ("Criticize or lecture myself," "Realize I brought the problem on myself") and to engage in planful problem solving ("Just concentrated on what I had to do next," "Draw on my past experiences; I was in a similar position before"). In general he tends to remain self-controlled and think about the problem rather than use escape–avoidance methods, engage in risky solutions, or seek social support and sympathy from others. The latter reflects his not being terribly forgiving of himself for getting into difficulty. Although there would appear to be some positive aspects to his coping, other responses indicate that he feels that he does not change or grow as a person as a result of these coping methods.

Goals

Jim was asked about his goals for the immediate future and for the long-range future. He felt that his immediate and long-term goals were pretty much the same: (1) getting to know his son and being a good parent; (2) becoming more accepting and less critical of his wife and others; and (3) feeling good about his professional work as a consultant. Generally he feels that there is a good chance of achieving these goals but he is guarded in that estimate, with some uncertainty about just how much he will be able to "get out of myself" and thereby be more able to give to his wife and child.

Summary

What, then, can be said about Jim from a social cognitive, information-processing point of view? In general Jim has a strong sense of self-efficacy in relation to intellectual and social skills, though he feels less efficacious in relation to creative thought and the ability to be loving, generous, and giving to people who are dear to him. He values money and financial success but has settled more on family intimacy and the quality of his work as a consultant as goals for the future. He has a strong sense of individual responsibility and belief in personal control over events. His attributions tend to be internal, stable, and global and there is a streak of pessimism and depression to him. He is bothered by concerns about the approval of others, by his perfectionism and impatience, and by a tendency to worry about things. He tends to be planful and self-controlled in coping with stress rather than avoiding problems or escaping from them. Generally he sees himself as a competent person and is guardedly optimistic about his chances of achieving his goals in the future.

Changes over Time, Views of the Approaches

The most important events over the past years for Jim have been his marriage, the birth of a child, and the stabilization of a professional identity. Prior to his marriage he was involved in lengthy relationships with two women. Though they were very different from one another, he found himself critical and discontented with each. He met his current wife about four years ago. He describes her as calm and peaceful, with a good sense of perspective on life. Although she is somewhat like one of the earlier women, he feels that he has changed in a way that makes a lasting relationship more possible: "I have a greater capacity for acceptance of the other and a clearer sense of boundaries between me and others — she is she and I am I. And, she accepts me, foibles and all."

Jim feels that he has made progress in what he calls "getting out of myself," but feels that his narcissism remains an important issue: "I'm selectively perfectionistic with myself, unforgiving of myself. If I lose money I punish myself. As a teenager I lost twenty dollars and went without lunches all summer long. I didn't need the money. My family has plenty of it. But what I did was unforgiveable. Is it perfectionistic or compulsive? I push myself all the time. I must read the newspaper thoroughly seven days a week. I feel imprisoned by it a lot of the time.

Can I give up these rituals and self-indulgences with the birth of a child? I must."

Jim read over the earlier assessment results and personality sketches and gave his impressions of them and changes in him. In relation to the psychoanalytic data, he felt that it did a good job of pointing up his compulsive and intellectual defenses and made sense as a picture of him at that time. However, he felt that was a time of considerable insecurity. He had gone from being a star in high shcool to an average person in a select college, with few meaningful relationships with women. Since then he feels that he has come a long way in his relations with women and sense of confidence in himself in that regard. The problems with uncertainty and being creative clearly remain. Although Jim did not mention the Count Dracula and vampire responses on the Rorschach, it is interesting that during much of the interview he bit on a plastic disk.

In relation to the phenomenological description, he noted that he felt he had changed considerably, becoming more expressive of warmth. Although still inhibited at times, this is true of him over a much narrower range of situations than was previously the case. He felt that many similarities to his father continue, but that he has now become more aware of similarities to his mother. Generally he feels that he has a less constricted view of the world than was represented on the Rep test, but that it presented an accurate picture of him at the time. Whereas he used few constructs in his relations with people at the time, and was very focused on how bright people were, he now takes a broader, more differentiated view of people.

As with the other approaches, he felt that the trait approach captured a part of him that was present at the time, and in relation to which there have been some changes. He feels he was more insecure twenty years ago than now, though he still has concerns about being liked and still has mood swings. Also, he still has difficulty in letting go of the issue of success.

What of the cognitive approach considered at this time? As a psychologist Jim was somewhat aware of this general orientation, but he was not very familiar with it. Thus, in a sense, this was a professional learning experience for him. At the same time, it should be noted that he came to the material with a mixed psychodynamic and humanist slant. Thus, he said of the cognitive, information-processing approach: "It picked up some interesting things but we're not cut from the same cloth. There's something valuable in it but I don't see it as a whole approach. It captures a part of the truth, a part of me, but somehow it seems like a denuded frame of reference. It misses some of the power and drama of life."

In the most general terms, we can see that over the years Jim has become more secure, more socially at ease, more expressive, and more differentiated in his views of the world. These are important gains. At the same time, he continues to have obsessive and compulsive characteristics, to struggle with his feelings toward his primary partner, to be sensitive to rejection, and to be bothered by mood swings and pessimism. Generally he is a happier person and optimistic about the future, though clearly he retains some personality features and concerns he had twenty years ago.

His overall view of the alternative approaches? In general Jim felt that the various approaches captured different aspects of him, highlighting different aspects of his personality while picking up some consistent themes. In addition, he commented that he felt that different approaches to therapy could be useful with different people or as different ways of gaining access to people.

PERSONALITY THEORY AND ASSESSMENT DATA: THE CASE OF JIM

By presenting the case of Jim we have been able to review the data gathered from a variety of assessment techniques. The attempt here has not been to learn all about any one instrument or to prove the validity of one or another instrument but to explore the personality of a single individual through the use of a variety of assessment devices and to compare the impressions gained from these devices. Our goal is further to appreciate differences in personality theories as they relate to the different kinds of data on which the theories are based.

What of the data that we have available to us? Clearly, there are important similarities but also significant differences. We began with the data from the projectives (Rorschach, TAT) and then moved to consideration of some phenomenological data (autobiography, semantic differential). How does what we have learned from one set of data compare with what we have learned from another set? The Rorschach suggested tension and anxiety behind a façade of poise. The semantic differential suggested tension and anxiety but not a façade of tact and poise. The projectives suggested considerable difficulty with women and a conflict between sexual preoccupation and hostility. The data were far less clear in the semantic differential, although we did observe what appears to be an ambivalent attitude toward his mother. There is some further suggestion of this in the autobiography, along with some defensiveness. "My relationship with my mother is superficial but mutually satisfactory. There is no depth of understanding on her part—she wants me to succeed in a very conventional way. I understand her for what she is—a loving, lovable woman. I hope this doesn't sound like I look down on her, because I respect her very much."

Although the projectives clearly suggest some confusion in sexual identity, the ratings on the semantic differential indicate that Jim perceives himself to be masculine and more identified with his father than with this mother. In his autobiography he writes: "My father and I have achieved a great deal more rapport. I have great, almost unlimited respect for him and I think he feels the same toward me. . . . I am much more like my father than my mother." Also, the semantic differential data indicate that Jim perceives himself to be weak and somewhat passive whereas the father and ideal self are perceived to be strong and active. In relation to the parents, one is tempted to ask why Jim was not able to identify with the warm, outgoing aspects of his mother or with the strong, active aspects of his father.

There is evidence in both the projectives and semantic differential of a lack of warmth in interpersonal relationships. However, what is clear is that percepts such as vampires and Count Dracula sucking blood do not appear on the semantic differential. These data, which have a clear primitive, oral quality to them, cannot be obtained from the semantic differential. In addition, the projectives gave far less suggestion of an individual who perceives himself as being deep, sensitive, kind, thoughtful, and basically good. Perhaps it is out of fear of expressing hostility that Jim remains inhibited. Perhaps he also confuses activity and assertiveness with hostility and thereby feels unable to be a strong man. In any case, he often is unable to be what he *feels*. This is something that is basic to Rogerian theory and is well expressed by Jim in the conclusion of his autobiography: "All in all, there is a great chasm between my intellectual and emotional estimates of myself, and I think this chasm must be closed before I can reach some kind of peace with myself."

The data from the semantic differential and the autobiography are not inconsistent with those from the projectives, but they are different. In both cases, there are expressions of anxiety and problems of warmth in interpersonal relationships. However, whereas in the projectives there are expressions of sadism and confusion in sexual identity, in the autobiography and semantic differential there are expressions of an individual who is not quite what he would like to be and who feels that he is not free to be himself. Thus he cannot be at peace with himself.

The data from the Kelly Rep test and from the Cattell 16 P.F. continue to tell the story of information obtained from other assessment devices that is not inconsistent with previous data and theoretical interpretations but is distinct and different from them. The trait of anxiety appears on the 16 P.F., and on the Kelly Rep test the construct insecurity was associated with the self. Similarly, both the 16 P.F. and the Rep test data suggest problems in interpersonal relationships. The projectives and semantic differential suggested a difficulty in being uninhibited with people or becoming involved. On the Rep test, Jim indicated that constructs such as Gives Love–Self-oriented, Sensitive–Insensitive, and Interested in People–Uninterested in People are important to him in interpreting his environment. The meaning of the construct Sensitive–Insensitive may be particularly critical since, in reading over the results of the 16 P.F., Jim noted that the reference to his being overly sensitive was fundamental to understanding his personality.

The use of the term *sensitive* is ambiguous. One can be a sensitive person in terms of being sensitive to the feelings and needs of others. This kind of sensitivity would suggest an empathic and warm individual. One can also be sensitive to art and music, which may or may not be related to an interpersonal, empathic sensitivity. Finally, one can be sensitive to others in terms of being dependent on them. Thus the individual who is buoyed by compliments and depressed by criticism is sensitive to others. Or the individual who is always searching to find out whether he has hurt someone's feelings may be viewed as sensitive to others. This type of sensitivity involves a concern with others but is not expressive of warmth. This distinction is of interest in relation to Jim's high score on the Tender-minded–Emotionality factor. The score suggests that Jim is easily discouraged and frustrated, sensitive to the subtleties of life, and often thinks too much. The score suggests that Jim is sensitive to people in that he is concerned with them but not necessarily that he is a warm individual. This helps us to understand how a "sensitive" individual can show signs of rigidity and inhibition on the projectives and on the 16 P.F. and still construe himself as being warm on the semantic differential and the Rep test.

The data from the social cognitive, information-processing approach helped to highlight Jim's cognitive world and ways in which he has changed as well as remained the same. These data allowed us to see Jim as someone with strong self-efficacy beliefs in the intellectual and social areas, though he is less creative and less generous and loving with his primary partner than he would like to be. His internal attributions fit with his belief in individual responsibility and desire for control. They also fit with a pessimistic–depressive streak that is tempered, however, by his attributions being even more internal for positive events than for negative events. His dysfunctional thoughts involve a need for approval, perfectionism, and impatience. He copes with stress through planful problem solving, self-control, and thought. His goals involve increased closeness to his wife and child and continued growth as a psychologist. These data tell us much about him, though Jim reports that the picture that emerges from them seems to lack a sense of vitality and life—it seems "denuded."

Concluding Comments

What, then, is the value of these comparisons of data from different tests of Jim? The attempt here has been to demonstrate, in an individual case, a theme that has been repeated throughout this book: Different theories of personality are based on different sets of observations and in turn lead to the investigation of different phenomena. Is Jim a Dracula, a person unable to be what he feels, a person "hung-up" on security and warmth, a person characterized by the scores on sixteen factor scales, or a respondent to reinforcers in the environment? Is Jim fixated at a pregenital stage of development, limited in his efforts toward self-actualization, limited by a constricted construct system, or inhibited in his responses by fears of failure and rejection by others? There is evidence that he is each of these, but also evidence that he is more than any one of them. Because of the nature of the theories and the data gained in relation to each, at various points Jim appears to be one more than the other. As Kelly (1963) has observed, the bias of the investigator influences the behavior he will look at, the observations he will be sensitive to, the questions he will ask, and how important he feels it is to report various kinds of data.

At the beginning of this chapter we asked: Are the observations obtained similar when techniques of assessment associated with the different theories are applied to the same individual? I think the answer is that the observations obtained are different in striking and important ways, but they are not inconsistent with one another. To conclude that one knows Jim or understands his personality from just one set of observations would undoubtedly put one in the same position as the blind man who examined a small portion of the elephant and was led to a wrong conclusion on the basis of his limited observations. In part the data suggest that at times the theories talk about the same phenomena in different terms. However, the data also strongly suggest that each set of observations and each theory represents an incomplete picture of the whole individual. In a certain sense, each represents a glimpse of the total complexity of human personality.

What is needed in the future is the study of the same individuals by psychologists of different orientations. In Kelly's terms, this would permit us to assess the likeness and differences of personality theories and to determine each one's range and focus of convenience.

Chapter Sixteen
An Overview of Personality Theory, Assessment, and Research

CHAPTER FOCUS: In this chapter we return to some of the major points covered in this book and consider the different theories of personality in relation to them. Our goal is a deeper understanding of the issues and, through the process of contrast and comparison, a greater appreciation of the theories. First, there is a return to some of the issues that divide personality theorists. Second, there is an overview of the concepts emphasized by each theory as it attempts to explain the what, how, and why of human behavior. Finally, attention is again drawn to relationships among theory, assessment, and research. Throughout the emphasis is on recognizing the distinctive contributions each approach can make toward a more complete understanding of human behavior.

> *What theorists believe people to be influences which determinants and mechanisms of human functioning they explore most thoroughly and which they leave unexamined. . . . The view of human nature embodied by psychological theories is more than just a philosophical issue.*
>
> BANDURA, 1986, p. 1

This book has been an adventure into a greater understanding of why people behave as they do and how we may, in the future, proceed toward a clearer understanding of this behavior. The major focus has been on how different theories of personality conceptualize human behavior. There has been, as well, discussion of alternative approaches to assessment and research. Finally, we have considered relationships among types of theories, assessment techniques, and styles of conducting research; in other words, how different theories of personality may lead to the study of different aspects of personality functioning and the use of different means for gathering data. In this final chapter, let us take stock of some of the ground that has been covered and consider some of the issues that remain open.

A RETURN TO SOME ISSUES THAT DIVIDE PERSONALITY THEORISTS

In the first chapter we considered some issues that divide personality theorists. It was suggested that personality theorists repeatedly have confronted certain basic issues. Their solutions to these issues in part reflected their own life experiences as well as social and scientific trends current at the time of their work. Beyond this, it was suggested that theoretical positions on these issues affected which aspects of human functioning were chosen for investigation and how these aspects of human functioning were investigated. Let us briefly return to these issues in the light of previous study of the major theoretical orientations current today.

Philosophical View of the Person

We have seen that implicit in most theories of personality is a general, philosophical view of human nature. Periodically an article or book appears in the literature that addresses this issue in clear and forthright terms. For example, one distinguished psychologist recently called for an increased emphasis on a view of humans as active, selecting, choosing organisms as opposed to a view of humans as passive organisms responding in a mechanical way to stimuli: "Individuals create themselves . . . it is development we must study, but it is the development of the shaper rather than the shaped" (Tyler, 1978, pp. 233–234).

The theorists covered in this text present a diversity of views: Freud's view of the person as an energy system; Rogers' view of the person as a self-actualizing organism; Kelly's view of the person as a scientist; the Skinnerian view of the person as responding to environmental reinforcement contingencies; the cognitive, social learning view of the person as a problem-solving organism; the computer model of the person as a complex information processor. Of course, other views are possible—and within any single orientation, such as trait theory, different views can emerge. Furthermore, such labels or capsule descriptions fail to do justice to the complexity inherent in each view. At the same time, these capsule descriptions capture a distinctive element in each theoretical perspective and help to make us aware of the differing views that do exist. Of particular interest here is the emphasis on cognition found in so many recent theoretical developments (psychoanalytic ego psychology, cognitive social learning theory, and cognitive information-processing personality theory).

Each view of the organism opens up certain avenues of thought, research, and analysis. Each also potentially closes off other important lines of emphasis and investigation. The early S–R view of the person inhibited recognition of the importance of higher-order cognitive functions. The current cognitive emphasis may serve to correct this imbalance, but it may also lead us to ignore other important areas of experience such as motivation and emotion. The point here is not that one view is right or wrong but that such views exist and that it is important to be aware of them in understanding each theory as well as in assessing its strengths and limitations.

Internal and External Causes of Behavior

A second, related issue, is whether the causes of behavior are inside the person or in the environment. In Chapter 1, Freud and Skinner were contrasted as representing extreme positions on this issue. There was also discussion of how in recent years attention was first directed to *whether* behavior is caused by the "person" or the "situation," then to *how much* behavior was caused by person and situation factors, and finally to *how* person and situation factors interact with one another to determine behavior.

In the theories covered, this issue came out most clearly in relation to trait theory and social cognitive theory. At one extreme, trait theory has been characterized as suggesting that people are consistent or stable in their behavior over time and across situations. Psychoanalytic theory, with its similar emphasis on personality structure, has been seen as emphasizing internal causes of behavior and general stability in personality functioning. At the other extreme, learning theory has been characterized as emphasizing environmental determinants of behavior and the variability or situational specificity of behavior. Such characterizations are to some extent accurate and useful in highlighting important theoretical differences. At the same time, it should be clear that none of these theories emphasizes only one set of causes. To a certain extent, they are all interactionist in their emphasis; they all emphasize the interaction between individual and environment, or person and situation, in determining behavior. Trait theory, for example, does recognize the importance of situational factors in affecting which traits are activated as well as affecting the moods of the individual. It is inconceivable that a trait theorist or a psychoanalytic theorist would expect a person to behave the same way in all situations. On the other hand, social cognitive theory recognizes the importance of person factors in terms of concepts such as plans–goals, cognitive and behavioral competencies, self-efficacy, and self-regulation. Indeed, the concept of reciprocal determinism or the mutually causal relationship between person and situation is a cornerstone of social cognitive theory.

As with other issues in the field, emphasis often shifts in one direction or another—in this case in terms of relative emphasis on internal, person factors or on external, environmental factors. At one point considerable evidence was presented to suggest that human behavior is quite variable over time and across situations. Such evidence was used to challenge traditional trait and psychodynamic views of personality structure and personality dispositions (Mischel, 1968). More recently, evidence has been presented to suggest that human behavior is more consistent, both over time and across situations, than had been suggested previously (Epstein, 1983; Pervin, 1985). Such consistency does not seem to be explained by unchanged environmental circumstances. Indeed, we often are impressed with how resistant some behavior is to change despite dramatic changes in environmental circumstances. Thus, whereas at one point situational determinants were emphasized, many psychologists are again emphasizing dispositions or reaction tendencies within individuals.

Although important differences remain in the relative emphasis on internal (person) and external (situation) causes, all theories of personality recognize that both are important in understanding behavior. Perhaps we can now expect to find theorists who increasingly will address questions in terms of both sets of causes rather than with an almost exclusive emphasis on one or another set of causes. All personality theorists recognize that there is both consistency and variability to individual behavior. The task, then, is to account for the pattern of stability and change that characterizes people.

The Unity of Behavior and the Concept of the Self

There is movement in human organisms, as living systems, toward integrated functioning and the reduction of conflict. Personality theories differ in the extent to which they emphasize the patterned, unified, system aspects of human functioning and efforts toward the reduction of conflict. An emphasis on the unity of behavior may be seen to be greatest in the clinical theories of Freud, Rogers, and Kelly. With the exception of Allport, it is much less present in trait theories and learning theories. Why should this be? Undoubtedly the reasons are complex and varied, but a number of points can be considered. First, clinical theories are based on observations of many behaviors of a single individual. The theories of Freud, Rogers, and Kelly evolved out of these clinical observations. Their efforts were directed toward understanding relationships among thoughts, behaviors, and feelings. Almost of necessity, they were struck with the issues of conflict and threats to the coherence of the system as reported to them by their patients. Although clinical approaches based on learning theory exist and are important, they evolved out of theories rather than initially serving as the basis for them.

A second point to be considered is the emphasis in trait theories, at least those based on factor analysis, and in learning theories on the systematic exploration of particular variables. The belief here is that an understanding of human behavior can come through the systematic study of particular variables or processes and then consideration of complex relationships among variables and processes. The strategy is to study phenomena systematically and to build from the simple to the complex. Pattern and organization become important when one has a clear enough grasp of the parts that constitute the pattern or organization.

The concept of self traditionally has been used to give expression to the patterned, organized aspects of personality functioning. In psychoanalytic theory, the concept of ego gives expression to the person's self-experiencing as well as to the "executive" or integrative aspects of system functioning. Although sometimes portrayed as a person or homunculus inside the individual ("The ego seeks to reduce conflict"), it really is descriptive of processes going on within the person. For both Rogers and Kelly the concept of self played an important integrative function. For Rogers, the person seeks self-actualization and to make the self and experience congruent with one another. For Kelly, the constructs associated with the self and how they are organized play a central role in the person's functioning. The emphasis on the concept of self as an organizing entity is perhaps most clearly expressed in the view of Allport. The concept of self, or proprium as he called it, gave testimony to the complex, organized aspects of the mature human system.

In their efforts to avoid the vague, romantic, and fanciful, many theorists have avoided the concept of self. In particular, the self as a homunculus within the person that determines action has been criticized. Still, as we have witnessed, recent developments in social cognitive theory place heavy emphasis on the concept of self. This is a somewhat different concept of self, however, involving standards for self-praise and self-criticism as well as other self-regulatory functions. Nevertheless, it is a self concept. The concept of efficacy, or ability to perform the behavior necessary for certain outcomes, an increasingly important part of Bandura's theory, involves cognitions or beliefs about the self. It is seen as a broadly integrative concept that can account for diverse findings. Thus, at this point social cognitive theory also has come to emphasize both the organized aspects of the human personality and the importance of the self concept in such organization. Finally, the organizing and directing functions of self-schemata are clearly articulated in the cognitive information-processing view. Just as any complex system may have higher-order control units, so the self may be viewed as consisting of schemata or constructs that organize and integrate the functioning of other parts of the system. It is noteworthy, however, to again emphasize the view of a multiplicity or family of selves rather than a single, all-encompassing self-concept.

Although the utility and necessity of the concept of self continues to be debated, theories of personality appear to be drawn to it continuously. Interpretations of it clearly differ from theory to theory, and theories differ in their emphasis on it. At the same time, in one form or another, the concept of self enters into most theories and attests to the important ways in which we experience ourselves, to the myriad ways in which we understand ourselves, and to the organized aspects of our functioning.

Varying States of Awareness and the Concept of the Unconscious

Interest in varying states of awareness and altered states of consciousness has been increasing in psychology. This probably is due in part to interest in "mind-expanding" drugs during the 1960s and to the broader interest in brain functioning. Such phenomena are fascinating, yet they represent complex problems for theory, assessment, and research.

As noted at the outset, many theorists are uncomfortable with the concept of the unconscious as formulated by Freud. The notion of things "buried in the unconscious" or of "unconscious forces striving for expression" is too metaphorical for most systematic thinkers. Yet, if we accept the view that we are not always aware of factors affecting our behavior, how are we to conceptualize such phenomena? Is it merely that we do not attend to them and that focusing of our attention "brings them into awareness"? Is it the case, as some cognitive theorists suggest, that what others view as unconscious processes actually consist of rehearsed behaviors that flow automatically, that they consist of overlearned inhibited responses? In other words, is there no need to consider special processes and label them as unconscious; rather, can we say that we do not think of certain things because there are stronger responses inhibiting such thoughts?

As we have seen, both Rogers and Kelly avoided the concept of the unconscious. Instead, they emphasized concepts that involve aspects of the person's functioning that are not available to awareness. Rogers stated the view that experiences incongruent with the self concept may be distorted and/or denied. Threatening feelings may be unavailable to awareness but experienced through the process of subception. Kelly suggested that one or both poles of a construct may be submerged and unavailable to awareness. Each of these theories describes a defensive process resulting in important aspects of personality functioning being unavailable to awareness. Though learning theorists such as Dollard and Miller accepted such processes and attempted to interpret them within the framework of Hullian theory, other learning theorists reject such concepts as vague and unnecessary. Although initially expressing little interest in unconscious processes, cognitive theorists have recently been concerned with them — albeit not necessarily in the terms suggested by psychoanalytic theorists.

The problem of evaluating the importance of such phenomena and conceptualizing them continues to be with us. If much of our behavior is governed by reinforcements, both from within ourselves as well as from others, are we always aware of what these reinforcers are? If not, why not? Is it because some of them were learned in infancy, prior to the development of verbal labels? Is it because some are so much a part of our daily lives that we no longer attend to them? Or is it because often we "choose" not to be aware of things that make us anxious and uncomfortable? How much attention is paid to these phenomena and how they are interpreted continue to be important issues upon which theories of personality differ.

Relationships among Cognition, Affect, and Overt Behavior

As we have seen, personality theories differ in the attention given to cognitive, affective, and behavioral processes. Understanding the intricate relations among them remains a significant task. Although Freud emphasized cognitive and drive processes, he assigned a central role to affects in his conceptualization of human behavior. This is seen most clearly in relation to the affect of anxiety, but he and his followers also were concerned with other affects such as anger, depression, guilt, shame, jealousy, and so on. There is interest in overt behavior but only as an expression or manifestation of the workings of thought and drive processes. Rogers and Kelly both emphasized the person as an active construer of events, but for Rogers the "felt experience" was central, whereas for Kelly emotions followed from cognitive interpretations. The latter emphasis also is found in current attribution and other cognitive theories. In these theories cognitive properties are central and primary to feelings and overt behavior. Radical behaviorism, of course, focused exclusively on overt behavior. However, behavior therapists increasingly have become concerned with cognitive processes and, even more recently, with the influences of affective processes.

Historically, many issues in psychology initially get framed in either–or terms. Is it heredity or environment? Person or situation? Then there is debate about which is more important. Finally, there is recognition that the issues are more complex than "either–or" and "more important than" solutions. There is recognition that multiple factors enter into complex functioning, the individual factors contributing to a greater or lesser amount at different times and in different situations. The critical question then becomes one of understanding relationships among variables rather than choosing among them. Thus, the question becomes how heredity and environment interact and how person and situation variables mutually affect one another. In a similar vein, we are coming to understand that people are always thinking, feeling, and behaving and what remains to be understood is how these processes interact in the ongoing stream of human functioning.

Influences of the Past, Present, and Future on Behavior

When we think of Freud, we almost automatically think of behavior being governed by the past. When we think of Kelly, we think of the person as striving to anticipate the future. Prediction becomes the key to understanding behavior. Skinner's emphasis on past reinforcement contingencies can be contrasted with social cognitive theory's emphasis on expectancies. Is behavior regulated by the past or by our expectations of the future? Is there a difference between the two?

This is yet another issue that divides personality theorists. Often the differences among theorists are subtle but important in their implications. For example, Bandura's suggestion that past reinforcements are important for what has been *learned* but that expectancies about future reinforcement are important for what is *performed* is a subtle but important distinction. It involves not only the important distinction between the acquisition and the performance of behavior but also an important emphasis on cognitive functioning. In fact, there appears to be a close relationship between an emphasis on the future and an emphasis on cognitive processes. This is not surprising, since the development of higher mental processes and the capacity for language are necessary for an organism to be able to construct a future world.

In reality, of course, past events and our anticipation of future events affect one another as well as our experiences in the present. How we anticipate the future is inevitably linked to our past. However, it is probably also the case that how we view the future influences our construction of the past. For example, if we are depressed about the future we may feel bound by our past, whereas if we are optimistic about the future we may perceive the past as having been liberating. Our views of the past, present, and future are all parts of our experience. An understanding of the relationships among these views, then, becomes the task of each theory of personality.

PERSONALITY THEORY AS AN ANSWER TO THE QUESTIONS OF WHAT, HOW, AND WHY

In Chapter 1 it was stated that a theory of personality should answer the questions of *what, how,* and *why.* In the chapters in this text, the concepts and principles used by various theorists to account for human personality were considered. A summary of some of the major concepts relevant to each theory is given in Figure 16.1. At this point, let us review some of these concepts, consider the similarities among the theories, and raise some remaining questions.

Personality Structure

Each theory that has been studied here suggests concepts relevant to the structure of personality; each theory presents conceptual units that can be used to describe individuals. The theories differ not only in the content of these units but also in their level of abstraction and in the complexity of the structural organization. Freud's structural units are at a very high level of abstraction. One cannot observe an id, ego, or super-ego, or a conscious, preconscious, or unconscious. Somewhat less abstract are the structural units used by Rogers and Kelly. Many problems remain

THEORIST OR THEORY	STRUCTURE	PROCESS	GROWTH AND DEVELOPMENT
FREUD	Id, ego, superego; unconscious, preconscious, conscious.	Life and death instincts; anxiety and the mechanisms of defense.	Erogenous zones; oral, anal, phallic stages of development; Oedipus complex
ROGERS	Self; ideal self	Self-actualization; congruence of self and experience; incongruence and defensive distortion and denial.	Congruence and self-actualization versus incongruence and defensiveness
KELLY	Constructs	Processes channelized by anticipation of events	Increased complexity and definition to construct system
CATTELL	Traits	Dynamic traits; ergs; sentiments.	age trends
LEARNING THEORY	Response	Classical conditioning; instrumental conditioning; operant conditioning	Imitation; schedules of reinforcement and successive approximations
SOCIAL COGNITIVE THEORY	Expectancies; standards; goals-plans; self-efficacy beliefs	Observational learning; vicarious conditioning; symbolic processes, self-evaluative and self-regulatory processes (standards)	Social learning through observation and direct experience; development of self-efficacy judgments and standards for self-regulation
COGNITIVE, INFORMATION-PROCESSING THEORY	Cognitive categories and schemata; attributions; generalized expectancies	Information-processing strategies; attributions	Development of cognitive competencies, self-schemata, expectancies, attributions

FIGURE 16.1 Summary of Major Theoretical Concepts.

in current definitions of the self, but the definitions offered by Rogers do suggest some methods of systematic investigation. Similarly, although the defining properties of constructs need to be clarified further, a technique for assessing the construct system of an individual is available to us.

The structural units of Cattell vary in their level of abstraction, with source traits being more abstract than surface traits. At the lowest level of

PATHOLOGY	CHANGE	ILLUSTRATIVE CASE
Infantile sexuality; fixation and regression; conflict; symptoms	Transference; conflict resolution; "Where id was, ego shall be"	Little Hans
Defensive maintenance of self; incongruence	Therapeutic atmosphere: congruence, unconditional positive regard, empathic understanding	Mrs. Oak
Disordered functioning of construct system	Psychological reconstruction of life; invitational mood; fixed-role therapy.	Ronald Barrett
Heredity and environment; conflict; anxiety.	Change in trait structure.	Jim
Maladaptive learned response patterns	Extinction; discrimination learning; counter-conditioning; positive reinforcement; imitation; systematic desensitization; behavior modification	Peter; Reinterpretation of Little Hans
Learned response patterns; excessive self-standards; problems in self-efficacy	Modeling; guided participation; increased self-efficacy	Reinterpretation of bombardier case
Unrealistic or maladaptive beliefs; errors in information-processing	Cognitive therapy— changes in irrational beliefs, dysfunctional thoughts, and maladaptive attributions	Jim

abstraction is the major structural unit used by learning theorists to describe behavior—the response. Whether it refers to a simple reflex or a complex behavior, the response is always external and observable. It is defined by the behavior. In this case, one does not go from the specific act to an abstract structural unit. The act itself is the structural unit. Instead of being internal to the organism and only indirectly observable, the response is part of the observable behavior of the organism.

Social cognitive theory started with a similar emphasis on the overt, behavioral response. The units of the person were concrete, clearly defined, and objectively measured. Variations in response were tied to equally clearly defined and objectively measured variations in the environment. With the development of an emphasis on cognitive activities and self-regulatory behavior, however, there was a shift toward emphasis on more abstract structural units. Concepts such as standards, self-efficacy judgments, and goals tend to be more abstract than the concept of a response. Furthermore, they require different tools of measurement and this has resulted in a defense of the use of verbal reports on the part of social cognitive theorists. At the same time, it should be clear that this movement toward an emphasis on different kinds of units has not lessened the concern for rigor, objectivity, and measurement. Social cognitive theorists continue to emphasize concepts that are clear in their meaning and specific in the appropriate method of measurement. This is equally true for psychologists emphasizing cognitive, information-processing approaches. These psychologists, often associated with social cognitive theorists, emphasize concepts such as attributions and schemata that are measured in systematic ways.

In addition to differences in their level of abstraction, theories also differ in the complexity of structural organization. This complexity may be considered in terms of the number of units involved and whether they are formed in some kind of *hierarchial arrangement* in relation to one another. Cattell's theory clearly involves a complex structural organization of personality. Not only are there many units but there is also a hierarchial arrangement of these units into surface traits, source traits, and second-order factors (types). Similarly, Eysenck emphasizes a hierarchical organization of structural units, starting with responses at the lowest level and progressing on up to habits, traits, and types. Kelly's system allows for a complex system of constructs—one in which there are many constructs, some superordinate and others subordinate. However, the complexity of organization is viewed as varying considerably with the individual personality. The psychoanalytic framework includes many structural units and almost unlimited possibilities for interrelationships among the units. Although no clear hierarchical structure is set forth, the concept of personality types clearly indicates layers of organization beyond that of specific behaviors.

In contrast to such a complexity of personality structure is the fairly simple structure described by most learning theorists. There are few categories of responses, no suggestion that behavior generally involves the expression of many units at the same time, and a definite bias against the concept of personality types, which implies a stable organization of many different responses. Indeed, it may again be noted that the social cognitive theorist Mischel was particularly critical of trait and psychoanalytic theories for their emphasis on a hierarchical organization of personality. Cognitive theory, particularly in its emphasis on category formation and prototypes, should provide for a hierarchical view of the organization of personality. However, this has not been the case since cognitive psychologists typically have been interested in information *processing* rather than in the *structural* organization of personality.

These differences in levels of abstraction and complexity of structural organization can be related to differences in the general importance attached to structure in behavior. The concept of structure generally is used to account for the more stable aspects of personality and for the consistency of individual behavior over time and over situations. To consider two extremes: psychoanalytic theory places great emphasis on the stability of behavior over time, whereas learning theory does not; psychoanalytic theory places great emphasis on the consistency of behavior across situations, whereas learning theory does not; psychoanalytic theory places great emphasis on individual differences, whereas learning theory does not. At one extreme, psychoanalytic theory involves abstract units and a complex structural organization. At the other extreme, learning theory involves concrete units and little emphasis on the organization of these units. In other words, there appears to be a relationship between the importance attributed to structure by a theory and the theory's emphasis on stability and consistency in human behavior.

Process

In our review of theories of personality, the major conceptions in psychology concerning the "why" of behavior have been identified. As indicated in Chapter 1, many theories of motivation emphasize the efforts on the part of the individual to *reduce tension*. The push toward tension reduction is clearly indicated in psychoanalytic theory, in Cattell's theory, and in Hull's approach to learning theory. For Freud, the individual's efforts are directed toward expressing the sexual and aggressive instincts and, thereby, toward the reduction of the tension associated with these instincts. For Cattell, the individual is directed toward the expression of ergs and the energy associated with them. For Hull, and for Dollard and Miller, reinforcement is associated with the satisfaction of primary or secondary drives and, thereby, with the reduction of drive-induced tension.

Rogers' theory gives expression to the motivational model suggesting that individuals often *seek tension*. Rogers suggests that individuals seek self-actualization, that they want to grow and to realize their inner potentials even at the cost of increased tension. However, Rogers also places emphasis on a third motivational force — *consistency*. The particular kind of consistency emphasized by Rogers is a congruence between self and experience. For Kelly, who also emphasizes consistency, the relevant variables are different. According to Kelly, it is important that the individual's constructs be consistent with one another, so that the predictions from one do not cancel out the predictions from another. It is also important that predictions be consistent with experiences, or, in other words, that events confirm and validate the construct system.

Although operant learning theory and social cognitive theory both emphasize the importance of reinforcement, they do not do so in terms of drive reduction as happens in Hullian stimulus–response theory. For Skinner, reinforcements affect the probability of a response, but there is no use of an internal concept of drive or tension. In social cognitive theory the emphasis is on cognitive processes and the development of expectancies. Reinforcers are critical for performance but not for the acquisition of behavior. Expectancies concerning reinforcement and evaluative standards guide and direct behavior. In this way they serve a motivational function. Finally, information-processing theorists suggest that many aspects of human performance attributed to motivational factors may, in fact, be better understood as the consequence of using particular cognitive strategies or heuristics.

Notice that these motivational models are only in conflict with one another if we assume that all behavior must follow the same motivational principles. In relation to structure, we need not assume that the individual only has drives, that one only has a concept of the self, or that one only has personal constructs. In the same way, we need not assume that the individual is always reducing tension, or always striving toward actualization, or always seeking consistency. It may be that all three models of motivation have something to say about human behavior. An individual may at some points be functioning to reduce tension, at other times to actualize the self, and at other times to achieve cognitive consistency. Another possibility is that, at one time, two kinds of motivation are operating, but they are in conflict with one another. For example, the individual may seek to relieve aggressive urges through hitting someone but also have fond feelings for the person involved and view this behavior as "out of character." A third possibility is that two kinds of motivation may combine to operate in support of one another. Thus, to make love to someone can represent the reduction of tension from sexual urges, an actualizing expression of the self, and an act consistent with the self-concept and with predictions from one's construct system. If room is left for more than one process model, it becomes the task of psychologists to define the conditions under which each type of motivation will occur and the ways in which the different types of motivation can combine to determine behavior. At the same time, we must be careful not to feel compelled to account for all behavior in terms of motivation. Certain processes are best understood in terms of their own characteristics, without necessarily bringing other explanatory principles into play.

Growth and Development

In Chapter 1 we considered the causes of personality—cultural, social class, familial, and genetic. None of the theories studied really gives adequate attention to the variety of factors that determine growth and development. Cattell has done important work on the influences of heredity and environment, and on age trends in personality development. Psychoanalytic theory gives attention to the role of biological and environmental factors in personality development, but in most cases this remains speculative. It is disappointing that Rogers and Kelly have so little to say in this area. Finally, although the learning theorists have done a great deal to interpret the processes through which cultural, social class, and familial influences are transmitted, there has been a serious neglect of biological factors. Also, until recently learning theorists tended to give insufficient attention to the important area of cognitive growth and development. Important contributions are, however, now being made by cognitive theorists. For example, Bandura has been doing research on observational learning and Mischel has been researching how children develop methods for tolerating increased delays in reinforcement. As personality psychologists increasingly emphasize cognitive variables, they are able to incorporate into their work the considerable body of research and theory devoted to cognitive development.

In considering the theorists covered in the text, differences concerning two questions about development become apparent. The first concerns the utility of the concept of stages of development and the second concerns the importance of early experiences for later personality development. Psychoanalytic theory attaches great importance to the concept of stages of development, and Cattell's work on age trends suggests that certain periods are critical for the formation of different traits. It is also true that psychoanalytic theory places the greatest emphasis on the early years of growth and development. There is impressive evidence that the early years are important for many personality characteristics. More specifically, the research suggests that the effects of the environment are greatest at the time of rapid change in a personality characteristic (Bloom, 1964; Scott, 1968). Since change and development are most rapid for many personality characteristics during the early years, it is during these years that environmental forces exert their greatest impact. This is not to say that the early years are critical for every characteristic. Different characteristics have different developmental curves, and for some the period of most rapid development may be during the teens or even later in life. Nor is this to suggest that the effects of early experiences are permanent. However, generally the early environment is of critical importance. This is true because often it is a period of rapid growth and because what is learned during these years sets the stage for later learning.

An understanding of the critical ages for different developments in personality is essential for theoretical progress and for progress in our efforts to correct various arrests in growth. Since it is not usually possible to make resources available to children over the course of many years, it would be extremely valuable to know at which ages the commitment of human resources would most make a difference. For example, if we are interested in the development of certain cognitive skills that develop most rapidly in prepuberty, the commitment of human resources to preschool children may be wasteful. On the other hand, if we know that the initial period for the development of an ability is between the ages of six and eight, the commitment of resources to children of a later age will not represent the most effective use of these resources.

Psychopathology

The forces producing psychopathology are interpreted differently by the theorists. However, the concept of conflict is essential to a number of them. This is most clearly the case in psychoanalytic theory. According to Freud, psychopathology occurs when the instinctive urges of the id come into conflict with the functioning of the ego. Although Rogers does not emphasize the importance of conflict, one can interpret the problem of incongruence in terms of a conflict between experience and the self-concept. Learning theory offers a number of explanations for psychopathology, and at least one of these explanations emphasizes the importance of approach–avoidance conflicts. And, although cognitive theorists do not emphasize the importance of conflict, one can think of the implications of goal conflicts and conflicting beliefs or expectancies.

The concept of conflict makes sense as a relevant variable in psychopathology. However, there is a need for a greater distinction between frustration and conflict. A drive being blocked does not represent conflict, though this may lead to a conflict situation. A state of conflict exists when two or more incompatible forces are striving for expression at the same time. The parts of a system are in conflict if the gratification of one part is achieved at the cost of frustration of another part of the system. In contrast, in an integrated system the parts are either functioning independently of each other or are in harmony with one another. In the latter case, the achievement of a goal leads to a variety of kinds of gratification.

Many complex questions concerning psychopathology remain unanswered. For example, we know that cultures vary in the incidence of various forms of psychopathology. Depression is rare in Africa, but is common in the United States. Why? Conversion symptoms, such as hysterical paralysis of the arm or leg, were quite common in Freud's time but are observed much less frequently today. Why? Are there important differences in the problems that people in different cultures face? Or do they face the same problems but cope with them differently? Or is it just that some problems are more likely to be reported than others and that this varies with the individual culture? If people today are more concerned with problems of identity than with problems of guilt, if they are more concerned with the problem of finding meaning than of relieving sexual urges, what are the implications for psychoanalysis and the other theories of personality? Although each of the theories of personality can offer some explanation for suicide, do all seem equally plausible? Can any of the theories account for the fact that the suicide rate for college students is higher than that for individuals of comparable age who are not in college and higher than that for any other age group?

We are at a point at which the whole question of the nature of psychopathology is under reexamination. Questions are being raised concerning the disease model of mental illness, the responsibilities of the person who is ill, and illness in society as opposed to illness in the individual. Whereas psychoanalytic theory suggests that someone is ill with a "sick personality," learning theory suggests that the individual has learned a maladaptive response. But how, within the scope of either of these theories, do we account for the prevalence of psychological disorders in current society? And how, within the scope of either of these theories, do we account for the situation wherein some seemingly mal-adaptive responses have, in reality, adaptive qualities? Thus, for example, in their book *Black Rage*, Grier and Cobbs (1968) describe how the mistrustful, almost paranoid behavior of many blacks is based on reality and has adaptive qualities. The answers to questions like these go beyond the theories of personality we have considered, but they are relevant to them.

Change

An analysis of the change concepts of the theorists suggests that, in some cases, the point of focus for one is different from that for another. For example, the following questions concerning change are given varying amounts of attention by each theorist: What is changed? What are the conditions for change? What is the process in change?

Psychoanalytic theory, in its emphasis on changes in the relation-ship between the unconscious and the conscious and between the ego and the id, is particularly concerned with structural change. Kelly, in his analysis of psychotherapy as the psychological reconstruction of life, is also concerned with structural change. In contrast, Rogers is most con-cerned with the conditions that make change possible. Although in his research he has attended to structural change (e.g., changes in self–ideal-self discrepancy), this has been for the purpose of having a criterion against which he could measure the effectiveness of different variables (e.g., congruence, unconditional positive regard, empathic understand-ing). Kelly pointed out the importance of an atmosphere of experimenta-tion and invitational mood, but there is little research to suggest the variables critical in establishing this atmosphere or mood. Psychoana-lysts have been quite concerned with the quality of the transference relationship as it affects change, but this has been, for the most part, from a practical standpoint and has had little impact on the theory as a whole.

The process of change is a particular focus of convenience for learning theory. The following learning processes are used to account for a wide range of changes related to a variety of forms of psychotherapy: extinction, discrimination learning, counterconditioning, positive reinforcement, and imitation. Whereas, initially, learning concepts were used to explain treatment effects associated with other theories, more recently these concepts have been used in the development of learning-based treatment methods. This development of technique out of a theory of the process of change is healthy. A clear illustration of therapeutic technique as an outgrowth of theory is Bandura's work on modeling and guided participation. It is also interesting to note here that although therapy or psychological change has not been a major aspect of social cognitive theory, it is becoming an increasingly important part of it. In fact, Bandura suggests that developments in this area may well serve as a test of the theory generally. Finally, approaches grouped under the cognitive therapy label are part of the cognitive revolution, though the extent to which they are closely tied to developments in cognitive science remains an open question. For the most part, theoretical developments and practical applications seem to have occurred somewhat independently as part of a more general development in the field.

There are, of course, basic and important differences in the theories concerning the potential for change. At one extreme would be psychoanalytic theory, which suggests that fundamental personality change is quite difficult. This view is related to the psychoanalytic emphasis on structure and the importance of early experiences. If structure is important and is developed early in life, it follows that basic change later in life is difficult. Many of the early learning theorists (e.g., Hull, Dollard, and Miller), particularly those who attempted to relate learning theory to psychoanalytic theory, were similarly pessimistic about the potential for change. However, the more recent developments in operant conditioning, social cognitive theory, and cognitive behavior therapy have led to much greater optimism for change. These theorists place little emphasis on structure and great emphasis on the potential to change behavior. With faith in their ability to shape behavior through the manipulation of external rewards or through changes in cognitive beliefs and attributions, these psychologists are at the other extreme from psychoanalysts.

Change, of course, is not limited to psychotherapy—it occurs at all levels and to varying degrees. Consider, for example, the following description of changes in a professional hockey player whose fortunes have risen and declined:

> As Gilbert stayed at home earlier this season, with little to do but consider his future, he saw that his entire personality was changing. "I didn't have any patience at all," Gilbert said. "I

realized not a long time ago I was reacting like it was not me. I'm always the type of guy who will laugh all the time. I don't worry about nothing."

"I was acting like I was always angry," he said. "It seemed like everything was bothering me. I was thinking too much about retiring. I love to play with my kids. I would sit at the table and say, 'Don't do that. Don't do this.' It was bad. I think I'm a great father, but all of a sudden I changed, day and night. My wife said, 'If you keep going that way, what will they think? You've changed so much.'"

NEW YORK TIMES, DECEMBER 4, 1982, p. 10

In considering the question of how people change, we again recognize the extent to which theories of personality emphasize different processes of change, different conditions for change, and change in different aspects of personality functioning. Some of these differences may well represent competing and conflicting points of view, and others merely various terms for similar processes. Finally, some differences may result from attending to different aspects of the person. Sorting these out represents a task for both students and professionals in the field.

RELATIONSHIPS AMONG THEORY, ASSESSMENT, AND RESEARCH

At various times in this book, theory, assessment, and research have been considered separately. However, throughout, the attempt has been made to keep in mind the intimate relationships among the three. Indeed, this has been a major theme throughout the book.

In Chapter 1, theory as an attempt to fit together and explain a wide variety of facts with a few assumptions was considered. In Chapter 2 the tools that personality psychologists use to observe and measure behavior in a systematic way were discussed. It is clear that research involves the use of assessment techniques to develop and test theory. What of the relationships among theory, assessment, and research? Here we can note a relationship between the assumptions basic to theories and the techniques of assessment generally associated with these theories. For example, a psychodynamic theory such as psychoanalysis is associated with the Rorschach, a phenomenological theory such as that of Rogers with the interview and measures of the self-concept, a factor-analytic theory such as that of Cattell with psychometric tests, a learning theory approach with objective tests, and cognitive theories with ways in which people process information and organize their worlds. Do different theories of personality tend to lead to different techniques of assessment and to different kinds of observations about individuals? Was such the case in our varied efforts to understand the case of Jim (Chapter 15)? Are such differences in theory and assessment then also related to strategies for research, leading to clinical and experimental attitudes? To what extent are these theories associated with a greater or lesser emphasis on naturalistic observation, questionnaire research, or laboratory experimentation?

The clinical approach emphasizes dynamics, individual differences, the entire personality, the history of the individual, flexibility in observation, prediction from an understanding of the individual, and theory that postulates internal processes and allows for concepts that cannot be verified directly. The experimental approach emphasizes consistency across individuals, changes in one or two responses under various experimental conditions rather than the pattern of many responses, tends to be ahistorical, emphasizes rigor in experimental design and theoretical conceptualization, and allows for the use of animals as subjects.

Do differences such as these exist among psychologists generally? In a study of the psychological value systems of psychologists, Thorndike (1954) obtained ratings from 200 psychologists on the contributions made by a number of outstanding people to psychology. An analysis of these ratings suggested two major dimensions along which the psychologists made their judgments. The first factor was labeled laboratory versus clinic, and indicated that some psychologists valued laboratory research, whereas others valued the clinical study of the individual. The second factor located by Thorndike was labeled psychometric versus verbal approach and distinguished between psychologists who value analytic study with psychometric (statistical) techniques and psychologists who value a global and typological approach to the study of behavior. A more recent study similarly finds two cultures in psychology—the scientific and humanistic. Although there are many differing aspects to these cultures, two are particularly relevant. One, called *setting for discovery*, concerns a preference for the laboratory and experimentation as opposed to field and case studies. The second, called *level of analysis*, involves an emphasis on parts as opposed to an emphasis on wholes. The suggestion once more is made that these two cultures represent differing and conflicting values, and that the prospects for bringing about harmony between them is not bright (Kimble, 1984).

If indeed such a theme runs throughout the study of personality, to what can it be attributed? In his review of the history of psychology, Boring (1950) noted that over time the experimentalists became more technical and electronically oriented, whereas the clinicians did not. He went on to suggest that clinicians usually liked other people, whereas "the experimentalists often did not, preferring rats for subjects as being less embarrassing socially or at any rate more pliant, convenient and exploitable than human subjects" (Boring, 1950, p. 578). Boring concluded that the split may be a result of personality differences between members of the two orientations.

Clearly the emphasis here is not on whether one or another approach to theory, assessment, and research is right or wrong. Rather it is on the strengths and limitations of each and the relationships among the three. Is it not possible that different aspects of one's personality may be studied with greater or lesser accuracy with different assessment devices? Is it not possible that some phenomena can be observed quite easily in the laboratory whereas others cannot? Is it not possible that each assessment device and research approach has its own potential sources of error or bias? Should we not be aware that limiting ourselves to one approach to assessment and research may restrict our observations to phenomena directly relevant to a specific theoretical position? In such circumstances we may be led to confuse accuracy in a few predictions with more general aspects concerning the quality of a theory. It may be useful to be aware of restrictive relationships among theory, assessment, and research and also appreciative of the contributions that different theories, assessment devices, and research procedures can make to our understanding of human behavior.

A FINAL SUMMING UP

In a certain sense, every person is a psychologist. Every person develops a view of human nature and a strategy for predicting events. The theory and research presented in this book represent the efforts of psychologists to systematize what is known about human personality and to suggest areas for future exploration. The attempt has been to focus on similarities in what these psychologists have been trying to do and on differences in what they view as being the best mode of operation. Although psychologists as a group are more explicit about their view of the person than is the average layperson, and although they are more systematic in their efforts to understand and predict human behavior, there are individual differences among them. In this book the theories of many psychologists have been considered in detail. They represent major theories in the field today although not the only theories, and they are representative of the diversity of approach that can be considered reasonable and useful.

An effort has been made in this text to demonstrate that theory, assessment, and research are related to one another. In most cases some consistency can be found in the nature of theory proposed, the types of tests used to obtain data, and the problems suggested for investigation. A distinction was drawn between the psychologists who emphasize individual differences and those who emphasize general principles, between the correlational approach and the experimental approach, between the psychologists who use projective tests and those who use objective tests, between those who emphasize stability and consistency in behavior and those who emphasize change and situational specificity, and between those who emphasize individuals and those who emphasize environments. Finally, we proposed that the theories of personality covered need not be considered mutually exclusive. In a very real sense, each represents a glimpse of the total picture. Human behavior is like a very complex jigsaw puzzle. The theories of personality considered have offered us many possible pieces for solution of the puzzle. Although some pieces may have to be discarded as not fitting the puzzle at all, and many remain outstanding, undoubtedly many of the pieces offered will be there when the final picture is put together.

ABA research. A Skinnerian variant of the experimental method consisting of one subject exposed to three experimental phases: (A) a baseline period, (B) introduction of reinforcers to change the frequency of specific behaviors, and (A) withdrawal of reinforcement and observation of whether the behaviors return to their earlier frequency (baseline period).

ABC approach. In behavioral assessment, an emphasis on the identification of antecedent (A) events and the consequences (C) of behavior (B); a functional analysis of behavior involving identification of the environmental conditions that regulate specific behaviors.

Ability, temperament, and dynamic traits. In Cattell's trait theory, the categories of traits that capture the major aspects of personality.

Acquiescence. A kind of response style or bias in which there is a tendency to agree with test items regardless of their content.

Acquisition. The learning of new behaviors, viewed by Bandura as independent of reward and contrasted with performance — which is seen as dependent on reward.

Aggression (Kelly). In Kelly's personal construct theory, the active expansion of the person's construct system.

Aggressive instincts. Freud's concept for those drives directed toward harm, injury, or destruction.

Anal character. Freud's concept for a personality type that expresses a fixation at the anal stage of development and relates to the world in terms of the wish for control or power.

Anal stage. Freud's concept for that period of life during which the major center of bodily excitation or tension is the anus.

Anxiety. An emotion expressing a sense of impending threat or danger. In Kelly's personal construct theory anxiety occurs when the person recognizes that his or her construct system does not apply to the events being perceived.

Approach–avoidance conflict. In S–R theory, the simultaneous presence of opposing drives to move toward an object and away from it.

Attributional style questionnaire. A questionnaire designed to measure attributions concerning learned helplessness along three dimensions: internal (personal)–external (universal), specific–global, and stable–unstable.

Behavior modification. The approach to therapeutic treatment (behavior change) based on Skinner's operant conditioning theory.

Behavior therapy. An approach to therapeutic treatment (behavior change) based on learning theory and focusing on specific behavioral difficulties.

Behavioral aftereffects. Behavioral effects that are a result of environmental conditions that do not show up during exposure to a condition but at some later point (e.g., Glass and Singer's conclusions regarding the consequences of adaptation to stress).

Behavioral assessment. The emphasis in assessment on specific behaviors that are tied to defined situational characteristics (e.g., ABC approach).

Behavioral competencies. Abilities to behave in particular ways, particularly emphasized in social cognitive theory in relation to performance, as in delay of gratification.

Behaviorism. An approach within psychology, developed by Watson, that restricts investigation to overt, observable behavior.

The big five. In trait factor theory, the five major trait categories including Emotionality, Activity, and Sociability factors.

Bivariate method. Cattell's description of the method of personality study that follows the classical experimental design of manipulating an independent variable and observing the effects on a dependent variable.

Cardinal trait. Allport's concept for a disposition that is so pervasive and outstanding in a person's life that virtually every act is traceable to its influence.

Castration anxiety. Freud's concept for the boy's fear, experienced during the phallic stage, that the father will cut off the son's penis because of their sexual rivalry for the mother.

Causal attribution. In the revised theory of learned helplessness and depression, attributions made on three dimensions: internal (personal)–external (universal), specific–global, and stable–unstable.

Central trait. Allport's concept for a disposition to behave in a particular way in a range of situations.

Classical conditioning. A process, emphasized by Pavlov, in which a previously neutral stimulus becomes capable of eliciting a response because of its association with a stimulus that automatically produces the same or a similar response.

Client-centered therapy. Rogers' term for his earlier approach to therapy in which the counselor's attitude is one of interest in the ways in which the client experiences the self and the world.

Clinical method. Cattell's description of the method of personality study in which there is an interest in complex patterns of behavior as they occur in life but variables are not assessed in a systematic way.

Cognition. The person's thought processes, including perception, memory, and language. The term is used to refer to the ways in which the organism processes information concerning the environment and the self.

Cognitive behavior assessment. An approach to assessment, associated with cognitive behavior therapy, that emphasizes the measurement of specific thoughts and self-statements made by the person, particularly in problematic situations.

Cognitive competencies. Abilities to think in a variety of ways, particularly emphasized in social cognitive theory in relation to the ability to delay gratification.

Cognitive complexity–simplicity. An aspect of a person's cognitive functioning that at one end is defined by the use of many constructs with many relationships to one another (complexity) and at the other end by the use of few constructs with limited relationships to one another (simplicity).

Cognitive strategies. Cognitive procedures individuals use to cope with stressful situations (e.g., self-handicapping and defensive pessimism).

Cognitive therapy. An approach to therapy in which changes in unrealistic and maladaptive thinking are emphasized.

Cognitive triad. Beck's description of the cognitive factors that lead to depression, involving a view of the self as a "loser," a view of the world as frustrating, and a view of the future as bleak.

Competence motivation. White's concept for motivation that emphasizes behavior directed toward dealing competently or effectively with the environment, even if this involves an increase in tension.

Conditioned emotional reaction. Watson and Rayner's term for the development of an emotional reaction to a previously neutral stimulus, as in Little Albert's fear of rats.

Congruence. Rogers' concept expressing an absence of conflict between the perceived self and experience. Also one of three therapist conditions suggested as essential for growth and therapeutic progress. (See **Empathic understanding** and **unconditional positive regard**)

Conscious. Those thoughts, experiences, and feelings of which we are aware.

Constriction. In Kelly's personal construct theory, the narrowing of the construct system so as to minimize incompatibilities.

Construct. In Kelly's theory, a way of perceiving, construing, or interpreting events.

Construct system. In Kelly's theory, the hierarchical arrangement of constructs.

Contrast pole. In Kelly's personal construct theory, the contrast pole of a construct is defined by the way in which a third element is perceived as different from two other elements that are used to form a similarity pole.

Core construct. In Kelly's personal construct theory, a construct that is basic to the person's construct system and cannot be altered without serious consequences for the rest of the system.

Correlational research. An approach to research, described by Cronbach, in which existing individual indifferences are measured and related to one another, in contrast with the experimental approach to research.

Counterconditioning. The conditioning or learning of responses that interfere with previously learned responses to stimuli, as in the counterconditioning of a pleasurable response to a previously fear-provoking stimulus.

Death instinct. Freud's concept for drives or sources of energy that are directed toward death or a return to an inorganic state.

Defense mechanisms. Freud's concept for those devices used by the person to reduce anxiety that result in the exclusion from awareness of some thought, wish, or feeling.

Defensive behaviors. Efforts on the part of the person, emphasized by both Freud and Rogers, to ward off anxiety.

Delay of gratification. The postponement of pleasure until the optimum or proper time, a concept particularly emphasized in social cognitive theory in relation to self-regulation.

Demand characteristics. Cues that are implicit (hidden) in the experimental setting and influence the subject's behavior.

Denial. A defense mechanism, emphasized by both Freud and Rogers, in which threatening feelings are not allowed into awareness.

Dilation. In Kelly's personal construct theory, the broadening of a construct system so that it will be more comprehensive.

Direct consequences. In social cognitive theory, the external events that follow behavior and influence future performance, contrasted with vicarious consequences and self-produced consequences.

Discrimination. In conditioning, the differential response to stimuli depending on whether they have been associated with pleasure, pain, or neutral events.

Disguised tests. Tests in which the subject is unaware of the purpose of the test and the ways in which responses will be interpreted.

Distortion. According to Rogers, a defensive process in which experience is changed so as to be brought into awareness in a form that is consistent with the self.

Dream interpretation. In psychoanalysis, the use of dreams to understand the person's unconscious wishes and fears.

Drive, primary. In Hull's theory, an innate internal stimulus that activates behavior (e.g., hunger drive).

Drive, secondary. In Hull's theory, a learned internal stimulus, acquired through association with the satisfaction of primary drives, that activates behavior (e.g., anxiety).

Dysfunctional expectancies. In social cognitive theory, maladaptive expectations concerning the consequences of specific behaviors.

Dysfunctional self-evaluation. In social cognitive theory, maladaptive standards for self-reward that have important implications for psychopathology.

Ego. Freud's structural concept for the part of personality that attempts to satisfy drives (instincts) in accordance with reality and the person's moral values.

Emitted behaviors. In Skinner's theory, behaviors or responses that cannot be associated with known preceding stimuli.

Empathic understanding. Rogers' term for the ability to perceive experiences and feelings and their meanings from the standpoint of another person. One of three therapist conditions essential for therapeutic progress. (See *also* **Congruence** and **Unconditional positive regard**)

Energy system. Freud's view of personality as involving the interplay among various forces (e.g., drives, instincts) or sources of energy.

Erg. Cattell's concept for innate biological drives that provide the basic motivating power for behavior.

Erogenous zones. According to Freud, those parts of the body that are the sources of tension or excitation.

Existentialism. An approach to understanding people and conducting therapy, associated with the human potential movement, that emphasizes phenomenology and concerns inherent in existing as a person. Derived from a more general movement in philosophy.

Expectancies. In social cognitive theory, what the individual anticipates or predicts will occur as the result of specific behaviors

in specific situations (anticipated consequences).

Experimental research. An approach to research, described by Cronbach, in which the experimenter manipulates the variable and is interested in general laws, in contrast with the correlational approach to research.

Experimenter expectancy effects. Unintended experimenter effects involving behaviors that lead subjects to respond in accordance with the experimenter's hypothesis.

Extinction. In conditioning, the progressive weakening of the association between a stimulus and a response; in classical conditioning because the conditioned stimulus is no longer followed by the unconditioned stimulus; and in operant conditioning because the response is no longer followed by reinforcement.

Extroversion. In Eysenck's theory, one end of the introversion–extroversion dimension of personality characterized by a disposition to be sociable, friendly, impulsive, and risk taking.

Factor analysis. A statistical method for determining those variables or test responses that increase and decrease together. Used in the development of personality tests and of some trait theories (e.g., Cattell, Eysenck).

Fear (Kelly). In Kelly's personal construct theory, fear occurs when a new construct is about to enter the person's construct system.

Fixation. Freud's concept expressing a developmental arrest or stoppage at some point in the person's psychosexual development.

Fixed-role therapy. Kelly's therapeutic technique that makes use of scripts or roles for people to try out, thereby encouraging people to behave in new ways and to perceive themselves in new ways.

Focus of convenience. In Kelly's personal construct theory, those events or phenomena that are best covered by a construct or by the construct system.

Free association. In psychoanalysis, the patient's reporting to the analyst of every thought that comes to mind.

Functional analysis. In behavioral approaches, particularly Skinnerian, the identification of the environmental stimuli that control behavior.

Functional autonomy. Allport's concept that a motive may become independent of its origins; in particular, motives in adults may become independent of their earlier basis in tension reduction.

Generalization. In conditioning, the association of a response with stimuli similar to the stimulus to which the response was originally conditioned or attached.

Generalized Expectancies that go beyond specific situations, as in Rotter's internal–external locus of control and Scheier and Carver's optimism–pessimism.

Generalized reinforcer. In Skinner's operant conditioning theory, a reinforcer that provides access to many other reinforcers (e.g., money).

Genuineness. Rogers' term for the ability of a person to be himself or herself and honest in relation to another person. One of three therapist conditions necessary for therapeutic progress.

Goals–plans. In social cognitive theory, desired future events that motivate the person over extended periods of time and enable the person to go beyond momentary influences.

Guided participation. A treatment approach emphasized in social cognitive theory in which a person is assisted in performing modeled behaviors.

Habit. In Hull's theory, an association between a stimulus and a response.

Hierarchy. The organization of things in a graded order or according to rank (e.g., Eysenck's conceptualization of personality and Kelly's view of the personal construct system).

Higher mental processes. In S–R theory, the central role of thought in behavior that allows organisms to go beyond reflexive responses to stimuli.

Hostility (Kelly). In Kelly's personal construct theory, making others behave in an expected way to validate one's own construct system.

Human potential movement. A group of psychologists, represented by Rogers and Maslow, who emphasize the actualization or fulfillment of individual potential, including an openness to experience.

Id. Freud's structural concept for the source of the instincts or all of the drive energy in people.

Ideal self. The self-concept the individual would most like to possess. A key concept in Rogers' theory.

Identification. The acquisition, as characteristics of the self, of personality characteristics perceived to be part of others (e.g., parents).

Idiographic approach. An approach emphasized by Allport in which particular attention is given to the intensive study of individuals and the organization of personality variables in each person.

Imitation. Behavior that is acquired through the observation of others. In S–R theory, the result of the process called matched-dependent behavior in which, for example, children match their behavior to that of their parents and this is followed by reward.

Impermeable construct. In Kelly's personal construct theory, a construct that does not allow new elements into it.

Implicit personality theory. The layperson's beliefs concerning the characteristics or traits of people that go together, implicit in that they are not made explicit and are not part of a formal theory of personality.

Incongruence. Rogers' concept for the existence of a discrepancy or conflict between the perceived self and experience.

Inefficacy. In social cognitive theory, the inability to cope with a perceived threat or other important situation.

Instrumental learning. In S–R theory, the learning of responses that are instrumental in bringing about a desirable situation.

Interactionism. The view within psychology that behavior can be understood in terms of relationships between variables that affect one another, as in person and situation variables, or interact to determine behavior.

Internal–external (I–E) scale. The personality scale developed by Rotter to measure the extent to which the person has developed a generalized expectancy that he or she has the ability to control life's events (i.e., internal locus of control) as opposed to the generalized expectancy that life's events are the result of external factors such as chance, luck, or fate (i.e., external locus of control).

Internal standards. A concept in social cognitive theory emphasizing how behavior may be regulated and maintained by learned standards for reinforcement (e.g., pride, shame) that are now part of the individual.

Introversion. In Eysenck's theory, one end of the introversion–extroversion dimension of personality characterized by a disposition to be quiet, reserved, reflective, and risk avoiding.

Intuitive social scientist. A view of ordinary people as trying to gather and organize information in the course of which certain rules or heuristics are used and errors made. The emphasis is on cognitive rather than motivational influences in personality functioning.

Jenkins activity survey. A personality questionnaire designed to measure Type A behavior patterns associated with increased risk of heart disease.

Laboratory research. Research conducted

in the laboratory that typically emphasizes experimenter control over the variables of interest and the investigation of cause–effect relationships among a few variables. (See **Experimental research**)

L-Data. In Cattell's theory, life-record data relating to behavior in everyday-life situations or to ratings of such behavior.

Learned helplessness. Seligman's concept expressing an animal's or person's learning that outcomes are not affected by his or her behavior.

Libido. Freud's concept for the energy of the life instincts directed toward sexual gratification and pleasure.

Life instinct. Freud's concept for drives or sources of energy (libido) directed toward the preservation of life and sexual gratification.

Locus of causality. In Weiner's scheme of causal attributions, a dimension that relates to whether the person perceives causes of events as coming from within (internal) or from outside (external).

Locus of control. Rotter's concept expressing a generalized expectancy or belief concerning the determinants of rewards and punishments. (See **Internal–External scale**)

Loosening. In Kelly's personal construct theory, the use of the same construct to make varied predictions.

Maintenance. Bandura's concept for the conditions that regulate behavior once it has been initiated.

Mechanisms of defense. (See **Defense mechanisms**)

Microanalytic research. Bandura's suggested research strategy concerning the concept of self-efficacy in which specific rather than global self-efficacy judgments are recorded.

Modeling. Bandura's concept for the process of reproducing behaviors learned through the observation of others.

Multivariate method. Cattell's description

of the method of personality study, favored by him, in which there is study of the interrelationships among many variables at once.

Naturalistic observation. An approach to research that involves the study of phenomena as they occur naturally (in their own environment) and without efforts toward experimental manipulation and control.

Need for positive regard. (See **Positive regard**)

Negative reinforcer. In Skinner's operant conditioning theory, the removal of an unpleasant or aversive stimulus that results in an increase in the probability of occurrence of the preceding response.

Neuroticism. In Eysenck's theory, a dimension of personality defined by stability and low anxiety at one end as opposed to instability and high anxiety at the other end.

Objective tests. Tests in which the subject is asked to give a correct response.

Observational learning. Bandura's concept for the process through which people learn merely by observing the behavior of others, called models.

Oedipus complex. Freud's concept expressing the boy's sexual attraction to the mother and fear of castration by the father who is seen as a rival.

Operant conditioning. Skinner's term for the process through which the characteristics of a response are determined by its consequences.

Operants. In Skinner's theory, behaviors that appear (are emitted) without being specifically associated with any prior (eliciting) stimuli and are studied in relation to the reinforcing events that follow them.

Oral character. Freud's concept for a personality type that expresses a fixation at the oral stage of development and who relates to the world in terms of the wish to be fed or to swallow.

Oral stage. Freud's concept for that period

of life during which the major center of bodily excitation or tension is the mouth.

OT-Data. In Cattell's theory, objective test data or information about personality obtained from observing behavior in miniature situations.

Own-control design. A Skinnerian variant of the experimental method in which one subject is used and serves as his or her own control while experimental conditions are varied. (See **ABA design**)

Paradigm. Kuhn's concept for a model that is commonly accepted by scientists in a field and that defines the field of observations and the methods to be used in research.

Performance. The production of learned behaviors, viewed by Bandura as dependent on rewards, in contrast to the acquisition of new behaviors, which is seen as independent of reward.

Peripheral construct. In Kelly's personal construct theory, a construct that is not basic to the construct system and can be altered without serious consequences for the rest of the system.

Permeable construct. In Kelly's personal construct system, a construct that allows new elements into it.

Person–situation controversy. A controversy between those psychologists who emphasize the importance of personal (internal) variables in determining behavior and those who emphasize the importance of situational (external) influences.

Personality. Those characteristics of the person, or of people generally, that account for consistent patterns of response to situations.

Phallic character. Freud's concept for a personality type that expresses a fixation at the phallic stage of development and who strives for success in competition with others.

Phallic stage. Freud's concept for that period of life during which excitation or tension begins to be centered in the genitals and during which there is an attraction to the parent of the opposite sex.

Phenomenology. An approach within psychology that focuses on how the person perceives and experiences the self and the world.

Pleasure principle. According to Freud, psychological functioning based on the pursuit of pleasure and the avoidance of pain.

Possible selves. Individuals' ideas of what they might become, would like to become, and are afraid of becoming.

Positive regard, need for. Rogers' concept expressing the need for warmth, liking, respect, and acceptance from others.

Positive reinforcer. In Skinner's operant conditioning theory, a stimulus that results in an increase in the probability of occurrence of the response that preceded it.

Preconscious. Freud's concept for those thoughts, experiences, and feelings of which we are momentarily unaware but can readily bring into awareness.

Preverbal construct. In Kelly's personal construct theory, a construct that is used but cannot be expressed in words.

Process. In personality theory, the concept of process refers to the motivational aspects of personality.

Projective test. A test that generally involves vague, ambiguous stimuli and allows subjects to reveal their personalities in terms of their distinctive responses (e.g., Rorschach, TAT).

Prototype. The pattern of characteristics that best illustrates or exemplifies membership in a category. The prototype represents an ideal type with members of the category not necessarily possessing all the characteristics of the prototype.

Psychoticism. In Eysenck's theory, a dimension of personality defined by a tendency to be solitary and insensitive at one end

as opposed to accepting social custom and being caring about others at the other end.

Q-Data. In Cattell's theory, personality data obtained from questionnaires.

Q-Sort. An assessment device in which the subject sorts statements into categories following a normal distribution. Used by Rogers as a measure of statements regarding the self and ideal self.

Range of convenience. In Kelly's personal construct theory, those events or phenomena that are covered by a construct or by the construct system.

Rational–emotive therapy. A therapeutic approach, developed by Albert Ellis, that emphasizes change in irrational beliefs that have destructive emotional and behavioral consequences.

Reality principle. According to Freud, psychological functioning based on reality in which pleasure is delayed until an optimum time.

Reciprocal determinism. The mutual effects of variables on one another (e.g., Bandura's emphasis on personal and environmental factors continuously affecting one another).

Regression. Freud's concept expressing a person's return to ways of relating to the world and self that were part of an earlier stage of development.

Reliability. In test construction, a measure of the consistency of scores derived from the test; a measure of the freedom from chance error of the obtained scores.

Rep test (Role construct repertory test). Kelly's test to determine the constructs used by a person, the relationships among constructs, and how the constructs are applied to specific people.

Response style. The tendency of some subjects to respond to test items in a consistent, patterned way that has to do with the form of the questions and/or answers rather than with their content.

Role. Behavior considered to be appropriate for a person's place or status in society. Emphasized by Cattell as one of a number of variables that limit the influence of personality variables on behavior relative to situational variables.

Sample approach. Mischel's description of assessment approaches in which there is an interest in the behavior itself and its relation to environmental conditions, in contrast to sign approaches that infer personality from test behavior.

Schedule of reinforcement. In Skinner's operant conditioning theory, the rate and interval of reinforcement of responses (e.g., response ratio schedule and time intervals).

Script. A series or pattern of behaviors considered to be appropriate for a situation.

Second signal system. Pavlov's concept emphasizing the importance of speech and thought in human classical conditioning.

Secondary disposition. Allport's concept for a disposition to behave in a particular way that is relevant to few situations.

Self. A concept many psychologists use to express pattern, organization, and consistency in personality functioning; in social cognitive theory, cognitive processes (schemata) associated by the person with the I or Me.

Self-actualization. The fundamental tendency on the part of the organism to actualize, maintain, and enhance itself. A concept emphasized by Rogers and other members of the human potential movement.

Self-concept. The perceptions and meaning associated with the self, Me, or I.

Self-conceptions. In social cognitive theory, cognitive evaluations of the self. Dysfunctional self-evaluations, for example, are viewed as being important in psychopathology.

Self-consistency. Rogers' concept expressing an absence of conflict among perceptions of the self.

Self-efficacy. In social cognitive theory, the perceived ability to cope with specific situations.

Self-efficacy expectations. In social cognitive theory, the expectations on the part of the person concerning his or her ability to perform specific behaviors in a situation.

Self-esteem. The person's evaluative regard for the self or personal judgment of worthiness.

Self-experience discrepancy. Rogers' emphasis on the potential for conflict between the concept of self and experience—the basis for psychopathology.

Self-monitoring. Snyder's concept defining the extent to which people monitor or regulate their behavior according to situational cues. High self-monitoring individuals are sensitive to cues of situational appropriateness and regulate their behavior accordingly whereas low self-monitoring individuals behave more in accord with internal feelings and attitudes.

Self-produced consequences. In social cognitive theory, the consequences to behavior that are produced personally (internally) by the individual and that play a vital role in self-regulation and self-control.

Self-regulation. Bandura's concept for the process through which the person regulates his or her own behavior.

Self-schemata. Cognitive generalizations about the self, derived from past experience, that organize and guide the processing of self-related information.

Semantic conditioning. The classical conditioning of responses to the meaning of words. Associated with Pavlov's emphasis on the second signal system.

Sentiment. Cattell's concept for environmentally determined patterns of behavior that are expressed in attitudes (i.e., readiness to act in a certain direction) and are linked to underlying ergs (i.e., innate biological drives).

Sexual instincts. Freud's concept for those drives directed toward sexual gratification or pleasure.

Shaping. In Skinner's operant conditioning theory, the modification of behavior in a specific direction through the reinforcement of specific responses.

Sign approach. Mischel's description of assessment approaches that infer personality from test behavior, in contrast with a sample approach to assessment.

Similarity pole. In Kelly's personal construct theory, the similarity pole of a construct is defined by the way in which two elements are perceived to be similar.

Situational specificity. The emphasis on behavior as varying according to the situation in opposition to the emphasis by trait theorists on consistency in behavior across situations.

Sixteen personality factor inventory (16 P.F.). Cattell's personality questionnaire, derived from the use of factor analysis, measuring personality on sixteen dimensions.

Social desirability. The perceived social value of a response to a test item that may lead to a subject responding in terms of the perceived acceptability (desirability) of a response rather than in terms of its actual relevance to the self.

Source trait. In Cattell's theory, behaviors that vary together to form an independent dimension of personality, which is discovered through the use of factor analysis.

State. Emotional and mood changes (e.g., anxiety, depression, fatigue) that Cattell suggested may influence the behavior of a person at a given time. The assessment of both traits and states is suggested to predict behavior.

Stress. The person's perception that circumstances exceed his or her resources and endanger well-being. In Lazarus' view this involves two stages of cognitive appraisal — primary appraisal and secondary appraisal.

Stress inoculating training. Meichenbaum's procedure for training individuals to cope with stress, involving the phases of Conceptualization, Skill Acquisition and Rehearsal, and Application–Follow-through.

Structure. In personality theory, the concept of structure refers to the more enduring and stable aspects of personality.

Structured interview. An interview that follows a set format, an illustration of which is the procedure used to measure individual differences in the Type A behavior pattern. In this case expressive style is measured in terms of characteristics such as speech speed, volume, and explosiveness.

Subception. A process emphasized by Rogers in which a stimulus is experienced without being brought into awareness.

Submerged construct. In Kelly's personal construct theory, a construct that once could be expressed in words but now either one or both poles of the construct cannot be verbalized.

Subordinate construct. In Kelly's personal construct theory, a construct that is lower in the construct system and is thereby included in the context of another (superordinate) construct.

Successive approximation. In Skinner's operant conditioning theory, the development of complex behaviors through the reinforcement of behaviors that increasingly resemble the final form of behavior to be produced.

Superego. Freud's structural concept for the part of personality that expresses our ideals and moral values.

Superordinate construct. In Kelly's personal construct theory, a construct that is higher in the construct system and thereby includes other constructs within its context.

Surface trait. In Cattell's theory, behaviors that appear to be linked to one another but do not in fact increase and decrease together.

Symptom. In psychopathology, the expression of psychological conflict or disordered psychological functioning. For Freud, a disguised expression of a repressed impulse.

Systematic desensitization. A technique in behavior therapy in which a competing response (relaxation) is conditioned to stimuli that previously aroused anxiety.

Target behaviors. In behavioral assessment, the identification of specific behaviors to be observed and measured in relation to changes in environmental events.

Tension-reduction model. A view of motivation that suggests that behavior is directed toward the reduction of tensions associated with drives or needs.

Theory. A set of assumptions and concepts used to explain existing empirical findings and suggest findings that are expected in the future.

Threat (Kelly). In Kelly's personal construct theory, threat occurs when the person is aware of an imminent, comprehensive change in his or her construct system.

Tightening. In Kelly's personal construct theory, the use of constructs to make the same predictions regardless of circumstances.

Token economy. Following Skinner's operant conditioning theory, an environment in which individuals are rewarded with tokens for desirable behaviors.

Trait. A disposition to behave in a particular way as expressed in a person's behavior over a range of situations.

Transference. In psychoanalysis, the patient's development toward the analyst of attitudes and feelings rooted in past experiences with parental figures.

Type. The classification of people into a few groups, each of which has its own defining characteristics (e.g., introverts and extroverts).

Type A behavior pattern. A pattern of personality characteristics or behaviors such as competitiveness, quick action, hostility, and a pressured way of life that are associated with increased risk of heart disease.

Unconditional positive regard. Rogers' term for the acceptance of a person in a total, unconditional way. One of three therapist conditions suggested as essential for growth and therapeutic progress. (See **Congruence** and **Empathic Understanding**)

Unconscious. Those thoughts, experiences, and feelings of which we are unaware. According to Freud this unawareness is the result of repression.

Validity. In test construction and evaluation, the extent to which a test measures what it claims to measure.

Verbal construct. In Kelly's personal construct theory, a construct that can be expressed in words.

Vicarious conditioning. Bandura's concept for the process through which emotional responses are learned through the observation of emotional responses in others.

Vicarious consequences. In social cognitive theory, the observed consequences to the behavior of others that influence future performance.

Zeitgeist. The prevailing mood or spirit within a field at a particular time.

Bibliography

ABRAMSON, L. Y., GARBER, J., & SELIGMAN, M. E. P. Learned helplessness in humans: An attributional analysis. In J. Garber & M. E. P. Seligman (Eds.), *Human helplessness.* New York: Academic, 1980.

ABRAMSON, L. Y., SELIGMAN, M. E. P. & TEASDALE, J. D. Learned helplessness in humans: Critique and reformulation. *Journal of Abnormal Psychology,* 1978, **87,** 49–74.

ACHENBACH, T., & ZIGLER, E. Social competence and self-image disparity in psychiatric and non-psychiatric patients. *Journal of Abnormal and Social Psychology,* 1963, **67,** 197–205.

ADAMS-WEBBER, J. R. Actual structure and potential chaos: Relational aspects of progressive variations within a personal construct system. In D. Bannister (Ed.), *Perspectives in personal construct theory.* New York: Academic Press, 1970. Pp. 31–46.

ADAMS-WEBBER, J. R. *Personal construct theory: Concepts and applications.* New York: Wiley, 1979.

ADAMS-WEBBER, J. R. Assimilation and contrast in personal judgment: The dichotomy corollary. In J. C. Mancuso & J. R. Adams-Webber (Eds.), *The construing person. New York:* Praeger, *1982.*

ADORNO, T. W., FRENKEL-BRUNSWIK, E., LEVINSON, D. J., & SANFORD, R. N. *The authoritarian personality.* New York: Harper, 1950.

AKERET, R. U. Interrelationships among various dimensions of the self concept. *Journal of Counseling Psychology,* 1959, **6,** 199–201.

ALEXANDER, F., & FRENCH, T. M. *Psychoanalytic therapy.* New York: Ronald, 1946.

ALKER, H. A. Is personality situationally specific or intrapsychically consistent? *Journal of Personality,* 1972, **40,** 1–16.

ALLPORT, F. H. & ALLPORT, G. W. Personality traits: Their classification and measurement. *Journal of Abnormal and Social Psychology,* 1921, **16,** 1–40.

ALLPORT, G. W. Personality: A psychological inter-pretation. New York: Holt, Rinehart & Winston, 1937.

ALLPORT, G. W. The trend in motivational theory. *American Journal of Orthopsychiatry,* 1953, **23,** 107–119.

ALLPORT, G. W. *Becoming.* New Haven, Conn.: Yale University Press, 1955.

ALLPORT, G. W. European and American theories of personality. In H. P. David & H. von Bracken (Eds.), *Perspectives in personality theory,* New York: Basic Books, 1957. Pp. 3–26.

ALLPORT, G. W. What units shall we employ? In G. Lindzey (Ed.), *Assessment of human motives.* New York: Holt, Rinehart & Winston, 1958. Pp. 239–260.

ALLPORT, G. W. *Pattern and growth in personality.* New York: Holt, Rinehart & Winston, 1961.

ALLPORT, G. W. The general and the unique in psychological science. *Journal of Personality,* 1962, **30,** 405–421.

ALLPORT, G. W. Autobiography. In E. G. Boring & G. Lindzey (Eds.), *A history of psychology in auto-biography.* New York: Appleton–Century–Crofts, 1967.

APA ETHICAL PRINCIPLES OF PSYCHOLOGISTS. *American Psychologist,* 1981, **36,** 633–638.

APA MONITOR The spreading case of fraud. 1982, **13,** p. 1.

ARGYLE, M. The experimental study of the basic features of situations. In D. Magnusson (Ed.), *Toward a psychology of situations.* Hillsdale, N.J.: Erlbaum, 1981.

ARONSON, E., & CARLSMITH, J. M. Performance expectancy as a determinant of actual performance. *Journal of Abnormal and Social Psychology,* 1962, **65,** 178–182.

ARONSON, E., & METTEE, D. R. Dishonest behavior as a function of differential levels of induced self-esteem. *Journal of Personality and Social Psychology,* 1968, **9,** 121–127.

ATTHOWE, J. M., JR., & KRASNER, L. A. A preliminary report of the application of contingent reinforcement procedures and token economy on a "chronic" psychiatric ward. *Journal of Abnormal Psychology*, 1968, **73**, 37–43.

AYLLON, T., & AZRIN, H. H. The measurement and reinforcement of behavior of psychotics. *Journal of the Experimental Analysis of Behavior*, 1965, **8**, 357–383.

BALDWIN, A., CRITELLI, J. W., STEVENS, L. C., & RUSSELL, S. Androgyny and sex role measurement: A personal construct approach. *Journal of Personality and Social Psychology*, 1986, **51**, 1081–1088.

BALDWIN, A. L. The effect of home environment on nursery school behavior. *Child Development*, 1949, **20**, 49–61.

BALDWIN, A. L. *Theories of child development.* New York: Wiley, 1968.

BANDURA, A. The Rorschach white space response and "oppositional" behavior. *Journal of Consulting Psychology*, 1954, **18**, 17–21.(a)

BANDURA, A. The Rorschach white space response and perceptual reversal. *Journal of Experimental Psychology*, 1954, **48**, 113–117.(b)

BANDURA, A. Psychotherapy as a learning process. *Psychological Bulletin*, 1961, **58**, 143–159.

BANDURA, A. Social learning through imitation. In M. R. Jones (Ed.), *Nebraska symposium on motivation.* Lincoln: University of Nebraska Press, 1962. Pp. 211–215.

BANDURA, A. Influence of models' reinforcement contingencies on the acquisition of imitative responses. *Journal of Personality and Social Psychology*, 1965, **1**, 589–595.

BANDURA, A. A social learning interpretation of psychological dysfunctions. In P. London & D. Rosenhan (Eds.), *Foundations of abnormal psychology.* New York: Holt, Rinehart & Winston, 1968. Pp. 293–344.

BANDURA, A. Social-learning theory of identificatory processes. In D. A. Goslin (Ed.), *Handbook of socialization theory and research.* Chicago: Rand McNally, 1969. Pp. 213–262.(a)

BANDURA, A. *Principles of behavior modification.* New York: Holt, Rinehart & Winston, 1969.(b)

BANDURA, A. Analysis of modeling processes. In A. Bandura (Ed.), *Psychological modeling.* Chicago: Aldine–Atherton, 1971. Pp. 1–62.(a)

BANDURA, A. Psychotherapy based upon modeling principles. In A. E. Bergin & S. Garfield (Eds.), *Handbook of psychotherapy and behavior change.* New York: Wiley, 1971. Pp. 653–708.(b)

BANDURA, A. The process and practice of participant modeling treatment. Paper presented at the Conference on the Behavioral Basis of Mental Health, Ireland, 1972.

BANDURA, A. Social learning perspective on behavior change. In A. Burton (Ed.), *What makes behavior change?* New York: Brunner/Mazel, 1976. Pp. 34–57.

BANDURA, A. *Social learning theory.* Englewood Cliffs, N.J.: Prentice–Hall, 1977.(a)

BANDURA, A. Self-efficacy: Toward a unified theory of behavioral change. *Psychological Review*, 1977, **84**, 191–215.(b)

BANDURA, A. On paradigms and recycled ideologies. *Cognitive Therapy and Research*, 1978, **2**, 79–103.(a)

BANDURA, A. The self system in reciprocal determinism. *American Psychologist*, 1978, **33**, 344–358.(b)

BANDURA, A. Psychological mechanisms of aggression. In M. Von Cranach, K. Foppa, W. LePenies, & D. Ploog (Eds.), *Human ethology: Claims and limits of a new discipline.* Cambridge: Cambridge University Press, 1979.

BANDURA, A. Self-referent thought: A developmental analysis of self-efficacy. In J. Flavell & L. Ross (Eds.), *Social cognitive development.* Cambridge: Cambridge University Press, 1981.

BANDURA, A. Self-efficacy mechanism in human agency. *American Psychologist*, 1982, **37**, 122–147.

BANDURA, A. *Social foundations of thought and action: A social cognitive theory.* Englewood Cliffs, N.J.: Prentice–Hall, 1986.

BANDURA, A. Self-regulation of motivation and action through goal systems. In L. A. Pervin (Ed.), *Goal concepts in personality and social psychology.* Hillsdale, N.J.: Erlbaum, 1988.

BANDURA, A., & ABRAMS, K. Self-regulatory mechanisms in motivating, apathetic, and despondent reactions to unfulfilled standards. Unpublished manuscript, 1986.

BANDURA, A., & ADAMS, N. E. Analysis of self-efficacy theory of behavioral change. *Cognitive Therapy and Research*, 1977, **1**, 287–310.

BANDURA, A., ADAMS, N. E., & BEYER, J. Cognitive processes mediating behavioral change. *Journal of Personality and Social Psychology*, 1977, **35**, 125–139. (Copyright © 1977 by the American Psychological Association. Reprinted by permission.)

BANDURA, A., & BARAB, P. G. Conditions governing nonreinforced imitation. *Developmental Psychology*, 1971, **5**, 244–255.

BANDURA, A., BLANCHARD, E. B., & RITTER, B. J. The relative efficacy of modeling therapeutic approaches for producing behavioral, attitudinal and affective changes. Unpublished manuscript, Stanford University, 1967.

BANDURA, A., & CERVONE, D. Self-evaluative and self-efficacy mechanisms governing the motivational effect of goal systems. *Journal of Personality and Social Psychology*, 1983, **45**, 1017–1028.

BANDURA, A., GRUSEC, J. E., & MENLOVE, F. L. Some social determinants of self-monitoring reinforcement systems. *Journal of Personality and Social Psychology*, 1967, **5**, 449–455.

BANDURA, A., & KUPERS, C. J. Transmission of patterns of self-reinforcement through modeling. *Journal of Abnormal and Social Psychology*, 1964, **69**, 1–9.

BANDURA, A., & MENLOVE, F. L. Factors determining vicarious extinction of avoidance behavior through symbolic modeling. *Journal of Personality and Social Psychology*, 1968, **8**, 99–108.

BANDURA, A., & MISCHEL, W. Modification of self-imposed delay of reward through exposure to live and symbolic models. *Journal of Personality and Social Psychology*, 1965, **2**, 698–705.

BANDURA, A., O'LEARY, A., TAYLOR, C. B., GAUTHIER, J., & GOSSARD, D. Perceived self-efficacy and pain control: Opioid and nonopoid mechanisms. *Journal of Personality and Social Psychology*, 1987, **53**, 563–571.

BANDURA, A., REESE, L., & ADAMS, N. E. Microanalysis of action and fear arousal as a function of differential levels of perceived self-efficacy. *Journal of Personality and Social Psychology*, 1982, **43**, 5–21.

BANDURA, A., & ROSENTHAL, T. L. Vicarious classical conditioning as a function of arousal level. *Journal of Personality and Social Psychology*, 1966, **3**, 54–62.

BANDURA, A., ROSS, D., & ROSS, S. Imitation of film-mediated aggressive models. *Journal of Abnormal and Social Psychology*, 1963, **66**, 3–11.(a)

BANDURA, A., ROSS, D., & ROSS, S. Vicarious reinforcement and imitative learning. *Journal of Abnormal and Social Psychology*, 1963, **67**, 601–607.(b)

BANDURA, A., & SCHUNK, D. H. Cultivating competence, self-efficacy, and intrinsic interest. *Journal of Personality and Social Psychology*, 1981, **41**, 586–598.

BANDURA, A., & WALTERS, R. H. *Adolescent aggression*. New York: Ronald, 1959.

BANDURA, A., & WALTERS, R. H. *Social learning and personality development*. New York: Holt, Rinehart & Winston, 1963.

BANNISTER, D. The nature and measurement of schizophrenic thought disorder. *Journal of Mental Science*, 1962, **108**, 825–842.

BANNISTER, D. (ED.) *New perspectives in personal construct theory*. New York: Academic Press, 1977.

BANNISTER, D., & AGNEW, J. The child's construing of self. *Nebraska symposium on motivation*, 1977, **24**, 99–126.

BANNISTER, D., & FRANSELLA, F. A grid test of schizophrenic thought disorder. *British Journal of Social and Clinical Psychology*, 1966, **5**, 95–102.

BANNISTER, D., & FRANSELLA, F. *Inquiring man: The theory of personal constructs*. Baltimore: Penguin, 1971.

BANNISTER, D., & FRANSELLA, F. *A manual for repertory grid technique*. New York: Academic Press, 1977.

BARBER, T. X. *Pitfalls in human research*. New York: Pergamon, 1976.

BARBU, Z. Studies in children's honesty. *Quarterly Bulletin of the British Psychological Society*, 1951, **2**, 53–57.

BARGH, J. A. Attention and automaticity in the processing of self-relevant information. *Journal of Personality and Social Psychology*, 1982, **43**, 425–436.

BARLOW, D. H., & WINCZE, J. P. Treatment of sexual deviations. In S. Leiblum & L. A. Pervin (Eds.),

Principles and practice of sex therapy. New York: Guilford, 1980.

BARON, R. A. Outlines of a grand theory. *Contemporary Psychology,* 1987, **32,** 413–415.

BARRATT, B. The development of peer perception: A content analysis with children from 8 to 14 years. Unpublished manuscript, Harvard University, 1977.

BATESON, G. A., JACKSON, D. D., HALEY, J., & WEAKLAND, J., JR. Toward a theory of schizophrenia. *Behavioral Science,* 1965, **1,** 251–264.

BAUMEISTER, R. F. A self-presentational view of social phenomena. *Psychological Bulletin,* 1982, **91,** 3–26.

BECK, A. T. *Cognitive therapy and the emotional disorders.* New York: International Universities Press, 1976.

BECK, A. T., RUSH, A. J., SHAW, B. F., & EMERY, G. *Cognitive therapy of depression.* New York: Guilford, 1979.

BECKER, W. C. Consequences of different kinds of parental discipline. In M. L. Hoffman & L. W. Hoffman (Eds.), *Review of Child Development Research,* Vol. 1. New York: Russell Stage Foundation, 1964. Pp. 169–208.

BEM, D. J., & ALLEN, A. On predicting some of the people some of the time: The search for cross-situational consistencies in behavior. *Psychological Review,* 1974, **81,** 506–520.

BENDER, M. P. Does construing people as similar involve similar behavior towards them? A subjective and objective replication. *British Journal of Social and Clinical Psychology,* 1976, **15,** 93–95.

BERGER, S. M. Conditioning through vicarious investigation. *Psychological Review,* 1962, **69,** 450–466.

BERGIN, A. E., & STRUPP, H. H. *Changing frontiers in the science of psychotherapy.* New York: Aldine–Atherton, 1972.

BERGLAS, S. Self-handicapping and self-handicappers: A cognitive-attributional model of interpersonal self-protective behavior. In B. Maher (Ed.), *Progress in experimental personality research.* New York: Academic, 1985.

BERGLAS, S., & JONES, E. E. Drug choice as an internalization strategy in response to noncontingent success. *Journal of Personality and Social Psychology,* 1978, **36,** 405–417.

BERGMANN, G., & SPENCE, K. W. Operationism and theory in psychology. *Psychological Review,* 1941, **48,** 1–14.

BERKOWITZ, L., & DONNERSTEIN, E. External validity is more than skin deep. *American Psychologist,* 1982, **37,** 245–257.

BIBRING, E. The mechanism of depression. In P. Greenacre (Ed.), *Affective disorders.* New York: International Universities Press, 1953.

BIERI, J. Changes in interpersonal perceptions following social interaction. *Journal of Abnormal and Social Psychology,* 1953, **48,** 61–66.

BIERI, J. Cognitive complexity–simplicity and predictive behavior. *Journal of Abnormal and Social Psychology,* 1955, **51,** 263–268.

BIERI, J. Complexity–simplicity as a personality variable in cognitive and preferential behavior. In D. W. Fiske & S. R. Maddi (Eds.), *Functions of varied experience.* Homewood, Ill.: Dorsey, 1961. Pp. 355–379.

BIERI, J. Beyond the grid principle. *Contemporary Psychology,* 1986, **31,** 672–673.

BIERI, J., ATKINS, A., BRIAR, S., LEAMAN, R. L., MILLER, H., & TRIPOLDI, T. *Clinical and social judgment.* New York: Wiley, 1966.

BIJOU, S. W. Experimental studies of child behavior, normal and deviant. In L. Krasner & L. P. Ullmann (Eds.), *Research in behavior modification.* New York: Holt, Rinehart & Winston, 1965. Pp. 56–81.

BIJOU, S. W. *Child development: The basic stage of early childhood.* Englewood Cliffs, N.J.: Prentice–Hall, 1976.

BINDRA, D., & SCHEIER, I. H. The relation between psychometric and experimental research in psychology. *American Psychologist,* 1954, **9,** 69–71.

BLOCK, J. Advancing the psychology of personality: Paradigmatic shift or improving the quality of research? In D. Magmusson & N. Endler (Eds.), *Personality at the crossroads.* Hillsdale, N.J.: Erlbaum, 1977.

BLOOM, B. S. *Stability and change in human characteristics.* New York: Wiley, 1964.

BLUM, G., & MILLER, D. R. Exploring the psychoanalytic theory of the "oral character." *Journal of Personality,* 1952, **20,** 287–304.

BONARIUS, H. The interaction model of communication: Through experimental research toward existential relevance. In A. W. Landfield (Ed.), *Nebraska symposium on motivation.* Lincoln: University of Nebraska Press, 1977. Pp. 291–343.

BONARIUS, H., HOLLAND, R., & ROSENBERG, S. (EDS.) *Personal construct psychology. Recent advances in theory and practice.* London: Macmillan & Co., 1981.

BOOTH-KEWLEY, S., & FRIEDMAN, H. S. Psychological predictors of heart disease: A quantitative review. *Psychological Bulletin,* 1987, **101,** 343–362.

BORING, E. G. *A history of experimental psychology.* New York: Appleton–Century–Crofts, 1950.

BORKENAU, P. Toward an understanding of trait interrelations: Acts as instances for several traits. *Journal of Personality and Social Psychology.* 1986, **51,** 371–381.

BORKENAU, P., & OSTENDORF, F. Retrospective estimates of act frequencies: How accurately do they reflect reality? *Journal of Personality and Social Psychology,* 1987, **52,** 626–638.

BOURNE, P. G. *Fidel: A biography of Fidel Castro.* New York: Dodd, Mead, 1986.

BOWER, G. H. Contacts of cognitive psychology with social learning theory. *Cognitive Therapy and Research,* 1978, **2,** 123–146.

BOWER, G. H. Mood and memory. *American Psychologist,* 1981, **36,** 129–148. (Copyright © 1981 by the American Psychological Association. Reprinted by permission.)

BRAMEL, D. Some determinants of defensive projection. Unpublished Ph.D. dissertation, Stanford University, 1960.

BRAMEL, D., & FRIEND, R. Hawthorne, the myth of the docile worker, and the class bias in psychology. *American Psychologist,* 1981, **36,** 867–878.

BREWER, W. F. There is no convincing evidence for operant or classical conditioning in adult humans. In W. B. Weimer & D. S. Palermo (Eds.), *Cognition and the symbolic processes.* Hillsdale, N.J.: Erlbaum, 1974.

BREWIN, C. R. Depression and causal attributions: What is their relation? *Psychological Bulletin,* 1985, **98,** 297–309.

BRIERLY, D. W. The use of personality constructs by children of three different ages. Unpublished Ph.D. thesis, London University, 1967.

BRIM, O. G., & KAGAN, J. (EDS.) *Continuity and change in human development.* Cambridge, Mass.: Harvard University Press, 1980.

BROWN, I. B., JR., & INOUYE, D. K. Learned helplessness through modeling: The role of perceived similarity in competence. *Journal of Personality and Social Psychology,* 1978, **36,** 900–908.

BROWN, N. O. *Life against death.* New York: Random House, 1959.

BRUNER, J. S. You are your constructs. *Contemporary Psychology,* 1956, **1,** 355–356.

BURGER, J. M., & COOPER, H. M. The desirability of control. *Motivation and Emotion,* 1979, **3,** 381–387.

BURTON, R. V. Generality of honesty revisited. *Psychological Review,* 1963, **70,** 481–499.

BURTON, R. V. Validity of retrospective reports assessed by the multitrait–multimethod analysis. *Developmental Psychology Monographs,* 1970, **3,** No. 3, Part 2.

BUSS, A. H., & PLOMIN, R. *Temperament: Early developing personality traits.* Hillsdale, N.J.: Erlbaum, 1984.

BUSS, D. M. Paradigm for personality? *Contemporary Psychology,* 1982, **27,** 341–342.

BUSS, D. M., & CRAIK, K. H. The act frequency approach to personality. *Psychological Review,* 1983, **90,** 105–126.

BUTLER, J. M., & HAIGH, G. V. Changes in the relation between self-concepts and ideal concepts consequent upon client centered counseling. In C. R. Rogers & R. F. Dymond (Eds.), *Psychotherapy and personality change.* Chicago: University of Chicago Press, 1954. Pp. 55–75.

CAMPBELL, J. B., & HAWLEY, C. W. Study habits and Eysenck's theory of extroversion–introversion. *Journal of Research in Personality,* 1982, **16,** 139–146.

CANTOR, N. A cognitive-social approach to personality. In N. Cantor & J. F. Kihlstrom (Eds.), *Personality, cognition, and social interaction.* Hillsdale, N.J.: Erlbaum, 1981.

CANTOR, N. & KIHLSTROM, J. F. *Personality and social intelligence.* Englewood Cliffs, N.J.: Prentice–Hall, 1987.

CANTOR, N., & MISCHEL, W. Prototypes in person perception. *Advances in Experimental Social Psychology,* 1979, **12,** 3–52.

CANTOR, N., MISCHEL, W., & SCHWARTZ, J. C. A

prototype analysis of psychological situations. *Cognitive Psychology*, 1982, **14,** 45–77.

CARLSON, E. R., & CARLSON, R. Male and female subjects in personality research. *Journal of Abnormal and Social Psychology*, 1960, **61,** 482–483.

CARLSON, R. Where is the person in personality research? *Psychological Bulletin,* 1971, **75,** 203–219.

CARR, A. C. An evaluation of nine nondirective psychotherapy cases by means of the Rorschach. *Journal of Consulting Psychology*, 1949, **13,** 196–205.

CARTWRIGHT, D. S. Self-consistency as a factor affecting immediate recall. *Journal of Abnormal and Social Psychology*, 1956, **52,** 212–218.

CARTWRIGHT, D. S., KIRTNER, W. L., & FISKE, D. W. Method factors in changes associated with psychotherapy. *Journal of Abnormal and Social Psychology*, 1963, **66,** 164–175.

CATTELL, R. B. The main personality factors in questionnaire, self-estimated material. *Journal of Social Psychology*, 1950, **31,** 3–38.

CATTELL, R. B. Personality and motivation theory based on structural measurement. In J. L. McCary (Ed.), *Psychology of personality.* New York: Logos, 1956. Pp. 63–120.(a)

CATTELL, R. B. Validation and interpretation of the 16 P.F. questionnaire. *Journal of Clinical Psychology*, 1956, **12,** 205–214.(b)

CATTELL, R. B. The dynamic calculus: Concepts and crucial experiments. In M. R. Jones (Ed.), *Nebraska symposium on motivation.* Lincoln: University of Nebraska Press, 1959. Pp. 84–134.(a)

CATTELL, R. B. Personality theory growing from multivariate quantitative research. In S. Koch (Ed.), *Psychology: The study of a science.* New York: McGraw–Hill, 1959. Pp. 257–327.(b)

CATTELL, R. B. Foundations of personality measurement theory in multivariate expressions. In B. M. Bass & I. A. Berg (Eds.), *Objective approaches to personality assessment.* Princeton, N.J.: Van Nostrand, 1959. Pp. 42–65.(c)

CATTELL, R. B. Personality measurement functionally related to source trait structure. In S. Messick & J. Ross (Eds.), *Measurement in personality and cognition.* New York: Wiley, 1962. Pp. 249–267.

CATTELL, R. B. Personality, role, mood, and situation perception: A unifying theory of modulators. *Psychological Review,* 1963, **70,** 1–18.(a)

CATTELL, R. B. The nature and measurement of anxiety. *Scientific American,* 1963, **208,** 96–104.(b)

CATTELL, R. B. *The scientific analysis of personality.* Baltimore: Penquin, 1965.

CATTELL, R. B. Psychological theory and scientific method. In R. B. Cattell (Ed.), *Handbook of multivariate experimental psychology.* Chicago: Rand McNally, 1966. Pp. 1–18.(a)

CATTELL, R. B. The principles of experimental design and analysis in relation to theory building. In R. B. Cattell (Ed.), *Handbook of multivariate experimental psychology.* Chicago: Rand McNally, 1966. Pp. 19–66.(b)

CATTELL, R. B. A more sophisticated look at structure: Perturbation, sampling, role, and observer trait-view theories. In R. B. Cattell, & R. M. Dreger (Eds.), *Handbook of modern personality theory.* Washington: Hemisphere, 1977. Pp. 166–220.

CATTELL, R. B. *Personality and learning theory.* New York: Springer Pub., 1979.

CATTELL, R. B. *Personality and learning theory. Vol. 2: A systems theory of maturation and structured learning.* New York: Springer Pub., 1980.

CATTELL, R. B. *Structured personality learning theory.* New York: Praeger, 1983.

CATTELL, R. B. *Human motivation and the dynamic calculus.* New York: Praeger, 1985.

CATTELL, R. B., & BAGGALEY, A. R. The objective measurement of motivation. I. Development and evaluation of principles and devices. *Journal of Personality*, 1956, **24,** 401–423.

CATTELL, R. B., BLEWETT, D., & BELOFF, J. The inheritance of personality: A multiple variance analysis of nature–nurture ratios for personality factors in Q-data. *American Journal of Human Genetics*, 1955, **7,** 122–146.

CATTELL, R. B., & CHILD, D. *Motivation and dynamic structure.* New York: Wiley, 1975.

CATTELL, R. B., & CROSS, P. Comparison of the ergic and self-sentiment structures found in dynamic traits by R- and P-techniques. *Journal of Personality*, 1952, **21,** 250–270.

CATTELL, R. B., & DELHEES, K. H. Seven missing

normal personality factors in the questionnaire primaries. *Multivariate Behavioral Research,* 1973, **8,** 173–194.

CATTELL, R. B., & DREGER, R. M. (EDS.) *Handbook of modern personality theory.* Washington: Hemisphere, 1977.

CATTELL, R. B., & EBER, H. W. *Handbook for the Sixteen Personality Factor Questionnaire: The 16 PF Test.* Champaign, Ill.: Institute for Personality and Ability Testing, 1957, 1962.

CATTELL, R. B., EBER, H. W., & TATSUOKA, M. M. *Handbook for the 16 PF Questionnaire.* Champaign, Ill.: IPAT, 1970.

CATTELL, R. B., & NICHOLS, K. E. An improved definition, from 10 researchers, of second order personality factors in Q-data (with cross-cultural checks). *Journal of Social Psychology,* 1972, **86,** 187–203.

CATTELL, R. B., RADCLIFFE, J. A., & SWEENEY, A. B. The nature and measurement of components of motivation. *Genetic Psychology Monographs,* 1963, **68,** 49–211.

CATTELL, R. B., RADCLIFFE, J. A., & SWEENEY, A. B. Components in motivation strength in children compared with those in adults. *Journal of Genetic Psychology,* 1964, **70,** 65–1112.

CATTELL, R. B., & RICKELS, K. Diagnostic power of IPAT objective anxiety neuroticism tests. *Archives of General Psychiatry,* 1964, **11,** 459–465.

CATTELL, R. B., RICKELS, K., WEISE, C., GRAY, B., & YEE, R. The effects of psychotherapy upon measured anxiety and regression. *American Journal of Psychotherapy,* 1966, **20,** 261–269.

CATTELL, R. B., & SCHEIER, I. H. *The meaning and measurement of neuroticism and anxiety.* New York: Ronald Press, 1961.

CATTELL, R. B., & STICE, G. F. *Handbook for the sixteen personality factor questionnaire.* Champaign, Ill.: Institute for Personality and Ability Testing, 1962.

CATTELL, R. B., & TATRO, D. F. The personality factors, objectively measured, which distinguish psychotics from normals. *Behavior Research and Therapy,* 1966, **4,** 39–51.

CAUTELA, J. R., & UPPER, D. The Behavioral Inventory Battery: The use of self-report measures in behavioral analysis and therapy. In M. Hersen &

A. Bellack (Eds.), *Behavioral assessment: A practical handbook.* New York: Pergamon, 1976.

CHAMPAGNE, B., & PERVIN, L. A. The relation of perceived situation similarity to perceived behavior similarity: Implications for social learning theory. *European Journal of Personality,* 1987, **1,** 79–92.

CHODORKOFF, B. Self perception, perceptual defense, and adjustment. *Journal of Abnormal and Social Psychology,* 1954, **49,** 508–512.

CIMINERO, A. R. Behavioral assessment: An overview. In A. R. Ciminero, K. S. Calhoun, & H. E. Adams (Eds.), *Handbook of behavioral assessment.* New York: Wiley, 1977. Pp. 3–14.

CIMINERO, A. R., CALHOUN, K. S., & ADAMS, H. E. (EDS.) *Handbook of behavioral assessment.* New York: Wiley, 1977.

CLEAVER, E. *Soul on ice.* New York: Dell, 1968.

COAN, R. W. Child personality and developmental psychology. In R. B. Cattell (Ed.), *Handbook of multivariate experimental psychology.* Chicago: Rand McNally, 1966. Pp. 732–752.

COAN, R. W. Dimensions of psychological theory. *American Psychologist,* 1968, **23,** 715–722.

COCHRAN, S. D., & HAMMEN, C. L. Perceptions of stressful life events and depression: A test of attributional models. *Journal of Personality and Social Psychology,* 1985, **48,** 1562–1571.

COLBY, K. M. Modeling a paranoid mind. *Behavioral and Brain Sciences,* 1981, **4,** 515–560.

COLE, J. K., LANDFIELD, A. W. (EDS.) *Personal construct psychology. Nebraska symposium on motivation.* Lincoln: University of Nebraska Press, 1976.

COMBS, A. W., & SUPER, D. W. The self, its derivative terms, and research. *Journal of Individual Psychology,* 1957, **13,** 134–145.

CONDON, T. J., & ALLEN, G. J. The role of psychoanalytic merging fantasies in systematic desensitization: A rigorous methodological examination. *Journal of Abnormal Psychology,* 1980, **89,** 437–443.

CONLEY, J. J. Longitudinal stability of personality traits: A multitrait-multimethod-multioccasion analysis. *Journal of Personality and Social Psychology,* 1985, **49,** 1266–1282.

COOPERSMITH, S. *The antecedents of self-esteem.* San Francisco: Freeman, 1967.

COVINGTON, M. V., & OMELICH, C. L. Are the causal attributions causal? A path analysis of the cognitive model of achievement motivation. *Journal of Personality and Social Psychology*, 1979, **37**, 1487–1504.

CROCKETT, W. H. Cognitive complexity and impression formation. In B. A. Maher (Ed.), *Progress in experimental personality research.* New York: Academic Press, 1965. Pp. 47–90.

CROCKETT, W. H. The organization of construct systems: The organization corollary. In J. C. Mancuso & J. R. Adams-Webber (Eds.), *The construing person.* New York: Praeger, 1982.

CRONBACH, L. J. The two disciplines of scientific psychology. *American Psychologist*, 1957, **12**, 671–684.

CRONBACH, L. J. *Essentials of psychological testing.* New York: Harper, 1960.

CRONBACH, L. J., & MEEHL, P. E. Construct validity in psychological tests. *Psychological Bulletin*, 1955, **52**, 281–302.

CROWNE, D. P. Review of R. B. Cattell, the scientific life, analysis of personality. *Contemporary Psychology*, 1967, **12**, 40–41.

CROWNE, D. P., & MARLOWE, D. *The approval motive: Studies in evaluative dependence.* New York: Wiley, 1964.

CURTIS, R. C., & MILLER, K. Believing another likes or dislikes you: Behaviors making the beliefs come true. *Journal of Personality and Social Psychology*, 1986, **51**, 284–290.

CUTRONA, C. E., RUSSELL, D., & JONES, R. D. Cross-situational consistency in causal attributions: Does attributional style exist? *Journal of Personality and Social Psychology*, 1985, **47**, 1043–1058.

DAMARIN, F. L., & CATTELL, R. B. Personality factors in early childhood and their relation to intelligence. *Monographs of the Society for Research in Child Development*, 1968, **33**, 1–95.

DANKER-BROWN, P., & BAUCOM, D. H. Cognitive influences on the development of learned helplessness. *Journal of Personality and Social Psychology*, 1982, **43**, 793–801.

DARLEY, J. M., & FAZIO, R. Expectancy confirmation processes arising in the social interaction sequence. *American Psychologist*, 1980, **35**, 867–881.

DASHIELL, J. F. Some rapproachments in contemporary psychology. *Psychological Bulletin*, 1939, **36**, 1–24.

DAVIS, P. J., & SCHWARTZ, G. E. Repression and the inaccessibility of affective memories. *Journal of Personality and Social Psychology*, 1987, **52**, 155–162.

DAVISON, G. C. Systematic desensitization as a counterconditioning process. *Journal of Abnormal Psychology*, 1968, **73**, 91–99.

DAVISON, G. C., & NEALE, J. M. *Abnormal psychology: An experimental clinical approach.* New York: Wiley, 1982.

DAVISON, G. C., & WILSON, T. Critique of desensitization: Social and cognitive factors underlying the effectiveness of Wolpe's procedure. *Psychological Bulletin*, 1972, **78**, 28–31.

DAVISON, G. C., & WILSON, G. T. Processes of fear-reduction in systematic desensitization: Cognitive and social reinforcement factors in humans. *Behavior Therapy*, 1973, **4**, 1–21.

DEAUX, K. *The behavior of women and men.* Monterey, Ca.: Brooks/Cole, 1976.

DEUTSCH, M., & KRAUSS, R. M. *Theories in social psychology.* New York: Basic Books, 1965.

DeVELLIS, R. F., DeVELLIS, B. M., & McCAULEY, C. Vicarious acquisition of learned helplessness. *Journal of Personality and Social Psychology*, 1978, **36**, 894–899.

DIGMAN, J. M., & INOUYE, J. Further specification of the five robust factors of personality. *Journal of Personality and Social Psychology*, 1986, **50**, 116–123.

DIVEN, K. Certain determinants in the conditioning of anxiety reactions. *Journal of Psychology*, 1937, **3**, 291–308.

DIXON, N. F. *Preconscious processing.* Chichester, England: Wiley, 1981.

DOLLARD, J., DOOB, L. W., MILLER, N. E., MOWRER, O. H., & SEARS, R. R. *Frustration and aggression.* New Haven, Conn.: Yale University Press, 1939.

DOLLARD, J., & MILLER, N. E. *Personality and psychotherapy.* New York: McGraw-Hill, 1950.

DREISER, T. *A gallery of women.* New York: Liveright, 1929.

DUCK, S. Two individuals in search of agreement: The commonality corollary. In J. C. Mancuso & J. R. Adams-Webber (Eds.), *The construing person.* New York: Praeger, 1982.

DWECK, C. S. Motivational processes affecting learning. *American Psychologist,* 1986, **41,** 1040–148.

DYMOND, R. F. Adjustment changes over therapy from self-sorts. In C. R. Rogers & R. F. Dymond (Eds.), *Psychotherapy and personality change.* Chicago: University of Chicago Press, 1954. Pp. 76–84.(a)

DYMOND, R. F. Adjustment changes over therapy from thematic apperception test ratings. In C. R. Rogers & R. F. Dymond (Eds.), *Psychotherapy and personality change.* Chicago: University of Chicago Press, 1954. Pp. 109–120.(b)

EAGLE, M., WOLITZKY, D. L., & KLEIN, G. S. Imagery: Effect of a concealed figure in a stimulus. *Science,* 1966, **18,** 837–839.

EDELSON, M. *Hypothesis and evidence in psychoanalysis.* Chicago: University of Chicago Press, 1984.

EDUCATIONAL AND INDUSTRIAL TESTING SERVICE. 1967 catalog of tests, books, and guidance materials. San Diego, Calif., 1967.

EDWARDS, A. L. The relationship between the judged desirability of a trait and the probability that the trait will be endorsed. *Journal of Applied Psychology,* 1953, **37,** 90–93.

EDWARDS, A. L. Social desirability and personality test construction. In B. M. Bass & I. A. Berg (Eds.), *Objective approaches to personality.* Princeton, N.J.: Van Nostrand, 1959. Pp. 101–116.

ELLIS, A., & HARPER, R. A. *A new guide to rational living.* North Hollywood, Calif.: Wilshire, 1975.

EMMONS, R. A. Narcissism: Theory and measurement. *Journal of Personality and Social Psychology,* 1987, **52,** 11–17.

ENDLER, N. S., HUNT, J. McV., & ROSENSTEIN, A. J. An S–R inventory of anxiousness. *Psychological Monographs,* 1962, **76** (17, Whole No. 536).

ENDLER, N. S., & MAGNUSSON, D. (EDS.) *Interactional psychology and personality.* Washington, D.C.: Hemisphere (Halsted–Wiley), 1976.

EPSTEIN, S. The stability of behavior. I. On predicting most of the people most of the time. *Journal of Personality and Social Psychology,* 1979, **37,** 1097–1126.

EPSTEIN, S. A research paradigm for the study of personality and emotions. In M. M. Page (Ed.), *Personality: Current theory and research.* Lincoln: University of Nebraska Press, 1983.

EPSTEIN, S., & O'BRIEN, E. J. The person–situation debate in historical and current perspective. *Psychological Bulletin,* 1985, **98,** 513–537.

EPTING, F. R. *Personal construct counseling and psychotherapy.* Chichester, England: Wiley, 1984.

ERDELYI, M. *Psychoanalysis: Freud's cognitive psychology.* New York: Freeman, 1984.

ERDELYI, M. H., & GOLDBERG, B. Let's not sweep repression under the rug: Toward a cognitive psychology of repression. In J. F. Kihlstrom & F. J. Evans (Eds.), *Functional disorders of memory.* Hillsdale, N.J.: Erlbaum, 1979.

ERICSSON, K. A., & SIMON, H. A. Verbal reports as data. *Psychological Review,* 1980, **87,** 215–251.

ERIKSON, E. *Childhood and society.* New York: Norton, 1950.

ERIKSON, E. H. *The life cycle completed: A review.* New York: Norton, 1982.

ERWIN, E. *Behavior therapy: Scientific, philosophical, and moral foundations.* New York: Cambridge University Press, 1978.

EVANS, G. W., PALSAÑE, M. N., & CARRERE, S. Type A behavior and occupational stress: A cross-cultural study of blue-collar workers. *Journal of Personality and Social Psychology,* 1987, **52,** 1002–1007.

EVANS, R. I. *The making of psychology.* New York: Knopf, 1976.

EYSENCK, H. J. *Dimensions of personality,* London: Routledge & Kegan Paul, 1947. (Reprinted by permission.)

EYSENCK, H. J. The organization of personality. *Journal of Personality,* 1951, **20,** 101–117.

EYSENCK, H. J. *The scientific study of personality.* London: Routledge & Kegan Paul, 1952.

EYSENCK, H. J. *Uses and abuses of psychology.* London: Penguin, 1953.

EYSENCK, H. J. A dynamic theory of anxiety and hysteria. *Journal of Mental Science,* 1955, **101,** 28–51.

EYSENCK, H. J. The inheritance of extraversion–

introversion. *Acta Psychologica*, 1956, **12**, 429–432.

EYSENCK, H. *Sense and nonsense in psychology*. Baltimore: Penguin, 1957.

EYSENCK, H. J. Learning theory and behavior therapy. *Journal of Mental Science*, 1959, **105**, 61–75.

EYSENCK, H. J. (ED.) *Handbook of abnormal psychology*. New York: Basic Books, 1961.

EYSENCK, H. J. *The structure of human personality*. London: Methuen, 1970. (Reprinted by permission.)

EYSENCK, H. J. *Eysenck on extraversion*. London: Crosby, Lockwood, Staples, 1973.

EYSENCK, H. J. *The inequality of man*. San Diego, Calif.: Edits Publishers, 1975.

EYSENCK, H. J. Personality and factor analysis: A reply to Guilford. *Psychological Bulletin*, 1977, **84**, 405–411.

EYSENCK, H. J. The conditioning model of neurosis. *Behavioral and Brain Sciences*, 1979, **2**, 155–199.

EYSENCK, H. J. *Personality genetics and behavior*. New York: Praeger, 1982.

EYSENCK, H. J., & BEECH, H. R. Counter conditioning and related methods. In A. E. Bergin & S. Garfield (Eds.), *Handbook of psychotherapy and behavior change*. New York: Wiley, 1971. Pp. 543–611.

EYSENCK, H. J., & EYSENCK, M. W. *Personality and individual differences: A natural science approach*. New York: Plenum, 1985.

EYSENCK, H. J., & RACHMAN, S. *The causes and cures of neurosis*. San Diego, Calif.: Knapp, 1965.

EYSENCK, H. J., & WILSON, G. D. *The experimental study of Freudian theories*. London: Methuen, 1973.

EYSENCK, S. B. G., & LONG, F. Y. A cross-cultural comparison of personality in adults and children: Singapore and England. *Journal of Personality and Social Psychology*, 1986, **50**, 124–130.

FARBEROW, N. J., & SHNEIDMAN, E. S. (EDS.) *The cry for help*. New York: McGraw–Hill, 1961.

FERSTER, C. B. Classification of behavioral pathology. In L. Krasner & L. P. Ullman (Eds.), *Research in behavior modification*. New York: Holt, Rinehart & Winston, 1965. Pp. 6–26.

FERSTER, C. B. A functional analysis of depression. *American Psychologist*, 1973, **28**, 857–870.

FESHBACH, S. The stimulating effects of a vicarious aggressive activity. *Journal of Abnormal and Social Psychology*, 1961, **63**, 381–385.

FESTINGER, L. *A theory of cognitive dissonance*. Evanston, Ill.: Row, Peterson, 1957.

FESTINGER, L., & BRAMEL, D. The reactions of humans to cognitive dissonance. In A. J. Bachrach (Ed.), *Experimental foundations of clinical psychology*. New York: Basic Books, 1962. Pp. 254–279.

FIEDLER, F. E. A comparison of therapeutic relationships in psychoanalytic, nondirective, and Adlerian therapy. *Journal of Counseling Psychology*, 1950, **14**, 436–445.

FIEDLER, F. E. Engineer the job to fit the manager. *Harvard Business Review*. 1965, **43**, 115–122.

FISHER, A. E. Unpublished doctoral dissertation, Pennsylvania State University, 1955.

FISHER, S., & FISHER, R. L. *Pretend the world is funny and forever: A psychological analysis of comedians, clowns, and actors*. Hillsdale, N.J.: Erlbaum, 1981.

FISHER, S., & GREENBERG, R. P. *The scientific credibility of Freud's theories and therapy*. New York: Basic Books, 1977.

FISKE, D. W. *Strategies for personality research*. San Francisco: Jossey–Bass, 1978.

FISKE, D. W., & GOODMAN, G. The post therapy period. *Journal of Abnormal Psychology*, 1965, **70**, 169–179.

FOLKMAN, S., LAZARUS, R. S., GRUEN, R. J., & DE-LONGIS, A. Appraisal, coping, health status, and psychological symptoms. *Journal of Personality and Social Psychology*, 1986, **50**, 571–579.

FONG, G. T., & MARKUS, H. Self-schemas and judgments about others. *Social Cognition*, 1982, **1**, 191–204.

FORD, D. H., & URBAN, H. B. *Systems of psychotherapy*. New York: Wiley, 1963.

FRANK, L. K. Projective methods for the study of personality. *Journal of Psychology*, 1939, **8**, 389–413.

FRANKL, V. E. *The doctor and the soul*. New York: Knopf, 1955.

FRANKL, V. E. On logotherapy and existential analysis. *American Journal of Psychoanalysis,* 1958, **18,** 28–37.

FRANKS, C. M., & WILSON, G. T. (EDS.) *Annual review of behavior therapy: Theory and practice.* New York: Brunner/Mazel, 1978.

FRANKS, C. M., & WILSON, G. T. (EDS.) *Annual review of behavior therapy: Theory and practice.* New York: Brunner/Mazel, 1980.

FRANKS, C. M., WILSON, G. T., KENDALL, P. C., & BROWNELL, K. D. *Annual review of behavior therapy: Theory and practice.* New York: Guilford, 1982.

FREUD, S. The interpretation of dreams. In *Standard edition,* Vols. 4 & 5. London: Hogarth Press, 1953. (First German edition, 1900.)

FREUD, S. *Three essays on sexuality.* London: Hogarth Press, 1953. (Original edition, 1905.)

FREUD, S. Analysis of a phobia in a five-year-old boy. In *Standard edition,* Vol. 10. London: Hogarth Press, 1959. (First German edition, 1909.)

FREUD, S. Psycho-analytic notes upon an autobiographical account of a case of paranoia (dementia paranoides). In *Collected Papers,* Vol. III. New York: Basic Books, 1959. (Original edition, 1911.)

FREUD, S. Instincts and their vicissitudes. In *Standard edition,* Vol. 14. London: Hogarth Press, 1957. (First German edition, 1915.)

FREUD, S. Beyond the pleasure principle. In *Standard edition,* Vol. 18. London: Hogarth Press, 1955. (First German edition, 1920.)

FREUD, S. *A general introduction to psychoanalysis.* New York: Permabooks, 1953. (Boni & Liveright edition, 1924.)

FREUD, S. *Civilization and its discontents.* London: Hogarth Press, 1949. (Original edition, 1930.)

FREUD, S. *New introductory lectures on psychoanalysis.* New York: Norton, 1933.

FREUD, S. An outline of psychoanalysis. *International Journal of Psychoanalysis,* 1940, **21,** 27–84.

FRIEDMAN, M. Alteration of Type A behavior and reduction in cardiac occurrences in postmyocardial infarction in patients. *American Heart Journal,* 1984, **108,** 237–248.

FRIEDMAN, M., & POWELL, L. H. The diagnosis and quantitative assessment of Type A behavior: Introduction and description of the video-taped structured interview. *Integrative Psychiatry,* 1984, 123–129.

FRIEDMAN, M., & ROSENMAN, R. H. *Type A behavior and your heart.* New York: Knopf, 1974.

FROMM, E. *Sigmund Freud's mission.* New York: Harper, 1959.

FUNDER, D. C., & OZER, D. J. Behavior as a function of the situation. *Journal of Personality and Social Psychology,* 1983, **44,** 107–112.

GAENSBAUER, T. J. The differentiation of discrete affects. *Psychoanalytic Study of the Child,* 1982, **37,** 29–66.

GAGE, N. L. Paradigms for research on teaching. In N. L. Gage (Ed.), *Handbook of research on teaching.* Chicago: Rand McNally, 1963.

GALLUP, G. G. Toward a comparative psychology of mind. In R. L. Mellgren (Ed.), *Animal cognition and behavior.* New York: Elsevier/North-Holland, 1986.

GARDNER, R. W., JACKSON, D. N., & MESSICK, S. J. Personality organization in cognitive controls and intellectual abilities. *Psychological Issues,* 1960, Monograph No. 8.

GARFIELD, S. L., & BERGIN, A. E. *Handbook of psychotherapy and behavior change,* 2d ed. New York: Wiley, 1978.

GEEN, R. G. Preferred stimulation levels in introverts and extroverts: Effects on arousal and performance. *Journal of Personality and Social Psychology,* 1984, **46,** 1303–1312.

GEER, J. H., & TURTELTAUB, A. Fear reduction following observation of a model. *Journal of Personality and Social Psychology,* 1967, **6,** 327–331.

GEISLER, C. The use of subliminal psychodynamic activation in the study of repression. *Journal of Personality and Social Psychology,* 1986, **51,** 844–851.

GENDLIN, E. T. Client-centered developments and work with schizophrenics. *Journal of Counseling Psychology,* 1962, **9,** 205–211.

GEWIRTZ, J. L. Conditional responding as a paradigm for observational, imitative learning and vicarious imitative learning and vicarious reinforcement. In H. W. Reese (Ed.), *Advances in child development and behavior.* New York: Academic Press, 1971. Pp. 274–304.

GILL, J. J. Reduction in Type A behavior in healthy middle-aged American military officers. *American Heart Journal*, 1985, **110,** 503–514.

GILMORE, J. Toward an understanding of imitation. In E. C. Simmerl, R. A. Hoppe, & G. A. Milton (Eds.), *Social facilitation and imitative behavior.* Boston: Allyn & Bacon, 1968. Pp. 217–238.

GLASS, D. C. *Behavior patterns, stress, and coronary disease.* Hillsdale, N.J.: Erlbaum, 1977.

GLASS, D. C., & CARVER, C. S. Helplessness and the coronary-prone personality. In J. Garber & M. E. P. Seligman (Eds.), *Human helplessness.* New York: Academic Press, 1980.

GLASS, D. C., & SINGER, J. E. *Urban stress.* New York: Academic Press, 1972.

GLUCKSBERG, S. General discussion of issues: Relationships between cognitive psychology and the psychology of personality. In N. Cantor and J. Kihlstrom (Eds.), *Personality, cognition, and social interaction.* Hillsdale, N.J.: Erlbaum, 1981.

GLUCKSBERG, S., & KING, L. J. Motivated forgetting mediated by implicit verbal chaining: A laboratory analog of repression. *Science,* October 27, 1967, 517–519.

GOFFMAN, E. *The presentation of self in everyday life.* Garden City, N.Y.: Doubleday, 1959.

GOLDSTEIN, K. *The organism.* New York: American Book, 1939.

GORDON, J. E. Review of R. B. Cattell's *Personality and social psychology. Contemporary Psychology,* 1966, **11,** 236–238.

GOTTESMAN, I. I. Heritability of personality: A demonstration. *Psychological Monographs,* 1963, **77** (9, Whole No. 572).

GOTTESMAN, I. I., & SHIELDS, J. Schizophrenia in twins: 16 years' consecutive admissions to a psychiatric clinic. *British Journal of Psychiatry,* 1966, **112,** 809–818.

GRAY, J. A. A critique of Eysenck's theory of personality. In H. J. Eysenck (Ed.), *A model for personality.* Berlin: Springer-Verlag, 1981.

GREENE, M. A. Client perception of the relationship as a function of worker–client cognitive styles. Unpublished doctoral dissertation, Columbia·University School of Social Work, 1972.

GREENSPAN, S. I. A consideration of some learning variables in the context of psychoanalytic learning perspective. *Psychological Issues,* 1975, **9,** Monograph No. 33.

GREENSPOON, J. The reinforcing effects of two spoken sounds on the frequency of two responses. *American Journal of Psychology,* 1955, **68,** 409–416.

GREENSPOON, J. Verbal conditioning and clinical psychology. In A. J. Bachrach (Ed.), *Experimental foundations of clinical psychology.* New York: Basic Books, 1962.

GREENSPOON, J., & LAMAL, P. A. Cognitive behavior modification—Who needs it? *Psychological Record,* 1978, **28,** 323–335.

GRIER, W. H., & COBBS, P. M. *Black rage.* New York: Bantam, 1968.

GRINKER, R. R., & SPIEGEL, J. P. *Men under stress.* Philadelphia: Blakiston, 1945.

GRODDECK, G. *The book of the it.* New York: Vintage, 1961. (Original edition 1923.)

GRUMMON, D. L., & JOHN, EVE S. Changes over client-centered therapy evaluated on psychoanalytically based TAT scales. In C. R. Rogers & R. F. Dymond (Eds.), *Psychotherapy and personality change.* Chicago: University of Chicago Press, 1954. Pp. 121–144.

GRUNBAUM, A. *Foundations of psychoanalysis: A philosophical critique.* Berkeley: University of California Press, 1984.

GUILFORD, J. P. Factors and factors of personality. *Psychological Bulletin,* 1975, **82,** 802–814.

GUMP, P. V. A statistical investigation of one psychoanalytic approach and a comparison of it with nondirective therapy. Unpublished M.A. thesis, Ohio State University, 1944.

GUR, R. C., & SACKEIM, H. A. Self-deception: A concept in search of a phenomenon. *Journal of Personality and Social Psychology,* 1979, **37,** 147–169.

GUTHRIE, E. R. *The psychology of learning.* New York: Harper, 1952.

HAIGH, G. Defensive behavior in client-centered therapy. *Journal of Consulting Psychology,* 1949, **13,** 181–189.

HAIMOWITZ, N. R. An investigation into some personality changes occurring in individuals undergoing client-centered therapy. Unpublished Ph.D. dissertation, University of Chicago, 1948.

HALKIDES, G. An experimental study of four conditions necessary for therapeutic change. Unpublished Ph.D. dissertation, University of Chicago, 1958.

HALL, C. S. *A primer of Freudian psychology.* New York: Mentor, 1954.

HALL, C. S., & LINDZEY, G. *Theories of personality.* New York: Wiley, 1957.

HALPERN, J. Projection: A test of the psychoanalytic hypothesis. *Journal of Abnormal Psychology,* 1977, **86,** 536–542.

HARRINGTON, D. M., BLOCK, J. H., & BLOCK, J. Testing aspects of Carl Rogers' theory of creative environments: Child-rearing antecedents of creative potential in young adolescents. *Journal of Personality and Social Psychology,* 1987, **52,** 851–856.

HARRIS, B. Whatever happened to Little Albert? *American Psychologist,* 1979, **34,** 151–160.

HARRIS, J. G., JR. Validity: The search for a constant in a universe of variables. In M. A. Rickers-Ovsiankina (Ed.), *Rorschach psychology.* New York: Wiley, 1960. Pp. 380–439.

HARRISON, R. Cognitive change and participation in a sensitivity-training laboratory. *Journal of Consulting Psychology,* 1966, **30,** 517–520.

HARTSHORNE, H., & MAY, M. A. *Studies in the nature of character: Studies in deceit.* New York: Macmillan, 1928.

HAUGHTON, E., & AYLLON, T. Production and elimination of symptomatic behavior. In L. P. Ullmann & L. Krasner (Eds.), *Case studies in behavior modification.* New York: Holt, Rinehart & Winston, 1965, Pp. 94–98.

HAVENER, P. H., & IZARD, C. E. Unrealistic self-enhancement in paranoid schizophrenics. *Journal of Consulting Psychology,* 1962, **26,** 65–68.

HAVENS, L. Review of D. Wyss, Psychoanalytic schools from the beginning to the present. *Psychotherapy and the Social Science Review,* July 13, 1973.

HAWKINS, R. P., PETERSON, R. F., SCHWEID, E., & BIJOU, S. W. Behavior therapy in the home: Amelioration of problem parent–child relations with the parent in a therapeutic role. *Journal of Experimental Child Psychology,* 1966, **4,** 99–107.

HAYDEN, B. C. Experience—A case for possible change: The modulation corollary. In J. C. Man-cuso & J. R. Adams-Webber (Eds.), *The construing person.* New York: Praeger, 1982.

HAZAN, C., & SHAVER, P. Romantic love conceptualized as an attachment process. *Journal of Personality and Social Psychology,* 1987, **52,** 511–524.

HEBB, D. O. The role of neurological ideas in psychology. *Journal of Personality,* 1951, **20,** 39–55.

HEILBRUN, K. Silverman's subliminal psychodynamic activation: A failure to replicate. *Journal of Abnormal Psychology,* 1980, **89,** 560–566.

HEINE, R. W. An investigation of the relationship between change in personality from psychotherapy as reported by patients and the factors seen by patients as producing change. Unpublished Ph.D. dissertation, University of Chicago, 1950.

HELPER, M. M. Parental evaluations of children and children's self-evaluations. *Journal of Abnormal and Social Psychology,* 1958, **56,** 190–194.

HENDRICK, I. *Facts and theories of psychoanalysis.* New York: Knopf, 1934.

HENDRICK, I. The discussion of the "instinct to master." *Psychoanalytic Quarterly,* 1943, **12,** 561–565.

HERRNSTEIN, R. J. The evolution of behaviorism. *American Psychologist,* 1977, **32,** 593–602.

HESSE, H. *Demian.* New York: Harper, 1965. (Originally published in 1925.)

HESSE, H. *Siddhartha.* New York: New Directions, 1951.

HIGGINS, E. T. Self-discrepancy: A theory relating self and affect. *Psychological Review,* 1987, **94,** 319–340.

HIGGINS, E. T., BOND, R. N., KLEIN, R., & STRAUMAN, T. Self-discrepancies and emotional vulnerability: How magnitude, accessibility, and type of discrepancy influence affect. *Journal of Personality and Social Psychology,* 1986, **51,** 5–15.

HILGARD, E. R. Human motives and the concept of self. *American Psychologist,* 1949, **4,** 374–382.

HILL, W. F. Learning theory and the acquisition of values. *Psychological Review,* 1960, **67,** 317–331.

HINKLE, D. N. The change of personal constructs from the viewpoint of a theory of implications. Unpublished Ph.D. dissertation, Ohio State University, 1965.

HIROTO, D. S. Locus of control and learned helplessness. *Journal of Experimental Psychology*, 1974, **102**, 187–193. (Copyright © 1974 by the American Psychological Association. Reprinted by permission.)

HIROTO, D. S., & SELIGMAN, M. E. P. Generality of learned helplessness in man. *Journal of Personality and Social Psychology*, 1975, **31**, 311–327.

HITT, W. D. Two models of man. *American Psychologist*, 1969, **24**, 651–658.

HOGAN, R. On adding apples and oranges in personality psychology. *Contemporary Psychology*, 1982, **27**, 851–852.

HOGAN, R. A socioanalytic theory of personality. In M. M. Page (Ed.), *Nebraska symposium on motivation*. Lincoln: University of Nebraska Press, 1983.

HOLLINGSHEAD, A. B., & REDLICH, F. C. *Social class and mental illness*. New York: Wiley, 1958.

HOLLON, S. D., & KENDALL, P. C. Cognitive self-statements in depression: Development of an Automatic Thoughts Questionnaire. *Cognitive Therapy and Research*, 1980, **4**, 383–395.

HOLMES, D. S. Existence of classical projection and the stress-reducing function of attribution projection: A reply to Sherwood. *Psychological Bulletin*, 1981, **90**, 460–466.

HOLT, R. R. A clinical-experimental strategy for research in personality. In S. Messick & J. Ross (Eds.), *Measurement in personality and cognition*. New York: Wiley, 1962. Pp. 269–283.(a)

HOLT, R. R. Individuality and generalization in the psychology of personality: An evaluation. *Journal of Personality*, 1962, **30**, 377–402.(b)

HOLT, R. R. *Methods in clinical psychology*. New York: Plenum, 1978.

HOLTZMAN, W. H. Methodological issues in P technique. *Psychological Bulletin*, 1962, **59**, 248–256.

HONESS, T. Children's implicit theories of their peers: A developmental analysis. *British Journal of Psychology*, 1979, **70**, 417–424.

HONESS, T. Self-reference in children's descriptions of peers: Egocentricity or collaboration? *Child Development*, 1980, **51**, 476–480.

HORN, J. L. Motivation and the dynamic calculus concepts from multivariate experiment. In R. B. Cattell (Ed.), *Handbook of multivariate experimental psychology*. Chicago: Rand McNally, 1966. Pp. 611–641.

HORNEY, K. *The neurotic personality of our time*. New York: Norton, 1937.

HORNEY, K. *Our inner conflicts*. New York: Norton, 1945.

HORNEY, K. *Feminine psychology*. New York: Norton, 1973.

HOWARTH, E. A. A factor analysis of selected markers for objective personality factors. *Multivariate Behavioral Research*, 1972, **7**, 451–476.

HOWE, M. J. A. Biographical evidence and the development of outstanding individuals. *American Psychologist*, 1982, **37**, 1071–1081.

HULL, C. L. *Mathematico-deductive theory of rote learning*. New Haven, Conn.: Yale University Press, 1940.

HULL, C. L. *Principles of behavior*. New York: Appleton, 1943.

HULL, C. L. Autobiography in E. G. Boring, H. S. Langfeld, H. Werner, & R. M. Yerkes (Eds.), *A history of psychology in autobiography*. Worcester, Mass.: Clark University Press, 1952, Pp. 143–162.

HULL, J. G., YOUNG, R. D., & JOURILES, E. Applications of the self-awareness model of alcohol consumption: Predicting patterns of use and abuse. *Journal of Personality and Social Psychology*, 1986, **51**, 790–796.

HUNDLEBY, J. D., PAWLIK, K., & CATTELL, R. B. *Personality factors in objective test devices: A critical integration of a quarter of a century's research*. San Diego: Calif.: Knapp, 1965.

HUNT, J. McV. Effects of infant feeding-frustration upon adult hoarding in the Albino rat. *Journal of Abnormal and Social Psychology*, 1941, **36**, 338–360.

HUNT, J. McV. Traditional personality theory in the light of recent evidence. *American Scientist*, 1965, **53**, 80–96.

HUNT, J. McV. Psychological development: Early experience. *Annual Review of Psychology*, 1979, **30**, 103–144.

HUNTLEY, C. W. Judgments of self based upon records of expressive behavior. *Journal of Abnormal and Social Psychology*, 1940, **35**, 398–427.

ICHHEISER, G. Misinterpretation of personality in everyday life and the psychologist's frame of reference. *Character and Personality*, 1943, **12,** 145–152.

INKELES, A. Sociology and psychology. In S. Koch (Ed.), *Psychology: A study of a science.* New York: McGraw–Hill, 1963.

JACKSON, D. N., & MESSICK, S. Content and style in personality assessment. *Psychological Bulletin,* 1958, **55,** 243–252.

JANIS, I. L. Psychodynamic aspects of stress tolerance. In S. Z. Klausner (Ed.), *The quest for self-control.* New York: Free Press, 1965, Pp. 215–247.

JANKOWICZ, A. D. Whatever became of George Kelly? *American Psychologist,* 1987, **42,** 481–487.

JASPARS, J. M. F. Individual cognitive structures. In *Proceedings of the seventeenth international congress of psychology.* Amsterdam: North-Holland, 1964.

JENKINS, C. D. The coronary-prone personality. In W. D. Gentry & R. B. Williams (Eds.), *Psychological aspects of myocardial infarction and coronary disease.* St. Louis: Mosby, 1979.

JENKINS, C. D., ROSEMAN, R. H., & ZYMANSKI, S. J. *The Jenkins Activity Survey for Health Prediction* (Form B). Boston: Authors, 1972.

JENSEN, A. R. Personality. *Annual Review of Psychology,* 1958, **9,** 295–322.

JENSEN, A. R. Review of the Maudsley Personality Inventory, In O. K. Buros (Ed.), *Sixth mental measurements yearbook.* Highland Park, N.J.: Gryphon Press, 1965. Pp. 288–291.

JONES, E. *The life and work of Sigmund Freud,* Vol. 1. New York: Basic Books, 1953; Vol. 2, 1955; Vol. 3, 1957.

JONES, E. E., & NISBETT, R. E. The actor and the observer: Divergent perceptions of the causes of behavior. In E. E. Jones, D. E. Kanouse, H. H. Kelley, R. E. Nisbett, S. Valins, & B. Weiner (Eds.), *Attribution: Perceiving the causes of behavior.* Morristown, N.J.: General Learning Press, 1971.

JONES, M. C. A laboratory study of fear. The case of Peter. *Pedagogical Seminar,* 1924, **31,** 308–315.

JONIETZ, A. K. A study of the phenomenological changes in perception after psychotherapy as exhibited in the content of Rorschach percepts. Unpublished Ph.D. dissertation, University of Chicago, 1950.

JOURARD, S. M., & REMY, R. M. Perceived parental

attitudes, the self, and security. *Journal of Consulting Psychology,* 1955, **19,** 364–366.

JUNG, C. G. *The integration of the personality.* New York: Farrar & Rinehart, 1939.

KAGAN, J. Personality development. In P. London and D. Rosenhan (Eds.), *Foundations of abnormal psychology.* New York: Holt, Rinehart & Winston, 1968. Pp. 117–173.

KAGAN, J. Emergent themes in human development. *American Scientist,* 1976, **64,** 186–196.

KAHN, M. W. Clinical and statistical prediction revisited. *Journal of Clinical Psychology,* 1960, **26,** 115–118.

KAHN, M., AND BAKER, B. Desensitization with minimal therapist contact, *Journal of Abnormal Psychology,* 1968, **73,** 198–200.

KAHNEMAN, D., & TVERSKY, A. Choices, values, and frames. *American Psychologist,* 1984, **39,** 341–350.

KALISH, H. I. Behavior therapy, In B. B. Wolman (Ed.), *Handbook of clinical psychology.* New York: McGraw–Hill, 1965.

KALLMANN, F. J. The genetic theory of schizophrenia. *American Journal of Psychiatry,* 1946, **103,** 309–322.

KAMIN, L. J. *The science and politics of I.Q.* Hillsdale, N.J.: Erlbaum, 1974.

KANFER, F. H., & KAROLY, P. Self-control: A behavioristic excursion into the lion's den. *Behavior Therapy,* 1972, **3,** 398–416.

KANFER, F. H., & PHILLIPS, J. S. *Learning foundations of behavior therapy.* New York: Wiley, 1970.

KANFER, F. H., & SASLOW, G. Behavioral analysis: An alternative to diagnostic classification. *Archives of General Psychiatry,* 1965, **12,** 519–538.

KATAHN, M., & KOPLIN, J. H. Paradigm clash. *Psychological Bulletin,* 1968, **69,** 147–148.

KAVANAGH, D. J., & BOWER, G. H. Mood and self-efficacy: Impact of joy and sadness on perceived capabilities. *Behavior Therapy and Research,* 1985, **9,** 507–525.

KAZDIN, A. E. *The token economy: A review and evaluation.* New York: Plenum, 1977.

KAZDIN, A. E., & BOOTZIN, R. R. The token economy: An evaluative review. *Journal of Applied Behavior Analysis,* 1972, **5,** 343–372.

KAZDIN, A. E., & ROGERS, T. On paradigms and

recycled ideologies: Analogue research revisited. *Cognitive Therapy and Research*, 1978, **2**, 105–117.

KAZDIN, A. E., & WILCOXON, L. A. Systematic desensitization and nonspecific treatment effects: A methodological evaluation. *Psychological Bulletin*, 1976, **83**, 729–758.

KAZDIN, A. E., & WILSON, G. T. *Evaluation of behavior theory: Issues, evidence, and research strategies*. Cambridge, Mass.: Ballinger, 1978.

KELLY, E. L. Consistency of the adult personality. *American Psychologist*, 1955, **10**, 659–681.

KELLY, G. A. *The psychology of personal constructs*. New York: Norton, 1955.

KELLY, G. A. Man's construction of his alternatives. In G. Lindzey (Ed.), *Assessment of human motives*. New York: Holt, Rinehart & Winston, 1958. Pp. 33–64.(a)

KELLY, G. A. The theory and technique of assessment. *Annual Review of Psychology*, 1958, **9**, 323–352.(b)

KELLY, G. A. Suicide: The personal construct point of view. In N. L. Faberow & E. S. Schneidman (Eds.), *The cry for help*. New York: McGraw–Hill, 1961. Pp. 255–280.

KELLY, G. A. Non-parametric factor analysis of personality theories. *Journal of Individual Psychology*, 1963, **19**, 115–147.

KELLY, G. A. The language of hypothesis: Man's psychological instrument. *Journal of Individual Psychology*, 1964, **20**, 137–152.

KENDALL, P. C. Behavioral assessment and methodology. In C. M. Franks, G. T. Wilson, P. C. Kendall, & K. D. Brownell (Eds.), *Annual Review of behavior therapy: Theory and practice*. New York: Guilford, 1982.

KIMBLE, G. A. Psychology's two cultures. *American Psychologist*, 1984, **39**, 833–839.

KIRSCHENBAUM, H. *On becoming Carl Rogers*. New York: Delacorte, 1979.

KLEIN, G. S. The personal world through perception. In R. R. Blake & G. V. Ramsey (Eds.), *Perception: An approach to personality*. New York: Ronald Press, 1951. Pp. 328–355.

KLEIN, G. S. Need and regulation. In M. R. Jones (Ed.), *Nebraska symposium on motivation*. Lincoln: Nebraska University Press, 1954. Pp. 224–274.

KLEIN, G. S. *Perception, motives and personality*. New York: Knopf, 1970.

KLEIN, G. S. *Psychoanalytic theory: An exploration of essentials*. New York: International Universities Press, 1976.

KLEIN, G. S., BARR, HARRIET L., & WOLITZKY, D. L. Personality. *Annual Review of Psychology*, 1967, **18**, 467–560.

KLEIN, G. S., & KRECH, D. The problem of personality and its theory. *Journal of Personality*, 1951, **20**, 2–23.

KLEINMUNTZ, B. *Personality measurement*. Homewood, Ill.: Dorsey, 1967.

KLINE, P. *Fact and fantasy in Freudian theory*, 2nd ed. London: Methuen, 1981.

KLUCKHOHN, C. *Mirror for man*. New York: McGraw–Hill, 1949.

KLUCKHOHN, C. Culture and behavior. In G. Lindzey (Ed.), *Handbook of social psychology*. Cambridge, Mass.: Addison–Wesley, 1954. Pp. 921–976.

KLUCKHOHN, C., & MORGAN, W. Some notes on Navaho dreams. In G. B. Wilbur & W. Muensterberger (Eds.), *Psychoanalysis and culture*. New York: International Universities Press, 1951. Pp. 120–131.

KLUCKHOHN, C., & MURRAY, H. A. Personality formation: The determinants. In C. Kluckhohn, H. Murray, & D. M. Schneider (Eds.), *Personality in nature, society, and culture*. New York: Knopf, 1953.

KOBASA, S. C. The hardy personality: Toward a social psychology of stress and health. In J. Suls & G. Sanders (Eds.), *The social psychology of health and illness*. Hillsdale, N.J.: Erlbaum, 1982.

KOBASA, S. C. Barriers to work stress: The "hardy" personality. In W. D. Gentry, H. Benson, & C. J. deWolff (Eds.), *Behavioral medicine: Work, stress, and health*. The Hague: Nijhoff, 1984.

KOHUT, H. *The analysis of the self*. New York: International Universities Press, 1971.

KOHUT, H. *The restoration of the self*. New York: International Universities Press, 1977.

KOHUT, H. *How does analysis cure?* Chicago: University of Chicago Press, 1984.

KRASNER, L. The behavioral scientist and social responsibilty: No place to hide. *Journal of Social Issues*, 1965, **21**, 9–30.

KRASNER, L. Token economy as an illustration of operant conditioning procedures with the aged, with youth, and with society. In D. J. Levis (Ed.), *Learning approaches to therapeutic behavior change.* Chicago: Aldine, 1970. Pp. 74–101.

KRASNER, L. Behavior therapy. In *Annual Review of Psychology.* Palo Alto, Calif.: Annual Reviews, 1971, Pp. 483–532.(a)

KRASNER, L. The operant approach in behavior therapy. In A. E. Bergin & S. L. Garfield (Eds.), *Handbook of psychotherapy and behavior change.* New York: Wiley, 1971. Pp. 612–652. (b)

KRASNER, L., & ULLMANN, L. P. *Behavior influence and personality.* New York: Holt, Rinehart & Winston, 1973.

KRECH, D., & CRUTCHFIELD, R. S. *Elements of psychology.* New York: Knopf, 1958.

KRIS, E. Danger and morale. *American Journal of Orthopsychiatry,* 1944, **14,** 147–155.

KUHN, T. S. *The structure of scientific revolutions,* 2d ed. Chicago: University of Chicago Press, 1970.

LACEY, J. I. The evaluation of autonomic responses: Toward a general solution. *Annals of the New York Academy of Science,* 1956, **67,** 123–164.

LAING, R. D. *The divided self.* London: Tavistock, 1959.

LAING, R. D. *The politics of experience.* New York: Ballantine, 1967.

LAMBERT, M. J., DeJULIO, S. S., & STEIN, D. M. Therapist interpersonal skills: Process, outcome, methodological considerations and recommendations for future research. *Psychological Bulletin,* 1978, **85,** 467–489.

LANDFIELD, A. W. *Personal construct systems in psychotherapy.* Chicago: Rand McNally, 1971.

LANDFIELD, A. W. (ED.) *1976 Nebraska symposium on motivation.* Lincoln: University of Nebraska Press, 1977.

LANDFIELD, A. W. A construction of fragmentation and unity. In J. C. Mancuso & J. R. Adams-Webber (Eds.), *The construing person.* New York: Praeger, 1982.

LANG, P. J. Stimulus control, response control, and the desensitization of fear. In D. J. Levis (Ed.), *Learning approaches to therapeutic behavior change.* Chicago: Aldine, 1970. Pp. 148–173.

LANG, P. J. The application of psychophysiological methods to the study of psychotherapy and be-havior modification. In A. E. Bergin & S. Garfield (Eds.), *Handbook of psychotherapy and behavior change.* New York: Wiley, 1971. Pp. 75–125.

LANGER, E. J., JANIS, I. L., & WOLFER, J. A. Reduction of psychological stress in surgical patients. *Journal of Experimental Social Psychology,* 1975, **11,** 155–165.

LANGER, E. J., & RODIN, J. The effects of choice and enhanced personal responsibility for the aged: A field experiment in an institutional setting. *Journal of Personality and Social Psychology,* 1978, **34,** 191–198.

LANGNER, T. S., & MICHAEL, S. T. *Life stress and mental health.* New York: Free Press, 1963.

LAU, R. R. Origins of health locus of control beliefs. *Journal of Personality and Social Psychology,* 1982, **42,** 322–324.

LAYNE, C. Painful truths about depressives' cognitions. *Journal of Clinical Psychology,* 1983, **39,** 848–853.

LAZARUS, A. A. Behavior therapy, incomplete treatment and symptom substitution. *Journal of Nervous and Mental Disease,* 1965, **140,** 80–86.

LAZARUS, A. A. Learning theory and the treatment of depression. *Behavior Research and Therapy,* 1968, **6,** 83–89.

LAZARUS, A. A., & DAVISON, G. C. Clinical innovation in research and practice. In A. E. Bergin & S. L. Garfield (Eds.), *Handbook of psychotherapy and behavior change.* New York: Wiley, 1971. Pp. 196–213.

LAZARUS, R. S. The costs and benefits of denial. In S. Breznitz (Ed.), *Denial of stress.* New York: International Universities Press, 1983.

LAZARUS, R. S., & FOLKMAN, S. *Stress, appraisal, and coping.* New York: Springer Pub., 1984.

LECKY, P. *Self-consistency: A theory of personality.* New York: Island, 1945.

LEDWIDGE, B. Cognitive behavior modification: A step in the wrong direction? *Psychological Bulletin,* 1978, **85,** 353–375.

LESTER, D., HVEZDA, J., SULLIVAN, S., & PLOURDE, R. Maslow's hierarchy of needs and psychological health. *Journal of General Psychology,* 1983, **109,** 83–85.

LEVINE, R. A. *Culture, behavior, and personality.* Chicago: Aldine, 1973.

LEVIS, D. J., & MALLOY, P. F. Research in infrahuman and human conditioning. In G. T. Wilson & C. M. Franks (Eds.), *Contemporary behavior therapy: Conceptual and empirical foundations.* New York: Guilford, 1982.

LEVY, S. M. The expression of affect and its biological correlates: Mediating mechanisms of behavior and disease. In C. VanDyke, L. Temoshok, & L. S. Zegans (Eds.), *Emotions in health and illness.* New York: Grune & Stratton, 1984.

LEWINSOHN, P. M., STEINMETZ, J. L., LARSON, D. W., & FRANKLIN, J. Depression-related cognitions: Antecedent or consequence. *Journal of Abnormal Psychology*, 1981, **90**, 213–219.

LEWIS, M. Newton, Einstein, Piaget and the concept of self: The role of the self in the process of knowing. In L. S. Liben (Ed.), *Piaget and the foundation of knowledge.* Hillsdale, N.J.: Erlbaum, 1982.

LEWIS, M., & BROOKS-GUNN, J. *Social cognition and the acquisition of self.* New York: Plenum, 1979.

LEWIS, M., FEIRING, C., McGUFFOG, C., & JASKIR, J. Predicting psychopathology in six year olds from early social relations. *Child Development*, 1984, **55**, 123–136.

LEWIS, M., YOUNG, G., BROOKS, J., & MICHALSON, L. The beginning of friendship. In M. Lewis & L. A. Rosenblum (Eds.), *Friendship and peer relations.* New York: Plenum, 1975. Pp. 27–66.

LIDDELL, H. S. Conditioned reflex method and experimental neurosis. In J. McV. Hunt (Ed.), *Personality and the behavior disorders.* New York: Ronald Press, 1944. Pp. 389–412.

LIEBERMAN, D. A. Behaviorism and the mind. *American Psychologist*, 1979, **34**, 319–333.

LIFTON, R. J. *Thought reform and the psychology of totalism.* New York: Norton, 1963.

LOCKSLEY, A., & LENAUER, M. Considerations for a theory of self-influence processes. In N. Cantor & J. F. Kihlstrom (Eds.), *Personality, cognition, and social interaction.* Hillsdale, N.J.: Erlbaum, 1981.

LOEHLIN, J. C. Rhapsody in G. *Contemporary Psychology*, 1982, **27**, 623.

LOEVINGER, J., & KNOLL, E. Personality: Stages, traits, and the self. *Annual Review of Psychology*, 1983, **34**, 195–222.

LORD, C. G. Predicting behavioral consistency from an individual's perception of situational sim-

ilarities. *Journal of Personality and Social Psychology*, 1982, **42**, 1076–1088.

LOVAAS, O. I., KOEGEL, R., SIMMONS, J. Q., & LONG, G. S. Some generalization and follow-up measures on autistic children in behavior therapy. *Journal of Applied Behavior Analysis*, 1973, **6**, 131–166.

LUNDIN, R. W. *Personality: An experimental approach.* New York: Macmillan Co., 1961

LYKKEN, D. T. Multiple factor analysis and personality research. *Journal of Experimental Research in Personality*, 1971, **5**, 161–170.

LYKKEN, D. T. Research with twins: The concept of emergenesis. *Psychophysiology*, 1982, **19**, 361–373.

MACKINNON, D. W., & DUKES, W. Repression. In L. Postman (Ed.), *Psychology in the making.* New York: Knopf, 1962. Pp. 662–744.

MACLEOD, R. B. The place of phenomenological analysis in social psychological theory. In J. H. Rohrer & M. Sherif (Eds.), *Social psychology at the crossroads,* New York: Harper, 1951. Pp. 215–241.

MACLEOD, R. B. Phenomenology: A challenge to experimental psychology. In T. W. Wann (Ed.), *Behaviorism and phenomenology.* Chicago: University of Chicago Press, 1964. Pp. 47–73.

MADISON, P. *Freud's concept of repression and defence: Its theoretical and observational language.* Minneapolis: University of Minnesota Press, 1961.

MAGNUSSON, D. Learned helplessness—Welfare for good or bad. *Skandina Viska Enskilda Barsken Quarterly Review*, 1980, **3–4**, 67–74.

MAGNUSSON, D., & ENDLER, N. S. (EDS.) *Personality at the crossroads: Current issues in interactional psychology.* Hillsdale, N.J.: Erlbaum, 1977.

MAHER, B. *Principles of psychopathology.* New York: McGraw–Hill, 1966.

MAHER, B. *Clinical psychology and personality: The selected papers of George Kelly.* New York: Wiley, 1969.

MAHONEY, M. J. *Cognition and behavior modification.* Cambridge, Mass.: Ballinger, 1974.

MAHONEY, M. J. Publication prejudices: An experimental study of confirmatory bias in the peer review system. *Cognitive Therapy and Research*, 1977, **1**, 161–175.

MAHONEY, M. J., & ARNKOFF, D. Cognitive and self-control therapies. In S. Garfield & A. E. Bergin

(Eds.), *Handbook of psychotherapy and behavior change*. New York: Wiley, 1978.

MAHONEY, M. J., & BANDURA, A. Self-reinforcement in pigeons. *Learning and motivation*, 1972, **3**, 293–303.

MAHONEY, M. J., KAZDIN, A. E., & KENIGSBERG, M. Getting published. *Cognitive Therapy and Research*, 1978, **2**, 69–70.

MAHONEY, M. J., & MAHONEY, K. *Permanent weight control*. New York: Norton, 1976.

MAIER, N. R. F. *Frustration: The study of behavior without a goal*. New York: McGraw–Hill, 1949.

MAIER, N. R. F. Maier's Law. *American Psychologist*, 1960, **15**, 208–212.

MANCUSO, J. C., & ADAMS-WEBBER, J. R. (EDS.) *The construing person*. New York: Praeger, 1982.

MANDEL, N. M., & SHRAUGER, J. S. The effects of self-evaluative statements on heterosocial approach in shy and nonshy males. *Cognitive Therapy and Research*, 1980, **4**, 369–381.

MARCIA, J. E., RUBIN, B. M., & EFRAN, J. S. Systematic desensitization: Expectancy change or counterconditioning? *Journal of Abnormal Psychology*, 1969, **74**, 382–387.

MARKS, J., SONODA, B., & SCHALOCK, R. Reinforcement versus relationship therapy for schizophrenics. *Journal of Abnormal Psychology*, 1968, **73**, 397–402.

MARKUS, H. Self-schemata and processing information about the self. *Journal of Personality and Social Psychology*, 1977, **35**, 63–78.

MARKUS, H., CRANE, M., BERNSTEIN, S., & SILADI, M. Self-schemas and gender. *Journal of Personality and Social Psychology*, 1982, **42**, 38–50.

MARKUS, H. Self-knowledge: An expanded view. *Journal of Personality*, 1983, **51**, 543–565.

MARKUS, H., & NURIUS, P. Possible selves. *American Psychologist*, 1986, **41**, 954–969.

MARKUS, H., & SMITH, J. The influence of self-schemata on the perception of others. In N. Cantor & J. F. Kihlstrom (Eds.), *Personality, cognition, and social interaction*. Hillsdale, N.J.: Erlbaum, 1981.

MARLATT, G. A., & GORDON, J. R. Determinants of relapse: Implications for the maintenance of behavior change. In P. O. Davidson & S. M. Davidson (Eds.), *Behavioral medicine: Changing health lifestyles*. New York: Brunner/Mazel, 1980.

MASLOW, A. H. *Motivation and personality*. New York: Harper, 1954.

MASLOW, A. H. *Toward a psychology of being*. Princeton, N.J.: Van Nostrand, 1968.

MASLOW, A. H. *The farther reaches of human nature*. New York: Viking, 1971.

MATTHEWS, K. A. Psychological perspectives on the Type A behavior pattern. *Psychological Bulletin*, 1982, **91**, 293–323.

MAY, M. A. Foreword. In J. W. Dollard, L. W. Doob, N. E. Miller, O. H. Mowrer, & R. R. Sears, *Frustration and aggression*. New Haven, Conn.: Yale University Press, 1939.

MAY, R. *The meaning of anxiety*. New York: Ronald Press, 1950.

MAYO, C. W., & CROCKETT, W. H. Cognitive complexity and primacy; recency effects in impression formation. *Journal of Abnormal and Social Psychology*, 1964, **68**, 335–338.

McARTHUR, C., WALDRON, E., & DICKINSON, J. The psychology of smoking. *Journal of Abnormal and Social Psychology*, 1958, **56**, 267–275.

McCLEARY, R. A., & LAZARUS, R. S. Autonomic discrimination without awareness. *Journal of Personality*, 1949, **18**, 171–179.

McCLELLAND, D. C. *The achieving society*. Princeton, N.J.: Van Nostrand, 1961.

McCOY, M. M. Positive and negative emotion: A personal construct theory interpretation. In H. Bonarius, R. Holland, & S. Rosenberg (Eds.), *Personal construct psychology: Recent advances in theory and practice*. London: Macmillan & Co., 1981.

McCRAE, R. R., & COSTA, P. T. Validation of the five-factor model of personality across instruments and observers. *Journal of Personality and Social Psychology*, 1987, **52**, 81–90.

McGINNIES, E. Emotionality and perceptual defense. *Psychological Review*, 1949, **56**, 244–251.

McGUIRE, W. J. Some impending reorientations in social psychology: Some thoughts provoked by Kenneth Ring. *Journal of Experimental Social Psychology*, 1967, **3**, 124–139.

McNEMAR, Q. At random: Sense and nonsense. *American Psychologist*, 1960, **15**, 295–300.

MEDINNUS, G. R., & CURTIS, F. J. The relation between maternal self-acceptance and child acceptance. *Journal of Consulting Psychology*, 1963, **27**, 542–544.

MEDNICK, S. A. A learning theory approach to research in schizophrenia. *Psychological Bulletin*, 1958, **55**, 316–327.

MEEHL, P. E. The dynamics of "structured" personality tests. *Journal of Clinical Psychology*, 1945, **1**, 296–303.

MEHRABIAN, A., & RUSSELL, J. A. *An approach to environmental psychology.* Cambridge, Mass.: MIT Press, 1974.

MEICHENBAUM, D. Cognitive modification of test anxious college students. *Journal of Consulting and Clinical Psychology*, 1972, **39**, 370–380. (Copyright © 1972 by the American Psychological Association. Reprinted by permission.)

MEICHENBAUM, D. Cognitive factors in behavior modification: Modifying what clients say to themselves. In C. M. Franks & G. T. Wilson (Eds.), *Annual review of behavior therapy.* New York: Brunner/Mazel, 1973. Pp. 416–431.

MEICHENBAUM, D. *Cognitive-behavior modification: An integrative approach.* New York: Plenum, 1977.

MEICHENBAUM, D. Cognitive behavior modification: The need for a fairer assessment. *Cognitive Therapy and Research*, 1979, **3**, 127–132.

MEICHENBAUM, D. *Stress inoculation training.* New York: Pergamon, 1985.

MEICHENBAUM, D., & CAMERON, R. Cognitive behavior therapy. In G. T. Wilson & C. M. Franks (Eds.), *Contemporary behavior therapy: Conceptual and empirical foundations.* New York: Guilford, 1982.

MEICHENBAUM, D., & GILMORE, J. B. The nature of unconscious processes: A cognitive-behavioral perspective. In K. Bowers & D. Meichenbaum (Eds.), *The unconscious reconsidered.* New York: Wiley, 1983.

MEICHENBAUM, D., TURK, D., & BURSTEIN, S. The nature of coping with stress. In I. G. Sarason & C. D. Spielberger (Eds.), *Stress and anxiety.* Washington, D. C.: Hemisphere, 1975. Pp. 337–360.

MELGES, F. T., & WEISZ, A. E. The personal future and suicidal ideation. *Journal of Nervous and Mental Disease*, 1971, **153**, 244–250.

MESSICK, S. Personality structure. In *Annual Review of Psychology.* Palo Alto, Calif.: Annual Reviews, 1961. Pp. 93–128.

MIGLER, B., & WOLPE, J. Automated self-desensitization: A case report. *Behavior Research and Therapy*, 1967, **5**, 133–135.

MILGRAM, N. A., & HELPER, M. M. The social desirability set in individual and grouped self-ratings. *Journal of Consulting Psychology*, 1961, **25**, 91.

MILGRAM, S. Some conditions of obedience and disobedience to authority. *Human Relations*, 1965, **18**, 57–76.

MILLER, G. Quoted in the *New York Times*, November 12, 1982, page C1.

MILLER, N. E. Theory and experiment relating psychoanalytic displacement to stimulus–response generalization. *Journal of Abnormal and Social Psychology*, 1948, **43**, 155–178.

MILLER, N. E. Comments on theoretical models: Illustrated by the development of a theory of conflict behavior. *Journal of Personality*, 1951, **20**, 82–100.

MILLER, N. E. Biofeedback and visceral learning. *Annual Review of Psychology*, 1978, **29**, 373–404.

MILLER, N. E. Behavioral medicine: Symbiosis between laboratory and clinic. *Annual Review of Psychology*, 1983, **34**, 1–31.

MILLER, N. E., & DOLLARD, J. *Social learning and imitation.* New Haven, Conn.: Yale University Press, 1941.

MILLER, R. C., & BERMAN, J. S. The efficacy of cognitive behavior therapies: A quantitative review of the research evidence. *Psychological Bulletin*, 1983, **94**, 39–53.

MILLER, S., & MANGAN, C. E. Interacting effects of information and coping style in adapting to gynecologic stress: Should the doctor tell all? *Journal of Personality and Social Psychology*, 1983, **45**, 223–236.

MINEKA, S., DAVIDSON, M., COOK, M., & KLEIR, R. Observational conditioning of snake fear in rhesus monkeys. *Journal of Abnormal Psychology*, 1984, **93**, 355–372.

MISCHEL, W. Delay of gratification, need for achievement, and acquiesence in another culture. *Journal of Abnormal and Social Psychology*, 1961, **62**, 543–552.

MISCHEL, W. *Personality assessment.* New York: Wiley, 1968.

MISCHEL, W. *Introduction to personality.* New York: Holt, Rinehart & Winston, 1971.

MISCHEL, W. Toward a cognitive social learning reconceptualization of personality. *Psychological Review*, 1973, **80**, 252–283.

MISCHEL, W. *Introduction to personality*. New York: Holt, Rinehart & Winston, 1976.

MISCHEL, W. Self-control and the self. In T. Mischel (Ed.), *The self: Psychological and philosophical issues*. Totowa, N.J.: Rowman & Littlefield, 1977. Pp. 31–64.

MISCHEL, W. Personality and cognition: Something borrowed, something new? In N. Cantor & J. F. Kihlstrom (Eds.), *Personality, cognition, and social interaction*. Hillsdale, N.J.: Erlbaum, 1981.

MISCHEL, W. A cognitive-social learning approach to assessment. In T. V. Merluzzi, C. R. Glass, & M. Genest (Eds.), *Cognitive assessment*. New York: Guilford, 1982.

MISCHEL, W., & GRUSEC, J. Determinants of the rehearsal and transmission of neutral and aversive behaviors. *Journal of Personality and Social Psychology*, 1966, **3**, 197–205.

MISCHEL, W., & LIEBERT, R. M. Effects of discrepancies between observed and imposed reward criteria on their acquisition and transmission. *Journal of Personality and Social Psychology*, 1966, **3**, 45–53.

MISCHEL, W., & LIEBERT, R. M. The role of power in the adoption of self-reward patterns. *Child Development*, 1967, **38**, 673–683.

MISCHEL, W., & PEAKE, P. K. Beyond déjà vu in the search for cross-situational consistency. *Psychological Review*, 1982, **89**, 730–755.

MISCHEL, W., & PEAKE, P. K. Analyzing the construction of consistency in personality. In M. M. Page (Ed.), *Personality: Current theory and research*. Lincoln: University of Nebraska Press, 1983.

MONSON, T. C., HESLEY, J. W., & CHERNICK, L. Specifying when personality traits can and cannot predict behavior: An alternative to abandoning the attempt to preduct single-act criteria. *Journal of Personality and Social Psychology*, 1982, **43**, 385–399.

MORGAN, C. D., & MURRAY, H. A. A method for investigating fantasies. *Archives of Neurology and Psychiatry*, 1935, **34**, 289–306.

MORGAN, M. Self-monitoring of attained subgoals in private study. *Journal of Educational Psychology*, 1985, **77**, 623–630.

MORGAN, W. G. Non-necessary conditions or useful procedures in desensitization: A reply to Wilkins. *Psychological Bulletin*, 1973, **79**, 373–375.

MORIN, S. F. Heterosexual bias in psychological research on lesbianism and male homosexuality. *American Psychologist*, 1977, **32**, 629–637.

MOROKOFF, P. J. Effects of sex, guilt, repression, sexual "arousability," and sexual experience on female sexual arousal during erotica and fantasy. *Journal of Personality and Social Psychology*, 1985, **49**, 177–187.

MORRISON, J. K., & COMETA, M. C. Variations in developing construct systems: The experience corollary. In J. C. Mancusco & J. R. Adams-Webber (Eds.), *The construing person*. New York: Praeger, 1982.

MOSS, P. D., & MCEVEDY, C. P. An epidemic of over-breathing among school-girls. *British Medical Journal*, Nov. 26, 1966, 1295–1300.

MOWRER, O. H., & MOWRER, W. A. Enuresis: A method for its study and treatment. *American Journal of Orthopsychiatry*, 1928, **8**, 436–447.

MUNROE, R. L. *Schools of psychoanalytic thought*. New York: Dryden, 1955.

MURRAY, E. J. A case study in a behavioral analysis of psychotherapy. *Journal of Abnormal and Social Psychology*, 1954, **49**, 305–310.

MURRAY, E. J., & BERKUN, M. M. Displacement as a function of conflict. *Journal of Abnormal and Social Psychology*, 1955, **51**, 47–50.

MURRAY, E. J., & JACOBSON, L. I. The nature of learning in traditional and behavioral psychotherapy. In A. E. Bergin & S. Garfield (Eds.), *Handbook of psychotherapy and behavior change*. New York: Wiley, 1971. Pp. 709–747.

MURRAY, H. A. *Explorations in personality*. New York: Oxford University Press, 1938.

MURRAY, H. A., & KLUCKHOHN, L. A conception of personality. In C. Kluckhohn, H. Murray, & D. M. Schneider (Eds.), *Personality in nature, society, and culture*. New York: Knopf, 1956. Pp. 3–49.

NATHAN, P. E. Aversion therapy in the treatment of alcoholism: Success and failure. *Annals of the New York Academy of Sciences*, 1985, **443**, 357–364.

NEISSER, U. Cognitive psychology. New York: Appleton–Century–Crofts, 1967.

NEISSER, U. On "social knowing." Personality and Social Psychology Bulletin, 1980, **6**, 601–605.

NESSELROADE, J. R., & BARTSCH, T. W. Multivariate perspectives in the construct validity of the trait–state distinction. In R. B. Cattell & R. M. Dreger (Eds.), Handbook of modern personality theory. Washington, D.C.: Hemisphere, 1977. Pp. 221–238.

NESSELROADE, J. R., & DELHEES, K. H. Methods and findings in experimentally based personality theory. In R. B. Cattell (Ed.), Handbook of multivariate experimental psychology. Chicago: Rand McNally, 1966. Pp. 563–610.

NEWCOMB, T. M., KOENING, K. E., FLACHS R., & WARWICK, D. P. Persistence and change. New York: Wiley, 1967.

NISBETT, R., & ROSS, L. Human inference: Strategies and shortcomings of social judgment. Englewood Cliffs, N.J.: Prentice–Hall, 1980.

NISBETT, R. E., & WILSON, T. D. Telling more than we know: Verbal reports on mental processes. Psychological Review, 1977, **84**, 231–279.

NOLEN-HOEKSEMA, S., GIRGUS, J. S., & SELIGMAN, M. E. P. Learned helplessness in children: A longitudinal study of depression, achievement, and explanatory style. Journal of Personality and Social Psychology, 1986, **51**, 435–442.

NOREM, J. K., & CANTOR, N. Defensive pessimism: "Harnessing" anxiety as motivation. Journal of Personality and Social Psychology, 1986, **51**, 1208–1217.

NORMAN, D. A. Twelve issues for cognitive science. Cognitive Science, 1980, **4**, 1–32.

NORMAN, W. T. Toward an adequate taxonomy of personality attributes. Journal of Abnormal and Social Psychology, 1963, **66**, 574–583.

OGILVIE, D. M. The undesired self: A neglected variable in personality research. Journal of Personality and Social Psychology, 1987, **52**, 379–385.

O'LEARY, A. Self-efficacy and health. Behavior Research and Therapy, 1985, **23**, 437–451.

O'LEARY, A., SHOOR, S., LORIG, K., & HOLMAN, H. R. A cognitive-behavioral treatment of rheumatoid arthritis. Manuscript submitted for publication, 1988.

O'LEARY, K. D. The assessment of psychopathology in children. In H. C. Quay & J. S. Werry (Eds.), Psychopathological disorders of childhood. New York: Wiley, 1972. Pp. 234–272.

O'LEARY, K. D., & WILSON, G. T. Behavior therapy: Application and outcome. Englewood Cliffs, N.J.: Prentice–Hall, 1987.

OLWEUS, D. The consistency issue in personality psychology revisited. British Journal of Social and Clinical Psychology, 1980, **19**, 377–390.

OLWEUS, D. Continuity in aggressive and withdrawn, inhibited behavior patterns. Psychiatry and Social Science, 1981, **1**, 141–159.

OPLER, M. K., & SINGER, J. L. Ethnic differences in behavior and psychopathology. International Journal of Social Psychiatry, 1956, **2**, 11–23.

ORNE, M. T. On the social psychology of the psychological experiment: With particular reference to demand characteristics and their implications. American Psychologist, 1962, **17**, 776–783.

ORNE, M. T., & SCHREIBE, K. E. The contribution of nondeprivation factors in the production of sensory deprivation effects: The psychology of the "panic button." Journal of Abnormal and Social Psychology, 1964, **68**, 3–13.

OSGOOD, C. E., & LURIA, Z. A blind analysis of a case of multiple personality using the semantic differential. Journal of Abnormal and Social Psychology, 1954, **49**, 579–591.

OSGOOD, C. E., SUCI, G. J., & TANNENBAUM, P. H. The measurement of meaning. Urbana, Ill.: University of Illinois Press, 1957.

PATTERSON, G. R. Behavioral intervention procedures in the classroom and in the home. In A. E. Bergin & S. L. Garfield (Eds.), Handbook of psychotherapy and behavior change. New York: Wiley, 1971. Pp. 751–775.

PAUL, G. L., & SHANNON, D. T. Treatment of anxiety through systematic desensitization in therapy groups. Journal of Abnormal Psychology, 1966, **71**, 124–135.

PAVLOV, I. P. Conditioned reflexes. London: Oxford University Press, 1927.

PAVLOV, I. P. Lectures on conditioned reflexes, Vol. 2. London: Oxford University Press, 1928.

PENNEBAKER, J. W. Traumatic experience and psychosomatic disease: Exploring the roles of behavioral inhibition, obsession, and confiding. *Canadian Psychology*, 1985, **26**, 82–95.

PERVIN, L. A. Rigidity in neurosis and general personality functioning. *Journal of Abnormal and Social Psychology*, 1960, **61**, 389–395.(a)

PERVIN, L. A. Existentialism, psychotherapy, and psychology. *American Psychologist*, 1960, **15**, 305–309.(b)

PERVIN, L. A. Predictive strategies and the need to confirm them: Some notes on pathological types of decisions. *Psychological Reports*, 1964, **15**, 99–105.

PERVIN, L. A. A twenty-college study of Student × College interaction using TAPE (Transactional Analysis of Personality and Environment): Rationale, reliability, and validity. *Journal of Educational Psychology*, 1967, **58**, 290–302.(a)

PERVIN, L. A. Satisfaction and perceived self-environment similarity: A semantic differential study of student–college interaction. *Journal of Personality*, 1967, **35**, 623–634.(b)

PERVIN, L. A. Performance and satisfaction as a function of individual–environment fit. *Psychological Bulletin*, 1968, **69**, 56–68.

PERVIN, L. A. A free-response description approach to the analysis of person–situation interaction. *Journal of Personality and Social Psychology*, 1976, **34**, 465–474.

PERVIN, L. A. The representative design of person–situation research. In D. Magnusson & N. S. Endler (Eds.), *Personality at the crossroads: Current issues in interactional psychology*. Hillsdale, N.J.: Erlbaum, 1977.

PERVIN, L. A. Definitions, measurements, and classifications of stimuli, situations, and environments. *Human Ecology*, 1978, **6**, 71–105.(a)

PERVIN, L. A. *Current controversies and issues in personality*. New York: Wiley, 1978. (Second edition, 1984.)(b)

PERVIN, L. A. Idiographic approaches to personality. In J. McV. Hunt & N. Endler (Eds.), *Personality and the behavior disorders*. New York: Wiley, 1983.

PERVIN, L. A. Personality: Current controversies, issues, and directions. *Annual Review of Psychology*, 1985, **36**, 83–114.

PERVIN, L. A. Affect and addiction. *International Journal of Addictive Behaviors*, 1988, **13**, 83–86.

PERVIN, L. A., & LEWIS, M. (EDS.) *Perspectives in interactional psychology*. New York: Plenum, 1978.

PERVIN, L. A., & LILLY, R. S. Social desirability and self–ideal self on the semantic differential. *Educational and Psychological Measurement*, 1967, **27**, 845–853.

PERVIN, L. A., & RUBIN, D. B. Student dissatisfaction with college and the college dropout: A transactional approach. *Journal of Social Psychology*, 1967, **72**, 285–295.

PESKIN, H. Unity of science begins at home: A study of regional factionalism in clinical psychology. *American Psychologist*, 1963, **18**, 96–100.

PETERSON, C., SCHWARTZ, S. M., & SELIGMAN, M. E. P. Self-blame and depressive symptoms. *Journal of Personality and Social Psychology*, 1981, **41**, 253–259.

PETERSON, C., & SELIGMAN, M. E. P. Causal explanations as a risk factor for depression: Theory and evidence. *Psychological Review*, 1984, **91**, 347–374.

PETERSON, C., SEMMEL, A., VON BAEYER, C., ABRAMSON, L. Y., METALSKY, G. I., & SELIGMAN, M. E. P. The Attributional Style Questionnaire. *Cognitive Therapy and Research*, 1982, **6**, 287–300.

PFUNGST, O. *Clever Hans: A contribution to experimental, animal, and human psychology*. New York: Holt, Rinehart & Winston, 1911.

PHARES, E. J. Locus of control. In H. London & J. E. Exner, Jr. (Eds.), *Dimensions of personality*. New York: Wiley, 1978. Pp. 263–304.

POCH, S. M. A study of changes in personal constructs as related to interpersonal prediction and its outcomes. Unpublished Ph.D. dissertation, Ohio State University, 1952.

POHL, R. L., & PERVIN, L. A. Academic performance as a function of task requirements and cognitive style. *Psychological Reports*, 1968, **22**, 1017–1020.

POLLACK, J. M. Obsessive-compulsive personality: A review. *Psychological Bulletin*, 1979, **86**, 225–241.

POSNER, M. Cognition and personality. In N. Cantor & J. F. Kihlstron (Eds.), *Personality, cognition,* and social interaction. Hillsdale, N.J.: Erlbaum, 1981.

POWER, M. J., & CHAMPION, L. A. Cognitive approaches to depression: A theoretical critique. *British Journal of Clinical Psychology*, 1986, **25**, 201–212.

RACHMAN, S. The primacy of affect: Some theoretical implications. *Behavior Research and Therapy*, 1981, **19**, 279–290.

RACHMAN, S. Irrational thinking, with special reference to cognitive therapy. *Advances in Behavior Research and Therapy*, 1983, **5**, 63–88.

RAIMY, V. C. Self-reference in counseling interviews. *Journal of Consulting Psychology*, 1948, **12**, 153–163.

RAPAPORT, D. A critique of Dollard and Miller's "Personality and Psychotherapy." *American Journal of Orthopsychiatry*, 1953, **23**, 204–208.

RASKIN, N. J. Analysis of six parallel studies of the therapeutic process. *Journal of Consulting Psychology*, 1949, **13**, 206–220.

RASKIN, R., & HALL, C. S. A narcissistic personality inventory. *Psychological Reports*, 1979, **45**, 590.

RASKIN, R., & HALL, C. S. The Narcissistic Personality Inventory: Alternate form reliability and further evidence of construct validity. *Journal of Personality Assessment*, 1981, **45**, 159–162.

RASKIN, R., & SHAW, R. Narcissism and the use of personal pronouns. Unpublished manuscript, 1987.

RASKIN, R., & TERRY, H. A factor-analytic study of the Narcissistic Personality Inventory and further evidence of its construct validity. Unpublished manuscript, 1987.

RAZRAN, G. A quantitative study of meaning by a conditioned salivary technique. *Science*, 1939, **90**, 89–91.

RESCORLA, R. A., & HOLLAND, P. C. Behavioral studies of associative learning in animals. *Annual Review of Psychology*, 1982, **33**, 265–308.

REYNOLDS, G. S. *A primer of operant conditioning.* Glenview, Ill.: Scott, Foresman, 1968.

RICKELS, K., & CATTELL, R. B. The clinical factor validity and trueness of the IPAT verbal and objective batteries for anxiety and repression. *Journal of Clinical Psychology*, 1965, **21**, 257–264.

RIESMAN, D. *The lonely crowd.* Garden City, N.Y.: Doubleday, 1950.

RING, K. Experimental social psychology: Some sober questions about some frivolous values. *Journal of Experimental-Social Psychology*, 1967, **3**, 113–123.

RODIN, J., & LANGER, E. Long-term effects of a control-relevant intervention with institutionalized aged. *Journal of Personality and Social Psychology*, 1977, **35**, 897–902.

ROGERS, C. R. *Counseling and psychotherapy.* Boston: Houghton Mifflin, 1942.

ROGERS, C. R. Significant aspects of client-centered therapy. In H. M. Ruitenbeek (Ed.), *Varieties of personality theory.* New York: Dutton, 1964. Pp. 168–183. (Originally published in 1946.)

ROGERS, C. R. Some observations on the organization of personality. *American Psychologist*, 1947, **2**, 358–368.

ROGERS, C. R. *Client-centered therapy.* Boston: Houghton Mifflin, 1951.

ROGERS, C. R. Some directions and end points in therapy. In O. H. Mowrer (Ed.), *Psychotherapy: Theory and research.* New York: Ronald Press, 1953. Pp. 44–68.

ROGERS, C. R. The case of Mrs. Oak: A research analysis. In C. R. Rogers & R. F. Dymond (Eds.), *Psychotherapy and personality change.* Chicago: University of Chicago Press, 1954. Pp. 259–348.

ROGERS, C. R. Some issues concerning the control of human behavior. *Science*, 1956, **124**, 1057–1066.

ROGERS, C. R. A process conception of psychotherapy. *American Psychologist*, 1958, **13**, 142–149.

ROGERS, C. R. A theory of therapy, personality, and interpersonal relationships as developed in the client-centered framework. In S. Koch (Ed.), *Psychology: A study of science.* New York: McGraw–Hill, 1959. Pp. 184–256.

ROGERS, C. R. *On Becoming a person.* Boston: Houghton Mifflin, 1961.(a)

ROGERS, C. R. A tentative scale for the measurement of process in psychotherapies. In M. P. Stein (Ed.), *Contemporary psychotherapies.* New York: Free Press, 1961, Pp. 113–127.(b)

ROGERS, C. R. The process equation in psychotherapy. *American Journal of Psychotherapy*, 1961, **15**, 27–45.(c)

ROGERS, C. R. The actualizing tendency in relation to "motives" and to consciousness. In M. R.

Jones (Ed.), *Nebraska symposium on motivation.* Lincoln: University of Nebraska, 1963. Pp. 1–24.

ROGERS, C. R. Toward a science of the person. In T. W. Wann (Ed.), *Behaviorism and phenomenology.* Chicago: University of Chicago Press, 1964. Pp. 109–133.

ROGERS, C. R. Client-centered therapy. In S. Arieti (Ed.), *American handbook of psychiatry.* New York: Basic Books, 1966. Pp. 183–200.

ROGERS, C. R. (ED.) *The therapeutic relationship and its impact: A study of psychotherapy with schizophrenics.* Madison: University of Wisconsin Press, 1967.

ROGERS, C. R. *On encounter groups.* New York: Harper, 1970.

ROGERS, C. R. *Becoming partners: Marriage and its alternatives.* New York: Delacorte, 1972.(a)

ROGERS, C. R. My personal growth. In A. Burton (Ed.), *Twelve therapists.* San Francisco: Jossey–Bass, 1972. Pp. 28–77.(b)

ROGERS, C. R. In retrospect: Forty-six years. Distinguished professional contribution award address. American Psychological Association Convention, Montreal, August 1973.

ROGERS, C. R. *Carl Rogers on personal power.* New York: Delacorte, 1977.

ROGERS, C. R. *A way of being.* Boston: Houghton Mifflin, 1980.

ROGERS, C. R., & DYMOND, R. F. (EDS.) *Psychotherapy and personality change.* Chicago: University of Chicago Press, 1954.

ROGERS, C. R., GENDLIN, E. T., KIESLER, D. J., & TRUAX, C. B. *The therapeutic relationship and its impact: A study of the psychotherapy of schizophrenics.* Madison: University of Wisconsin Press, 1967.

ROGERS, C. R., & SKINNER, B. F. Some issues concerning the control of human behavior: A symposium. *Science,* 1956, **124,** 1057–1066.

ROGERS, T. B., KUIPER, N. A., & KIRKER, W. S. Self-reference and the encoding of personal information. *Journal of Personality and Social Psychology,* 1977, **35,** 677–688.

RORSCHACH, H. *Psychodiagnostics.* Bern: Huber, 1921.

ROSCH, E. Principles of categorization. In E. Rosch & B. B. Lloyd (Eds.), *Cognition and categorization.* Hillsdale, N.J.: Erlbaum, 1978.

ROSCH, E., MERVIS, C., GRAY, W., JOHNSON, D., & BOYES-BRAEM, P. Basic objects in natural categories. *Cognitive Psychology,* 1976, **8,** 382–439.

ROSEN, E. Differences between volunteers and non-volunteers for psychological studies. *Journal of Applied Psychology,* 1951, **35,** 185–193.

ROSENBAUM, M., & HADARI, D. Personal efficacy, external locus of control, and perceived contingency of parental reinforcement among depressed, paranoid, and normal subjects. *Journal of Personality and Social Psychology,* 1985, **49,** 539–547.

ROSENBERG, S. Personal constructs in person perception. *Nebraska Symposium on Motivation,* 1977, **24,** 179–242.

ROSENBERG, S. A theory in search of its zeitgeist. *Contemporary Psychology,* 1980, **25,** 898–900.

ROSENBERG, S., & JONES, R. A. A method of investigating and representing a person's implicit theory of personality: Theodore Dreiser's view of people. *Journal of Personality and Social Psychology,* 1972, **22,** 372–386.

ROSENBERG, S., & SEDLAK, A. Structural representations of implicit personality theory. *Advances in Experimental Social Psychology,* 1972, **6,** 235–297.

ROSENBLATT, A. D., & THICKSTUN, G. T. Modern psychoanalytic concepts in a general psychology. *Psychological Issues,* 1977, **11,** Monograph No. 42–43.

ROSENHAN, D. Some origins of concern for others. M. P. Mussen (Ed.), *New directions in child psychology.* New York: Holt, Rinehart & Winston, 1969. Pp. 134–154.

ROSENMAN, R. H. Health consequences of anger and implications for treatment. In M. A. Chesney & R. H. Rosenman (Eds.), *Anger and hostility in cardiovascular and behavioral disorders.* New York: Hemisphere, 1985.

ROSENTHAL, R. The effect of the experimenter on the results of psychological research. In B. A. Maher (Ed.), *Progress in experimental personality research,* Vol. 1. New York: Academic Press, 1964. Pp. 80–114.

ROSENTHAL, R., & JACOBSON, L. *Pygmalion in the classroom.* New York: Holt, Rinehart & Winston, 1968.

ROSENTHAL, R., & ROSNOW, R. L. (EDS.) *Artifact in*

behavioral research. New York: Academic Press, 1969.

ROSENTHAL, R., & RUBIN, D. Interpersonal expectancy effects: The first 345 studies. *Behavioral and Brain Sciences*, 1978, **3**, 377–415.

ROSENTHAL, T., & BANDURA, A. Psychological modeling: Theory and practice. In S. L. Garfield & A. E. Bergin (Eds.), *Handbook of psychotherapy and behavior change*. New York: Wiley, 1978. Pp. 621–658.

ROSENZWEIG, S. Need-persistive and ego-defensive reactions to frustration as demonstrated by an experiment on repression. *Psychological Review*, 1941, **48**, 347–349.

ROSS, L. The "intuitive scientist" formulation and its developmental implications. In J. H. Flavell & L. Ross (Eds.), *Social cognitive development*. Cambridge, England: Cambridge University Press, 1981.

ROTTER, J. B. *Social learning and clinical psychology*. Englewood Cliffs, N.J.: Prentice–Hall, 1954.

ROTTER, J. B. The role of the psychological situation in determining the direction of human behavior. In M. R. Jones (Ed.), *Nebraska symposium on motivation*. Lincoln: University of Nebraska Press, 1955.

ROTTER, J. B. Generalized expectancies for internal versus external control of reinforcement. *Psychological Monographs*, 1966, 80 (Whole No. 609).

ROTTER, J. B. External control and internal control. *Psychology Today*, 1971, **5**, 37–42.

ROTTER, J. B. *The development and application of social learning theory*. New York: Praeger, 1982.

ROWE, D. C. Resolving the person–situation debate. *American Psychologist*, 1987, **42**, 218–227.

ROZIN, P., & ZELLNER, D. The role of Pavlovian conditioning in the acquisition of food likes and dislikes. *Annals of the New York Academy of Sciences*, 1985, **443**, 189–202.

RUBINSTEIN, E. A. Warning: The surgeon general's research program may be dangerous to preconceived notions. *Journal of Social Issues*, 1976, **32**, 18–34.

RUDIN, S. A., & STAGNER, R. Figure-ground phenomena in the perception of physical and social stimuli. *Journal of Psychology* 1958, **45**, 213–225.

RUSHTON, J. P., & ERDLE, S. Evidence for aggressive (and delinquent) personality. *British Journal of Social Psychology*, 1987, **26**, 87–89.

RUSHTON, J. P., RUSSELL, R. J. H., & WELLS, P. A. Personality and genetic similarity theory. *Journal of Social and Biological Structures*, 1985, **8**, 63–86.

SACKEIM, H. A., & GUR, R. C. Self-deception, other-deception, and self-reported psychopathology. *Journal of Consulting and Clinical Psychology*, 1979, **47**, 213–215.

SALMON, P. A psychology of personal growth. In D. Bannister (Ed.), *Perspectives in personal construct theory*. New York: Academic Press, 1970. Pp. 197–221.

SANDLER, J. Masochism: An empirical analysis. *Psychological Bulletin*, 1964, **62**, 197–204.

SANFORD, N. Personality: Its place in psychology. In S. Koch (Ed.), *Psychology: A study of a science*. New York: McGraw–Hill, 1963, Pp. 488–592.

SARASON, I. G. *Personality: An objective approach*. New York: Wiley, 1966.

SARNOFF, I. Identification with the aggressor: Some personality correlates of anti-Semitism among Jews. Unpublished Ph.D. dissertation, U. Michigan, 1951.

SCHACHTER, S. The interaction of cognitive and physiological determinants of emotional state. In L. Berkowitz (Ed.), *Advances in experimental social psychology*. New York: Academic Press, 1964. Pp. 49–80.

SCHACHTER, S., & SINGER, J. Cognitive, social, and physiological determinants of emotional state. *Psychological Review*, 1962, **69**, 379–399.

SCHAFER, R. *Psychoanalytic interpretation in Rorschach testing*. New York: Grune & Stratton, 1954.

SCHAFER, R. *A new language for psychoanalysis*. New Haven, Conn.: Yale University Press, 1976.

SCHAFER, R. *Language and insight*. New Haven, Conn.: Yale University Press, 1978.

SCHAFER, R. The pursuit of failure and the idealization of unhappiness. *American Psychologist*, 1984, **39**, 398–405.

SCHANK, R., & ABELSON, R. *Scripts, plans, goals, and understanding*. Hillsdale, N.J.: Erlbaum, 1977.

SCHEIER, M. F., & CARVER, C. S. Optimism, coping, and health: Assessment and implications of generalized outcome expectancies. *Health Psychology*, 1985, **4**, 219–247.

SCHEIER, M. F., & CARVER, C. S. Dispositional optimism and physical well-being: The influence of generalized outcome expectancies on health. *Journal of Personality*, 1987, **55**, 169–210.

SCHNEIDER, D. J. Personal construct psychology: An international menu. *Contemporary Psychology*, 1982, **27**, 712–713.

SCHNEIDER, J. A., O'LEARY, A., & AGRAS, W. S. The role of perceived self-efficacy in recovery from bulimia: A preliminary examination. *Behavior Research and Therapy*, in press.

SCHNEIDER, J. M. College students' belief in personal control. *Journal of Individual Psychology*, 1971, **27**, 188.

SCHUNK, D. H., & COX, P. D. Strategy training and attributional feedback with learning disabled students. *Journal of Educational Psychology*, 1986, **78**, 201–209.

SCHWARTZ, G. E. Integrating psychobiology and behavior therapy: A systems perspective. In G. T. Wilson & C. M. Franks (Eds.), *Contemporary behavior therapy: Conceptual and empirical foundations*. New York: Guilford, 1982.

SCHWARTZ, R. M., & GOTTMAN, J. M. Toward a task analysis of assertive behavior. *Journal of Consulting and Clinical Psychology*, 1976, **44**, 910–920.

SCOTT, J. P. *Early experience and the organization of behavior*. Belmont, Calif.: Wadsworth, 1968.

SEARS, R. R. Experimental studies of projection. I. Attribution of traits. *Journal of Social Psychology*, 1936, **7**, 151–163.

SEARS, R. R. Relation of fantasy aggression to interpersonal aggression. *Child Development*, 1950, **21**, 5–6.

SEARS, R. R., RAU, L., & ALPERT, R. *Identification and child-rearing*. Stanford, Calif.: Stanford University Press, 1965.

SECHREST, L. The psychology of personal constructs. In J. M. Wepman & R. W. Heine (Eds.), *Concepts of personality*. Chicago: Aldine, 1963. Pp. 206–233.

SECHREST, L. J. Personal constructs theory. In R. J. Corsini (Ed.), *Current personality theories*. Itasca, Ill.: Peacock, 1977. Pp. 203–241.

SECHREST, L. A passion for theory. *Contemporary Psychology*, 1979, **24**, 19–20.

SECHREST, L., & JACKSON, D. N. Social intelligence and accuracy of interpersonal predictions. *Journal of Personality*, 1961, **29**, 167–182.

SEEMAN, J. Perspectives in client-centered therapy. In B. B. Wolman (Ed.), *Handbook of clinical psychology*. New York: McGraw–Hill, 1965. Pp. 1215–1229.

SELIGMAN, M. E. P. *Helplessness*. San Francisco: Freeman, 1975.

SELIGMAN, M. E. P., & SCHULMAN, P. Explanatory style as a predictor of productivity and quitting among life insurance agents. *Journal of Personality and Social Psychology*, 1986, **50**, 832–838.

SHERWOOD, G. G. Consciousness and stress reduction in defensive projection: A reply to Holmes. *Psychological Bulletin*, 1982, **91**, 372–375.

SHEVRIN, H., & DICKMAN, S. The psychological unconscious: A necessary assumption for all psychological theory? *American Psychologist*, 1980, **35**, 421–434.

SHIELDS, J. Heredity and environment. In H. J. Eysenck & G. D. Wilson (Eds.), *A textbook of human psychology*. Baltimore: University Park Press, 1976.

SHIELDS, S. Functionalism, Darwinism, and the psychology of women: A study in social myth. *American Psychologist*, 1975, **30**, 739–754.

SHONTZ, F. C. *Research methods in personality*. Englewood Cliffs, N.J.: Prentice–Hall, 1965.

SHOTWELL, A. M., HURLEY, J. R., & CATTELL, R. B. Motivational structure of a hospitalized mental defective. *Journal of Personality*, 1961, **62**, 422–426.

SHWEDER, R. A. Fact and artifact in trait perception: The systematic distortion hypothesis. *Progress in Experimental Personality Research*, 1982, **11**, 65–100.

SIGEL, I. E. Social experience in the development of representational thought: Distancing theory. In I. E. Sigel, D. Brodzinsky, & R. Golinkoff (Eds.), *New directions in Piagetian theory and practice*. Hillsdale, N.J.: Erlbaum, 1981.

SILVERMAN, L. H. Psychoanalytic theory: The reports of its death are greatly exaggerated. *American Psychologist*, 1976, **31**, 621–637.

SILVERMAN, L. H. A comment on two subliminal psychodynamic activation studies. *Journal of Abnormal Psychology*, 1982, **91**, 126–130.

SILVERMAN, L. H., ROSS, D. L., ADLER, J. M., & LUSTIG, D. A. Simple research paradigm for demonstrating subliminal psychodynamic activation:

Effects of oedipal stimuli on dart-throwing accuracy in college men. *Journal of Abnormal Psychology*, 1978, **87**, 341–357. (Copyright © 1978 by the American Psychological Association. Adapted by permission.)

SIXTEEN PERSONALITY FACTOR INVENTORY. Champaign, Ill.: Institute for Personality and Ability Testing, 1962.

SKINNER, B. F. *Walden two.* New York: Macmillan Co., 1948.

SKINNER, B. F. Are theories of learning necessary? *Psychological Review*, 1950, **57**, 193–216.

SKINNER, B. F. *Science and human behavior.* New York: Macmillan Co., 1953.

SKINNER, B. F. A case history in the scientific method. *American Psychologist*, 1956, **11**, 221–233.

SKINNER, B. F. *Cumulative record.* New York: Appleton–Century–Crofts, 1959.

SKINNER, B. F. Behaviorism at fifty. *Science*, 1963, **140**, 951–958.

SKINNER, B. F. Autobiography. In E. G. Boring & G. Lindzey (Eds.), *A history of psychology in autobiography.* New York: Appleton–Century–Crofts, 1967. Pp. 385–414.

SKINNER, B. F. *Beyond freedom and dignity.* New York: Knopf, 1971.

SKINNER, B. F. I have been misunderstood. *The Center Magazine*, 1972, March–April, 63–65.

SKINNER, B. F. *About behaviorism.* New York: Knopf, 1974

SKINNER, B. F. What is wrong with daily life in the western world? *American Psychologist*, 1986, **41**, 568–574.

SKINNER, B. F., & ROGERS, C. R. Some issues concerning the control of human behavior: A symposium. *Science*, 1965, **124**, 1057–1066.

SKOLAICK, A. Motivational imagery and behavior over twenty years. *Journal of Consulting Psychology*, 1966, **30**, 463–478.

SMITH, E. R., & KLUEGEL, J. R. Cognitive and social bases of emotional experience: Outcome, attribution, and affect. *Journal of Personality and Social Psychology*, 1982, **43**, 1129–1141.

SMITH, T. W., SNYDER, C. R., & PERKINS, S. C. The self-serving function of hypochondriacal complaints. *Journal of Personality and Social Psychology*, 1983, **44**, 787–797.

SNYDER, M. Self-monitoring of expressive behavior. *Journal of Personality and Social Psychology*, 1974, **30**, 526–537.

SNYDER, M. Self-monitoring processes. *Advances in Experimental Social Psychology*, 1979, **12**, 85–128.

SNYDER, M. On the influence of individuals on situations. In N. Cantor & J. F. Kihlstrom (Eds.), *Personality, cognition, and social interaction.* Hillsdale, N.J.: Erlbaum, 1981.

SNYDER, W. U. An investigation of the nature of non-directive psychotherapy. *Journal of General Psychology*, 1945, **33**, 193–223.

SOLYOM, L., & MILLER, S. A. Differential conditioning procedure as the initial phase of the behavior therapy of homosexuality. *Behavioral Research Therapy*, 1965, **3**, 147–160.

SPENCE, K. W. A theory of emotionally based drive (D) and its relation to performance in simple, learning situations. *American Psychologist*, 1958, **13**, 131–141.

STAATS, A. Q., & BURNS, G. L. Emotional personality repertoire as cause of behavior: Specification of personality and interaction principles. *Journal of Personality and Social Psychology*, 1982, **43**, 873–886.

STEINER, J. F. *Treblinka.* New York: Simon & Schuster, 1966.

STEPHAN, W. G., & GOLLWITZER, P. M. Affect as a mediator of attributional egotism. *Journal of Experimental Social Psychology*, 1981, **17**, 443–458.

STEPHENSON, W. *The study of behavior.* Chicago: University of Chicago Press, 1953.

STEVENS, S. S. The operational definition of psychological concepts. *Psychological Review*, 1935, **42**, 517–527.

STRELAU, J. *Temperament, personality, activity.* London: Academic Press, 1983.

SUEDFELD, P., & RANK, A. D. Revolutionary leaders: Long-term success as a function of changes in conceptual complexity. *Journal of Personality and Social Psychology*, 1976, **34**, 169–178.

SUEDFELD, P., & TETLOCK, P. Integrative complexity of communications in international crises. *Journal of Conflict Resolution*, 1977, **21**, 169–184.

SUEDFELD, P., TETLOCK, P., & RAMIREZ, C. War,

peace, and integrative complexity. *Journal of Conflict Resolution*, 1977, **21**, 427–442.

SUINN, R. M., OSBORNE, D., & WINFREE, P. The self concept and accuracy of recall of inconsistent self-related information. *Journal of Clinical Psychology*, 1962, **18**, 473–474.

SULLIVAN, H. S. *The interpersonal theory of psychiatry.* New York: Norton, 1953.

SULLOWAY, F. J. *Freud: Biologist of the mind.* New York: Basic Books, 1979.

SURWIT, R. S., WILLIAMS, R. B., & SHAPIRO, D. *Behavioral approaches to cardiovascular disease.* New York: Academic Press, 1982.

SWANBERG, W. A. *Dreiser.* New York: Scribner's, 1965.

SWANN, W. B., JR. Self-verification: Bringing social reality into harmony with the self. In J. Suls & A. G. Greenwald (Eds.), *Social psychological perspectives on the self.* Hillsdale, N.J.: Erlbaum, 1983.

SWANN, W. B., & HILL, C. A. When our identities are mistaken: Reaffirming self-conceptions through social interaction. *Journal of Personality and Social Psychology*, 1982, **43**, 59–66.

SWANN, W. B., & READ, S. J. Acquiring self-knowledge: The search for feedback that fits. *Journal of Personality and Social Psychology*, 1981, **41**, 1119–1128.

SZASZ, T. S. *The myth of mental illness.* New York: Harper, 1961.

TAGIURI, R. Person perception. In G. Lindzey & E. Aronson (Eds.), *Handbook of social psychology.* Reading, Mass.: Addison–Wesley, 1969.

TAYLOR, J. A. Drive theory and manifest anxiety. *Psychological Bulletin*, 1956, **53**, 303–320.

TAYLOR, S. E. Social cognition and health. *Personality and Social Psychology Bulletin*, 1982, **8**, 549–562.

TEMOSHOK, L. The relationship of psychosocial factors to prognostic indicators in cutaneous malignant melanoma. *Journal of Psychosomatic Research*, 1985, **29**, 139–153.

THARP, R. G., & WETZEL, R. J. *Behavior modification in the natural environment.* New York: Academic Press, 1969.

THEORELL, T., & RAHE, R. H. Life change events, ballistocardiography, and coronary death. *Journal of Human Stress*, 1975, **1**, 18–24.

THORNDIKE, R. L. The psychological value systems of psychologists. *American Psychologist*, 1954, **9**, 787–790.

TOBACYK, J. J., & DOWNS, A. Personal construct threat and irrational beliefs as cognitive predictors of increases in musical performance anxiety. *Journal of Personality and Social Psychology*, 1986, **51**, 779–782.

TOMKINS, S. S. Commentary. The ideology of research strategies. In S. Messick & J. Ross (Eds.), *Measurement in personality and cognition.* New York: Wiley, 1962. Pp. 285–294.

TRIPOLDI, T., & BIERI, J. Cognitive complexity as a function of own and provided constructs. *Psychological Reports*, 1963, **13**, 26.

TRUAX, C. B. Reinforcement and nonreinforcement in Rogerian psychotherapy. *Journal of Abnormal Psychology*, 1966, **71**, 1–9.

TURKAT, I. D., & FOREHAND, R. The future of behavior therapy. *Progress in Behavior Modification*, 1980, **9**, 1–47.

TVERSKY, A., & KAHNEMAN, D. Judgment under uncertainty: Heuristics and biases. *Science*, 1974, **185**, 1124–1131.

TYLER, L. E. *The psychology of human differences.* New York: Appleton–Century–Crofts, 1965.

TYLER, L. E. *Individuality.* San Francisco: Jossey–Bass, 1978.

TYRER, P., LEWIS, P., & LEE, I. Effects of subliminal and supraliminal stress on symptoms on anxiety. *Journal of Nervous and Mental Disease*, 1978, **166**, 88–95.

ULLMANN, L. P., & KRASNER, L. (Eds.) *Case studies in behavior modification.* New York: Holt, Rinehart & Winston, 1965.

ULLMANN, L. P. & KRASNER, L. *A psychological approach to abnormal behavior.* Englewood Cliffs, N.J.: Prentice–Hall, 1969.

ULLMANN, L. P., & KRASNER, L. *A psychological approach to abnormal behavior.* Englewood Cliffs, N.J.: Prentice–Hall, 1975.

VALINS, S., & RAY, A. A. Effects of cognitive desensitization on avoidance behavior. *Journal of Personality and Social Psychology*, 1967, **7**, 345–350.

VANDENBERG, S. G. The hereditary abilities study: Hereditary components in a psychological test battery. *American Journal of Human Genetics*, 1962, **14**, 220–237.

VAN KAAM, A. *Existential foundations of psychology*. Pittsburgh: Duquesne University Press, 1966.

VARGAS, M. J. Changes in self-awareness during client-centered therapy. In C. R. Rogers & R. F. Dymond (Eds.), *Psychotherapy and personality change*. Chicago: University of Chicago Press, 1954. Pp. 145–166.

VERNON, P. E. *Personality assessment*. New York: Wiley, 1963.

WACHTEL, P. L. Psychodynamics, behavior therapy, and the implacable experimenter: An inquiry into the consistency of personality. *Journal of Abnormal Psychology*, 1973, **82**, 324–334.

WALKER, A. M., RABLEN, R. A., & ROGERS, C. R. Development of a scale to measure process changes in psycho-therapy. *Journal of Clinical Psychology*, 1960, **16**, 79–85.

WALTERS, R. H. Some conditions facilitating the occurrence of imitative behavior. In E. C. Simmel, R. A. Hoppe, & G. A. Milton (Eds.), *Social facilitation and imitative behavior*. Boston: Allyn & Bacon, 1968. Pp. 7–30.

WALTERS, R. H., & PARKE, R. D. Influence of the response consequences to a social model on resistance to deviation. *Journal of Experimental Child Psychology*, 1964, **1**, 269–280.

WATSON, J. B. *Behavior*. New York: Holt, Rinehart & Winston, 1914.

WATSON, J. B. *Psychology from the standpoint of a behaviorist*. Philadelphia: Lippincott, 1919.

WATSON, J. B. *Behaviorism*. New York: People's Institute Publishing Co., 1924.

WATSON, J. B. Autobiography. In C. Murchison (Ed.), *A history of psychology in autobiography*. Worcester, Mass.: Clark University Press, 1936. Pp. 271–282.

WATSON, J. B., & RAYNER, R. Conditioned emotional reactions. *Journal of Experimental Psychology*, 1920, **3**, 1–14.

WATSON, J. D. *The double helix*. New York: Atheneum, 1968.

WEBB, W. B. The choice of the problem. *American Psychologist*, 1961, **16**, 223–227.

WEBER, S. J., & COOK, T. D. Subject effects in laboratory research: An examination of subject roles, demand characteristics, and valid inference. *Psychological Bulletin*, 1972, **77**, 273–295.

WEINER, B. A theory of motivation for some classroom experiences. *Journal of Educational Psychology*, 1979, **71**, 3–25.

WEINER, B. An attributional theory of achievement motivation and emotion. *Psychological Review*, 1985, **92**, 548–573.

WEINER, B., & LITMAN-ADIZES, T. An attributional, expectancy-value analysis of learned helplessness and depression. In J. Garber & M. E. P. Seligman (Eds.), *Human helplessness*. New York: Academic Press, 1980.

WEISS, J. M. Effects of coping response on stress. *Journal of Comparative and Physiological Psychology*, 1968, **65**, 251–260.

WEISS, J. M. Somatic effects of predictable and unpredictable shock. *Psychosomatic Medicine*, 1970, **32**, 397–409.

WEISSMAN, A. E., & RICKS, D. F. *Mood and personality*. New York: Holt, Rinehart & Winston, 1966.

WEITZ, J. Criteria for criteria. *American Psychologist*, 1961, **16**, 228–231.

WHITE, B. J. The relation of self-concept and parental identification to women's vocational interests. *Journal of Counseling Psychology*, 1959, **6**, 202–206.

WHITE, P. Limitations of verbal reports of internal events: A refutation of Nisbett and Wilson and of Bem. *Psychological Review*, 1980, **87**, 105–112.

WHITE, R. W. Motivation reconsidered: The concept of competence. *Psychological Review*, 1959, **66**, 297–333.

WHITE, R. W. Competence and the psychosexual stages of development. In M. R. Jones (Ed.), *Nebraska symposium on motivation*. Lincoln: University of Nebraska Press, 1960.

WIGGINS, J. S. *Personality and prediction: Principles of personality assessment*. New York: Addison–Wesley, 1973.

WIGGINS, J. S. Cattell's system from the perspective of mainstream personality theory. *Multivariate Behavioral Research*, 1984, **19**, 176–190.

WILKINS, W. Desensitization: Social and cognitive factors underlying the effectiveness of Wolpe's procedure. *Psychological Bulletin*, 1971, **76**, 311–317.

WILLIAMS, J. R. A test of the validity of the P-technique in the measurement of internal conflict. *Journal of Personality*, 1959, **27**, 418–437.

WILSON, G. Introversion/extroversion. In H. London & J. E. Exner (Eds.), *Dimensions of personality.* New York: Wiley, 1978. Pp. 217–261.

WILSON, G. T. Adult disorders. In G. T. Wilson & C. M. Franks (Eds.), *Contemporary behavior therapy: Conceptual and empirical foundations.* New York: Guilford, 1982.

WILSON, G. T., & FRANKS, C. M. (Eds.) *Contemporary behavior therapy: Conceptual and empirical foundations.* New York: Guilford, 1982.

WILSON, T. D., HULL, J. G., & JOHNSON, J. Awareness and self-perception: Verbal reports on internal states. *Journal of Personality and Social Psychology,* 1981, **40,** 53–71.

WILSON, T. D., & LINVILLE, P. W. Improving the performance of college freshmen with attributional techniques. *Journal of Personality and Social Psychology,* 1985, **49,** 287–293.

WINETT, R. A., & WINKLER, R. C. Current behavior modification in the classroom: Be still, be quiet, be docile. *Journal of Applied Behavior Analysis,* 1972, **5,** 499–504.

WING, C. W., JR. Measurement of personality. In D. K. Whitla (Ed.), *Handbook of measurement and assessment in behavioral sciences.* Reading, Mass.: Addison–Wesley, 1968. Pp. 315–347.

WOLF, S. "Irrationality" in a psychoanalytic psychology of the self. In T. Mischel (Ed.), *The self: Psychological and philosophical issues.* Totowa, N.J.: Rowman & Littlefield, 1977. Pp. 203–223.

WOLPE, J. The systematic desensitization treatment of neuroses. *Journal of Nervous and Mental Disorders,* 1961, **132,** 189–203.

WOLPE, J. *The practice of behavior therapy.* New York: Pergamon, 1969.

WOLPE, J., & LAZARUS, A. A. *Behavior therapy techniques: A guide to the treatment of neuroses.* New York: Pergamon, 1966.

WOLPE, J., & RACHMAN, S. Psychoanalytic "evidence." A critique based on Freud's case of Little Hans. *Journal of Nervous and Mental Disease,* 1960, **130,** 135–148.

WYLIE, R. C. *The self-concept.* Lincoln: University of Nebraska Press, 1961.

WYLIE, R. C. The present status of self theory. In E. F. Borgatta & W. W. Lambert (Eds.), *Handbook of personality theory and research.* Chicago: Rand McNally, 1968. Pp. 728–787.

WYLIE, R. C. *The self-concept,* rev. ed. Lincoln: University of Nebraska Press, 1974.

YARMEY, A. D., & JOHNSON, J. Evidence for the self as an imaginal prototype. *Journal of Research in Personality,* 1982, **16,** 238–246.

ZIMBARDO, P. G. On the ethics of intervention in human psychological research: With special reference to the Stanford prison experiment. *Cognition,* 1973, **2,** 243–256.

Photo Credits

Chapter 13

Opener: Hank Morgan/Photo Researchers.   Page 432: Robert Schochet.   Page 437: Courtesy Dodge/Chrysler Corporation.   Page 450: Hazel Hankin.

Chapter 14

Opener: Arthur Tress/Photo Researchers.   Page 470: Teri Leigh Stratford/Photo Researchers.   Page 472: Sidney Harris.   Page 476: Cartoon by Gil Eisner, by The New York Times Company.   Page 474: Courtesy Dr. Donald Meichenbaum.   Page 477: Courtesy Dr. Aaron T. Beck.

Chapter 15

Opener: Timothy Egan/Woodfin Camp.

Chapter 16

Opener: Ethan Hoffman/Archive Photos.

Index

Functional autonomy, 571
Functioning, 3–6, 18
  cognitive, 396–401, 403
  dynamics, 89–90, 251–253, 281
  flexible–rigid, 212–213
  mechanical, 212
  societal, and learned
    helplessness, 66
  trait approach, 294–298
Future and personality theory, 19,
  102–106, 528–529

Gallery of Women, A, 435
Generalization, cognitive, *see*
  Self-schemata
Generalization of concepts, 336,
  350, 472
Genetic influence, 315–319
  criminality, 316
  factors of personality variance,
    298–299, 311
  and neuroticism, 311
Genital stage, 106
Glass, D. C., 37–39, 42, 50, 53
Global system, 272
Goal-oriented identification, 105
Goals, 388, 392–396, 512–513
  research, 56–64
Goldstein, Kurt, 212–213
Good–bad evaluation judgment,
  434–435, 444
Good–evil preoccupation, 128
Good-me, 154
Greek temperamental types,
  294–295
Grinker–Spiegel study, 33–35, 37,
  414, 417
Group behavior, 66
Group therapy, person-centered
  theory, 210–211
Growth and development in
  personality theory, 10–13
  behavioral approach, 344–345,
    352, 364–365
  character (personality), 100–115
  personal construct theory,
    253–255
  personality theory, 10–13
  person-centered theory, 192–196
  psychoanalytic theory, 100–115
  social cognitive theory, 396–401
  summary of theory concepts,
    530, 535–536
  trait approach, 310–311
Guided participation therapy
  techniques, 410–411

Guilt, 225, 263, 397
Guilty–innocent construct, 240

Habit, 7, 362
Hardiness and Type A behavior, 216
Hard–soft trait characteristics, 435
Health:
  and personality dynamics, 134
  and self-efficacy, 408
Helplessness, 34–56. *See also*
    Learned helplessness; Stress
  and anxiety, 34
  questionnaires, 42–56, 67–68
  research, 38–39, 41–56, 67–68
Heredity, 310–311, 315–319. *See
    also* Genetic influence
Hierarchical category structures,
  436–442
Hierarchical organization of
    personality, 287–288, 313
Hierarchy of needs, 215
Horney, Karen, 150–153
Hostility construct, 263
Hull, Clark L., 60, 202, 293,
  358–360, 381
  biography, 359–360
  stimulus–response theory,
    361–367
Human characteristics, 5
Human potential movement,
  212–219
  existentialism, 216–219
  Goldstein, Kurt, 212–213
  Maslow, Abraham H., 213–216
Hypnosis, 81
  cathartic hypnosis, 136
Hysterical personality, 132

Id, 86, 88–90, 138
  and ego, 135
  sexual and aggressive instincts,
    90–91
Ideal, unattainability of, 149
Ideal self, 181, 462
Identification, 105. *See also*
    Parent–child relationship
Identity, adolescence, 106–107
Ideographic approach, 59, 291–292
If–then causal relationship, 67
Imagery and action, 476
Imitative behavior, 352, 364
Immigration policy, 66
Implicit personality theory, 433,
  478–480
Impressionist observation, 276
Incongruence, 188–190

Independent–dependent
    personality dimension, 458
Index of Self-actualization, 187
Individual, uniqueness of, 217, 275,
  291, 435, 446–452
Individual differences, 297–298,
  300, 349
Individuality of behavior, 6
Individual psychology, 173–174
Individual Psychology School of
    personality theory, 145–148
Inefficacy, 393–396
Inferiority feelings, 146
Information organization:
  events, 452–458
  people, 442–443
  situations, 442–452
Information processing:
  compared to traditional theories,
    479–481
  in decision-making, 457
  sex differences, 459–460
Initiation rites, 106
Innate tendencies, 309–310
Instincts:
  aggressive, 78, 86, 90, 396–398
  aim-inhibited, 91
  life and death, 76, 86, 90–92
  sex, *see* Sex instinct
  vs. social cognitive theory, 397
Instrumental learning, 353–364
Integrated system, 272
Intellectualization, 93
Intensity, trait property, 290
Intensity score, 262
Intentions, 398
Interaction, 385
Internal–external causal
    attribution, 44–45, 524–525
  controversy, 16, 368
Internal–External Scale (I–E
    Scale), 43
Internal forces, 15–16, 43–45,
  524–525
  behavioral approach, 356–357,
    368
  learning theory, 384–385,
    392–393
  trait theory, 332
Internal standards, 392–393, 398,
  407–409, 420, 426–427
Interpersonal relationships, 11–12,
  150–151, 240
Interpersonal Theory of Psychiatry,
  153–155
Interpretation of Dreams, 75

INDEX

Printed and bound in Singapore by
Chong Moh Offset Printing Pte. Ltd.

10th Edn available
2007.

SUMMARY OF MAJOR THEORETICAL CONCEPTS

THEORIST OR THEORY	STRUCTURE	PROCESS	GROWTH AND DEVELOPMENT
FREUD	Id, ego, superego; unconscious, preconscious, conscious.	Life and death instincts; cathexes and anticathexes; anxiety and the mechanisms of defense.	Erogenous zones; oral, anal, phallic stages of development; Oedipus complex.
ROGERS	Self; ideal self	Self-actualization; congruence of self and experience; incongruence and defensive distortion and denial.	Congruence and self-actualization versus incongruence and defensiveness.
KELLY	Constructs	Processes channelized by anticipation of events.	Increased complexity and definition to construct system.
CATTEL	Traits	Attitudes; motives; ergs; sentiments.	Multiple abstract variance analysis (MAVA); age trends.
LEARNING THEORY	Response	Classical conditioning; instrumental conditioning; operant conditioning.	Imitation; schedules of reinforcement and successive approximations.
SOCIAL LEARNING THEORY	Expectancies; standards; goals–plans; self-efficacy	Observational learning; vicarious conditioning; symbolic processes, self-evaluative and self-regulatory processes.	Social learning through observation and direct experience; development of self-efficacy judgments and standards for self-regulation.